Rogers Cadenhead
Laura Lemay

Sams Teach Yourself

Java 2

IN 21 DAYS

THIRD EDITION

SAMS

201 West 103rd St., Indianapolis, Indiana, 46290 USA

Sams Teach Yourself Java 2 in 21 Days, Third Edition

Copyright © 2003 by Sams Publishing

International Standard Book Number: 0-672-32370-2

Library of Congress Catalog Card Number: 2001098207

Printed in the United States of America

First Printing: August 2002

05   04   03   02   4   3   2   1

Trademarks

Warning and Disclaimer

ACQUISITIONS EDITORS
Katie Purdum
Mark Taber

DEVELOPMENT EDITOR
Scott Meyers

MANAGING EDITOR
Charlotte Clapp

PROJECT EDITOR
Matthew Purcell

COPY EDITOR
Publication Services, Inc.

PRODUCTION EDITOR
Publication Services, Inc.

INDEXER
Publication Services, Inc.

PROOFREADER
Publication Services, Inc.

TECHNICAL EDITOR
John Purdum

TEAM COORDINATOR
Amy Patton

INTERIOR DESIGNER
Gary Adair

COVER DESIGNER
Aren Howell

PAGE LAYOUT
Publication Services, Inc.

GRAPHICS
Tammy Graham
Oliver Jackson

Contents at a Glance

Contents

Day 7 Threads and Exceptions

About the Authors

ROGERS CADENHEAD is the author of 12 books on Internet-related topics, including *Sams Teach Yourself Java 2 in 24 Hours* and *Sams Teach Yourself Microsoft FrontPage 2002 in 24 Hours*, but not *Teach Yourself to Tell Time in 10 Minutes*. Cadenhead is also a Web application developer and the publisher of sites that receive more than 7 million visits a year. He maintains this book's official World Wide Web site at `http://www.java21days.com`.

LAURA LEMAY is a technical writer and author. After spending six years writing software documentation for various computer companies in Silicon Valley, she decided that writing books would be much more fun. In her spare time, she collects computers, e-mail addresses, interesting hair colors, and non-running motorcycles. She is also the perpetrator of *Sams Teach Yourself Web Publishing with HTML in a Week* and *Sams Teach Yourself Perl in 21 Days*.

Dedication

To Rita Craker (a.k.a. "Nana") and Mary Cadenhead (a.k.a. "Mimi"). Everyone should have grandmothers as loving, supportive, and fun to be around as these two. I love them dearly, even though they didn't get me the pony I really, really wanted when I was five. —Rogers

To Eric, for all the usual reasons (moral support, stupid questions, comfort in dark times, brewing big pots of coffee). —LL

Acknowledgments

From Rogers Cadenhead:

Thanks to the people at Sams Publishing who contributed so much to the book, including Trish Barker, Arlene Brown, Jerome Colburn, Mike Kopp, Jessica Matthews, Scott Meyers, Peter Nelson, Matt Purcell, John Purdum, Katie Purdum, Molly Redenbaugh, and Mark Taber. Thanks to the people at the Studio B agency who represent me, including David and Sherry Rogelberg, Neil Salkind, and Jessica Richardson. Thanks to my coauthor Laura Lemay, whose books helped inspire me to start writing for Sams in 1996. And thanks to my wife Mary Moewe and my sons, Max, Eli, and Sam, who make me happier than a first-generation American immigrant at the end of a Frank Capra movie who is in such a state of bliss that he must express his feelings in song.

I'd also like to thank readers who have sent helpful comments about corrections, typos, and suggested improvements regarding this book and its prior editions. The list includes the following people: Dave Barton, Patrick Benson, Lawrence Chang, Jim DeVries, Ryan Esposto, Kim Farr, Bruce Franz, Owen Gailar, Rich Getz, Bob Griesemer, Jenny Guriel, Ben Hensley, Jon Hereng, Drew Huber, John R. Jackson, Bleu Jaegel, Natalie Kehr, Mark Lehner, Stephen Loscialpo, Brad Kaenel, Chris McGuire, Paul Niedenzu, Chip Pursell, Pranay Rajgarhia, Peter Riedlberger, Darrell Roberts, Luke Shulenburger, Mike Tomsic, John Walker, Joseph Walsh, Mark Weiss, P.C. Whidden, Chen Yan, Kyu Hwang Yeon, and J-F. Zurcher.

From Laura Lemay:

To the folks on Sun's Java team, for all their hard work on Java, the language, and on the browser, and particularly to Jim Graham, who demonstrated Java and HotJava to me on very short notice in May 1995 and planted the idea for this book. To everyone who bought my previous books and liked them: Buy this one, too.

Tell Us What You Think!

As the reader of this book, *you* are our most important critic and commentator. We value your opinion and want to know what we're doing right, what we could do better, what areas you'd like to see us publish in, and any other words of wisdom you're willing to pass our way.

You can e-mail or write me directly to let me know what you did or didn't like about this book, as well as what we can do to make our books stronger.

Please note that I cannot help you with technical problems related to the topic of this book, and that due to the high volume of mail I receive, I might not be able to reply to every message.

When you write, please be sure to include this book's title and author as well as your name and contact information. I will carefully review your comments and share them with the author and editors who worked on the book.

Fax: 317-581-4770

E-mail: webdev@samspublishing.com

Mail: Mark Taber
           Associate Publisher
           Sams Publishing
           201 West 103rd Street
           Indianapolis, IN 46290 USA

Introduction

Some revolutions catch the world completely by surprise. The World Wide Web, the Linux operating system, and personal digital assistants all rose to prominence unexpectedly and against conventional wisdom.

The remarkable success of the Java programming language, on the other hand, caught no one by surprise. Java has been the source of great expectations since its introduction more than seven years ago. When Sun Microsystems, Inc. launched Java by incorporating it into Web browsers, a torrent of publicity welcomed the arrival of the new language. Anyone who passed within eyesight of a World Wide Web page, computer magazine, or newspaper business section knew about Java and how it was expected to change the way software is developed.

Sun cofounder Bill Joy didn't hedge his bets at all when describing the company's new language. "This represents the end result of nearly 15 years of trying to come up with a better programming language and environment for building simpler and more reliable software," he proclaimed.

In the years that have passed, Java has lived up to a considerable amount of its hype. The language is becoming as much a part of software development as the beverage of the same name. One kind of Java keeps programmers up nights, whereas the other kind enables programmers to rest easier once they have developed their software.

Java was originally considered a technology for enhancing Web sites, and it's still being put to that use today; the AltaVista search engine reports that more than 4.6 million Web pages contain a Java program.

Each new release of Java strengthens its capabilities as a general-purpose programming language for environments other than a Web browser. Today, Java is being put to use in desktop applications, Internet servers, middleware, personal digital assistants, embedded devices, and many other environments.

Now in its fifth major release—Java 2 version 1.4—the Java language is a full-featured competitor to other general-purpose development languages, such as C++, Perl, Visual Basic, Delphi, and Microsoft C#.

You might be familiar with Java programming tools, such as WebGain Visual Café, Borland JBuilder, and Sun ONE Studio. These programs make it possible to develop functional Java programs, and you also can use Sun's Java 2 Software Development Kit. The kit, which is available for free on the Web at http://java.sun.com, is a set of command-line tools for writing, compiling, and testing Java programs.

This is where *Sams Teach Yourself Java 2 in 21 Days, Third Edition,* comes in. You'll be introduced to all aspects of Java software development using the most current version of the language and the best available techniques.

By the time you're done, you'll be well acquainted with the reasons Java has become the most talked-about programming language of the past decade, and why it's the most popular language today.

How This Book Is Organized

Sams Teach Yourself Java 2 in 21 Days covers the Java language and its class libraries in 21 days, organized as three separate weeks. Each week covers a broad area of developing Java applets and applications.

In the first week you will learn about the Java language itself:

- Day 1 is the basic introduction—what Java is, why to learn the language, and how to create programs using a style of development called object-oriented programming. You will also create your first Java application.
- On Day 2, you will start getting down to details with the basic Java building blocks—data types, variables, and expressions such as arithmetic and comparisons.
- Day 3 goes into detail about how to deal with objects in Java—how to create them, how to access their variables and call their methods, and how to compare and copy them. You will also get your first glance at the Java class libraries.
- On Day 4, you'll learn more about Java with arrays, conditional statements, and loops.
- Day 5 fully explores the creation of classes—the basic building blocks of any Java program.
- On Day 6, you will discover more about interfaces and packages, which are useful for grouping classes and organizing a class hierarchy.
- Day 7 covers two of the most powerful features of Java—*exceptions,* the ability to recognize and respond to errors as a program is running, and *threads,* the ability to separate parts of a program so that they run simultaneously.

Week 2 is dedicated to the most useful classes created by Sun for use in your own Java programs:

- On Day 8, you will be introduced to data structures that you can use as an alternative to strings and arrays—vectors, stacks, maps, hash tables, and bit sets.
- Day 9 begins a five-day exploration of visual programming. You will learn how to create a graphical user interface using *Swing,* a set of classes introduced in Java 2 that greatly expands Java's user-interface capabilities.

- Day 10 covers more than a dozen interface components that you can use in a Java program, including buttons, text fields, sliders, scrolling text areas, and icons.

- Day 11 explains how to make a user interface look good using *layout managers,* a set of classes that determine how components on an interface will be arranged.

- Day 12 concludes the coverage of Swing with *event-handling classes,* which enable a program to respond to mouse clicks and other user interactions.

- On Day 13, you will learn about drawing shapes and characters on a user interface component such as an applet window—including coverage of the Java2D classes introduced in Java 2.

- Day 14 provides the basics of applets—how they differ from applications, how to create them, and how to use the Java Plug-in to run Java 2 applets in Netscape Navigator, Microsoft Internet Explorer, and other browsers.

Week 3 includes advanced topics such as JavaBeans and Java Database Connectivity:

- Day 15 covers input and output using *streams,* a set of classes that enable file access, network access, and other sophisticated data handling.

- Day 16 introduces object *serialization,* a way to make your objects exist even when no program is running. You will learn to save them to a storage medium, such as a hard disk, read them into a program, and then use them again as objects.

- On Day 17, you'll extend your knowledge of streams to write programs that communicate with the Internet, including socket programming and URL handling.

- Day 18 adds another layer of multimedia with Java's sound capabilities. You will add sounds to applets and applications, and you'll work with JavaSound, an extensive new class library for playing, recording, and mixing sound.

- Day 19 covers *JavaBeans,* a way to develop Java programs using the rapid application techniques that are so popular in tools such as Microsoft Visual Basic.

- Day 20 explores how data are handled in Java. You will connect to databases using Java Database Connectivity (JDBC) and JDBC-ODBC, and you'll learn how to read XML data, one of the new features of Java 2 introduced in version 1.4.

- On Day 21, you will finish with one of the most exciting areas of new Java development—*servlets,* programs that run on Web servers to deliver dynamic Web applications. You will create servlets and Java Server Pages, which are Web pages that include Java statements along with HTML tags.

About This Book

This book teaches you about the Java language and how to use it to create applications for any computing environment and applets that run in Web browsers. By the time you have finished *Sams Teach Yourself Java 2 in 21 Days, Third Edition*, you'll have a well-rounded knowledge of Java and the Java class libraries and you will be able to develop your own programs for tasks such as data retrieval over the Internet, database connectivity, interactive gaming, and client/server programming.

You learn by doing in this book, as you create several programs each day that demonstrate the topics being introduced. The source code for all these programs is available on this book's official Web site at http://www.java21days.com, along with other supplemental material such as answers to reader questions.

Who Should Read This Book

This book teaches the Java language to three groups:

- Novices who are relatively new to programming
- People who have been introduced to earlier versions of Java such as Java 1.1 or 1.0
- Experienced developers in other languages, such as Visual C++, Visual Basic, or Delphi

You will learn how to develop *applets,* interactive Java programs that run as part of a World Wide Web page, and *applications,* programs that run everywhere else. When you've finished *Sams Teach Yourself Java 2 in 21 Days, Third Edition,* you'll be able to tackle any aspect of the language, and you'll be comfortable enough with Java to dive into your own ambitious programming projects—both on and off the Web.

If you're still new to programming, or if you have never written a program before, you might be wondering whether this is the right book to tackle. Because all the concepts in this book are illustrated with working programs, you'll be able to work your way through the subject regardless of your experience level. If you understand what variables, loops, and functions are, you'll be able to benefit from this book. You are among those who might want to read this book if any of the following rings true:

- You're a real whiz at HTML, you understand CGI programming in Perl, Visual Basic, or some other language, and you want to move on to the next level in Web page design.
- You had some BASIC or Pascal in school, have a grasp of what programming is, and you've heard Java is easy to learn, powerful, and cool.

- You've programmed in C and C++ for a few years, you keep hearing accolades for Java, and you want to see whether it lives up to its hype.

- You've heard that Java is great for Web programming and you want to see how well it can be used for other software development.

If you have never been introduced to object-oriented programming, which is the style of programming embodied by Java, you don't have to worry. This book assumes that you have no background in object-oriented design, and you'll get a chance to learn this groundbreaking development strategy as you're learning Java.

If you're a complete beginner in programming, this book might move a little fast for you. Java is a good language to start with, though, and if you take it slowly and work through all the examples, you can still pick up Java and start creating your own programs.

How This Book Is Structured

This book is most effective when read over the course of three weeks. During each week, you will read seven chapters that present concepts related to the Java language and the creation of applets and applications.

Conventions

Note

A *Note* presents interesting, sometimes technical, pieces of information related to the surrounding discussion.

Tip

A *Tip* offers advice or an easier way to do something.

Caution

A *Caution* advises you of potential problems and helps you to steer clear of disaster.

 NEW TERM A new term is accompanied by a New Term icon, with the new term in *italics*.

Text that you type and text that should appear on your screen is presented in monospace type:

```
It will look like this.
```

This font mimics the way text looks on your screen. Placeholders for variables and expressions appear in `monospace italic`.

The end of each lesson offers commonly asked questions about that day's subject matter with answers from the authors, a chapter-ending quiz to test your knowledge of the material, and two exercises that you can try on your own. Solutions to the exercises may be found on this book's official Web site at `http://www.java21days.com`.

WEEK 1

The Java Language

1

2

3

4

5

6

7

DAY 1

Getting Started with Java

> Big companies like IBM are embracing Java far more than most people real-
> ize. Half of IBM is busy recoding billions of lines of software to Java. The
> other half is working to make Java run well on all platforms, and great on all
> future platforms.
>
> —*PBS technology commentator Robert X. Cringely*

When Sun Microsystems first released the Java programming language in
1995, it was an inventive toy for the World Wide Web that had the potential to
be much more.

The word "potential" is an unusual compliment because it comes with an expiration date. Sooner or later, potential must be realized or new words are used in
its place such as "letdown," "waste," and "major disappointment to your mother
and me."

As you develop your skills during the 21 one-day tutorials in *Sams Teach
Yourself Java 2 in 21 Days, Third Edition*, you'll be in a good position to judge
whether the language has lived up to years of hype.

You'll also become a Java programmer with a lot of potential.

The Java Language

Now in its fifth major release with Java 2 version 1.4, Java appears to have lived up to the expectations that accompanied its arrival. More than two million programmers have learned the language and are using it in places such as NASA, IBM, Kaiser Permanente, ESPN, and New York's Museum of Modern Art. It's a standard part of the academic curriculum at many computer science departments around the world. More than 1,700 books have been written about it, according to the most recent *JavaWorld Magazine* count.

First used to create simple programs on World Wide Web pages, Java can be found today in each of the following places and many more:

- Web servers
- Relational databases
- Mainframe computers
- Telephones
- Orbiting telescopes
- Personal digital assistants
- Credit card–sized "smartcards"

Over the next 21 days, you will write Java programs that reflect how the language is being used in the 21st century. In some cases, this is very different from how it was originally envisioned.

Although Java remains useful for Web developers trying to enliven sites, it extends far beyond the Web browser. Java is now a popular general-purpose programming language.

History of the Language

The story of the Java language has become well known by this point. James Gosling and other developers at Sun were working on an interactive TV project in the mid-1990s when Gosling became frustrated with the language being used—C++, an object-oriented programming language developed by Bjarne Stroustrup at AT&T Bell Laboratories 10 years earlier as an extension of the C language.

Gosling holed up in his office and created a new language that was suitable for his project and addressed some of the things that frustrated him about C++.

Sun's interactive TV effort failed, but its work on the language had unforeseen applicability to a new medium that was becoming popular at the same time: the World Wide Web.

Java was released by Sun in fall 1995 through a free development kit that could be downloaded from the company's Web site. Although most of the language's features were extremely primitive compared with C++ (and Java today), Java programs called applets could be run as part of Web pages on the Netscape Navigator browser.

This functionality—the first interactive programming available on the Web—helped publicize the new language and attract several hundred thousand developers in its first six months.

Even after the novelty of Java Web programming wore off, the overall benefits of the language became clear and the programmers stuck around. Some surveys indicate that there are more professional Java programmers today than C++ programmers.

Introduction to Java

Java is an object-oriented, platform-neutral, secure language that was designed to be easier to learn than C++ and harder to misuse than C and C++.

Object-oriented programming (OOP) is a software development methodology in which a program is conceptualized as a group of objects that work together. Objects are created using templates called classes, and they contain data and the statements required to use that data. Java is completely object-oriented, as you'll see later today when you create your first class and use it to create objects.

Platform neutrality is the ability of a program to run without modification in different computing environments. Java programs are compiled into a format called bytecode that is run by any operating system, software, or device with a Java interpreter. You can create a Java program on a Windows XP machine that runs on a Linux Web server, Apple Mac using OS X, and Palm personal digital assistant. As long as a platform has a Java interpreter, it can run the bytecode.

Note
> This feature has typically been touted as a way to "write once, run anywhere" by Java admirers, including the authors of this book, on numerous occasions. However, practical experience with Java shows that there are always some inconsistencies and bugs in the implementation of the language on different platforms. For this reason, a more derisive slogan has been coined among some less-than-admirers: "write once, debug everywhere." Even so, the platform neutrality of Java makes it much easier to develop software that isn't locked into a single operating system or computing environment.

Though the ease of learning one language over another is always a point of contention among programmers, Java was designed to be easier than C++ primarily in the following ways:

- Java automatically takes care of memory allocation and deallocation, freeing programmers from this tedious and complex task.

- Java doesn't include pointers, a powerful feature of use primarily to experienced programmers that can be easily misused.
- Java includes only single inheritance in object-oriented programming.

The lack of pointers and the presence of automatic memory management are two of the key elements to the security of Java. Another is the way that Java programs running on Web pages are limited to a subset of the language to prevent malicious code from harming a user's computer.

Language features that could easily be employed for harmful purposes—such as the abilities to write data to a disk and delete files—cannot be executed by a program when it is run by a World Wide Web browser's Java interpreter.

For a longer discussion of Java's history and the strong points of the language, read Appendix A, "Choosing Java."

Selecting a Development Tool

Now that you've been introduced to Java as a spectator, it's time to put some of these concepts into play and create your first Java program.

If you work your way through the 21 days of this book, you'll become well versed in Java's capabilities, including graphics, file input and output, user-interface design, event handling, JavaBeans, and database connectivity. You will write programs that run on Web pages and others that run on your personal computer, Web servers, and other computing environments.

Before you can get started, you must have software on your computer that can be used to edit, compile, and run Java programs that use the most up-to-date version of the language: Java 2 version 1.4.

There are several popular integrated development environments for Java that support version 1.4, including Borland JBuilder, WebGain Visual Café, Sun ONE Studio, and IBM VisualAge for Java.

These are each well recommended by Java developers, but if you are learning to use these tools at the same time as you are learning Java, it can be a daunting task. Most integrated development environments are aimed primarily at experienced programmers who want to be more productive, not new people who are taking their first foray into a new language.

For this reason, unless you are comfortable with a development tool before picking up this book, you should probably use the simplest tool for Java development: the Java 2 Software Development Kit, which is free and can be downloaded from Sun's Java Web site at http://java.sun.com.

The Software Development Kit

Whenever Sun releases a new version of Java, it also makes a free development kit available over the Web to support that version. The current release is the Java 2 Software Development Kit, Standard Edition, Version 1.4.

Although the authors of a book like this have no business poking fun at long-winded titles, Sun has given its most popular Java development tool a name that's longer than most celebrity marriages.

For the sake of a few trees, in this book the language will usually be referred to simply as Java and the kit as SDK 1.4. You might see the kit referred to elsewhere as Java Development Kit 1.4.

If you will be using the Software Development Kit to create the tutorial programs in this book, you can find out how to get started with the software in Appendix B, "Using the Java 2 Software Development Kit." The appendix covers how to download and install the kit and use it to create a sample Java program.

Once you have a Java development tool on your computer that supports Java 2 version 1.4, you're ready to dive into the language.

Object-Oriented Programming

The biggest challenge for a new Java programmer is learning object-oriented programming at the same time as the Java language.

Although this might sound daunting if you are unfamiliar with this style of programming, think of it as a two-for-one discount for your brain. You will learn object-oriented programming by learning Java. There's no other way to make use of the language.

Object-oriented programming is an approach to building computer programs that mimics how objects are assembled in the physical world.

By using this style of development, you will be able to create programs that are more reusable, reliable, and understandable.

To get to that point, you first must explore how Java embodies the principles of object-oriented programming. The following topics are covered:

- Organizing programs into elements called classes
- Learning how these classes are used to create objects
- Defining a class by two aspects of its structure: how it should behave and what its attributes are

- Connecting classes to each other in a way that one class inherits functionality from another class
- Linking classes together through packages and interfaces

If you already are familiar with object-oriented programming, much of today's lesson will be a review for you. Even if you skim over the introductory material, you should create the sample program to get some experience developing, compiling, and running Java programs.

There are many different ways to conceptualize a computer program. One way is to think of a program as a series of instructions carried out in sequence, and this is commonly called *procedural programming*. Most programmers start by learning a procedural language such as Pascal or one of the many versions of BASIC.

Procedural languages mirror the way a computer carries out instructions, so the programs you write are tailored to the computer's manner of doing things. One of the first things a procedural programmer must learn is how to break down a problem into a series of simple steps.

Object-oriented programming looks at a computer program from a different angle, focusing on the task for which you are using the computer rather than the way a computer handles tasks.

In object-oriented programming, a computer program is conceptualized as a set of objects that work together to accomplish a task. Each object is a separate part of the program, interacting with the other parts in specific, highly controlled ways.

For a real-life example of object-oriented design, consider a stereo system. Most systems are built by hooking together a bunch of different objects, which are more commonly called components, such as the following:

- Speaker components play midrange and high-frequency sounds.
- Subwoofer components play low, bass-frequency sounds.
- Tuner components receive radio broadcast signals.
- CD player components read audio data from CDs.

These components are designed to interact with each other using standard input and output connectors. Even if you bought the speakers, subwoofer, tuner, and CD player from different companies, you can combine them to form a stereo system as long as they have standard connectors.

Object-oriented programming works under the same principle: You put together a program by combining newly created objects and existing objects in standard ways. Each object serves a specific role in the overall program.

 An *object* is a self-contained element of a computer program that represents a related group of features and is designed to accomplish specific tasks.

Objects and Classes

Object-oriented programming is modeled on the observation that in the physical world, objects are made up of many kinds of smaller objects. However, the capability to combine objects is only one aspect of object-oriented programming. Another important feature is the use of classes.

 A *class* is a template used to create an object. Every object created from the same class will have similar, if not identical, features.

Classes embody all features of a particular set of objects. When you write a program in an object-oriented language, you don't define individual objects. Instead, you define classes used to create those objects.

For example, you could create a Modem class that describes the features of all computer telephone modems. Most modems have the following common features:

- They use RS-232 protocol to communicate with other modems.
- They send and receive information.
- They dial phone numbers.

The Modem class serves as an abstract model for the concept of a modem. To actually have something concrete you can manipulate in a program, you must use the Modem class to create a Modem object. The process of creating an object from a class is called *instantiation*, which is why objects are also called *instances*.

A Modem class can be used to create lots of different Modem objects in a program, and each of these objects could have different features, such as the following:

- Some are internal modems and others are external modems.
- Some use the COM1 port and others use the COM2 port.
- Some have error control and others don't.

Even with these differences, two Modem objects still have enough in common to be recognizable as related objects. Figure 1.1 shows a Modem class and several objects created from that template.

FIGURE 1.1

The Modem class and several Modem objects.

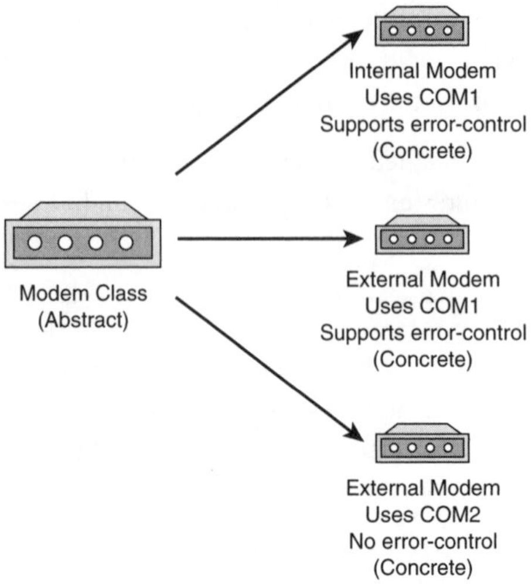

Modem Class
(Abstract)

Internal Modem
Uses COM1
Supports error-control
(Concrete)

External Modem
Uses COM1
Supports error-control
(Concrete)

External Modem
Uses COM2
No error-control
(Concrete)

Object Reuse

Here's another example: Using Java, you could create a class to represent all command buttons—those clickable boxes that show up on windows, dialog boxes, and other parts of a program's graphical user interface.

When the CommandButton class is developed, it could define these features:

- The text that identifies the button's purpose
- The size of the button
- Aspects of its appearance, such as whether it has a 3D shadow

The CommandButton class also could define how a button behaves, deciding the following things:

- Whether the button needs a single-click or a double-click to use
- Whether it should ignore mouse clicks entirely
- What it does when successfully clicked

After you define the CommandButton class, you can create instances of that button—in other words, CommandButton objects. The objects all take on the basic features of a clickable button as defined by the class, but each one could have a different appearance and slightly different behavior depending on what you need that object to do.

By creating a `CommandButton` class, you don't have to keep rewriting the code for each command button that you want to use in your programs. In addition, you can reuse the `CommandButton` class to create different kinds of buttons as you need them, both in this program and in others.

Note

> One of Java's standard classes, `javax.swing.JButton`, encompasses all the functionality of this hypothetical `CommandButton` example and more. You get a chance to work with it during Day 9, "Working with Swing."

When you write a Java program, you design and construct a set of classes. When your program runs, objects are instantiated from those classes and used as needed. Your task as a Java programmer is to create the right set of classes to accomplish what your program needs to accomplish.

Fortunately, you don't have to start from scratch. The Java language includes hundreds of classes that implement most of the basic functionality you will need. These classes are called the Java 2 class library, and they are installed along with a development tool such as SDK 1.4.

When you're talking about using the Java language, you're actually talking about using this class library and some standard keywords and operators that are recognized by Java compilers.

The class library handles numerous tasks, such as mathematical functions, text handling, graphics, sound, user interaction, and networking. Working with these classes is no different from working with classes you create.

For complicated Java programs, you might create a whole set of new classes with defined interactions among them. These classes could be used to form your own class library for use in other programs.

Reuse is one of the fundamental benefits of object-oriented programming.

Attributes and Behavior

A Java class consists of two distinct types of information: attributes and behavior.

Both of these are present in `VolcanoRobot`, a project you will implement today as a class. This project, a computer simulation of a volcanic exploration vehicle, is patterned after the Dante II robot used by NASA's Telerobotics Research program to do research inside volcanic craters.

Attributes of a Class of Objects

Attributes are the data that differentiate one object from another. They can be used to determine the appearance, state, and other qualities of objects that belong to that class.

A volcanic exploration vehicle could have the following attributes:

- Status—exploring, moving, returning home
- Speed—measured in miles per hour
- Temperature—measured in Fahrenheit degrees

In a class, attributes are defined by variables—places to store information in a computer program. Instance variables are attributes that have values that differ from one object to another.

NEW TERM   An *instance variable* defines an attribute of one particular object. The object's class defines what kind of attribute it is, and each instance stores its own value for that attribute. Instance variables also are called *object variables*.

Each class attribute has a single corresponding variable; you change that attribute in an object by changing the value of the variable.

For example, the VolcanoRobot class could define a speed instance variable. This must be an instance variable because each robot travels at different speeds depending on the circumstances of the environment. The value of a robot's speed instance variable could be changed to make the robot move more quickly or slowly.

Instance variables can be given a value when an object is created and then stay constant throughout the life of the object. They also can be given different values as the object is used in a running program.

For other variables, it makes more sense to have one value shared by all objects of that class. These attributes are called class variables.

NEW TERM   A *class variable* defines an attribute of an entire class. The variable applies to the class itself and to all of its instances, so only one value is stored no matter how many objects of that class have been created.

An example of a class variable for the VolcanoRobot class would be a variable that holds the current time. If an instance variable were created to hold the time, each object could have a different value for this variable, which could cause problems if the robots are supposed to perform tasks in conjunction with each other.

Using a class variable prevents this problem because all objects of that class share the same value automatically. Each VolcanoRobot object would have access to that variable.

Behavior of a Class of Objects

Behavior refers to the things that a class of objects can do to themselves and other objects. Behavior can be used to change the attributes of an object, receive information from other objects, and send messages to other objects asking them to perform tasks.

A volcano robot could have the following behavior:

- Check current temperature
- Begin a survey
- Report its current location

Behavior for a class of objects is implemented using methods.

NEW TERM   *Methods* are groups of related statements in a class of objects that handle a task. They are used to accomplish specific tasks on their own objects and on other objects, and they are used in the way that functions and subroutines are used in other programming languages.

Objects communicate with each other using methods. A class or an object can call methods in another class or object for many reasons, including the following:

- To report a change to another object
- To tell the other object to change something about itself
- To ask another object to do something

For example, two volcano robots could use methods to report their locations to each other and avoid collisions, and one robot could tell another to stop so it could pass by.

Just as there are instance and class variables, there are also instance and class methods. *Instance methods,* which are so common they're usually just called *methods*, are used when you are working with an object of the class. If a method makes a change to an individual object, it must be an instance method. *Class methods* apply to a class itself.

Creating a Class

To see classes, objects, attributes, and behavior in action, you will develop a `VolcanoRobot` class, create objects from that class, and work with them in a running program.

Note   The main purpose of this project is to explore object-oriented programming. You'll leearn more about Java programming syntax during Day 2, "The ABCs of Programming."

To begin creating a class, open the text editor you're using to create Java programs and create a new file. Enter the text of Listing 1.1, and save the file as `VolcanoRobot.java` in a folder you are using to work on programs from this book.

LISTING 1.1 The Full Text of `VolcanoRobot.java`

```
 1: class VolcanoRobot {
 2:     String status;
 3:     int speed;
 4:     float temperature;
 5:
 6:     void checkTemperature() {
 7:         if (temperature > 660) {
 8:             status = "returning home";
 9:             speed = 5;
10:         }
11:     }
12:
13:     void showAttributes() {
14:         System.out.println("Status: " + status);
15:         System.out.println("Speed: " + speed);
16:         System.out.println("Temperature: " + temperature);
17:     }
18: }
```

The `class` statement in line 2 of Listing 1.1 defines and names the `VolcanoRobot` class. Everything contained between the bracket on line 1 and the bracket on line 18 is part of this class.

The `VolcanoRobot` class contains three instance variables and two instance methods.

The instance variables are defined in lines 2–4:

```
String status;
int speed;
float temperature;
```

The variables are named `status`, `speed`, and `temperature`. Each will be used to store a different type of information:

- `status` holds a `String` object, a group of letters, numbers, punctuation, and other characters.
- `speed` holds an `int`, an integer value.
- `temperature` holds a `float`, a floating-point number.

`String` objects are created from the `String` class, which is part of the Java class library and can be used in any Java program.

> **Note** As you might have noticed from the use of `String` in this program, a class can use objects as instance variables.

The first instance method in the `VolcanoRobot` class is defined in lines 6–11:

```
void checkTemperature() {
    if (temperature > 660) {
        status = "returning home";
        speed = 5;
    }
}
```

Methods are defined in a manner similar to a class. They begin with a statement that names the method, the kind of information the method produces, and other things.

The `checkTemperature()` method is contained within the brackets on Lines 6 and 11 of Listing 1.1. This method can be called on a `VolcanoRobot` object to find out its temperature.

This method checks to see whether the object's `temperature` instance variable has a value greater than `660`. If it does, two other instance variables are changed:

- The `status` is changed to the text `"returning home"`, indicating that the temperature is too hot and the robot is heading back to its base.

- The `speed` is changed to 5. (Presumably, this is as fast as the robot can travel.)

The second instance method, `showAttributes()`, is defined in lines 13–17:

```
void showAttributes() {
    System.out.println("Status: " + status);
    System.out.println("Speed: " + speed);
    System.out.println("Temperature: " + temperature);
}
```

This method uses `System.out.println()` to display the values of three instance variables along with some text explaining what each value represents.

Running the Program

If you compiled the `VolcanoRobot` class at this point, you couldn't actually use it to simulate the actions of these exploratory robots. The class you have created defines what a `VolcanoRobot` object would be like if it were used in a program, but it doesn't use one of these objects yet.

There are two ways to put this VolcanoRobot class to use:

- Create a separate Java program that uses this class.

- Add a special class method called main() to the VolcanoRobot class so that it can be run as an application, and then use VolcanoRobot objects in that method.

The latter is done for this exercise. Open VolcanoRobot.java again in your text editor and insert a blank line directly above the last line of the program (line 18 in Listing 1.1).

In the space created by this blank line, insert the following class method:

```
public static void main(String[] arguments) {
    VolcanoRobot dante = new VolcanoRobot();
    dante.status = "exploring";
    dante.speed = 2;
    dante.temperature = 510;

    dante.showAttributes();
    System.out.println("Increasing speed to 3.");
    dante.speed = 3;
    dante.showAttributes();
    System.out.println("Changing temperature to 670.");
    dante.temperature = 670;
    dante.showAttributes();
    System.out.println("Checking the temperature.");
    dante.checkTemperature();
    dante.showAttributes();
}
```

With the main() method in place, the VolcanoRobot class can now be used as an application. Save the file as VolcanoRobot.java and compile the program.

If you are using the Software Development Kit, you can do the following to compile the program: Go to a command line or open a command-line window, open the folder where VolcanoRobot.java was saved, and then compile the program by typing the following command at the command line:

```
javac VolcanoRobot.java
```

Listing 1.2 shows the final VolcanoRobot.java source file.

Note If you encounter problems compiling or running any program in this book with SDK 1.4, you can find a copy of the source file and other related files on the book's official Web site at http://www.java21days.com.

LISTING 1.2   The Final Text of `VolcanoRobot.java`

```
 1: class VolcanoRobot {
 2:     String status;
 3:     int speed;
 4:     float temperature;
 5:
 6:     void checkTemperature() {
 7:         if (temperature > 660) {
 8:             status = "returning home";
 9:             speed = 5;
10:         }
11:     }
12:
13:     void showAttributes() {
14:         System.out.println("Status: " + status);
15:         System.out.println("Speed: " + speed);
16:         System.out.println("Temperature: " + temperature);
17:     }
18:
19:     public static void main(String[] arguments) {
20:         VolcanoRobot dante = new VolcanoRobot();
21:         dante.status = "exploring";
22:         dante.speed = 2;
23:         dante.temperature = 510;
24:
25:         dante.showAttributes();
26:         System.out.println("Increasing speed to 3.");
27:         dante.speed = 3;
28:         dante.showAttributes();
29:         System.out.println("Changing temperature to 670.");
30:         dante.temperature = 670;
31:         dante.showAttributes();
32:         System.out.println("Checking the temperature.");
33:         dante.checkTemperature();
34:         dante.showAttributes();
35:     }
36: }
```

After you have compiled the VolcanoRobot application, run the program.

Using the SDK, you can run the VolcanoRobot application by opening the folder containing the VolcanoRobot.class file at a command line and using this command:

```
java VolcanoRobot
```

When you run the VolcanoRobot class, the output should be the following:

```
Status: exploring
Speed: 2
Temperature: 510.0
```

```
Increasing speed to 3.
Status: exploring
Speed: 3
Temperature: 510.0
Changing temperature to 670.
Status: exploring
Speed: 3
Temperature: 670.0
Checking the temperature.
Status: returning home
Speed: 5
Temperature: 670.0
```

Using Listing 1.2 as a guide, the following things take place in the main() class method:

- Line 19—The main() method is created and named. All main() methods take this format, and you'll learn more about them during Day 5, "Creating Classes and Methods." For now, the most important thing to note is the static keyword. This indicates that the method is a class method.

- Line 20—A new VolcanoRobot object is created using that class as a template. The object is given the name dante.

- Lines 21–23—Three instance variables of the dante object are given values: status is set to the text "exploring", speed is set to 2, and temperature is set to 510.

- Line 25—On this line and several that follow, the showAttributes() method of the dante object is called. This method displays the current values of the instance variables status, speed, and temperature.

- Line 26—On this line and others that follow, a System.out.println() statement is used to display the text within the parentheses.

- Line 27—The speed instance variable is set to the value 3.

- Line 30—The temperature instance variable is set to the value 670.

- Line 33—The checkTemperature() method of the dante object is called. This method checks to see whether the temperature instance variable is greater than 660. If it is, status and speed are assigned new values.

Organizing Classes and Class Behavior

An introduction to object-oriented programming in Java isn't complete without looking at three more concepts: inheritance, interfaces, and packages.

These three things are all mechanisms for organizing classes and class behavior. The Java class library uses these concepts, and the classes you create for your own programs also need them.

Inheritance

Inheritance is one of the most crucial concepts in object-oriented programming, and it has a direct effect on how you design and write your own Java classes.

 Inheritance is a mechanism that enables one class to inherit all the behavior and attributes of another class.

Through inheritance, a class immediately has all the functionality of an existing class. Because of this, you must define only how the new class is different from an existing class.

With inheritance, all classes—those you create and those from the Java class library and other libraries—are arranged in a strict hierarchy.

New Term A class that inherits from another class is called a *subclass*. The class that gives the inheritance is called a *superclass*.

A class can have only one superclass, but each class can have an unlimited number of subclasses. Subclasses inherit all the attributes and behavior of their superclasses.

In practical terms, this means that if the superclass has behavior and attributes that your class needs, you don't have to redefine it or copy that code to have the same behavior and attributes. Your class automatically receives these things from its superclass, the superclass gets them from its superclass, and so on, all the way up the hierarchy. Your class becomes a combination of its own features and all the features of the classes above it in the hierarchy.

The situation is comparable to the way you inherited all kinds of things from your parents, such as your height, hair color, love of ska music, and reluctance to ask for directions. They inherited some of these things from their parents, who inherited from theirs, and backward through time to the Garden of Eden, Big Bang, or *insert personal cosmological belief here*.

Figure 1.2 shows the way a hierarchy of classes is arranged.

FIGURE 1.2

A class hierarchy.

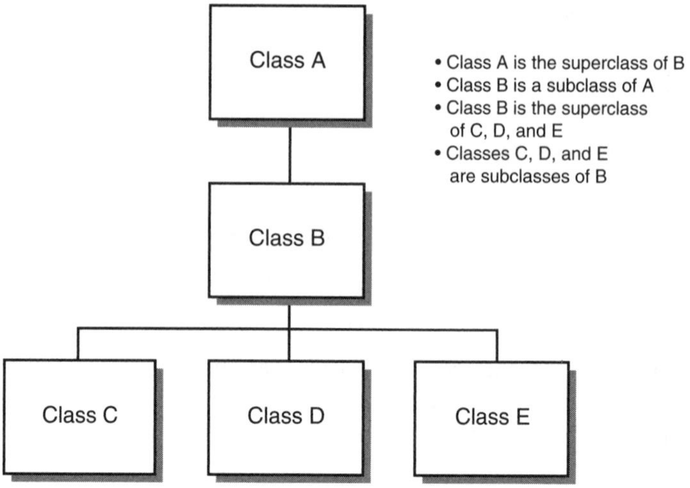

- Class A is the superclass of B
- Class B is a subclass of A
- Class B is the superclass of C, D, and E
- Classes C, D, and E are subclasses of B

At the top of the Java class hierarchy is the class `Object`—all classes inherit from this one superclass. `Object` is the most general class in the hierarchy, and it defines behavior inherited by all the classes in the Java class library. Each class further down the hierarchy becomes more tailored to a specific purpose. A class hierarchy defines abstract concepts at the top of the hierarchy. Those concepts become more concrete farther down the line of subclasses.

Often when you create a new class in Java, you will want all the functionality of an existing class with some modifications of your own creation. For example, you might want a version of a `CommandButton` that makes a sound when clicked.

To receive all the `CommandButton` functionality without doing any work to re-create it, you can define your class as a subclass of `CommandButton`. Your class then would automatically inherit behavior and attributes defined in `CommandButton`, as well as the behavior and attributes defined in the superclasses of `CommandButton`. All you have to worry about are the things that make your new class different from `CommandButton` itself. Subclassing is the mechanism for defining new classes as the differences between those classes and their superclass.

NEW TERM   *Subclassing* is the creation of a new class that inherits from an existing class. The only task in the subclass is to indicate the differences in behavior and attributes between itself and its superclass.

If your class defines an entirely new behavior and isn't a subclass of another class, you can inherit directly from the Object class. This allows it to fit neatly into the Java class hierarchy. In fact, if you create a class definition that doesn't indicate a superclass, Java assumes that the new class is inheriting directly from Object. The VolcanoRobot class you created earlier inherited from the Object class.

Creating a Class Hierarchy

If you're creating a large set of classes, it makes sense for your classes to inherit from the existing class hierarchy and to make up a hierarchy themselves. Organizing your classes this way takes significant planning, but the advantages include the following:

- Functionality that is common to multiple classes can be put into a superclass, which enables it to be used repeatedly in all classes below it in the hierarchy.

- Changes to a superclass automatically are reflected in all its subclasses, their subclasses, and so on. There is no need to change or recompile any of the lower classes; they receive the new information through inheritance.

For example, imagine that you have created a Java class to implement all the features of a volcanic exploratory robot. (This shouldn't take much imagination.)

The VolcanoRobot class is completed and works successfully, and everything is copacetic. Now you want to create a Java class called MarsRobot.

These two kinds of robots have similar features; both are research robots that work in hostile environments and conduct research. Your first impulse might be to open up the VolcanoRobot.java source file and copy a lot of it into a new source file called MarsRobot.java.

A better plan is to figure out the common functionality of MarsRobot and VolcanoRobot and organize it into a more general class hierarchy. This might be a lot of work just for the classes VolcanoRobot and MarsRobot, but what if you also want to add MoonRobot, UnderseaRobot, and DesertRobot? Factoring common behavior into one or more reusable superclasses significantly reduces the overall amount of work that must be done.

To design a class hierarchy that might serve this purpose, start at the top with the class Object, the pinnacle of all Java classes. The most general class to which these robots belong might be called Robot. A robot, generally, could be defined as a self-controlled exploration device. In the Robot class, you define only the behavior that qualifies something to be a device, self-controlled, and designed for exploration.

There could be two classes below Robot: WalkingRobot and DrivingRobot. The obvious thing that differentiates these classes is that one travels by foot and the other by wheel.

The behavior of walking robots might include bending over to pick something up, ducking, running, and the like. Driving robots would behave differently. Figure 1.3 shows what you have so far.

FIGURE 1.3

The basic Robot *hierarchy.*

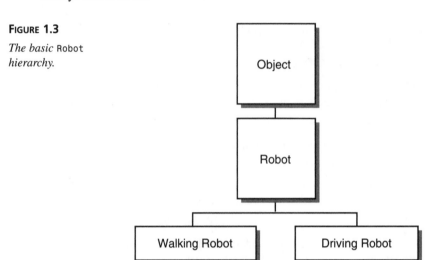

Now, the hierarchy can become even more specific. With WalkingRobot, you might have several classes: ScienceRobot, GuardRobot, SearchRobot, and so on. As an alternative, you could factor out still more functionality and have intermediate classes for TwoLegged and FourLegged robots, with different behaviors for each (see Figure 1.4).

Finally, the hierarchy is done, and you have a place for VolcanoRobot. It can be a subclass of ScienceRobot, which is a subclass of WalkingRobot, which is a subclass of Robot, which is a subclass of Object.

Where do qualities such as status, temperature, or speed come in? They come in at the place they fit into the class hierarchy most naturally. Because all robots have a need to keep track of the temperature of their environment, it makes sense to define temperature as an instance variable in Robot. All subclasses would have that instance variable as well. Remember that you need to define a behavior or attribute only once in the hierarchy, and it automatically is inherited by each subclass.

FIGURE 1.4

Two-legged and four-legged walking robots.

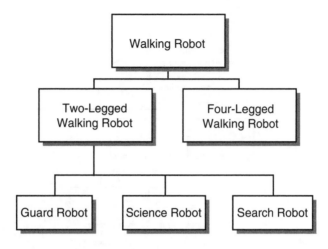

Note Designing an effective class hierarchy involves a lot of planning and revision. As you attempt to put attributes and behavior into a hierarchy, you're likely to find reasons to move some classes to different spots in the hierarchy. The goal is to reduce the number of repetitive features that are needed.

Inheritance in Action

Inheritance in Java works much more simply than it does in the real world. There are no executors of a will, judges, or courts of any kind required in Java.

When you create a new object, Java keeps track of each variable defined for that object and each variable defined for each superclass of the object. In this way, all of the classes combine to form a template for the current object, and each object fills in the information appropriate to its situation.

Methods operate similarly: A new object has access to all method names of its class and superclass. This is determined dynamically when a method is used in a running program. If you call a method of a particular object, the Java interpreter first checks the object's class for that method. If the method isn't found, the interpreter looks for it in the super-class of that class, and so on, until the method definition is found. This is illustrated in Figure 1.5.

Figure 1.5

How methods are located in a class hierarchy.

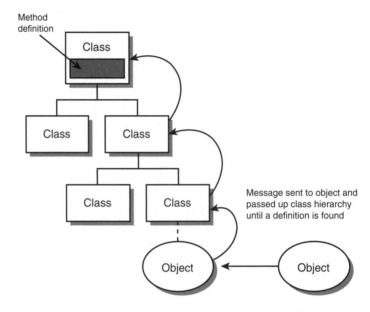

Things get complicated when a subclass defines a method that has the same name, return type, and arguments that a method defined in a superclass has. In this case, the method definition that is found first (starting at the bottom of the hierarchy and working upward) is the one that is used. Because of this, you can create a method in a subclass that prevents a method in a superclass from being used. To do this, you give the method with the same name, return type, and arguments as the method in the superclass. This procedure is called *overriding* (see Figure 1.6).

Single and Multiple Inheritance

Java's form of inheritance is called *single inheritance* because each Java class can have only one superclass (although any given superclass can have multiple subclasses).

In other object-oriented programming languages, such as C++, classes can have more than one superclass, and they inherit combined variables and methods from all those superclasses. This is called *multiple inheritance,* and it provides the means to create classes that encompass just about any imaginable behavior. However, it significantly complicates class definitions and the code needed to produce them. Java makes inheritance simpler by allowing only single inheritance.

FIGURE 1.6

Overriding methods.

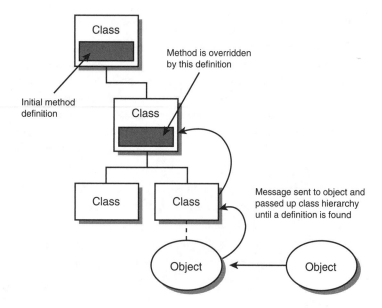

Interfaces

Single inheritance makes the relationship between classes and the functionality those classes implement easier to understand and to design. However, it also can be restrictive, especially when you have similar behavior that needs to be duplicated across different branches of a class hierarchy. Java solves the problem of shared behavior by using interfaces.

NEW TERM An *interface* is a collection of methods that indicate that a class has some behavior in addition to what it inherits from its superclasses. The methods included in an interface do not define this behavior; that task is left for the classes that implement the interface.

For example, the `Comparable` interface contains a method that compares two objects of the same class to see which one should appear first in a sorted list. Any class that implements this interface can determine the sorting order for objects of that class. This behavior would not be available to the class without the interface.

You learn about interfaces during Day 6, "Packages, Interfaces, and Other Class Features."

Packages

Packages in Java are a way of grouping related classes and interfaces. Packages enable groups of classes to be available only if they are needed, and they eliminate potential conflicts among class names in different groups of classes.

For now, there are only a few things you need to know:

- *The class libraries in Java are contained in a package called* java. The classes in the java package are guaranteed to be available in any Java implementation and are the only classes guaranteed to be available across different implementations. The java package contains smaller packages that define specific subsets of the Java language's functionality, such as standard features, file handling, graphical user interface support, and many other things. Classes in other packages such as sun often are available only in specific implementations.

- *By default, your Java classes have access to only the classes in* java.lang *(basic language features).* To use classes from any other package, you have to refer to them explicitly by package name or import them in your source file.

- *To refer to a class within a package, you must normally use the full package name.* For example, because the Color class is contained in the java.awt package, you refer to it in your programs with the notation java.awt.Color.

Summary

If today was your first exposure to object-oriented programming, it probably seems theoretical and a bit overwhelming.

That's understandable. When your brain has just been stuffed with OOP concepts and terminology for the first time, you may be worried that there's no room left for the Java lessons of the remaining 20 days.

At this point, you should have a basic understanding of classes, objects, attributes, and behavior. You also should be familiar with instance variables and methods. You'll be using these right away tomorrow.

The other aspects of object-oriented programming, such as inheritance and packages, will be covered in more detail on upcoming days.

To summarize today's material, here's a glossary of terms and concepts that were covered:

Class—A template for an object that contains variables to describe the object and methods to describe how the object behaves. Classes can inherit variables and methods from other classes.

Object—An instance of a class. Multiple objects that are instances of the same class have access to the same methods but often have different values for their instance variables.

Instance—The same thing as an object. Each object is an instance of some class.

Method—A group of statements in a class that defines how the class's objects will behave. Methods are analogous to functions in other languages but must always be located inside a class.

Class method—A method that operates on a class itself rather than on specific instances of a class.

Instance method—A method of an object that operates on that object by manipulating the values of its instance variables. Because instance methods are much more common than class methods, they often are just called methods.

Class variable—A variable that describes an attribute of a class instead of specific instances of the class.

Instance variable—A variable that describes an attribute of an instance of a class instead of the class itself.

Interface—A specification of abstract behavior that individual classes can then implement.

Package—A collection of classes and interfaces. Classes from packages other than `java.lang` must be explicitly imported or referred to by their full package and class name.

Subclass—A class further down the class hierarchy than another class, its superclass. Creating a new class that inherits from an existing one is often called subclassing. A class can have as many subclasses as necessary.

Superclass—A class further up the class hierarchy than another class, its subclass. A class can have only one superclass immediately above it, but that class also can have a superclass, and so on.

Q&A

Q In effect, methods are functions that are defined inside classes. If they look like functions and act like functions, why aren't they called functions?

A Some object-oriented programming languages do call them functions. (C++ calls them member functions.) Other object-oriented languages differentiate between functions inside and outside a body of a class or object because in those languages the use of the separate terms is important to understanding how each function works. Because the difference is relevant in other languages and because the term *method* is now in common use in object-oriented terminology, Java uses the term as well.

Q What's the distinction between instance variables and methods and their counterparts, class variables and methods?

A Almost everything you do in a Java program will involve instances (also called objects) rather than classes. However, some behavior and attributes make more sense if stored in the class itself rather than in the object. For example, the `Math` class in the `java.lang` package includes a class variable called `PI` that holds the approximate value of pi. This value does not change, so there's no reason different objects of that class would need their own individual copy of the `PI` variable. On the other hand, every `String` object contains a method called `length()` that reveals the number of characters in that `String`. This value can be different for each object of that class, so it must be an instance method.

Quiz

Review today's material by taking this three-question quiz.

Questions

1. What is another word for a class?

    (a.) Object

    (b.) Template

    (c.) Instance

2. When you create a subclass, what must you define about that class?

    (a.) It already is defined.

    (b.) Things that are different from its superclass.

    (c.) Everything about the class.

3. What does an instance method of a class represent?

    (a.) The attributes of that class.

    (b.) The behavior of that class.

    (c.) The behavior of an object created from that class.

Answers

1. (b.) A class is an abstract template used to create objects that are similar to each other.

2. (b.) You define how the subclass is different from its superclass. The things that are similar are already defined for you because of inheritance. Answer (a.) is technically correct, but if everything in the subclass is identical to the superclass, there's no reason to create the subclass at all.

3. (c.) Instance methods refer to a specific object's behavior. Class methods refer to the behavior of all objects belonging to that class.

Certification Practice

The following question is the kind of thing you could expect to be asked on a Java programming certification test. Answer it without looking at today's material.

Which of the following statements is true?

(a.) All objects created from the same class must be identical.

(b.) All objects created from the same class can be different from each other.

(c.) An object inherits attributes and behavior from the class used to create it.

(d.) A class inherits attributes and behavior from its subclass.

The answer is available on the book's Web site at http://www.java21days.com. Visit the Day 1 page and click the Certification Practice link.

Exercises

To extend your knowledge of the subjects covered today, try the following exercises:

- In the main() method of the VolcanoRobot class, create a second VolcanoRobot robot named virgil, set up its instance variables, and display them.

- Create an inheritance hierarchy for the pieces of a chess set. Decide where the instance variables color, startingPosition, forwardMovement, and sideMovement should be defined in the hierarchy.

Where applicable, exercise solutions are offered on the book's Web site at http://www.java21days.com.

DAY 2

The ABCs of Programming

A Java program is made up of classes and objects, which in turn are made up of methods and variables. Methods are made up of statements and expressions, which are made up of operators.

At this point, you might be afraid that Java is like the Russian nesting *matryoshka* dolls. Every one of those dolls seems to have a smaller doll inside it that is as intricate and detailed as its larger companion.

This day clears away the big dolls to reveal the smallest elements of Java programming. You'll leave classes, objects, and methods alone for a day and examine the basic things you can do in a single line of Java code.

The following subjects are covered:

- Java statements and expressions
- Variables and data types
- Constants

- Comments
- Literals
- Arithmetic
- Comparisons
- Logical operators

 Note Because Java was inspired by C and C++, much of the material in this day will look familiar to programmers who are well versed in those languages.

Statements and Expressions

All tasks that you want to accomplish in a Java program can be broken down into a series of statements.

NEW TERM A *statement* is a simple command, written in a programming language, that causes something to happen.

Statements represent a single action taken in a Java program. All of the following are simple Java statements:

```
int weight = 295;

System.out.println("Free the bound periodicals!");

song.duration = 230;
```

Some statements can convey a value, such as when you add two numbers together in a program or evaluate whether two variables are equal to each other. This kind of statement is called an expression.

NEW TERM An *expression* is a statement that results in the production of a value. The value can be stored for later use in the program, used immediately in another statement, or disregarded. The value produced by a statement is called its *return value*.

Some expressions produce a numerical return value, as in the example of adding two numbers together. Others produce a Boolean value—true or false—or can even produce a Java object. They are discussed later today.

Although many Java programs list one statement per line, this is a formatting decision that does not determine where one statement ends and another one begins. Each statement in Java is terminated with a semicolon character (;). A programmer can put more than one statement on a line, and it will compile successfully, as in the following example:

```
dante.speed = 2; dante.temperature = 510;
```

Statements in Java are grouped using the opening curly brace ({) and closing curly brace (}). A group of statements organized between these characters is called a *block* or a *block statement*, and you learn more about them during Day 4, "Lists, Logic, and Loops."

Variables and Data Types

In the `VolcanoRobot` application you created during Day 1, "Getting Started with Java," you used variables to keep track of information.

NEW TERM   A *variable* is a place where information can be stored while a program is running. The value can be changed at any point in the program—hence the name.

To create a variable, you must give it a name and identify what type of information it will store. You also can give a variable an initial value at the same time you create it.

There are three kinds of variables in Java: instance variables, class variables, and local variables. *Instance variables*, as you learned yesterday, are used to define an object's attributes. *Class variables* define the attributes of an entire class of objects and apply to all instances of it.

Local variables are used inside method definitions or even smaller blocks of statements within a method. You can use them only while the method or block is being executed by the Java interpreter. They cease to exist afterward.

Although all three kinds of variables are created in much the same way, class and instance variables are used in a different manner than local variables. You will learn about local variables today and cover instance and class variables during Day 3, "Working with Objects."

 Note   Unlike other languages, Java does not have *global variables*, variables that can be used in all parts of a program. Instance and class variables communicate information from one object to another, so they replace the need for global variables.

Creating Variables

Before you can use a variable in a Java program, you must create the variable by declaring its name and the type of information it will store. The type of information is listed first, followed by the name of the variable. The following are all examples of variable declarations:

```
int loanLength;

String message;

boolean gameOver;
```

Note

> You learn about variable types later today, but you might be familiar with the `int` type represents integers, `String` is a special variable type for storing text, and `boolean` is used for true/false values.

Local variables can be declared at any place inside a method, just like any other Java statement, but they must be declared before they can be used. The normal place for variable declarations is immediately after the statement that names and identifies the method.

In the following example, three variables are declared at the top of a program's `main()` method:

```
public static void main(String[] arguments) {
    int total;
    String reportTitle;
    boolean active;
}
```

If you are creating several variables of the same type, you can declare all of them in the same statement by separating the variable names with commas. The following statement creates three `String` variables named `street`, `city`, and `state`:

```
String street, city, state;
```

Variables can be assigned a value when they are created by using an equal sign (=) followed by the value. The following statements create new variables and give them initial values:

```
int zipCode = 02134;

int box = 350;

boolean pbs = true;

String name = "Zoom", city = "Boston", state = "MA";
```

As the last statement indicates, you can assign values to multiple variables of the same type by using commas to separate them.

You must give values to local variables before you use them in a program, or the program won't compile successfully. For this reason, it is good practice to give initial values to all local variables.

Instance and class variable definitions are given an initial value depending on the type of information they hold, as in the following:

- Numeric variables: `0`
- Characters: `'\0'`

- Booleans: `false`
- Objects: `null`

Naming Variables

Variable names in Java must start with a letter, an underscore character (_), or a dollar sign ($). They cannot start with a number. After the first character, variable names can include any combination of letters or numbers.

> **Note**
>
> In addition, the Java language uses the Unicode character set, which includes the standard character set plus thousands of other sets to represent international alphabets. Accented characters and other symbols can be used in variable names so long as they have a Unicode character number.

When naming a variable and using it in a program, it's important to remember that Java is case sensitive—the capitalization of letters must be consistent. Because of this, a program can have a variable named X and another named x—and Rose is not a rose is not a ROSE.

In programs in this book and elsewhere, Java variables are given meaningful names that include several words joined together. To make it easier to spot the words, the following rule of thumb is used:

- The first letter of the variable name is lowercase.
- Each successive word in the variable name begins with a capital letter.
- All other letters are lowercase.

The following variable declarations follow this rule of naming:

```
Button loadFile;

int localAreaCode;

boolean quitGame;
```

Variable Types

In addition to a name, a variable declaration must include the type of information being stored. The type can be any of the following:

- One of the basic data types
- The name of a class or interface
- An array

You learn how to declare and use array variables on Day 4. Today's lesson focuses on the other variable types.

Data Types

There are eight basic variable types for the storage of integers, floating-point numbers, characters, and Boolean values. These often are called *primitive types* because they are built-in parts of the Java language rather than objects, which makes them more efficient to use. These data types have the same size and characteristics no matter what operating system and platform you're on, unlike some data types in other programming languages.

There are four data types you can use to store integers. Which one you use depends on the size of the integer, as indicated in Table 2.1.

TABLE 2.1 Integer Types

Type	Size	Values That Can Be Stored
byte	8 bits	–128 to 127
short	16 bits	–32,768 to 32,767
int	32 bits	–2,147,483,648 to 2,147,483,647
long	64 bits	–9,223,372,036,854,775,808 to 9,223,372,036,854,775,807

All these types are signed, which means that they can hold either positive or negative numbers. The type used for a variable depends on the range of values it might need to hold. None of these integer variables can reliably store a value that is too large or too small for its designated variable type, so you should take care when designating the type.

Another type of number that can be stored is a floating-point number, which has the type float or double. *Floating-point numbers* are numbers with a decimal point. The float type should be sufficient for most uses because it can handle any number from 1.4E-45 to 3.4E+38. If not, the double type can be used for more precise numbers ranging from 4.9E-324 to 1.7E+308.

The char type is used for individual characters, such as letters, numbers, punctuation, and other symbols.

The last of the eight basic data types is boolean. As you have learned, this data type holds either true or false in Java.

All these variable types are listed in lowercase, and you must use them as such in programs. There are classes with the same names as some of these data types but different capitalization—for example, Boolean and Char. These have different functionality in a Java program, so you can't use them interchangeably. Tomorrow you will see how to use these special classes.

Class Types

In addition to the eight basic data types, a variable can have a class as its type, as in the following examples:

```
String lastName = "Hopper";

Color hair;

VolcanoRobot vr;
```

2

When a variable has a class as its type, the variable refers to an object of that class or one of its subclasses.

The last example in the preceding list, VolcanoRobot vr;, creates a variable named vr that is reserved for a VolcanoRobot object, although the object itself might not exist yet. You'll learn tomorrow how to associate objects with variables.

Referring to a superclass as a variable type is useful when the variable might be one of several different subclasses. For example, consider a class hierarchy with a CommandButton superclass and three subclasses: RadioButton, CheckboxButton, and ClickButton. If you create a CommandButton variable called widget, it could refer to a RadioButton, CheckboxButton, or ClickButton object.

Declaring a variable of type Object means that it can be associated with any kind of object.

 Note   Java does not have anything comparable to the typedef statement from C and C++. To declare a new type in Java, a new class is declared, and variables can use that class as their type.

Assigning Values to Variables

After a variable has been declared, a value can be assigned to it with the assignment operator, which is an equal sign (=). The following are examples of assignment statements:

```
idCode = 8675309;

accountOverdrawn = false;
```

Constants

Variables are useful when you need to store information that can be changed as a program runs.

If the value should never change during a program's runtime, you can use a special type of variable called a constant.

NEW TERM   A *constant,* which is also called a *constant variable,* is a variable with a value that never changes. This might seem like an oxymoron, given the meaning of the word *variable.*

Constants are useful in defining shared values for all methods of an object—in other words, for giving meaningful names to unchanging values that an entire object must have access to. In Java you can create constants for all kinds of variables: instance, class, and local.

To declare a constant, use the `final` keyword before the variable declaration and include an initial value for that variable, as in the following:

```
final float PI = 3.141592;

final boolean DEBUG = false;

final int PENALTY = 25;
```

In the preceding statements, the names of the constants are capitalized: `PI`, `DEBUG`, and `PENALTY`. This isn't required, but it is a convention used by many Java programmers—Sun uses it in the Java class library. The capitalization makes it clear that you're using a constant.

Constants can be handy for naming various states of an object and then testing for those states. Suppose you have a program that takes directional input from the numeric keypad on the keyboard—push 8 to go up, 4 to go left, and so on. You can define those values as constant integers:

```
final int LEFT = 4;
final int RIGHT = 6;
final int UP = 8;
final int DOWN = 2;
```

Constants often make a program easier to understand. To illustrate this point, consider which of the following two statements is more informative as to its function?

```
this.direction = 4;

this.direction = LEFT;
```

Comments

One of the most important ways to improve the readability of your program is to use comments.

NEW TERM   *Comments* are information included in a program strictly for the benefit of humans trying to figure out what's going on in the program. The Java compiler ignores comments entirely when preparing a runnable version of a Java source file.

There are three different kinds of comments you can use in Java programs, and you can use each of them at your discretion. The first way to add a comment to a program is to precede it with two slash characters (//). Everything from the slashes to the end of the line is considered a comment and is disregarded by a Java compiler, as in the following statement:

```
int creditHours = 3; // set up credit hours for course
```

If you need to make a comment that takes up more than one line, you can begin it with the text /* and end it with the text */. Everything between these two delimiters is considered a comment, as in the following:

```
/* This program occasionally deletes all files on
your hard drive and renders it completely unusable
when you spellcheck a document. */
```

The final type of comment is meant to be computer-readable as well as human-readable. If you begin a comment with the text /** (instead of /*) and end it with */, the comment is interpreted to be official documentation on how the class and its public methods work.

This kind of comment then can be read by utilities such as the javadoc tool included with the SDK. The javadoc program uses official comments to create a set of HTML records that document the program, its class hierarchy, and its methods.

All the official documentation on Java's class library comes from javadoc-style comments. You can view current Java 2 documentation on the Web at http://java.sun.com/j2se/1.4/docs/api/.

Literals

In addition to variables, you can use literals in a Java statement.

NEW TERM A *literal* is any number, text, or other information that directly represents a value.

Literal is a programming term that essentially means that what you type is what you get. The following assignment statement uses a literal:

```
int year = 2000;
```

The literal is 2000 because it directly represents the integer value 2000. Numbers, characters, and strings all are examples of literals.

Although the meaning and usage of literals will seem intuitive most of the time, Java has some special types of literals that represent different kinds of numbers, characters, strings, and Boolean values.

Number Literals

Java has several integer literals. The number 4, for example, is an integer literal of the int variable type. It also can be assigned to byte and short variables because the number is small enough to fit into those integer types. An integer literal larger than an int can hold is automatically considered to be of the type long. You also can indicate that a literal should be a long integer by adding the letter L (L or l) to the number. For example, the following statement treats the value 4 as a long integer:

```
pennyTotal = pennyTotal + 4L;
```

To represent a negative number as a literal, prepend a minus sign (-) to the literal, as in -45.

If you need to use a literal integer with octal numbering, prepend a 0 to the number. For example, the octal number 777 would be the literal 0777. Hexadecimal integers are used as literals by prepending the number with 0x, as in 0x12 or 0xFF.

> **Note**
>
> Octal and hexadecimal numbering systems are convenient for many advanced programming purposes but are unlikely to be needed by beginners. *Octal numbers* are a base-8 numbering system, which means they can represent only the values 0 through 7 as a single digit. The eighth number in octal is 10 (or 010 as a Java literal).
>
> *Hexadecimal* is a base-16 numbering system that can represent each of 16 numbers as a single digit. The letters A through F represent the last six digits, so the first 16 numbers are 0, 1, 2, 3, 4, 5, 6, 7, 8, 9, A, B, C, D, E, F.
>
> The octal and hexadecimal systems are better suited for certain tasks in programming than the normal decimal system is. If you have ever used HTML to set a Web page's background color, you might have used hexadecimal numbers.

Floating-point literals use a period character (.) for the decimal point, as you would expect. The following statement uses a literal to set up a double variable:

```
double myGPA = 2.25;
```

All floating-point literals are considered of the double variable type instead of float. To specify a literal of float, add the letter F (F or f) to the literal, as in the following example:

```
float piValue = 3.1415927F;
```

You can use exponents in floating-point literals by using the letter e or E followed by the exponent, which can be a negative number. The following statements use exponential notation:

```
double x = 12e22;
double y = 19E-95;
```

Boolean Literals

The Boolean values `true` and `false` also are literals. These are the only two values you can use when assigning a value to a `boolean` variable type or using a Boolean in a statement in other ways.

If you have used another language, such as C, you might expect that a value of 1 is equivalent to `true`, and 0 is equivalent to `false`. This isn't the case in Java; you must use the values `true` or `false` to represent Boolean values. The following statement sets a `boolean` variable:

```
boolean chosen = true;
```

Note that the literal `true` does not have quotation marks around it. If it did, the Java compiler would assume that it was a string of characters.

Character Literals

Character literals are each expressed by a single character surrounded by single quotation marks, such as `'a'`, `'#'`, and `'3'`. You might be familiar with the ASCII character set, which includes 128 characters, including letters, numerals, punctuation, and other characters useful in computing. Java supports thousands of additional characters through the 16-bit Unicode standard.

Some character literals represent characters that are not readily printable or accessible through a keyboard. Table 2.2 lists the special codes that can represent these special characters as well as characters from the Unicode character set. The letter d in the octal, hex, and Unicode escape codes represents a number or a hexadecimal digit (a–f or A–F).

TABLE 2.2 Character Escape Codes

Escape	Meaning
\n	New line
\t	Tab
\b	Backspace
\r	Carriage return
\f	Formfeed
\\	Backslash
\'	Single quotation mark
\"	Double quotation mark
\d	Octal
\xd	Hexadecimal
\ud	Unicode character

> **Note**
>
> C and C++ programmers should note that Java does not include character codes for \a (bell) or \v (vertical tab).

String Literals

The final literal that you can use in a Java program represents strings of characters. A string in Java is an object rather than being a basic data type, and strings are not stored in arrays, as they are in languages such as C.

Because string objects are real objects in Java, methods are available to combine strings, modify strings, and determine whether two strings have the same value.

String literals consist of a series of characters inside double quotation marks, as in the following statements:

```
String quitMsg = "Are you sure you want to quit?";

String password = "swordfish";
```

Strings can include the character escape codes listed previously in Table 2.2, as shown here:

```
String example = "Socrates asked, \"Hemlock is poison?\"";

System.out.println("Sincerely,\nMillard Fillmore\n");

String title = "Sams Teach Yourself Rebol While You Sleep\u2122"
```

In the last example above, the Unicode code sequence \u2122 produces a ™ symbol on systems that have been configured to support Unicode.

> **Caution**
>
> Most users in English-speaking countries aren't likely to see Unicode characters when they run Java programs. Although Java supports the transmission of Unicode characters, the user's system also must support it for the characters to be displayed. Unicode support provides a way to encode its characters for systems that support the standard. Although Java 1.0 supported only the Latin subset of Unicode, Java 1.1 and subsequent versions support the display of any Unicode character that can be represented by a host font.
>
> For more information about Unicode, visit the Unicode Consortium Web site at http://www.unicode.org.

Although string literals are used in a manner similar to other literals in a program, they are handled differently behind the scenes.

With a string literal, Java stores that value as a String object. You don't have to explicitly create a new object, as you must do when working with other objects, so they are as easy to work with as basic data types. Strings are unusual in this respect—none of the basic types is stored as an object when used. You learn more about strings and the `String` class later today and tomorrow.

Expressions and Operators

An *expression* is a statement that can convey a value. Some of the most common expressions are mathematical, such as in the following source code example:

```
int x = 3;
int y = x;
int z = x * y;
```

All three of these statements can be considered expressions; they convey values that can be assigned to variables. The first assigns the literal 3 to the variable x. The second assigns the value of the variable x to the variable y. The multiplication operator * is used to multiply the x and y integers, and the expression produces the result of the multiplication. This result is stored in the z integer.

An expression can be any combination of variables, literals, and operators. They also can be method calls because methods can send back a value to the object or class that called the method.

The value conveyed by an expression is called a *return value*, as you have learned. This value can be assigned to a variable and used in many other ways in your Java programs.

Most of the expressions in Java use operators such as *.

 Operators are special symbols used for mathematical functions, some types of assignment statements, and logical comparisons.

Arithmetic

There are five operators used to accomplish basic arithmetic in Java. These are shown in Table 2.3.

TABLE 2.3 Arithmetic Operators

Operator	Meaning	Example
+	Addition	3 + 4
-	Subtraction	5 - 7
*	Multiplication	5 * 5
/	Division	14 / 7
%	Modulus	20 % 7

Each operator takes two operands, one on either side of the operator. The subtraction operator can also be used to negate a single operand, which is equivalent to multiplying that operand by -1.

One thing to be mindful of when using division is the kind of numbers you're dealing with. If you store a division operation into an integer, the result will be truncated to the next lower whole number because the int data type can't handle floating-point numbers. As an example, the expression 31 / 9 results in 3 if stored as an integer.

Modulus division, which uses the % operator, produces the remainder of a division operation. Using 31 % 9 results in 4 because 31 divided by 9, with the whole number result of 3, leaves a remainder of 4.

Note that many arithmetic operations involving integers produce an int regardless of the original type of the operands. If you're working with other numbers, such as floating-point numbers or long integers, you should make sure that the operands have the same type you're trying to end up with.

Listing 2.1 is an example of simple arithmetic in Java.

LISTING 2.1   The Source File Weather.java

```
 1: class Weather {
 2:     public static void main(String[] arguments) {
 3:         float fah = 86;
 4:         System.out.println(fah + " degrees Fahrenheit is ...");
 5:         // To convert Fahrenheit into Celsius
 6:         // Begin by subtracting 32
 7:         fah = fah - 32;
 8:         // Divide the answer by 9
 9:         fah = fah / 9;
10:         // Multiply that answer by 5
11:         fah = fah * 5;
12:         System.out.println(fah + " degrees Celsius\n");
13:
14:         float cel = 33;
15:         System.out.println(cel + " degrees Celsius is ...");
16:         // To convert Celsius into Fahrenheit
17:         // Begin by multiplying it by 9
18:         cel = cel * 9;
19:         // Divide the answer by 5
20:         cel = cel / 5;
21:         // Add 32 to that answer
22:         cel = cel + 32;
23:         System.out.println(cel + " degrees Fahrenheit");
24:     }
25: }
```

If you run this Java application, it produces the following output:

```
86.0 degrees Fahrenheit is ...
30.0 degrees Celsius

33.0 degrees Celsius is ...
91.4 degrees Fahrenheit
```

In lines 3–12 of this Java application, a temperature in Fahrenheit is converted to Celsius using the arithmetic operators:

- Line 3—The floating-point variable fah is created with a value of 86.
- Line 4—The current value of fah is displayed.
- Line 5—The first of several comments for the benefit of people trying to figure out what the program is doing. The Java compiler ignores these comments.
- Line 7—fah is set to its current value minus 32.
- Line 9—fah is set to its current value divided by 9.
- Line 11—fah is set to its current value multiplied by 5.
- Line 12—Now that fah has been converted to a Celsius value, fah is displayed again.

A similar thing happens in lines 14–23 but in the reverse direction. A temperature in Celsius is converted to Fahrenheit.

This program also makes use of System.out.println() in several statements. The System.out.println() method is used in an application to display strings and other information to the standard output device, which usually is the screen.

System.out.println() takes a single argument within its parentheses: a string. To present more than one variable or literal as the argument to println(), you can use the + operator to combine these elements into a single string.

There's also a System.out.print() method, which displays a string without terminating it with a newline character. You can call print() instead of println() to display several strings on the same line.

You learn more about this use of the + operator later today.

More About Assignment

Assigning a value to a variable is an expression because it produces a value. Because of this feature, you can string assignment statements together the following way:

```
x = y = z = 7;
```

In this statement, all three variables end up with the value of 7.

The right side of an assignment expression is always calculated before the assignment takes place. This makes it possible to use an expression statement as in the following code example:

```
int x = 5;
x = x + 2;
```

In the expression x = x + 2, the first thing that happens is that x + 2 is calculated. The result of this calculation, 7, is then assigned to x.

Using an expression to change a variable's value is an extremely common task in programming. There are several operators used strictly in these cases. Table 2.4 shows these assignment operators and the expressions they are functionally equivalent to.

TABLE 2.4 Assignment Operators

Expression	Meaning
x += y	x = x + y
x -= y	x = x - y
x *= y	x = x * y
x /= y	x = x / y

Caution

These shorthand assignment operators are functionally equivalent to the longer assignment statements for which they substitute. If either side of your assignment statement is part of a complex expression, however, there are cases where the operators are not equivalent. For example, if x equals 20 and y equals 5, the following two statements do not produce the same value:

```
x = x / y + 5;
x /= y + 5;
```

When in doubt, simplify an expression by using multiple assignment statements and don't use the shorthand operators.

Incrementing and Decrementing

Another common task is to add or subtract 1 from an integer variable. There are special operators for these expressions, which are called increment and decrement operations.

NEW TERM   *Incrementing* a variable means to add 1 to its value, and *decrementing* a variable means to subtract 1 from its value.

The increment operator is ++, and the decrement operator is --. These operators are placed immediately after or immediately before a variable name, as in the following code example:

```
int x = 7;
x++;
```

In this example, the statement x++ increments the x variable from 7 to 8.

These increment and decrement operators can be placed before or after a variable name, and this affects the value of expressions that involve these operators.

NEW TERM   Increment and decrement operators are called *prefix* operators if listed before a variable name and *postfix* operators if listed after a name.

In a simple expression such as standards--;, using a prefix or postfix operator produces the same result, making the operators interchangeable. When increment and decrement operations are part of a larger expression, however, the choice between prefix and postfix operators is important.

Consider the following two expressions:

```
int x, y, z;
x = 42;
y = x++;
z = ++x;
```

These two expressions yield very different results because of the difference between prefix and postfix operations. When you use postfix operators, as in y=x++, y receives the value of x before it is incremented by one. When using prefix operators, as in z = ++x, x is incremented by one before the value is assigned to z. The end result of this example is that y equals 42, z equals 44, and x equals 44.

If you're still having some trouble figuring this out, here's the example again with comments describing each step:

```
int x, y, z; // x, y, and z are all declared
x = 42;      // x is given the value of 42
y = x++;     // y is given x's value (42) before it is incremented
             // and x is then incremented to 43
z = ++x;     // x is incremented to 44, and z is given x's value
```

Caution

As with shorthand operators, increment and decrement operators in extremely complex expressions can produce results you might not have expected. The concept of "assigning x to y before x is incremented" isn't precisely right because Java evaluates everything on the right side of an expression before assigning its value to the left side. Java stores some values before handling an expression in order to make postfix work the way it has been described in this section. When you're not getting the results you expect from a complex expression that includes prefix and postfix operators, try to break the expression into multiple statements to simplify it.

Comparisons

Java has several operators for making comparisons among variables, variables and literals, or other types of information in a program. These operators are used in expressions that return Boolean values of `true` or `false`, depending on whether the comparison being made is true or not. Table 2.5 shows the comparison operators.

TABLE 2.5 Comparison Operators

Operator	Meaning	Example
==	Equal	x == 3
!=	Not equal	x != 3
<	Less than	x < 3
>	Greater than	x > 3
<=	Less than or equal to	x <= 3
>=	Greater than or equal to	x >= 3

The following example shows a comparison operator in use:

```
boolean hip;
int age = 33;
hip = age < 25;
```

The expression `age < 25` produces a result of either `true` or `false`, depending on the value of the integer `age`. Because `age` is 33 in this example (which is not less than 25), `hip` is given the Boolean value `false`.

Logical Operators

Expressions that result in Boolean values, such as comparison operations, can be combined to form more complex expressions. This is handled through logical operators, which are used for the logical combinations AND, OR, XOR, and logical NOT.

For AND combinations, the & or && logical operators are used. When two Boolean expressions are linked by the & or && operators, the combined expression returns a `true` value only if both Boolean expressions are true.

Consider this example, taken directly from the film *Harold & Maude*:

```
boolean unusual = (age < 21) & (girlfriendAge > 78);
```

This expression combines two comparison expressions: `age < 21` and `girlfriendAge > 78`. If both of these expressions are true, the value `true` is assigned to the variable `unusual`. In any other circumstance, the value `false` is assigned to `unusual`.

The difference between `&` and `&&` lies in how much work Java does on the combined expression. If `&` is used, the expressions on either side of the `&` are evaluated no matter what. If `&&` is used and the left side of the `&&` is false, the expression on the right side of the `&&` never is evaluated.

For OR combinations, the `|` or `||` logical operators are used. These combined expressions return a `true` value if either Boolean expression is true.

Consider this *Harold & Maude*–inspired example:

```
boolean unusual = (grimThoughts > 10) || (girlfriendAge > 78);
```

This expression combines two comparison expressions: `grimThoughts > 10` and `girlfriendAge > 78`. If either of these expressions is true, the value `true` is assigned to the variable `unusual`. Only if both of these expressions are false will the value `false` be assigned to `unusual`.

Note the use of `||` instead of `|`. Because of this usage, if `grimThoughts > 10` is true, `unusual` is set to `true` and the second expression is never evaluated.

The XOR combination has one logical operator, `^`. This results in a `true` value only if both Boolean expressions it combines have opposite values. If both are true or both are false, the `^` operator produces a `false` value.

The NOT combination uses the `!` logical operator followed by a single expression. It reverses the value of a Boolean expression the same way that a minus symbol reverses the positive or negative sign on a number. For example, if `age < 30` returns a `true` value, `!(age < 30)` returns a `false` value.

These logical operators can seem completely illogical when encountered for the first time. You get plenty of chances to work with them in subsequent days, especially on Day 5, "Creating Classes and Methods."

Operator Precedence

When more than one operator is used in an expression, Java has an established precedence hierarchy to determine the order in which operators are evaluated. In many cases, this precedence determines the overall value of the expression.

For example, consider the following expression:

```
y = 6 + 4 / 2;
```

The y variable receives the value 5 or the value 8, depending on which arithmetic operation is handled first. If the 6 + 4 expression comes first, y has the value of 5. Otherwise, y equals 8.

In general, the order from first to last is the following:

- Increment and decrement operations
- Arithmetic operations
- Comparisons
- Logical operations
- Assignment expressions

If two operations have the same precedence, the one on the left in the actual expression is handled before the one on the right. Table 2.6 shows the specific precedence of the various operators in Java. Operators farther up the table are evaluated first.

TABLE 2.6 Operator Precedence

Operator	Notes
. [] ()	Parentheses (()) are used to group expressions; a period (.) is used for access to methods and variables within objects and classes (discussed tomorrow); square brackets ([]) are used for arrays. (This operator is discussed later in the week.)
++ -- ! ~ instanceof	The instanceof operator returns true or false based on whether the object is an instance of the named class or any of that class's subclasses (discussed tomorrow).
new (type)expression	The new operator is used for creating new instances of classes; () in this case are for casting a value to another type. (You learn about both of these tomorrow.)
* / %	Multiplication, division, modulus.
+ -	Addition, subtraction.
<< >> >>>	Bitwise left and right shift.
< > <= >=	Relational comparison tests.
== !=	Equality.
&	AND
^	XOR
|	OR

TABLE 2.6   Continued

Operator	Notes
&&	Logical AND
||	Logical OR
? :	Shorthand for `if...then...else` (discussed on Day 4).
= += -= *= /= %= ^=	Various assignments.
&= |= <<= >>= >>>=	More assignments.

Returning to the expression y = 6 + 4 / 2, Table 2.6 shows that division is evaluated before addition, so the value of y will be 8.

To change the order in which expressions are evaluated, place parentheses around the expressions that should be evaluated first. You can nest one set of parentheses inside another to make sure that expressions are evaluated in the desired order; the innermost parenthetic expression is evaluated first.

The following expression results in a value of 5:

```
y = (6 + 4) / 2
```

The value of 5 is the result because 6 + 4 is calculated first, and then the result, 10, is divided by 2.

Parentheses also can improve the readability of an expression. If the precedence of an expression isn't immediately clear to you, adding parentheses to impose the desired precedence can make the statement easier to understand.

String Arithmetic

As stated earlier today, the + operator has a double life outside the world of mathematics. It can concatenate two or more strings.

NEW TERM   *Concatenate* means to link two things together. For reasons unknown, it is the verb of choice when describing the act of combining two strings—winning out over *paste, glue, affix, combine, link,* and *conjoin.*

In several examples, you have seen statements that look something like this:

```
String firstName = "Raymond";
System.out.println("Everybody loves " + firstName);
```

These two lines result in the display of the following text:

```
Everybody loves Raymond
```

The + operator combines strings, other objects, and variables to form a single string. In the preceding example, the literal `Everybody loves` is concatenated to the value of the `String` object `firstName`.

Working with the concatenation operator is easy in Java because of the way the operator can handle any variable type and object value as if it were a string. If any part of a concatenation operation is a `String` or `String` literal, all elements of the operation will be treated as if they were strings:

```
System.out.println(4 + " score and " + 7 + " years ago.");
```

This produces the output text `4 score and 7 years ago.`, as if the integer literals 4 and 7 were strings.

There is also a shorthand += operator to add something to the end of a string. For example, consider the following expression:

```
myName += " Jr.";
```

This expression is equivalent to the following:

```
myName = myName + " Jr.";
```

In this example, it changes the value of `myName`, which might be something like `Efrem Zimbalist`, by adding `Jr.` at the end (`Efrem Zimbalist Jr.`).

Summary

Anyone who pops open a set of *matryoshka* dolls has to be a bit disappointed to reach the smallest doll in the group. Advances in microengineering should enable Russian artisans to create ever smaller and smaller dolls, until someone reaches the subatomic threshold and is declared the winner.

You have reached Java's smallest nesting doll today, but it shouldn't be a letdown. Using statements and expressions enables you to begin building effective methods, which make effective objects and classes possible.

Today you learned about creating variables and assigning values to them; using literals to represent numeric, character, and string values; and working with operators. Tomorrow you put these skills to use as you develop objects for Java programs.

To summarize today's material, Table 2.7 lists the operators you learned about. Be a doll and look them over carefully.

TABLE 2.7 Operator Summary

Operator	Meaning
+	Addition
-	Subtraction
*	Multiplication
/	Division
%	Modulus
<	Less than
>	Greater than
<=	Less than or equal to
>=	Greater than or equal to
==	Equal
!=	Not equal
&&	Logical AND
||	Logical OR
!	Logical NOT
&	AND
|	OR
^	XOR
=	Assignment
++	Increment
--	Decrement
+=	Add and assign
-=	Subtract and assign
*=	Multiply and assign
/=	Divide and assign
%=	Modulus and assign

Q&A

Q What happens if you assign an integer value to a variable that is too large for that variable to hold?

A Logically, you might think that the variable is converted to the next larger type, but this isn't what happens. Instead, an *overflow* occurs—a situation in which the number wraps around from one size extreme to the other. An example of overflow would be a `byte` variable that goes from `127` (acceptable value) to `128` (unacceptable). It would wrap around to the lowest acceptable value, which is `-128`, and start counting upward from there. Overflow isn't something you can readily deal with in a program, so you should be sure to give your variables plenty of living space in their chosen data type.

Q Why does Java have all these shorthand operators for arithmetic and assignment? It's really hard to read that way.

A Java's syntax is based on C++, which is based on C (more Russian nesting doll behavior). C is an expert language that values programming power over readability, and the shorthand operators are one of the legacies of that design priority. Using them in a program isn't required because effective substitutes are available, so you can avoid them in your own programming, if you prefer.

Quiz

Review today's material by taking this quiz.

Questions

1. Which of the following is a valid value for a `boolean` variable?

    (a.) `"false"`

    (b.) `false`

    (c.) `10`

2. Which of these is not a convention for naming variables in Java?

    (a.) After the first word in the variable name, each successive word begins with a capital letter.

    (b.) The first letter of the variable name is lowercase.

    (c.) All letters are capitalized.

3. Which of these data types holds numbers from -32,768 to 32,767?

    (a.) `char`

    (b.) `byte`

    (c.) `short`

Answers

1. (b.) In Java, a `boolean` can be only `true` or `false`. If you put quotation marks around the value, it will be treated like a `String` rather than one of the two `boolean` values.

2. (c.) Only constant names are capitalized to make them stand out from other variables.

3. (c.)

Certification Practice

The following question is the kind of thing you could expect to be asked on a Java programming certification test. Answer it without looking at today's material.

Which of the following data types can hold the number 3,000,000,000 (three billion)?

(a.) `short, int, long, float`

(b.) `int, long, float`

(c.) `long, float`

(d.) `byte`

The answer is available on this book's Web site at `http://www.java21days.com`. Visit the Day 2 page and click the Certification Practice link.

Exercises

To extend your knowledge of the subjects covered today, try the following exercises:

- Create a program that calculates how much a $14,000 investment would be worth if it increased in value by 40% during the first year, lost $1,500 in value the second year, and increased 12% in the third year.

- Write a program that displays two numbers and uses the / and % operators to display the result and remainder after they are divided. Use the \t character escape code to separate the result and remainder in your output.

Where applicable, exercise solutions are offered on this book's Web site at `http://www.java21days.com`.

DAY 3

Working with Objects

Java is a heavily object-oriented programming language. When you do work in Java, you use objects to get the job done. You create objects, modify them, move them around, change their variables, call their methods, and combine them with other objects. You develop classes, create objects out of those classes, and use them with other classes and objects.

Today you will work extensively with objects. The following topics are covered:

- Creating objects (also called instances)
- Testing and modifying class and instance variables in those objects
- Calling an object's methods
- Converting objects and other types of data from one class to another

Creating New Objects

When you write a Java program, you define a set of classes. As you learned during Day 1, "Getting Started with Java," classes are templates that are used to create objects. These objects, which are also called instances, are self-contained elements of a program with related features and data. For the most part, you use the class merely to create instances and then work with those instances. In this section, therefore, you will learn how to create a new object from any given class.

Remember strings from yesterday? You learned that using a *string literal* (a series of characters enclosed in double quotation marks) creates a new instance of the class String with the value of that string.

The String class is unusual in that respect. Although it's a class, there's an easy way to create instances of that class using a literal. To create instances of other classes, the new operator is used.

Note

> What about the literals for numbers and characters—don't they create objects, too? Actually, they don't. The primitive data types for numbers and characters create numbers and characters, but for efficiency they actually aren't objects. You can put object wrappers around them, though, if you need to treat them like objects (which you learn to do on Day 5, "Creating Classes and Methods").

Using new

To create a new object, you use the new operator with the name of the class you want to create an instance of, followed by parentheses:

```
String name = new String();
URL address = new URL("http://www.java21days.com");
VolcanoRobot robbie = new VolcanoRobot();
```

The parentheses are important; don't leave them off. The parentheses can be empty, in which case the most simple, basic object is created, or the parentheses can contain arguments that determine the initial values of instance variables or other initial qualities of that object.

The following examples show objects being created with arguments:

```
Random seed = new Random(6068430714);

Point pt = new Point(0,0);
```

The number and type of arguments you can use inside the parentheses with new are defined by the class itself using a special method called a *constructor*. (You'll learn more about constructors later today.) If you try to create a new instance of a class with the wrong number or type of arguments (or if you give it no arguments and it needs some), you get an error when you try to compile your Java program.

Here's an example of creating different types of objects with different numbers and types of arguments: the StringTokenizer class, part of the java.util package, divides a string into a series of shorter strings called *tokens*.

A string is divided into tokens by applying some kind of character or characters as a delimiter. For example, the text "02/20/67" could be divided into three tokens—02, 20, and 67—using the slash character ("/") as a delimiter.

Listing 3.1 is a Java program that creates StringTokenizer objects by using new in two different ways and then displays each token the objects contain.

LISTING 3.1   The Full Text of ShowTokens.java

```
 1: import java.util.StringTokenizer;
 2:
 3: class ShowTokens {
 4:
 5:     public static void main(String[] arguments) {
 6:         StringTokenizer st1, st2;
 7:
 8:         String quote1 = "VIZY 3 -1/16";
 9:         st1 = new StringTokenizer(quote1);
10:         System.out.println("Token 1: " + st1.nextToken());
11:         System.out.println("Token 2: " + st1.nextToken());
12:         System.out.println("Token 3: " + st1.nextToken());
13:
14:         String quote2 = "NPLI@9 27/32@3/32";
15:         st2 = new StringTokenizer(quote2, "@");
16:         System.out.println("\nToken 1: " + st2.nextToken());
17:         System.out.println("Token 2: " + st2.nextToken());
18:         System.out.println("Token 3: " + st2.nextToken());
19:     }
20: }
```

When you compile and run the program, the output should resemble the following:

```
Token 1: VIZY
Token 2: 3
Token 3: -1/16

Token 1: NPLI
Token 2: 9 27/32
Token 3: 3/32
```

In this example, two different StringTokenizer objects are created using different arguments to the constructor listed after new.

The first instance (line 9) uses `new StringTokenizer()` with one argument, a `String` object named `quote1`. This creates a `StringTokenizer` object that uses the default delimiters: blank spaces, tab, newline, carriage return, or formfeed characters.

If any of these characters is contained in the string, it is used to divide the tokens. Because the `quote1` string contains spaces, these are used as delimiters dividing each token. Lines 10–12 display the values of all three tokens: `VIZY`, `3`, and `-1/16`.

The second `StringTokenizer` object in this example has two arguments when it is constructed in line 14—a `String` object named `quote2` and an at-sign character (`"@"`). This second argument indicates that the `"@"` character should be used as the delimiter between tokens. The `StringTokenizer` object created in line 15 contains three tokens: `NPLI`, `9 27/32`, and `3/32`.

What new Does

Several things happen when you use the `new` operator—the new instance of the given class is created, memory is allocated for it, and a special method defined in the given class is called. This special method is called a constructor.

NEW TERM   A *constructor* is a special method for creating and initializing a new instance of a class. A constructor initializes the new object and its variables, creates any other objects that the object needs, and performs any other operations that the object needs to initialize itself.

Multiple constructor definitions in a class can each have a different number, or type, of arguments. When you use `new`, you can specify different arguments in the argument list, and the correct constructor for those arguments will be called. Multiple constructor definitions are what enabled the `ShowTokens()` class in the previous example to accomplish different things with the different uses of the `new` operator. When you create your own classes, you can define as many constructors as you need to implement the behavior of the class.

A Note on Memory Management

If you are familiar with other object-oriented programming languages, you might wonder whether the `new` statement has an opposite that destroys an object when it is no longer needed.

Memory management in Java is dynamic and automatic. When you create a new object, Java automatically allocates the right amount of memory for that object. You don't have to allocate any memory for objects explicitly. Java does it for you.

Because Java memory management is automatic, you do not need to de-allocate the memory an object uses when you're done using the object. Under most circumstances, when you are finished with an object you have created, Java will be able to determine that the object no longer has any live references to it. (In other words, the object won't be assigned to any variables still in use or stored in any arrays.)

As a program runs, Java periodically looks for unused objects and reclaims the memory that those objects are using. This process is called *garbage collection*, and it's entirely automatic. You don't have to explicitly free the memory taken up by an object; you just have to make sure you're not still holding onto an object you want to get rid of.

Accessing and Setting Class and Instance Variables

3

At this point, you could create your own object with class and instance variables defined in it, but how do you work with those variables? Easy! Class and instance variables are used in largely the same manner as the local variables you learned about yesterday. You can use them in expressions, assign values to them in statements, and the like. You just refer to them slightly differently from how you refer to regular variables in your code.

Getting Values

To get to the value of an instance variable, you use dot notation, with which an instance or class variable name has two parts: a reference to an object or class on the left side of the dot and a variable on the right side of the dot.

 Dot notation is a way to refer to an object's instance variables and methods using a dot (.) operator.

For example, if you have an object named myCustomer, and that object has a variable called orderTotal, you refer to that variable's value like this:

```
myCustomer.orderTotal;
```

This form of accessing variables is an expression (that is, it returns a value), and both sides of the dot are also expressions. That means you can nest instance variable access. If the orderTotal instance variable itself holds an object, and that object has its own instance variable called layaway, you could refer to it like this:

```
myCustomer.orderTotal.layaway;
```

Dot expressions are evaluated from left to right, so you start with myCustomer's variable orderTotal, which points to another object with the variable layaway. You end up with the value of that layaway variable.

Changing Values

Assigning a value to that variable is equally easy; just tack on an assignment operator to the right side of the expression:

```
myCustomer.orderTotal.layaway = true;
```

This example sets the value of the layaway variable to true.

Listing 3.2 is an example of a program that tests and modifies the instance variables in a Point object. Point, a part of the java.awt package, refers to a coordinate point with x and y values.

LISTING **3.2**   The Full Text of SetPoints.java

```
 1: import java.awt.Point;
 2:
 3: class SetPoints {
 4:
 5: public static void main(String[] arguments) {
 6:     Point location = new Point(4, 13);
 7:
 8:     System.out.println("Starting location:");
 9:     System.out.println("X equals " + location.x);
10:     System.out.println("Y equals " + location.y);
11:
12:     System.out.println("\nMoving to (7, 6)");
13:     location.x = 7;
14:     location.y = 6;
15:
16:     System.out.println("\nEnding location:");
17:     System.out.println("X equals " + location.x);
18:     System.out.println("Y equals " + location.y);
19:     }
20: }
```

When you run this application, the output should be the following:

```
Starting location:
X equals 4
Y equals 13

Moving to (7, 6)

Ending location:
X equals 7
Y equals 6
```

In this example, you first create an instance of Point where x equals 4 and y equals 13 (line 6). Lines 9 and 10 display these individual values using dot notation. Lines 13 and 14 change the values of x to 7 and y to 6, respectively. Finally, lines 17 and 18 display the values of x and y again to show how they have changed.

Class Variables

Class variables, as you have learned, are variables that are defined and stored in the class itself. Their values apply to the class and all its instances.

With instance variables, each new instance of the class gets a new copy of the instance variables that the class defines. Each instance then can change the values of those instance variables without affecting any other instances. With class variables, only one copy of that variable exists. Changing the value of that variable changes it for all instances of that class.

You define class variables by including the static keyword before the variable itself. For example, consider the following partial class definition:

```
class FamilyMember {
    static String surname = "Mendoza";
    String name;
    int age;
}
```

Each instance of the class FamilyMember has its own values for name and age. The class variable surname, however, has only one value for all family members: "Mendoza". Change the value of surname, and all instances of FamilyMember are affected.

 Note

Calling these static variables refers to one of the meanings of the word *static*: fixed in one place. If a class has a static variable, every object of that class has the same value for that variable.

To access class variables, you use the same dot notation as with instance variables. To retrieve or change the value of the class variable, you can use either the instance or the name of the class on the left side of the dot. Both lines of output in this example display the same value:

```
FamilyMember dad = new FamilyMember();
System.out.println("Family's surname is: " + dad.surname);
System.out.println("Family's surname is: " + FamilyMember.surname);
```

Because you can use an instance to change the value of a class variable, it's easy to become confused about class variables and where their values are coming from. Remember that the value of a class variable affects all its instances. For this reason, it's a good idea to use the name of the class when you refer to a class variable. It makes your code easier to read and makes strange results easier to debug.

Calling Methods

Calling a method in an object is similar to referring to its instance variables: Dot notation is used. The object whose method you're calling is on the left side of the dot, and the name of the method and its arguments are on the right side of the dot:

```
myCustomer.addToOrder(itemNumber, price, quantity);
```

Note that all methods must have parentheses after them, even if the method takes no arguments:

```
myCustomer.cancelAllOrders();
```

Listing 3.3 shows an example of calling some methods defined in the String class. Strings include methods for string tests and modification, similar to what you would expect in a string library in other languages.

LISTING 3.3   The Full Text of CheckString.java

```
 1: class CheckString {
 2:
 3:     public static void main(String[] arguments) {
 4:         String str = "Nobody ever went broke by buying IBM";
 5:         System.out.println("The string is: " + str);
 6:         System.out.println("Length of this string: "
 7:             + str.length());
 8:         System.out.println("The character at position 5: "
 9:             + str.charAt(5));
10:         System.out.println("The substring from 26 to 32: "
11:             + str.substring(26, 32));
12:         System.out.println("The index of the character v: "
13:             + str.indexOf('v'));
14:         System.out.println("The index of the beginning of the "
15:             + "substring \"IBM\": " + str.indexOf("IBM"));
16:         System.out.println("The string in upper case: "
17:             + str.toUpperCase());
18:     }
19: }
```

The following is displayed on your system's standard output device when you run the program:

```
The string is: Nobody ever went broke by buying IBM
Length of this string: 36
The character at position 5: y
```

```
The substring from 26 to 32: buying
The index of the character v: 8
The index of the beginning of the substring "IBM": 33
The string in upper case: NOBODY EVER WENT BROKE BY BUYING IBM
```

In line 4, you create a new instance of `String` by using a string literal. The remainder of the program simply calls different string methods to do different operations on that string:

- Line 5 prints the value of the string you created in line 4: `"Nobody ever went broke by buying IBM"`.

- Line 7 calls the `length()` method in the new `String` object. This string has 36 characters.

- Line 9 calls the `charAt()` method, which returns the character at the given position in the string. Note that string positions start at position `0` rather than `1`, so the character at position `5` is y.

- Line 11 calls the `substring()` method, which takes two integers indicating a range and returns the substring with those starting and ending points. The `substring()` method can also be called with only one argument, which returns the substring from that position to the end of the string.

- Line 13 calls the `indexOf()` method, which returns the position of the first instance of the given character (here, `'v'`). Character literals are surrounded by single quotation marks; if double quotation marks had surrounded the v in line 13, the literal would be considered a `String`.

- Line 15 shows a different use of the `indexOf()` method, which takes a string argument and returns the index of the beginning of that string.

- Line 17 uses the `toUpperCase()` method to return a copy of the string in all uppercase.

Nesting Method Calls

A method can return a reference to an object, a primitive data type, or no value at all. In the `CheckString` program, all the methods called on the `String` object `str` returned values that were displayed; for example, the `charAt()` method returned a character at a specified position in the string.

The value returned by a method also can be stored in a variable:

```
String label = "From";
String upper = label.toUpperCase();
```

In the preceding example, the `String` object `upper` contains the value returned by calling `label.toUpperCase()`—the text `"FROM"`, an uppercase version of `"From"`.

If the method returns an object, you can call the methods of that object in the same statement. This makes it possible for you to nest methods as you would variables.

Earlier today, you saw an example of a method called with no arguments:

```
myCustomer.cancelAllOrders();
```

If the `cancelAllOrders()` method returns an object, you can call methods of that object in the same statement:

```
myCustomer.cancelAllOrders().talkToManager();
```

This statement calls the `talkToManager()` method, which is defined in the object returned by the `cancelAllOrders()` method of the `myCustomer` object.

You can combine nested method calls and instance variable references, as well. In the next example, the `putOnLayaway()` method is defined in the object stored by the `orderTotal` instance variable, which itself is part of the `myCustomer` object:

```
myCustomer.orderTotal.putOnLayaway(itemNumber, price, quantity);
```

`System.out.println()`, the method you've been using in all program examples to display information, is an example of nesting variables and methods.

The `System` class, part of the `java.lang` package, describes behavior specific to the system on which Java is running. `System.out` is a class variable that contains an instance of the class `PrintStream`. This `PrintStream` object represents the standard output of the system, which is normally the screen but can be redirected to a printer or file. `PrintStream` objects have a `println()` method that sends a string to that output stream.

Class Methods

Class methods, like class variables, apply to the class as a whole and not to its instances. Class methods are commonly used for general utility methods that might not operate directly on an instance of that class but do fit with that class conceptually. For example, the `String` class contains a class method called `valueOf()`, which can take one of many different types of arguments (integers, Booleans, other objects, and so on). The `valueOf()` method then returns a new instance of `String` containing the string value of the argument. This method doesn't operate directly on an existing instance of `String`, but getting a string from another object or data type is definitely a `String`-like operation, and it makes sense to define it in the `String` class.

Class methods can also be useful for gathering general methods together in one place (the class). For example, the `Math` class, defined in the `java.lang` package, contains a large set of mathematical operations as class methods; there are no instances of the class

Math, but you still can use its methods with numeric or Boolean arguments. For example, the class method Math.max() takes two arguments and returns the larger of the two. You don't need to create a new instance of Math; it can be called anywhere you need it, as in the following:

```
int maximumPrice = Math.max(firstPrice, secondPrice);
```

Dot notation is used to call a class method. As with class variables, you can use either an instance of the class or the class itself on the left side of the dot. For the same reasons noted in the discussion on class variables, however, using the name of the class makes your code easier to read. The last two lines in this example produce the same result—the string 5:

```
String s, s2;
s = "item";
s2 = s.valueOf(5);
s2 = String.valueOf(5);
```

References to Objects

As you work with objects, it's important to understand references.

NEW TERM   A *reference* is an address that indicates where an object's variables and methods are stored.

You aren't actually using objects when you assign an object to a variable or pass an object to a method as an argument. You aren't even using copies of the objects. Instead, you're using references to those objects.

To better illustrate the difference, Listing 3.4 shows how references work.

LISTING 3.4   The Full Text of ReferencesTest.java

```
 1: import java.awt.Point;
 2:
 3: class ReferencesTest {
 4:     public static void main (String[] arguments) {
 5:         Point pt1, pt2;
 6:         pt1 = new Point(100, 100);
 7:         pt2 = pt1;
 8:
 9:         pt1.x = 200;
10:         pt1.y = 200;
11:         System.out.println("Point1: " + pt1.x + ", " + pt1.y);
12:         System.out.println("Point2: " + pt2.x + ", " + pt2.y);
13:     }
14: }
```

Here is this program's output:

```
Point1: 200, 200
Point2: 200, 200
```

The following takes place in the first part of this program:

- Line 5—Two Point variables are created.

- Line 6—A new Point object is assigned to pt1.

- Line 7—The value of pt1 is assigned to pt2.

Lines 9–12 are the tricky part. The x and y variables of pt1 are both set to 200, and then all variables of pt1 and pt2 are displayed onscreen.

You might expect pt1 and pt2 to have different values. However, the output shows this is not the case. As you can see, the x and y variables of pt2 also were changed, even though nothing in the program explicitly changes them. This happens because line 7 creates a reference from pt2 to pt1, instead of creating pt2 as a new object copied from pt1.

pt2 is a reference to the same object as pt1; this is shown in Figure 3.1. Either variable can be used to refer to the object or to change its variables.

FIGURE 3.1

References to objects.

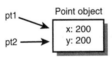

If you wanted pt1 and pt2 to refer to separate objects, separate new Point() statements could be used on lines 6 and 7 to create separate objects, as shown in the following:

```
pt1 = new Point(100, 100);
pt2 = new Point(100, 100);
```

References in Java become particularly important when arguments are passed to methods. You learn more about this later today.

Note

There are no explicit pointers or pointer arithmetic in Java, as there are in C and C++. By using references and Java arrays, however, most pointer capabilities are duplicated without many of their drawbacks.

Casting and Converting Objects and Primitive Types

One thing you discover quickly about Java is how finicky it is about the information it will handle. Like Morris, the perpetually hard-to-please cat in the 9Lives™ Cat Food commercials, Java expects things to be a certain way and won't put up with alternatives.

When you are sending arguments to methods or using variables in expressions, you must use variables of the right data types. If a method requires an `int`, the Java compiler responds with an error if you try to send a `float` value to the method. Likewise, if you're setting up one variable with the value of another, they must be of the same type.

Note

> There is one area where Java's compiler is decidedly un–Morris-like: `Strings`. String handling in `println()` methods, assignment statements, and method arguments is simplified by the concatenation operator (+). If any variable in a group of concatenated variables is a string, Java treats the whole thing as a `String`. This makes the following possible:
>
> ```
> float gpa = 2.25F;
> System.out.println("Honest, dad, my GPA is a " + (gpa+1.5));
> ```

3

Sometimes you'll have a value in your Java program that isn't the right type for what you need. It might be the wrong class or the wrong data type, such as a `float` when you need an `int`.

You use casting to convert a value from one type to another.

NEW TERM *Casting* is the process of producing a new value that has a different type than its source. The word's meaning is similar to that regarding acting, where a character on a TV show can be recast with another actor after a salary dispute or an unfortunate public lewdness arrest.

Although the concept of casting is reasonably simple, the usage is complicated by the fact that Java has both primitive types (such as `int`, `float`, and `boolean`) and object types (`String`, `Point`, `ZipFile`, and the like). There are three forms of casts and conversions to talk about in this section:

- Casting between primitive types, such as `int` to `float`, or `float` to `double`
- Casting from an instance of a class to an instance of another class
- Casting primitive types to objects and then extracting primitive values from those objects

When discussing casting, it can be easier to think in terms of sources and destinations. The source is the variable being cast into another type. The destination is the result.

Casting Primitive Types

Casting between primitive types enables you to convert the value of one type to another primitive type. It most commonly occurs with the numeric types, and there's one primitive type that can never be used in a cast. Boolean values must be either `true` or `false` and cannot be used in a casting operation.

In many casts between primitive types, the destination can hold larger values than the source, so the value is converted easily. An example would be casting a `byte` into an `int`. Because a `byte` holds values from –128 to 127 and an `int` holds from –2100000 to 2100000, there's more than enough room to cast a `byte` into an `int`.

You can often automatically use a `byte` or a `char` as an `int`; you can use an `int` as a `long`, an `int` as a `float`, or anything as a `double`. In most cases, because the larger type provides more precision than the smaller, no loss of information occurs as a result. The exception is casting integers to floating-point values; casting an `int` or a `long` to a `float`, or a `long` to a `double`, can cause some loss of precision.

 Note

> A character can be used as an `int` because each character has a corresponding numeric code that represents its position in the character set. If the variable i has the value 65, the cast `(char)i` produces the character value `'A'`. The numeric code associated with a capital A is 65, according to the ASCII character set, and Java adopted this as part of its character support.

You must use an explicit cast to convert a value in a large type to a smaller type, or else converting that value might result in a loss of precision. Explicit casts take the following form:

```
(typename)value
```

In the preceding example, *typename* is the name of the data type you're converting to, such as `short`, `int`, or `float`. *value* is an expression that results in the value of the source type. For example, the value of x is divided by the value of y, and the result is cast into an `int` in the following expression:

```
(int)(x / y);
```

Note that because the precedence of casting is higher than that of arithmetic, you have to use parentheses here; otherwise, the value of x would be cast into an `int` first and then divided by y, which could easily produce a different result.

Casting Objects

Instances of classes also can be cast into instances of other classes, with one restriction: The source and destination classes must be related by inheritance; one class must be a subclass of the other.

Analogous to converting a primitive value to a larger type, some objects might not need to be cast explicitly. In particular, because a subclass contains all the same information as its superclass, you can use an instance of a subclass anywhere a superclass is expected.

For example, consider a method that takes two arguments, one of type Object and another of type Window. You can pass an instance of any class for the Object argument because all Java classes are subclasses of Object. For the Window argument, you can pass in its subclasses, such as Dialog, FileDialog, and Frame.

This is true anywhere in a program, not just inside method calls. If you had a variable defined as class Window, you could assign objects of that class or any of its subclasses to that variable without casting.

This is true in the reverse, and you can use a superclass when a subclass is expected. There is a catch, however: Because subclasses contain more behavior than their super-classes, there's a loss in precision involved. Those superclass objects might not have all the behavior needed to act in place of a subclass object. For example, if you have an operation that calls methods in objects of the class Integer, using an object of class Number won't include many methods specified in Integer. Errors occur if you try to call methods that the destination object doesn't have.

To use superclass objects where subclass objects are expected, you must cast them explicitly. You won't lose any information in the cast, but you gain all the methods and variables that the subclass defines. To cast an object to another class, you use the same operation as for primitive types:

```
(classname)object
```

In this case, classname is the name of the destination class, and object is a reference to the source object. Note that casting creates a reference to the old object of the type classname; the old object continues to exist as it did before.

The following example casts an instance of the class VicePresident to an instance of the class Employee; VicePresident is a subclass of Employee with more information, which here defines that the VicePresident has executive washroom privileges:

```
Employee emp = new Employee();
VicePresident veep = new VicePresident();
emp = veep; // no cast needed for upward use
veep = (VicePresident)emp; // must cast explicitly
```

Casting one object is necessary whenever you use Java2D graphics operations. You must cast a `Graphics` object to a `Graphics2D` object before you can draw onscreen. The following example uses a `Graphics` object called `screen` to create a new `Graphics2D` object called `screen2D`:

```
Graphics2D screen2D = (Graphics2D)screen;
```

`Graphics2D` is a subclass of `Graphics`, and both are in the `java.awt` package. You explore the subject fully during Day 13, "Color, Fonts, and Graphics."

In addition to casting objects to classes, you also can cast objects to interfaces, but only if an object's class or one of its superclasses actually implements the interface. Casting an object to an interface means that you can call one of that interface's methods even if that object's class does not actually implement that interface.

Converting Primitive Types to Objects and Vice Versa

One thing you can't do under any circumstance is cast from an object to a primitive data type, or vice versa.

Primitive types and objects are very different things in Java, and you can't automatically cast between the two or use them interchangeably.

As an alternative, the `java.lang` package includes classes that correspond to each primitive data type: `Float`, `Boolean`, `Byte`, and so on. Most of these classes have the same names as the data types, except that the class names begin with a capital letter (`Short` instead of `short`, `Double` instead of `double`, and the like). Also, two classes have names that differ from the corresponding data type: `Character` is used for `char` variables and `Integer` for `int` variables.

Java treats the data types and their class versions very differently, and a program won't compile successfully if you use one when the other is expected.

Using the classes that correspond to each primitive type, you can create an object that holds the same value. The following statement creates an instance of the `Integer` class with the integer value 7801:

```
Integer dataCount = new Integer(7801);
```

After you have an object created in this manner, you can use it as you would any object (although you cannot change its value). When you want to use that value again as a primitive value, there are methods for that, as well. For example, if you wanted to get an `int` value from a `dataCount` object, the following statement would be apt:

```
int newCount = dataCount.intValue(); // returns 7801
```

A common translation you need in programs is converting a String to a numeric type, such as an integer. When you need an int as the result, this can be done by using the parseInt() class method of the Integer class. The String to convert is the only argument sent to the method, as in the following example:

```
String pennsylvania = "65000";
int penn = Integer.parseInt(pennsylvania);
```

The following classes can be used to work with objects instead of primitive data types: Boolean, Byte, Character, Double, Float, Integer, Long, Short, and Void.

Caution If you try to use the preceding example in a program, your program won't compile. The parseInt() method is designed to fail with a NumberFormatException error if the argument to the method is not a valid numeric value. In order to deal with errors of this kind, you must use special error-handling statements, which are introduced during Day 7, "Threads and Exceptions."

Comparing Object Values and Classes

In addition to casting, there are three other common tasks you will often perform that involve objects:

- Comparing objects
- Finding out the class of any given object
- Testing to see whether an object is an instance of a given class

Comparing Objects

Yesterday you learned about operators for comparing values—equal, not equal, less than, and so on. Most of these operators work only on primitive types, not on objects. If you try to use other values as operands, the Java compiler produces errors.

The exceptions to this rule are the operators for equality: == (equal) and != (not equal). When applied to objects, these operators don't do what you might first expect. Instead of checking whether one object has the same value as the other object, they determine whether both sides of the operator refer to the same object.

To compare instances of a class and have meaningful results, you must implement special methods in your class and call those methods.

A good example of this is the String class. It is possible to have two different String objects that contain the same values. If you were to employ the == operator to compare these objects, however, they would be considered unequal. Although their contents match, they are not the same object.

To see whether two String objects have matching values, a method of the class called equals() is used. The method tests each character in the string and returns true if the two strings have the same values. Listing 3.5 illustrates this.

LISTING 3.5   The Full Text of EqualsTest.java

```
 1: class EqualsTest {
 2:     public static void main(String[] arguments) {
 3:         String str1, str2;
 4:         str1 = "Free the bound periodicals.";
 5:         str2 = str1;
 6:
 7:         System.out.println("String1: " + str1);
 8:         System.out.println("String2: " + str2);
 9:         System.out.println("Same object? " + (str1 == str2));
10:
11:         str2 = new String(str1);
12:
13:         System.out.println("String1: " + str1);
14:         System.out.println("String2: " + str2);
15:         System.out.println("Same object? " + (str1 == str2));
16:         System.out.println("Same value? " + str1.equals(str2));
17:     }
18: }
```

This program's output is as follows:

```
String1: Free the bound periodicals.
String2: Free the bound periodicals.
Same object? true
String1: Free the bound periodicals.
String2: Free the bound periodicals.
Same object? false
Same value? true
```

The first part of this program (lines 3–5) declares two variables (str1 and str2), assigns the literal Free the bound periodicals. to str1, and then assigns that value to str2. As you learned earlier, str1 and str2 now point to the same object, and the equality test at line 9 proves that.

In the second part of this program, you create a new String object with the same value as str1 and assign str2 to that new String object. Now you have two different string objects in str1 and str2, both with the same value. Testing them to see whether they're

the same object by using the == operator (line 15) returns the expected answer: false—
they are not the same object in memory. Testing them using the equals() method in
line 16 also returns the expected answer: true—they have the same values.

Note

> Why can't you just use another literal when you change str2, rather than
> using new? String literals are optimized in Java; if you create a string using a
> literal and then use another literal with the same characters, Java knows
> enough to give you the first String object back. Both strings are the same
> objects; you have to go out of your way to create two separate objects.

Determining the Class of an Object

Want to find out what an object's class is? Here's the way to do it for an object assigned
to the variable key:

```
String name = key.getClass().getName();
```

What does this do? The getClass() method is defined in the Object class and is therefore available for all objects. The result of that method is a Class object (where Class is
itself a class) that has a method called getName(). In turn, getName() returns a string
representing the name of the class.

Another test that might be useful is the instanceof operator. instanceof has two
operands: a reference to an object on the left and a class name on the right. The expression returns true or false based on whether the object is an instance of the named class
or any of that class's subclasses:

```
"Texas" instanceof String // true
Point pt = new Point(10, 10);
pt instanceof String // false
```

The instanceof operator can also be used for interfaces. If an object implements an interface, the instanceof operator with that interface name on the right side returns true.

Summary

Now that you have spent three days exploring how object-oriented programming is
implemented in Java, you're in a better position to decide how useful it can be in your
own programming.

If you are a "glass is half empty" person, object-oriented programming is a level of
abstraction that gets in the way of what you're trying to use a programming language for.
You will learn more about why OOP is thoroughly ingrained in Java in the coming days.

If you are a "glass is half full" person, object-oriented programming is worth using because of the benefits it offers: improved reliability, reusability, and maintenance.

Today you learned how to deal with objects: creating them, reading their values and changing them, and calling their methods. You also learned how to cast objects from one class to another or from a data type to a class.

At this point you possess the skills to handle most simple tasks in the Java language. All that remains are arrays, conditionals, and loops (which are covered tomorrow), and how to define and use classes on Day 5.

Q&A

Q I'm confused about the differences between objects and the primitive data types, such as int and boolean.

A The primitive types (byte, short, int, long, float, double, boolean, and char) represent the smallest things in the language. They are not objects, although in many ways they can be handled like objects: They can be assigned to variables and passed in and out of methods. Most of the operations that work exclusively on objects, however, will not work with primitive types.

Objects are instances of classes and, as such, are usually much more complex data types than simple numbers and characters, often containing numbers and characters as instance or class variables.

Q The length() and charAt() methods in Listing 3.3 don't appear to make sense. If length() says that a string is 36 characters long, shouldn't the characters be numbered from 1 to 36 when charAt() is used to display characters in the string?

A The two methods look at strings a little differently. The length() method counts the characters in the string, with the first character counting as 1, the second as 2, and so on. The string "Charlie Brown" has 13 characters. The charAt() method considers the first character in the string to be located at position number 0. This is the same numbering system used with array elements in Java. The string Charlie Brown has characters ranging from position 0 (the letter "C") to position 12 (the letter "n").

Q No pointers in Java? If you don't have pointers, how are you supposed to do something like linked lists, where you have a pointer from one nose to another so you can traverse them?

A It's untrue to say Java has no pointers at all; it just has no explicit pointers. Object references are, effectively, pointers. To create something like a linked list, you would create a class called Node, which would have an instance variable also of type Node. To link together node objects, assign a node object to the instance variable of the object immediately before it in the list. Because object references are pointers, linked lists set up this way behave as you would expect them to.

Quiz

Review today's material by taking this quiz.

Questions

1. What operator do you use to call an object's constructor method and create a new object?

    (a.) +

    (b.) new

    (c.) instanceof

2. What kinds of methods apply to all objects of a class rather than an individual object?

    (a.) Universal methods

    (b.) Instance methods

    (c.) Class methods

3. If you have a program with objects named obj1 and obj2, what happens when you use the statement obj2 = obj1?

    (a.) The instance variables in obj2 are given the same values as obj1.

    (b.) obj2 and obj1 are considered to be the same object.

    (c.) Neither (a.) nor (b.).

Answers

1. (b.)

2. (c.)

3. (b.) The = operator does not copy values from one object to another. Instead, it makes both variables refer to the same object.

Certification Practice

The following question is the kind of thing you could expect to be asked on a Java programming certification test. Answer it without looking at today's material.

Given:

```java
public class AyeAye {
    int i = 40;
    int j;

    public AyeAye() {
        setValue(i++);
    }

    void setValue(int inputValue) {
        int i = 20;
        j = i + 1;
        System.out.println("j = " + j);
    }
}
```

What is the value of the j variable at the time it is displayed inside the setValue() method?

(a.) 42

(b.) 40

(c.) 21

(d.) 20

The answer is available on this book's Web site at http://www.java21days.com. Visit the Day 3 page and click the Certification Practice link.

Exercises

To extend your knowledge of the subjects covered today, try the following exercises:

- Create a program that turns a birthday in MM/DD/YYYY format (such as 8/23/2002) into three individual strings.

- Create a class with instance variables for height, weight, and depth, making each an integer. Create a Java application that uses your new class, sets each of these values in an object, and displays the values.

Where applicable, exercise solutions are offered on this book's Web site at http://www.java21days.com.

DAY 4

Lists, Logic, and Loops

Today, you will learn about three of the most boring features in the Java language:

- How to make part of a Java program repeat itself by using loops
- How to make a program decide whether to do something based on logic
- How to organize groups of the same class or data type into lists called arrays

If these features don't sound boring to you, they shouldn't. Most of the significant work that you will accomplish with your Java software will make heavy use of all three.

These topics are boring for computers because they enable software to do one of the things at which it excels: taking care of tedious and repetitive tasks by doing them over and over.

Arrays

At this point, you have dealt with only a few variables in each Java program. In some cases, it's manageable to use individual variables to store information.

What if you had 20 items of related information to keep track of? You could create 20 different variables and set up their initial values, but that becomes progressively more cumbersome as you deal with larger amounts of information. What if there were 100 items, or even 1,000?

Arrays are a way to store a list of items that have the same primitive data type, the same class, or a common parent class. Each item on the list goes into its own numbered slot, so that you can easily access the information.

Arrays can contain any type of information that is stored in a variable, but once the array is created, you can use it for that information type only. For example, you can have an array of integers, an array of String objects, or an array of arrays, but you can't have an array that contains both String objects and integers.

Java implements arrays differently than some other languages do—as objects that are treated just like other objects.

To create an array in Java, you must do the following:

1. Declare a variable to hold the array.

2. Create a new array object and assign it to the array variable.

3. Store information in that array.

Declaring Array Variables

The first step in array creation is to declare a variable that will hold the array. Array variables indicate the object or data type that the array will hold and the name of the array. To differentiate from regular variable declarations, a pair of empty brackets ([ ]) is added to the object or data type, or to the variable name.

The following statements are examples of array variable declarations:

```
String[] requests;

Point[] targets;

float[] donations;
```

You also can declare an array by putting the brackets after the variable name instead of the information type, as in the following statements:

```
String requests[];

Point targets[];

float donations[];
```

Note

The choice of which style to use is a matter of personal preference. The sample programs in this book place the brackets after the information type rather than after the variable name.

Creating Array Objects

After you declare the array variable, the next step is to create an array object and assign it to that variable. To do this

- Use the new operator.
- Initialize the contents of the array directly.

Because arrays are objects in Java, you can use the new operator to create a new instance of an array, as in the following statement:

```
String[] players = new String[10];
```

This statement creates a new array of strings with 10 slots that can contain String objects. When you create an array object by using new, you must indicate how many slots the array will hold. This statement does not put actual String objects in the slots; you must do that later.

Array objects can contain primitive types, such as integers or Booleans, just as they can contain objects:

```
int[] temps = new int[99];
```

When you create an array object using new, all its slots automatically are given an initial value (0 for numeric arrays, false for Booleans, '\0' for character arrays, and null for objects).

Note

The Java keyword null refers to a null object (and can be used for any object reference). It is not equivalent to zero or the '\0' character as the NULL constant is in C.

You also can create and initialize an array at the same time by enclosing the elements of the array inside braces, separated by commas:

```
Point[] markup = { new Point(1,5), new Point(3,3), new Point(2,3) };
```

Each of the elements inside the braces must be the same type as the variable that holds the array. When you create an array with initial values in this manner, the array will be the same size as the number of elements you have included within the braces. The preceding example creates an array of Point objects named markup that contains three elements.

Because String objects can be created and initialized without the new operator, you can do the same when creating an array of strings:

```
String[] titles = { "Mr.", "Mrs.", "Ms.", "Miss", "Dr." };
```

The preceding statement creates a five-element array of String objects named titles.

Accessing Array Elements

After you have an array with initial values, you can retrieve, change, and test the values in each slot of that array. The value in a slot is accessed with the array name followed by a subscript enclosed within square brackets. This name and subscript can be put into expressions, as in the following:

```
testScore[40] = 920;
```

The preceding statement sets the 41st element of the testScore array to a value of 920. The testScore part of this expression is a variable holding an array object, although it also can be an expression that results in an array. The subscript expression specifies the slot to access within the array.

The first element of an array has a subscript of 0 rather than 1, so an array with 12 elements has array slots that are accessed by using subscripts 0 through 11.

All array subscripts are checked to make sure that they are inside the array's boundaries, as specified when the array was created. In Java, it is impossible to access or assign a value to an array slot outside the array's boundaries. This helps to avoid problems that result from overrunning the bounds of an array in C-type languages. Note the following two statements:

```
float[] rating = new float[20];

rating[20] = 3.22F;
```

A program with the preceding two lines of code produces a compilation error when rating[20] is used. The error occurs because the rating array does not have a slot 20; it has 20 slots that begin at 0 and end at 19. The Java compiler would make note of this by displaying an ArrayIndexOutOfBoundsException error.

The Java interpreter produces an error if the array subscript is calculated when the program is running and the subscript is outside the array's boundaries. To be technically correct, the interpreter flags this error by generating an exception. You will learn more about exceptions and how to use them on Day 7, "Threads and Exceptions."

One way to avoid accidentally overrunning the end of an array in your programs is to use the length instance variable, which is part of all array objects, regardless of type. The length variable contains the number of elements in the array. The following statement displays the number of elements in the rating object:

```
System.out.println("Elements: " + rating.length);
```

Changing Array Elements

As you saw in the previous examples, you can assign a value to a specific slot in an array by putting an assignment statement after the array name and subscript, as in the following:

```
temperature[4] = 85;

day[0] = "Sunday";

manager[2] = manager[0];
```

An important thing to note is that an array of objects in Java is an array of references to those objects. When you assign a value to a slot in that kind of array, you are creating a reference to that object. When you move values around inside arrays, you are reassigning the reference rather than copying a value from one slot to another. Arrays of a primitive data type, such as int or float, do copy the values from one slot to another, as do elements of a String array, even though they are objects.

Arrays are reasonably simple to create and modify, and they provide an enormous amount of functionality for Java. Listing 4.1 shows a simple program that creates, initializes, and displays elements of three arrays.

4

LISTING 4.1   The Full Text of HalfDollars.java

```
 1: class HalfDollars {
 2:     public static void main(String[] arguments) {
 3:         int[] denver = { 15000006, 18810000, 20752110 };
 4:         int[] philadelphia = new int[denver.length];
 5:         int[] total = new int[denver.length];
 6:         int average;
 7:
 8:         philadelphia[0] = 15020000;
 9:         philadelphia[1] = 18708000;
10:         philadelphia[2] = 21348000;
11:
12:         total[0] = denver[0] + philadelphia[0];
13:         total[1] = denver[1] + philadelphia[1];
14:         total[2] = denver[2] + philadelphia[2];
15:         average = (total[0] + total[1] + total[2]) / 3;
16:
17:         System.out.println("1993 production: " + total[0]);
18:         System.out.println("1994 production: " + total[1]);
```

continues

LISTING 4.1   Continued

```
19:            System.out.println("1995 production: " + total[2]);
20:            System.out.println("Average production: "+ average);
21:        }
22: }
```

The HalfDollars application uses three integer arrays to store production totals for U.S. half-dollar coins produced at the Denver and Philadelphia mints. The output of the program is as follows:

```
1993 production: 30020006
1994 production: 37518000
1995 production: 42100110
Average production: 36546038
```

The class that is created here, HalfDollars, has three instance variables that hold arrays of integers.

The first, which is named denver, is declared and initialized on line 3 to contain three integers: 15000006 in element 0, 18810000 in element 1, and 20752110 in element 2. These figures are the total half-dollar production at the Denver mint for three years.

The second and third instance variables, philadelphia and total, are declared in lines 4–5. The philadelphia array contains the production totals for the Philadelphia mint, and total is used to store the overall production totals.

No initial values are assigned to the slots of the philadelphia and total arrays in lines 4–5. For this reason, each element is given the default value for integers: 0.

The denver.length variable is used to give both of these arrays the same number of slots as the denver array; every array contains a length variable that you can use to keep track of the number of elements it contains.

The rest of the main() method of this application performs the following:

- Line 6 creates an integer variable called average.
- Lines 8–10 assign new values to the three elements of the philadelphia array: 15020000 in element 0, 18708000 in element 1, and 21348000 in element 2.
- Lines 12–14 assign new values to the elements of the total array. In line 12, total element 0 is given the sum of denver element 0 and philadelphia element 0. Similar expressions are used in lines 13 and 14.

- Line 15 sets the value of the `average` variable to the average of the three `total` elements. Because `average` and the three `total` elements are integers, the average will be expressed as an integer rather than a floating-point number.

- Lines 17–20 display the values stored in the `total` array and the `average` variable, along with some explanatory text.

One last note about Listing 4.1 concerns lines 12–14 and lines 17–19. These lines demonstrate an inefficient way to use arrays in a program. The statements are almost identical, except for the subscripts that indicate which array element you are referring to. If the `HalfDollars` application was being used to track 100 years of production totals instead of three years, your program would contain a lot of repetitive code.

When dealing with arrays, you can use loops to cycle through an array's elements rather than dealing with each element individually. This makes the code a lot shorter and easier to read. When you learn about loops later today, you will see a rewrite of the current example.

Multidimensional Arrays

If you have used arrays in other languages, you might be expecting Java to support *multidimensional arrays,* which are arrays that contain more than one subscript and can store information in multiple dimensions.

A common use of a multidimensional array is to represent the data in an x,y grid of array elements.

Java does not support multidimensional arrays, but you can achieve the same functionality by declaring an array of arrays. Those arrays can also contain arrays, and so on, for as many dimensions as needed.

For example, consider a program that needs to accomplish the following tasks:

- Record an integer value each day for a year
- Organize those values by week

One way to organize this data is to create a 52-element array in which each element contains a 7-element array:

```
int[][] dayValue = new int[52][7];
```

This array of arrays contains a total of 364 integers, one for each day in 52 weeks. You could set the value for the first day of the 10th week with the following statement:

```
dayValue[9][0] = 14200;
```

You can use the `length` variable with these arrays as you would any other. The following statement contains a three-dimensional array of integers and displays the number of elements in each dimension:

```
int[][][] century = new int[100][52][7];
System.out.println("Elements in the first dimension: " + century.length);
System.out.println("Elements in the second dimension: " +
        century[0].length);
System.out.println("Elements in the third dimension: " +
        century[0][0].length);
```

Block Statements

Statements in Java are grouped into blocks. The beginning and ending of a block are noted with brace characters—an opening brace ({) for the beginning and a closing brace (}) for the ending.

You already have used blocks throughout the programs during the first four days. You've used them for the following:

- To contain the variables and methods in a class definition
- To define the statements that belong in a method

Blocks are also called *block statements* because an entire block can be used anywhere a single statement could be used (they're called *compound statements* in C and other languages). Each statement inside the block is then executed from top to bottom.

You can put blocks inside other blocks, just as you do when you put a method inside of a class definition.

An important thing to note about using a block is that it creates a scope for the local variables that are created inside the block.

NEW TERM *Scope* is the part of a program in which a variable exists and can be used. If you try to use a variable outside of its scope, an error will occur.

In Java, the scope of a variable is the block in which it was created. When you can declare and use local variables inside a block, those variables cease to exist after the block is finished executing. For example, the following `testBlock()` method contains a block:

```
void testBlock() {
    int x = 10;
    { // start of block
        int y = 40;
        y = y + x;
    } // end of block
}
```

There are two variables defined in this method: x and y. The scope of the y variable is the block it's in, and it can be used only within that block. An error would result if you tried to use the y variable in another part of the testBlock() method. The x variable was created inside the method but outside of the inner block, so it can be used anywhere in the method. You can modify the value of x anywhere within the method, and this value will be retained.

Block statements usually are not used alone in a method definition, as they are in the preceding example. You use them throughout class and method definitions, as well as in the logic and looping structures you will learn about next.

if Conditionals

One of the key aspects of programming is a program's capability to decide what it will do. This is handled through a special type of statement called a *conditional*.

NEW TERM   A *conditional* is a programming statement that is executed only if a specific condition is met.

The most basic conditional is the if keyword. The if conditional uses a Boolean expression to decide whether a statement should be executed. If the expression returns a true value, the statement is executed.

Here's a simple example that displays the message "You call that a haircut?" on only one condition: if the value of the age variable is greater than 39:

```
if (age > 39)
    System.out.println("You call that a haircut?");
```

If you want something else to happen in the case when the if expression returns a false value, then an optional else keyword can be used. The following example uses both if and else:

```
if (blindDateIsAttractive == true)
    restaurant = "Benihana's";
else
    restaurant = "Taco Bell";
```

The if conditional executes different statements based on the result of a single Boolean test.

Note   A difference between if conditionals in Java and those in C or C++ is that Java requires the test to return a Boolean value (true or false). In C and C++, the test can return an integer.

Using if, you can include only a single statement as the code to execute if the test expression is true, and another statement if the expression is false.

However, as you learned earlier today, a block can appear anywhere in Java that a single statement can appear. If you want to do more than just one thing as a result of an if statement, you can enclose those statements inside a block. Note the following snippet of code, which was used on Day 1, "Getting Started with Java":

```
if (temperature > 660) {
    status = "returning home";
    speed = 5;
}
```

The if statement in this example contains the test expression temperature > 660. If the temperature variable contains a value higher than 660, the block statement is executed and two things occur:

- The status variable is given the value returning home.
- The speed variable is set to 5.

All if and else statements use Boolean tests to determine whether statements will be executed. You can use a boolean variable itself for this test, as in the following:

```
if (outOfGas)
    status = "inactive";
```

The preceding example uses a boolean variable called outOfGas. It functions exactly like the following:

```
if (outOfGas == true)
    status = "inactive";
```

switch Conditionals

A common programming practice in any language is to test a variable against some value, and if it doesn't match, test it again against a different value, and so on. This process can become unwieldy if you're using only if statements, depending on how many different values you have to test. For example, you might end up with a set of if statements something like the following:

```
if (operation == '+')
    add(object1, object2);
else if (operation == '-')
    subtract(object1, object2);
else if (operation == '*')
    multiply(object1, object2);
else if (operation == '/')
    divide(object1, object2);
```

This use of `if` statements is called a *nested `if` statement* because each `else` statement contains another `if` until all possible tests have been made.

In some programming languages, a shorthand mechanism that you can use for nested `if` statements is to group tests and actions together in a single statement. In Java, you can group actions together with the `switch` statement, which behaves as it does in C. The following is an example of `switch` usage:

```java
switch (grade) {
    case 'A':
        System.out.println("Great job!");
        break;
    case 'B':
        System.out.println("Good job!");
        break;
    case 'C':
        System.out.println("You can do better!");
        break;
    default:
        System.out.println("Consider cheating!");
}
```

The `switch` statement is built on a test; in the preceding example, the test is on the value of the `grade` variable, which holds a `char` value. The test variable, which can be any of the primitive types `byte`, `char`, `short`, or `int`, is compared in turn with each of the `case` values. If a match is found, the statement or statements after the test are executed.

If no match is found, the `default` statement or statements are executed. Providing a `default` statement is optional—if it is omitted and there is no match for any of the `case` statements, the `switch` statement completes without executing anything.

The Java implementation of `switch` is limited; tests and values can be only simple primitive types that can be cast to an `int`. You cannot use larger primitive types such as `long` or `float`, strings, or other objects within a `switch`, nor can you test for any relationship other than equality. These restrictions limit `switch` to the simplest cases. In contrast, nested `if` statements can work for any kind of test on any possible type.

The following is a revision of the nested `if` example shown previously. It has been rewritten as a `switch` statement:

```java
switch (operation) {
    case '+':
        add(object1, object2);
        break;
    case '*':
        subtract(object1, object2);
```

```
            break;
        case '-':
            multiply(object1, object2);
            break;
        case '/':
            divide(object1, object2);
            break;
    }
```

There are two things to be aware of in this example: The first is that after each case, you can include a single result statement or more; in fact, you can include as many as you need. Unlike with `if`, you don't need to surround multiple statements with braces in order for it to work.

The second thing to note about this example is the `break` statement that is included with each `case` section. Without a `break` statement in a `case` section, after a match is made, the statements for that match and all the statements farther down the `switch` are executed until a `break` or the end of the switch is found. In some cases, this might be exactly what you want to do. However, in most cases, you should include the `break` to ensure that only the right code is executed. `break`, which you will learn about in the section "Breaking Out of Loops," stops execution at the current point and jumps to the code outside of the next closing bracket (}).

One handy use of falling through without a `break` occurs when multiple values need to execute the same statements. To accomplish this task, you can use multiple `case` lines with no result; the `switch` will execute the first statement that it finds. For example, in the following `switch` statement, the string `x is an even number.` is printed if x has the values of 2, 4, 6, or 8. All other values of x cause the string `x is an odd number.` to be printed.

```
switch (x) {
    case 2:
    case 4:
    case 6:
    case 8:
        System.out.println("x is an even number.");
        break;
    default: System.out.println("x is an odd number.");
}
```

In Listing 4.2, the `DayCounter` application takes two arguments, a month and a year, and displays the number of days in that month. A `switch` statement, `if` statements, and `else` statements are used.

LISTING 4.2 The Full Text of `DayCounter.java`

```
 1: class DayCounter {
 2:     public static void main(String[] arguments) {
 3:         int yearIn = 2002;
 4:         int monthIn = 12;
 5:         if (arguments.length > 0)
 6:             monthIn = Integer.parseInt(arguments[0]);
 7:         if (arguments.length > 1)
 8:             yearIn = Integer.parseInt(arguments[1]);
 9:         System.out.println(monthIn + "/" + yearIn + " has "
10:             + countDays(monthIn, yearIn) + " days.");
11:     }
12:
13:     static int countDays(int month, int year) {
14:         int count = -1;
15:         switch (month) {
16:             case 1:
17:             case 3:
18:             case 5:
19:             case 7:
20:             case 8:
21:             case 10:
22:             case 12:
23:                 count = 31;
24:                 break;
25:             case 4:
26:             case 6:
27:             case 9:
28:             case 11:
29:                 count = 30;
30:                 break;
31:             case 2:
32:                 if (year % 4 == 0)
33:                     count = 29;
34:                 else
35:                     count = 28;
36:                 if ((year % 100 == 0) & (year % 400 != 0))
37:                     count = 28;
38:         }
39:         return count;
40:     }
41: }
```

This application uses command-line arguments to specify the month and year to check. The first argument is the month, which should be expressed as a number from 1 to 12. The second argument is the year, which should be expressed as a full four-digit year.

After compiling the program, type the following at a command line to see the number of days in April 2003:

```
java DayCounter 4 2003
```

The output will be the following:

```
4/2003 has 30 days.
```

If you run it without arguments, the default month of December 2002 will be used and the output will be the following:

```
12/2002 has 31 days.
```

The DayCounter application uses a switch statement to count the days in a month. This statement is part of the countDays() method in lines 13–40 of Listing 4.2.

The countDays() method has two int arguments: month and year. The number of days will be stored in the count variable, which is given an initial value of -1 that will be replaced by the correct count later.

The switch statement that begins on line 15 uses month as its conditional value.

The number of days in a month is easy to determine for 11 months of the year. January, March, May, July, August, October, and December have 31 days. April, June, September, and November have 30 days.

The count for these 11 months is handled in lines 16–30 of Listing 4.2. Months are numbered from 1 (January) to 12 (December), as you would expect. When one of the case statements has the same value as month, every statement after that will be executed until break or the end of the switch statement is reached.

February is a little more complex, and is handled in lines 31–37 of the program. Every leap year has 29 days in February, whereas other years have 28. A leap year must meet either of the following conditions:

- The year must be evenly divisible by 4 and not evenly divisible by 100, or
- The year must be evenly divisible by 400.

As you learned on Day 2, "The ABCs of Programming," the modulus operator % returns the remainder of a division operation. This is used with several if-else statements to determine how many days there are in February, depending on what year it is.

The if-else statement in lines 32–35 sets count to 29 when the year is evenly divisible by 4 and sets it to 28 otherwise.

The if statement in lines 36–37 uses the & operator to combine two conditional expressions: year % 100 == 0 and year % 400 != 0. If both of these conditions are true, count is set to 28.

The countDays method ends by returning the value of count in line 39.

When you run the DayCounter application, the main() method in lines 2–11 is executed.

In all Java applications, command-line arguments are stored in an array of String objects. This array is called arguments in DayCounter. The first command-line argument is stored in argument[0], the second in argument[1], and upward until all arguments have been stored. If the application is run with no arguments, the array will be created with no elements.

Lines 3–4 create yearIn and monthIn, two integer variables to store the year and month that should be checked. They are given the initial values of 2002 and 12 (meaning December 2002), respectively.

The if statement in line 5 uses arguments.length to make sure the arguments array has at least one element. If it does, line 6 is executed.

Line 6 calls parseInt(), a class method of the Integer class, with argument[0] as an argument. This method takes a String object as an argument, and if the string could be a valid integer, it returns that value as an int. This converted value is stored in monthIn. A similar thing happens in line 7; parseInt() is called with argument[1], and this is used to set yearIn.

The output of the program is displayed in lines 9–10. As part of the output, the countDays() method is called with monthIn and yearIn, and the value returned by this method is displayed.

Note At this point, you may want to know how to collect input from a user in a program rather than using command-line arguments to receive it. There isn't a method comparable to System.out.println() that receives input. Instead, you must learn a bit more about Java's input and output classes before you can receive input in a program without a graphical user interface. This topic is covered during Day 15, "Working with Input and Output."

for Loops

A for loop is used to repeat a statement until a condition is met. Although for loops frequently are used for simple iteration in which a statement is repeated a certain number of times, for loops can be used for just about any kind of loop.

The for loop in Java looks roughly like the following:

```
for (initialization; test; increment) {
    statement;
}
```

The start of the for loop has three parts:

- *initialization* is an expression that initializes the start of the loop. If you have a loop index, this expression might declare and initialize it, such as int i = 0. Variables that you declare in this part of the for loop are local to the loop itself; they cease to exist after the loop is finished executing. You can initialize more than one variable in this section by separating each expression with a comma. The statement int i = 0, int j = 10 in this section would declare the variables i and j, and both would be local to the loop.

- *test* is the test that occurs before each pass of the loop. The test must be a Boolean expression or a function that returns a boolean value, such as i < 10. If the test is true, the loop executes. Once the test is false, the loop stops executing.

- *increment* is any expression or function call. Commonly, the increment is used to change the value of the loop index to bring the state of the loop closer to returning false and stopping the loop. The increment takes place after each pass of the loop. Similar to the *initialization* section, you can put more than one expression in this section by separating each expression with a comma.

The *statement* part of the for loop is the statement that is executed each time the loop iterates. As with if, you can include either a single statement or a block statement. The previous example used a block because that is more common. The following example is a for loop that sets all slots of a String array to the value Mr.:

```
String[] salutation = new String[10];
int i; // the loop index variable

for (i = 0; i < salutation.length; i++)
    salutation[i] = "Mr.";
```

In this example, the variable i serves as a loop index; it counts the number of times the loop has been executed. Before each trip through the loop, the index value is compared with salutation.length, the number of elements in the salutation array. When the index is equal to or greater than salutation.length, the loop is exited.

The final element of the for statement is i++. This causes the loop index to increment by 1 each time the loop is executed. Without this statement, the loop would never stop.

The statement inside the loop sets an element of the salutation array equal to "Mr.". The loop index is used to determine which element is modified.

Any part of the for loop can be an empty statement; in other words, you can include a semicolon with no expression or statement and that part of the for loop will be ignored. Note that if you do use an empty statement in your for loop, you might have to initialize or increment any loop variables or loop indexes yourself elsewhere in the program.

You also can have an empty statement as the body of your for loop if everything you want to do is in the first line of that loop. For example, the following for loop finds the first prime number higher than 4,000. (It employs a method called notPrime(), which returns a Boolean value, presumably to indicate whether i is prime or not.)

```
for (i = 4001; notPrime(i); i += 2)
    ;
```

A common mistake in for loops is to accidentally put a semicolon at the end of the line that includes the for statement:

```
for (i = 0; i < 10; i++);
    x = x * i; // this line is not inside the loop!
```

In this example, the first semicolon ends the loop without executing x = x * i as part of the loop. The x = x * i line will be executed only once because it is outside the for loop entirely. Be careful not to make this mistake in your Java programs.

To finish up for loops, the HalfDollar application will be rewritten using for loops to remove redundant code. The original example is long and repetitive and works only with an array that is three elements long. This version, shown in Listing 4.3, is shorter and more flexible (but it returns the same output).

LISTING 4.3 The Full Text of HalfLoop.java

```
 1: class HalfLoop {
 2:     public static void main(String[] arguments) {
 3:         int[] denver = { 15000006, 18810000, 20752110 };
 4:         int[] philadelphia = { 15020000, 18708000, 21348000 };
 5:         int[] total = new int[denver.length];
 6:         int sum = 0;
 7:
 8:         for (int i = 0; i < denver.length; i++) {
 9:             total[i] = denver[i] + philadelphia[i];
10:             System.out.println((i + 1993) + " production: "
11:                 + total[i]);
12:             sum += total[i];
13:         }
14:
15:         System.out.println("Average production: "
16:             + (sum / denver.length));
17:     }
18: }
```

4

The output of the program is as follows:

```
1993 production: 30020006
1994 production: 37518000
1995 production: 42100110
Average production: 36546038
```

Instead of going through the elements of the three arrays one by one, this example uses a for loop. The following things take place in the loop, which is contained in lines 8–13 of Listing 4.3:

- Line 8: The loop is created with an int variable called i as the index. The index will increment by 1 for each pass through the loop and stop when i is equal to or greater than denver.length, the total number of elements in the denver array.
- Lines 9–11: The value of one of the total elements is set using the loop index and then displayed with some text identifying the year.
- Line 12: The value of a total element is added to the sum variable, which will be used to calculate the average yearly production.

Using a more general-purpose loop to iterate over an array enables you to use the program with arrays of different sizes and still have it assign correct values to the elements of the total array and display those values.

while and do Loops

The remaining types of loops are while and do. As with for loops, *while* and *do loops* enable a block of Java code to be executed repeatedly until a specific condition is met. Whether you use a for, while, or do loop is mostly a matter of your programming style.

while Loops

The while loop is used to repeat a statement as long as a particular condition is true. The following is an example of a while loop:

```
while (i < 10) {
    x = x * i++; // the body of the loop
}
```

The condition that accompanies the while keyword is a Boolean expression—i < 10 in the preceding example. If the expression returns true, the while loop executes the body of the loop and then tests the condition again. This process repeats until the condition is false. Although the preceding loop uses opening and closing braces to form a block statement, the braces are not needed because the loop contains only one statement: x = x * i++. Using the braces does not create any problems though, and the braces will be required if you add another statement inside the loop later on.

Listing 4.4 shows an example of a `while` loop that copies the elements of an array of integers (in `array1`) to an array of float variables (in `array2`), casting each element to a `float` as it goes. The one catch is that if any of the elements in the first array is 1, the loop will immediately exit at that point.

LISTING 4.4 The Full Text of `CopyArrayWhile.java`

```
 1: class CopyArrayWhile {
 2:     public static void main(String[] arguments) {
 3:         int[] array1 = { 7, 4, 8, 1, 4, 1, 4 };
 4:         float[] array2 = new float[array1.length];
 5:
 6:         System.out.print("array1: [ ");
 7:         for (int i = 0; i < array1.length; i++) {
 8:             System.out.print(array1[i] + " ");
 9:         }
10:         System.out.println("]");
11:
12:         System.out.print("array2: [ ");
13:         int count = 0;
14:         while ( count < array1.length && array1[count] != 1) {
15:             array2[count] = (float) array1[count];
16:             System.out.print(array2[count++] + " ");
17:         }
18:         System.out.println("]");
19:     }
20: }
```

The output of the program is as follows:

```
array1: [ 7 4 8 1 4 1 4 ]
array2: [ 7.0 4.0 8.0 ]
```

Here is what's going on in the `main()` method:

- Lines 3–4 declare the arrays; `array1` is an array of integers, which are initialized to some suitable numbers. `array2` is an array of floating-point numbers that is the same length as `array1` but doesn't have any initial values.

- Lines 6–10 are for output purposes; they simply iterate through `array1` using a `for` loop to print out its values.

- Lines 13–17 are where the interesting stuff happens. This bunch of statements both assigns the values of `array2` (converting the numbers to floating-point numbers along the array) and prints it out at the same time. You start with a `count` variable, which keeps track of the array index elements. The test in the `while` loop keeps track of the two conditions for exiting the loop, where those two conditions are running out of elements in array1 or encountering a 1 in array1. (Remember, that was part of the original description of what this program does.)

You can use the logical conditional && to keep track of the test; remember that && makes sure both conditions are true before the entire expression is true. If either one is false, the expression returns false and the loop exits.

The program's output shows that the first four elements in array1 were copied to array2 but that there was a 1 in the middle that stopped the loop from going any farther. Without the 1, array2 should end up with all the same elements as array1. If the while loop's test initially is false the first time it is tested (for example, if the first element in that first array is 1), the body of the while loop will never be executed. If you need to execute the loop at least once, you can do one of two things:

- Duplicate the body of the loop outside the while loop.
- Use a do loop (which is described in the following section).

The do loop is considered the better solution of the two.

do…while Loops

The *do loop* is just like a while loop with one major difference—the place in the loop when the condition is tested. A while loop tests the condition before looping, so if the condition is false the first time it is tested, the body of the loop never will execute. A do loop executes the body of the loop at least once before testing the condition, so that if the condition is false the first time it is tested, the body of the loop already will have executed once.

It's the difference between asking Dad to borrow the car and telling him later that you borrowed it. If Dad nixes the idea in the first case, you don't get to borrow it. If he nixes the idea in the second case, you already have borrowed it once.

The following example uses a do loop to keep doubling the value of a long integer until it is larger than 3 trillion:

```
long i = 1;
do {
    i *= 2;
    System.out.print(i + " ");
} while (i < 3000000000000L);
```

The body of the loop is executed once before the test condition, i < 3000000000000L, is evaluated; then, if the test evaluates as true, the loop runs again. If it is false, the loop exits. Keep in mind that the body of the loop executes at least once with do loops.

Breaking Out of Loops

In all of the loops, the loop ends when a tested condition is met. There might be times when something occurs during execution of a loop, and you want to exit the loop early. In that case, you can use the break and continue keywords.

You already have seen break as part of the switch statement; break stops execution of the switch statement, and the program continues. The break keyword, when used with a loop, does the same thing—it immediately halts execution of the current loop. If you have nested loops within loops, execution picks up with the next outer loop. Otherwise, the program simply continues executing the next statement after the loop.

For example, recall the while loop that copied elements from an integer array into an array of floating-point numbers until either the end of the array or a 1 was reached. You can test for the latter case inside the body of the while loop and then use break to exit the loop:

```
int count = 0;
while (count < array1.length) {
    if (array1[count] == 1)
        break;
    array2[count] = (float) array2[count++];
}
```

The continue keyword starts the loop over at the next iteration. For do and while loops, this means that the execution of the block statement starts over again; with for loops, the increment expression is evaluated and then the block statement is executed. The continue keyword is useful when you want to make a special case out of elements within a loop. With the previous example of copying one array to another, you could test for whether the current element is equal to 1 and use continue to restart the loop after every 1 so that the resulting array never will contain zero. Note that because you're skipping elements in the first array, you now have to keep track of two different array counters:

```
int count = 0;
int count2 = 0;
while (count++ <= array1.length) {
    if (array1[count] == 1)
        continue;

    array2[count2++] = (float)array1[count];
} >
```

Labeled Loops

Both break and continue can have an optional label that tells Java where to resume execution of the program. Without a label, break jumps outside the nearest loop to an enclosing loop or to the next statement outside the loop. The continue keyword restarts the loop it is enclosed within. Using `break` and `continue` with a label enables you to use `break` to go to a point outside a nested loop or to use `continue` to go to a loop outside the current loop.

To use a labeled loop, add the label before the initial part of the loop, with a colon between the label and the loop. Then, when you use `break` or `continue`, add the name of the label after the keyword itself, as in the following:

```
out:
    for (int i = 0; i <10; i++) {
        while (x < 50) {
            if (i * x++ > 400)
                break out;
            // inner loop here
        }
        // outer loop here
    }
```

In this snippet of code, the label `out` labels the outer loop. Then, inside both the `for` and `while` loops, when a particular condition is met, a `break` causes the execution to break out of both loops. Without the label `out`, the `break` statement would exit the inner loop and resume execution with the outer loop.

The Conditional Operator

An alternative to using the `if` and `else` keywords in a conditional statement is to use the conditional operator, sometimes called the *ternary operator*. The *conditional operator* is called a ternary operator because it has three operands.

The conditional operator is an expression, meaning that it returns a value—unlike the more general `if`, which can result in only a statement or block being executed. The conditional operator is most useful for short or simple conditionals and looks like the following line:

```
test ? trueresult : falseresult;
```

The `test` is an expression that returns `true` or `false`, just like the test in the `if` statement. If the `test` is true, the conditional operator returns the value of `trueresult`. If the `test` is false, the conditional operator returns the value of `falseresult`. For example, the following conditional tests the values of `myScore` and `yourScore`, returns the larger of the two as a value, and assigns that value to the variable `ourBestScore`:

```
int ourBestScore = myScore > yourScore ? myScore : yourScore;
```

This use of the conditional operator is equivalent to the following `if-else` code:

```
int ourBestScore;
if (myScore > yourScore)
    ourBestScore = myScore;
else
    ourBestScore = yourScore;
```

The conditional operator has a very low precedence—usually it is evaluated only after all its subexpressions are evaluated. The only operators lower in precedence are the assignment operators. For a refresher on operator precedence, refer to Table 3.7 in Day 3, "Working with Objects."

> The ternary operator is of primary benefit to experienced programmers creating complex expressions. Its functionality is duplicated in simpler use of `if-else` statements, so there's no need to use this operator while you're beginning to learn the language. The main reason it's introduced in this book is because you'll encounter it in the source code of other Java programmers.

Summary

Now that you have been introduced to lists, loops, and logic, you can make a computer decide whether to repeatedly display the contents of an array.

You learned how to declare an array variable, assign an object to it, and access and change elements of the array. With the `if` and `switch` conditional statements, you can branch to different parts of a program based on a Boolean test. You learned about the `for`, `while`, and `do` loops, and you learned that each enables a portion of a program to be repeated until a given condition is met.

It bears repeating: You'll use all three of these features frequently in your Java programs.

You'll use all three of these features frequently in your Java programs.

Q&A

Q I declared a variable inside a block statement for an `if`. When the `if` was done, the definition of that variable vanished. Where did it go?

A In technical terms, block statements form a new *lexical scope*. What this means is that if you declare a variable inside a block, it's visible and usable only inside that block. When the block finishes executing, all the variables you declared go away.

It's a good idea to declare most of your variables in the outermost block in which they'll be needed—usually at the top of a block statement. The exception might be very simple variables, such as index counters in for loops, where declaring them in the first line of the for loop is an easy shortcut.

Q Why can't you use switch with strings?

A Strings are objects in Java, and switch works only for the primitive types byte, char, short, and int. To compare strings, you have to use nested if statements, which enable more general expression tests, including string comparison.

Quiz

Review today's material by taking this quiz.

Questions

1. Which loop is used to execute the statements in the loop at least once before the conditional expression is evaluated?

   (a.) do-while

   (b.) for

   (c.) while

2. Which operator returns the remainder of a division operation?

   (a.) /

   (b.) %

   (c.) ?

3. Which instance variable of an array is used to find out how big it is?

   (a.) size

   (b.) length

   (c.) MAX_VALUE

Answers

1. (a.) In a do-while loop, the while conditional statement appears at the end of the loop. Even if it is initially false, the statements in the loop will be executed once.

2. (b.) The modulus operator ("%").

3. (b.)

Certification Practice

The following question is the kind of thing you could expect to be asked on a Java programming certification test. Answer it without looking at today's material or using the Java compiler to test the code.

Given:

```
public class Cases {
    public static void main(String[] arguments) {
        float x = 9;
        float y = 5;
        int z = (int)(x / y);
        switch (z) {
            case 1:
                x = x + 2;
            case 2:
                x = x + 3;
            default:
                x = x + 1;
        }
        System.out.println("Value of x: " + x);
    }
}
```

What will be the value of x when it is displayed?

(a.) 9.0

(b.) 11.0

(c.) 15.0

(d.) The program will not compile.

The answer is available on this book's Web site at http://www.java21days.com. Visit the Day 4 page and click the Certification Practice link.

Exercises

To extend your knowledge of the subjects covered today, try the following exercises:

- Using the countDays() method from the DayCounter application, create an application that displays every date in a given year in a single list from January 1 to December 31.

- Create a class that takes words for the first 10 numbers (one up to ten) and converts them into a single long integer. Use a switch statement for the conversion and command-line arguments for the words.

Where applicable, exercise solutions are offered on this book's Web site at http://www.java21days.com.

4

DAY 5

Creating Classes and Methods

If you're coming to Java from another programming language, you might be struggling with the meaning of the term *class*. It seems synonymous to the term *program*, but you may be uncertain of the relationship between the two.

In Java, a program is made up of a main class and any other classes that are needed to support the main class. These support classes include any of those in Java's class library you might need (such as String, Math, and the like).

Today, the meaning of *class* will be clarified as you create classes and methods, which define the behavior of an object or class. You will undertake each of the following:

- The parts of a class definition
- The creation and use of instance variables
- The creation and use of methods
- The main() method used in Java applications

- The creation of overloaded methods that share the same name but have different signatures and definitions
- The creation of constructor methods that are called when an object is created

Defining Classes

Because you have created classes during each of the previous days, you should be familiar with the basics of class definition at this point. A class is defined via the `class` keyword and the name of the class, as in the following example:

```
class Ticker {
    // body of the class
}
```

By default, classes inherit from the `Object` class. It's the superclass of all classes in the Java class hierarchy.

The `extends` keyword is used to indicate the superclass of a class. Look at the following subclass of `Ticker`:

```
class SportsTicker extends Ticker {
    // body of the class
}
```

Creating Instance and Class Variables

Whenever you create a class, you define behavior that makes the new class different from its superclass.

This behavior is defined by specifying the variables and methods of the new class. In this section, you will work with three kinds of variables: class variables, instance variables, and local variables. The next section covers methods.

Defining Instance Variables

On Day 2, "The ABCs of Programming," you learned how to declare and initialize local variables, which are variables inside method definitions. Instance variables are declared and defined in almost the same way local variables are. The main difference is their location in the class definition. Variables are considered instance variables if they are declared outside a method definition and are not modified by the `static` keyword. By programming custom, most instance variables are defined right after the first line of the class definition. Listing 5.1 contains a simple class definition for the class `VolcanoRobot`, which inherits from its superclass, `ScienceRobot`.

LISTING 5.1   The Full Text of `VolcanoRobot.java`

```
1: class VolcanoRobot extends ScienceRobot {
2:
3:     String status;
4:     int speed;
5:     float temperature;
6:     int power;
7: }
```

This class definition contains four variables. Because these variables are not defined inside a method, they are instance variables. The variables are as follows:

- `status`—A string indicating the current activity of the robot (for example, `exploring` or `returning home`)
- `speed`—An integer that indicates the robot's current rate of travel
- `temperature`—A floating-point number that indicates the current temperature of the environment the robot is in
- `power`—An integer indicating the robot's current battery power

Class Variables

As you learned in previous days, class variables apply to a class as a whole, rather than being stored individually in objects of the class.

Class variables are good for communicating among different objects of the same class or for keeping track of class-wide information among a set of objects.

The `static` keyword is used in the class declaration to declare a class variable, as in the following:

```
static int sum;
static final int maxObjects = 10;
```

Creating Methods

As you learned on Day 3, "Working with Objects," methods define an object's behavior—that is, anything that happens when the object is created as well as the various tasks the object can perform during its lifetime.

This section introduces method definition and how methods work. Tomorrow's lesson has more detail about advanced things you can do with methods.

5

Defining Methods

Method definitions have four basic parts:

- The name of the method
- A list of parameters
- The type of object or primitive type returned by the method
- The body of the method

The first two parts of the method definition form what is called the method's *signature*.

 Note

> To keep things simpler today, two optional parts of the method definition have been left out: a modifier, such as public or private, and the throws keyword, which indicates the exceptions a method can throw. You learn about these parts of method definition during Day 6, "Packages, Interfaces, and Other Class Features."

In other languages, the name of the method, which might be called a function, subroutine, or procedure, is enough to distinguish it from other methods in the program.

In Java, you can have several methods in the same class with the same name but differences in signatures. This practice is called *method overloading,* and you will learn more about it tomorrow.

Here's what a basic method definition looks like:

```
returnType methodName(type1 arg1, type2 arg2, type3 arg3 ...) {
    // body of the method
}
```

The `returnType` is the primitive type or class of the value returned by the method. It can be one of the primitive types, a class name, or void if the method does not return a value at all.

Note that if this method returns an array object, the array brackets can go after either the `returnType` or the parameter list. Because the former way is easier to read, it is used in this book's examples as in the following:

```
int[] makeRange(int lower, int upper) {
    // body of this method
}
```

The method's parameter list is a set of variable declarations that are separated by commas and set inside parentheses. These parameters become local variables in the body of the method, receiving their values when the method is called.

You can have statements, expressions, method calls on other objects, conditionals, loops, and so on inside the body of the method.

Unless a method has been declared with void as its return type, the method returns some kind of value when it is completed. This value must be explicitly returned at some exit point inside the method, using the return keyword.

Listing 5.2 shows an example of a class that defines a makeRange() method. makeRange() takes two integers—a lower boundary and an upper boundary—and creates an array that contains all the integers between those two boundaries. The boundaries themselves are included in the array of integers.

LISTING 5.2 The Full Text of RangeClass.java

```
 1: public class RangeClass {
 2:     int[] makeRange(int lower, int upper) {
 3:         int arr[] = new int[ (upper - lower) + 1 ];
 4:
 5:         for (int i = 0; i < arr.length; i++) {
 6:             arr[i] = lower++;
 7:         }
 8:         return arr;
 9:     }
10:
11:     public static void main(String[] arguments) {
12:         int theArray[];
13:         RangeClass theRange = new RangeClass();
14:
15:         theArray = theRange.makeRange(1, 10);
16:         System.out.print("The array: [ ");
17:         for (int i = 0; i < theArray.length; i++) {
18:             System.out.print(theArray[i] + " ");
19:         }
20:         System.out.println("]");
21:     }
22:
23: }
```

The output of the program is the following:

```
The array: [ 1 2 3 4 5 6 7 8 9 10 ]
```

The main() method in this class tests the makeRange() method by creating a range where the lower and upper boundaries of the range are 1 and 10, respectively, and then uses a for loop to print the new array's values in lines 5–7.

The `this` Keyword

In the body of a method definition, you might want to refer to the current object—the object the method was called on. This can be done to use that object's instance variables or to pass the current object as an argument to another method.

To refer to the current object in these cases, use the `this` keyword where you normally would refer to an object's name.

The `this` keyword refers to the current object, and you can use it anywhere a reference to an object might appear: in dot notation, as an argument to a method, as the return value for the current method, and so on. The following are some examples of using `this`:

```
t = this.x;            // the x instance variable for this object

this.resetData(this); // call the resetData method, defined in
                       // this class, and pass it the current
                       // object

return this;           // return the current object
```

In many cases, you might not need to explicitly use the `this` keyword because it will be assumed. For instance, you can refer to both instance variables and method calls defined in the current class simply by name because the `this` is implicit in those references. Therefore, you could write the first two examples as the following:

```
t = x;              // the x instance variable for this object

resetData(this); // call the resetData method, defined in this
                 // class
```

> **Note**
>
> The viability of omitting the `this` keyword for instance variables depends on whether variables of the same name are declared in the local scope. You will see more on this subject in the next section.

Because `this` is a reference to the current instance of a class, you should use it only inside the body of an instance method definition. Class methods—which are declared with the `static` keyword—cannot use `this`.

Variable Scope and Method Definitions

One of the things you must know in order to use a variable is its scope.

 Scope is the part of a program in which a variable or another type of information can be used. When the part defining the scope has completed execution, the variable ceases to exist.

When you declare a variable in Java, that variable always has a limited scope. A variable with local scope, for example, can be used only inside the block in which it was defined. Instance variables have a scope that extends to the entire class, so they can be used by any of the instance methods within that class.

When you refer to a variable within a method definition, Java checks for a definition of that variable first in the current scope (which might be a block), next in each outer scope, and finally, in the current method definition. If the variable is not a local variable, Java then checks for a definition of that variable as an instance or class variable in the current class. If Java still does not find the variable definition, it searches each superclass in turn.

Because of the way Java checks for the scope of a given variable, it is possible for you to create a variable in a lower scope that hides (or replaces) the original value of that variable and introduces subtle and confusing bugs into your code.

For example, consider the following Java application:

```java
class ScopeTest {
    int test = 10;

    void printTest () {
        int test = 20;
        System.out.println("Test: " + test);
    }

    public static void main(String arguments[]) {
        ScopeTest st = new ScopeTest();
        st.printTest();
    }
}
```

In this class, you have two variables with the same name and definition. The first, an instance variable, has the name test and is initialized with the value 10. The second is a local variable with the same name, but with the value 20.

The local variable test within the printTest() method hides the instance variable test. When the printTest() method is called from within the main() method, it displays that test equals 20, even though there's a test instance variable that equals 10. You can avoid this problem by using this.test to refer to the instance variable and using just test to refer to the local variable, but a better solution is to avoid the duplication of variable names and definitions.

A more insidious example occurs when you redefine a variable in a subclass that already occurs in a superclass. This can create subtle bugs in your code; for example, you might call methods that are intended to change the value of an instance variable, but the wrong variable is changed. Another bug might occur when you cast an object from one class to another; the value of your instance variable might mysteriously change because it was getting that value from the superclass instead of your class.

The best way to avoid this behavior is to be aware of the variables defined in all your class's superclasses. This awareness prevents you from duplicating a variable that's used higher in the class hierarchy.

Passing Arguments to Methods

When you call a method with object parameters, the objects you pass into the body of the method are passed by reference. Whatever you do to the objects inside the method affects the original objects. Keep in mind that such objects include arrays and all objects that are contained in arrays. When you pass an array into a method and modify its contents, the original array is affected. Primitive types, on the other hand, are passed by value.

Listing 5.3 demonstrates how this works.

LISTING 5.3   The PassByReference Class

```
 1: public class PassByReference {
 2:     int onetoZero(int arg[]) {
 3:         int count = 0;
 4:
 5:         for (int i = 0; i < arg.length; i++) {
 6:             if (arg[i] == 1) {
 7:                 count++;
 8:                 arg[i] = 0;
 9:             }
10:         }
11:         return count;
12:     }
13:
14:     public static void main(String[] arguments) {
15:         int arr[] = { 1, 3, 4, 5, 1, 1, 7 };
16:         PassByReference test = new PassByReference();
17:         int numOnes;
18:
19:         System.out.print("Values of the array: [ ");
20:         for (int i = 0; i < arr.length; i++) {
21:             System.out.print(arr[i] + " ");
22:         }
23:         System.out.println("]");
24:
25:         numOnes = test.onetoZero(arr);
26:         System.out.println("Number of Ones = " + numOnes);
27:         System.out.print("New values of the array: [ ");
```

LISTING 5.3 Continued

```
28:         for (int i = 0; i < arr.length; i++) {
29:             System.out.print(arr[i] + " ");
30:         }
31:         System.out.println("]");
32:     }
33: }
```

The following is this program's output:

```
Values of the array: [ 1 3 4 5 1 1 7 ]
Number of Ones = 3
New values of the array: [ 0 3 4 5 0 0 7 ]
```

Note the method definition for the onetoZero() method in lines 2–12, which takes a single array as an argument. The onetoZero() method does two things:

- It counts the number of 1s in the array and returns that value.

- For every 1 in the array, it substitutes a 0 in its place.

The main() method in the PassByReference class tests the use of the onetoZero() method. Go over the main() method line by line so that you can see what is going on and why the output shows what it does.

Lines 15–17 set up the initial variables for this example. The first one is an array of integers; the second one is an instance of the class PassByReference, which is stored in the variable test. The third is a simple integer to hold the number of 1s in the array.

Lines 19–23 print the initial values of the array; you can see the output of these lines in the first line of the output.

Line 25 is where the real work takes place; this is where you call the onetoZero() method defined in the object test and pass it the array stored in arr. This method returns the number of 1s in the array, which you then assign to the variable numOnes. It returns 3, as you would expect.

The last section of lines prints the array values. Because a reference to the array object is passed to the method, changing the array inside that method changes that array's original copy. Printing the values in lines 28–31 proves this; that last line of output shows that all the 1s in the array have been changed to 0s.

Class Methods

The relationship between class and instance variables is directly comparable to how class and instance methods work.

Class methods are available to any instance of the class itself and can be made available to other classes. In addition, unlike an instance method, a class does not require an instance of the class for its methods to be called.

For example, the Java class libraries include a class called Math. The Math class defines a set of math operations that you can use in any program or any of the various number types, as in the following:

```
double root = Math.sqrt(453.0);

System.out.print("The larger of x and y is " + Math.max(x, y));
```

To define class methods, use the static keyword in front of the method definition, just as you would use static in front of a class variable. For example, the class method max() used in the preceding example might have the following signature:

```
static int max(int arg1, int arg2) {
    // body of the method
}
```

Java supplies wrapper classes for each of the base types; for example, Java supplies Integer, Float, and Boolean classes. By using class methods defined in those classes, you can convert objects to primitive types and convert primitive types to objects.

For example, the parseInt() class method in the Integer class can be used with a string. The string is sent to the method as an argument, and this is used to calculate a return value to send back as an int.

The following statement shows how the parseInt() method can be used:

```
int count = Integer.parseInt("42");
```

In the preceding statement, the String value "42" is returned by parseInt() as an integer with a value of 42, and this is stored in the count variable.

The lack of a static keyword in front of a method name makes it an instance method. Instance methods operate in a particular object, rather than a class of objects. On Day 1, "Getting Started with Java," you created an instance method called checkTemperature() that checked the temperature in the robot's environment.

> **Tip**
>
> Most methods that operate on or affect a particular object should be defined as instance methods. Methods that provide some general capability but do not directly affect an instance of the class, should be declared as class methods.

Creating Java Applications

Now that you know how to create classes, objects, class and instance variables, and class and instance methods, you can put it all together into a Java program.

To refresh your memory, *applications* are Java programs that run on their own. Applications are different from *applets,* which require a Java-enabled browser to view them. The projects you have created up to this point have been Java applications. (You will get a chance to dive into applets during Day 14, "Writing Java Applets.")

A Java application consists of one or more classes and can be as large or as small as you want it to be. Although all the Java applications you've created up to this point do nothing but output some characters to the screen or to a window, you also can create Java applications that use windows, graphics, and user-interface elements.

The only thing you need in order to make a Java application run, however, is one class that serves as the starting point for the rest of your Java program.

The starting-point class for your application needs only one thing: a main() method. When the application is run, the main() method is the first thing that is called. None of this should be much of a surprise to you at this point; you've been creating Java applications with main() methods all along.

The signature for the main() method takes the following form:

```
public static void main(String[] arguments) {
    // body of method
}
```

Here's a rundown of the parts of the main() method:

- public means that this method is available to other classes and objects. The main() method must be declared public. You will learn more about public and private methods during Day 6, "Packages, Interfaces, and Other Class Features."

- static means that main() is a class method.

- void means that the main() method doesn't return a value.

- main() takes one parameter, which is an array of strings. This argument is used for program arguments, which you will learn about in the next section.

The body of the main() method contains any code you need to start your application, such as the initialization of variables or the creation of class instances.

When Java executes the main() method, keep in mind that main() is a class method. An instance of the class that holds main() is not created automatically when your program runs. If you want to treat that class as an object, you have to create an instance of it in the main() method.

5

Helper Classes

Your Java application can have only one class, or in the case of most larger programs, it might be made up of several classes, where different instances of each class are created and used while the application is running. You can create as many classes as you want for your program.

 Note   If you're using the Java 2 SDK, the classes must be accessible from a folder that's listed in your CLASSPATH.

As long as Java can find the class, your program will use it when it runs. Note, however, that only the starting-point class needs a main() method. After it is called, the methods inside the various classes and objects used in your program take over. Although you can include main() methods in helper classes, they will be ignored when the program actually runs.

Java Applications and Command-Line Arguments

Because Java applications are standalone programs, it's useful to pass arguments or options to an application. You did this on Day 4, "Lists, Logic, and Loops," in the DayCounter project.

You can use arguments to determine how an application is going to run or to enable a generic application to operate on different kinds of input. You can use program arguments for many different purposes, such as to turn on debugging input or to indicate a filename to load.

Passing Arguments to Java Applications

How you pass arguments to a Java application varies based on the platform you're running Java on and the development tool you are using.

To pass arguments to a Java program using the SDK, the arguments should be appended to the command line when the program is run. For example:

```
java EchoArgs April 450 -10
```

In the preceding example, three arguments were passed to a program: April, 450, and -10. Note that a space separates each of the arguments.

To group arguments that include spaces, the arguments should be surrounded with quotation marks. For example, note the following command line:

```
java EchoArgs Wilhelm Niekro Hough "Tim Wakefield" 49
```

Putting quotation marks around `Tim Wakefield` causes that text to be treated as a single argument. The `EchoArgs` program would receive five arguments: `Wilhelm`, `Niekro`, `Hough`, `Tim Wakefield`, and `49`. The quotation marks prevent the spaces from being used to separate one argument from another; they are not included as part of the argument when it is sent to the program and received using the `main()` method.

 Caution   One thing the quotation marks are not used for is to identify strings. Every argument passed to an application is stored in an array of `String` objects, even if it has a numeric value (such as `450`, `-10`, and `49` in the preceding examples).

Handling Arguments in Your Java Application

When an application is run with arguments, Java stores the arguments as an array of strings and passes the array to the application's `main()` method. Take another look at the signature for `main()`:

```
public static void main(String[] arguments) {
    // body of method
}
```

Here, *arguments* is the name of the array of strings that contains the list of arguments. You can call this array anything you like.

Inside the `main()` method, you then can handle the arguments your program was given by iterating over the array of arguments and handling them in some manner. For example, Listing 5.4 is a simple Java program that takes any number of numeric arguments and returns the sum and the average of those arguments.

LISTING 5.4   The Full Text of SumAverage.java

```
1: class SumAverage {
2:     public static void main(String[] arguments) {
3:         int sum = 0;
4:
5:         if (arguments.length > 0) {
6:             for (int i = 0; i < arguments.length; i++) {
7:                 sum += Integer.parseInt(arguments[i]);
8:             }
9:             System.out.println("Sum is: " + sum);
```

continues

5

LISTING 5.4   Continued

```
10:                     System.out.println("Average is: " +
11:                         (float)sum / arguments.length);
12:             }
13:         }
14: }
```

The SumAverage application makes sure in line 5 that at least one argument was passed to the program. This is handled through length, the instance variable that contains the number of elements in the arguments array.

You must always do things like this when dealing with command-line arguments. Otherwise, your programs will crash with ArrayIndexOutOfBoundsException errors whenever the user supplies fewer command-line arguments than you were expecting.

If at least one argument was passed, the for loop in lines 6–8 iterates through all the strings stored in the arguments array.

Because all command-line arguments are passed to a Java application as String objects, you must convert them to numeric values before using them in any mathematical expressions. The parseInt() class method of the Integer class is used on line 6. It takes a String object as input and returns an int.

If you can run Java classes on your system with a command line, type the following:

```
java SumAverage 1 4 13
```

You should see the following output:

```
Sum is: 18
Average is: 6.0
```

Note

> The array of arguments in Java is not analogous to argv in C and Unix. In particular, arg[0] or arguments[0], the first element in the array of arguments, is the first command-line argument after the name of the class—not the name of the program, as it would be in C. Be careful of this as you write your Java programs.

Creating Methods with the Same Name, Different Arguments

When you work with Java's class library, you often encounter classes that have numerous methods with the same name.

Two things differentiate methods with the same name:

- The number of arguments they take
- The data type or objects of each argument

These two things are part of a method's signature. Using several methods with the same name and different signatures is called *overloading*.

Method overloading can eliminate the need for entirely different methods that do essentially the same thing. Overloading also makes it possible for methods to behave differently based on the arguments they receive.

When you call a method in an object, Java matches the method name and arguments in order to choose which method definition to execute.

To create an overloaded method, you create different method definitions in a class, each with the same name but different argument lists. The difference can be the number, the type of arguments, or both. Java allows method overloading as long as each argument list is unique for the same method name.

Caution

Java does not consider the return type when differentiating among overloaded methods. If you attempt to create two methods with the same signature and different return types, the class won't compile. In addition, the variable names that you choose for each argument to the method are irrelevant. The number and the type of arguments are the two things that matter.

5

The next project is creating an overloaded method. It begins with a simple class definition for a class called MyRect, which defines a rectangular shape with four instance variables to define the upper-left and lower-right corners of the rectangle, x1, y1, x2, and y2:

```
class MyRect {
    int x1 = 0;
    int y1 = 0;
    int x2 = 0;
    int y2 = 0;
}
```

When a new instance of the MyRect class is created, all of its instance variables are initialized to 0.

A buildRect() instance method sets the variables to their correct values:

```
MyRect buildRect(int x1, int y1, int x2, int y2) {
    this.x1 = x1;
    this.y1 = y1;
```

```
        this.x2 = x2;
        this.y2 = y2;
        return this;
    }
```

This method takes four integer arguments and returns a reference to the resulting `MyRect` object. Because the arguments have the same names as the instance variables, the keyword `this` is used inside the method when referring to the instance variables.

This method can be used to create rectangles, but what if you wanted to define a rectangle's dimensions in a different way? An alternative would be to use `Point` objects rather than individual coordinates because `Point` objects contain both an x and y value as instance variables.

You can overload `buildRect()` by creating a second version of the method with an argument list that takes two `Point` objects:

```
MyRect buildRect(Point topLeft, Point bottomRight) {
    x1 = topLeft.x;
    y1 = topLeft.y;
    x2 = bottomRight.x;
    y2 = bottomRight.y;
    return this;
}
```

For the preceding method to work, the `java.awt.Point` class must be imported so that the Java compiler can find it.

Another possible way to define the rectangle is to use a top corner, a height, and a width:

```
MyRect buildRect(Point topLeft, int w, int h) {
    x1 = topLeft.x;
    y1 = topLeft.y;
    x2 = (x1 + w);
    y2 = (y1 + h);
    return this;
}
```

To finish this example, a `printRect()` is created to display the rectangle's coordinates and a `main()` method tries everything out. Listing 5.5 shows the completed class definition.

LISTING 5.5   The Full Text of `MyRect.java`

```
1: import java.awt.Point;
2:
3: class MyRect {
4:     int x1 = 0;
5:     int y1 = 0;
6:     int x2 = 0;
```

LISTING 5.5 Continued

```
 7:     int y2 = 0;
 8:
 9:     MyRect buildRect(int x1, int y1, int x2, int y2) {
10:         this.x1 = x1;
11:         this.y1 = y1;
12:         this.x2 = x2;
13:         this.y2 = y2;
14:         return this;
15:     }
16:
17:     MyRect buildRect(Point topLeft, Point bottomRight) {
18:         x1 = topLeft.x;
19:         y1 = topLeft.y;
20:         x2 = bottomRight.x;
21:         y2 = bottomRight.y;
22:         return this;
23:     }
24:
25:     MyRect buildRect(Point topLeft, int w, int h) {
26:         x1 = topLeft.x;
27:         y1 = topLeft.y;
28:         x2 = (x1 + w);
29:         y2 = (y1 + h);
30:         return this;
31:     }
32:
33:     void printRect(){
34:         System.out.print("MyRect: <" + x1 + ", " + y1);
35:         System.out.println(", " + x2 + ", " + y2 + ">");
36:     }
37:
38:     public static void main(String[] arguments) {
39:         MyRect rect = new MyRect();
40:
41:         System.out.println("Calling buildRect with coordinates 25,25,
                    50,50:");
42:         rect.buildRect(25, 25, 50, 50);
43:         rect.printRect();
44:         System.out.println("***");
45:
46:         System.out.println("Calling buildRect with points (10,10),
                    (20,20):");
47:         rect.buildRect(new Point(10,10), new Point(20,20));
48:         rect.printRect();
49:         System.out.println("***");
50:
51:         System.out.print("Calling buildRect with 1 point (10,10),");
52:         System.out.println(" width (50) and height (50):");
53:
```

5

continues

LISTING 5.5 Continued

```
54:          rect.buildRect(new Point(10,10), 50, 50);
55:          rect.printRect();
56:          System.out.println("***");
57:    }
58: }
```

The following is this program's output:

```
Calling buildRect with coordinates 25,25, 50,50:
MyRect: <25, 25, 50, 50>
***
Calling buildRect with points (10,10), (20,20):
MyRect: <10, 10, 20, 20>
***
Calling buildRect with 1 point (10,10), width (50) and height (50):
MyRect: <10, 10, 60, 60>
***
```

You can define as many versions of a method as you need to implement the behavior that is needed for that class.

When you have several methods that do similar things, using one method to call another is a shortcut technique to consider. For example, the buildRect() method in lines 17–23 can be replaced with the following, much shorter method:

```
MyRect buildRect(Point topLeft, Point bottomRight) {
    return buildRect(topLeft.x, topLeft.y,
        bottomRight.x, bottomRight.y);
}
```

The return statement in this method calls the buildRect() method in lines 9–15 with four integer arguments, producing the same result in fewer statements.

Constructor Methods

You also can define constructor methods in your class definition that are called automatically when objects of that class are created.

NEW TERM   A *constructor method* is a method that is called on an object when it is created—in other words, when it is constructed.

Unlike other methods, a constructor cannot be called directly. Java does three things when new is used to create an instance of a class:

- Allocates memory for the object
- Initializes that object's instance variables, either to initial values or to a default (0 for numbers, null for objects, false for Booleans, or '\0' for characters)
- Calls the constructor method of the class, which might be one of several methods

If a class doesn't have any constructor methods defined, an object still is created when the new operator is used in conjunction with the class. However, you might have to set its instance variables or call other methods that the object needs to initialize itself.

By defining constructor methods in your own classes, you can set initial values of instance variables, call methods based on those variables, call methods on other objects, and set the initial properties of an object. You also can overload constructor methods, as you can do with regular methods, to create an object that has specific properties based on the arguments you give to new.

Basic Constructors Methods

Constructors look a lot like regular methods, with three basic differences:

- They always have the same name as the class.
- They don't have a return type.
- They cannot return a value in the method by using the return statement.

For example, the following class uses a constructor method to initialize its instance variables based on arguments for new:

```
class VolcanoRobot {
    String status;
    int speed;
    int power;

    VolcanoRobot(String in1, int in2, int in3) {
        status = in1;
        speed = in2;
        power = in3;
    }
}
```

You could create an object of this class with the following statement:

```
VolcanoRobot vic = new VolcanoRobot("exploring", 5, 200);
```

The status instance variable would be set to exploring, speed to 5, and power to 200.

Calling Another Constructor Method

If you have a constructor method that duplicates some of the behavior of an existing constructor method, you can call the first constructor from inside the body of the second constructor. Java provides a special syntax for doing this. Use the following code to call a constructor method defined in the current class:

```
this(arg1, arg2, arg3);
```

The use of this with a constructor method is similar to how this can be used to access a current object's variables. In the preceding statement, the arguments with this() are the arguments for the constructor method.

For example, consider a simple class that defines a circle using the (x,y) coordinate of its center and the length of its radius. The class, MyCircle, could have two constructors: one where the radius is defined, and one where the radius is set to a default value of 1:

```
class MyCircle {
    int x, y, radius;

    MyCircle(int xPoint, int yPoint, int radiusLength) {
        this.x = xPoint;
        this.y = yPoint;
        this.radius = radiusLength;
    }

    MyCircle(int xPoint, int yPoint) {
        this(xPoint, yPoint, 1);
    }
}
```

The second constructor in MyCircle takes only the x and y coordinates of the circle's center. Because no radius is defined, the default value of 1 is used—the first constructor is called with the arguments xPoint, yPoint, and the integer literal 1.

Overloading Constructor Methods

Like regular methods, constructor methods also can take varying numbers and types of parameters. This capability enables you to create an object with exactly the properties you want it to have, or lets the object calculate properties from different kinds of input.

For example, the buildRect() methods that you defined in the MyRect class earlier today would make excellent constructor methods because they are being used to initialize an object's instance variables to the appropriate values. So, instead of the original buildRect() method that you defined (which took four parameters for the coordinates of the corners), you could create a constructor.

Listing 5.6 shows a new class, MyRect2, that has the same functionality of the original MyRect, except that it uses overloaded constructor methods instead of overloaded buildRect() methods.

LISTING 5.6   The Full Text of `MyRect2.java`

```
 1: import java.awt.Point;
 2:
 3: class MyRect2 {
 4:     int x1 = 0;
 5:     int y1 = 0;
 6:     int x2 = 0;
 7:     int y2 = 0;
 8:
 9:     MyRect2(int x1, int y1, int x2, int y2) {
10:         this.x1 = x1;
11:         this.y1 = y1;
12:         this.x2 = x2;
13:         this.y2 = y2;
14:     }
15:
16:     MyRect2(Point topLeft, Point bottomRight) {
17:         x1 = topLeft.x;
18:         y1 = topLeft.y;
19:         x2 = bottomRight.x;
20:         y2 = bottomRight.y;
21:     }
22:
23:     MyRect2(Point topLeft, int w, int h) {
24:         x1 = topLeft.x;
25:         y1 = topLeft.y;
26:         x2 = (x1 + w);
27:         y2 = (y1 + h);
28:     }
29:
30:     void printRect() {
31:         System.out.print("MyRect: <" + x1 + ", " + y1);
32:         System.out.println(", " + x2 + ", " + y2 + ">");
33:     }
34:
35:     public static void main(String[] arguments) {
36:         MyRect2 rect;
37:
38:         System.out.println("Calling MyRect2 with coordinates 25,25 50,50:");
39:         rect = new MyRect2(25, 25, 50,50);
40:         rect.printRect();
41:         System.out.println("***");
42:
43:         System.out.println("Calling MyRect2 with points (10,10), (20,20):");
44:         rect= new MyRect2(new Point(10,10), new Point(20,20));
45:         rect.printRect();
46:         System.out.println("***");
47:
48:         System.out.print("Calling MyRect2 with 1 point (10,10)");
49:         System.out.println(" width (50) and height (50):");
```

5

continues

LISTING 5.6   Continued

```
50:            rect = new MyRect2(new Point(10,10), 50, 50);
51:            rect.printRect();
52:            System.out.println("***");
53:
54:    }
55: }
```

Overriding Methods

When you call an object's method, Java looks for that method definition in the object's class. If it doesn't find one, it passes the method call up the class hierarchy until a method definition is found. Method inheritance enables you to define and use methods repeatedly in subclasses without having to duplicate the code.

However, there might be times when you want an object to respond to the same methods but have different behavior when that method is called. In that case, you can override the method. To override a method, define a method in a subclass with the same signature as a method in a superclass. Then, when the method is called, the subclass method is found and executed instead of the one in the superclass.

Creating Methods That Override Existing Methods

To override a method, all you have to do is create a method in your subclass that has the same signature (name, return type, and argument list) as a method defined by your class's superclass. Because Java executes the first method definition it finds that matches the signature, the new signature hides the original method definition.

Here's a simple example; Listing 5.7 contains two classes: `PrintClass`, which contains a method called `printMe()` that displays information about objects of that class, and `PrintSubClass`, a subclass that adds a z instance variable to the class.

LISTING 5.7   The Full Text of `PrintClass.java`

```
1: class PrintClass {
2:     int x = 0;
3:     int y = 1;
4:
5:     void printMe() {
6:         System.out.println("x is " + x + ", y is " + y);
7:         System.out.println("I am an instance of the class " +
8:         this.getClass().getName());
9:     }
```

LISTING 5.7   Continued

```
10: }
11:
12: class PrintSubClass extends PrintClass {
13:     int z = 3;
14:
15:     public static void main(String[] arguments) {
16:         PrintSubClass obj = new PrintSubClass();
17:         obj.printMe();
18:     }
19: }
```

After compiling this file, run `PrintSubClass` with the Java interpreter to see the following output:

```
x is 0, y is 1
I am an instance of the class PrintSubClass
```

Caution

Make sure that you run `PrintSubClass` with the interpreter rather than `PrintClass`. The `PrintClass` class does not have a `main()` method, so it cannot be run as an application.

A `PrintSubClass` object was created and the `printMe()` method was called in the `main()` method of `PrintSubClass`. Because the `PrintSubClass` does not define the `printMe()` method, Java looks for it in the superclasses of `PrintSubClass`, starting with `PrintClass`. `PrintClass` has a `printMe()` method, so it is executed. Unfortunately, this method does not display the z instance variable, as you can see from the preceding output.

To correct the problem, you could override the `printMe()` method of `PrintClass` in `PrintSubClass`, adding a statement to display the z instance variable:

```
void printMe() {
    System.out.println("x is " + x + ", y is " + y +
        ", z is " + z);
    System.out.println("I am an instance of the class " +
        this.getClass().getName());
}
```

5

Calling the Original Method

Usually, there are two reasons why you want to override a method that a superclass already has implemented:

- To replace the definition of that original method completely
- To augment the original method with additional behavior

Overriding a method and giving the method a new definition hides the original method definition. There are times, however, when behavior should be added to the original definition instead of replacing it completely, particularly when behavior is duplicated in both the original method and the method that overrides it. By calling the original method in the body of the overriding method, you can add only what you need.

Use the super keyword to call the original method from inside a method definition. This keyword passes the method call up the hierarchy, as shown in the following:

```
void myMethod (String a, String b) {
    // do stuff here
    super.myMethod(a, b);
    // do more stuff here
}
```

The super keyword, similar to the this keyword, is a placeholder for the class's superclass. You can use it anywhere that you use this, but super refers to the superclass rather than the current object.

Overriding Constructors

Technically, constructor methods cannot be overridden. Because they always have the same name as the current class, new constructor methods are created instead of being inherited. This system is fine much of the time; when your class's constructor method is called, the constructor method with the same signature for all your superclasses is also called. Therefore, initialization can happen for all parts of a class that you inherit.

However, when you are defining constructor methods for your own class, you might want to change how your object is initialized, not only by initializing new variables added by your class, but also by changing the contents of variables that are already there. To do this, explicitly call the constructor methods of the superclass and subsequently change whatever variables need to be changed.

To call a regular method in a superclass, you use super.*methodname*(*arguments*). Because constructor methods don't have a method name to call, the following form is used:

```
super(arg1, arg2, ...);
```

Note that Java has a specific rule for the use of super(): It must be the very first statement in your constructor definition. If you don't call super() explicitly in your constructor, Java does it for you—using super() with no arguments. Because a call to a super() method must be the first statement, you can't do something like the following in your overriding constructor:

```
if (condition == true)
    super(1,2,3); // call one superclass constructor
else
    super(1,2); // call a different constructor
```

Similar to using this() in a constructor method, super() calls the constructor method for the immediate superclass (which might, in turn, call the constructor of its super-class, and so on). Note that a constructor with that signature has to exist in the super-class for the call to super() to work. The Java compiler checks this when you try to compile the source file.

You don't have to call the constructor in your superclass that has the same signature as the constructor in your class; you have to call the constructor only for the values you need initialized. In fact, you can create a class that has constructors with entirely differ-ent signatures from any of the superclass's constructors.

Listing 5.8 shows a class called NamedPoint, which extends the class Point from the java.awt package. The Point class has only one constructor, which takes an x and a y argument and returns a Point object. NamedPoint has an additional instance variable (a string for the name) and defines a constructor to initialize x, y, and the name.

LISTING 5.8 The NamedPoint Class

```
1: import java.awt.Point;
2:
3: class NamedPoint extends Point {
4:     String name;
5:
6:     NamedPoint(int x, int y, String name) {
7:         super(x,y);
8:         this.name = name;
9:     }
10:
11:     public static void main(String[] arguments) {
12:         NamedPoint np = new NamedPoint(5, 5, "SmallPoint");
13:         System.out.println("x is " + np.x);
14:         System.out.println("y is " + np.y);
15:         System.out.println("Name is " + np.name);
16:     }
17: }
```

The output of the program is as follows:

```
x is 5
y is 5
Name is SmallPoint
```

The constructor method defined here for `NamedPoint` calls `Point`'s constructor method to initialize the instance variables of `Point` (x and y). Although you can just as easily initialize x and y yourself, you might not know what other things `Point` is doing to initialize itself. Therefore, it is always a good idea to pass constructor methods up the hierarchy to make sure everything is set up correctly.

Finalizer Methods

Finalizer methods are almost the opposite of constructor methods. A *constructor method* is used to initialize an object, whereas *finalizer methods* are called just before the object is collected for garbage and has its memory reclaimed.

The finalizer method is `finalize()`. The `Object` class defines a default finalizer method that does nothing. To create a finalizer method for your own classes, override the `finalize()` method using this signature:

```
protected void finalize() throws Throwable {
    super.finalize();
}
```

 Note

> The `throws Throwable` part of this method definition refers to the errors that might occur when this method is called. Errors in Java are called *exceptions*; you learn more about them on Day 7, "Threads and Exceptions." For now, all you need to do is include these keywords in the method definition.

Include any cleaning up that you want to do for that object inside the body of that `finalize()` method. You also can call `super.finalize()` to enable your class's superclasses to finalize the object if necessary.

You can call the `finalize()` method yourself at any time; it's a method just like any other. However, calling `finalize()` does not trigger an object to be collected in the garbage. Only removing all references to an object causes it to be marked for deletion.

Finalizer methods are valuable for optimizing the removal of an object—for example, by removing references to other objects. In most cases, you don't need to use `finalize()` at all.

Summary

After finishing today's lesson, you should have a pretty good idea of the relationship among classes in Java and programs you create using the language.

Everything you create in Java involves the use of a main class that interacts with other classes as needed. It's a different programming mindset than you might be used to with other languages.

Today you put together everything you have learned about creating Java classes. Each of the following topics was covered:

- Instance and class variables, which hold the attributes of a class and objects created from it.

- Instance and class methods, which define the behavior of a class. You learned how to define methods—including the parts of a method signature, how to return values from a method, how arguments are passed to methods, and how to use the `this` keyword to refer to the current object.

- The `main()` method of Java applications, and how to pass arguments to it from the command line.

- Overloaded methods, which reuse a method name by giving it different arguments.

- Constructor methods, which define the initial variables and other starting conditions of an object.

Q&A

Q **In my class, I have an instance variable called `origin`. I also have a local variable called `origin` in a method, which, because of variable scope, gets hidden by the local variable. Is there any way to access the instance variable's value?**

A The easiest way to avoid this problem is to give your local variables different names than your instance variables have. Otherwise, you can use `this.origin` to refer to the instance variable and `origin` to refer to the local variable.

Q **I created two methods with the following signatures:**

```
int total(int arg1, int arg2, int arg3) {...}
float total(int arg1, int arg2, int arg3) {...}
```

The Java compiler complains when I try to compile the class with these method definitions, but their signatures are different. What have I done wrong?

A Method overloading in Java works only if the parameter lists are different—either in number or type of arguments. Return type is not relevant for method overloading. Think about it; if you had two methods with exactly the same parameter list, how would Java know which one to call?

Q I wrote a program to take four arguments, but when I give it too few arguments, it crashes with a runtime error. Why?

A Testing for the number and type of arguments your program expects is up to you in your Java program; Java won't do it for you. If your program requires four arguments, test that you have indeed been given four arguments, and return an error message if you haven't.

Quiz

Review today's material by taking this quiz.

Questions

1. If a local variable has the same name as an instance variable, how can you refer to the instance variable in the scope of the local variable?

    (a.) You can't; you should rename one of the variables.

    (b.) Use the keyword `this` before the instance variable name.

    (c.) Use the keyword `super` before the name.

2. Where are instance variables declared in a class?

    (a.) Anywhere in the class

    (b.) Outside of all methods in the class

    (c.) After the class declaration and above the first method

3. How can you send an argument to a program that includes a space character?

    (a.) Surround it with quotes

    (b.) Separate the arguments with commas

    (c.) Separate the arguments with period characters

Answers

1. (b.) Answer (a.) is a good idea, though. Variable name conflicts can be a source of subtle errors in your Java programs.

2. (b.) Customarily, instance variables are declared right after the class declaration and before any methods. It's necessary only that they be outside of all methods.

3. (a.) The quotation marks will not be included in the argument when it is passed to the program.

Certification Practice

The following question is the kind of thing you could expect to be asked on a Java programming certification test. Answer it without looking at today's material or using the Java compiler to test the code.

Given:

```java
public class BigValue {
    float result;

    public BigValue(int a, int b) {
        result = calculateResult(a, b);
    }

    float calculateResult(int a, int b) {
        return (a * 10) + (b * 2);
    }

    public static void main(String[] arguments) {
        BiggerValue bgr = new BiggerValue(2, 3, 4);
        System.out.println("The result is " + bgr.result);
    }
}

class BiggerValue extends BigValue {

    BiggerValue(int a, int b, int c) {
        super(a, b);
        result = calculateResult(a, b, c);
    }

    // answer goes here
        return (c * 3) * result;
    }
}
```

What statement should replace `// answer goes here` so that the `result` variable equals 312.0?

```
(a.) float calculateResult(int c) {
(b.) float calculateResult(int a, int b) {
(c.) float calculateResult(int a, int b, int c) {
(d.) float calculateResult() {
```

The answer is available on this book's Web site at `http://www.java21days.com`. Visit the Day 5 page and click the Certification Practice link.

Exercises

To extend your knowledge of the subjects covered today, try the following exercises:

- Modify the `VolcanoRobot` project from Day 1 so that it includes constructor methods.

- Create a class for four-dimensional points called `FourDPoint` that is a subclass of `Point` from the `java.awt` package.

Where applicable, exercise solutions are offered on this book's Web site at `http://www.java21days.com`.

DAY 6

Packages, Interfaces, and Other Class Features

Java has a lot of class.

Classes, the templates used to create objects that can store data and accomplish tasks, turn up in everything you do with the language. Consequently, you must spend a lot of time learning how to use them.

Today, you will extend your knowledge of classes by learning more about how to create them, use them, organize them, and establish rules for how others can use them.

The following subjects will be covered:

- Controlling access to methods and variables from outside a class
- Finalizing classes, methods, and variables so that their values or definitions cannot be subclasses or cannot be overridden
- Creating abstract classes and methods for factoring common behavior into superclasses

- Grouping classes into packages
- Using interfaces to bridge gaps in a class hierarchy

Modifiers

The techniques for programming that you will learn today involve different strategies and ways of thinking about how a class is organized. The one thing all these techniques have in common is that they all use special modifier keywords in the Java language.

During this week, you have learned how to define classes, methods, and variables in Java. *Modifiers* are keywords that you add to those definitions in order to change their meanings.

The Java language has a wide variety of modifiers, including

- Modifiers for controlling access to a class, method, or variable: `public`, `protected`, and `private`
- The `static` modifier, for creating class methods and variables
- The `final` modifier, for finalizing the implementations of classes, methods, and variables
- The `abstract` modifier, for creating abstract classes and methods
- The `synchronized` and `volatile` modifiers, which are used for threads

To use a modifier, you include its keyword in the definition of the class, method, or variable that is being modified. The modifier precedes the rest of the statement, as in the following examples:

```
public class MyApplet extends javax.swing.JApplet {
    // ...
}

private boolean offline;

static final double weeks = 9.5;

protected static final int MEANING_OF_LIFE = 42;

public static void main(String[] arguments) {
    // ...
}
```

If you're using more than one modifier in a statement, you can place them in any order, as long as all modifiers precede the element they are modifying. Make sure to avoid treating a method's return type—such as void—as if it were one of the modifiers.

Modifiers are optional—which you may realize, after using very few of them in the preceding six days. You can come up with many good reasons to use them, though, as you'll see.

Access Control for Methods and Variables

The modifiers that you will use the most often in your programs are the ones that control access to methods and variables: `public`, `private`, and `protected`. These modifiers determine which variables and methods of a class are visible to other classes.

By using access control, you can control how other classes will use your class. Some variables and methods in a class will be of use only within the class itself, and they should be hidden from other classes that might interact with the class. This process is called encapsulation: An object controls what the outside world can know about it and how the outside world can interact with it.

NEW TERM   *Encapsulation* is the process that prevents class variables from being read or modified by other classes. The only way to use these variables is by calling methods of the class, if they are available.

The Java language provides four levels of access control: public, private, protected, and a default level that is specified by using no modifier.

Default Access

Variables and methods can be declared without any modifiers, as in the following examples:

```
String version = "0.7a";

boolean processOrder() {
    return true;
}
```

A variable or method that is declared without any access control modifier is available to any other class in the same package. The Java class library is organized into packages such as `java.awt`, which are windowing classes for use primarily in graphical user interface programming, and `java.util`, a useful collection of utility classes.

Any variable declared without a modifier can be read or changed by any other class in the same package. Any method declared the same way can be called by any other class in the same package. No other classes can access these elements in any way.

This level of access control doesn't control much access. When you begin to consider how other classes will use your class, you'll choose one of the three modifiers more often than the default control option.

6

Note

The preceding discussion raises the question about what package your own classes have been in up to this point. As you'll see later today, you can make your class a member of a package by using the package declaration. If you don't use this approach, the class is put into a package with all other classes that don't belong to any other packages.

Private Access

To completely hide a method or variable from being used by any other classes, you use the `private` modifier. The only place these methods or variables can be seen is from within their own class.

A private instance variable, for example, can be used by methods in its own class but not by objects of any other class. In the same vein, private methods can be called by other methods in their own class but cannot be called by any others. This restriction also affects inheritance: Neither private variables nor private methods are inherited by subclasses.

Private variables are extremely useful in two circumstances:

- When other classes have no reason to use that variable
- When another class could wreak havoc by changing the variable in an inappropriate way

For example, consider a Java class called `SlotMachine` that generates bingo numbers for an Internet gambling site. A variable in that class called `winRatio` could control the number of winners and losers that are generated. As you can imagine, this variable has a big impact on the bottom line at the site. If the variable were changed by other classes, the performance of `SlotMachine` would change greatly. To guard against this scenario, you can declare the `winRatio` variable as `private`.

The following class uses private access control:

```java
class Writer {
    private boolean writersBlock = true;
    private String mood;
    private int income = 0;

    private void getIdea(Inspiration in) {
        // ...
    }

    Manuscript createManuscript(int numDays, long numPages) {
        // ...
    }
}
```

In this code example, the internal data to the class Writer (the variables writersBlock, mood, and income and the method getIdea()) are all private. The only method accessible from outside the Writer class is the createManuscript() method. createManuscript() is the only task other objects can ask the Writer object to perform. Editor and Publisher objects might prefer a more direct means of extracting a Manuscript object from the Writer, but they don't have the access to do so.

Using the private modifier is the main way that an object encapsulates itself. You can't limit the ways in which a class is used without using private in many places to hide variables and methods. Another class is free to change the variables inside a class and call its methods in many possible ways if you don't control access.

Public Access

In some cases, you might want a method or variable in a class to be completely available to any other class that wants to use it. Think of the class variable black from the Color class. This variable is used when a class wants to use the color black, so black should have no access control at all.

Class variables often are declared to be public. An example would be a set of variables in a Football class that represent the number of points used in scoring. The TOUCHDOWN variable could equal 7, the FIELD_GOAL variable could equal 3, and so on. If these variables are public, other classes could use them in statements such as the following:

```
if (position < 0) {
    System.out.println("Touchdown!");
    score = score + Football.TOUCHDOWN;
}
```

The public modifier makes a method or variable completely available to all classes. You have used it in every application you have written so far, with a statement such as the following:

```
public static void main(String[] arguments) {
    // ...
}
```

The main() method of an application has to be public. Otherwise, it could not be called by a Java interpreter (such as java) to run the class.

Because of class inheritance, all public methods and variables of a class are inherited by its subclasses.

6

Protected Access

The third level of access control is to limit a method and variable to use by the following two groups:

- Subclasses of a class
- Other classes in the same package

You do so by using the `protected` modifier, as in the following statement:

```
protected boolean outOfData = true;
```

 Note

You might be wondering how these two groups are different. After all, aren't subclasses part of the same package as their superclass? Not always. An example is the `JApplet` class. It is a subclass of `java.applet.Applet` but is actually in the `javax.swing` package. Protected access differs from default access this way; protected variables are available to subclasses, even if they aren't in the same package.

This level of access control is useful if you want to make it easier for a subclass to implement itself. Your class might use a method or variable to help the class do its job. Because a subclass inherits much of the same behavior and attributes, it might have the same job to do. Protected access gives the subclass a chance to use the helper method or variable, while preventing a non-related class from trying to use it.

Consider the example of a class called `AudioPlayer` that plays a digital audio file. `AudioPlayer` has a method called `openSpeaker()`, which is an internal method that interacts with the hardware to prepare the speaker for playing. `openSpeaker()` isn't important to anyone outside the `AudioPlayer` class, so at first glance you might want to make it `private`. A snippet of `AudioPlayer` might look something like this:

```
class AudioPlayer {

    private boolean openSpeaker(Speaker sp) {
        // implementation details
    }
}
```

This code works fine if `AudioPlayer` isn't going to be subclassed. But what if you were going to create a class called `StreamingAudioPlayer` that is a subclass of `AudioPlayer`? That class would want access to the `openSpeaker()` method so that it can override it and provide streaming audio-specific speaker initialization. You still don't want the method generally available to random objects (and so it shouldn't be `public`), but you want the subclass to have access to it.

Comparing Levels of Access Control

The differences among the various protection types can become very confusing, particularly in the case of `protected` methods and variables. Table 6.1, which summarizes exactly what is allowed where, helps clarify the differences from the least restrictive (`public`) to the most restrictive (`private`) forms of protection.

TABLE 6.1 The Different Levels of Access Control

Visibility	public	protected	default	private
From the same class	yes	yes	yes	yes
From any class in the same package	yes	yes	yes	no
From any class outside the package	yes	no	no	no
From a subclass in the same package	yes	yes	yes	no
From a subclass outside the same package	yes	yes	no	no

Access Control and Inheritance

One last issue regarding access control for methods involves subclasses. When you create a subclass and override a method, you must consider the access control in place on the original method.

As a general rule, you cannot override a method in Java and make the new method more controlled than the original. You can, however, make it more public. The following rules for inherited methods are enforced:

- Methods declared `public` in a superclass must also be `public` in all subclasses of that class.
- Methods declared `protected` in a superclass must either be `protected` or `public` in subclasses; they cannot be `private`.
- Methods declared without access control (no modifier was used) can be declared more private in subclasses.

Methods declared `private` are not inherited at all, so the rules don't apply.

6

Accessor Methods

In many cases, you may have an instance variable in a class that has strict rules for the values it can contain. An example would be a `zipCode` variable. A ZIP Code in the United States must be a number that is five digits long.

To prevent an external class from setting the `zipCode` variable incorrectly, you can declare it `private` with a statement such as the following:

```
private int zipCode;
```

However, what if other classes must be able to set the `zipCode` variable for the class to be useful? In that circumstance, you can give other classes access to a private variable by using an accessor method inside the same class as `zipCode`.

An accessor method is so named because it provides access to something that otherwise would be off-limits. By using a method to provide access to a private variable, you can control how that variable is used. In the ZIP Code example, the class could prevent anyone else from setting `zipCode` to an incorrect value.

Often, separate accessor methods to read and write a variable are available. Reading methods have a name beginning with `get`, and writing methods have a name beginning with `set`, as in `setZipCode(int)` and `getZipCode(int)`.

Note

> This convention is becoming more standard with each version of Java. You might want to use the same naming convention for your own accessor methods as a means of making the class more understandable.

Using methods to access instance variables is a frequently used technique in object-oriented programming. This approach makes classes more reusable because it guards against a class being used improperly.

Static Variables and Methods

A modifier that you already have used in programs is `static`, which was introduced during Day 5, "Creating Classes and Methods." The `static` modifier is used to create class methods and variables, as in the following example:

```
public class Circle {
    public static float PI = 3.14159265F;

    public float area(float r) {
        return PI * r * r;
    }
}
```

Class variables and methods can be accessed using the class name followed by a dot and the name of the variable or method, as in `Color.black` or `Circle.PI`. You also can use the name of an object of the class, but for class variables and methods, using the class name is better. This approach makes clearer what kind of variable or method you're working with; instance variables and methods can never be referred to by a class name.

The following statements use class variables and methods:

```
float circumference = 2 * Circle.PI * getRadius();
float randomNumber = Math.random();
```

Tip

For the same reason that holds true for instance variables, class variables can benefit from being private and limiting their use to accessor methods only.

Listing 6.1 shows a class called `CountInstances` that uses class and instance variables to keep track of how many instances of that class have been created.

LISTING 6.1   The Full Text of `CountInstances.java`

```
 1: public class CountInstances {
 2:     private static int numInstances = 0;
 3:
 4:     protected static int getNumInstances() {
 5:         return numInstances;
 6:     }
 7:
 8:     private static void addInstance() {
 9:         numInstances++;
10:     }
11:
12:     CountInstances() {
13:         CountInstances.addInstance();
14:     }
15:
16:     public static void main(String[] arguments) {
17:         System.out.println("Starting with " +
18:             CountInstances.getNumInstances() + " instances");
19:         for (int  i = 0; i < 10; ++i)
20:             new CountInstances();
21:         System.out.println("Created " +
22:             CountInstances.getNumInstances() + " instances");
23:     }
24: }
```

6

The output of this program is as follows:

```
Started with 0 instances
Created 10 instances
```

This example has a number of features. In line 2, you declare a `private` class variable to hold the number of instances (called `numInstances`). It is a class variable (declared `static`) because the number of instances is relevant to the class as a whole, not to any one instance. And it's private so that it follows the same rules as instance variables' accessor methods.

Note the initialization of `numInstances` in that same line. Just as an instance variable is initialized when its instance is created, a class variable is initialized when its class is created. This class initialization happens essentially before anything else can happen to that class, or its instances, so that the class in the example will work as planned.

In lines 4–6, you create a `get` method for that private instance variable to get its value (`getNumInstances()`). This method is also declared as a class method because it applies directly to the class variable. The `getNumInstances()` method is declared `protected`, as opposed to `public`, because only this class and perhaps its subclasses will be interested in that value; other random classes are therefore restricted from seeing it.

Note that you don't have an accessor method to set the value. The reason is that the value of the variable should be incremented only when a new instance is created; it should not be set to any random value. Instead of creating an accessor method, therefore, you create a special private method called `addInstance()` in lines 8–10 that increments the value of `numInstances` by 1.

Lines 12–14 create the constructor method for this class. Remember, constructors are called when a new object is created, which makes this the most logical place to call `addInstance()` and to increment the variable.

Finally, the `main()` method indicates that you can run this as a Java application and test all the other methods. In the `main()` method, you create ten instances of the `CountInstances` class, reporting after you're done the value of the `numInstances` class variable (which, predictably, prints `10`).

Final Classes, Methods, and Variables

The `final` modifier is used with classes, methods, and variables to indicate that they will not be changed. It has different meanings for each thing that can be made final, as follows:

- A `final` class cannot be subclassed.
- A `final` method cannot be overridden by any subclasses.
- A `final` variable cannot change in value.

Variables

Final variables are often called constant variables (or just constants) because they do not change in value at any time.

With variables, the `final` modifier often is used with `static` to make the constant a class variable. If the value never changes, you don't have much reason to give each object in the same class its own copy of the value. They all can use the class variable with the same functionality.

The following statements are examples of declaring constants:

```
public static final int TOUCHDOWN = 7;
static final String TITLE = "Captain";
```

In Java 1.0, a local variable could not be final, but that was changed as part of the addition of inner classes to the language. As of Java 2, any kind of variable can be a final variable: class, instance, or local variables.

Methods

Final methods are those that can never be overridden by a subclass. You declare them using the `final` modifier in the class declaration, as in the following example:

```
public final void getSignature() {
    // ...
}
```

The most common reason to declare a method `final` is to make the class run more efficiently. Normally, when a Java runtime environment such as the `java` interpreter runs a method, it checks the current class to find the method first, checks its superclass second, and onward up the class hierarchy until the method is found. This process sacrifices some speed in the name of flexibility and ease of development.

If a method is `final`, the Java compiler can put the executable bytecode of the method directly into any program that calls the method. After all, the method won't ever change because of a subclass that overrides it.

When you are first developing a class, you won't have much reason to use `final`. However, if you need to make the class execute more quickly, you can change a few methods into `final` methods to speed up the process. Doing so removes the possibility of the method being overridden in a subclass later on, so consider this change carefully before continuing.

The Java class library declares many of the commonly used methods `final` so that they can be executed more quickly when utilized in programs that call them.

6

Note Private methods are final without being declared that way because they can't be overridden in a subclass under any circumstance.

Classes

You finalize classes by using the `final` modifier in the declaration for the class, as in the following:

```
public final class ChatServer {
    // ....
}
```

A final class cannot be subclassed by another class. As with final methods, this process introduces some speed benefits to the Java language at the expense of flexibility.

If you're wondering what you're losing by using final classes, you must not have tried to subclass something in the Java class library yet. Many of the popular classes are final, such as `java.lang.String`, `java.lang.Math`, and `java.net.InetAddress`. If you want to create a class that behaves like strings but with some new changes, you can't subclass `String` and define only the behavior that is different. You have to start from scratch.

All methods in a final class automatically are final themselves, so you don't have to use a modifier in their declarations.

Because classes that can bequeath their behavior and attributes to subclasses are much more useful, you should strongly consider whether the benefit of using `final` on one of your classes is outweighed by the cost.

Abstract Classes and Methods

In a class hierarchy, the higher the class, the more abstract its definition. A class at the top of a hierarchy of other classes can define only the behavior and attributes that are common to all the classes. More specific behavior and attributes are going to fall somewhere lower down the hierarchy.

When you are factoring out common behavior and attributes during the process of defining a hierarchy of classes, you might at times find yourself with a class that doesn't ever need to be instantiated directly. Instead, such a class serves as a place to hold common behavior and attributes shared by their subclasses.

These classes are called abstract classes, and they are created using the abstract modifier. The following is an example:

```
public abstract class Palette {
    // ...
}
```

An example of an abstract class is java.awt.Component, the superclass of graphical user interface components. Because numerous components inherit from this class, it contains methods and variables useful to each of them. However, there's no such thing as a generic component that can be added to an interface, so you would never need to create a Component object in a program.

Abstract classes can contain anything a normal class can, including constructor methods, because their subclasses might need to inherit the methods. Abstract classes also can contain abstract methods, which are method signatures with no implementation. These methods are implemented in subclasses of the abstract class. Abstract methods are declared with the abstract modifier. You cannot declare an abstract method in a non-abstract class. If an abstract class has nothing but abstract methods, you're better off using an interface, as you'll see later today.

Packages

Using packages, as mentioned previously, is a way of organizing groups of classes. A package contains any number of classes that are related in purpose, in scope, or by inheritance.

If your programs are small and use a limited number of classes, you might find that you don't need to explore packages at all. But the more Java programming you create, the more classes you'll find you have. And although those classes might be individually well designed, reusable, encapsulated, and might have specific interfaces to other classes, you may discover the need for a bigger organizational entity that enables you to group your packages.

Packages are useful for several broad reasons:

- Packages enable you to organize your classes into units. Just as you have folders or directories on your hard disk to organize your files and applications, packages enable you to organize your classes into groups so that you use only what you need for each program.

- Packages reduce problems with conflicts in names. As the number of Java classes grows, so does the likelihood that you'll use the same class name as someone else, opening up the possibility of naming clashes and error messages if you try to integrate groups of classes into a single program. Packages enable you to "hide" classes so that conflicts can be avoided.

6

- Packages enable you to protect classes, variables, and methods in larger ways than on a class-by-class basis, as you learned today. You'll learn more about protections with packages later.
- Packages can be used to identify your classes. For example, if you implement a set of classes to perform some task, you could name a package of those classes with a unique identifier that identifies you or your organization.

Although a package is most typically a collection of classes, packages can also contain other packages, forming yet another level of organization somewhat analogous to the inheritance hierarchy. Each "level" usually represents a smaller, more specific grouping of classes. The Java class library itself is organized along these lines. The top level is called java; the next level includes names such as io, net, util, and awt. The last of them has an even lower level, which includes the package image.

Using Packages

You've been using packages all along in this book. Every time you use the import command, and every time you refer to a class by its full package name (java.awt.Color, for example), you are using packages.

To use a class contained in a package, you can use one of three mechanisms:

- If the class you want to use is in the package java.lang (for example, System or Date), you can simply use the class name to refer to that class. The java.lang classes are automatically available to you in all your programs.
- If the class you want to use is in some other package, you can refer to that class by its full name, including any package names (for example, java.awt.Font).
- For classes that you use frequently from other packages, you can import individual classes or a whole package of classes. After a class or a package has been imported, you can refer to that class by its class name.

If you don't declare that your class belongs to a package, it is put into an unnamed default package. You can refer to that class simply by its class name from anywhere in your code.

Full Package and Class Names

To refer to a class in some other package, you can use its full name, which is the class name preceded by any package names. You do not have to import the class or the package to use it this way:

```
java.awt.Font f = new java.awt.Font()
```

For classes that you use only once or twice in your program, using the full name makes sense. If, however, you use that class multiple times, or if the package name is very long with lots of subpackages, you should import that class instead to save yourself some typing.

When you begin creating your own packages, you'll place all files in a package in the same folder. Each element of a package name corresponds to its own subfolder.

Consider the example of a `TransferBook` class that is part of the `com.prefect.library` package.

The following line should be the first statement in the source code of the class:

```
package com.prefect.library;
```

After you compile the `TransferBook` class, you must store it in a folder that corresponds with the package name. If you're using the Software Development Kit, the Java interpreter and other tools will look for the `TransferBook.class` file in several different places:

- The `com\prefect\library` subfolder of the folder where the `java` command was entered (for example, if the command was made from the `C:\J21work` folder, the `TransferBook.class` file could be run successfully if it was in the `C:\J21work\com\prefect\library` folder)
- The `com\prefect\library` subfolder of any folder in your `CLASSPATH` setting

One way to manage your own packages and any others you use is to add a folder to your `CLASSPATH` that serves as the root folder for any packages you create, such as `C:\javapackages` or something similar. After creating subfolders that correspond to the name of a package, place the package's class files in the correct subfolder.

The `import` Declaration

To import classes from a package, use the `import` declaration, as you've used throughout the examples in this book. You can either import an individual class, like this:

```
import java.util.Vector;
```

Or you can import an entire package of classes, using an asterisk (*) to replace the individual class names, like this:

```
import java.awt.*
```

6

> **Note**
>
> To be technically correct, this declaration doesn't import all the classes in a package; it imports only the classes that have been declared `public`, and even then it imports only those classes that the code itself refers to. You'll learn more about this topic in the section titled "Packages and Class Access Control."

Note that the asterisk (*) in this example is not like the one you might use at a command prompt to specify the contents of a folder or to indicate multiple files. For example, if you ask to list the contents of the directory `classes/java/awt/*`, that list includes all the `.class` files and subdirectories, such as `image` and `peer`. Writing `import java.awt.*` imports all the public classes in that package but does not import subpackages such as `image` and `peer`. To import all the classes in a complex package hierarchy, you must explicitly import each level of the hierarchy by hand. Also, you cannot indicate partial class names (for example, `L*` to import all the classes that begin with L). Your only options when using an `import` declaration are to load all the classes in a package or just a single class.

The `import` declarations in your class definition go at the top of the file, before any class definitions (but after the package declaration, as you'll see in the next section).

Should you take the time to import classes individually or simply import them as a group? The answer depends on how specific you want to be. Importing a group of classes does not slow down your program or make it any larger; only the classes that you actually use in your code are loaded as they are needed. Admittedly, importing a package does make it a little more confusing for readers of your code to figure out where your classes are coming from. Using individual `import` declaration or importing packages is mostly a question of your own coding style.

> **Note**
>
> If you're coming to Java from C or C++, you might expect the `import` declaration to work like `#include`, which results in a very large program because it includes source code from another file. This isn't the case; `import` indicates only where the Java compiler can find a class. It doesn't do anything to expand the size of a class.

Name Conflicts

After you have imported a class or a package of classes, you can usually refer to a class name simply by its name, without the package identifier. In one case, you might have to be more explicit: when you have multiple classes with the same name from different packages.

Here's an example. Assume that you import the classes from two packages:

```
import com.naviseek.web.*;
import com.prefect.http.*;
```

Inside the `com.naviseek.web` package is a class called `FTP`. Unfortunately, inside the `com.prefect.http` package, you also find a class called `FTP` that has an entirely different meaning and implementation. You might wonder which version of `FTP` is used if you refer to the `FTP` class in your own program like this:

```
FTP out = new FTP();
```

The answer is neither; the Java compiler will not compile your program because of the naming conflict. In this case, despite the fact that you imported both classes, you still have to refer to the appropriate `FTP` class by its full package name, as follows:

```
com.prefect.http.FTP out = new
    com.prefect.http.FTP();
```

A Note About CLASSPATH and Where Classes Are Located

For Java to be able to use a class, it has to be able to find that class on the file system. Otherwise, you get an error message indicating that the class does not exist. Java uses two elements to find classes: the package name itself and the directories listed in your CLASSPATH variable.

First, the package names: Package names map to directory names on the file system, so that the class `com.naviseek.Mapplet` is found in the `naviseek` directory, which in turn is inside the `com` directory (in other words, `com\naviseek\Mapplet.class`).

Java looks for those directories, in turn, inside the directories listed in your CLASSPATH variable, if one is provided in your configuration. If you installed the SDK, you used the CLASSPATH variable to point to the various places where your Java classes live. If no CLASSPATH is provided, the SDK looks only in the current folder for classes.

When Java looks for a class that you've referenced in your source, it looks for the package and class name in each of those directories and returns an error message if it can't find the class file. Most `class not found` error messages result because of misconfigured CLASSPATH variables.

Creating Your Own Packages

Creating a package for some of your classes in Java is not much more complicated than creating a class. You must follow three basic steps, as outlined next.

6

Picking a Package Name

The first step is to decide on a name. The name you choose for your package depends on how you will be using those classes. Perhaps you will name your package after yourself or perhaps you will name the package after the part of the Java system you're working on (such as graphics or messaging). If you intend to distribute your package to the Net at large or as part of a commercial product, you should use a package name that uniquely identifies the author.

A convention for naming packages recommended by Sun Microsystems, Inc. is to use your Internet domain name with the elements reversed. If your Internet domain name is naviseek.com, your package name might be com.naviseek. You might want to lengthen the name by adding something that describes the classes in the package, such as com.naviseek.canasta.

Note Sun has not followed this recommendation with three of its own Java packages—java, the package that comprises the Java class library; javax, the classes that extend the library; and sun, which consists of additional classes that are not part of the Java class library.

The idea is to make sure your package name is unique. Although packages can hide conflicting class names, the protection stops there. You cannot make sure that your package won't conflict with someone else's package if you both use the same package name.

By convention, package names tend to begin with a lowercase letter to distinguish them from class names. For example, in the full name of the built-in String class, java.lang.String, you can more easily separate the package name from the class name visually. This convention helps reduce name conflicts.

Creating the Folder Structure

Step two in creating packages is to create a folder structure on your hard drive that matches the package name. If your package has just one name (myPackage), you must create a folder for that one name only. If the package name has several parts, you have to create folders within folders. For the package name com.naviseek.canasta, for example, you need to create a com folder, a naviseek folder inside com, and a canasta folder inside naviseek. Your classes and source files can then go inside the canasta directory.

Adding a Class to a Package

The final step to putting your class inside packages is to add a statement to the class file above any import declarations that are being used. The package declaration is used along with the name of the package, as in the following:

```
package com.naviseek.canasta;
```

The single package declaration, if any, must be the first line of code in your source file, after any comments or blank lines and before any import declarations.

After you start using packages, you should make sure that all your classes belong to some package to reduce the chance of confusion about where your classes belong.

Packages and Class Access Control

Previously, you learned about access control modifiers for methods and variables. You also can control access to classes, as you might have noticed when the public modifier was used in some class declarations on past projects.

Classes have the default access control if no modifier is specified, which means that the class is available to all other classes in the same package but is not visible or available outside that package—not even to subpackages. It cannot be imported or referred to by name; classes with package protection are hidden inside the package in which they are contained.

Package protection comes about when you define a class as you have throughout this book, like this:

```
class TheHiddenClass extends AnotherHiddenClass {
    // ...
}
```

To allow a class to be visible and importable outside your package, you can give it public protection by adding the public modifier to its definition:

```
public class TheVisibleClass {
    // ...
}
```

Classes declared as public can be imported by other classes outside the package.

Note that when you use an import statement with an asterisk, you import only the public classes inside that package. Hidden classes remain hidden and can be used only by the other classes in that package.

Why would you want to hide a class inside a package? For the same reasons that you want to hide variables and methods inside a class: so that you can have utility classes and behavior that are useful only to your implementation, or so that you can limit the interface

6

of your program to minimize the effect of larger changes. As you design your classes, you should take the whole package into consideration and decide which classes you want to declare public and which you want to be hidden.

Think of protections not as hiding classes entirely, but more accurately as checking the permissions of a given class to use other classes, variables, and methods.

Creating a good package consists of defining a small, clean set of public classes and methods for other classes to use, and then implementing them by using any number of hidden support classes. You'll see another use for hidden classes later today.

Interfaces

Interfaces, like abstract classes and methods, provide templates of behavior that other classes are expected to implement. Interfaces, however, provide far more functionality to Java and to class and object design than do simple abstract classes and methods.

The Problem of Single Inheritance

After some deeper thought or more complex design experience, you might discover that the pure simplicity of the class hierarchy is restrictive, particularly when you have some behavior that needs to be used by classes in different branches of the same tree.

Look at an example that will make the problems clearer. Assume that you have a biological hierarchy with Animal at the top, and the classes Mammal and Bird underneath. Things that define a mammal include bearing live young and having fur. Behavior or features of birds include having a beak and laying eggs. So far, so good, right? So, how do you go about creating a class for the platypus, which has fur and a beak, and lays eggs? You would need to combine behavior from two classes to form the Platypus class. And, because classes can have only one immediate superclass in Java, this sort of problem simply cannot be solved elegantly.

Other object-oriented programming (OOP) languages include the concept of multiple inheritance, which solves this problem. With multiple inheritance, a class can inherit from more than one superclass and get behavior and attributes from all its superclasses at once. A problem with multiple inheritance is that it makes a programming language far more complex to learn, to use, and to implement. Questions of method invocation and how the class hierarchy is organized become far more complicated with multiple inheritance, and more open to confusion and ambiguity. Because one of the goals for Java was that it be simple, multiple inheritance was rejected in favor of the simpler single inheritance.

How do you solve the problem of needing common behavior that doesn't fit into the strict class hierarchy? Java has another hierarchy altogether separate from the main class hierarchy, which is a hierarchy of mixable behavior classes. Then, when you create a new class, that class has only one primary superclass, but it can pick and choose different common behaviors from the other hierarchy. This other hierarchy is the interface hierarchy. A Java interface is a collection of abstract behavior that can be mixed into any class to add to that class's behavior that is not supplied by its superclasses. Specifically, a Java interface contains nothing but abstract method definitions and constants—but no instance variables and no method implementations.

Interfaces are implemented and used throughout the Java class library whenever a behavior is expected to be implemented by a number of disparate classes. Later today, you'll use one of the interfaces in the Java class hierarchy, `java.lang.Comparable.`.

Interfaces and Classes

Classes and interfaces, despite their different definitions, have a great deal in common. Interfaces, like classes, are declared in source files and are compiled using the Java compiler into `.class` files. And, in most cases, anywhere you can use a class (as a data type for a variable, as the result of a cast, and so on) you can also use an interface.

You can substitute an interface name for a class name in almost every example in this book. Java programmers often say "class" when they actually mean "class or interface." Interfaces complement and extend the power of classes, and the two can be treated almost the same, but an interface cannot be instantiated: `new` can create an instance of only a non-abstract class.

Implementing and Using Interfaces

You can do two things with interfaces: use them in your own classes and define your own. For now, start with by using them in your own classes.

To use an interface, you include the `implements` keyword as part of your class definition:

```
public class AnimatedSign extends javax.swing.JApplet
    implements Runnable {
    //...
}
```

In this example, `javax.swing.JApplet` is the superclass, but the `Runnable` interface extends the behavior that it implements.

Because interfaces provide nothing but abstract method definitions, you then have to implement those methods in your own classes, using the same method signatures from the interface. Note that after you include an interface, you have to implement all the methods in that interface; you can't pick and choose the methods you need. By implementing an interface, you're telling users of your class that you support the entire interface.

6

After your class implements an interface, subclasses of your class inherit those new methods (and can override or overload them) just as if your superclass had actually defined them. If your class inherits from a superclass that implements a given interface, you don't have to include the `implements` keyword in your own class definition.

Examine one simple example now—creating the new class `Orange`. Suppose that you already have a good implementation of the class `Fruit` and an interface, `Fruitlike`, that represents what a `Fruit` is expected to be able to do. You want an orange to be a fruit, but you also want it to be a spherical object that can be tossed, rotated, and so on. Here's how to express it all. (Don't worry about the definitions of these interfaces for now; you'll learn more about them later today.)

```
interface  Fruitlike {
    void   decay();
    void   squish();
    // ...
}

class  Fruit implements Fruitlike {
    private Color myColor;
    private int daysTilIRot;
    // ...
}

interface  Spherelike {
    void   toss();
    void   rotate();
    // ...
}

class  Orange extends Fruit implements Spherelike {
    // toss()ing may squish() me (unique to me)
}
```

Note that the class `Orange` doesn't have to say `implements Fruitlike` because, by extending `Fruit`, it already has! One of the nice things about this structure is that you can change your mind about what class `Orange` extends (if a really great `Sphere` class is suddenly implemented, for example) yet class `Orange` still understands the same two interfaces:

```
class  Sphere implements Spherelike {
   // extends Object
    private float  radius;
    // ...
}

class  Orange extends Sphere implements Fruitlike {
    // ... users of Orange never need know about the change!
}
```

Implementing Multiple Interfaces

Unlike with the singly inherited class hierarchy, you can include as many interfaces as you need in your own classes, and your class will implement the combined behavior of all the included interfaces. To include multiple interfaces in a class, just separate their names with commas:

```
public class AnimatedSign extends javax.swing.JApplet
    implements Runnable, Observable {

    // ...
}
```

Note that complications might arise from implementing multiple interfaces. What happens if two different interfaces both define the same method? You can solve this problem in three ways:

- If the methods in each of the interfaces have identical signatures, you implement one method in your class and that definition satisfies both interfaces.

- If the methods have different parameter lists, it is a simple case of method overloading; you implement both method signatures, and each definition satisfies its respective interface definition.

- If the methods have the same parameter lists but differ in return type, you cannot create a method that satisfies both. (Remember that method overloading is triggered by parameter lists, not by return type.) In this case, trying to compile a class that implements both interfaces produces a compiler error message. Running across this problem suggests that your interfaces have some design flaws that you might need to reexamine.

Other Uses of Interfaces

Remember that almost everywhere that you can use a class, you can use an interface instead. For example, you can declare a variable to be of an interface type:

```
Runnable aRunnableObject = new MyAnimationClass()
```

When a variable is declared to be of an interface type, it simply means that any object the variable refers to is expected to have implemented that interface; that is, it is expected to understand all the methods that the interface specifies. It assumes that a promise made between the designer of the interface and its eventual implementers has been kept. In this case, because aRunnableObject contains an object of the type Runnable, the assumption is that you can call aRunnableObject.run().

The important point to realize here is that although aRunnableObject is expected to be able to have the run() method, you could write this code long before any classes that

6

qualify are actually implemented (or even created!). In traditional object-oriented programming, you are forced to create a class with "stub" implementations (empty methods, or methods that print silly messages) to get the same effect. You can also cast objects to an interface, just as you can cast objects to other classes. So, for example, go back to that definition of the Orange class, which implemented both the Fruitlike interface (through its superclass, Fruit) and the Spherelike interface. Here you can cast instances of Orange to both classes and interfaces:

```
Orange anOrange = new Orange();
Fruit aFruit = (Fruit)anOrange;
Fruitlike aFruitlike = (Fruitlike)anOrange;
Spherelike aSpherelike = (Spherelike)anOrange;

aFruit.decay(); // fruits decay
aFruitlike.squish(); //  and squish

aFruitlike.toss(); // things that are fruitlike do not toss
aSpherelike.toss(); // but things that are spherelike do

anOrange.decay(); // oranges can do it all
anOrange.squish();
anOrange.toss();
anOrange.rotate();
```

In this example, declarations and casts are used to restrict an orange's behavior to acting more like a mere fruit or sphere.

Finally, note that although interfaces are usually used to mix in behavior to other classes (method signatures), interfaces also can be used to mix in generally useful constants. For example, if an interface defines a set of constants, and then multiple classes use those constants, the values of those constants could be globally changed without having to modify multiple classes. This is yet another example of a case in which the use of interfaces to separate design from implementation can make your code more general and more easily maintainable.

Creating and Extending Interfaces

After you use interfaces for a while, the next step is to define your own interfaces. Interfaces look a lot like classes; they are declared in much the same way and can be arranged into a hierarchy. However, you must follow certain rules for declaring interfaces.

New Interfaces

To create a new interface, you declare it like this:

```
interface Growable {
    // ...
}
```

This declaration is, effectively, the same as a class definition, with the word `interface` replacing the word `class`. Inside the interface definition, you have methods and constants. The method definitions inside the interface are `public` and `abstract` methods; you can either declare them explicitly as such, or they will be turned into `public` and `abstract` methods if you do not include those modifiers. You cannot declare a method inside an interface to be either `private` or `protected`. So, for example, here's a `Growable` interface with one method explicitly declared `public` and `abstract` (`growIt()`) and one implicitly declared as (`growItBigger()`):

```
public interface Growable {
    public abstract void growIt(); // explicitly public and abstract
    void growItBigger(); // effectively public and abstract
}
```

Note that, as with abstract methods in classes, methods inside interfaces do not have bodies. Remember, an interface is pure design; no implementation is involved.

In addition to methods, interfaces also can have variables, but those variables must be declared `public`, `static`, and `final` (making them constant). As with methods, you can explicitly define a variable to be `public`, `static`, and `final`, or it is implicitly defined as such if you don't use those modifiers. Here's that same `Growable` definition with two new variables:

```
public interface Growable {
    public static final int increment = 10;
    long maxnum = 1000000; // becomes public static and final

    public abstract void growIt(); //explicitly public and abstract
    void growItBigger(); // effectively public and abstract
}
```

Interfaces must have either public or package protection, just like classes. Note, however, that interfaces without the `public` modifier do not automatically convert their methods to `public` and `abstract` or their constants to `public`. A non-public interface also has non-public methods and constants that can be used only by classes and other interfaces in the same package.

Interfaces, like classes, can belong to a package. Interfaces can also import other interfaces and classes from other packages, just as classes can.

Methods Inside Interfaces

Here's one trick to note about methods inside interfaces: Those methods are supposed to be abstract and apply to any kind of class, but how can you define parameters to those methods? You don't know what class will be using them! The answer lies in the fact that

6

you use an interface name anywhere a class name can be used, as you learned earlier. By defining your method parameters to be interface types, you can create generic parameters that apply to any class that might use this interface.

Consider the interface Fruitlike, which defines methods (with no arguments) for decay() and squish(). You might also have a method for germinateSeeds(), which has one argument: the fruit itself. Of what type is that argument going to be? It can't be simply Fruit because you may have a class that's Fruitlike (that is, one that implements the Fruitlike interface) without actually being a fruit. The solution is to declare the argument as simply Fruitlike in the interface:

```
public interface Fruitlike {
    public abstract germinate(Fruitlike self) {
        // ...
    }
}
```

Then, in an actual implementation for this method in a class, you can take the generic Fruitlike argument and cast it to the appropriate object:

```
public class Orange extends Fruit {

public germinate(Fruitlike self) {
    Orange theOrange = (Orange)self;
    // ...
    }
}
```

Extending Interfaces

As you can do with classes, you can organize interfaces into a hierarchy. When one interface inherits from another interface, that "subinterface" acquires all the method definitions and constants that its "superinterface" declared. To extend an interface, you use the extends keyword just as you do in a class definition:

```
interface Fruitlike extends Foodlike {
    // ...
}
```

Note that, unlike classes, the interface hierarchy has no equivalent of the Object class; this hierarchy is not rooted at any one point. Interfaces can either exist entirely on their own or inherit from another interface.

Note also that, unlike the class hierarchy, the inheritance hierarchy is multiply inherited. For example, a single interface can extend as many classes as it needs to (separated by commas in the extends part of the definition), and the new interface will contain a combination of all its parent's methods and constants. Here's an interface definition for an interface called `BusyInterface` that inherits from a whole lot of other interfaces:

```
public interface BusyInterface extends Runnable, Growable, Fruitlike,
    Observable {

    // ...
}
```

In multiply inherited interfaces, the rules for managing method name conflicts are the same as for classes that use multiple interfaces; methods that differ only in return type result in a compiler error message.

Creating an Online Storefront

To explore all the topics covered up to this point today, the `Storefront` application uses packages, access control, interfaces, and encapsulation. This application manages the items in an online storefront, handling two main tasks:

- Calculating the sale price of each item depending on how much of it is presently in stock
- Sorting items according to sale price

The `Storefront` application consists of two classes, `Storefront` and `Item`. These classes will be organized as a new package called `com.prefect.ecommerce`, so the first task is to define a directory structure on your system where this package's classes will be stored.

SDK 1.4 and other Java development tools look for packages in the folders listed in the system's `CLASSPATH`. The package name is also taken into account, so if `c:\jdk1.4` is in your `CLASSPATH`, `Storefront.class` and `Item.class` could be stored in `c:\jdk1.4\com\prefect\ecommerce`.

One way to manage your own packages is to create a new folder that will contain packages, and then add a reference to this folder when setting your `CLASSPATH`.

After you have created a folder where this package's files will be stored, create `Item.java` from Listing 6.2.

LISTING 6.2 The Full Text of `Item.java`

```
1: package com.prefect.ecommerce;
2:
3: import java.util.*;
4:
5: public class Item implements Comparable {
6:     private String id;
```

continues

LISTING 6.2 Continued

```
 7:         private String name;
 8:         private double retail;
 9:         private int quantity;
10:         private double price;
11:
12:         Item(String idIn, String nameIn, String retailIn, String quanIn) {
13:             id = idIn;
14:             name = nameIn;
15:             retail = Double.parseDouble(retailIn);
16:             quantity = Integer.parseInt(quanIn);
17:
18:             if (quantity > 400)
19:                 price = retail * .5D;
20:             else if (quantity > 200)
21:                 price = retail * .6D;
22:             else
23:                 price = retail * .7D;
24:             price = Math.floor( price * 100 + .5 ) / 100;
25:         }
26:
27:         public int compareTo(Object obj) {
28:             Item temp = (Item)obj;
29:             if (this.price < temp.price)
30:                 return 1;
31:             else if (this.price > temp.price)
32:                 return -1;
33:             return 0;
34:         }
35:
36:         public String getId() {
37:             return id;
38:         }
39:
40:         public String getName() {
41:             return name;
42:         }
43:
44:         public double getRetail() {
45:             return retail;
46:         }
47:
48:         public int getQuantity() {
49:             return quantity;
50:         }
51:
52:         public double getPrice() {
53:             return price;
54:         }
55: }
```

The Item class is a support class that represents a product sold by an online store. There are private instance variables for the product ID code, name, how many are in stock (quantity), and the retail and sale prices.

Because all the instance variables of this class are private, no other class can set or retrieve their values. Simple accessor methods are created in lines 36–54 of Listing 6.2 to provide a way for other programs to retrieve these values. Each method begins with get followed by the capitalized name of the variable, which is standard in the Java class library. For example, getPrice() returns a double containing the value of price. No methods are provided for setting any of these instance variables—that will be handled in the constructor method for this class.

Line 1 establishes that the Item class is part of the com.prefect.ecommerce package.

Note   Prefect.com is the personal domain of this book's co-author, so this project follows Sun's package-naming convention by beginning with a top-level domain (com), following it with the developer's domain name (prefect), and then by a name that describes the purpose of the package (ecommerce).

The Item class implements the Comparable interface (line 5), which makes it easy to sort a class's objects. This interface has only one method, compareTo(Object), which returns an integer.

The compareTo() method compares two objects of a class: the current object and another object passed as an argument to the method. The value returned by the method defines the natural sorting order for objects of this class:

- If the current object should be sorted above the other object, return -1.
- If the current object should be sorted below the other object, return 1.
- If the two objects are equal, return 0.

You determine in the compareTo() method which of an object's instance variables to consider when sorting. Lines 27–34 override the compareTo() method for the Item class, sorting on the basis of the price variable. Items are sorted by price from highest to lowest.

After you have implemented the Comparable interface for an object, there are two class methods that can be called to sort an array, linked list, or other collection of those objects. You will see this when Storefront.class is created.

The Item() constructor in lines 12–25 takes four String objects as arguments and uses them to set up the id, name, retail, and quantity instance variables. The last two must

6

be converted from strings to numeric values using the `Double.parseDouble()` and `Integer.parseInt()` class methods, respectively.

The value of the `price` instance variable depends on how much of that item is presently in stock:

- If there are more than 400 in stock, `price` is 50 percent of `retail` (lines 18–19).
- If there are between 201 and 400 in stock, `price` is 60 percent of `retail` (lines 20–21).
- For everything else, `price` is 70 percent of `retail` (lines 22–23).

Line 24 rounds off `price` so that it contains two or fewer decimal points, turning a price such as $6.92999999999999 to $6.99. The `Math.floor()` method rounds off decimal numbers to the next lowest mathematical integer, returning them as double values.

After you have compiled `Item.class`, you're ready to create a class that represents a storefront of these products. Create `Storefront.java` from Listing 6.3.

LISTING 6.3 The Full Text of `Storefront.java`

```
 1: package com.prefect.ecommerce;
 2:
 3: import java.util.*;
 4:
 5: public class Storefront {
 6:     private LinkedList catalog = new LinkedList();
 7:
 8:     public void addItem(String id, String name, String price,
 9:         String quant) {
10:
11:         Item it = new Item(id, name, price, quant);
12:         catalog.add(it);
13:     }
14:
15:     public Item getItem(int i) {
16:         return (Item)catalog.get(i);
17:     }
18:
19:     public int getSize() {
20:         return catalog.size();
21:     }
22:
23:     public void sort() {
24:         Collections.sort(catalog);
25:     }
26: }
```

The `Storefront.class` is used to manage a collection of products in an online store. Each product is an `Item` object, and they are stored together in a `LinkedList` instance variable named `catalog` (line 6).

The `addItem()` method in lines 8–13 creates a new `Item` object based on four arguments sent to the method: the ID, name, price, and quantity in stock of the item. After the item is created, it is added to the `catalog` linked list by calling its `add()` method with the `Item` object as an argument.

The `getItem()` and `getSize()` methods provide an interface to the information stored in the private `catalog` variable. The `getSize()` method in lines 19–21 calls the `catalog.size()` method, which returns the number of objects contained in `catalog`.

Because objects in a linked list are numbered like arrays and other data structures, you can retrieve them using an index number. The `getItem()` method in lines 15–17 calls `catalog.get()` with an index number as an argument, returning the object stored at that location in the linked list.

The `sort()` method in lines 23–25 is where you benefit from the implementation of the `Comparable` interface in the `Item` class. The class method `Collections.sort()` will sort a linked list and other data structures based on the natural sort order of the objects they contain, calling the object's `compareTo()` method to determine this order.

After you have created the `Storefront` class, you're ready to develop a program that actually makes use of the `com.prefect.ecommerce` package. Open the folder on your system where you've been creating the programs of this book (such as `\J21work`) and create `GiftShop.java` from Listing 6.4.

 Caution

> Don't save `GiftShop.java` in the same folder on your system where the classes of the `com.prefect.ecommerce` package are stored. It's not part of the package (as you'll note by the absence of a `package com.prefect.ecommerce` statement). The Java compiler will exit with an error message because it wasn't expecting to find `Storefront.class` in the same folder as the `GiftShop` application.

6

LISTING 6.4 The Full Text of `Giftshop.java`

```
1: import com.prefect.ecommerce.*;
2:
3: public class GiftShop {
4:     public static void main(String[] arguments) {
5:         Storefront store = new Storefront();
```

continues

LISTING 6.4 Continued

```
 6:          store.addItem("C01", "MUG", "9.99", "150");
 7:          store.addItem("C02", "LG MUG", "12.99", "82");
 8:          store.addItem("C03", "MOUSEPAD", "10.49", "800");
 9:          store.addItem("D01", "T SHIRT", "16.99", "90");
10:          store.sort();
11:
12:          for (int i = 0; i < store.getSize(); i++) {
13:              Item show = (Item)store.getItem(i);
14:              System.out.println("\nItem ID: " + show.getId() +
15:                  "\nName: " + show.getName() +
16:                  "\nRetail Price: $" + show.getRetail() +
17:                  "\nPrice: $" + show.getPrice() +
18:                  "\nQuantity: " + show.getQuantity());
19:          }
20:      }
21: }
```

The `GiftShop` class demonstrates each part of the public interface that the `Storefront` and `Item` classes make available. You can do each of the following:

- Create an online store
- Add items to it
- Sort the items by sale price
- Loop through a list of items to display information about each one

 Caution

> If you have created the `Item.class` and `Storefront.class` files in the same folder as `Giftshop.java`, you might not be able to compile the program because the Java compiler expects to find those files in their package folder. Move those files to the `com\prefect\ecommerce` folder and compile `Giftshop.java` in another folder, such as `\J21work`.

The output of this program is the following:

```
Item ID: D01
Name: T SHIRT
Retail Price: $16.99
Price: $11.89
Quantity: 90

Item ID: C02
Name: LG MUG
Retail Price: $12.99
Price: $9.09
Quantity: 82
```

```
Item ID: C01
Name: MUG
Retail Price: $9.99
Price: $6.99
Quantity: 150

Item ID: C03
Name: MOUSEPAD
Retail Price: $10.49
Price: $5.25
Quantity: 800
```

Many of the implementation details of these classes are hidden from GiftShop and other classes that would make use of the package.

For instance, the programmer who developed GiftShop doesn't need to know that Storefront uses a linked list to hold all the store's product data. If the developer of Storefront decided later to use a different data structure, as long as getSize() and getItem() returned the expected values, GiftShop would continue to work correctly.

Inner Classes

The classes you have worked with thus far are all members of a package, either because you specified a package name with the package declaration or because the default package was used. Classes that belong to a package are known as *top-level* classes. When Java was introduced, they were the only classes supported by the language.

Beginning with Java 1.1, you could define a class inside a class, as if it were a method or a variable. These types of classes are called *inner* classes. Listing 6.5 contains the DisplayResult application, which uses an inner class called Squared to square a floating-point number and store the result.

LISTING 6.5   The Full Text of DisplayResult.java

```
 1: public class DisplayResult {
 2:     public DisplayResult(String input) {
 3:         try {
 4:             float in = Float.parseFloat(input);
 5:             Squared sq = new Squared(in);
 6:             float result = sq.value;
 7:             System.out.println("The square of " + input + " is " + result);
 8:         } catch (NumberFormatException nfe) {
 9:             System.out.println(input + " is not a valid number.");
10:         }
11:     }
12:
13:     class Squared {
```

6

continues

LISTING 6.5 Continued

```
14:          float value;
15:
16:          Squared(float x) {
17:              value = x * x;
18:          }
19:      }
20:
21:      public static void main(String[] arguments) {
22:          if (arguments.length < 1) {
23:              System.out.println("Usage: java DisplayResult number");
24:          } else {
25:              DisplayResult dr = new DisplayResult(arguments[0]);
26:          }
27:      }
28: }
```

After compiling this application, run it with a floating-point number as an argument. For example, with the SDK you could enter the following at a command line:

```
java DisplayResult 13.0
```

Here's the output for that example:

```
The square of 13.0 is 169.0
```

If you run it without any arguments, the following text is displayed before the program exits:

```
Usage: java DisplayResult number
```

In this application, the Squared class isn't functionally different from a helper class that is included in the same source file as a program's main class file. The only difference is that the helper is defined inside the class file, which has several advantages:

- Inner classes are invisible to all other classes, which means that you don't have to worry about name conflicts between them and other classes.

- Inner classes can have access to variables and methods within the scope of a top-level class that they would not have as a separate class.

In many cases, an inner class is a short class file that exists only for a limited purpose. In the DisplayResult application, because the Squared class doesn't contain a lot of complex behavior and attributes, it is well suited for implementation as an inner class.

The name of an inner class is associated with the name of the class in which it is contained, and it is assigned automatically when the program is compiled. In the example of the Squared class, it is given the name DisplayResult$Squared.class by the Java compiler.

When you're using inner classes, you must be even more careful to include all .class files when making a program available. Each inner class has its own class file, and these class files must be included along with any top-level classes.

Inner classes, although seemingly a minor enhancement, actually represent a significant modification to the language.

Rules governing the scope of an inner class closely match those governing variables. An inner class's name is not visible outside its scope, except in a fully qualified name, which helps in structuring classes within a package. The code for an inner class can use simple names from enclosing scopes, including class and member variables of enclosing classes, as well as local variables of enclosing blocks.

In addition, you can define a top-level class as a static member of another top-level class. Unlike an inner class, a top-level class cannot directly use the instance variables of any other class. The ability to nest classes in this way allows any top-level class to provide a package-style organization for a logically related group of secondary top-level classes.

Summary

Today, you learned how to encapsulate an object by using access control modifiers for its variables and methods. You also learned how to use other modifiers such as `static`, `final`, and `abstract` in the development of Java classes and class hierarchies.

To further the effort of developing a set of classes and using them, you learned how to group classes into packages. These groupings better organize your programs and enable the sharing of classes with the many other Java programmers who are making their code publicly available.

Finally, you learned how to implement interfaces and inner classes, two structures that are helpful when designing a class hierarchy.

Q&A

Q Won't using accessor methods everywhere slow down my Java code?

A Not always. As Java compilers improve and can create more optimizations, they will be able to make accessor methods fast automatically, but if you're concerned about speed, you can always declare accessor methods to be `final`, and they'll be comparable in speed to direct instance variable accesses under most circumstances.

6

Q Based on what I've learned, `private abstract` methods and `final abstract` methods or classes don't seem to make sense. Are they legal?

A Nope, they're compile-time error messages, as you have guessed. To be useful, `abstract` methods must be overridden, and `abstract` classes must be subclassed, but neither of those two operations would be legal if they were also `private` or `final`.

Quiz

Review today's material by taking this quiz.

Questions

1. What packages are automatically imported into your Java classes?

   (a.) None

   (b.) The classes stored in the folders of your `CLASSPATH`

   (c.) The classes in the `java.lang` package

2. According to the convention for naming packages, what should be the first part of the name of a package you create?

   (a.) Your name followed by a period

   (b.) Your top-level Internet domain followed by a period

   (c.) The text `java` followed by a period

3. If you create a subclass and override a `public` method, what access modifiers can you use with that method?

   (a.) `public` only

   (b.) `public` or `protected`

   (c.) `public`, `protected`, or default access

Answers

1. (c.) All other packages must be imported if you want to use short class names such as `LinkedList` instead of full package and class names such as `java.util.LinkedList`.

2. (b.) This convention assumes that all Java package developers will own an Internet domain or have access to one so that the package can be made available for download.

3. (a.) All `public` methods must remain `public` in subclasses.

Certification Practice

The following question is the kind of thing you could expect to be asked on a Java programming certification test. Answer it without looking at today's material or using the Java compiler to test the code.

Given:

```
package com.prefect.bureau;

public class Information {
    public int duration = 12;
    protected float rate = 3.15F;
    float average = 0.5F;
}
```

And:

```
package com.prefect.bureau;

import com.prefect.bureau.*;

public class MoreInformation extends Information {
    public int quantity = 8;
}
```

And:

```
package com.prefect.bureau.us;

import com.prefect.bureau.*;

public class EvenMoreInformation extends MoreInformation {
    public int quantity = 9;

    EvenMoreInformation() {
        super();
        int i1 = duration;
        float i2 = rate;
        float i3 = average;
    }
}
```

Which instance variables are visible in the EvenMoreInformation class?

(a.) quantity, duration, rate, and average

(b.) quantity, duration, and rate

(c.) quantity, duration, and average

(d.) quantity, rate, and average

6

The answer is available on this book's Web site at `http://www.java21days.com`. Visit the Day 6 page and click the Certification Practice link.

Exercises

To extend your knowledge of the subjects covered today, try the following exercises:

- Create a modified version of the `Storefront` project that includes a `noDiscount` variable for each item. When this variable is `true`, sell the item at the retail price.
- Create a `ZipCode` class that uses access control to ensure that its `zipCode` instance variable always has a five-digit value.

Where applicable, exercise solutions are offered on the book's Web site at `http://www.java21days.com`.

DAY 7

Threads and Exceptions

Today, you will complete your weeklong journey through the Java language by learning about two of its most powerful elements:

- *Threads*, which are objects that implement the `Runnable` interface and can run simultaneously with other parts of a Java program
- *Exceptions,* which are objects that are used to handle errors that may occur as a Java program is running

Both of these features become most useful while a Java program is running.

Threads enable your programs to make more efficient use of its resources by separating the computing-intensive parts of a program so that they don't slow down the rest of the program.

Exceptions enable your programs to recognize errors and respond to them. Exceptions even assist your programs to correct the conditions if possible.

You'll start with exceptions, because they're one of the things that you will use when developing threads.

Exceptions

Programmers in any language endeavor to write bug-free programs, programs that never crash, programs that can handle any situation with grace, and that can recover from unusual situations without causing the user any undue stress. Good intentions aside, programs like this don't exist.

In real programs, errors occur either because the programmer didn't anticipate every situation the code would get into (or didn't have the time to test the program enough), or because of situations out of the programmer's control—including but not limited to bad data from users, corrupt files that don't have the right data in them, network connections that don't connect, hardware devices that don't respond, sun spots, gremlins, whatever.

In Java, these sorts of strange events that might cause a program to fail are called exceptions. Java defines a number of language features that deal with exceptions, including the following:

- How to handle exceptions in your code and recover gracefully from potential problems
- How to tell Java and your methods' users that you're expecting a potential exception
- How to create an exception if you detect one
- How your code is limited, yet made more robust by exceptions

With most programming languages, handling error conditions requires much more work than handling a program that is running properly. It can require a very confusing structure of statements, similar in functionality to Java's if...else and switch blocks, to deal with errors that might occur.

As an example, consider the following statements, which show the structure of how a file might be loaded from disk. Loading a file is something that can be problematic because of a number of different circumstances such as disk errors, file-not-found errors, and the like. If the program must have the data from the file in order to operate properly, it must deal with all of these circumstances before continuing.

Here's the structure of one possible solution:

```
int status = loadTextfile();
if (status != 1) {
    // something unusual happened, describe it
    switch (status) {
        case 2:
            // file not found
            break;
        case 3:
            // disk error
            break;
        case 4:
```

```
                // file corrupted
                break;
            default:
                // other error
        }
    } else {
        // file loaded OK, continue with program
    }
```

This code tries to load a file with a method call to `loadTextfile()`, which has been defined elsewhere in the program. This method returns an integer that indicates whether the file loaded properly (`status == 1`) or an error occurred (`status` equals anything other than 1).

Depending on the error that occurs, the program uses a `switch` statement to try to work around it. The end result is an elaborate block of code in which the most common circumstance—a successful file load—can be lost amid the error-handling code. This is the result of handling only one possible error. If other errors take place later in the program, you might end up with more nested `if...else` and `switch-case` blocks.

Error management can become a major problem after you start creating larger systems. Different programmers use different special values for handling errors, and they might not document them well, if at all. You might inconsistently use errors in your own programs. Code to manage these kinds of errors can often obscure the program's original intent, making the code difficult to read and maintain. Finally, if you try to deal with errors in this manner, there's no easy way for the compiler to check for consistency the way it can check to make sure that you called a method with the right arguments.

Although the previous example uses Java syntax, you don't have to deal with errors that way in your programs. The language introduces a better method to deal with exceptional circumstances in a program: through the use of a group of classes called exceptions.

Exceptions include errors that could be fatal to your program, but also include other unusual situations. By managing exceptions, you can manage errors and possibly work around them.

Errors and other unusual conditions in Java programs can be much more easily managed through a combination of special language features, consistency checking at compile time, and a set of extensible exception classes.

Given these features, you can now add a whole new dimension to the behavior and design of your classes, your class hierarchy, and your overall system. Your class and interface definitions describe how your program is supposed to behave given the best circumstances. By integrating exception handling into your program design, you can consistently describe how the program will behave when circumstances are not ideal, and allow people who use your classes to know what to expect in those cases.

7

Exception Classes

At this point in the book, it's likely that you've run into at least one Java exception—perhaps you mistyped a method name or made a mistake in your code that caused a problem. Maybe you tried to run a Java applet that was written using version 2 of the language in a browser that doesn't support it yet, and saw a `Security Exception` message on the browser's status line.

Chances are, a program quit and spewed a bunch of mysterious errors to the screen. Those errors are exceptions. When your program quits, it's because an exception was thrown. Exceptions can be thrown by the system, thrown by classes you use, or intentionally thrown in your own programs.

The term *thrown* is fitting because exceptions also can be caught. Catching an exception involves dealing with the exceptional circumstance so that your program doesn't crash—you will learn more about this later. "An exception was thrown" is the proper Java terminology for "an error happened."

The heart of the Java exception system is the exception itself. Exceptions in Java are actual objects, that is, they are instances of classes that inherit from the class `Throwable`. An instance of a `Throwable` class is created when an exception is thrown.

`Throwable` has two subclasses: `Error` and `Exception`. Instances of `Error` are internal errors in the Java runtime environment (the virtual machine). These errors are rare and usually fatal; there's not much that you can do about them (either to catch them or to throw them yourself), but they exist so that if they are needed, Java can use them.

The class `Exception` is more interesting. Subclasses of `Exception` fall into two general groups:

- Runtime exceptions (subclasses of the class `RuntimeException`) such as `ArrayIndexOutofBounds`, `SecurityException`, and `NullPointerException`
- Other exceptions such as `EOFException` and `MalformedURLException`

Runtime exceptions usually occur because of code that isn't very robust. An `ArrayIndexOutofBounds` exception, for example, should never be thrown if you're properly checking to make sure that your code stays within the bounds of an array. `NullPointerException` exceptions won't happen unless you try to use a variable before it has been set up to hold an object.

 Caution | If your program is causing runtime exceptions under any circumstances, you should fix those problems before you even begin dealing with exception management.

The final group of exceptions is the most interesting because these are the exceptions that indicate something very strange and out of control is happening. EOFExceptions, for example, happen when you're reading from a file and the file ends before you expected it to end. A MalformedURLException happens when an URL isn't in the right format (perhaps your user typed it wrong). This group includes exceptions that you create to signal unusual cases that might occur in your own programs.

Exceptions are arranged in a hierarchy just as other classes are, where the Exception superclasses are more general errors and the subclasses are more specific errors. This organization becomes more important to you as you deal with exceptions in your own code.

Most of the exception classes are part of the java.lang package (including Throwable, Exception, and RuntimeException). Many of the other packages define other exceptions, and those exceptions are used throughout the class library. For example, the java.io package defines a general exception class called IOException, which is subclassed not only in the java.io package for input and output exceptions (EOFException and FileNotFoundException), but also in the java.net classes for networking exceptions such as MalformedURLException.

Managing Exceptions

Now that you know what an exception is, how do you deal with one in your own code? In many cases, the Java compiler enforces exception management when you try to use methods that use exceptions; you need to deal with those exceptions in your own code or it simply won't compile. In this section, you will learn about consistency checking and how to use the try, catch, and finally language keywords to deal with exceptions that might occur.

Exception Consistency Checking

The more you work with the Java class libraries, the more likely it is that you'll run into a compiler error (an exception!) similar to this one:

```
XMLParser.java:32: Exception java.lang.InterruptedException
must be caught or it must be declared in the throws clause
of this method.
```

In Java, a method can indicate the kinds of errors it might possibly throw. For example, methods that read from files might potentially throw IOException errors, so that those methods are declared with a special modifier that indicates potential errors. When you use those methods in your own Java programs, you have to protect your code against those exceptions. This rule is enforced by the compiler itself, in the same way that it checks to make sure that you're using methods with the correct number of arguments and that all your variable types match what you're assigning to them.

7

Why is this check in place? It makes your programs less likely to crash with fatal errors because you know, up front, the kind of exceptions that can be thrown by the methods a program uses. You no longer have to carefully read the documentation or the code of an object you're going to use to ensure that you've dealt with all the potential problems— Java does the checking for you. On the other side, if you define your methods so that they indicate the exceptions they can throw, Java can tell your objects' users to handle those errors.

Protecting Code and Catching Exceptions

Assume that you've been happily coding and you run into that exception message during a test compile. According to the message, you have to either catch the error or declare that your method throws it. Deal with the first case: catching potential exceptions.

You do two things to catch an exception:

- You protect the code that contains the method that might throw an exception inside a try block.
- You deal with an exception inside a catch block.

What try and catch effectively mean is, "Try this bit of code that might cause an exception. If it executes okay, go on with the program. If the code doesn't execute, catch the exception and deal with it."

You've seen try and catch before, when you first dealt with threads. On Day 6, "Packages, Interfaces, and Other Class Features," you used code when using a String value to create an integer:

```
try {
    float in = Float.parseFloat(input);
} catch (NumberFormatException nfe) {
    System.out.println(input + " is not a valid number.");
}
```

Here's what's happening in these statements: The Float.parseFloat() class method could potentially throw an exception of type NumberFormatException, which signifies that the thread has been interrupted for some reason.

To handle this exception, the call to parseFloat() is placed inside a try block and an associated catch block has been set up. This catch block receives any NumberFormatException objects that are thrown within the try block.

The part of the catch clause inside the parentheses is similar to a method definition's argument list. It contains the class of exception to be caught and a variable name. You can use the variable to refer to that exception object inside the catch block.

One common use for this object is to call its getMessage() method. This method is present in all exceptions, and it displays a detailed error message describing what happened.

Another useful method is printStackTrace(), which displays the sequence of method calls that led to the statement that generated the exception.

The following example is a revised version of the try-catch statement used on Day 6:

```
try {
    float in = Float.parseFloat(input);
} catch (NumberFormatException nfe) {
    System.out.println("Oops: " + nfe.getMessage());
}
```

The examples you have seen thus far catch a specific type of exception. Because exception classes are organized into a hierarchy and you can use a subclass anywhere that a superclass is expected, you can catch groups of exceptions within the same catch statement.

As an example, when you start writing programs that handle input and output from files, Internet servers, and other places, you will deal with several different types of IOException exceptions (the "IO" stands for input/output). These exceptions include two of its subclasses, EOFException and FileNotFoundException. By catching IOException, you also catch instances of any IOException subclass.

To catch several different exceptions that aren't related by inheritance, you can use multiple catch blocks for a single try, like this:

```
try {
    // code that might generate exceptions
} catch (IOException e) {
    // handle IO exceptions
} catch (ClassNotFoundException e) {
    // handle class not found exceptions
} catch (InterruptedException e) {
    // handle interrupted exceptions
}
```

In a multiple catch block, the first catch block that matches will be executed and the rest ignored.

Caution You can run into unexpected problems by using an Exception superclass in a catch block followed by one or more of its subclasses in their own catch blocks. For example, the input-output exception IOException is the superclass of the end-of-file exception EOFException. If you put an IOException block above an EOFException block, the subclass will never catch any exceptions.

7

The `finally` Clause

Suppose that there is some action in your code that you absolutely must do, no matter what happens, whether an exception is thrown or not. This is usually to free some external resource after acquiring it, to close a file after opening it, or something similar. Although you could put that action both inside a `catch` block and outside it, that would be duplicating the same code in two different places. Instead, put one copy of that code inside a special optional part of the `try...catch` block called `finally`. The following example shows how a `try...catch...finally` block is structured:

```
try {
    readTextfile();
} catch (IOException e) {
    // deal with IO errors
} finally {
    closeTextfile();
}
```

The `finally` statement is actually useful outside exceptions; you can also use it to execute cleanup code after a `return`, a `break`, or a `continue` inside loops. For the latter cases, you can use a `try` statement with a `finally` but without a `catch` statement.

The next project, shown in Listing 7.1, shows how a `finally` statement can be used inside a method.

LISTING 7.1   The Full Text of `HexRead.java`

```
 1: class HexRead {
 2:     String[] input = { "000A110D1D260219 ",
 3:         "78700F1318141E0C ",
 4:         "6A197D45B0FFFFFF " };
 5:
 6:     public static void main(String[] arguments) {
 7:         HexRead hex = new HexRead();
 8:         for (int i = 0; i < hex.input.length; i++)
 9:             hex.readLine(hex.input[i]);
10:     }
11:
12:     void readLine(String code) {
13:         try {
14:             for (int j = 0; j + 1 < code.length(); j += 2) {
15:                 String sub = code.substring(j, j+2);
16:                 int num = Integer.parseInt(sub, 16);
17:                 if (num == 255)
18:                     return;
19:                 System.out.print(num + " ");
20:             }
21:         } finally {
```

LISTING 7.1   Continued

```
22:                System.out.println("**");
23:            }
24:        return;
25:    }
26: }
```

The output of this program is as follows:

```
0 10 17 13 29 38 2 25 **
120 112 15 19 24 20 30 12 **
106 25 125 69 176 **
```

The HexRead application reads sequences of two-digit hexadecimal numbers and displays their decimal values. There are three sequences to read:

- 000A110D1D260219

- 78700F1318141E0C

- 6A197D45B0FFFFFF

As you learned on Day 2, "The ABCs of Programming," hexadecimal is a base-16 numbering system where the single-digit numbers range from 00 (decimal 0) to 0F (decimal 15) and double-digit numbers range from 10 (decimal 16) to FF (decimal 255).

Line 15 of the program reads two characters from code, the string that was sent to the readLine() method, by calling the string's substring(int, int) method.

Note

In the substring() method of the String class, you select a substring in a somewhat counterintuitive way. The first argument specifies the index of the first character to include in the substring, but the second argument does not specify the last character. Instead, the second argument indicates the index of the last character plus 1. A call to substring(2, 5) for a string would return the characters from index position 2 to index position 4.

The two-character substring contains a hexadecimal number stored as a String. The Integer class method parseInt can be used with a second argument to convert this number into an integer. Use 16 as the argument for a hexadecimal (base 16) conversion, 8 for an octal (base 8) conversion, and so on.

In the HexRead application, the hexadecimal FF is used to fill out the end of a sequence and should not be displayed as a decimal value. This is accomplished by using a try-finally block in lines 13–23 of Listing 7.1.

7

The `try...finally` block causes an unusual thing to happen when the `return` statement is encountered at line 18. You would expect `return` to cause the `readLine()` method to be exited immediately.

Because it is within a `try...finally` block, the statement within the `finally` block is executed no matter how the `try` block is exited. The text `"**"` is displayed at the end of a line of decimal values.

Declaring Methods that Might Throw Exceptions

In previous examples, you learned how to deal with methods (by protecting code and catching any exceptions that occur) that might throw exceptions. The Java compiler checks to make sure that you've dealt with a method's exceptions—but how did it know which exceptions to tell you about in the first place?

The answer is that the original method indicated in its signature contains the exceptions that it might possibly throw. You can use this mechanism in your own methods—in fact, it's good style to do so to make sure that your classes' other users are alerted to the errors your methods may come across.

To indicate that a method may possibly throw an exception, you use a special clause in the method definition called `throws`.

The `throws` Clause

To indicate that some code in your method's body may throw an exception, simply add the `throws` keyword after the signature for the method (before the opening brace) with the name or names of the exception that your method throws:

```
public boolean myMethod (int x, int y) throws NumberFormatException {
    // ...
}
```

If your method may throw multiple kinds of exceptions, you can put them all in the `throws` clause, separated by commas:

```
public boolean myOtherMethod (int x, int y)
    throws NumberFormatException, EOFException, InterruptedException {
        // ...
}
```

Note that, as with `catch`, you can use a superclass of an exceptions group to indicate that your method may throw any subclass of that exception:

```
public void YetAnotherMethod() throws IOException {
    // ...
}
```

Keep in mind that adding a `throws` method to your method definition simply means that the method might throw an exception if something goes wrong, not that it actually will. The `throws` clause simply provides extra information to your method definition about potential exceptions and allows Java to make sure that other people are using your method correctly.

Think of a method's overall description as a contract between the designer of that method (or class) and the caller of the method. (You can be on either side of that contract, of course.) Usually the description indicates the types of a method's arguments, what it returns, and the general semantics of what it normally does. By using `throws`, you are adding information about the abnormal things the method can do. This new part of the contract helps separate and make explicit all the places where exceptional conditions should be handled in your program, and that makes large-scale design easier.

Which Exceptions Should You Throw?

After you decide to declare that your method might throw an exception, you must decide which exceptions it might throw (and actually throw them or call a method that will throw them—you'll learn about throwing your own exceptions in the next section). In many instances, this is apparent from the operation of the method itself. Perhaps you're already creating and throwing your own exceptions, in which case, you'll know exactly which exceptions to throw.

You don't really have to list all the possible exceptions that your method could throw; some exceptions are handled by the runtime itself and are so common (not common per se, but ubiquitous) that you don't have to deal with them. In particular, exceptions of either class `Error` or `RuntimeException` (or any of their subclasses) do not have to be listed in your `throws` clause. They get special treatment because they can occur anywhere within a Java program and are usually conditions that you, as the programmer, did not directly cause. One good example is `OutOfMemoryError`, which can happen anywhere, at any time, and for any number of reasons. These two types of exceptions are called *implicit exceptions*, and you don't have to worry about them.

Implicit exceptions are exceptions that are `RuntimeException` and `Error` subclasses. Implicit exceptions are usually thrown by the Java runtime itself. You do not have to declare that your method throws them.

7

Note   You can, of course, choose to list these errors and runtime exceptions in your throws clause if you like, but your method's callers will not be forced to handle them; only non-runtime exceptions must be handled.

All other exceptions are called *explicit exceptions* and are potential candidates for a throws clause in your method.

Passing on Exceptions

There are times when it doesn't make sense for your method to deal with an exception. It might be better for the method that calls your method to deal with that exception. There's nothing wrong with this; it's a fairly common occurrence that you will pass an exception back to the method that calls your method.

For example, consider the hypothetical example of WebRetriever, a class that loads a Web page using its URL address and stores it in a file. As you'll learn on Day 17, "Communicating Across the Internet," you can't work with URLs without dealing with MalformedURLException, the exception that is thrown when an URL isn't in the right format.

To use WebRetriever, another class calls its constructor method with the URL as an argument. If the URL specified by the other class isn't in the right format, a MalformedURLException will be thrown. Instead of dealing with this, the WebRetriever class has the following definition:

```
public WebRetriever() throws MalformedURLException {
    // ...
}
```

This forces any class that would use WebRetriever to deal with MalformedURLException errors (or pass the buck with their own throws clause, of course).

One thing is true at all times: It's better to pass on exceptions to calling methods than to catch them and ignore them.

In addition to declaring methods that throw exceptions, there's one other instance in which your method definition may include a throws clause: You want to use a method that throws an exception, but you don't want to catch or deal with that exception.

Rather than using the try and catch clauses in your method's body, you can declare your method with a throws clause such that it, too, might possibly throw the appropriate exception. It's then the responsibility of the method that calls your method to deal with that exception. This is the other case that satisfies the Java compiler that you have done something with a given method. Here's another way of implementing an example that converts a string into a `float` value:

```
public void readFloat(String input) throws NumberFormatException {
    float in = Float.parseFloat(input);
}
```

This example is similar to an example used previously today; remember that the `parseFloat()` method was declared to throw a `NumberFormatException`, so that you had to use `try` and `catch` to use it. After you declare your method to throw an exception, however, you can use other methods that also throw those exceptions inside the body of this method, without needing to protect the code or catch the exception.

Note

> You can, of course, deal with other exceptions using `try` and `catch` in the body of your method in addition to passing on the exceptions you listed in the `throws` clause. You also can both deal with the exception in some way and then rethrow it so that your method's calling method has to deal with it anyhow. You will learn how to throw methods in the next section.

throws and Inheritance

If your method definition overrides a method in a superclass that includes a `throws` clause, there are special rules for how your overridden method deals with `throws`. Unlike other parts of the method signature that must mimic those of the method it is overriding, your new method does not require the same set of exceptions listed in the `throws` clause.

Because there's a possibility that your new method might deal better with exceptions other than just throwing them, your method can potentially throw fewer types of exceptions. It could even throw no exceptions at all. That means that you can have the following two class definitions and things will work just fine:

```
public class RadioPlay {
    public void startPlaying() throws SoundException {
        // ...
    }
}

public class StereoPlay extends RadioPlay {
    public void startPlaying() {
        // ...
    }
}
```

7

The converse of this rule is not true: A subclass method cannot throw more exceptions (either exceptions of different types or more general exception classes) than its superclass method.

Creating and Throwing Your Own Exceptions

There are two sides to every exception: the side that throws the exception and the side that catches it. An exception can be tossed around a number of times to a number of methods before it's caught, but eventually it will be caught and dealt with.

Who does the actual throwing? Where do exceptions come from? Many exceptions are thrown by the Java runtime or by methods inside the Java classes themselves. You can also throw any of the standard exceptions that the Java class libraries define, or you can create and throw your own exceptions. This section describes all these things.

Throwing Exceptions

Declaring that your method throws an exception is useful only to your method's users and to the Java compiler, which checks to make sure that all your exceptions are being dealt with—but the declaration itself doesn't do anything to actually throw that exception should it occur; you have to do that yourself in the body of the method.

Remember that exceptions are all instances of some exception class, of which there are many defined in the standard Java class library. You need to create a new instance of an exception class to throw an exception. After you have that instance, use the throw statement to throw it. The simplest way to throw an exception is like this:

```
NotInServiceException() nis = new NotInServiceException();
throw nis;
```

 Note

You can throw only objects that are subclasses of Throwable. This is different from C++'s exceptions, which enable you to throw objects of any type.

Depending on the exception class you're using, the exception also may have arguments to its constructor that you can use. The most common of these is a string argument, which enables you to describe the problem in greater detail (which can be very useful for debugging purposes). Here's an example:

```
NotInServiceException() nis = new
    NotInServiceException("Exception: Database Not in Service");
throw nis;
```

After an exception is thrown, the method exits immediately, without executing any other code (other than the code inside `finally`, if that block exists) and without returning a value. If the calling method does not have a `try` or `catch` surrounding the call to your method, the program might very well exit based on the exception you threw.

Creating Your Own Exceptions

Although there are a fair number of exceptions in the Java class library that you can use in your own methods, you might need to create your own exceptions to handle the different kinds of errors that your programs run into. Fortunately, creating new exceptions is easy.

Your new exception should inherit from some other exception in the Java hierarchy. All user-created exceptions should be part of the `Exception` hierarchy rather than the `Error` hierarchy, which is reserved for errors involving the Java virtual machine. Look for an exception that's close to the one you're creating; for example, an exception for a bad file format would logically be an `IOException`. If you can't find a closely related exception for your new exception, consider inheriting from `Exception`, which forms the "top" of the exception hierarchy for explicit exceptions. (Remember that implicit exceptions, which include subclasses of `Error` and `RuntimeException`, inherit from `Throwable`.)

Exception classes typically have two constructors: The first takes no arguments and the second takes a single string as an argument. In the latter case, you should call `super()` in that constructor to make sure that the string is applied to the right place in the exception.

Beyond those three rules, exception classes look just like other classes. You can put them in their own source files and compile them just as you would other classes:

```
public class SunSpotException extends Exception {
    public SunSpotException() {}
    public SunSpotException(String msg) {
        super(msg);
    }
}
```

Combining `throws`, `try`, and `throw`

What if you want to combine all the approaches shown so far? You'd like to handle incoming exceptions yourself in your method, but also you'd like the option to pass the exception up to your caller. Simply using `try` and `catch` doesn't pass on the exception, and simply adding a `throws` clause doesn't give you a chance to deal with the exception. If you want to both manage the exception and pass it on to the caller, use all three mechanisms: the `throws` clause, the `try` statement, and a `throw` statement to explicitly rethrow the exception.

7

```
public void readMessage() throws IOException {
    MessageReader mr = new MessageReader();

    try {
        mr.loadHeader();
    } catch (IOException e) {
        // do something to handle the
        // IO exception
        throw e; // rethrow the exception
    }
}
```

This works because exception handlers can be nested. You handle the exception by doing something responsible with it, but decide that it is too important to not give an exception handler that might be in your caller a chance to handle it as well. Exceptions float all the way up the chain of method callers this way (usually not being handled by most of them) until, at last, the system itself handles any uncaught exceptions by aborting your program and printing an error message. This is not such a bad idea in a standalone program, but it can cause the browser to crash in an applet. Most browsers protect themselves from this disaster by catching all exceptions themselves whenever they run an applet, but you can never tell. If it's possible for you to catch an exception and do something intelligent with it, you should.

When to and When Not to Use Exceptions

Because throwing, catching, and declaring exceptions are related concepts and can be very confusing, here's a quick summary of when to do what.

When to Use Exceptions

You can do one of three things if your method calls another method that has a throws clause:

- Deal with the exception by using try and catch statements
- Pass the exception up the calling chain by adding your own throws clause to your method definition
- Perform both of the preceding methods by catching the exception using catch and then explicitly rethrowing it using throw

In cases where a method throws more than one exception, you can handle each of those exceptions differently. For example, you might catch some of those exceptions while allowing others to pass up the calling chain.

If your method throws its own exceptions, you should declare that it throws those methods using the throws statement. If your method overrides a superclass method that has a throws statement, you can throw the same types of exceptions or subclasses of those exceptions; you cannot throw any different types of exceptions.

Finally, if your method has been declared with a throws clause, don't forget to actually throw the exception in the body of your method using the throw statement.

When Not to Use Exceptions

Although they might seem appropriate at the time, there are several cases in which you should not use exceptions.

First, you should not use exceptions if the exception is something that you expect and could avoid easily with a simple expression. For example, although you can rely on an ArrayIndexOutofBounds exception to indicate when you've gone past the end of the array, it's easy in most circumstances to use the array's length variable to prevent you from going out of bounds.

In addition, if your users will enter data that must be an integer, testing to make sure that the data is an integer is a much better idea than throwing an exception and dealing with it somewhere else.

Exceptions take up a lot of processing time for your Java program. A simple test or series of tests will run much faster than exception handling and make your program more efficient. Exceptions should be used only for truly exceptional cases that are out of your control.

It's also easy to get carried away with exceptions and to try to make sure that all your methods have been declared to throw all the possible exceptions that they can possibly throw. This makes your code more complex; in addition, if other people will be using your code, they'll have to deal with handling all the exceptions that your methods might throw.

You're making more work for everyone involved when you get carried away with exceptions. Declaring a method to throw either few or lots of exceptions is a trade-off; the more exceptions your method can throw, the more complex that method is to use. Declare only the exceptions that have a reasonably fair chance of happening and that make sense for the overall design of your classes.

Bad Style Using Exceptions

When you first start using exceptions, it might be appealing to work around the compiler errors that result when you use a method that declared a throws statement. Although it is legal to add an empty catch clause or to add a throws statement to your own method (and there are appropriate reasons for doing so), intentionally dropping exceptions without dealing with them subverts the checks that the Java compiler does for you.

The Java exception system was designed so that if an error can occur, you're warned about it. Ignoring those warnings and working around them makes it possible for fatal errors to occur in your program—errors that you could have avoided with a few lines of code. Even worse, adding `throws` statements to your methods to avoid exceptions means that the users of your methods (objects further up in the calling chain) will have to deal with them. You've just made your methods more difficult to use.

Compiler errors regarding exceptions are there to remind you to reflect on these issues. Take the time to deal with the exceptions that might affect your code. This extra care will richly reward you as you reuse your classes in later projects and in larger and larger programs. Of course, the Java class library has been written with exactly this degree of care, and that's one of the reasons it's robust enough to be used in constructing all your Java projects.

Assertions

Exceptions are one way to improve the reliability of your Java programs. Java 2 version 1.4 introduces support for another—assertions.

An *assertion* is an expression that represents a condition that a programmer believes to be true at a specific place in a program. If it isn't true, an error results.

In Java 2 version 1.4, the `assert` keyword has been added so programmers can make assertions. Here's an example of its use:

```
assert price > 0;
```

In this example, the `assert` statement claims that a variable named `price` has a value greater than 0. Assertions are a way to assure yourself that a program is running correctly.

The `assert` keyword must be followed by one of three things: an expression that is true or false, a `boolean` variable, or a method that returns a `boolean`.

If the assertion that follows the `assert` keyword is not true, an `AssertionError` exception is thrown. To make the error message associated with an assertion more meaningful, you can specify a string in an `assert` statement, as in the following example:

```
assert price > 0 : "Price less than 0.";
```

In this example, if `price` is less than 0 when the assert statement is executed, an `AssertionError` exception is thrown with the error message "Price less than 0."

You can catch these exceptions or leave them for the Java interpreter to deal with. Here's an example of how the SDK's interpreter responds when an `assert` statement is false:

```
Exception in thread "main" java.lang.AssertionError
    at AssertTest.main(AssertTest.java:14)
```

Here's an example when an assert statement with a descriptive error message is false:

```
Exception in thread "main" java.lang.AssertionError: Price less than 0.
        at AssertTest.main(AssertTest.java:14)
```

Although assertions are an official part of the Java language with version 1.4, they are not supported by default by the tools included with the SDK, and the same may be true with other Java development tools.

To enable assertions with the SDK, you must use command-line arguments when running the compiler and interpreter.

To compile a class that contains assert statements, use the -source 1.4 argument, as in the following example:

```
javac -source 1.4 PriceChecker.java
```

When the -source 1.4 argument is used, the compiler includes support for assertions in the class file (or files) that it produces. If you did not use that argument, the class would not compile successfully.

There are several ways to turn on assertions in the SDK's Java interpreter.

To enable assertions in all classes except those in the Java class library, use the -ea argument, as in this example:

```
java -ea PriceChecker
```

To enable assertions only in one class, follow -ea with a colon (":") and the name of the class, like this:

```
java -ea:PriceChecker PriceChecker
```

You can also enable assertions for a specific package by following -ea: with the name of the package (or ... for the default package).

Tip

> There's also an -esa flag that enables assertions in the Java class library. There isn't much reason for you to do this because you're probably not testing the reliability of that code.

7

Because Java has added the assert keyword, you must not use it as the name of a variable in your programs, even if they are not compiled with support for assertions enabled.

Assertions are an unusual feature of the Java language because under most circumstances they cause absolutely nothing to happen. They're a means of expressing in a class the conditions under which it is running correctly (and the things you assume to be true as it runs).

If you make liberal use of them in a class, it will either be more reliable or you'll learn that some of your assumptions are incorrect, which is useful knowledge in its own right.

Threads

One of the things to consider in Java programming is how system resources are being used. Graphics, complex mathematical computations, and other intensive tasks can take up a lot of processor time.

This is especially true of programs that have a graphical user interface, which is a style of software that you'll be learning about next week.

If you write a graphical Java program that is doing something that consumes a lot of the computer's time, you might find that the program's graphical user interface responds slowly—drop-down lists take a second or more to appear, button clicks are recognized slowly, and so on.

To solve this problem, you can segregate the processor-hogging functions in a Java program so that they run separately from the rest of the program.

This is possible through the use of a feature of the Java language called threads. *Threads* are parts of a program that are set up to run on their own while the rest of the program does something else. This also is called *multitasking* because the program can handle more than one task simultaneously.

Threads are ideal for anything that takes up a lot of processing time and runs continuously.

By putting the workload of the program into a thread, you are freeing up the rest of the program to handle other things. You also make handling the program easier for the run-time environment because all the intensive work is isolated into its own thread.

Writing a Threaded Program

Threads are implemented in Java with the Thread class in the java.lang package.

The simplest use of threads is to make a program pause in execution and stay idle during that time. To do this, call the Thread class method sleep(*long*) with the number of milliseconds to pause as the only argument.

This method throws an exception, InterruptedException, whenever the paused thread has been interrupted for some reason. (One possible reason: The user closes the program while it is sleeping.)

The following statements stop a program in its tracks for 3 seconds:

```
try {
    Thread.sleep(3000);
catch (InterruptedException ie) {
    // do nothing
}
```

The catch block does nothing, which is typical when you're using sleep().

One way to make use of threads is to put all the time-consuming behavior into its own class.

To modify a class so that it uses threads, the class must implement the Runnable interface in the java.lang package. To do this, add the keyword implements to the class declaration followed by the name of the interface, as in the following example:

```
public class StockTicker implements Runnable {
    public void run() {
        // ...
    }
}
```

When a class implements an interface, it must include all methods of that interface. The Runnable interface contains only one method, run(), so it's included in the preceding example. You will see how to use this method in a moment.

The first step in creating a thread is to create a reference to an object of the Thread class:

```
Thread runner;
```

This statement creates a reference to a thread, but no Thread object has been assigned to it yet. Threads are created by calling the constructor Thread(Object) with the threaded object as an argument. You could create a threaded StockTicker object with the following statement:

```
StockTicker tix = new StockTicker();
Thread tickerThread = new Thread(tix);
```

Three good places to create threads are the constructor method for an application, the constructor for a component (such as a panel), or the start() method of an applet.

A thread is begun by calling its start() method, as in the following statement:

```
tixThread.start();
```

7

The following statements can be used inside a threaded object's class definition to start the thread:

```
Thread runner;
if (runner == null) {
    runner = new Thread(this);
    runner.start();
}
```

The this keyword used in the Thread() constructor refers to the object in which these statements are contained. The runner variable has a value of null before any object is assigned to it, so the if statement is used to make sure that the thread is not started more than once.

To run a thread, its start() method is called, as in this statement from the preceding example:

```
runner.start();
```

Calling a thread's start() method causes another method to be called—namely, the run() method that must be present in the threaded object.

The run() method is the heart of a threaded class. In an animated program, it can be used to make changes that would affect what is drawn in a paint method. (Looking back at the Headlines application, the scroll() method would require few changes to be suitable as a run() method.)

A Threaded Application

Threaded programming requires a lot of interaction among different objects, so it should become clearer when you see it in action.

Listing 7.2 contains a class that finds a specific prime number in a sequence, such as the 10th prime, 100th prime, or 1,000th prime. This can take some time, especially for numbers beyond 100,000, so the search for the right prime takes place in its own thread.

Enter the text of Listing 7.2 in your Java editor and save it as PrimeFinder.java.

LISTING 7.2   The Full Text of PrimeFinder.java

```
1: public class PrimeFinder implements Runnable {
2:     public long target;
3:     public long prime;
4:     public boolean finished = false;
5:     private Thread runner;
6:
7:     PrimeFinder(long inTarget) {
8:         target = inTarget;
```

LISTING 7.2 Continued

```
 9:              if (runner == null) {
10:                  runner = new Thread(this);
11:                  runner.start();
12:              }
13:          }
14:
15:      public void run() {
16:          long numPrimes = 0;
17:          long candidate = 2;
18:          while (numPrimes < target) {
19:              if (isPrime(candidate)) {
20:                  numPrimes++;
21:                  prime = candidate;
22:              }
23:              candidate++;
24:          }
25:          finished = true;
26:      }
27:
28:      boolean isPrime(long checkNumber) {
29:          double root = Math.sqrt(checkNumber);
30:          for (int i = 2; i <= root; i++) {
31:              if (checkNumber % i == 0)
32:                  return false;
33:          }
34:          return true;
35:      }
36: }
```

Compile the `PrimeFinder` class when you're done. This class doesn't have a `main()` method, so you can't run it as an application. You'll create a program that uses this class next.

The `PrimeFinder` class implements the `Runnable` interface, so it can be run as a thread.

There are three public instance variables:

- `target`—A Long that indicates when the specified prime in the sequence has been found. If you're looking for the 5,000th prime, `target` equals 5000.

- `prime`—A Long that holds the last prime number found by this class.

- `finished`—A Boolean that indicates when the target has been reached.

There is also a private instance variable called `runner` that holds the `Thread` object that this class will run in. This object should be equal to `null` before the thread has been started.

7

The `PrimeFinder` constructor method in lines 7–13 sets the `target` instance variable and starts the thread if it hasn't already been started. When the thread's `start()` method is called, it in turn calls the `run()` method of the threaded class.

The `run()` method is in lines 15–26. This method does most of the work of the thread, which is typical of threaded classes. You want to put the most computing-intensive tasks in their own thread so that they don't bog down the rest of the program.

This method uses two new variables: `numPrimes`, the number of primes that have been found, and `candidate`, the number that might possibly be prime. The `candidate` variable begins at the first possible prime number, which is 2.

The `while` loop in lines 18–24 continues until the right number of primes have been found.

First, it checks whether the current `candidate` is prime by calling the `isPrime(long)` method, which returns `true` if the number is prime and `false` otherwise.

If the `candidate` is prime, `numPrimes` increases by one and the `prime` instance variable is set to this prime number.

The `candidate` variable is then incremented by one and the loop continues.

Once the right number of primes has been found, the `while` loop ends and the `finished` instance variable is set to `true`. This indicates that the `PrimeFinder` object has found the right prime number and is done searching.

The end of the `run()` method is reached in line 26 and the thread is no longer doing any work.

The `isPrime()` method is contained in lines 28–35. This method determines whether a number is prime by using the `%` operator, which returns the remainder of a division operation. If a number is evenly divisible by 2 or any higher number (leaving a remainder of 0), it is not a prime number.

Listing 7.3 contains an application that makes use of the `PrimeFinder` class. Enter the text of Listing 7.3 and save the file as `PrimeThreads.java`.

LISTING 7.3   The Full Text of `PrimeThreads.java`

```
1: public class PrimeThreads {
2:     public static void main(String[] arguments) {
3:         PrimeFinder[] finder = new PrimeFinder[arguments.length];
4:         for (int i = 0; i < arguments.length; i++) {
5:             try {
6:                 long count = Long.parseLong(arguments[i]);
7:                 finder[i] = new PrimeFinder(count);
```

LISTING 7.3 Continued

```
 8:                    System.out.println("Looking for prime " + count);
 9:                } catch (NumberFormatException nfe) {
10:                    System.out.println("Error: " + nfe.getMessage());
11:                }
12:            }
13:            boolean complete = false;
14:            while (!complete) {
15:                complete = true;
16:                for (int j = 0; j < finder.length; j++) {
17:                    if (!finder[j].finished)
18:                        complete = false;
19:                }
20:                try {
21:                    Thread.sleep(1000);
22:                } catch (InterruptedException ie) {
23:                    // do nothing
24:                }
25:            }
26:            for (int j = 0; j < finder.length; j++) {
27:                System.out.println("Prime " + finder[j].target
28:                    + " is " + finder[j].prime);
29:            }
30:        }
31: }
```

Save and compile the file when you're finished.

The `PrimeThreads` application can be used to find one or more prime numbers in sequence. Specify the prime numbers that you're looking for as command-line arguments, and include as many as you like.

If you're using the SDK, here's an example of how you can run the application:

```
java PrimeThreads 1 10 100 1000
```

This produces the following output:

```
Looking for prime 1
Looking for prime 10
Looking for prime 100
Looking for prime 1000
Prime 1 is 2
Prime 10 is 29
Prime 100 is 541
Prime 1000 is 7919
```

7

The for loop in lines 4–12 of the PrimeThreads application creates one PrimeFinder object for each command-line argument specified when the program is run.

Because arguments are Strings and the PrimeFinder constructor requires long values, the Long.parseLong(*String*) class method is used to handle the conversion. Because all of the number-parsing methods throw NumberFormatException exceptions, you must enclose them in try-catch blocks to deal with arguments that are not numeric.

When a PrimeFinder object has been created, the object starts running in its own thread (as specified in the PrimeFinder constructor).

The while loop in lines 14–25 checks to see if all of the PrimeFinder threads have completed. This is accomplished by using a Boolean variable called complete that is set to true in line 15 and changed to false if any of the threads are not finished.

The call to Thread.sleep(1000) in line 21 causes the while loop to pause for one second during each pass through the loop. A slowdown in loops helps keep the Java interpreter from executing statements at such a furious pace that it becomes bogged down.

After all of the threads have completed, the for loop in lines 26–29 displays the prime numbers found by each thread.

Stopping a Thread

Stopping a thread is a little more complicated than starting one. The Thread class includes a stop() method that can be called to stop a thread, but it has been deprecated in Java 2 because it creates instabilities in Java's runtime environment and can introduce hard-to-detect errors into a program.

Another way to stop a thread is to make a loop in the thread's run() method end if a variable changes in value, as in the following example:

```
public void run() {
    while (okToRun == true) {
        // ...
    }
}
```

The okToRun variable could be an instance variable of the thread's class, and if it is changed to false, the loop inside the run() method will end.

Another option you can use to stop a thread is to only loop in the run() method while the currently running thread has a variable that references it.

In previous examples, a Thread object called runner has been used to hold the current thread.

A class method, `Thread.currentThread()`, can be called in a thread to return a reference to the current thread.

The following `run()` method loops as long as `runner` and `currentThread()` refer to the same object:

```
public void run() {
    Thread thisThread = Thread.currentThread();
    while (runner == thisThread) {
        // ...
    }
}
```

If you use a loop like this, you can stop the thread anywhere in the class with the following statement:

```
runner = null;
```

Summary

Exceptions and threads aid your program's design and robustness.

Exceptions enable you to manage potential errors in your programs. By using `try`, `catch`, and `finally`, you can protect code that might result in exceptions by handling those exceptions as they occur.

Handling exceptions is only half of the equation; the other half is generating and throwing exceptions. A `throws` clause tells a method's users that the method might throw an exception. It also can be used to pass on an exception from a method call in the body of your method.

You learned how to actually create and throw your own methods by defining new exception classes and by throwing instances of any exception classes using `throw`.

Threads enable you to run the most processor-intensive parts of a Java class separately from the rest of the class. This is especially useful when the class is doing something computing-intensive such as animation, complex mathematics, or looping through a large amount of data quickly.

You also can use threads to do several things at once and to start and stop threads externally.

Threads implement the `Runnable` interface, which contains one method: `run()`. When you start a thread by calling its `start()` method, the thread's `run()` method is called automatically.

7

Q&A

Q **I'm still not sure I understand the differences among exceptions, errors, and runtime exceptions. Is there another way of looking at them?**

A Errors are caused by dynamic linking or virtual machine problems, and are thus too low-level for most programs to care about—or be able to handle even if they did care about them. Runtime exceptions are generated by the normal execution of Java code, and although they occasionally reflect a condition you will want to handle explicitly, more often they reflect a coding mistake made by the programmer, and thus simply need to print an error to help flag that mistake. Exceptions that are non-runtime exceptions (`IOException` exceptions, for example) are conditions that, because of their nature, should be explicitly handled by any robust and well thought-out code. The Java class library has been written using only a few of these, but those few are extremely important to using the system safely and correctly. The compiler helps you handle these exceptions properly via its `throws` clause checks and restrictions.

Q **Is there any way to get around the strict restrictions placed on methods by the `throws` clause?**

A Yes. Suppose that you have thought long and hard and have decided that you need to circumvent this restriction. This is almost never the case because the right solution is to go back and redesign your methods to reflect the exceptions that you need to throw. Imagine, however, that for some reason a system class has you in a bind. Your first solution is to subclass `RuntimeException` to make up a new, exempt exception of your own. Now you can throw it to your heart's content because the `throws` clause that was annoying you does not need to include this new exception. If you need a lot of such exceptions, an elegant approach is to mix in some novel exception interfaces with your new `Runtime` classes. You're free to choose whatever subset of these new interfaces you want to `catch` (none of the normal `Runtime` exceptions need to be caught), while any leftover `Runtime` exceptions are allowed to go through that otherwise annoying standard method in the library.

Quiz

Review today's material by taking this quiz.

Questions

1. What keyword is used to jump out of a `try` block and into a `finally` block?

    (a.) `catch`

    (b.) `return`

    (c.) `while`

2. What class should be the superclass of any exceptions you create in Java?

    (a.) `Throwable`

    (b.) `Error`

    (c.) `Exception`

3. If a class implements the `Runnable` interface, what methods must the class contain?

    (a.) `start()`, `stop()`, and `run()`

    (b.) `actionPerformed()`

    (c.) `run()`

Answers

1. (b.)

2. (c.) `Throwable` and `Error` are of use primarily by Java. The kinds of errors you'll want to note in your programs belong in the `Exception` hierarchy.

3. (c.) The `Runnable` interface requires only the `run()` method.

Certification Practice

The following question is the kind of thing you could expect to be asked on a Java programming certification test. Answer it without looking at today's material or using the Java compiler to test the code.

The `AverageValue` application is supposed to take up to 10 floating-point numbers as command-line arguments and display their average.

7

Given:

```java
public class AverageValue {
    public static void main(String[] arguments) {
        float[] temps = new float[10];
        float sum = 0;
        int count = 0;
        int i;
        for (i = 0; i < arguments.length & i < 10; i++) {
            try {
                temps[i] = Float.parseFloat(arguments[i]);
                count++;
            } catch (NumberFormatException nfe) {
                System.out.println("Invalid input: " + arguments[i]);
            }
            sum += temps[i];
        }
        System.out.println("Average: " + (sum / i));
    }
}
```

Which statement contains an error?

(a.) `for (i = 0; i < arguments.length & i < 10; i++) {`

(b.) `sum += temps[i];`

(c.) `System.out.println("Average: " + (sum / i));`

(d.) None; the program is correct.

The answer is available on this book's Web site at `http://www.java21days.com`. Visit the Day 7 page and click the Certification Practice link.

Exercises

To extend your knowledge of the subjects covered today, try the following exercises:

- Modify the `PrimeFinder` class so that it throws a new exception, `NegativeNumberException`, if a negative number is sent to the constructor.

- Modify the `PrimeThreads` application so it can handle the new `NegativeNumberException` error.

Where applicable, exercise solutions are offered on this book's Web site at `http://www.java21days.com`.

WEEK 2

The Java Class Library

8

9

10

11

12

13

14

DAY 8

Data Structures and Strings

During the first week, you learned about the core elements of the Java language: objects, classes, interfaces, and the keywords, statements, expressions, and operators that you can use inside them.

For the second week, the focus shifts from the classes you create to the ones that have been created for you: the Java class library, a set of standard packages from Sun Microsystems, Inc. that includes more than 1,000 classes that you can use in your own Java programs.

Today, you'll start with classes that you can use to represent data.

Data Structures

Many Java programs that you create will rely on some means of storing and manipulating data within a class. Up to this point, you have used three structures for storing and retrieving data: variables, String objects, and arrays.

If you don't understand the full range of programming options in terms of data structures, you'll find yourself trying to use arrays or strings when other options would be more efficient or easier to implement.

A solid understanding of data structures and when to use them will be useful throughout your Java programming efforts.

Outside of primitive data types and strings, arrays are the simplest data structures supported by Java. An *array* is simply a series of data elements of the same primitive type or objects of any class. It's treated as a single entity, just as a primitive data type is, but contains multiple elements that can be accessed independently. Arrays are useful whenever you need to store and access related information.

The glaring limitation of arrays is that they can't adjust in size to accommodate additional or fewer elements. That means that you can't add new elements to an array that's already full. Because linked lists and vectors do not have this limitation, these objects can be used as an alternative.

The Java class library provides a set of data structures in the java.util package that gives you more flexibility in approaching the organization and manipulation of data.

 Note

Unlike the data structures provided by the java.util package, arrays are considered such a core component of Java that they are implemented in the language itself. Therefore, you can use arrays in Java without importing any packages.

Java Data Structures

The data structures provided by the java.util package are very powerful and perform a wide range of functions. These data structures consist of the Iterator interface, the Map interface, and classes such as the following:

- BitSet
- Vector
- Stack
- Hashtable

Each of these data structures provides a way to store and retrieve information in a well-defined manner. The Iterator interface itself isn't a data structure, but it defines a means to retrieve successive elements from a data structure. For example, Iterator defines a method called next() that gets the next element in a data structure that contains multiple elements.

Note | Iterator is an expanded and improved version of the Enumeration interface that was added in Java 2. Although Enumeration is still supported, Iterator has simpler method names and support for removing items.

8

The BitSet class implements a group of bits, or flags, that can be set and cleared individually. This class is very useful when you need to keep up with a set of Boolean values; you simply assign a bit to each value and set or clear it as appropriate.

NEW TERM A *flag* is a Boolean value that represents one of a group of on/off type states in a program.

The Vector class is similar to a traditional Java array, except that it can grow as necessary to accommodate new elements. Like an array, elements of a Vector object can be accessed via an index into the vector. The nice thing about using the Vector class is that you don't have to worry about setting it to a specific size upon creation; it automatically shrinks and grows when necessary.

The Stack class implements a last-in-first-out stack of elements. You can think of a stack literally as a vertical stack of objects; when you add a new element, it's stacked on top of the others. When you pull an element off the stack, it comes off the top. In other words, the last element you added to the stack is the first one to come back off. That element is removed from the stack completely, unlike a structure such as an array, where the elements are always available.

The Dictionary class is an abstract class that defines a data structure for mapping keys to values. This is useful when you want to access data through a particular key rather than an integer index. Because the Dictionary class is abstract, it provides only the framework for a key-mapped data structure rather than a specific implementation.

NEW TERM A *key* is an identifier used to reference, or look up, a value in a data structure.

An actual implementation of a key-mapped data structure is provided by the Hashtable class, which organizes data based on some user-defined key structure. For example, in an address list hash table, you could store and sort data based on a key such as ZIP Code rather than on a person's name. The specific meaning of keys in a hash table is totally dependent on how the table is used and the data it contains.

The next section looks at the data structures provided by the java.util package in more detail to show how they work.

Iterator

The Iterator interface provides a standard means of iterating through a list of elements in a defined sequence, which is a common task for many data structures. Even though you can't use the interface outside a particular data structure, understanding how the Iterator interface works will help you understand other Java data structures.

With that in mind, take a look at the methods defined by the Iterator interface:

```
public boolean hasNext();

public Object next();

public void remove();
```

The hasNext() method determines whether the structure contains any more elements. You will typically call this method to see whether you can continue iterating through a structure. An example of this is calling hasNext() in the conditional clause of a while loop that is iterating through a list.

The next() method retrieves the next element in a structure. If there are no more elements, next() will throw a NoSuchElementException exception. To avoid generating this exception, use hasNext() in conjunction with next() to make sure there is another element to retrieve.

The following is a while loop that uses these two methods to iterate through a data structure object called users that implements the Iterator interface:

```
while (users.hasNext()) {
    Object ob = users.next();
    System.out.println(ob);
}
```

This sample code displays the contents of each list item by using the hasNext() and next() methods.

 Note

Because Iterator is an interface, you'll never use it directly as a data structure. Rather, you'll use the methods defined by Iterator within the context of other data structures. The significance of this architecture is that it provides a consistent interface for many of the standard data structures, which makes them easier to learn and use.

Bit Sets

The `BitSet` class is useful whenever you need to represent a large amount of binary data, that is, bit values that can be equal only to 0 or 1. These are also called on-or-off values (with 1 representing on and 0 off) or Boolean values.

The nice thing about using the `BitSet` class is that you can use individual bits to store Boolean values without requiring bitwise operations to extract bit values. You simply refer to each bit using an index. Another nice feature is that it automatically grows to represent the number of bits required by a program. Figure 8.1 shows the logical organization of a bit set data structure.

FIGURE 8.1

The logical organization of a bit set data structure.

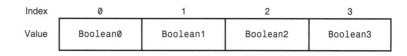

For example, you can use `BitSet` as an object with a number of attributes that can easily be modeled by Boolean values. Because the individual bits in a bit set are accessed via an index, you can define each attribute as a constant index value:

```
class ConnectionAttributes {
    public static final int READABLE = 0;
    public static final int WRITEABLE = 1;
    public static final int STREAMABLE = 2;
    public static final int FLEXIBLE = 3;
}
```

Notice that the attributes are assigned increasing values, beginning with 0. You can use these values to get and set the appropriate bits in a bit set. But first, you need to create a `BitSet` object:

```
BitSet connex = new BitSet();
```

This constructor creates a bit set with no specified size. You can also create a bit set with a specific size:

```
BitSet connex = new BitSet(4);
```

This creates a bit set containing four Boolean bit fields. Regardless of the constructor used, all bits in new bit sets are initially set to `false`. After you have a bit set created, you can set and clear the bits by using the `set` and `clear` methods along with the bit constants you defined:

```
connex.set(ChannelAttributes.WRITEABLE);
connex.set(ChannelAttributes.STREAMABLE);
connex.set(ChannelAttributes.FLEXIBLE);

connex.clear(ChannelAttributes.WRITEABLE);
```

In this code, the WRITEABLE, STREAMABLE, and FLEXIBLE attributes are set, and then the WRITEABLE bit is cleared. Notice that the class name is used for each attribute because the variables are declared as static in the ChannelAttributes class.

You can get the value of individual bits in a bit set by using the get method:

```
boolean isWriteable = connex.get(ChannelAttributes.WRITEABLE);
```

You can find out how many bits are being represented by a bit set by using the size method:

```
int numBits = connex.size();
```

The BitSet class also provides other methods for performing comparisons and bitwise operations on bit sets, such as AND, OR, and XOR. All these methods take a BitSet object as their only argument.

Today's first project is HolidaySked, a Java class that uses a bit set to keep track of which days in a year are holidays—something that would be useful in payroll, work scheduling, and other employment software.

A bit set is useful here because HolidaySked must be able to take any day of the year and answer the same yes/no question: Are you a holiday?

Enter the text of Listing 8.1 into your editor and save the file as HolidaySked.java.

LISTING 8.1   The Full Text of HolidaySked.java

```
 1: import java.util.*;
 2:
 3: public class HolidaySked {
 4:     BitSet sked;
 5:
 6:     public HolidaySked() {
 7:         sked = new BitSet(365);
 8:         int[] holiday = { 1, 20, 43, 48, 53, 115, 131, 146, 165, 166,
 9:             185, 244, 286, 315, 327, 359 };
10:         for (int i = 0; i < holiday.length; i++) {
11:             addHoliday(holiday[i]);
12:         }
13:     }
14:
15:     public void addHoliday(int dayToAdd) {
16:         sked.set(dayToAdd);
```

LISTING 8.1 Continued

```
17:      }
18:
19:      public boolean isHoliday(int dayToCheck) {
20:          boolean result = sked.get(dayToCheck);
21:          return result;
22:      }
23:
24:      public static void main(String[] arguments) {
25:          HolidaySked cal = new HolidaySked();
26:          if (arguments.length > 0) {
27:              try {
28:                  int whichDay = Integer.parseInt(arguments[0]);
29:                  if (cal.isHoliday(whichDay)) {
30:                      System.out.println("Day number " + whichDay + " is a
                            holiday.");
31:                  } else {
32:                      System.out.println("Day number " + whichDay + " is not a
                            holiday.");
33:                  }
34:              } catch (NumberFormatException nfe) {
35:                  System.out.println("Error: " + nfe.getMessage());
36:              }
37:          }
38:      }
39: }
```

Save HolidaySked.java and compile the class.

The HolidaySked class contains only one instance variable: sked, a BitSet that will hold values for each day in a year.

The constructor method of the class is in lines 6–13. The constructor creates the sked bit set with 365 positions, each set initially to 0. All bit sets are filled with 0 values when they are created.

Next, an integer array called holiday is created. This array holds the number of each work holiday in the year, beginning with 1 (New Year's Day) and ending with 359 (Christmas).

The holiday array is used to add each holiday to the sked bit set. A for loop in lines 10–12 iterates through the holiday array and calls the method addHoliday(int) with each one.

The addHoliday(int) method is defined in lines 15–17. The argument represents the day that should be added. The bit set's set(int) method is called to set the bit at the specified position to 1. For example, if set(359) was called, the bit at position 359 would be given the value 1.

The HolidaySked class also has the ability to determine whether a specified day is a holiday or not. This is handled by the isHoliday(*int*) method in lines 19–22. The method calls the bit set's get(*int*) method, which returns true if the specified position has the value 1 and false otherwise.

This class can be run as an application because of the main() method in lines 24–38. The application takes a single command-line argument: a number from 1 to 365 that represents one of the days of the year. The application displays whether that day is a holiday according to the schedule of the HolidaySked class. Test the program with values such as 20 (Martin Luther King Day) or 103 (my 36th birthday). The application should respond that day 20 is a holiday but day 103, sadly, is not.

Vectors

The Vector class implements an expandable array of objects. Because the Vector class is responsible for expanding as necessary to support more elements, it has to decide when and how much to grow as new elements are added. You can easily control this aspect of vectors upon creation.

Before getting into that, take a look at how to create a basic vector:

```
Vector v = new Vector();
```

This constructor creates a default vector containing no elements. All vectors are empty upon creation. One of the attributes that determines how a vector sizes itself is its initial capacity, or the number of elements it allocates memory for by default.

NEW TERM   The *size* of a vector is the number of elements currently stored in it.

NEW TERM   The *capacity* of a vector is the amount of memory allocated to hold elements, and
            it is always greater than or equal to the size.

The following code shows how to create a vector with a specified capacity:

```
Vector v = new Vector(25);
```

This vector will allocate enough memory to support 25 elements. Once 25 elements have been added, however, the vector must decide how to expand to accept more elements. You can specify the value by which a vector grows using another Vector constructor:

```
Vector v = new Vector(25, 5);
```

This vector has an initial size of 25 elements and will expand in increments of 5 elements when more than 25 elements are added to it. That means that the vector will jump to 30 elements in size, and then 35, and so on. A smaller growth value results in greater memory management efficiency, but at the cost of more execution overhead because more memory allocations are taking place. A larger growth value results in fewer memory allocations, although memory might be wasted if you don't use all the extra space created.

You can't just use square brackets ([]) to access the elements in a vector, as you can in an array. You must use methods defined in the Vector class. Use the add() method to add an element to a vector, as in the following example:

```
v.add("Watson");
v.add("Palmer");
v.add("Nicklaus");
```

This code shows how to add some strings to a vector. To retrieve the last string added to the vector, you can use the lastElement() method:

```
String s = (String)v.lastElement();
```

Notice that you have to cast the return value of lastElement() because the Vector class is designed to work with the Object class. Although lastElement() certainly has its uses, you will probably find more value in the get() method, which enables you to retrieve a vector element using an index.

The following is an example of the get() method:

```
String s1 = (String)v.get(0);
String s2 = (String)v.get(2);
```

Because vectors are zero-based, the first call to get() retrieves the "Watson" string and the second call retrieves the "Palmer" string. Just as you can retrieve an element at a particular index, you can also add and remove elements at an index by using the add() and remove() methods:

```
v.add(1, "Hogan");
v.add(0, "Jones");
v.remove(3);
```

The first call to add() inserts an element at index 1, between the "Watson" and "Palmer" strings. The "Palmer" and "Nicklaus" strings are moved up an element in the vector to accommodate the inserted "Hogan" string. The second call to add() inserts an element at index 0, which is the beginning of the vector. All existing elements are moved up one space in the vector to accommodate the inserted "Jones" string. At this point, the contents of the vector look like this:

- "Jones"
- "Watson"
- "Hogan"
- "Palmer"
- "Nicklaus"

The call to `remove()` removes the element at index 3, which is the `"Palmer"` string. The resulting vector consists of the following strings:

- `"Jones"`
- `"Watson"`
- `"Hogan"`
- `"Nicklaus"`

You can use the `set()` method to change a specific element:

```
v.set(1, "Woods");
```

This method replaces the `"Watson"` string with the `"Woods"` string, resulting in the following vector:

- `"Jones"`
- `"Woods"`
- `"Hogan"`
- `"Nicklaus"`

If you want to clear out the vector completely, you can remove all the elements with the `clear()` method:

```
v.clear();
```

The `Vector` class also provides some methods for working with elements without using indexes. These methods actually search through the vector for a particular element. The first of these methods is the `contains()` method, which simply checks if an element is in the vector:

```
boolean isThere = v.contains("O'Meara");
```

Another method that works in this manner is the `indexOf()` method, which finds the index of an element based on the element itself:

```
int i = v.indexOf("Nicklaus");
```

The `indexOf()` method returns the index of the element in question if it is in the vector or -1 if not. The `removeElement()` method works similarly, removing an element based on the element itself rather than on an index:

```
v.removeElement("Woods");
```

If you're interested in working sequentially with all the elements in a vector, you can use the `iterator()` method, which returns a list of the elements you can iterate through:

```
Iterator it = v.iterator();
```

8

As you learned earlier today, you can use an iterator to step through elements sequentially. In this example, you can work with the `it` list using the methods defined by the `Iterator` interface.

At some point, you might want to experiment with the size of a vector. Fortunately, the `Vector` class provides a few methods for determining and manipulating a vector's size. First, the `size` method determines the number of elements in the vector:

```
int size = v.size();
```

If you want to explicitly set the size of the vector, you can use the `setSize()` method:

```
v.setSize(10);
```

The `setSize()` method expands or truncates the vector to the size specified. If the vector is expanded, null elements are inserted as the newly added elements. If the vector is truncated, any elements at indexes beyond the specified size are discarded.

Recall that vectors have two different attributes relating to size: size and capacity. The size is the number of elements in the vector, and the capacity is the amount of memory allocated to hold all the elements. The capacity is always greater than or equal to the size. You can force the capacity to exactly match the size by using the `trimToSize()` method:

```
v.trimToSize();
```

You can also check to see what the capacity is by using the `capacity()` method:

```
int capacity = v.capacity();
```

Stacks

Stacks are a classic data structure used to model information that is accessed in a specific order. The `Stack` class in Java is implemented as a last-in-first-out (LIFO) stack, which means that the last item added to the stack is the first one to be removed. Figure 8.2 shows the logical organization of a stack.

FIGURE 8.2

The logical organization of a stack data structure.

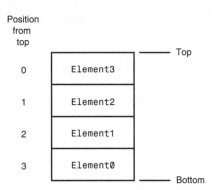

You may wonder why the numbers of the elements don't match their positions from the top of the stack. Keep in mind that elements are added to the top, so Element0, which is on the bottom, was the first element added to the stack. Likewise, Element3, which is on top, was the last element added. Also, because Element3 is at the top of the stack, it will be the first to be removed.

The Stack class defines only one constructor, which is a default constructor that creates an empty stack. You use this constructor as follows to create a stack:

```
Stack s = new Stack();
```

You add new elements to a stack by using the push() method, which pushes an element onto the top of the stack:

```
s.push("One");
s.push("Two");
s.push("Three");
s.push("Four");
s.push("Five");
s.push("Six");
```

This code pushes six strings onto the stack, with the last string ("Six") remaining on top. You pop elements back off the stack by using the pop() method:

```
String s1 = (String)s.pop();
String s2 = (String)s.pop();
```

This code pops the last two strings off the stack, leaving the first four strings. This code results in the s1 variable containing the "Six" string and the s2 variable containing the "Five" string.

If you want to get the top element on the stack without actually popping it off the stack, you can use the peek() method:

```
String s3 = (String)s.peek();
```

This call to peek() returns the "Four" string but leaves the string on the stack. You can search for an element on the stack by using the search() method:

```
int i = s.search("Two");
```

The search() method returns the distance from the top of the stack of the element if it is found or -1 if not. In this case, the "Two" string is the third element from the top, so the search() method returns 2 (zero-based).

8

Note As in all Java data structures that deal with indexes or lists, the Stack class reports element position in a zero-based fashion. This means that the top element in a stack has a location of 0, and the fourth element down has a location of 3.

The only other method defined in the Stack class is empty, which determines whether a stack is empty:

```
boolean isEmpty = s.empty();
```

Although the Stack class isn't quite as useful as the Vector class, it provides the functionality for a very common and established data structure.

Map

The Map interface defines a framework for implementing a *key-mapped data structure*, a place to store objects that are each referenced by a key. The key serves the same purpose as an element number in an array—it's a unique value that's used to access the data stored at a position in the data structure.

You can put the key-mapped approach to work by using the Hashtable class, which implements the Map interface, or by creating your own class that uses the interface. You'll learn about the Hashtable class in the next section.

The Map interface defines a means of storing and retrieving information based on a key. This is similar in some ways to the Vector class, in which elements are accessed through an index, which is a specific type of key. However, keys in the Map interface can be just about anything. You can create your own classes to use as the keys for accessing and manipulating data in a dictionary. Figure 8.3 shows how keys map to data in a dictionary.

FIGURE 8.3

The logical organization of a key-mapped data structure.

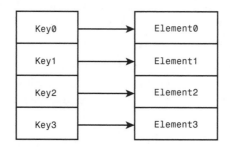

The Map interface declares a variety of methods for working with the data stored in a dictionary. Implementing classes will have to implement all of those methods to be truly useful. The put and get methods are used to put objects in the dictionary and get them back. Assuming look is a class that implements the Map interface, the following code shows how to use the put method to add elements:

```
Rectangle r1 = new Rectangle(0, 0, 5, 5);
look.put("small", r1);
Rectangle r2 = new Rectangle(0, 0, 15, 15);
look.put("medium", r2);
Rectangle r3 = new Rectangle(0, 0, 25, 25);
look.put("large", r3);
```

This code adds three rectangles to the dictionary, using strings as the keys. To get an element, use the get method and specify the appropriate key:

```
Rectangle r = (Rectangle)look.get("medium");
```

You also can remove an element with a key by using the remove() method:

```
look.remove("large");
```

You can find out how many elements are in the structure by using the size() method, much as you did with the Vector class:

```
int size = look.size();
```

You also can check whether the structure is empty by using the isEmpty() method:

```
boolean isEmpty = look.isEmpty();
```

Hash Tables

The Hashtable class is derived from Dictionary, implements the Map interface, and provides a complete implementation of a key-mapped data structure. Hash tables enable you to store data based on some type of key and have an efficiency defined by the load factor of the table. The *load factor* is a number between 0.0 and 1.0 that determines how and when the hash table allocates space for more elements.

Like vectors, hash tables have a capacity, or an amount of allocated memory. Hash tables allocate memory by comparing the current size of the table with the product of the capacity and the load factor. If the size of the hash table exceeds this product, the table increases its capacity by rehashing itself.

Load factors that are closer to 1.0 result in a more efficient use of memory at the expense of a longer lookup time for each element. Similarly, load factors closer to 0.0 result in more efficient lookups but tend to be more wasteful with memory. Determining the load factor for your own hash tables will depend on how you use each hash table and whether your priority is performance or memory efficiency.

You can create hash tables in any one of three ways. The first constructor creates a default hash table:

```
Hashtable hash = new Hashtable();
```

The second constructor creates a hash table with the specified initial capacity:

```
Hashtable hash = new Hashtable(20);
```

Finally, the third constructor creates a hash table with the specified initial capacity and load factor:

```
Hashtable hash = new Hashtable(20, 0.75F);
```

All the abstract methods defined in Map are implemented in the Hashtable class. In addition, the Hashtable class implements a few others that perform functions specific to supporting hash tables. One of these is the clear() method, which clears a hash table of all its keys and elements:

```
hash.clear();
```

The contains() method checks whether an object is stored in the hash table. This method searches for an object value in the hash table rather than searching for a key. The following code shows how to use the contains() method:

```
boolean isThere = hash.contains(new Rectangle(0, 0, 5, 5));
```

Similar to contains(), the containsKey() method searches a hash table but is based on a key rather than a value:

```
boolean isThere = hash.containsKey("Small");
```

As mentioned earlier, a hash table will rehash itself when it determines that it must increase its capacity. You can force a rehash yourself by calling the rehash() method:

```
hash.rehash();
```

The practical use of a hash table is actually in its ability to represent data that are too time-consuming to search or reference by value. In other words, hash tables come in handy when you're working with complex data and it's more efficient to access the data by simply using a key rather than comparing the data objects themselves.

Furthermore, hash tables typically compute a key for elements, which is called a hash code. For example, a string can have an integer hash code computed for it that uniquely represents the string. When a bunch of strings are stored in a hash table, the table can access the strings by using integer hash codes as opposed to using the contents of the strings themselves. This results in much more efficient searching and retrieving capabilities.

NEW TERM A *hash code* is a computed key that uniquely identifies each element in a hash table.

This technique of computing and using hash codes for object storage and reference is exploited heavily throughout the Java system. The parent of all classes, `Object`, defines a `hashCode()` method that is overridden in most standard Java classes. Any class that defines a `hashCode()` method can be efficiently stored and accessed in a hash table. A class that wants to be hashed must also implement the `equals()` method, which defines a way of telling whether two objects are equal. The `equals()` method usually just performs a straight comparison of all the member variables defined in a class.

The last project you will undertake today uses tables for a shopping application.

The `ComicBooks` application prices collectible comic books according to their base value and their condition. The condition is described as one of the following: mint, near mint, very fine, fine, good, or poor.

Each condition has a specific effect on a comic's value:

- "mint" books are worth 3 times their base price
- "near mint" books are worth 2 times their base price
- "very fine" books are worth 1.5 times their base price
- "fine" books are worth their base price
- "good" books are worth 0.5 times their base price
- "poor" books are worth 0.25 times their base price

To associate text such as "mint" or "very fine" with a numeric value, it must be put into a hash table. The keys to the hash table are the condition descriptions, and the values are floating-point numbers, such as 3.0, 1.5, and 0.25.

Enter the text of Listing 8.2 in your Java editor, and then save it as `ComicBooks.java` when you're done.

LISTING 8.2   The Full Text of `ComicBooks.java`

```
 1: import java.util.*;
 2:
 3: public class ComicBooks {
 4:
 5:     public ComicBooks() {
 6:     }
 7:
 8:     public static void main(String[] arguments) {
 9:         // set up hashtable
10:         Hashtable quality = new Hashtable();
11:         Float price1 = new Float(3.00F);
12:         quality.put("mint", price1);
13:         Float price2 = new Float(2.00F);
14:         quality.put("near mint", price2);
```

LISTING 8.1 Continued

```
15:            Float price3 = new Float(1.50F);
16:            quality.put("very fine", price3);
17:            Float price4 = new Float(1.00F);
18:            quality.put("fine", price4);
19:            Float price5 = new Float(0.50F);
20:            quality.put("good", price5);
21:            Float price6 = new Float(0.25F);
22:            quality.put("poor", price6);
23:            // set up collection
24:            Comic[] comix = new Comic[3];
25:            comix[0] = new Comic("Amazing Spider-Man", "1A", "very fine",
26:                5400.00F);
27:            comix[0].setPrice( (Float)quality.get(comix[0].condition) );
28:            comix[1] = new Comic("Incredible Hulk", "181", "near mint",
29:                770.00F);
30:            comix[1].setPrice( (Float)quality.get(comix[1].condition) );
31:            comix[2] = new Comic("Cerebus", "1A", "good", 260.00F);
32:            comix[2].setPrice( (Float)quality.get(comix[2].condition) );
33:            for (int i = 0; i < comix.length; i++) {
34:                System.out.println("Title: " + comix[i].title);
35:                System.out.println("Issue: " + comix[i].issueNumber);
36:                System.out.println("Condition: " + comix[i].condition);
37:                System.out.println("Price: $" + comix[i].price + "\n");
38:            }
39:        }
40: }
41:
42: class Comic {
43:      String title;
44:      String issueNumber;
45:      String condition;
46:      float basePrice;
47:      float price;
48:
49:      Comic(String inTitle, String inIssueNumber, String inCondition,
50:          float inBasePrice) {
51:
52:          title = inTitle;
53:          issueNumber = inIssueNumber;
54:          condition = inCondition;
55:          basePrice = inBasePrice;
56:      }
57:
58:      void setPrice(Float factor) {
59:          float multiplier = factor.floatValue();
60:          price = basePrice * multiplier;
61:      }
62: }
```

When you run the `ComicBooks` application, it produces the following output:

```
Title: Amazing Spider-Man
Issue: 1A
Condition: very fine
Price: $8100.0

Title: Incredible Hulk
Issue: 181
Condition: near mint
Price: $1540.0

Title: Cerebus
Issue: 1A
Condition: good
Price: $130.0
```

The `ComicBooks` application is implemented as two classes: an application class called `ComicBooks` and a helper class called `Comic`.

In the application, the hash table is created in lines 9–22.

First, the hash table is created in line 9.

Next, a `Float` object called `price1` is created that represents the floating-point value 3.00. This value is added to the hash table and associated with the key "mint."

> **Note**
>
> If you're wondering why a `Float` object is being used rather than a `float` data type, it's because hash tables can be used only to hold objects. You can't call a table's `put` method with `float` or any of the other primitive data types.

The process is repeated for each of the other comic book conditions from "near mint" to "poor."

After the hash table has been set up, an array of `Comic` objects called `comix` is created to hold each comic book that is currently for sale.

The `Comic` constructor is called with four arguments: the book's title, issue number, condition, and base price. The first three are strings, and the last is a `float`.

After a `Comic` has been created, its `setPrice(Float)` method is called to set the book's price based on its condition. Here's an example (line 27):

```
comix[0].setPrice( (Float)quality.get(comix[0].condition) );
```

The hash table's `get(String)` method is called with the condition of the book, a `String` that is one of the keys in the table. An `Object` is returned that represents the value associated with that key. (In line 27, because `comix[0].condition` is equal to "very fine," `get()` returns an `Object` that holds the floating-point number 3.00F.)

Because `get()` returns an `Object`, it must be cast as a `Float`.

This process is repeated for two more books.

In lines 33–38, information about each comic book in the `comix` array is displayed.

The `Comic` class is defined in lines 42–62. There are five instance variables—the `String` objects `title`, `issueNumber`, and `condition`, and the floating-point values `basePrice` and `price`.

The constructor method of the class, located in lines 49–56, sets the value of four instance variables to the arguments sent to the constructor.

The `setPrice(Float)` method in lines 58–60 sets the price of a comic book. The argument sent to the method is a `Float` object that is converted to the equivalent `float` value in line 59. In the next line, the price of a comic is calculated by multiplying this `float` by the base price of the comic. Consequently, if a book is worth $1000 and its multiplier is 2.0, the book is priced at $2000.

Hash tables are an extremely powerful data structure that should probably be integrated into some of your programs that manipulate large amounts of data. The fact that hash tables are so widely supported in the Java class library via the `Object` class should give you a clue as to their importance in Java programming.

Summary

Today you learned about several data structures you can use in your Java programs:

- Bit sets—Large sets of Boolean on-or-off values
- Stacks—Structures in which the last item added is the first item removed
- Vectors—Arrays that can change in size dynamically and be shrunken or expanded as needed
- Hash tables—Objects that are stored and retrieved using unique keys

These data structures are part of the `java.util` package, a collection of useful classes for handling data, dates, strings, and other things.

Learning about the ways you can organize data in Java has benefits in all aspects of software development. Whether you're learning the language to write servlets, console programs, consumer software with a graphical user interface, or something else entirely, you will need to represent data in numerous ways.

Q&A

Q The `HolidaySked` project from today could be implemented as an array of **Boolean** values. Is one way preferable to the other?

A That depends. One thing you'll find as you work with data structures is that there are often many different ways to implement something. Bit sets are somewhat preferable to a `boolean` array when the size of your program matters because a bit set is smaller. An array of a primitive type such as `boolean` is preferable when the speed of your program matters because arrays are somewhat faster. In the example of the `HolidaySked` class, it's so small that the difference is negligible, but as you develop your own robust, real-world applications, these kinds of decisions can make a difference.

Quiz

Review today's material by taking this quiz.

Questions

1. Which of the following kinds of data cannot be stored in a hash table?

    (a.) `String`

    (b.) `int`

    (c.) `Object`

2. A vector is created and three strings called `Tinker`, `Evers`, and `Chance` are added to it. The method `removeElement("Evers")` is called. Which of the following `Vector` methods will retrieve the "Chance" string ?

    (a.) `get(1);`

    (b.) `get(2);`

    (c.) `get("Chance");`

3. Which of these classes implements the `Map` interface?

(a.) `Stack`

(b.) `Hashtable`

(c.) `Bitset`

Answers

1. (b.) Primitive data types cannot be stored in a hash table. In order to store them in a table, you must use the objects that represent them (such as `Integer` for integers).

2. (a.) The index numbers of each item in a vector can change as items are added or removed. Because "Chance" becomes the second item in the `Vector` after "Evers" is removed, it is retrieved by calling `get(1)`.

3. (b.)

Certification Practice

The following question is the kind of thing you could expect to be asked on a Java programming certification test. Answer it without looking at today's material or using the Java compiler to test the code.

Given:

```java
public class Recursion {
    public int dex = -1;

    public Recursion() {
        dex = getValue(17);
    }

    public int getValue(int dexValue) {
        if (dexValue > 100)
            return dexValue;
        else
            return getValue(dexValue * 2);
    }

    public static void main(String[] arguments) {
        Recursion r = new Recursion();
        System.out.println(r.dex);
    }
}
```

What will be the output of this application?

(a.) -1

(b.) 17

(c.) 34

(d.) 136

The answer is available on this book's Web site at http://www.java21days.com. Visit the Day 8 page and click the Certification Practice link.

Exercises

To extend your knowledge of the subjects covered today, try the following exercises:

- Add two more conditions to the ComicBooks application: "pristine mint" for books that should sell at five times their base price and "coverless" for books that should sell at one-tenth of their base price.
- Create an application that uses a vector as a shopping cart that holds Fruit objects. Each Fruit object should have a name, a quantity, and a price.

Where applicable, exercise solutions are offered on this book's Web site at http://www.java21days.com.

DAY 9

Working with Swing

During the next four days you will work with a set of classes called Swing, which can implement a user-interface style called Metal. (Sounds like somebody at Sun Microsystems is either a music buff or a frustrated musician.)

Swing provides a way to offer a graphical user interface in your Java programs and accept user input with the keyboard, mouse, and other input devices.

The Swing library is an extension of the Abstract Windowing Toolkit, the package that offered limited graphical programming support in Java 1.0. Swing offers much-improved functionality over its predecessor—new components, expanded component features, better event handling, and a selectable look and feel.

Today you will use Swing to create applications that feature a graphical user interface, using each of these components:

- Frames—windows that can include a title bar and menu bar, as well as maximize, minimize, and close buttons
- Containers—interface elements that can hold other components

- Buttons—clickable regions with text or graphics indicating their purpose
- Labels—text or graphics that provide information
- Text fields and text areas—windows that accept keyboard input and allow text to be edited
- Drop-down lists—groups of related items that can be selected from drop-down menus or scrolling windows
- Check boxes and radio buttons—small windows or circles that can be selected or deselected

Creating an Application

The expression "look and feel" is used often when describing interface programming. As you might have guessed, it describes how a graphical user interface looks and feels to a user.

Swing enables you to create a Java program with an interface that uses the style of the native operating system, such as Windows or Solaris, or a new style, dubbed Metal, which is unique to Java.

Swing components, unlike their predecessors in previous versions of Java, are implemented entirely in Java. This makes them more compatible across different platforms than the AWT.

All elements of Swing are part of the `javax.swing` package, a standard part of the Java 2 class library. To use a Swing class, you must use either an `import` statement with that class or a catch-all statement such as the following:

```
import javax.swing.*;
```

 Caution

> The Swing package had several names before Sun settled on `javax.swing`. If you come across one of the older names in a program's source code—`com.sun.java.swing` or `java.awt.swing`—changing the package name might be all that's required to update the code for Java 2.

Two other packages that are used with graphical user interface programming are `java.awt`, the Abstract Windowing Toolkit, and `java.awt.event`, event-handling classes that handle user input.

When you use a Swing component, you work with objects of that component's class. You create the component by calling its constructor method and then calling methods of the component as needed for proper setup.

All Swing components are subclasses of the abstract class JComponent, which includes methods to set the size of a component, change the background color, define the font used for any displayed text, and set up *tooltips*—explanatory text that appears when a user hovers over the component for a few seconds.

Caution Swing classes inherit from many of the same superclasses as the Abstract Windowing Toolkit, so it is possible to use Swing and AWT components together in the same interface. However, in some cases the two types of components will not be rendered correctly in a container. To avoid these problems, it's best to use Swing components unless you are writing an applet that should be limited to Java 1.0 or 1.1 functionality—there's a Swing version of every AWT component.

Before components can be displayed in a user interface, they must be added to a *container:* a component that can hold other components. Swing containers, which can often be placed in other containers, are subclasses of java.awt.Container, a class in the Abstract Windowing Toolkit. This class includes methods to add and remove components from a container, arrange components using an object called a layout manager, and set up empty insets around the inside edges of a container.

Creating an Interface

The first step in creating a Swing application is to create a class that represents the graphical user interface. An object of this class serves as a container that holds all the other components to be displayed.

In many projects, the main interface object is either a simple window (the JWindow class) or a more specialized window called a frame (the JFrame class).

A window is a container that can be displayed on a user's desktop. A simple window does not have a title bar; maximize, minimize, or close buttons; or other features you see on most windows that open in a graphical user interface operating system. Windows that do have these window management features are called *frames.*

In a graphical environment such as Windows or MacOS, users expect to have the ability to move, resize, and close the windows of programs that they run. The main place a simple window, rather than a frame, turns up is when programs are loading—there is sometimes a "title screen" with the program's name, logo, and other information.

One way to create a graphical Swing application is to make the interface a subclass of JFrame, as in the following class declaration:

```
public class Lookup extends JFrame {
    // ...
}
```

This leaves only a few things to do in the constructor method of the class:

- Call a constructor method of the superclass to handle any of its setup procedures.
- Set the size of the frame's window, in pixels.
- Decide what to do if a user closes the window.
- Display the frame.

The JFrame class has two constructors: JFrame() and JFrame(*String*). One sets the frame's title bar to the specified text and the other leaves the title bar empty. You can also set the title by calling the frame's setTitle(*String*) method.

The size of a frame can be established by calling the setSize(*int, int*) method with the width and height as arguments. The size of a frame is indicated in pixels, so if you called setSize(600, 600), the frame would take up almost all of a screen at 800×600 resolution once it is displayed.

Note

> You also can call the method setSize(*Dimension*) to set up a frame's size. Dimension is a class in the java.awt package that represents the width and height of a user interface component. Calling the Dimension(*int, int*) constructor creates a Dimension object representing the width and height specified as arguments.

Another thing you can do to set the size of a frame is to fill the frame with the components it will contain and then call the frame's pack() method. This resizes the frame based on the size of the components inside it. If the frame is bigger than it needs to be, pack() shrinks it to the minimum size required to display the components. If the frame is too small (or the size has not been set at all), pack() expands it to the required size.

Frames are invisible when they are created. You can make them visible by calling the frame's show() method with no arguments or setVisible(*boolean*) with the literal true as an argument.

If you want a frame to be displayed when it is created, call one of these methods in the constructor method. You also can leave the frame invisible, requiring any class that uses the frame to make it visible by calling show() or setVisible(true). (There are also methods of hiding a frame—call either the hide() method or setVisible(false).)

When a frame is displayed, the default behavior is for it to be positioned in the upper left corner of the computer's desktop. You can specify a different location by calling the setBounds(*int, int, int, int*) method. The first two arguments to this method are the (x,y) position of the frame's upper left corner on the desktop, and the last two arguments set the width and height of the frame.

The following class represents a 400 × 100 frame with "Edit Payroll" in the title bar:

```
public class Payroll extends javax.swing.JFrame {
    public Payroll() {
        super("Edit Payroll");
        setSize(300, 100);
        show();
    }
}
```

Every frame has maximize, minimize, and close buttons on the title bar at the user's control—the same controls present in the interface of other software running on your system. In Java, the normal behavior when a frame is closed is for the application to keep running. To change this, you must call a frame's setDefaultCloseOperation() method with one of four static variables of the JFrame class as an argument:

- EXIT_ON_CLOSE—Exit the program when the frame is closed.
- DISPOSE_ON_CLOSE—Close the frame, dispose of the frame object, and keep running the application.
- DO_NOTHING_ON_CLOSE—Keep the frame open and continue running.
- HIDE_ON_CLOSE—Close the frame and continue running.

To prevent a user from closing a frame at all, add the following statement to the frame's constructor method:

```
setDefaultCloseOperation(JFrame.DO_NOTHING_ON_CLOSE);
```

If you are creating a frame to serve as an application's main user interface, the expected behavior is probably EXIT_ON_CLOSE, which shuts down the application along with the frame.

Developing a Framework

Listing 9.1 contains a simple application that displays a frame 300 × 100 pixels in size. This class can serve as a framework—pun unavoidable—for any applications you create that use a graphical user interface.

LISTING 9.1   The Full Text of `SimpleFrame.java`

```
 1: import javax.swing.JFrame;
 2:
 3: public class SimpleFrame extends JFrame {
 4:     public SimpleFrame() {
 5:         super("Frame Title");
 6:         setSize(300, 100);
 7:         setDefaultCloseOperation(JFrame.EXIT_ON_CLOSE);
 8:         setVisible(true);
 9:     }
10:
11:     public static void main(String[] arguments) {
12:         SimpleFrame sf = new SimpleFrame();
13:     }
14:
15: }
```

When you compile and run the application, you should see the frame displayed in Figure 9.1.

FIGURE 9.1

Displaying a frame.

The `SimpleFrame` application isn't much to look at—this graphical user interface contains no components a user can actually interface with, aside from the standard maximize, minimize, and close ("X") buttons on the title bar shown in Figure 9.1. You will add components later today.

A `SimpleFrame` object is created in the `main()` method in lines 11–13. If you had not displayed the frame when it was constructed, you could call `sf.setVisible(true)` in the `main()` method to display the frame represented by `sf`.

The work involved in creating the frame's user interface takes place in the `SimpleFrame()` constructor method. If you were adding components to this frame, they could be created and added to the frame within this constructor.

Creating a window using `JWindow` is very similar to working with frames in Swing. The only things you can't do involve features that simple windows don't support—titles, closing a window, and so on.

Listing 9.2 contains an application that creates and opens a window, displays the first 10,000 integers in the command-line window, and then closes the window.

LISTING 9.2   The Full Text of `SimpleWindow.java`

```
 1: import javax.swing.JWindow;
 2:
 3: public class SimpleWindow extends JWindow {
 4:     public SimpleWindow() {
 5:         super();
 6:         setBounds(250, 225, 300, 150);
 7:     }
 8:
 9:     public static void main(String[] arguments) {
10:         SimpleWindow sw = new SimpleWindow();
11:         sw.setVisible(true);
12:         for (int i = 0; i < 10000; i++)
13:             System.out.print(i + " ");
14:         sw.setVisible(false);
15:         System.exit(0);
16:     }
17:
18: }
```

Figure 9.2 shows this application running with the `SimpleWindow` container visible over the Java command-line window in Windows.

FIGURE 9.2

Displaying a window.

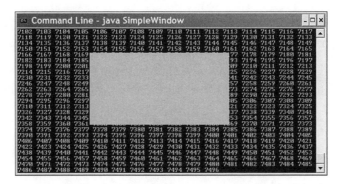

Because of the call to `setBounds(250, 225, 300, 150)` in line 6 of Listing 9.2, the window is 300 × 150 in size and displayed with its upper left corner at the (x,y) position 250, 225.

The `for` loop in lines 12–13 is included simply to take up a little time. An alternate way to do this would be to call the `sleep()` method of the `Thread` class, which you learned about during Day 7, "Threads and Exceptions."

Closing a Window

Prior to the introduction of the `setDefaultCloseOperation()` method in Java 2, the only way to close a graphical application after a user closed a window was to deal with the occurrence explicitly.

To do this, the window must be monitored to see whether the user has done anything to close it, such as clicking a title bar close button. When this is done, a program can respond by exiting the program, closing the window, keeping it open, or something else appropriate to the situation.

Monitoring for user interaction requires the use of event-handling classes—features that you will explore in great detail on Day 12, "Responding to User Input." The term *event-handling* in Java describes objects that wait for something to occur—such as a button click or typing text into a field—and then call methods in response to that occurrence.

All of Java's event-handling classes belong to the `java.awt.event` package.

 Note

> Although this technique isn't necessary in Java 2, it is introduced here because you will see it in many existing Swing applications. It also provides a first look at how Java handles user input in a Swing interface.

To monitor a window in a user interface, your program must do three things:

- Create an object to monitor the state of the window.
- Implement an interface in the object that handles each way the window can change.
- Associate the window with your user interface.

A window can be monitored by an object that implements the `WindowListener` interface. As you learned on Day 6, "Packages, Interfaces, and Other Class Features," an interface is a set of methods that indicate a class supports more behavior than it has inherited from its superclass.

In this example, a class that implements the `WindowListener` interface has behavior to keep track of what a user is doing to a window.

To implement an interface, a class must include all the methods in that interface. Classes that support WindowListener must have the following seven methods:

- windowActivated()—The window associated with this object is becoming the active window, which means that it will be able to receive keyboard input.
- windowDeactivated()—The window is about to become inactive, which means that it won't be able to receive keyboard input.
- windowClosed()—The window has been closed.
- windowClosing()—The window is being closed.
- windowOpened()—The window has been made visible.
- windowIconified()—The window has been minimized.
- windowDeiconified()—The window has been maximized.

As you can see, each method has something to do with how a user interacts with the window.

Another class in the java.awt.event package, WindowAdapter, implements this interface with seven empty methods that do nothing. By creating a subclass of WindowAdapter, you can override methods pertaining to the user interaction events that you want to deal with, as shown in Listing 9.3.

LISTING 9.3 The Full Text of ExitWindow.java

```
1: import java.awt.event.*;
2:
3: public class ExitWindow extends WindowAdapter {
4:     public void windowClosing(WindowEvent e) {
5:         System.exit(0);
6:     }
7: }
```

The ExitWindow class inherits from WindowAdapter, which implements the WindowListener interface. As a result, ExitWindow objects can be used to monitor frames.

An ExitWindow object has only one job: Wait to see whether a window is being closed, an event that causes the windowClosing() method to be called automatically.

Line 5 of Listing 9.3 calls a class method of java.lang.System, exit(), which shuts down the currently running application. The integer argument to exit() should be 0 if the program ended normally, or any other value if it ended because of an error of some kind.

Once you have created an object that can monitor a window, you associate it with that window by calling the component's addWindowListener() method, as in the following example:

```
JFrame main = new JFrame("Main Menu");
ExitWindow exit = new ExitWindow();
main.addWindowListener(exit);
```

This example associates the ExitWindow object with a frame called main.

You can use this ExitWindow class with the primary window of any application, provided that the program should shut down and do nothing else after the user closes the window.

Listing 9.4 contains the SimpleFrame application rewritten to use this technique.

LISTING 9.4   The Full Text of ExitFrame.java

```
 1: import javax.swing.JFrame;
 2:
 3: public class ExitFrame extends JFrame {
 4:     public ExitFrame() {
 5:         super("Frame Title");
 6:         setSize(300, 100);
 7:         ExitWindow exit = new ExitWindow();
 8:         addWindowListener(exit);
 9:         setVisible(true);
10:     }
11:
12:     public static void main(String[] arguments) {
13:         ExitFrame sf = new ExitFrame();
14:     }
15:
16: }
```

This application must have access to ExitWindow.class in order to compile and run successfully. The easiest way to do this is to compile both programs in the same folder.

Creating a Component

Creating a graphical user interface is a great way to get experience working with objects in Java because each component of the interface is represented by its own class.

You have already worked with the container classes JFrame and JWindow and the event-handling class WindowAdapter.

To use an interface component in Java, you create an object of that component's class. One of the simplest to employ is JButton, the class that embodies clickable buttons.

In most programs, buttons trigger an action—click Install to begin installing software, click a smiley button to begin a new game of Minesweeper, click the minimize button to prevent your boss from seeing Minesweeper running, and so on.

A Swing button can feature a text label, a graphical icon, or a combination of both.

Constructor methods you can use for buttons include the following:

- JButton(*String*)—A button labeled with the specified text
- JButton(*Icon*)—A button that displays the specified icon
- JButton(*String*, *Icon*)—A button with the specified text and icon

The following statements create three buttons:

```
JButton play = new JButton("Play");
JButton stop = new JButton("Stop");
JButton rewind = new JButton("Rewind");
```

Adding Components to a Container

Before you can display a user interface component such as a button in a Java program, you must add it to a container and display that container.

To add a component to a simple container, you call the container's add(*Component*) method with the component as the argument (all user interface components in Swing inherit from java.awt.Component).

The simplest Swing container is the panel (the JPanel class). The following example creates a button and adds it to a panel:

```
JButton quit = new JButton("Quit");
JPanel panel = new JPanel();
panel.add(quit);
```

Most other Swing containers, including frames, windows, applets, and dialog boxes, do not allow components to be added in this manner. Those containers are broken down into *panes,* a kind of container within a container. Ordinarily, components are added to the container's *content pane*.

You can add components to a container's content pane using the following steps:

1. Create a panel.
2. Add components to the panel using its add(*Component*) method.
3. Call setContentPane(*Container*) with the panel as an argument.

The program in Listing 9.5 uses the application framework created earlier in this chapter and extends it to add buttons to the frame's content pane.

LISTING 9.5   The Full Text of Buttons.java

```
 1: import javax.swing.*;
 2:
 3: public class Buttons extends JFrame {
 4:     JButton abort = new JButton("Abort");
 5:     JButton retry = new JButton("Retry");
 6:     JButton fail = new JButton("Fail");
 7:
 8:     public Buttons() {
 9:         super("Buttons");
10:         setSize(80, 140);
11:         setDefaultCloseOperation(JFrame.EXIT_ON_CLOSE);
12:         JPanel pane = new JPanel();
13:         pane.add(abort);
14:         pane.add(retry);
15:         pane.add(fail);
16:         setContentPane(pane);
17: }
18:
19:     public static void main(String[] arguments) {
20:         Buttons rb = new Buttons();
21:         rb.show();
22:     }
23: }
```

When you run the application, a small frame opens that contains the three buttons (see Figure 9.3).

FIGURE 9.3

The Buttons
application.

The Buttons class has three instance variables: the abort, retry, and fail JButton objects.

In lines 12–15, a new JPanel object is created, and the three buttons are added to the panel by calls to its add() method. When the panel is complete, the frame's setContentPane() method is called in line 16 with the panel as an argument, making it the frame's content pane.

Note

> If you click the buttons, absolutely nothing happens. Doing something in response to a button click will be covered on Day 12, "Responding to User Input."

Working with Components

9

Swing offers more than two dozen different user interface components in addition to the buttons and containers you have used thus far. You will work with many of these components for the rest of today and on Day 10, "Building a Swing Interface."

All Swing components share a common superclass, `javax.swing.JComponent`, from which they inherit several methods you will find useful in your own programs.

The `setEnabled(boolean)` method enables a component if the argument is `true` and disables it if the argument is `false`. Components are enabled by default, and they must be enabled in order to receive user input. Many disabled components change in appearance to indicate that they are not presently usable—for instance, a disabled `JButton` has light gray borders and gray text. If you want to check whether a component is enabled, you can call the `isEnabled()` method, which returns a `boolean` value.

The `setVisible(boolean)` method works for all components the way it does for containers. Use `true` to display a component and `false` to hide it. There's also a `boolean` `isVisible()` method.

The `setSize(int, int)` resizes the component to the width and height specified as arguments, and `setSize(Dimension)` uses a `Dimension` object to do the same thing. For most components, you do not need to set a size—the default is usually acceptable. To find out the size of a component, call its `getSize()` method, which returns a `Dimension` object with the dimensions in `height` and `width` instance variables.

As you will see, similar Swing components also have other methods in common, such as `setText()` and `getText()` for text components and `setValue()` and `getValue()` for components that store a numeric value.

Image Icons

Earlier today, you created button components that were labeled with text. Swing also supports the use of `ImageIcon` objects on buttons and other components in which a label can be provided. An *icon* is a small graphic that can be placed on a button, label, or other user interface element to identify it. Current operating systems have icons everywhere—garbage cans and recycling bins for deleting files, folder icons for storing files, mailbox icons for e-mail programs, and hundreds of others. Icons used on the Web are usually stored as GIF files.

An ImageIcon object can be created by specifying the filename of a graphic as the only argument to the constructor. The following example loads an icon from the file zap.gif and creates a JButton with the icon as its label:

```
ImageIcon zap = new ImageIcon("zap.gif");
JButton button = new JButton(zap);
JPanel pane = new JPanel();
pane.add(button);
setContentPane(pane);
```

Listing 9.6 contains a Java application that uses the same ImageIcon to create 24 buttons, add them to a panel, and then designate the panel as a frame's content pane.

LISTING 9.6   The Full Text of Icons.java

```
 1: import javax.swing.*;
 2:
 3: public class Icons extends JFrame {
 4:     JButton[] buttons = new JButton[24];
 5:
 6:     public Icons() {
 7:         super("Icons");
 8:         setSize(335, 318);
 9:         setDefaultCloseOperation(JFrame.EXIT_ON_CLOSE);
10:         JPanel pane = new JPanel();
11:         ImageIcon icon = new ImageIcon("3dman.gif");
12:         for (int i = 0; i < 24; i++) {
13:             buttons[i] = new JButton(icon);
14:             pane.add(buttons[i]);
15:         }
16:         setContentPane(pane);
17:         show();
18:     }
19:
20:     public static void main(String[] arguments) {
21:         Icons ike = new Icons();
22:     }
23: }
```

Figure 9.4 shows the result.

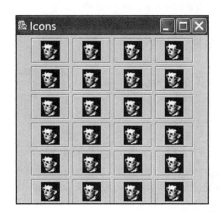

The icon graphic referred to in line 11 can be found on this book's official Web site at `http://www.java21days.com` on the Day 9 page under the filename `3dman.gif`.

> **Note**
>
> The 3D moviegoer icon is from Jeffrey Zeldman's *Pardon My Icons!* collection, which includes hundreds of icons you can use in your own projects as long as you give Zeldman credit. If you're looking for icons to experiment with in Swing applications, you can find *Pardon My Icons!* at the following address:
>
> `http://www.zeldman.com/icon.html`

Labels

A label is a user component that contains informative text, an icon, or both. Labels, which are created from the `JLabel` class, are often used to identify the purpose of other components on an interface. They cannot be directly edited by a user.

To create a label, you can use the following constructors:

- `JLabel(String)`—A label with the specified text
- `JLabel(String, int)`—A label with the specified text and alignment
- `JLabel(String, Icon, int)`—A label with the specified text, icon, and alignment

The alignment of a label determines how its text or icon is aligned in relation to the area taken up by the window. Three static class variables of the `SwingConstants` interface are used to specify alignment: `LEFT`, `CENTER`, and `RIGHT`.

The contents of a label can be set with setText(*String*) or setIcon(*Icon*) methods. You also can retrieve these things with getText() and getIcon() methods.

The following statements create three labels with left, center, and right alignment, respectively:

```
JLabel tinker = new JLabel("Tinker", SwingConstants.LEFT);
JLabel evers = new JLabel("Evers", SwingConstants.CENTER);
JLabel chance = new JLabel("Chance", SwingConstants.RIGHT);
```

Text Fields

A *text field* is a location on an interface where a user can enter and modify text through the keyboard. Text fields are represented by the JTextField class and can each handle one line of input. Later in this section you will see a similar component, called a text area, that can handle multiple lines.

Constructor methods for text fields include the following:

- JTextField()—An empty text field
- JTextField(*int*)—A text field with the specified width
- JTextField(*String*, *int*)—A text field with the specified text and width

A text field's width attribute has relevance only if the interface is organized in a manner that does not resize components. You will get more experience with this when you work with layout managers on Day 11, "Arranging Components on a User Interface."

The following statements create an empty text field that has enough space for roughly 30 characters and a text field of the same size with the starting text "Puddin N. Tane":

```
JTextField name = new JTextField(30);
JTextField name2 = new JTextField("Puddin N. Tane", 30);
```

Text fields and text areas both inherit from the superclass JTextComponent and share many common methods.

The setEditable(*boolean*) method determines whether a text component can be edited (an argument of true) or not (false). There's also an isEditable() method that returns a corresponding boolean value.

The setText(*String*) method changes the text to the specified string, and the getText() method returns the component's current text as a string. Another method retrieves only the text that a user has highlighted in the getSelectedText() component.

Password fields are text fields that hide the characters a user is typing into the field. They are represented by the JPasswordField class, a subclass of JTextField. The JPasswordField constructor methods take the same arguments as those of its parent class.

Once you have created a password field, call its setEchoChar(*char*) method to obscure input by replacing each input character with the specified character.

> **Note**
>
> The *TextField* class in the Abstract Windowing Toolkit supports obscured text with the setEchoCharacter(*char*) method. This method is not supported in the JTextField class—improvements in Java's security necessitated the creation of a new class for obscured text.

The following statements create a password field and set its echo character to #:

```
JPasswordField codePhrase = new JPasswordField(20);
codePhrase.setEchoChar('#');
```

Text Areas

Text areas, editable text fields that can handle more than one line of input, are implemented with the JTextArea class.

JTextArea includes the following constructor methods:

- JTextArea(*int*, *int*)—A text area with the specified number of rows and columns
- JTextArea(*String*, *int*, *int*)—A text area with the specified text, rows, and columns

You can use the getText(), getSelectedText(), and setText(*String*) methods with text areas as you would text fields. Also, an append(*String*) method adds the specified text at the end of the current text and an insert(*String*, *int*) method inserts the specified text at the indicated position.

The setLineWrap(*boolean*) method determines whether text will wrap to the next line when it reaches the far edge of the component. Call setLineWrap(true) to cause line wrapping to occur.

The setWrapStyleWord(*boolean*) method determines what wraps to the next line—either the current word (an argument of true) or the current character (false).

The next project you will create, the Form application in Listing 9.7, uses several Swing components to collect user input: a text field, a password field, and a text area. Labels also are used to indicate the purpose of each text component.

LISTING 9.7   The Full Text of `Form.java`

```
 1: import javax.swing.*;
 2:
 3: public class Form extends javax.swing.JFrame {
 4:     JTextField username = new JTextField(15);
 5:     JPasswordField password = new JPasswordField(15);
 6:     JTextArea comments = new JTextArea(4, 15);
 7:
 8:     public Form() {
 9:         super("Feedback Form");
10:         setSize(260, 160);
11:         setDefaultCloseOperation(EXIT_ON_CLOSE);
12:
13:         JPanel pane = new JPanel();
14:         JLabel usernameLabel = new JLabel("Username: ");
15:         JLabel passwordLabel = new JLabel("Password: ");
16:         JLabel commentsLabel = new JLabel("Comments: ");
17:         comments.setLineWrap(true);
18:         comments.setWrapStyleWord(true);
19:         pane.add(usernameLabel);
20:         pane.add(username);
21:         pane.add(passwordLabel);
22:         pane.add(password);
23:         pane.add(commentsLabel);
24:         pane.add(comments);
25:         setContentPane(pane);
26:
27:         show();
28:     }
29:
30:     public static void main(String[] arguments) {
31:         Form input = new Form();
32:     }
33: }
```

Figure 9.5 shows the result.

FIGURE 9.5

The Form *application.*

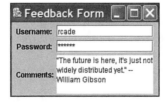

Scrolling Panes

Text areas in Swing do not include horizontal or vertical scrollbars, and there's no way to add them using this component alone. That's a difference between Swing text areas and their counterparts in the Abstract Windowing Toolkit.

The reason for the change is that Swing introduces a new container that can be used to hold any component that can be scrolled: JScrollPane.

A scrolling pane is associated with a component in the pane's constructor method. You can use either of the following constructors:

- JScrollPane(*Component*)—A scrolling pane that contains the specified component
- JScrollPane(*Component*, *int*, *int*)—A scrolling pane with the specified component, vertical scrollbar configuration, and horizontal scrollbar configuration

Scrollbars are configured using static class variables of the ScrollPaneConstants interface. You can use each of the following for vertical scrollbars:

- VERTICAL_SCROLLBAR_ALWAYS
- VERTICAL_SCROLLBAR_AS_NEEDED
- VERTICAL_SCROLLBAR_NEVER

There also are three similarly named variables for horizontal scrollbars.

After you create a scrolling pane containing a component, the pane should be added to containers in place of that component.

The following example creates a text area with a vertical scrollbar and no horizontal scrollbar, and then adds it to a content pane:

```
JPanel pane = new JPanel();
JTextArea letter = new JTextArea(5, 15);
JScrollPane scroll = new JScrollPane(letter,
    ScrollPaneConstants.VERTICAL_SCROLLBAR_ALWAYS,
    ScrollPaneConstants.HORIZONTAL_SCROLLBAR_NEVER);
pane.add(scroll);
setContentPane(pane);
```

Scrollbars

Scrollbars are components that enable a part of a large display to be selected for viewing. They are often used on text areas that contain more lines than a graphical user interface has space to display. A user can move to a particular location by dragging a box (the *knob*) between two arrows. The user can also move the view region a short distance (such as a line) by clicking one of the arrows, or a longer distance by clicking between an arrow and the knob.

Some Swing components have built-in scrollbar functionality, including scrolling panes and lists. You can also create a scrollbar by itself.

Scrollbars are normally created by specifying the minimum and maximum values that can be set using the component.

You can use the following constructor methods:

- JScrollBar(*int*)—A scrollbar with the specified orientation
- JScrollBar(*int*, *int*, *int*, *int*, *int*)—A scrollbar with the specified orientation, starting value, scroll box size, minimum value, and maximum value

The orientation is indicated by either of two JScrollBar class constants: HORIZONTAL or VERTICAL.

The initial value of the scrollbar should be equal to or between the minimum and maximum values of the bar. The default value is the minimum.

The third argument is the overall amount of material that can appear at one time in the display to which the scrollbar applies. If the scrollbar applies to a text area, for example, the third argument to the constructor is the number of lines the area can show. The default value is 10.

The fourth and fifth arguments are the minimum and maximum values of the scrollbar. The defaults are 0 and 100.

The following statement creates a vertical scrollbar with a minimum value of 10, a maximum value of 50, and an initial value of 33.

```
JScrollBar bar = new JScrollBar(JScrollBar.HORIZONTAL,
    33, 0, 10, 50);
```

Check Boxes and Radio Buttons

The next two components you will learn about, check boxes and radio buttons, are both components that have only two possible values: selected or not selected. The difference between them is that radio buttons are supposed to be grouped together so that only one of the buttons in a group can be selected at a time, like preset station selector buttons on a radio. Check boxes are typically used to make simple yes-no or on-off choices in a program.

Check boxes (the JCheckBox class) appear as labeled or unlabeled boxes that contain a check mark when they are selected and nothing otherwise. Radio buttons (the JRadioButton class) appear as circles that contain a dot when selected and are also empty otherwise.

Both the JCheckBox and JRadioButton classes have several useful methods inherited from their common superclass:

- setSelected(*boolean*)—Select the component if the argument is true and deselect it otherwise.
- isSelected()—Return a boolean indicating whether the component is currently selected.

The following constructors are available for the JCheckBox class:

- JCheckBox(*String*)—A check box with the specified text label
- JCheckBox(*String, boolean*)—A check box with the specified text label that is selected if the second argument is true
- JCheckBox(*Icon*)—A check box with the specified icon label
- JCheckBox(*Icon, boolean*)—A check box with the specified icon label that is selected if the second argument is true
- JCheckBox(*String, Icon*)—A check box with the specified text label and icon label
- JCheckBox(*String, Icon, boolean*)—A check box with the specified text label and icon label that is selected if the third argument is true

The JRadioButton class has constructors with the same arguments and functionality.

Check boxes and radio buttons by themselves are *nonexclusive,* meaning that if you have five check boxes in a container, all five can be checked or unchecked at the same time. To make them exclusive, as radio buttons should be, you must organize related components into groups.

To organize several radio buttons into a group, allowing only one to be selected at a time, create a ButtonGroup class object, as demonstrated in the following statement:

```
ButtonGroup choice = new ButtonGroup();
```

The ButtonGroup object keeps track of all radio buttons in its group. Call the group's add(*Component*) method to add the specified component to the group.

The following example creates a group and two radio buttons that belong to it:

```
ButtonGroup betterDarrin = new ButtonGroup();
JRadioButton r1 = new JRadioButton ("Dick York", true);
betterDarrin.add(r1);
JRadioButton r2 = new JRadioButton ("Dick Sargent", false);
betterDarrin.add(r2);
```

9

The betterDarrin object is used to group together the r1 and r2 radio buttons. The r1 object, which has the label "Dick York", is selected. Only one member of the group can be selected at a time—if one component is selected, the ButtonGroup object will make sure that all others in the group are deselected.

Listing 9.8 contains an application with four radio buttons in a group.

LISTING 9.8   The Full Text of ChooseTeam.java

```
 1: import javax.swing.*;
 2:
 3: public class ChooseTeam extends JFrame {
 4:     JRadioButton[] teams = new JRadioButton[4];
 5:
 6:     public ChooseTeam() {
 7:         super("Choose Team");
 8:         setSize(140, 190);
 9:         setDefaultCloseOperation(JFrame.EXIT_ON_CLOSE);
10:         teams[0] = new JRadioButton("Colorado");
11:         teams[1] = new JRadioButton("Dallas", true);
12:         teams[2] = new JRadioButton("New Jersey");
13:         teams[3] = new JRadioButton("Philadelphia");
14:         JPanel pane = new JPanel();
15:         ButtonGroup group = new ButtonGroup();
16:         for (int i = 0; i < teams.length; i++) {
17:             group.add(teams[i]);
18:             pane.add(teams[i]);
19:         }
20:         setContentPane(pane);
21:         show();
22:     }
23:
24:     public static void main(String[] arguments) {
25:         ChooseTeam ct = new ChooseTeam();
26:     }
27: }
```

Figure 9.6 shows the application running. The four JRadioButton objects are stored in an array, and in the for loop in lines 16–19 each element is first added to a button group, and then added to a panel. After the loop ends, the panel is used for the application's content pane.

FIGURE 9.6

The ChooseTeam *application.*

Drop-Down Lists and Combo Boxes

The Swing class JComboBox can be used to create two kinds of user interface components: drop-down lists and combo boxes.

Drop-down lists, also called *choice lists*, are components that enable a single item to be picked from a list. The list can be configured to appear only when a user clicks on the component, taking up less space in a graphical user interface.

Combo boxes are drop-down lists with an extra feature: a text field that also can be used to provide a response.

The following steps show how a drop-down list can be created:

1. The JComboBox() constructor is used with no arguments.
2. The combo box's addItem(*Object*) method adds items to the list.

In a drop-down list, users will be able to select only one of the items in the list. If the component's setEditable() method is called with true as an argument, it becomes a combo box rather than a drop-down list.

In a combo box, the user can enter text into the field instead of using the drop-down list to pick an item. This combination gives combo boxes their name.

The JComboBox class has several methods that can be used to control a drop-down list or combo box:

- getItemAt(*int*)—Return the text of the list item at the index position specified by the integer argument. As with arrays, the first item of a choice list is at index position 0, the second at position 1, and so on.
- getItemCount()—Return the number of items in the list.
- getSelectedIndex()—Return the index position of the currently selected item in the list.
- getSelectedItem()—Return the text of the currently selected item.
- setSelectedIndex(*int*)—Select the item at the indicated index position.

- setSelectedIndex(`Object`)—Select the specified object in the list.
- setMaximumRowCount(`int`)—Set the number of rows in the combo box that are displayed at one time.

The `Expiration` application in Listing 9.9 contains an application that uses drop-down lists to enter an expiration date, something you might use on an interface that conducts a credit-card transaction.

LISTING 9.9   The Full Text of `Expiration.java`

```
 1: import javax.swing.*;
 2:
 3: public class Expiration extends JFrame {
 4:     JComboBox monthBox = new JComboBox();
 5:     JComboBox yearBox = new JComboBox();
 6:
 7:     public Expiration() {
 8:         super("Expiration Date");
 9:         setSize(220, 90);
10:         setDefaultCloseOperation(JFrame.EXIT_ON_CLOSE);
11:         JPanel pane = new JPanel();
12:         JLabel exp = new JLabel("Expiration Date:");
13:         pane.add(exp);
14:         for (int i = 1; i < 13; i++)
15:             monthBox.addItem("" + i);
16:         for (int i = 2000; i < 2010; i++)
17:             yearBox.addItem("" + i);
18:         pane.add(monthBox);
19:         pane.add(yearBox);
20:         setContentPane(pane);
21:         show();
22:     }
23:
24:     public static void main(String[] arguments) {
25:         Expiration ct = new Expiration();
26:     }
27: }
```

Figure 9.7 shows the application after a date has been selected.

FIGURE 9.7

The Expiration
application.

Summary

Today you began working with Swing: the package of classes that enables you to offer a graphical user interface in your Java programs.

You used more than a dozen classes today, creating interface components such as buttons, labels, and text fields. You put each of these into containers: components that include panels, frames, and windows.

Programming of this kind can be complex, and Swing represents the largest package of classes that a new Java programmer must deal with in learning the language.

However, as you have experienced with components such as text areas and text fields, Swing components have many superclasses in common. This makes it easier to extend your knowledge into new components and containers, as well as the other aspects of Swing programming you will explore over the next three days.

Q&A

Q Can an application be created without Swing?

A Certainly. Swing is just an expansion of the Abstract Windowing Toolkit, and you can continue to use the AWT for applications with Java 2. However, event handling is different between the AWT and Swing, and there are many things in Swing that have no counterpart in the windowing toolkit. With Swing, you can use many more components and control them in more sophisticated ways.

Q Is there a way to change the font of text that appears on a button and other components?

A The JComponent class includes a setFont(Font) method that can be used to set the font for text displayed on that component. You will work with Font objects, color, and more graphics in Day 13, "Color, Fonts, and Graphics."

Q How can I find out what components are available in Swing and how to use them?

A This is the first of two days spent introducing user interface components, so you will learn more about them tomorrow. If you have Web access, you can find out what classes are in the Swing package by visiting Sun's online documentation for Java at the Web address http://java.sun.com/j2se/1.4/docs/api/.

Q **The SimpleFrame application compiles successfully, but when I try to run it (or any other Swing application), I get this error: "java.lang.UnsatisfiedLinkError: no fontmanager in java.library.path." What's the problem?**

A I can't reproduce this error myself, but after looking through Sun's Java bug database and support forums, it appears to be a problem with font support on your computer.

On a Windows system, the Java font manager is in a file called `fontmanager.dll`. To see all the folders in your library path, call `System.getProperty("java.library.path")` in a Java application and display the string that it returns (a short application that does this, `SeeLibraryPath`, is available from the Day 9 page of the book's Web site at `http://www.java21days.com`). Check to see if `fontmanager.dll` is in one of the folders in the library path. If it isn't, you need to remove and reinstall the Java 2 SDK and the Java 2 runtime.

If `fontmanager.dll` is in the right place, Borland's tech support forum for JBuilder offers another tip for a fontmanager problem: You should remove each shortcut from your `\Windows\Fonts` or `\Winnt\Fonts` folder and replace it with the actual font to which the shortcut refers.

Q **The combo box in the `Expiration` application does not allow the entry of text. How do I get it to accept text entry?**

A The `Expiration` application uses a drop-down list instead of a combo box. To change a `JComboBox` component so that it can receive text input, call the component's `setEditable(boolean)` method with an argument of `true` before you add the component to a container.

Quiz

Review today's material by taking this three-question quiz.

Questions

1. Which of the following user interface components is not a container?

   (a.) `JScrollPane`

   (b.) `JScrollBar`

   (c.) `JWindow`

2. Which container does not require the use of a content pane when adding components to it?

(a.) `JPanel`

(b.) `JWindow`

(c.) `JFrame`

3. If you use `setSize()` on an application's main frame or window, where will it appear on your desktop?

(a.) At the center of the desktop

(b.) At the same spot the last application appeared

(c.) At the upper left corner of the desktop

9

Answers

1. (b.)

2. (a.) `JPanel` is one of the simple containers that is not subdivided into panes, so you can call its `add(Component)` method to add components directly to the panel.

3. (c.) This is a trick question—calling `setSize()` has nothing to do with a window's position on the desktop. You must call `setBounds()` instead of `setSize()` to choose where a frame will appear.

Certification Practice

The following question is the kind of thing you could expect to be asked on a Java programming certification test. Answer it without looking at today's material or using the Java compiler to test the code.

Given:

```
import javax.swing.*;

public class Display extends JFrame {
    public Display() {
        super("Display");
        // answer goes here
        JLabel hello = new JLabel("Hello");
        JPanel pane = new JPanel();
        pane.add(hello);
        setContentPane(pane);
        pack();
        setVisible(true);
    }
```

```
        public static void main(String[] arguments) {
            Display ds = new Display();
        }
    }
```

What statement needs to replace // answer goes here in order to make the application function properly?

(a.) setSize(300, 200);

(b.) setDefaultCloseOperation(JFrame.EXIT_ON_CLOSE);

(c.) Display ds = new Display();

(d.) No statement is needed.

The answer is available on the book's Web site at http://www.java21days.com. Visit the Day 9 page and click the Certification Practice link.

Exercises

To extend your knowledge of the subjects covered today, try the following exercises:

- Create an application with a frame that includes all of the VCR controls as individual components: play, stop/eject, rewind, fast-forward, and pause. Choose a size for the window that enables all the components to be displayed on a single row.

- Create a frame that opens a smaller frame with fields asking for a username and password.

Where applicable, exercise solutions are offered on the book's Web site at http://www.java21days.com.

DAY **10**

Building a Swing Interface

With the popularity of Apple MacOS and Microsoft Windows, most computer users expect software to feature a graphical user interface and things they can control with a mouse. These software amenities are user friendly but programmer unfriendly in many languages. Windowing software can be one of the more challenging tasks for a novice developer.

As you learned yesterday, Java 2 has simplified the process with Swing, a set of classes for the creation and usage of graphical user interfaces.

Swing offers the following features:

- Common user interface components—buttons, text fields, text areas, labels, check boxes, radio buttons, scrollbars, lists, menu items, and sliders
- Containers—Interface components that can be used to hold other components, including containers—frames, panels, windows, menus, menu bars, and tabbed panes

- Adjustable look and feel—The ability to change the style of an entire interface to resemble Windows, MacOS, or other distinctive designs

Swing Features

Most of the components and containers you learned about yesterday were Swing versions of classes that were part of the Abstract Windowing Toolkit, the original Java package for graphical user interface programming.

Swing offers many features that are completely new, including a definable look and feel, keyboard mnemonics, tooltips, and standard dialog boxes.

Setting the Look and Feel

One of the more unusual features in Swing is the ability to define the look and feel of components—the way that the buttons, labels, and other elements of a graphical user interface are rendered onscreen.

Management of look and feel is handled by UIManager, a user interface manager class in the javax.swing package. The choices for look and feel vary depending on the Java development environment you're using. The following are available with Java 2 on a Windows platform:

- A Windows look and feel
- A Motif X Window system look and feel
- Swing's new cross-platform Java look and feel, also called Metal

Figures 10.1, 10.2, and 10.3 show the same graphical user interface under each of these look and feel designs.

FIGURE 10.1

An application using the Java look and feel (Metal).

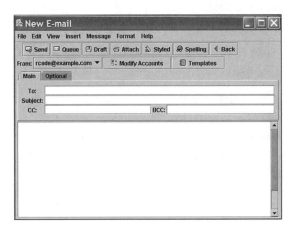

FIGURE 10.2

An application using the Windows look and feel.

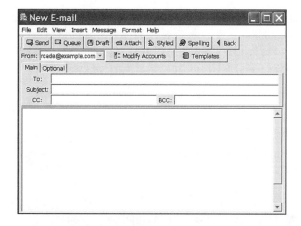

FIGURE 10.3

An application using the Motif look and feel.

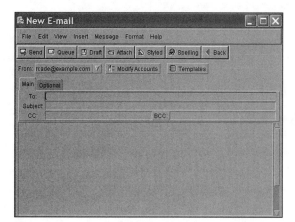

The UIManager class has a setLookAndFeel(*LookAndFeel*) method that is used to choose a program's look and feel. To get a LookAndFeel object that you can use with setLookAndFeel(), use one of the following UIManager methods:

- getCrossPlatformLookAndFeelClassName()—This method returns a LookAndFeel object representing Java's cross-platform Metal look and feel.

- getSystemLookAndFeelClassName()—This method returns a LookAndFeel object representing your system's look and feel.

The setLookAndFeel() method throws an UnsupportedLookAndFeelException if it can't set the look and feel.

After you call this method, you must tell every component in an interface to update its appearance with the new look and feel. Call the `SwingUtilities` class method `updateComponentTreeUI`(*Component*) with the main interface component (such as a `JFrame` object) as the argument.

Under most circumstances you should call `setLookAndFeel()` only after every component has been added to your graphical user interface (in other words, right before you make the interface visible).

The following statements set up a component to employ the Java look and feel:

```
try {
    UIManager.setLookAndFeel(
        UIManager.getCrossPlatformLookAndFeelClassName());
    SwingUtilities.updateComponentTreeUI(this);
    } catch (Exception e) {
        System.err.println("Can't set look and feel: " + e);
}
```

The `this` keyword refers to the class that contains these statements. If you used it at the end of the constructor method of a `JFrame`, every component on that frame would be displayed with the Java look and feel.

To select your system's look and feel, use `getSystemLookAndFeelClassName()`, which is inside the `setLookAndFeel()` method call in the preceding example. This produces different results on different operating systems. A Windows user would get that platform's look and feel by using `getSystemLookAndFeelClassName()`. A Unix user would get the Motif look and feel, and a Mac user would get the Aqua look and feel.

If you're not sure which look and feel designs are available on your operating system, you can list them with the following statements:

```
UIManager.LookAndFeelInfo[] laf = UIManager.getInstalledLookAndFeels();
for (int i = 0; i < laf.length; i++) {
    System.out.println("Class name: " + laf[i].getClassName());
    System.out.println("Name: " + laf[i].getName() + "\n");
}
```

On a Windows or Linux system, these statements produce the following output:

```
Name: Metal
Class name: javax.swing.plaf.metal.MetalLookAndFeel

Name: CDE/Motif
Class name: com.sun.java.swing.plaf.motif.MotifLookAndFeel

Name: Windows
Class name: com.sun.java.swing.plaf.windows.WindowsLookAndFeel
```

> **Caution** The presence of the Windows look and feel on a Linux installation appears to be a bug. For copyright reasons, neither the Windows nor the MacOS look and feel design is supposed to appear on a machine that isn't running the corresponding operating system.

Standard Dialog Boxes

The JOptionPane class offers several methods that can be used to create standard dialog boxes: small windows that ask a question, warn a user, or provide a brief, important message. Figure 10.4 shows a dialog box with the Metal look and feel.

FIGURE 10.4

A standard dialog box.

You have doubtlessly seen dialog boxes of this kind. When your system crashes, a dialog box appears and breaks the bad news. When you delete files, a dialog box might pop up to make sure that you really want to do that. These windows are an effective way to communicate with a user without creating a new class to represent the window, adding components to it, and writing event-handling methods to take input. All these things are handled automatically when one of the standard dialog boxes offered by JOptionPane is used.

The four standard dialog boxes are as follows:

- ConfirmDialog—Asks a question, with buttons for Yes, No, and Cancel responses
- InputDialog—Prompts for text input
- MessageDialog—Displays a message
- OptionDialog—Comprises all three of the other dialog box types

Each of these dialog boxes has its own method in the JOptionPane class.

If you are setting up a look and feel to use with any of these dialog boxes, it must be established before you open the box.

Confirm Dialog Boxes

The easiest way to create a Yes/No/Cancel dialog box is with the showConfirmDialog(*Component*, *Object*) method call. The *Component* argument specifies the container that should be considered to be the parent of the dialog box, and this

10

information is used to determine where on the screen the dialog window should be displayed. If null is used instead of a container, or if the container is not a JFrame object, the dialog box will be centered onscreen.

The second argument, *Object*, can be a string, a component, or an Icon object. If it's a string, that text will be displayed in the dialog box. If it's a component or an Icon, that object will be displayed in place of a text message.

This method returns one of three possible integer values, each a class constant of JOptionPane: YES_OPTION, NO_OPTION, and CANCEL_OPTION.

The following example uses a confirm dialog box with a text message and stores the response in the response variable:

```
int response;
response = JOptionPane.showConfirmDialog(null,
    "Should I delete all of your irreplaceable personal files?");
```

Figure 10.5 shows this dialog box.

FIGURE 10.5

A confirm dialog box.

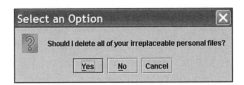

Another method offers more options for the confirm dialog: showConfirmDialog (*Component*, *Object*, *String*, *int*, *int*). The first two arguments are the same as those in other showConfirmDialog() methods. The last three arguments are the following:

- A string that will be displayed in the dialog box's title bar
- An integer that indicates which option buttons will be shown; it should be equal to one of the class constants: YES_NO_CANCEL_OPTION or YES_NO_OPTION.
- An integer that describes the kind of dialog box it is, using the class constants ERROR_MESSAGE, INFORMATION_MESSAGE, PLAIN_MESSAGE, QUESTION_MESSAGE, or WARNING_MESSAGE (this argument is used to determine which icon to draw in the dialog box along with the message)

For example:

```
int response = JOptionPane.showConfirmDialog(null,
    "Error reading file. Want to try again?",
    "File Input Error",
    JOptionPane.YES_NO_OPTION,
    JOptionPane.ERROR_MESSAGE);
```

Figure 10.6 shows the resulting dialog box with the Windows look and feel.

FIGURE 10.6

A confirm dialog box with Yes and No buttons.

Input Dialog Boxes

An input dialog box asks a question and uses a text field to store the response. Figure 10.7 shows an example with the Motif look and feel.

FIGURE 10.7

An input dialog box.

The easiest way to create an input dialog is with a call to the showInputDialog(*Component*, *Object*) method. The arguments are the parent component and the string, component, or icon to display in the box.

The input dialog method call returns a string that represents the user's response. The following statement creates the input dialog box shown in Figure 10.7:

```
String response = JOptionPane.showInputDialog(null,
    "Enter your name:");
```

You also can create an input dialog box with the showInputDialog(*Component*, *Object*, *String*, *int*) method. The first two arguments are the same as the shorter method call, and the last two are the following:

- The title to display in the dialog box title bar
- One of five class constants describing the type of dialog box: ERROR_MESSAGE, INFORMATION_MESSAGE, PLAIN_MESSAGE, QUESTION_MESSAGE, or WARNING_MESSAGE

The following statement uses this method to create an input dialog box:

```
String response = JOptionPane.showInputDialog(null,
    "What is your ZIP code?",
    "Enter ZIP Code",
    JOptionPane.QUESTION_MESSAGE);
```

10

Message Dialog Boxes

A message dialog box is a simple window that displays information. Figure 10.8 shows an example with the Metal look and feel.

FIGURE **10.8**

A message dialog box.

A message dialog box can be created with a call to the showMessageDialog(*Component*, *Object*) method. As with other dialog boxes, the arguments are the parent component and the string, component, or icon to display.

Unlike the other dialog boxes, message dialog boxes do not return any kind of response value. The following statement creates the message dialog shown in Figure 10.8:

```
JOptionPane.showMessageDialog(null,
        "The program has been uninstalled.");
```

You also can create a message input dialog box with the showMessageDialog(*Component*, *Object*, *String*, *int*) method. The use is identical to the showInputDialog() method, with the same arguments, except that showMessageDialog() does not return a value.

The following statement creates a message dialog box using this method:

```
JOptionPane.showMessageDialog(null,
        "An asteroid has destroyed the Earth.",
        "Asteroid Destruction Alert",
        JOptionPane.WARNING_MESSAGE);
```

Option Dialog Boxes

The most complex of the dialog boxes is the option dialog box, which combines the features of all the other dialogs. It can be created with the showOptionDialog(*Component*, *Object*, *String*, *int*, *int*, *Icon*, *Object[]*, *Object*) method.

The arguments to this method are as follows:

- The parent component of the dialog
- The text, icon, or component to display
- A string to display in the title bar
- The type of box, using the class constants YES_NO_OPTION or YES_NO_CANCEL_OPTION, or the literal 0 if other buttons will be used instead

- The icon to display, using the class constants ERROR_MESSAGE, INFORMATION_MESSAGE, PLAIN_MESSAGE, QUESTION_MESSAGE, or WARNING_MESSAGE, or the literal 0 if none of these should be used

- An Icon object to display instead of one of the icons in the preceding argument

- An array of objects holding the components or other objects that represent the choices in the dialog box, if YES_NO_OPTION and YES_NO_CANCEL_OPTION are not being used

- The object representing the default selection if YES_NO_OPTION and YES_NO_CANCEL option are not being used

The last two arguments enable you to create a wide range of choices for the dialog box. You can create an array of buttons, labels, text fields, or even a mixture of different components as an object array.

The following example creates an option dialog box that uses an array of JButton objects for the options in the box and the gender[2] element as the default selection:

```
JButton[] gender = new JButton[3];
gender[0] = new JButton("Male");
gender[1] = new JButton("Female");
gender[2] = new JButton("None of Your Business");
int response = JOptionPane.showOptionDialog(null,
        "What is your gender?",
        "Gender",
        0,
        JOptionPane.INFORMATION_MESSAGE,
        null,
        gender,
        gender[2]);
```

Figure 10.9 shows the resulting dialog box with the Motif look and feel.

FIGURE 10.9

An option dialog box.

An Example: The Info Application

The next project shows a series of dialog boxes in a working program. The Info application uses dialogs to get information from the user; that information is then placed into text fields in the application's main window.

Enter Listing 10.1 and compile the result.

LISTING 10.1 The Full Text of `Info.java`

```
 1: import java.awt.GridLayout;
 2: import java.awt.event.*;
 3: import javax.swing.*;
 4:
 5: public class Info extends JFrame {
 6:     private JLabel titleLabel = new JLabel("Title: ",
 7:         SwingConstants.RIGHT);
 8:     private JTextField title;
 9:     private JLabel addressLabel = new JLabel("Address: ",
10:         SwingConstants.RIGHT);
11:     private JTextField address;
12:     private JLabel typeLabel = new JLabel("Type: ",
13:         SwingConstants.RIGHT);
14:     private JTextField type;
15:
16:     public Info() {
17:         super("Site Information");
18:         setDefaultCloseOperation(JFrame.EXIT_ON_CLOSE);
19:         setLookAndFeel();
20:         // Site name
21:         String response1 = JOptionPane.showInputDialog(null,
22:             "Enter the site title:");
23:         title = new JTextField(response1, 20);
24:
25:         // Site address
26:         String response2 = JOptionPane.showInputDialog(null,
27:             "Enter the site address:");
28:         address = new JTextField(response2, 20);
29:
30:         // Site type
31:         String[] choices = { "Personal", "Commercial", "Unknown" };
32:         int response3 = JOptionPane.showOptionDialog(null,
33:             "What type of site is it?",
34:             "Site Type",
35:             0,
36:             JOptionPane.QUESTION_MESSAGE,
37:             null,
38:             choices,
39:             choices[0]);
40:         type = new JTextField(choices[response3], 20);
41:
42:         JPanel pane = new JPanel();
43:         pane.setLayout(new GridLayout(3, 2));
44:         pane.add(titleLabel);
45:         pane.add(title);
46:         pane.add(addressLabel);
```

LISTING 10.1 Continued

```
47:            pane.add(address);
48:            pane.add(typeLabel);
49:            pane.add(type);
50:            setContentPane(pane);
51:            pack();
52:            setLookAndFeel();
53:            setVisible(true);
54:        }
55:
56:        private void setLookAndFeel() {
57:            try {
58:                UIManager.setLookAndFeel(
59:                    UIManager.getSystemLookAndFeelClassName());
60:                SwingUtilities.updateComponentTreeUI(this);
61:            } catch (Exception e) {
62:                System.err.println("Couldn't use the system "
63:                    + "look and feel: " + e);
64:            }
65:        }
66:
67:        public static void main(String[] arguments) {
68:            Info frame = new Info();
69:        }
70: }
```

10

Figure 10.10 shows one of the three dialog boxes that appear when this application is run. After you fill in the fields in each dialog, you will see the application's main window, which is displayed in Figure 10.11 with the Windows look and feel. Three text fields have values supplied by dialog boxes.

FIGURE 10.10

The site address input dialog box.

FIGURE 10.11

The main window of the Info *application.*

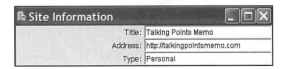

Much of this application is boilerplate code that can be used with any Swing application. The following lines relate to the dialog boxes:

- In lines 21–23, an input dialog asks the user to enter a site title. This title is used in the constructor for a JTextField object, which puts the title in the text field.
- In lines 26–28, a similar input dialog asks for a site address, which is used in the constructor for another JTextField object. Figure 10.10 shows this option dialog box.
- In line 31, an array of String objects called choices is created, and three elements are given values.
- In lines 32–39, an option dialog box asks for the site type. The choices array is the seventh argument, which sets up three buttons on the dialog labeled with the strings in the array: "Personal", "Commercial", and "Unknown". The last argument, choices[0], designates the first array element as the default selection in the dialog.
- In line 40, the response to the option dialog, an integer identifying the array element that was selected, is stored in a JTextField component called type.

The look and feel, which is established in the setLookAndFeel() method in lines 56–65, is called at the beginning and end of the frame's constructor method. Because you're opening several dialog boxes in the constructor, you must set up the look and feel before opening them.

Sliders

Sliders, which are implemented in Swing with the JSlider class, enable the user to set a number by sliding a control within the range of a minimum and maximum value. In many cases, a slider can be used for numeric input instead of a text field, and it has the advantage of restricting input to a range of acceptable values.

Figure 10.12 shows an example of a JSlider component.

FIGURE 10.12

A JSlider component.

Sliders are horizontal by default. The orientation can be explicitly set using two class constants of the SwingConstants interface: HORIZONTAL or VERTICAL.

You can use the following constructor methods:

- JSlider(*int*, *int*)—A slider with the specified minimum value and maximum value
- JSlider(*int*, *int*, *int*)—A slider with the specified minimum value, maximum value, and starting value
- JSlider(*int*, *int*, *int*, *int*)—A slider with the specified orientation, minimum value, maximum value, and starting value

Slider components have an optional label that can be used to indicate the minimum value, maximum value, and two different sets of tick marks ranging between the values. The default values are a minimum of 0, maximum of 100, starting value of 50, and horizontal orientation.

The elements of this label are established by calling several methods of JSlider:

- setMajorTickSpacing(*int*)—This method separates major tick marks by the specified distance. The distance is not in pixels, but in values between the minimum and maximum values represented by the slider.
- setMinorTickSpacing(*int*)—This method separates minor tick marks by the specified distance. Minor ticks are displayed as half the height of major ticks.
- setPaintTicks(*boolean*)—This method determines whether the tick marks should be displayed (a true argument) or not (a false argument).
- setPaintLabels(*boolean*)—This method determines whether the numeric label of the slider should be displayed (true) or not (false).

These methods should be called on the slider before it is added to a container.

Listing 10.2 contains the Slider.java source code; the application is shown in Figure 10.11.

LISTING 10.2   The Full Text of Slider.java

```
 1: import java.awt.event.*;
 2: import javax.swing.*;
 3:
 4: public class Slider extends JFrame {
 5:
 6:     public Slider() {
 7:         super("Slider");
 8:         setDefaultCloseOperation(JFrame.EXIT_ON_CLOSE);
 9:         JSlider pickNum = new JSlider(JSlider.HORIZONTAL, 0, 30, 5);
10:         pickNum.setMajorTickSpacing(10);
```

continues

LISTING 10.2 Continued

```
11:              pickNum.setMinorTickSpacing(1);
12:              pickNum.setPaintTicks(true);
13:              pickNum.setPaintLabels(true);
14:              JPanel pane = new JPanel();
15:              pane.add(pickNum);
16:
17:              setContentPane(pane);
18:      }
19:
20:      public static void main(String[] args) {
21:              Slider frame = new Slider();
22:              frame.pack();
23:              frame.setVisible(true);
24:      }
25: }
```

Lines 9–17 contain the code that's used to create a JSlider component, set up its tick marks to be displayed, and add the component to a container. The rest of the program is a basic framework for an application that consists of a main JFrame container with no menus.

In lines 20–24, a new Slider object is created, a call to the object's pack() method sets its size to the preferred size of its components, and the object is made visible.

 Note

It may seem strange for the pack() and setVisible() methods to be called outside the constructor method of the frame. However, there's no difference between calling these (and other) methods inside or outside of an interface component's class.

Scroll Panes

As you learned in yesterday's lesson, in early versions of Java, some components (such as text areas) had a built-in scrollbar. The bar could be used when the text in the component took up more space than the component could display. Scrollbars could be used in either the vertical or horizontal direction to scroll through the text.

One of the most common examples of scrolling is in a Web browser, where a scrollbar can be used on any page that is bigger than the browser's display area.

Swing changes the rules for scrollbars to the following:

* For a component to be able to scroll, it must be added to a JScrollPane container.
* This JScrollPane container is added to a container in place of the scrollable component.

Scroll panes can be created using the ScrollPane(*Object*) constructor, where *Object* represents the component that can be scrolled.

The following example creates a text area in a scroll pane and adds the scroll pane, scroller, to a container called mainPane:

```
textBox = new JTextArea(7, 30);
JScrollPane scroller = new JScrollPane(textBox);
mainPane.add(scroller);
```

As you're working with scroll panes, it can often be useful to indicate the size you would like them to occupy on the interface. This is done by calling the setPreferredSize(*Dimension*) method of the scroll pane before it is added to a container. The Dimension object represents the width and height of the preferred size, represented in pixels.

The following code builds on the previous example by setting the preferred size of scroller:

```
Dimension pref = new Dimension(350, 100);
scroller.setPreferredSize(pref);
```

This should be handled before scroller is added to a container.

Caution   This is one of many situations in Swing where you must do something in the proper order for it to work correctly. For most components, the order is the following: Create the component, set up the component fully, then add the component to a container.

By default, a scroll pane does not display scrollbars unless they are needed. If the component inside the pane is no larger than the pane itself, the bars won't appear. In the case of components such as text areas, where the component size might increase as the program is used, the bars automatically appear when they're needed and disappear when they are not.

To override this behavior, you can set a *policy* for a JScrollBar component when you create it. You set the policy by using one of several ScrollPaneConstants class constants:

- HORIZONTAL_SCROLLBAR_ALWAYS
- HORIZONTAL_SCROLLBAR_AS_NEEDED
- HORIZONTAL_SCROLLBAR_NEVER
- VERTICAL_SCROLLBAR_ALWAYS
- VERTICAL_SCROLLBAR_AS_NEEDED
- VERTICAL_SCROLLBAR_NEVER

These class constants are used with the JScrollPane(*Object*, *int*, *int*) constructor, which specifies the component in the pane, the vertical scrollbar policy, and the horizontal scrollbar policy.

Toolbars

A *toolbar*, created in Swing with the JToolBar class, is a container that groups several components into a row or column. These components are most often buttons.

If you have used software such as Microsoft Word, Netscape Navigator, or Lotus WordPro, you are probably familiar with the concept of toolbars. In these programs and many others, the most commonly used program options are grouped together as a series of buttons. You can click these buttons as an alternative to using pull-down menus or shortcut keys.

Toolbars are horizontal by default, but the orientation is explicitly set with the HORIZONTAL or VERTICAL class variables of the SwingConstants interface.

Constructor methods include the following:

- JToolBar()—Creates a new toolbar
- JToolBar(*int*)—Creates a new toolbar with the specified orientation

Once you have created a toolbar, you can add components to it by using the toolbar's add(*Object*) method, where *Object* represents the component to place on the toolbar.

Many programs that use toolbars enable the user to move the bars. These are called *dockable toolbars* because you can dock them along an edge of the screen, similar to docking a boat to a pier. Swing toolbars can also be docked into a new window, separate from the original.

For best results, a dockable JToolBar component should be arranged in a container using the BorderLayout manager. A border layout divides a container into five areas: north, south, east, west, and center. Each of the directional components takes up whatever space it needs, and the rest are allocated to the center.

The toolbar should be placed in one of the directional areas of the border layout. The only other area of the layout that can be filled is the center. (You'll learn more about layout managers such as border layout in tomorrow's chapter, "Arranging Components on a User Interface.")

Figure 10.13 shows a dockable toolbar occupying the north area of a border layout. A text area has been placed in the center.

FIGURE 10.13

*A dockable toolbar
and a text area.*

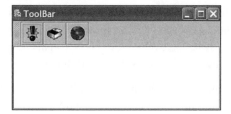

Listing 10.3 contains the source code used to produce this application.

LISTING 10.3   The Full Text of `ToolBar.java`

```
 1: import java.awt.*;
 2: import java.awt.event.*;
 3: import javax.swing.*;
 4:
 5: public class ToolBar extends JFrame {
 6:
 7:     public ToolBar() {
 8:         super("ToolBar");
 9:         setDefaultCloseOperation(JFrame.EXIT_ON_CLOSE);
10:         ImageIcon image1 = new ImageIcon("button1.gif");
11:         JButton button1 = new JButton(image1);
12:         ImageIcon image2 = new ImageIcon("button2.gif");
13:         JButton button2 = new JButton(image2);
14:         ImageIcon image3 = new ImageIcon("button3.gif");
15:         JButton button3 = new JButton(image3);
16:         JToolBar bar = new JToolBar();
17:         bar.add(button1);
18:         bar.add(button2);
19:         bar.add(button3);
20:         JTextArea edit = new JTextArea(8,40);
21:         JScrollPane scroll = new JScrollPane(edit);
22:         JPanel pane = new JPanel();
23:         BorderLayout bord = new BorderLayout();
24:         pane.setLayout(bord);
25:         pane.add("North", bar);
26:         pane.add("Center", scroll);
27:
28:         setContentPane(pane);
29:     }
30:
31:     public static void main(String[] arguments) {
32:         ToolBar frame = new ToolBar();
33:         frame.pack();
34:         frame.setVisible(true);
35:     }
36: }
```

10

This application uses three images to represent the graphics on the buttons: button1.gif, button2.gif, and button3.gif. You can find these on this book's official World Wide Web site at http://www.java21days.com on the Day 10 page. You also can use graphics from your own system, although they must be in GIF format and reasonably small.

The toolbar in this application can be grabbed by its handle—the area immediately to the left of the exclamation button in Figure 10.13. If you drag it within the window, you can dock it along different edges of the application window. When you release the toolbar, the application is rearranged using the border layout manager. You also can drag the toolbar out of the application window entirely.

Although toolbars are most commonly used with graphical buttons, they can contain textual buttons, combo boxes, and other components.

> **Tip**
>
> Sun MicroSystems has a Java look-and-feel design team that offers a repository of icon graphics that you can use in your own programs. To view the graphics and find out more about this look and feel, visit the Web page http://java.sun.com/developer/techDocs/hi/repository/.

Progress Bars

Anyone who has ever installed computer software is undoubtedly familiar with *progress bars*. These components are commonly used with long tasks to show the user how much time is left before the task is complete.

Progress bars are implemented in Swing through the JProgressBar class. A sample Java program that makes use of this component is shown in Figure 10.14.

FIGURE 10.14

A progress bar in a frame.

Progress bars are used to track the progress of a task that can be represented numerically. They are created by specifying a minimum and a maximum value that represent the points at which the task is beginning and ending.

A software installation that consists of 335 different files is a good example of a task that can be numerically quantified. The number of files transferred can be used to monitor the progress of the task. The minimum value is 0 and the maximum value 335.

Constructor methods include the following:

- `JProgressBar()`—Creates a new progress bar
- `JProgressBar(int, int)`—Creates a new progress bar with the specified minimum value and maximum value
- `JProgressBar(int, int, int)`—Creates a new progress bar with the specified orientation, minimum value, and maximum value

The orientation of a progress bar can be established with the `SwingConstants.VERTICAL` and `SwingConstants.HORIZONTAL` class constants. Progress bars are horizontal by default.

The minimum and maximum values can also be set up by calling the progress bar's `setMinimum(int)` and `setMaximum(int)` values with the indicated values.

To update a progress bar, you call its `setValue(int)` method with a value indicating how far along the task is at that moment. This value should be somewhere between the minimum and maximum values established for the bar. The following example tells the `install` progress bar in the previous example of a software installation how many files have been uploaded thus far:

```
int filesDone = getNumberOfFiles();
install.setValue(filesDone);
```

In this example, the `getNumberOfFiles()` method represents some code that would be used to keep track of how many files have been copied so far during the installation. When this value is passed to the progress bar by the `setValue()` method, the bar is immediately updated to represent the percentage of the task that has been completed.

Progress bars often include a text label in addition to the graphic of an empty box filling up. This label displays the percentage of the task that has become completed, and you can set it up for a bar by calling the `setStringPainted(boolean)` method with a value of `true`. A `false` argument turns this label off.

Listing 10.4 contains `Progress`, the application shown at the beginning of this section in Figure 10.10.

LISTING 10.4 The Full Text of `Progress.java`

```
1: import java.awt.*;
2: import java.awt.event.*;
3: import javax.swing.*;
4:
5: public class Progress extends JFrame {
6:
```

continues

LISTING 10.4 Continued

```
 7:     JProgressBar current;
 8:     JTextArea out;
 9:     JButton find;
10:     Thread runner;
11:     int num = 0;
12:
13:     public Progress() {
14:         super("Progress");
15:
16:         setDefaultCloseOperation(JFrame.EXIT_ON_CLOSE);
17:         JPanel pane = new JPanel();
18:         pane.setLayout(new FlowLayout());
19:         current = new JProgressBar(0, 2000);
20:         current.setValue(0);
21:         current.setStringPainted(true);
22:         pane.add(current);
23:         setContentPane(pane);
24:     }
25:
26:
27:     public void iterate() {
28:         while (num < 2000) {
29:             current.setValue(num);
30:             try {
31:                 Thread.sleep(1000);
32:             } catch (InterruptedException e) { }
33:             num += 95;
34:         }
35:     }
36:
37:     public static void main(String[] arguments) {
38:         Progress frame = new Progress();
39:         frame.pack();
40:         frame.setVisible(true);
41:         frame.iterate();
42:     }
43: }
```

The Progress application uses a progress bar to track the value of the num variable. The progress bar is created in line 19 with a minimum value of 0 and a maximum value of 2000.

The iterate() method in lines 27–35 loops while num is less than 2000 and increases num by 95 each iteration. The progress bar's setValue() method is called in line 29 of the loop with num as an argument, causing the bar to use that value when charting progress.

Using a progress bar is a way to make a program more user friendly when it is going to be busy for more than a few seconds. Software users like progress bars because they indicate how much more time something's going to take. This information can be a deciding factor in whether to wait at the computer, launch an expedition for something to drink, or take advantage of your employer's lax policy in regard to personal long-distance calls. (If the task is especially time-consuming, a progress bar is essential—artists who create 3D computer scenes have become accustomed to tasks that take 12 hours or more to complete.)

Progress bars also provide another essential piece of information: proof that the program is still running and has not crashed.

Menus

One of the ways you can enhance the usability of a frame is to give it a menu bar—a series of pull-down menus that are used to perform tasks. Menus often duplicate the same tasks you could accomplish by using buttons and other user interface components, giving someone using your program two ways to get work done.

10

Menus in Java are supported by three components that work in conjunction with each other:

- `JMenuItem`—an item on a menu
- `JMenu`—a drop-down menu that contains one or more `JMenuItem` components, other interface components, and *separators*, lines that are displayed between items
- `JMenuBar`—a container that holds one or more JMenu components and displays their names

A `JMenuItem` component is like a button and can be set up using the same constructor methods as a `JButton` component. Call it with `JMenuItem(String)` for a text item, `JMenuItem(Icon)` for an item that displays a graphics file, or `JMenuItem(String, Icon)` for both.

The following statements create seven menu items:

```
JMenuItem j1 = new JMenuItem("Open");
JMenuItem j2 = new JMenuItem("Save");
JMenuItem j3 = new JMenuItem("Save as Template");
JMenuItem j4 = new JMenuItem("Page Setup");
JMenuItem j5 = new JMenuItem("Print");
JMenuItem j6 = new JMenuItem("Use as Default Message Style");
JMenuItem j7 = new JMenuItem("Close");
```

A `JMenu` container holds all of the menu items for a drop-down menu. To create it, call the `JMenu(String)` constructor with the name of the menu as an argument. This name will appear on the menu bar.

After you have created a JMenu container, call its add(*JMenuItem)* to add a menu item to it. New items are placed at the end of the menu.

The item you put on a menu doesn't have to be a menu item. Call the add(*Component*) method with a user interface component as the argument. One that often appears on a menu is a check box (the JCheckBox class in Java).

To add a line separator to the end of the menu, call the addSeparator() method. Separators are often used to group several related items visually on a menu.

You also can add text to a menu that serves as a label of some kind. Call the add(*String*) method with the text as an argument.

Using the seven menu items from the preceding example, the following statements create a menu and fill it with all of those items and three separators:

```
JMenu m1 = new JMenu("File");
m1.add(j1);
m1.add(j2);
m1.add(j3);
m1.addSeparator();
m1.add(j4);
m1.add(j5);
m1.addSeparator();
m1.add(j6);
m1.addSeparator();
m1.add(j7);
```

A JMenuBar container holds one or more JMenu containers and displays each of their names. The most common place to see a menu bar is directly below an application's title bar.

To create a menu bar, call the JMenuBar() constructor method with no arguments. Add menus to the end of a bar by calling its add(*JMenu*) method.

Once you have created all your items, added them to menus, and added the menus to a bar, you're ready to add them to a frame. Call the frame's setJMenuBar(*JMenuBar)* method.

The following statement finishes off the current example by creating a menu bar, adding a menu to it, then placing the bar on a frame called gui:

```
JMenuBar bar = new JMenuBar();
bar.add(m7);
gui.setJMenuBar(bar);
```

Figure 10.15 shows what this menu looks like on an otherwise empty frame.

Figure 10.15

A frame with a menu bar.

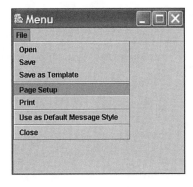

Though you can open and close a menu and select items, nothing happens in response. You'll learn how to receive user input for this component and others during Day 12, "Responding to User Input."

Tabbed Panes

Tabbed panes, a group of stacked panels in which only one panel can be viewed at a time, are implemented in Swing by the `JTabbedPane` class.

To view a panel, you click the tab that contains its name. Tabs can be arranged horizontally across the top or bottom of the component or vertically along the left or right side.

Tabbed panes are created with the following three constructor methods:

- `JTabbedPane()`—Create a vertical tabbed pane along the top that does not scroll.
- `JTabbedPane(int)`—Create a tabbed pane that does not scroll and has the specified placement.
- `JTabbedPane(int, int)`—Create a tabbed pane with the specified placement (first argument) and scrolling policy (second argument).

The placement of a tabbed pane is the position where its tabs are displayed in relation to the panels. Use one of four class variables as the argument to the constructor: `JTabbedPane.TOP`, `JTabbedPane.BOTTOM`, `JTabbedPane.LEFT`, or `JTabbedPane.RIGHT`.

The scrolling policy determines how tabs will be displayed when there are more tabs than the interface can hold. A tabbed pane that does not scroll displays extra tabs on their own line, which can be set up using the `JTabbedPane.WRAP_TAB_LAYOUT` class variable. A tabbed pane that scrolls displays scrolling arrows beside the tabs. This can be set up with `JTabbedPane.SCROLL_TAB_LAYOUT`.

After you create a tabbed pane, you can add components to it by calling the pane's `addTab(String, Component)` method. The `String` argument will be used as the label of the tab. The second argument is the component that will make up one of the tabs on the pane. It's common to use a JPanel object for this purpose, but not required.

The following statements create five empty panels and add them to a tabbed pane:

```
JPanel mainSettings = new JPanel();
JPanel advancedSettings = new JPanel();
JPanel privacySettings = new JPanel();
JPanel emailSettings = new JPanel();
JPanel securitySettings = new JPanel();
JTabbedPane tabs = new JTabbedPane();
tabs.addTab("Main", mainSettings);
tabs.addTab("Advanced", advancedSettings);
tabs.addTab("Privacy", privacySettings);
tabs.addTab("E-mail", emailSettings);
tabs.addTab("Security", securitySettings);
```

After adding all the panels and other components to a tabbed pane, the pane can be added to another container. Figure 10.16 shows what the example looks like when added to a frame.

FIGURE 10.16

A tabbed pane with five tabs displayed along the top edge.

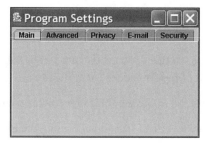

Summary

You now know how to paint a user interface onto a Java application window using the components of the Swing package.

Swing includes classes for many of the buttons, bars, lists, and fields you would expect to see on a program, along with more advanced components, such as sliders, dialog boxes, progress bars, and menu bars. Interface components are implemented by creating an instance of their class and adding it to a container using the container's add() method or a similar method specific to the container, such as the tabbed pane's addTab() method.

Today you developed components and added them to an interface. During the next two days, you will learn about two things required to make a graphical interface usable: how to arrange components together to form a whole interface and how to receive input from a user through these components.

Q&A

Q Can an application be created without Swing?

A Certainly. Swing is just an expansion on the Abstract Windowing Toolkit, and if you are developing an applet for Java 1.0, you could use only AWT classes to design your interface and receive input from a user. Whether you should create an application without Swing is another issue. There's no comparison between Swing's capabilities and those offered by the AWT. With Swing, you can use many more components and control them in more sophisticated ways.

Q In the Info application, what does the pack() statement on line 51 do?

A Every interface component has a preferred size, though this is often disregarded by the layout manager used to arrange the component within a container. Calling a frame or window's pack() method causes it to be resized to fit the preferred size of the components that it contains. Because the Info application does not set a size for the frame, calling pack() sets it to an adequate size before the frame is displayed.

Quiz

Review today's material by taking this three-questionquiz.

Questions

1. What is the default look and feel in a Java application?

    (a.) Motif

    (b.) Windows

    (c.) Metal

2. Which user interface component is commonplace in software installation programs?

    (a.) Sliders

    (b.) Progress bars

    (c.) Dialog boxes

3. Which Java class library includes a class for clickable buttons?

    (a.) Abstract Windowing Toolkit

    (b.) Swing

    (c.) Both

10

Answers

1. (c.) If you want to use a look and feel other than Metal, you must explicitly establish that look and feel using a method of the `javax.swing.UIManager` class.

2. (b.) Progress bars are useful when used to display the progress of a file-copying or file-extracting activity.

3. (c.) Swing duplicates all the simple user interface components that are included in the Abstract Windowing Toolkit.

Certification Practice

The following question is the kind of thing you could expect to be asked on a Java programming certification test. Answer it without looking at today's material or using the Java compiler to test the code.

Given:

```java
import java.awt.*;
import javax.swing.*;

public class AskFrame extends JFrame {
    public AskFrame() {
        setDefaultCloseOperation(JFrame.EXIT_ON_CLOSE);
        Container pane = getContentPane();
        JSlider value = new JSlider(0, 255, 100);
        pane.add(value);
        setSize(450, 150);
        setVisible(true);
        setContentPane(pane);
        super();
    }

    public static void main(String[] arguments) {
        AskFrame af = new AskFrame();
    }
}
```

What will happen when you attempt to compile and run this source code?

(a.) It compiles without error and runs correctly.

(b.) It compiles without error but does not display anything in the frame.

(c.) It does not compile because of the `super()` statement.

(d.) It does not compile because of the `setContentPane()` statement.

The answer is available on this book's Web site at `http://www.java21days.com`. Visit the Day 10 page and click the Certification Practice link.

Exercises

To extend your knowledge of the subjects covered today, try the following exercises:

- Create an input dialog that can be used to set the title of the frame that loaded the dialog.

- Create a modified version of the Progress application that also displays the value of the num variable in a text field.

Where applicable, exercise solutions are offered on this book's Web site at http://www.java21days.com.

10

WEEK 2

DAY 11

Arranging Components on a User Interface

If designing a graphical user interface were comparable to painting, you could currently produce only one kind of art: abstract expressionism. You can put components onto an interface, but you don't have much control over where they go.

In order to impose some kind of form on an interface in Java, you must use a set of classes called *layout managers*.

Today you will learn how to use five layout managers to arrange components into an interface. You'll take advantage of the flexibility of Swing, which was designed to be presentable on the many different platforms that support the language.

You will also learn how to put several different layout managers to work on the same interface when one arrangement doesn't suit what you have in mind for a program.

You will start with the basic layout managers.

Basic Interface Layout

As you learned yesterday, a graphical user interface designed with Swing is a very fluid thing. Resizing a window can wreak havoc on your interface because components move to places on a container that you might not have intended.

This fluidity is necessary. Java is implemented on many different platforms, and there are subtle differences in the way each platform displays buttons, scrollbars, and so on.

With programming languages such as Microsoft Visual Basic, a component's location on a window is precisely defined by its x,y coordinates. Some Java development tools allow similar control over an interface through the use of their own windowing classes (and there's a way to do that in Java).

When using Swing, a programmer gains more control over the layout of an interface by using layout managers.

Laying Out an Interface

A layout manager determines how components will be arranged when they are added to a container.

The default layout manager for panels is the FlowLayout class. This class lets components flow from left to right in the order that they are added to a container. When there's no more room, a new row of components begins immediately below the first, and the left-to-right order continues.

Java includes the FlowLayout, GridLayout, BorderLayout, CardLayout, and GridBagLayout layout managers. To create a layout manager for a container, call the layout manager's constructor, as in the following example:

```
FlowLayout flo = new FlowLayout();
```

After you create a layout manager, you make it the layout manager for a container by using the container's setLayout() method. The layout manager must be established before any components are added to the container. If no layout manager is specified, its default layout will be used—FlowLayout for panels and BorderLayout for frames and windows.

The following statements represent the starting point for a frame that creates a layout manager and uses setLayout() so that it controls the arrangement of all the components that will be added to the frame:

```
public class Starter extends javax.swing.JFrame {

    public Starter() {
        Container pane = getContentPane();
        FlowLayout lm = new FlowLayout();
        pane.setLayout(lm);
        // add components here
        setContentPane(pane);
    }
}
```

After the layout manager is set, you can start adding components to the container that it manages. For some of the layout managers, such as `FlowLayout`, the order in which components are added is significant. You learn more in today's subsequent sections as you work with each of the managers.

Flow Layout

The `FlowLayout` class is the simplest of the layout managers. It lays out components in a manner similar to the way words are laid out on a page—from left to right until there's no more room, and then on to the next row.

By default, the components on each row will be centered when you use the `FlowLayout()` constructor with no arguments. If you want the components to be aligned along the left or right edge of the container, the `FlowLayout.LEFT` or `FlowLayout.RIGHT` class variable should be the constructor's only argument, as in the following statement:

```
FlowLayout righty = new FlowLayout(FlowLayout.RIGHT);
```

The `FlowLayout.CENTER` class variable is used to specify centered components.

The application in Listing 11.1 displays six buttons that are arranged by the flow layout manager. Because the `FlowLayout.LEFT` class variable was used in the `FlowLayout()` constructor, the components are lined up along the left side of the application window.

LISTING 11.1 The Full Text of `Alphabet.java`

```
 1: import java.awt.*;
 2: import java.awt.event.*;
 3: import javax.swing.*;
 4:
 5: class Alphabet extends JFrame {
 6:     JButton a = new JButton("Alibi");
 7:     JButton b = new JButton("Burglar");
 8:     JButton c = new JButton("Corpse");
 9:     JButton d = new JButton("Deadbeat");
10:     JButton e = new JButton("Evidence");
11:     JButton f = new JButton("Fugitive");
```

continues

LISTING 11.1   Continued

```
12:
13:     Alphabet() {
14:         super("Alphabet");
15:         setSize(360, 120);
16:         setDefaultCloseOperation(JFrame.EXIT_ON_CLOSE);
17:         JPanel pane = new JPanel();
18:         FlowLayout lm = new FlowLayout(FlowLayout.LEFT);
19:         pane.setLayout(lm);
20:         pane.add(a);
21:         pane.add(b);
22:         pane.add(c);
23:         pane.add(d);
24:         pane.add(e);
25:         pane.add(f);
26:         setContentPane(pane);
27:         setVisible(true);
28:     }
29:
30:     public static void main(String[] arguments) {
31:         JFrame frame = new Alphabet();
32:         frame.show();
33:     }
34: }
```

Figure 11.1 shows the application running.

FIGURE 11.1

Six buttons arranged in flow layout.

In the Alphabet application, the flow layout manager uses the default gap of five pixels between each component on a row and a gap of five pixels between each row. You also can change the horizontal and vertical gap between components with some extra arguments to the FlowLayout() constructor.

The FlowLayout(*int*, *int*, *int*) constructor takes the following three arguments, in order:

- The alignment, which must be FlowLayout.CENTER, FlowLayout.LEFT, or FlowLayout.RIGHT
- The horizontal gap between components, in pixels
- The vertical gap, in pixels

The following constructor creates a flow layout manager with centered components, a horizontal gap of 30 pixels, and a vertical gap of 10:

```
FlowLayout flo = new FlowLayout(FlowLayout.CENTER, 30, 10);
```

Tip

Often, the only reason you need to create a layout manager object is to apply it to a frame's content pane. After that, you have no more need for the object. To give the Java interpreter one less object to keep track of, you can use a new statement to create the layout manager inside the setLayout() method. Both of the following examples accomplish the same thing—setting a frame's content pane to use flow layout:

```
Container pane = getContentPane();
FlowLayout fl = new FlowLayout();
pane.setLayout(fl);

Container pane = getContentPane();
pane.setLayout(new FlowLayout());
```

Grid Layout

The grid layout manager arranges components into a grid of rows and columns. Components are added first to the top row of the grid, beginning with the leftmost grid cell and continuing to the right. When all the cells in the top row are full, the next component is added to the leftmost cell in the second row of the grid—if there is a second row—and so on.

Grid layouts are created with the GridLayout class. Two arguments are sent to the GridLayout constructor—the number of rows in the grid and the number of columns. The following statement creates a grid layout manager with 10 rows and 3 columns:

```
GridLayout gr = new GridLayout(10, 3);
```

As with flow layout, you can specify a vertical and a horizontal gap between components with two extra arguments. The following statement creates a grid layout with 10 rows and 3 columns, a horizontal gap of 5 pixels, and a vertical gap of 8 pixels:

```
GridLayout gr2 = new GridLayout(10, 3, 5, 8);
```

The default gap between components under grid layout is 0 pixels in both vertical and horizontal directions.

11

Listing 11.2 contains an application that creates a grid with 3 rows, 3 columns, and a 10-pixel gap between components in both the vertical and horizontal directions.

LISTING 11.2   The Full Text of `Bunch.java`

```
 1: import java.awt.*;
 2: import java.awt.event.*;
 3: import javax.swing.*;
 4:
 5: class Bunch extends JFrame {
 6:     JButton marcia = new JButton("Marcia");
 7:     JButton carol = new JButton("Carol");
 8:     JButton greg = new JButton("Greg");
 9:     JButton jan = new JButton("Jan");
10:     JButton alice = new JButton("Alice");
11:     JButton peter = new JButton("Peter");
12:     JButton cindy = new JButton("Cindy");
13:     JButton mike = new JButton("Mike");
14:     JButton bobby = new JButton("Bobby");
15:
16:     Bunch() {
17:         super("Bunch");
18:         setSize(260, 260);
19:         setDefaultCloseOperation(JFrame.EXIT_ON_CLOSE);
20:         JPanel pane = new JPanel();
21:         GridLayout family = new GridLayout(3, 3, 10, 10);
22:         pane.setLayout(family);
23:         pane.add(marcia);
24:         pane.add(carol);
25:         pane.add(greg);
26:         pane.add(jan);
27:         pane.add(alice);
28:         pane.add(peter);
29:         pane.add(cindy);
30:         pane.add(mike);
31:         pane.add(bobby);
32:         setContentPane(pane);
33:     }
34:
35:     public static void main(String[] arguments) {
36:         JFrame frame = new Bunch();
37:         frame.show();
38:     }
39: }
```

Figure 11.2 shows this application.

FIGURE **11.2**

Nine buttons arranged in a 3 × 3 grid layout.

One thing to note about the buttons in Figure 11.2 is that they expanded to fill the space available to them in each cell. This is an important difference between grid layout and some of the other layout managers.

Border Layout

Border layouts, which are created by using the BorderLayout class, divide a container into five sections: north, south, east, west, and center. The five areas of Figure 11.3 show how these sections are arranged.

FIGURE **11.3**

Component arrangement under border layout.

Under border layout, the components in the four compass points will take up as much space as they need—the center gets whatever space is left over. Ordinarily, this will result in an arrangement with a large central component and four thin components around it.

A border layout is created with either the BorderLayout() or BorderLayout(*int, int*) constructors. The first constructor creates a border layout with no gap between any of the components. The second constructor specifies the horizontal gap and vertical gap, respectively.

11

After you create a border layout and set it up as a container's layout manager, components are added using a call to the add() method that's different from what you have seen previously:

```
add(String, component)
```

The first argument is a string indicating which part of the border layout to assign the component to. There are five possible values: "North", "South", "East", "West", or "Center".

The second argument to this method is the component that should be added to the container.

The following statement adds a button called quitButton to the north portion of a border layout:

```
add("North", quitButton);
```

Listing 11.3 contains the application used to produce Figure 11.3.

LISTING 11.3   The Full Text of Border.java

```
 1: import java.awt.*;
 2: import java.awt.event.*;
 3: import javax.swing.*;
 4:
 5: class Border extends JFrame {
 6:     JButton north = new JButton("North");
 7:     JButton south = new JButton("South");
 8:     JButton east = new JButton("East");
 9:     JButton west = new JButton("West");
10:     JButton center = new JButton("Center");
11:
12:     Border() {
13:         super("Border");
14:         setSize(240, 280);
15:         setDefaultCloseOperation(JFrame.EXIT_ON_CLOSE);
16:         JPanel pane = new JPanel();
17:         pane.setLayout(new BorderLayout());
18:         pane.add("North", north);
19:         pane.add("South", south);
20:         pane.add("East", east);
21:         pane.add("West", west);
22:         pane.add("Center", center);
23:         setContentPane(pane);
24:     }
25:
26:     public static void main(String[] arguments) {
27:         JFrame frame = new Border();
28:         frame.show();
29:     }
30: }
```

Mixing Layout Managers

At this point, you might be wondering how Java's layout managers can be useful for the graphical user interfaces you want to design. Choosing a layout manager is an experience akin to Goldilocks checking out the home of the three bears—"This one is too square! This one is too disorganized! This one is too strange!"

To find the layout that is just right, you often have to combine more than one manager on the same interface.

This is done by putting several containers inside a larger container (such as a frame) and giving each smaller container its own layout manager.

The container to use for these smaller containers is the *panel*, which is created from the JPanel class. Panels are containers that are used to group components together. There are two things to keep in mind when working with panels:

- The panel is filled with components before it is put into a larger container.
- The panel has its own layout manager.

Panels are created with a simple call to the constructor of the JPanel class, as shown in the following example:

```
JPanel pane = new JPanel();
```

The layout method is set for a panel by calling the setLayout() method on that panel.

The following statements create a layout manager and apply it to a JPanel object called pane:

```
FlowLayout flo = new FlowLayout();
pane.setLayout(flo);
```

Components are added to a panel by calling the panel's add() method, which works the same for panels as it does for some other containers.

The following statements create a text field and add it to a Panel object called pane:

```
JTextField nameField = new JTextField(80);
pane.add(nameField);
```

You'll see several examples of panel use in the rest of today's example programs.

Card Layout

Card layouts differ from the other layouts because they hide some components from view. A *card layout* is a group of containers or components that are displayed one at a

11

time, in the same way that a blackjack dealer reveals one card at a time from a deck. Each container in the group is called a *card*.

If you have used software such as HyperCard on the Macintosh or a tabbed dialog box such as the System Properties portion of the Windows Control Panel, you have worked with a program that uses card layout.

The most common way to use a card layout is to use a panel for each card. Components are added to the panels first, and then the panels are added to the container that is set to use card layout.

A card layout is created from the CardLayout class with a simple constructor call:

```
CardLayout cc = new CardLayout();
```

The setLayout() method is used to make this the layout manager for the container, as in the following statement:

```
setLayout(cc);
```

After you set a container to use the card layout manager, you must use a slightly different add() method call to add cards to the layout.

The method to use is add(*String*, *container*). The second argument specifies the container or component that is the card. If it is a container, all components must have been added to it before the card is added.

The first argument to the add() method is a string that represents the name of the card. This can be anything you want to call the card. You might want to number the cards in some way and use the number in the name, as in "Card 1", "Card 2", "Card 3", and so on.

The following statement adds a panel called options to a container and gives this card the name "Options Card":

```
add("Options Card", options);
```

After you have added a card to the main container for an interface, you can use the show() method of your card layout manager to display a card. The show() method takes two arguments:

- The container that all the cards have been added to
- The name that was given to the card

The following statement calls the show() method of a card layout manager called cc:

```
cc.show(this, "Fact Card");
```

The `this` keyword refers to the object that this statement is appearing in, and `"Fact Card"` is the name of the card to reveal. When a card is shown, the previously displayed card will be obscured. Only one card in a card layout can be viewed at a time.

In a program that uses the card layout manager, a card change will usually be triggered by a user's action. For example, in a program that displays mailing addresses on different cards, the user could select a card for display by selecting an item in a scrolling list.

Grid Bag Layout

The last of the layout managers available through Java is grid bag layout, which is an extension of the grid layout manager. A grid bag layout differs from grid layout in the following ways:

- A component can take up more than one cell in the grid.
- The proportions between different rows and columns do not have to be equal.
- Components inside grid cells can be arranged in different ways.

To create a grid bag layout, you use the `GridBagLayout` class and a helper class called `GridBagConstraints`. `GridBagLayout` is the layout manager, and `GridBagConstraints` is used to define the properties of each component to be placed into the cell—its placement, dimensions, alignment, and so on. The relationship among the grid bag, the constraints, and each component defines the overall layout.

In its most general form, creating a grid bag layout involves the following steps:

1. Creating a `GridBagLayout` object and defining it as the current layout manager, as you would for any other layout manager
2. Creating a new instance of `GridBagConstraints`
3. Setting up the constraints for a component
4. Telling the layout manager about the component and its constraints
5. Adding the component to the container

The following example adds a single button to a container that makes use of the grid bag layout. (Don't worry about the various values for the constraints; they are covered later in this section.)

```
// set up layout
GridBagLayout gridbag = new GridBagLayout();
GridBagConstraints constraints = new GridBagConstraints();
getContentPane().setLayout(gridbag);

// define constraints for the button
JButton btn = new JButton("Save");
constraints.gridx = 0;
```

11

```
constraints.gridy = 0;
constraints.gridwidth = 1;
constraints.gridheight = 1;
constraints.weightx = 30;
constraints.weighty = 30;
constraints.fill = GridBagConstraints.NONE;
constraints.anchor = GridBagConstraints.CENTER;

// attach constraints to layout, add button
gridbag.setConstraints(btn, constraints);
getContentPane().add(btn);
```

As you can see from this example, you have to set all the constraints for every component you want to add to the panel. Given the numerous constraints, it helps to have a plan and to deal with each kind of constraint one at a time.

Designing the Grid

The first place to start in the grid bag layout is on paper. Sketching out your user interface design beforehand—before you even write a single line of code—will help enormously in the long run with trying to figure out where everything goes. Put your editor aside for a second, pick up a piece of paper and a pencil, and build the grid.

Figure 11.4 shows the panel layout you'll be building for this project's application. Figure 11.5 shows the same layout with a grid imposed on top of it. Your layout will have a grid similar to this one, with rows and columns forming individual cells.

FIGURE 11.4

A grid bag layout.

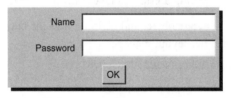

FIGURE 11.5

The grid bag layout from Figure 11.4, with grid imposed.

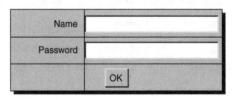

As you draw your grid, keep in mind that each component must have its own cell. You cannot put more than one component into the same cell. The reverse is not true, however; one component can span multiple cells in the x or y directions (as in the OK button in the bottom row, which spans two columns). In Figure 11.5, note that the labels and text fields have their own grids and that the button spans two column cells.

Label the cells with x and y coordinates while you're still working on paper; this will help you later. They aren't pixel coordinates; rather, they're cell coordinates. The top-left cell is 0,0. The next cell to the right of it in the top row is 1,0. The cell to the right of that one is 2,0. Moving to the next row, the leftmost cell is 1,0, the next cell in the row is 1,1, and so on. Label your cells on the paper with these numbers; you'll need them later when you do the code for this example. Figure 11.6 shows the numbers for each of the cells in this example.

FIGURE 11.6

The grid bag layout from Figure 11.5, with cell coordinates.

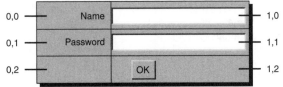

Creating the Grid

Now go back to Java and start implementing the layout you've just drawn on paper. Initially, you're going to focus exclusively on the layout—getting the grid and the proportions right. For that, it might be easier to use buttons as placeholders for the actual elements in the layout. They're easy to create, and they clearly define the space that a component will take up in the layout manager—or managers—that are in use. When everything is set up correctly, the buttons can be replaced with the right elements.

To cut down on the amount of typing you have to do to set up all those constraints, you can start by defining a helper method that takes several values and sets the constraints for those values. The buildConstraints() method takes seven arguments: a GridBagConstraints object and six integers representing the GridBagConstraints instance variables gridx, gridy, gridwidth, gridheight, weightx, and weighty. You'll learn later what these actually do; for now, here's the code to the helper method that you'll use later in this example:

```
void buildConstraints(GridBagConstraints gbc, int gx, int gy,
    int gw, int gh, int wx, int wy) {

    gbc.gridx = gx;
    gbc.gridy = gy;
    gbc.gridwidth = gw;
    gbc.gridheight = gh;
    gbc.weightx = wx;
    gbc.weighty = wy;
}
```

Now, move on to the application's constructor method, where all the layout actually occurs. Here's the basic method definition, where you'll define the GridBagLayout to be the initial layout manager and create a constraints object (an instance of GridBagConstraints):

```
public NamePass() {
    super("Username and Password");
    setSize(290, 110);
    setDefaultCloseOperation(JFrame.EXIT_ON_CLOSE);
    GridBagLayout gridbag = new GridBagLayout();
    GridBagConstraints constraints = new GridBagConstraints();
    JPanel pane = new JPanel();
    pane.setLayout(gridbag);

    constraints.fill = GridBagConstraints.BOTH;
    setContentPane(pane);
}
```

One more small note of explanation: The second-to-last line, which sets the value of constraints.fill, will be removed (and explained) later. It's there so that the components will fill the entire cell in which they're contained, which helps you see what's going on. Add it for now; you'll get a clearer idea of what it's for later.

Now add the button placeholders to the layout. (Remember that you're focusing on basic grid organization at the moment, so you'll use buttons as placeholders for the actual user interface elements you'll add later.) Start with a single button so that you can get a feel for setting its constraints. This code will go into the constructor method just after the setLayout line:

```
// Name label
buildConstraints(constraints, 0, 0, 1, 1, 100, 100);
JButton label1 = new JButton("Name:");
gridbag.setConstraints(label1, constraints);
pane.add(label1);
```

These four lines set up the constraints for an object, create a new button, attach the constraints to the button, and then add it to the panel. Note that constraints for a component are stored in the GridBagConstraints object, so the component doesn't even have to exist to set up its constraints.

Now you can get down to details: Just what are the values for the constraints that you've plugged into the helper method buildConstraints()?

The first two integer arguments are the gridx and gridy values of the constraints. They are the cell coordinates of the cell containing this component. Remember how you wrote these components down on paper in step one? With the cells neatly numbered on paper, all you have to do is plug in the right values. Note that if you have a component that spans multiple cells, the cell coordinates are those of the cell in the top left corner.

This button is in the top left corner, so its `gridx` and `gridy` (the first two arguments to `buildConstraints()`) are `0` and `0`, respectively.

The second two integer arguments are the `gridwidth` and `gridheight`. They are not the pixel widths and heights of the cells; rather, they are the number of cells this component spans: `gridwidth` for the columns and `gridheight` for the rows. Here this component spans only one cell, so the values for both are `1`.

The last two integer arguments are for `weightx` and `weighty`. They are used to set up the proportions of the rows and columns—that is, how wide or deep they will be. Weights can become very confusing, so for now, set both values to `100`. Weights are dealt with in step three.

After the constraints have been built, you can attach them to an object using the `setConstraints()` method. `setConstraints()`, which is a method defined in `GridBagLayout`, takes two arguments: the component (here a button) and the constraints for that component. Finally, you can add the button to the panel.

After you've set and assigned the constraints to one component, you can reuse that `GridBagConstraints` object to set up the constraints for the next object. You, therefore, duplicate these four lines for each component in the grid, with different values for the `buildConstraints()` method. To save space, the `buildConstraints()` methods will be shown only for the last four cells.

The second cell to add is the one to hold the text box for the name. The cell coordinates for this one are 1,0 (second column, first row); it too spans only one cell, and the weights (for now) are both `100`:

```
buildConstraints(constraints, 1, 0, 1, 1, 100, 100);
```

The next two components, which will be a label and a text field, are nearly identical to the previous two; the only difference is in their cell coordinates. The password label is at 0,1 (first column, second row), and the password text field is at 1,1 (second column, second row):

```
buildConstraints(constraints, 0, 1, 1, 1, 100, 100);
buildConstraints(constraints, 1, 1, 1, 1, 100, 100);
```

Finally, you need the OK button, which is a component that spans two cells in the bottom row of the panel. Here the cell coordinates are those of the top left cell, where the span starts (0,2). Here, unlike the previous components, you'll set `gridwidth` and `gridheight` to be something other than `1` because this cell spans multiple columns. The `gridweight` is `2` (it spans two cells) and the `gridheight` is `1` (it spans only one row):

```
buildConstraints(constraints, 0, 2, 2, 1, 100, 100);
```

11

You've set the placement constraints for all the components that will be added to the grid layout. You also need to assign each component's constraints to the layout manager and then add each component to the panel. Figure 11.7 shows the result at this point. Note that you're not concerned about exact proportions here, or about making sure everything lines up. At this point, make sure that the grid is working, you have the right number of rows and columns, the spans are correct, and nothing strange is going on (such as cells in the wrong place, cells overlapping, and that kind of thing).

FIGURE **11.7**

Grid bag layout, first pass.

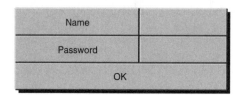

Determining the Proportions

The next step is to determine the proportions of the rows and columns in relation to other rows and columns. For example, in this case you'll want the labels (name and password) to take up less space than the text boxes. You might want the OK button at the bottom to be only half the height of the two text boxes above it. You can arrange the proportions of the cells within your layout by using the `weightx` and `weighty` constraints.

The easiest way to think of `weightx` and `weighty` is that their values are either percentages of the total width and height of the panel, or 0 if the weight or height has been set by some other cell. The values of `weightx` and `weighty` for all your components, therefore, should add up to 100.

Note

> Actually, the `weightx` and `weighty` values are not percentages; they're simply proportions—they can have any value whatsoever. When the proportions are calculated, all the values in a direction are added up so that each individual value is in proportion to that total. Thinking about the weights as percentages simply makes this process easier to understand: If you make sure that they add up to 100, you can be sure everything is coming out right.

Which cells get values and which cells get 0? Cells that span multiple rows or columns should always be 0 in the direction they span. Beyond that, deciding is simply a question of picking one cell to have a value, and then assigning all the other cells in that row or column a value of 0.

Look at the five calls to `buildConstraints()` made in the preceding step:

```
buildConstraints(constraints, 0, 0, 1, 1, 100, 100); //name
buildConstraints(constraints, 1, 0, 1, 1, 100, 100); //name text
buildConstraints(constraints, 0, 1, 1, 1, 100, 100); //password
buildConstraints(constraints, 1, 1, 1, 1, 100, 100); //password text
buildConstraints(constraints, 0, 2, 2, 1, 100, 100); //OK button
```

You'll be changing those last two arguments in each call to `buildConstraints` to be either a value or 0. Start with the x direction (the proportions of the columns), which is the second-to-last argument in the preceding list.

If you look back to Figure 11.5 (the picture of the panel with the grid imposed), note that the second column is much larger than the first. If you were going to pick theoretical percentages for those columns, you might say that the first is 10% and the second is 90%. (This is a guess; that's all you need to do as well.) With these two guesses, you can assign them to cells. You don't want to assign any values to the cell with the OK button because that cell spans both columns, and percentages wouldn't work there. Add them to the first two cells, the name label and the name text field, as in the following:

```
buildConstraints(constraints, 0, 0, 1, 1, 10, 100); //name
buildConstraints(constraints, 1, 0, 1, 1, 90, 100); //name text
```

What about the values of the remaining two cells, the password label and text field? Because the name label and field have already set the proportions of the columns, you don't have to reset them here. Give both of these cells as well as the one for the OK box 0 values:

```
buildConstraints(constraints, 0, 1, 1, 1, 0, 100); //password
buildConstraints(constraints, 1, 1, 1, 1, 0, 100); //password text
buildConstraints(constraints, 0, 2, 2, 1, 0, 100); //OK button
```

Note here that a 0 value does not mean that the cell has 0 width. These values are proportions, not pixel values. A 0 simply means that the proportion has been set somewhere else; all 0 says is "stretch it to fit."

Now that the totals of all the `weightx` constraints are 100, you can move on to the `weighty` arguments. Here you have three rows. Glancing over the grid you drew, it looks like the button has about 20% and the text fields have the rest (40% each). As with the x values, you have to set the value of only one cell per row (the two labels and the button), with all the other cells having a `weightx` of 0.

Here are the final five calls to `buildConstraints()` with the weights in place:

```
buildConstraints(constraints, 0, 0, 1, 1, 10, 40); //name
buildConstraints(constraints, 1, 0, 1, 1, 90, 0); //name text
```

11

```
buildConstraints(constraints, 0, 1, 1, 1, 0, 40); //password
buildConstraints(constraints, 1, 1, 1, 1, 0, 0); //password text
buildConstraints(constraints, 0, 2, 2, 1, 0, 20); //OK button
```

Figure 11.8 shows the result with the correct proportions.

FIGURE 11.8

Grid bag layout, second pass.

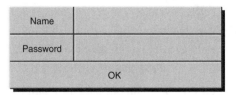

At this step, the goal is to try to come up with some basic proportions for how the rows and cells will be spaced on the screen. You can make some elementary estimates based on how big you expect the various components to be, but chances are you're going to use a lot of trial and error in this part of the process.

Adding and Arranging the Components

With the layout and the proportions in place, you can now replace the button placeholders with actual labels and text fields. Because you set up everything already, it should all work perfectly, right? Well, almost. Figure 11.9 shows what you get if you use the same constraints as before and replace the buttons with actual components.

FIGURE 11.9

Grid bag layout, almost there.

This layout is close, but it's weird. The text boxes are too tall, and the OK button stretches across the width of the cell.

What is missing are the constraints that arrange the components inside the cell. There are two of them: `fill` and `anchor`.

The `fill` constraint determines—for components that can stretch in either direction—in which direction to stretch the components (such as text boxes and buttons). `fill` can have one of the following four values, defined as class variables in the `GridBagConstraints` class:

- `GridBagConstraints.BOTH`—Stretches the component to fill the cell in both directions

- GridBagConstraints.NONE—Causes the component to be displayed in its smallest size

- GridBagConstraints.HORIZONTAL—Stretches the component in the horizontal direction

- GridBagConstraints.VERTICAL—Stretches the component in the vertical direction

Note

Keep in mind that this layout is dynamic. You're not going to set up the actual pixel dimensions of any components; rather, you're telling these elements in which direction they can grow, given a panel that can be of any size.

By default, the fill constraint for all components is NONE. Why are the text fields and labels filling the cells if this is the case? If you remember way back to the start of the code for this example, this line was added to the constructor method:

```
constraints.fill = GridBagConstraints.BOTH;
```

Now you know what it does. For the final version of this application, you'll want to remove that line and add fill values for each independent component.

The second constraint that affects how a component appears in the cell is anchor. This constraint applies only to components that aren't filling the whole cell, and it tells Java where inside the cell to place the component. The possible values for the anchor constraint are GridBagConstraints.CENTER, which aligns the component both vertically and horizontally inside the cell, or one of the following eight direction values:

GridBagConstraints.NORTH	GridBagConstraints.NORTHEAST
GridBagConstraints.EAST	GridBagConstraints.SOUTHEAST
GridBagConstraints.SOUTH	GridBagConstraints.SOUTHWEST
GridBagConstraints.WEST	GridBagConstraints.NORTHWEST

The default value of anchor is GridBagConstraints.CENTER.

You set these constraints the same way you did all the other ones: by changing instance variables in the GridBagConstraints object. Here you can change the definition of buildConstraints() to take two more arguments (they're integers), or you could just set them in the body of the init() method. The latter is used on this project.

Be careful with defaults. Keep in mind that because you're reusing the same GridBagConstraints object for each component, you might have some values left over when you're done with one component. On the other hand, if a fill or anchor from one object is the same as the one before it, you don't have to reset that object.

For this example, the following three changes are going to be made to the `fill` and `anchor` values of the components:

- The labels will have no `fill` and will be aligned `EAST` (so they hug the right side of the cell).
- The text fields will be filled horizontally (so they start one line high, but stretch to the width of the cell).
- The button will have no `fill` and will be center-aligned.

This is reflected in the full code at the end of this section.

Making Adjustments

As you work with your own programs and grid bag layouts, you'll notice that the resulting layout often requires some tinkering. You might need to play with various values of the constraints to get an interface to come out right. There's nothing wrong with that; the goal of following the previous steps is to get things fairly close to the final positions, not to come out with a perfect layout every time.

Listing 11.4 shows the complete code for the layout you've been building up in this section. If you had trouble following the discussion up to this point, you might find it useful to go through this code line by line to make sure that you understand the various parts.

LISTING 11.4   The Full Text of `NamePass.java`

```
 1: import java.awt.*;
 2: import javax.swing.*;
 3: import java.awt.event.*;
 4:
 5: public class NamePass extends JFrame {
 6:
 7:     void buildConstraints(GridBagConstraints gbc, int gx, int gy,
 8:         int gw, int gh, int wx, int wy) {
 9:
10:         gbc.gridx = gx;
11:         gbc.gridy = gy;
12:         gbc.gridwidth = gw;
13:         gbc.gridheight = gh;
14:         gbc.weightx = wx;
15:         gbc.weighty = wy;
16:     }
17:
18:     public NamePass() {
19:         super("Username and Password");
20:         setSize(290, 110);
21:         setDefaultCloseOperation(JFrame.EXIT_ON_CLOSE);
```

LISTING 11.4 Continued

```
22:          GridBagLayout gridbag = new GridBagLayout();
23:          GridBagConstraints constraints = new GridBagConstraints();
24:          JPanel pane = new JPanel();
25:          pane.setLayout(gridbag);
26:
27:          // Name label
28:          buildConstraints(constraints, 0, 0, 1, 1, 10, 40);
29:          constraints.fill = GridBagConstraints.NONE;
30:          constraints.anchor = GridBagConstraints.EAST;
31:          JLabel label1 = new JLabel("Name:", JLabel.LEFT);
32:          gridbag.setConstraints(label1, constraints);
33:          pane.add(label1);
34:
35:          // Name text field
36:          buildConstraints(constraints, 1, 0, 1, 1, 90, 0);
37:          constraints.fill = GridBagConstraints.HORIZONTAL;
38:          JTextField tfname = new JTextField();
39:          gridbag.setConstraints(tfname, constraints);
40:          pane.add(tfname);
41:
42:          // password label
43:          buildConstraints(constraints, 0, 1, 1, 1, 0, 40);
44:          constraints.fill = GridBagConstraints.NONE;
45:          constraints.anchor = GridBagConstraints.EAST;
46:          JLabel label2 = new JLabel("Password:", JLabel.LEFT);
47:          gridbag.setConstraints(label2, constraints);
48:          pane.add(label2);
49:
50:          // password text field
51:          buildConstraints(constraints, 1, 1, 1, 1, 0, 0);
52:          constraints.fill = GridBagConstraints.HORIZONTAL;
53:          JPasswordField tfpass = new JPasswordField();
54:          tfpass.setEchoChar('*');
55:          gridbag.setConstraints(tfpass, constraints);
56:          pane.add(tfpass);
57:
58:          // OK Button
59:          buildConstraints(constraints, 0, 2, 2, 1, 0, 20);
60:          constraints.fill = GridBagConstraints.NONE;
61:          constraints.anchor = GridBagConstraints.CENTER;
62:          JButton okb = new JButton("OK");
63:          gridbag.setConstraints(okb, constraints);
64:          pane.add(okb);
65:
66:          // Content Pane
67:          setContentPane(pane);
68:          setVisible(true);
69:      }
70:
```

11

continues

LISTING 11.4 Continued

```
71:     public static void main(String[] arguments) {
72:         NamePass frame = new NamePass();
73:     }
74: }
```

Cell Padding and Insets

Before you finish up with grid bag layouts, two more constraints deserve mentioning:
`ipadx` and `ipady`. These two constraints control the *padding* (the extra space around an
individual component). By default, no components have extra space around them (which
is easiest to see in components that fill their cells).

`ipadx` adds space to either side of the component, and `ipady` adds it above and below.

The horizontal and vertical gaps that appear when you create a new layout manager (or
use `ipadx` and `ipady` in grid bag layouts) are used to determine the amount of space
between components in a panel. *Insets*, however, are used to determine the amount of
space around the panel itself. The `Insets` class includes values for the top, bottom, left,
and right insets, which are then used when the panel itself is drawn.

Insets determine the amount of space between the edges of a panel and that panel's
components.

To include an `inset` for your layout, override the `getInsets()` method.

Inside the `getInsets()` method, create a new `Insets` object, where the constructor to the
`Insets` class takes four integer values representing the insets on the top, left, bottom, and
right of the panel. The `getInsets()` method should then return that `Insets` object.
Here's some code to add insets for a grid layout: 10 to the top and bottom and 30 to the
left and right.

```
public Insets getInsets() {
    return new Insets(10, 30, 10, 30);
}
```

Summary

Abstract expressionism goes only so far, as you have seen today. Layout managers
require some adjustment for people who are used to more precise control over the place
that components appear on an interface.

You now know how to use the five different layout managers and panels. As you work with the Abstract Windowing Toolkit, you'll find that it can approximate any kind of interface through the use of nested containers and different layout managers.

Once you master the development of a user interface in Java, your programs can offer something that most other visual programming languages can't: an interface that works on multiple platforms without modification.

Q&A

Q I really dislike working with layout managers; they're either too simplistic or too complicated (the grid bag layout, for example). Even with a whole lot of tinkering, I can never get my user interface to look like I want it to. All I want to do is define the sizes of my components and put them at an x,y position on the screen. Can I do this?

A It's possible, but very problematic. Java was designed in such a way that a program's graphical user interface could run equally well on different platforms and with different screen resolutions, fonts, screen sizes, and the like. Relying on pixel coordinates can cause a program that looks good on one platform to be unusable on others, where layout disasters such as components overlapping each other or getting cut off by the edge of a container may result. Layout managers, by dynamically placing elements on the screen, get around these problems. Although there might be some differences among the end results on different platforms, the differences are less likely to be catastrophic.

If none of that is persuasive, here's how to ignore my advice: Set the content pane's layout manager with `null` as the argument, create a `Rectangle` object (from the `java.awt` package) with the x,y position, width, and height of the component as arguments, and then call the component's setBounds(Rectangle) method with that rectangle as the argument.

The following application displays a 300 × 300 pixel frame with a "Click Me" button at the (x,y) position 10, 10 that is 120 pixels wide and 30 pixels tall:

```
import java.awt.*;
import javax.swing.*;

public class Absolute extends JFrame {
    public Absolute() {
        super("Example");
        setSize(300, 300);
        Container pane = getContentPane();
        pane.setLayout(null);
        JButton myButton = new JButton("Click Me");
```

11

```
                    myButton.setBounds(new Rectangle(10, 10, 120, 30));
                    pane.add(myButton);
                    setContentPane(pane);
                    setVisible(true);
            }

            public static void main(String[] arguments) {
                Absolute ex = new Absolute();
            }
        }
```

You can find out more about setBounds() in the Component class. The documentation for the Java class library can be found on the Web at http://java.sun.com/j2se/1.4/docs/api/.

Quiz

Review today's material by taking this quiz.

Questions

1. What is the default layout manager for a panel in Java?

   (a.) None

   (b.) BorderLayout

   (c.) FlowLayout

2. Which layout manager uses a compass direction or a reference to the center when adding a component to a container?

   (a.) BorderLayout

   (b.) MapLayout

   (c.) FlowLayout

3. If you want a grid layout in which a component can take up more than one cell of the grid, which layout should you use?

   (a.) GridLayout

   (b.) GridBagLayout

   (c.) None; it isn't possible to do that.

Answers

1. (c.)

2. (a.)

3. (b.)

Certification Practice

The following question is the kind of thing you could expect to be asked on a Java programming certification test. Answer it without looking at today's material or using the Java compiler to test the code.

Given:

```java
import java.awt.*;
import javax.swing.*;

public class ThreeButtons extends JFrame {
    public ThreeButtons() {
        super("Program");
        setSize(350, 225);
        setDefaultCloseOperation(JFrame.EXIT_ON_CLOSE);
        JButton alpha = new JButton("Alpha");
        JButton beta = new JButton("Beta");
        JButton gamma = new JButton("Gamma");
        Container content = getContentPane();
        // answer goes here
        content.add(alpha);
        content.add(beta);
        content.add(gamma);
        setContentPane(content);
        pack();
        setVisible(true);
    }

    public static void main(String[] arguments) {
        ThreeButtons b3 = new ThreeButtons();
    }
}
```

Which statement should replace `// answer goes here` to make the frame display all three buttons side by side?

(a.) `content.setLayout(null);`

(b.) `content.setLayout(new FlowLayout());`

(c.) `content.setLayout(new GridLayout(3,1));`

(d.) `content.setLayout(new BorderLayout());`

The answer is available on the book's Web site at `http://www.java21days.com`. Visit the Day 9 page and click the Certification Practice link.

11

Exercises

To extend your knowledge of the subjects covered today, try the following exercises:

- Create a user interface that displays a calendar for a single month, including headings for the seven days of the week and a title of the month across the top.
- Create an interface that incorporates more than one layout manager.

Where applicable, exercise solutions are offered on the book's Web site at `http://www.java21days.com`.

DAY 12

Responding to User Input

In order to turn a working Java interface into a working Java program, you must make the interface receptive to user events.

Swing handles events with a set of interfaces called *event listeners*. You create a listener object and associate it with the user interface component being listened to.

Today you will learn how to add listeners of all kinds to your Swing programs, including those that handle action events, mouse events, and other interactions.

When you're done, you'll celebrate by completing a full Java application using the Swing set of classes.

Event Listeners

NEW TERM   If a class wants to respond to a user event under the Java 2 event-handling system, it must implement the interface that deals with the events. These interfaces are called *event listeners*.

Each listener handles a specific kind of event. A class can implement as many of them as needed.

The event listeners in Java include the following interfaces:

- `ActionListener`—*Action events*, which are generated by a user taking an action on a component, such as a click on a button
- `AdjustmentListener`—*Adjustment events*, which are generated when a component is adjusted, such as when the knob of a scrollbar is moved
- `FocusListener`—*Keyboard focus events*, which are generated when a component such as a text field gains or loses the focus
- `ItemListener`—*Item events*, which are generated when an item such as a check box is changed
- `KeyListener`—*Keyboard events*, which occur when a user enters text on the keyboard
- `MouseListener`—*Mouse events*, which are generated by mouse clicks, a mouse entering a component's area, and a mouse leaving a component's area
- `MouseMotionListener`—*Mouse movement events*, which track all movement by a mouse over a component
- `WindowListener`—*Window events*, which are generated by a window (such as the main application window) being maximized, minimized, moved, or closed

The following class is declared so it can handle both action and text events:

```
public class Suspense extends JFrame implements ActionListener,
    TextListener {
    // ...
}
```

The `java.awt.event` package contains all the basic event listeners, as well as the objects that represent specific events. In order to use these classes in your programs, you can import them individually or use a statement such as the following:

```
import java.awt.event.*;
```

Setting Up Components

When you make a class an event listener, you have to first set up a specific type of event to be heard by that class. This will never happen if you don't follow up with a second step: A matching listener must be added to the component. That listener generates the events when the component is used.

After a component is created, you can call one of the following methods on the component to associate a listener with it:

- `addActionListener()`—JButton, JCheckBox, JComboBox, JTextField, JRadioButton, and JMenuItem components

- addAdjustmentListener()—JScrollBar components

- addFocusListener()—All Swing components

- addItemListener()—JButton, JCheckBox, JComboBox, and JRadioButton components

- addKeyListener()—All Swing components

- addMouseListener()—All Swing components

- addMouseMotionListener()—All Swing components

- addWindowListener()—All JWindow and JFrame components

Caution

> Modifying a component after adding it to a container is an easy mistake to make in a Java program. You must add listeners to a component and handle any other configuration before the component is added to any containers; otherwise these settings are disregarded when the program is run.

The following example creates a JButton object and associates an action event listener with it:

```
JButton zap = new JButton("Zap");
zap.addActionListener(this);
```

All the add methods take one argument: the object that is listening for events of that kind. Using this indicates that the current class is the event listener. You could specify a different object, as long as its class implements the right listener interface.

Event-Handling Methods

When you associate an interface with a class, the class must handle all the methods contained in the interface.

In the case of event listeners, each of the methods is called automatically by the windowing system when the corresponding user event takes place.

The ActionListener interface has only one method: actionPerformed(). All classes that implement ActionListener must have a method with a structure similar to the following:

```
public void actionPerformed(ActionEvent evt) {
    // handle event here
}
```

12

If only one component in your program's graphical user interface has a listener for action events, this `actionPerformed()` method can be used to respond to an event generated by that component.

If more than one component has an action event listener, you must use the method to figure out which component was used and act accordingly in your program.

In the `actionPerformed()` method, you might have noticed that an `ActionEvent` object is sent as an argument when the method is called. This object can be used to discover details about the component that generated the event.

`ActionEvent` and all other event objects are part of the `java.awt.event` package, and they are subclasses of the `EventObject` class.

Every event-handling method is sent an event object of some kind. The object's `getSource()` method can be used to determine the component that sent the event, as in the following example:

```
public void actionPerformed(ActionEvent evt) {
    Object src = evt.getSource();
}
```

The object returned by the `getSource()` method can be compared with components by using the `==` operator. The following statements can be used inside the preceding `actionPerformed()` example:

```
if (src == quitButton)
    quitProgram();
else if (src == sortRecords)
    sortRecords();
```

This example calls the `quitProgram()` method if the `quitButton` object generated the event and the `sortRecords()` method if the `sortRecords` object generated the event.

Many event-handling methods call a different method for each kind of event or component. This makes the event-handling method easier to read. In addition, if there is more than one event-handling method in a class, each one can call the same methods to get work done.

Using the `instanceof` operator inside an event-handling method is another useful technique for checking what kind of component generated the event. The following example can be used in a program with one button and one text field, each of which generates an action event:

```
void actionPerformed(ActionEvent evt) {
    Object src = evt.getSource();
    if (src instanceof JTextField)
```

```
              calculateScore();
          else if (src instanceof JButton)
              quitProgram();
     }
```

The program in Listing 12.1 uses the application framework to create a JFrame and add components to it. The program itself sports two JButton components, which are used to change the text on the frame's title bar.

LISTING 12.1 The Full Text of ChangeTitle.java

```
 1: import java.awt.event.*;
 2: import javax.swing.*;
 3: import java.awt.*;
 4:
 5: public class ChangeTitle extends JFrame implements ActionListener {
 6:     JButton b1 = new JButton("Rosencrantz");
 7:     JButton b2 = new JButton("Guildenstern");
 8:
 9:     public ChangeTitle() {
10:         super("Title Bar");
11:         setDefaultCloseOperation(JFrame.EXIT_ON_CLOSE);
12:         b1.addActionListener(this);
13:         b2.addActionListener(this);
14:         JPanel pane = new JPanel();
15:         pane.add(b1);
16:         pane.add(b2);
17:         setContentPane(pane);
18:         pack();
19:         setVisible(true);
20:     }
21:
22:     public static void main(String[] arguments) {
23:         JFrame frame = new ChangeTitle();
24:     }
25:
26:     public void actionPerformed(ActionEvent evt) {
27:         Object source = evt.getSource();
28:         if (source == b1)
29:             setTitle("Rosencrantz");
30:         else if (source == b2)
31:             setTitle("Guildenstern");
32:         repaint();
33:     }
34: }
```

12

After you run this application with the Java interpreter, the program's interface should resemble Figure 12.1.

FIGURE **12.1**

The ChangeTitle *application.*

Only 11 lines were needed to respond to action events in this application:

- Line 1 imports the java.awt.event package.
- Lines 12 and 13 add action listeners to both JButton objects.
- Lines 26–33 respond to action events that occur from the two JButton objects. The evt object's getSource() method determines the source of the event. If it is equal to the b1 button, the title of the frame is set to Rosencrantz; if it is equal to b2, the title is set to Guildenstern. A call to repaint() is needed so the frame is redrawn after any title change that might have occurred in the method.

Working with Methods

The following sections detail the structure of each event-handling method and the methods that can be used within them.

In addition to the methods described, the getSource() method can be used on any event object to determine which object generated the event.

Action Events

Action events occur when a user completes an action using one of the following components: JButton, JCheckBox, JComboBox, JTextField, or JRadioButton.

A class must implement the ActionListener interface in order to handle these events. In addition, the addActionListener() method must be called on each component that should generate an action event—unless you want to ignore that component's action events.

The actionPerformed(ActionEvent) method is the only method of the ActionListener interface. It takes the following form:

```
public void actionPerformed(ActionEvent evt) {
    // ...
}
```

In addition to the getSource() method, you can use the getActionCommand() method on the ActionEvent object to discover more information about the event's source.

The action command, by default, is the text associated with the component, such as the label on a JButton. You also can set a different action command for a component by calling its setActionCommand(*String*) method. The string argument should be the action command's desired text.

For example, the following statements create a JButton and a JTextField and give both of them the action command "Sort Files":

```
JButton sort = new JButton("Sort");
JTextField name = new JTextField();
sort.setActionCommand("Sort Files");
name.setActionCommand("Sort Files");
```

Note

Action commands are useful in a program in which more than one component should cause the same thing to happen. A program with a Quit button and a Quit option on a pull-down menu is an example of this. By giving both components the same action command, you can handle them with the same code in an event-handling method.

Adjustment Events

Adjustment events occur when a JScrollBar component is moved by using the arrows on the bar or on the box, or by clicking anywhere on the bar. To handle these events, a class must implement the AdjustmentListener interface.

The adjustmentValueChanged(*AdjustmentEvent*) method is the only method in the AdjustmentListener interface. It takes the following form:

```
public void adjustmentValueChanged(AdjustmentEvent evt) {
    // ...
}
```

To see what the current value of the JScrollBar is within this event-handling method, the getValue() method can be called on the AdjustmentEvent object. This method returns an integer representing the scrollbar's value.

You can also determine the way the user moved the scrollbar by using the AdjustmentEvent object's getAdjustmentType() method. This returns one of five values, each of which is a class variable of the Adjustment class:

- UNIT_INCREMENT—A value increase of 1, which can be caused by clicking a scrollbar arrow or using a cursor key
- UNIT_DECREMENT—A value decrease of 1
- BLOCK_INCREMENT—A larger value increase, caused by clicking the scrollbar in the area between the box and the arrow
- BLOCK_DECREMENT—A larger value decrease
- TRACK—A value change caused by moving the box

12

The program in Listing 12.2 illustrates the use of the AdjustmentListener interface. A scrollbar and an uneditable text field are added to a frame, and messages are displayed in the field whenever the scrollbar is moved.

LISTING 12.2   The Full Text of WellAdjusted.java

```
 1: import java.awt.event.*;
 2: import javax.swing.*;
 3: import java.awt.*;
 4:
 5: public class WellAdjusted extends JFrame implements AdjustmentListener {
 6:     JTextField value = new JTextField("50", 30);
 7:     JScrollBar bar = new JScrollBar(SwingConstants.HORIZONTAL,
 8:         50, 10, 0, 100);
 9:
10:     public WellAdjusted() {
11:         super("Well Adjusted");
12:         setSize(350, 100);
13:         setDefaultCloseOperation(JFrame.EXIT_ON_CLOSE);
14:         bar.addAdjustmentListener(this);
15:         value.setHorizontalAlignment(SwingConstants.CENTER);
16:         value.setEditable(false);
17:         JPanel pane = new JPanel();
18:         pane.setLayout(new BorderLayout());
19:         pane.add(value, "Center");
20:         pane.add(bar, "South");
21:         setContentPane(pane);
22:     }
23:
24:     public static void main(String[] arguments) {
25:         JFrame frame = new WellAdjusted();
26:         frame.show();
27:     }
28:
29:     public void adjustmentValueChanged(AdjustmentEvent evt) {
30:         Object source = evt.getSource();
31:         if (source == bar) {
32:             int newValue = bar.getValue();
33:             value.setText("" + newValue);
34:         }
35:         repaint();
36:     }
37: }
```

Figure 12.2 shows a screen capture of the application after it has been run with the Java interpreter.

FIGURE 12.2

The output of the WellAdjusted *application.*

> **Tip**
>
> You might be wondering why there's an empty set of quotation marks in the call to setText() in line 33 of this program. The empty quotation is called a null *string,* and it is concatenated to the newValue integer to turn the argument into a string. As you might recall, if a string and nonstring are concatenated, Java always treats the result as a string. The null string is a shortcut when you want to display something that isn't already a string.

Focus Events

Focus events occur when any component gains or loses input focus on a graphical user interface. *Focus* describes the component that is active for keyboard input. If one of the fields has the focus (in a user interface with several editable text fields), a cursor will blink in the field. Any text entered goes into this component.

Focus applies to all components that can receive input. In a JButton object, a dotted outline appears on the button that has the focus.

To handle a focus event, a class must implement the FocusListener interface. There are two methods in the interface: focusGained(*FocusEvent*) and focusLost(*FocusEvent*). They take the following forms:

```
public void focusGained(FocusEvent evt) {
    // ...
}

public void focusLost(FocusEvent evt) {
    // ...
}
```

To determine which object gained or lost the focus, the getSource() method can be called on the FocusEvent object and sent as an argument to the focusGained() and focusLost() methods.

Item Events

Item events occur when an item is selected or deselected on any of the following components: JButton, JCheckBox, JComboBox, or JRadioButton. A class must implement the ItemListener interface in order to handle these events.

12

itemStateChanged(ItemEvent) is the only method in the ItemListener interface. It takes the following form:

```
void itemStateChanged(ItemEvent evt) {
    // ...
}
```

To determine in which item the event occurred, the getItem() method can be called on the ItemEvent object.

You also can determine whether the item was selected or deselected by using the getStateChange() method. This method returns an integer that will equal either the class variable ItemEvent.DESELECTED or ItemEvent.SELECTED.

The use of item events is illustrated in Listing 12.3. The SelectItem application displays the choice from a combo box in a text field.

LISTING 12.3   The Full Text of SelectItem.java

```
 1: import java.awt.event.*;
 2: import javax.swing.*;
 3: import java.awt.*;
 4:
 5: public class SelectItem extends JFrame implements ItemListener {
 6:     BorderLayout bord = new BorderLayout();
 7:     JTextField result = new JTextField(27);
 8:     JComboBox pick = new JComboBox();
 9:
10:     public SelectItem() {
11:         super("Select Item");
12:         setDefaultCloseOperation(JFrame.EXIT_ON_CLOSE);
13:         pick.addItemListener(this);
14:         pick.addItem("Navigator");
15:         pick.addItem("Internet Explorer");
16:         pick.addItem("Opera");
17:         pick.setEditable(false);
18:         result.setHorizontalAlignment(SwingConstants.CENTER);
19:         result.setEditable(false);
20:         JPanel pane = new JPanel();
21:         pane.setLayout(bord);
22:         pane.add(result, "South");
23:         pane.add(pick, "Center");
24:         setContentPane(pane);
25:         pack();
26:         setVisible(true);
27:     }
28:
29:     public static void main(String[] arguments) {
30:         JFrame frame = new SelectItem();
```

LISTING 12.3   Continued

```
31:        }
32:
33:        public void itemStateChanged(ItemEvent evt) {
34:            Object source = evt.getSource();
35:            if (source == pick) {
36:                Object newPick = evt.getItem();
37:                result.setText(newPick.toString() + " is the selection.");
38:            }
39:            repaint();
40:        }
41: }
```

Figure 12.3 shows this application with the combo box open. The object's toString()
method is used to retrieve the object's text returned by getItem().

FIGURE 12.3

The output of the
SelectItem
application.

Key Events

Key events occur when a key is pressed on the keyboard. Any component can generate
these events, and a class must implement the KeyListener interface to support them.

There are three methods in the KeyListener interface. They include
keyPressed(*KeyEvent*), keyReleased(*KeyEvent*), and keyTyped(*KeyEvent*). They take
the following forms:

```
public void keyPressed(KeyEvent evt) {
    // ...
}

public void keyReleased(KeyEvent evt) {
    // ...
}

public void keyTyped(KeyEvent evt) {
    // ...
}
```

KeyEvent's getKeyChar() method returns the character of the key associated with the
event. If there is no Unicode character that can be represented by the key, getKeyChar()
returns a character value equal to the class variable KeyEvent.CHAR_UNDEFINED.

12

Mouse Events

Mouse events are generated by the following types of user interaction:

- A mouse click
- A mouse entering a component's area
- A mouse leaving a component's area

Any component can generate these events, which are implemented by a class through the `MouseListener` interface. This interface has five methods:

- `mouseClicked(`*MouseEvent*`)`
- `mouseEntered(`*MouseEvent*`)`
- `mouseExited(`*MouseEvent*`)`
- `mousePressed(`*MouseEvent*`)`
- `mouseReleased(`*MouseEvent*`)`

Each takes the same basic form as `mouseReleased (`*MouseEvent*`)`:

```
public void mouseReleased(MouseEvent evt) {
    // ...
}
```

The following methods can be used on `MouseEvent` objects:

- `getClickCount()`—Returns the number of times the mouse was clicked as an integer
- `getPoint()`—Returns the x,y coordinates within the component where the mouse was clicked as a `Point` object
- `getX()`—Returns the x position
- `getY()`—Returns the y position

Mouse Motion Events

Mouse motion events occur when a mouse is moved over a component. As with other mouse events, any component can generate mouse motion events. A class must implement the `MouseMotionListener` interface in order to support them.

There are two methods in the `MouseMotionListener` interface: `mouseDragged(MouseEvent)` and `mouseMoved(MouseEvent)`. They take the following forms:

```
public void mouseDragged(MouseEvent evt) {
    // ...
}

public void mouseMoved(MouseEvent evt) {
    // ...
}
```

Unlike the other event-listener interfaces you have dealt with up to this point, MouseMotionListener does not have its own event type. Instead, MouseEvent objects are used.

Because of this, you can call the same methods you would for mouse events: getClick(), getPoint(), getX(), and getY().

Window Events

Window events occur when a user opens or closes a window object, such as a JFrame or a JWindow. Any component can generate these events, and a class must implement the WindowListener interface in order to support them.

There are seven methods in the WindowListener interface:

- windowActivated(*WindowEvent*)
- windowClosed(*WindowEvent*)
- windowClosing(*WindowEvent*)
- windowDeactivated(*WindowEvent*)
- windowDeiconified(*WindowEvent*)
- windowIconified(*WindowEvent*)
- windowOpened(*WindowEvent*)

They all take the same form as the windowOpened() method:

```
public void windowOpened(WindowEvent evt) {
    // ...
}
```

The windowClosing() and windowClosed() methods are similar, but one is called as the window is closing and the other is called after it is closed. In fact, you can take action in a windowClosing() method to stop the window from being closed.

There's also an adapter class that implements the WindowListener interface called WindowAdapter. This class was used in the ExitWindow project during Day 9, "Working with Swing."

Creating a Swing Application

As an opportunity to put the past several days' material to more use, the following application demonstrates layout creation, nested panels, interface creation, and event handling.

Figure 12.4 shows the SwingColorTest application, which enables a user to pick colors based on the sRGB or HSB color spaces—systems that describe colors based on their red, green, and blue content or hue, saturation, and brightness values, respectively.

12

FIGURE 12.4

The SwingColorTest application.

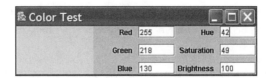

The SwingColorTest application has three main parts: a colored box on the left side and two groups of text fields on the right. The first group indicates RGB values; the second group, HSB. If you change any of the values in any of the text boxes, the colored box is updated to the new color, as are the values in the other group of text boxes.

This application uses three classes:

- SwingColorTest, which inherits from JFrame and is the main class for the application itself.
- SwingColorControls, which inherits from JPanel. You create this class to represent a group of three text fields and to handle actions from them. Two instances of this class, one for the sRGB values and one for the HSB ones, are created and added to the application.

The code for this application is shown at the end of this section.

Designing the Layout

The first step in a Swing project is to worry about the layout first and the functionality second. When dealing with the layout, you should start with the outermost panel first and work inward.

Making a sketch of your user-interface design can help you figure out how to organize the panels inside your application to best take advantage of layout and space. Paper designs are helpful even when you're not using grid bag layouts and are doubly so when you are. (You'll be using a simple grid layout for this application.)

Figure 12.5 shows the SwingColorTest application with a grid drawn over it so you can get an idea of how the panels and embedded panels work.

FIGURE 12.5

SwingColorTest *panels and components.*

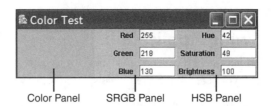

Start with the outermost panel—a JFrame component. This frame has three parts: the color box on the left, the RGB text fields in the middle, and the HSB fields on the right.

Because the outermost panel is the frame itself, the SwingColorTest class will inherit from JFrame. You also import the Swing, AWT, and event-handling classes here. (Note that because you use so many of them in this program, importing the entire package is easiest.)

```
import java.awt.*;
import java.awt.event.*;
import javax.swing.*;

public class SwingColorTest extends JFrame {
    // ...
}
```

This frame has three main elements to keep track of: the color box and the two subpanels. Each of the subpanels refers to different things, but they're extremely similar in how they look and the information they contain. Rather than duplicate a lot of code in this class, you can take this opportunity to create another class strictly for the subpanels, use instances of that class in the frame, and communicate using methods. The new class, called SwingColorControls, will be defined in a bit.

For now, however, you know you need to keep a handle on all three parts of the application so you can update them when they change. Create three instance variables: one of type JPanel for the color box and the other two of type SwingColorControls for the control panels:

```
SwingColorControls RGBcontrols, HSBcontrols;
JPanel swatch;
```

Now you can move onto the frame's constructor method, where all the basic initialization and layout of the application takes place, in the following steps:

1. Set up the class and create the layout for the big parts of the panel. Although a flow layout would work, creating a grid layout with one row and three columns is a better idea.

2. Create and initialize the three components of this application: a panel for the color box and two subpanels for the text fields.

3. Add these components to the application.

The first statement in the constructor method of a subclass should be a call to a constructor of the superclass. The JFrame(String) constructor sets the text of the frame's title bar to the indicated String. It will be used here:

```
super("Color Test");
```

12

Next, a panel is created and its layout is set to a grid layout with a gap of 10 points to separate each of the components:

```
JPanel pane = new JPanel();
GridLayout grid = new GridLayout(1, 3, 5, 15);
pane.setLayout(grid);
```

This panel, pane, will be set up completely and then used to create the frame's content pane—the portion of the frame that can contain other components.

The first component that will be added to pane is the color box, swatch. It is created as a JPanel and given the background color black:

```
swatch = new JPanel();
swatch.setBackground(Color.black);
```

You also need to create two instances of the currently nonexistent SwingColorControls panels here. Because you haven't created the class yet, you don't know what the constructors to that class will look like. Put in some placeholder constructors here; you can fill in the details later.

```
RGBcontrols = new SwingColorControls( ... );
HSBcontrols = new SwingColorControls( ... );
```

Once all the components have been created, they are added to the panel, which is then used to set up the frame's content pane:

```
pane.add(swatch);
pane.add(RGBcontrols);
pane.add(HSBcontrols);
setContentPane(pane);
```

At this point your class should contain three instance variables, a constructor method, incomplete constructors for RGBControls and HSBControls, and a getInsets() method. Move on to creating the subpanel layout in the SwingColorControls class, which will enable you to fill in the incomplete constructors and finish the layout.

Defining the Subpanels

The SwingColorControls class will have behavior for laying out and handling the subpanels that represent the RGB and HSB values for a color. SwingColorControls inherits from JPanel, a simple component that can contain other components:

```
class SwingColorControls extends JPanel {
    // ...
}
```

The SwingColorControls class needs a number of instance variables so information from the panel can get back to the application. The first of these instance variables is a hook back to the class that contains this panel. Because the outer application class controls the updating of each panel, this panel needs a way to tell the application that something has changed. To call a method in that application, you need a reference to the object; instance variable number one is a reference to an instance of the class `SwingColorTest`:

```
SwingColorTest frame;
```

If you figure that the `frame` class is updating everything, that class will be interested in the individual text fields in this subpanel. You create instance variables for these text fields:

```
JTextField[] setting = new JTextField[3];
```

Now you can move on to the constructor method for this class. You establish the layout for the subpanel, create the text fields, and add them to the panel's content pane inside the constructor.

The goal here is to make the `SwingColorControls` class generic enough so you can use it for both the panel of RGB fields and the panel of HSB fields. These two panels differ in only one respect: the labels for the text—that's three values to get before you can create the object. You can pass these three values in through the constructors in `SwingColorTest`. You also need one more: the reference to the enclosing application, which you can get from the constructor as well.

You now have two arguments to the basic constructor for the `SwingColorControls` class—a reference to the parent class and a `String` array containing the text field labels. Here's the signature for the constructor:

```
SwingColorControls(SwingColorTest parent, String[] label) {
    // ..
}
```

Start this constructor by first setting the value of `parent` to the `frame` instance variable:

```
frame = parent;
```

Next, create the layout for this panel. You can also use a grid layout for these subpanels, as you did for the application frame, but this time the grid will have three rows (one for each of the text field and label pairs) and two columns (one for the labels and one for the fields). Also, define a 10-point gap between the components in the grid:

```
GridLayout cGrid = new GridLayout(3, 2, 10, 10);
setLayout(cGrid);
```

Now you can create and add the components to the panel. First create a `for` loop named `i` that can iterate three times:

```
for (int i = 0; i < 3; i++) {
    // ...
}
```

12

Inside this loop, each text field and label will be created and added to a container. First, a text field will be initialized to the string "0" and assigned to the appropriate instance variable:

```
tfield[i] = new JTextField("0");
```

Next, the text field and a label are added to the panel using the String array sent to the SwingColorControls constructor as the text for the labels:

```
JLabel settingLabel = new JLabel(label[i], JLabel.RIGHT);
add(settingLabel);
add(setting[i]);
```

Now that a SwingColorControls class has been completed, you can fix the placeholder constructors in SwingColorTest for the subpanel.

The constructor for SwingColorControls that you just created now has two arguments: the SwingColorTest object and an array of strings containing three labels. Replace the RGBcontrols and HSBcontrols placeholder constructors in SwingColorTest so the array labels are created and used in calls to the SwingColorTest constructor:

```
String[] rgbLabels = { "Red", "Green", "Blue" };
RGBcontrols = new SwingColorControls(this, rgbLabels);
String[] hsbLabels = { "Hue", "Saturation", "Brightness" };
HSBcontrols = new SwingColorControls(this, hsbLabels);
```

The this keyword is used to pass the SwingColorTest object to these constructors.

Note The number 0 (actually, the string "0") is used for the initial value of all the text fields in this example. For the color black, both the RGB and the HSB values are 0, which is why this assumption can be made. If you want to initialize the application to some other color, you might want to rewrite the SwingColorControls class to use initializer values as well as to initialize labels.

Converting Between sRGB and HSB

At this point, the SwingColorTest application will compile successfully, and you can take a look at the layout. It's common to do this in a programming project, resolving all issues with the interface before spending any time writing code to make the interface function.

This application's main purpose is to convert between sRGB and HSB values, and vice versa. When the value in a text field is changed, the color box updates to the new color and the value of the fields in the opposite subpanel changes to reflect the new color.

The SwingColorTest class will be made responsible for actually doing the updating when a user has changed a value. A new method will be added to handle this: update().

This `update()` method takes a single argument: the `SwingColorControls` instance that contains the changed value. (You will get this argument from event-handling methods in the `SwingColorControls` object.)

> **Note**
>
> Won't this `update()` method interfere with the system's `update()` method? No. Remember, methods can have the same name, but different signatures and definitions. Because this `update()` has a single argument of type `SwingColorControls`, it doesn't interfere with the other version of `update()`.

The `update()` method is responsible for updating all the panels in the application. To know which panel to update, you need to know which panel changed. You can find out by testing to see whether the argument you got passed from the panel is the same as the subpanels you have stored in the `RGBcontrols` and `HSBcontrols` instance variables:

```
void update(SwingColorControls control) {

    if (control == RGBcontrols) {
        // RGB has changed, update HSB
    } else {
        // HSB has changed, update RGB
    }
}
```

This test is the heart of the `update()` method. Start with the first case—a number has been changed in the RGB text fields. Now, based on these new sRGB values, you have to generate a new `Color` object and update the values on the HSB panel. You can create a few local variables to hold some basic values in order to reduce the amount of typing you have to do. In particular, the values of the text fields are strings whose values you can get using the `getText()` method defined in the `JTextField` objects of the `SwingColorControls` object. Because most of the time you'll want to deal with these values as integers in this method, you can get these string values, convert them to integers, and store them in an array of integers, called `value`. Here's the code to take care of this job:

```
int[] value = new int[3];
for (int i = 0; i < 3; i++) {
    value[i] = Integer.parseInt(control.setting[i].getText());
    if ( (value[i] < 0) || (value[i] > 255) ) {
        value[i] = 0;
        control.setting[i].setText("" + value[i]);
    }
}
```

Each of the values collected from the `JTextField` objects is checked to see whether it is less than 0 or greater than 255 (sRGB and HSB values are represented as integers from 0 to 255). If the value is out of that range, the text field is set back to its initial value, `"0"`.

While you're defining local variables, you also need one for the new `Color` object:

```
Color c;
```

Now assume that one of the text fields in the RGB side of the application has changed and add the code to the `if` part of the `update()` method. You need to create a new `Color` object and update the HSB side of the panel. The first part is easy. Given the three sRGB values, you can create a new `Color` object using these values as arguments to the constructor:

```
c = new Color(value[0], value[1], value[2]);
```

Now you convert the sRGB values to HSB. Standard algorithms can convert an sRGB-based color to an HSB color, but you don't have to look them up. The `Color` class has a class method called `RGBtoHSB()` that you can use. This method does the work for you—most of it, at least. The `RGBtoHSB()` method poses two problems, however:

- The `RGBtoHSB()` method returns an array of the three HSB values, so you have to extract these values from the array.

- The HSB values are measured in floating-point values from `0.0` to `1.0`. I prefer to think of HSB values as integers, where the hue is a degree value around a color wheel (`0` through `360`), and saturation and brightness are percentages from `0` to `100`.

Neither of these problems is insurmountable; you just have to add some extra lines of code. Start by calling `RGBtoHSB()` with the new RGB values you have. The return type of that method is an array of `float` values, so you create a local variable (`HSB`) to store the results of the `RBGtoHSB()` method. (Note that you also need to create and pass in an empty `float` array as the fourth argument to `RGBtoHSB()`.)

```
float[] hsbValues = new float[3];
float[] HSB = Color.RGBtoHSB(value[0], value[1], value[2],
    hsbValues);
```

Now convert these floating-point values that range from `0.0` to `1.0` to values that range from `0` and `100` (for the saturation and brightness) and `0` to `360` (for the hue) by multiplying the appropriate numbers and reassigning the value back to the array:

```
HSB[0] *= 360;
HSB[1] *= 100;
HSB[2] *= 100;
```

Now you have the numbers you want. The last part of the update puts these values back into the text fields. Of course, these values are still floating-point numbers, so you have to cast them to `ints` before turning them into strings and storing them:

```
for (int i = 0; i < 3; i++) {
    HSBcontrols.setting[i].setText( String.valueOf((int)HSB[i]) );
```

The next part of the application updates the sRGB values when a text field on the HSB side has changed. This is the `else` in the big `if-else` that defines this method and determines what to update, given a change.

Generating sRGB values from HSB values is actually easier than the other way around. A class method in the `Color` class, `getHSBColor()`, creates a new `Color` object from three HSB values. After you have a `Color` object, you can easily pull the RGB values out of it. The catch, of course, is that `getHSBColor` takes three floating-point arguments, and the values you have are integer values. In the call to `getHSBColor`, you'll have to cast the integer values from the text fields to `float` values and divide them by the proper conversion factor. The result of `getHSBColor` is a `Color` object. Therefore you can simply assign the object to the c local variable so you can use it again later:

```
c = Color.getHSBColor( (float)value[0] / 360,
    (float)value[1] / 100, (float)value[2] / 100 );
```

With the `Color` object set, updating the RGB values involves extracting these values from that `Color` object. The `getRed()`, `getGreen()`, and `getBlue()` methods, defined in the `Color` class, will do that job:

```
RGBcontrols.setting[0].setText( String.valueOf(c.getRed()) );
RGBcontrols.setting[1].setText( String.valueOf(c.getGreen()) );
RGBcontrols.setting[2].setText( String.valueOf(c.getBlue()) );
```

Finally, regardless of whether the sRGB or HSB value has changed, you need to update the color box on the left to reflect the new color. Because you have a new `Color` object stored in the variable c, you can use the `setBackground` method to change the color. Also note that `setBackground` doesn't automatically repaint the screen, so fire off a `repaint()` as well:

```
swatch.setBackground(c);
swatch.repaint();
```

Handling User Events

Two classes are created for this project: `SwingColorTest` and `SwingColorControls`. `SwingColorTest` contains the application window and the `main()` method that is used to set up the window. `SwingColorControls`, a helper class, is a panel that holds three labels and three text fields used to choose a color.

All the user input in this program takes place on the color controls; the text fields are used to define sRGB or HSB values.

Because of this, all the event-handling behaviors are added to the `SwingColorControls` class.

12

The first thing to do is make the SwingColorControls class handle two kinds of events: action events and focus events. The extends clause should be added to the class declaration statement, as shown here, so the ActionListener and FocusListener interfaces are implemented:

```
class SwingColorControls extends JPanel
     implements ActionListener, FocusListener {
```

Action and focus listeners must next be added to the three text fields in the class, which are referenced using the setting array. These listeners must be added after the text fields are created but before they are added to a container. The following statements can be used in a for loop called i that iterates through the setting array:

```
setting[i].addFocusListener(this);
setting[i].addActionListener(this);
```

Finally, you must add all the methods that are defined in the three interfaces this class implements: actionPerformed(*ActionEvent*), focusLost(*FocusEvent*), and focusGained(*FocusEvent*).

The color controls enter a numeric value for a color, and this causes the color to be drawn on a panel. This also causes the other color controls to be updated to reflect the color change.

There are two ways a user can finalize a new color choice—by pressing Enter inside a text field, which generates an action event, or by leaving the field to edit a different field, which generates a focus event.

The following statements compose the actionPerformed() and focusLost() methods that should be added to the class:

```
public void actionPerformed(ActionEvent evt) {
    if (evt.getSource() instanceof JTextField)
        frame.update(this);
}
public void focusLost(FocusEvent evt) {
    frame.update(this);
}
```

One of these, focusGained(), doesn't need to be handled. Because of this, an empty method definition should be added:

```
public void focusGained(FocusEvent evt) { }
```

The event-handling methods added to SwingColorControls call a method in its parent class, update(*SwingColorControls*).

This method doesn't contain any event-handling behavior—it updates the color swatch and all the color controls to reflect a color change.

Listing 12.4 contains the application, including the `SwingColorTest` and `SwingColorControls` classes.

LISTING 12.4   The Full Text of `SwingColorTest.java`

```
 1: import java.awt.*;
 2: import java.awt.event.*;
 3: import javax.swing.*;
 4:
 5: public class SwingColorTest extends JFrame {
 6:     SwingColorControls RGBcontrols, HSBcontrols;
 7:     JPanel swatch;
 8:
 9:     public SwingColorTest() {
10:         super("Color Test");
11:         setSize(400, 100);
12:         setDefaultCloseOperation(JFrame.EXIT_ON_CLOSE);
13:         JPanel pane = new JPanel();
14:         GridLayout grid = new GridLayout(1, 3, 5, 15);
15:         pane.setLayout(grid);
16:         swatch = new JPanel();
17:         swatch.setBackground(Color.black);
18:         String[] rgbLabels = { "Red", "Green", "Blue" };
19:         RGBcontrols = new SwingColorControls(this, rgbLabels);
20:         String[] hsbLabels = { "Hue", "Saturation", "Brightness" };
21:         HSBcontrols = new SwingColorControls(this, hsbLabels);
22:         pane.add(swatch);
23:         pane.add(RGBcontrols);
24:         pane.add(HSBcontrols);
25:         setContentPane(pane);
26:         pack();
27:         setVisible(true);
28:     }
29:
30:     public static void main(String[] arguments) {
31:         JFrame frame = new SwingColorTest();
32:     }
33:
34:     void update(SwingColorControls control) {
35:         Color c;
36:         // get string values from text fields, convert to ints
37:         int[] value = new int[3];
38:         for (int i = 0; i < 3; i++) {
39:             value[i] = Integer.parseInt(control.setting[i].getText());
40:             if ( (value[i] < 0) || (value[i] > 255) ) {
41:                 value[i] = 0;
42:                 control.setting[i].setText("" + value[i]);
43:             }
44:         }
45:         if (control == RGBcontrols) {
```

12

continues

LISTING 12.4 Continued

```
46:                   // RGB has changed, update HSB
47:                   c = new Color(value[0], value[1], value[2]);
48:
49:                   // convert RGB values to HSB values
50:                   float[] hsbValues = new float[3];
51:                   float[] HSB = Color.RGBtoHSB(value[0], value[1], value[2],
52:                       hsbValues);
53:                   HSB[0] *= 360;
54:                   HSB[1] *= 100;
55:                   HSB[2] *= 100;
56:
57:                   // reset HSB fields
58:                   for (int i = 0; i < 3; i++) {
59:                      HSBcontrols.setting[i].setText(String.valueOf( (int)HSB[i])
                               );
60:                   }
61:            } else {
62:                   // HSB has changed, update RGB
63:                   c = Color.getHSBColor( (float)value[0] / 360,
64:                       (float)value[1] / 100, (float)value[2] / 100 );
65:
66:                   // reset RGB fields
67:                   RGBcontrols.setting[0].setText( String.valueOf(c.getRed()) );
68:                   RGBcontrols.setting[1].setText( String.valueOf(c.getGreen()) );
69:                   RGBcontrols.setting[2].setText( String.valueOf(c.getBlue()) );
70:            }
71:
72:            // update swatch
73:            swatch.setBackground(c);
74:            swatch.repaint();
75:      }
76: }
77:
78: class SwingColorControls extends JPanel
79:      implements ActionListener, FocusListener {
80:
81:      SwingColorTest frame;
82:      JTextField[] setting = new JTextField[3];
83:
84:      SwingColorControls(SwingColorTest parent, String[] label) {
85:
86:          frame = parent;
87:          GridLayout cGrid = new GridLayout(3, 2, 10, 10);
88:          setLayout(cGrid);
89:          for (int i = 0; i < 3; i++) {
90:              setting[i] = new JTextField("0");
91:              setting[i].addFocusListener(this);
92:              setting[i].addActionListener(this);
93:              JLabel settingLabel = new JLabel(label[i], JLabel.RIGHT);
94:              add(settingLabel);
```

LISTING **12.4**   Continued

```
 95:                add(setting[i]);
 96:            }
 97:            setVisible(true);
 98:        }
 99:
100:        public void actionPerformed(ActionEvent evt) {
101:            if (evt.getSource() instanceof JTextField)
102:                frame.update(this);
103:        }
104:
105:        public void focusLost(FocusEvent evt) {
106:            frame.update(this);
107:        }
108:
109:        public void focusGained(FocusEvent evt) { }
110:
111: }
```

Summary

The event-handling system used with Swing is added to a program through the same steps:

- A listener interface is added to the class that will contain the event-handling methods.
- A listener is added to each component that will generate the events to handle.
- The methods are added, each with an EventObject class as the only argument to the method.
- Methods of that EventObject class, such as getSource(), are used to learn which component generated the event and what kind of event it was.

Once you know these steps, you can work with each of the different listener interfaces and event classes. You also can learn about new listeners as they are added to Swing with new components.

Q&A

Q Can a program's event-handling behavior be put into its own class instead of including it with the code that creates the interface?

A It can, and many programmers will tell you that this is a good way to design your programs. Separating interface design from your event-handling code enables the two to be developed separately—the SwingColorTest application today shows the alternative approach. This makes it easier to maintain the project; related behavior is grouped and isolated from unrelated behavior.

12

Q **Is there a way of differentiating between the buttons on a `mouseClicked()` event?**

A You can, using a feature of mouse events that wasn't covered today because right and middle mouse buttons are platform-specific features that aren't available on all systems where Java programs run.

All mouse events send a `MouseEvent` object to their event-handling methods. Call the `getModifiers()` method of the object to receive an integer value that indicates which mouse button generated the event.

Check the value against three class variables. It equals `MouseEvent.BUTTON1_MASK` if the left button was clicked, `MouseEvent.BUTTON2_MASK` if the middle button was clicked, and `MouseEvent.BUTTON3_MASK` if the right button was clicked. See `MouseTest.java` and `MouseTest.class` on the Day 12 page of the book's Web site at `http://www.java21days.com` for an example that implements this technique.

For more information, see the Java class library documentation for the `MouseEvent` class: Visit the Web page `http://java.sun.com/j2se/1.4/docs/api/` and click the `java.awt.event` hyperlink to view the classes in that package.

Quiz

Review today's material by taking this three-question quiz.

Questions

1. If you use `this` in a method call, such as `addActionListener(this)`, what object is being registered as a listener?

   (a.) An adapter class

   (b.) The current object

   (c.) No class

2. What is the benefit of subclassing an adapter class such as `WindowAdapter` (which implements the `WindowListener` interface)?

   (a.) You inherit all the behavior of that class.

   (b.) The subclass automatically becomes a listener.

   (c.) You don't need to implement any `WindowListener` methods you won't be using.

3. What kind of event is generated when you press Tab to leave a text field?

   (a.) `FocusEvent`

   (b.) `WindowEvent`

   (c.) `ActionEvent`

Answers

1. (b.) The current object must implement the correct listener interface and the required methods.

2. (c.) Because most listener interfaces contain more methods than you will need, using an adapter class as a superclass saves the hassle of implementing empty methods just to implement the interface.

3. (a.) A user interface component loses focus when the user stops editing that component and moves to a different part of the interface.

Certification Practice

The following question is the kind of thing you could expect to be asked on a Java programming certification test. Answer it without looking at today's material or using the Java compiler to test the code.

Given:

```
import java.awt.event.*;
import javax.swing.*;
import java.awt.*;

public class Interface extends JFrame implements ActionListener {
    public boolean deleteFile;

    public Interface() {
        super("Interface");
        JLabel commandLabel = new JLabel("Do you want to delete the
                file?");
        JButton yes = new JButton("Yes");
        JButton no = new JButton("No");
        yes.addActionListener(this);
        no.addActionListener(this);
        Container cp = getContentPane();
        cp.setLayout( new BorderLayout() );
        JPanel bottom = new JPanel();
        bottom.add(yes);
        bottom.add(no);
        cp.add("North", commandLabel);
        cp.add("South", bottom);
        setContentPane(cp);
        pack();
        setVisible(true);
    }

    public void actionPerformed(ActionEvent evt) {
        JButton source = (JButton) evt.getSource();
        // answer goes here
```

12

```
              deleteFile = true;
         else
              deleteFile = false;
    }

    public static void main(String[] arguments) {
        new Interface();
    }
}
```

Which of the following statements should replace // answer goes here to make the application function correctly?

(a.) if (source instanceof JButton)

(b.) if (source.getActionCommand().equals("yes"))

(c.) if (source.getActionCommand().equals("Yes"))

(d.) if source.getActionCommand() == "Yes"

The answer is available on the book's Web site at http://www.java21days.com. Visit the Day 12 page and click the Certification Practice link.

Exercises

To extend your knowledge of the subjects covered today, try the following exercises:

- Create an application that uses FocusListener to make sure a text field's value is multiplied by -1 and redisplayed any time a user changes it to a negative value.

- Create a simple calculator that adds the contents of two text fields whenever a button is clicked and displays the result as a label.

Where applicable, exercise solutions are offered on the book's Web site at http://www.java21days.com.

DAY **13**

Color, Fonts, and Graphics

Today you will work with Java classes that add graphics to a graphical user interface.

This achievement requires Java2D, a set of classes that supports high-quality two-dimensional graphics, images, color, and text.

Java2D, which includes classes in the `java.awt` and `javax.swing` packages of the Java class library, can be used to draw text and shapes such as circles and polygons; use different fonts, colors, and line widths; and work with colors and patterns.

The `Graphics2D` Class

Java2D begins with the `Graphics2D` class in the `java.awt` package, which represents an environment in which something can be drawn. A `Graphics2D` object may represent a component on a graphical user interface, printer, or another display device.

Graphics2D is a subclass of the Graphics class, which includes extended features required by Java2D.

 Note   Prior versions of Java included rudimentary support for graphics in the Graphics class, but these methods have been supplanted by more sophisticated and efficient alternatives in Java2D.

Before you can start using the Graphics2D class, you need something on which to draw.

Several user-interface components can act as a canvas for graphical operations: panels, windows, even Java applet windows (as you will see in Day 14, "Writing Java Applets").

Once you have an interface component to use as a canvas, you can draw text, lines, ovals, circles, arcs, and rectangles and other polygons on that object.

One component that's suitable for this purpose is JPanel in the javax.swing package. This class represents panels in a graphical user interface that can be empty or contain other components.

The following example creates a frame and a panel, then adds the panel to the frame window:

```
JFrame main = new JFrame("Main Menu");
JPanel pane = new JPanel();
Container content = main.getContentPane();
content.add(pane);
```

The frame's getContentPane() method returns a Container object representing the portion of the frame that can contain other components. The container's add() method is called to add the panel to the frame.

Like many other user-interface components in Java, JPanel objects have a paintComponent(Graphics) method that is called automatically whenever the component should be redisplayed.

Several things could cause paintComponent() to be called, including the following:

- The graphical user interface containing the component is displayed for the first time.
- A window that was displayed on top of the component is closed.
- The graphical user interface containing the component is resized.

By creating a subclass of JPanel, you can override the panel's paintComponent() method and put all of your graphical operations in this method.

As you may have noticed, a `Graphics` object is sent to an interface component's `paintComponent()` method, not a `Graphics2D` object. To create a `Graphics2D` object that represents the component's drawing surface, you must use casting to convert it, as in the following example:

```
public void paintComponent(Graphics comp) {
    Graphics2D comp2D = (Graphics2D)comp;
}
```

The `comp2D` object in this example was produced via casting.

The Graphics Coordinate System

Java2D classes make use of the same x,y coordinate system you have used when setting the size of frames.

Java's coordinate system uses pixels as its unit of measure. The origin coordinate 0,0 is in the upper-left corner of a component.

The value of x coordinates increases to the right of 0,0, and y coordinates increase downward.

When you set the size of a frame by calling its `setSize(int,int)` method, the frame's upper-left corner is at 0,0 and its lower-right corner is at the two arguments sent to `setSize()`.

For example, the following statement creates a frame 425 pixels wide and 130 pixels tall with its lower-right corner at 425,130:

```
setSize(425,130);
```

 Caution This differs from other drawing systems in which the 0,0 origin is at the lower left and y values increase in an upward direction.

13

All pixel values are integers; you can't use decimal numbers to display something at a position between two integer values.

Figure 13.1 depicts Java's graphical coordinate system visually, with the origin at 0,0. Two of the points of a rectangle are at 20,20 and 60,60.

FIGURE 13.1

The Java graphics coordinate system.

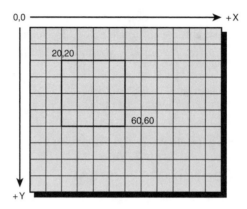

Drawing Text

The easiest thing to draw on an interface component is text.

To draw text, call a Graphics2D object's drawString() method with three arguments:

- the String to display
- the x coordinate where it should be displayed
- the y coordinate where it should be displayed

The x,y coordinates used in the drawString() method represent the pixel at the lower-left corner of the string.

The following paintComponent() method draws the string "Free the bound periodicals." at the coordinate 22,100.

```
public void paintComponent(Graphics comp) {
    Graphics2D comp2D = (Graphics2D)comp;
    comp2D.drawString("Free the bound periodicals.", 22, 100);
}
```

The preceding example uses a default font. To use a different font, you must create an object of the Font class in the java.awt package.

Font objects represent the name, style, and point size of a font.

A Font object is created by sending three arguments to its constructor:

- The font's name
- The font's style
- The font's point size

The name of the font can be the name of a TrueType font, such as Arial, Courier New, Garamond, or Kaiser. If the font is present on the system on which the Java program is running, it will be used. If the font is not present, the default font will be used.

The name also can be one of five generic fonts: Dialog, DialogInput, Monospaced, SanSerif, or Serif. These fonts can be used to specify the kind of font to use without requiring a specific font. This is often a better choice because some font families might not be present on all implementations of Java.

Three Font styles can be selected by using static class variables: Font.PLAIN, Font.BOLD, and Font.ITALIC. These constants are integers, and you can add them to combine effects.

The following statement creates a 24-point Dialog font that is bold and italicized.

```
Font f = new Font("Dialog", Font.BOLD + Font.ITALIC, 24);
```

After you have created a font, you can use it by calling the setFont(*Font*) method of the Graphics2D class with the font as the method argument.

The setFont() method sets the font that will be used for subsequent calls to the drawString() method on the same Graphics2D object. You can call it again later to change the font and draw more text.

The following paintComponent() method creates a new Font object, sets the current font to that object, and draws the string "I'm very font of you." at the coordinate 10,100.

```
public void paintComponent(Graphics comp) {
    Graphics2D comp2D = (Graphics2D)comp;
    Font f = new Font("Arial Narrow", Font.PLAIN, 72);
    comp2D.setFont(f);
    comp2D.drawString("I'm very font of you.", 10, 100);
}
```

Finding Information About a Font

To make text look good in a graphical user interface, you often must figure out how much space the text is taking up on an interface component.

The FontMetrics class in the java.awt package provides methods to determine the size of the characters being displayed with a specified font, which can be used for things like formatting and centering text.

The FontMetrics class can be used for detailed information about the current font, such as the width or height of characters it can display.

To use this class's methods, a FontMetrics object must be created using the getFontMetrics() method. The method takes a single argument: a Font object.

13

Table 13.1 shows some of the information you can find using font metrics. All these methods should be called on a `FontMetrics` object.

TABLE 13.1   Font Metrics Methods

Method Name	Action
stringWidth(String)	Given a string, returns the full width of that string in pixels
charWidth(char)	Given a character, returns the width of that character
getHeight()	Returns the total height of the font

Listing 13.1 shows how the `Font` and `FontMetrics` classes can be used. The `SoLong` application displays a string at the center of a frame, using `FontMetrics` to measure the string's width using the current font.

LISTING 13.1   The Full Text of `SoLong.java`

```
 1: import java.awt.*;
 2: import java.awt.event.*;
 3: import javax.swing.*;
 4:
 5: public class SoLong extends JFrame {
 6:     public SoLong() {
 7:         super("So Long");
 8:         setSize(425, 150);
 9:         setDefaultCloseOperation(JFrame.EXIT_ON_CLOSE);
10:         SoLongPane sl = new SoLongPane();
11:         Container content = getContentPane();
12:         content.add(sl);
13:         setVisible(true);
14:     }
15:
16:     public static void main(String[] arguments) {
17:         SoLong frame = new SoLong();
18:     }
19:
20: }
21:
22: class SoLongPane extends JPanel {
23:     public void paintComponent(Graphics comp) {
24:         Graphics comp2D = (Graphics2D)comp;
25:         Font f = new Font("Monospaced", Font.BOLD, 18);
26:         FontMetrics fm = getFontMetrics(f);
27:         comp2D.setFont(f);
28:         String s = "So long, and thanks for all the fish.";
29:         int x = (getSize().width - fm.stringWidth(s)) / 2;
30:         int y = getSize().height / 2;
```

LISTING 13.1   Continued

```
31:          comp2D.drawString(s, x, y);
32:      }
33: }
34:
```

Figure 13.2 shows the SoLong application. Resize the application to see how the text moves so it remains centered.

FIGURE 13.2

Displaying centered text in a graphical user interface.

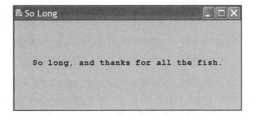

The SoLong application consists of two classes: a frame and a panel subclass called SoLongPane. The text is drawn on the panel by overriding the paintComponent(*Graphics*) method and calling drawing methods of the Graphics2D class inside the method.

The getSize() method in lines 29 and 30 uses the width and height of the panel to determine where the text should be displayed. When the application is resized, the panel is also resized and paintComponent() is called automatically.

Color

The Color and ColorSpace classes of the java.awt package can be used to make your programs more colorful. With these classes you can set the color for use in drawing operations, as well as the background color of an interface component and other windows. You also can translate a color from one color-description system into another.

By default, Java uses colors according to a color-description system called sRGB. In this system, a color is described by the amounts of red, green, and blue it contains—that's what the R, G, and B stand for. Each of the three components can be represented as an integer between 0 and 255. Black is 0,0,0—the complete absence of any red, green, or blue. White is 255,255,255—the maximum amount of all three. You also can represent sRGB values using three floating-point numbers ranging from 0 to 1.0. Java can represent millions of colors between the two extremes using sRGB.

13

A color-description system is called a *color space*, and sRGB is only one such space. There is also CMYK, a system used by printers that describes colors by the amount of cyan, magenta, yellow, and black they contain. Java 2 supports the use of any color space desired, as long as a `ColorSpace` object is used that defines the description system. You also can convert from any color space to sRGB, and vice versa.

Java's internal representation of colors using sRGB is just one color space that's being used in a program. An output device such as a monitor or printer also has its own color space.

When you display or print something of a designated color, the output device might not support the designated color. In this circumstance, a different color will be substituted or a *dithering* pattern will be used to approximate the unavailable color. This happens frequently on the World Wide Web, when an unavailable color is replaced by a dithering pattern of two or more colors that approximate the missing color.

The practical reality of color management is that the color you designate with sRGB will not be available on all output devices. If you need more precise control of the color, you can use `ColorSpace` and other classes in the `java.awt.color` package introduced in Java 2.

For most programs, the built-in use of sRGB to define colors will be sufficient.

Using `Color` Objects

To set the current drawing color, either a `Color` object must be created that represents it, or you must use one of the standard colors available from the `Color` class.

There are two ways to call the `Color` constructor method to create a color:

- Using three integers that represent the sRGB value of the desired color
- Using three floating-point numbers that represent the desired sRGB value

You can specify a color's sRGB value using either three `int` or three `float` values. The following statements show examples of each:

```
Color c1 = new Color(0.807F,1F,0F);

Color c2 = new Color(255,204,102);
```

The c1 object describes a neon green color and c2 is butterscotch.

Note

It's easy to confuse floating-point literals like 0F and 1F with hexadecimal numbers, which were discussed on Day 2, "The ABCs of Programming." Colors are often expressed in hexadecimal, such as when a background color is set for a Web page using the HTML <BODY> tag. The Java classes and methods you work with don't take hexadecimal arguments, so when you see a literal such as 1F or 0F, you're dealing with floating-point numbers.

Testing and Setting the Current Colors

The current color for drawing is designated by using the Graphics class's setColor() method. This method must be called on the Graphics or Graphics2D object that represents the area you're drawing to.

One way to set the color is to use one of the standard colors available as class variables in the Color class.

These colors use the following Color variables (with sRGB values indicated within parentheses):

```
black (0,0,0)                blue (0,0,255)
cyan (0,255,255)             darkGray (64,64,64)
gray (128,128,128)           green (0,255,0)
lightGray (192,192,192)      magenta (255,0,255)
orange (255,200,0)           pink (255,175,175)
red (255,0,0)                white (255,255,255)
yellow (255,255,0)
```

The following statement sets the color for the comp2D object using one of the standard class variables:

```
comp2D.setColor(Color.pink);
```

If you have created a Color object, it can be set in a similar fashion:

```
Color brush = new Color(255,204,102);
comp2D.setColor(brush);
```

After you set the current color, all drawing operations will occur in that color.

You can set the background color for a component, such as a panel or frame, by calling the component's setBackground() and setForeground() methods.

The setBackground() method sets the component's background color. It takes a single argument, a Color object:

```
setBackground(Color.white);
```

There is also a setForeground() method that is called on user-interface components instead of Graphics objects. It works the same as setColor() but changes the color of an interface component, such as a button or a window.

You can use setForeground() in the init() method to set the color for drawing operations. This color is used until another color is chosen with either setForeground() or setColor().

If you want to find out what the current color is, you can use the getColor() method on a Graphics object, or the getForeground() or getBackground() methods on the component.

13

The following statement sets the current color of comp2D—a Graphics2D object—to the same color as a component's background:

```
comp2D.setColor(getBackground());
```

Drawing Lines and Polygons

All the basic drawing commands you learn about today will be Graphics2D methods that are called within a component's paintComponent() method.

This is an ideal place for all drawing operations because paintComponent() is automatically called any time the component needs to be redisplayed.

If another program's window overlaps the component and it needs to be redrawn, putting all the drawing operations in paintComponent() makes sure that no part of the drawing is left out.

Java2D features include the following:

- The capability to draw polygons that are empty and polygons that are filled with a solid color
- Special fill patterns, such as gradients and patterns
- Strokes that define the width and style of a drawing stroke
- Anti-aliasing to smooth edges of drawn objects

User and Device Coordinate Spaces

One of the concepts introduced with Java2D is the difference between an output device's coordinate space and the coordinate space you refer to when drawing an object.

NEW TERM *Coordinate space* is any 2D area that can be described using x,y coordinates.

For all drawing operations prior to Java 2, the only coordinate space used was the *device coordinate space*. You specified the x,y coordinates of an output surface, such as a panel, and those coordinates were used to draw text and other elements.

Java2D requires a second coordinate space that you refer to when creating an object and actually drawing it. This is called the *user coordinate space*.

Before any 2D drawing has occurred in a program, the device space and user space have the 0,0 coordinate in the same place—the upper-left corner of the drawing area.

The user space's 0,0 coordinate can move as a result of the 2D drawing operations being conducted. The x- and y-axes can even shift because of a 2D rotation. You will learn more about the two coordinate systems as you work with Java2D.

Specifying the Rendering Attributes

The next step in 2D drawing is to specify how a drawn object will be rendered. Drawings that are not 2D can select only one attribute: color.

Java2D offers a wide range of attributes for designating color, including line width, fill patterns, transparency, and many other features.

Fill Patterns

Fill patterns control how a drawn object will be filled in. With Java2D, you can use a solid color, gradient fill, texture, or a pattern of your own devising.

A fill pattern is defined by using the `setPaint()` method of `Graphics2D` with a `Paint` object as its only argument. Any class that can be a fill pattern, including `GradientPaint`, `TexturePaint`, and `Color`, can implement the `Paint` interface. The third might surprise you, but using a `Color` object with `setPaint()` is the same thing as using a solid color as the pattern.

NEW TERM A *gradient fill* is a gradual shift from one color at one coordinate point to another color at a different coordinate point. The shift can occur once between the points, which is called an *acyclic gradient*, or it can happen repeatedly, which is a *cyclic gradient*.

Figure 13.3 shows examples of acyclic and cyclic gradients between white and a darker color. The arrows indicate the points that the colors shift between.

FIGURE 13.3

Acyclic and cyclic gradient shifts.

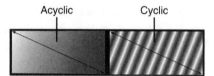

The coordinate points in a gradient do not refer directly to points on the `Graphics2D` object being drawn onto. Instead, they refer to user space and can even be outside the object being filled with a gradient.

Figure 13.4 illustrates this. Both rectangles are filled using the same `GradientPaint` object as a guide. One way to think of a gradient pattern is as a piece of fabric that has been spread over a flat surface. The shapes being filled with a gradient are the patterns cut from the fabric, and more than one pattern can be cut from the same piece of cloth.

13

FIGURE 13.4

*Two rectangles using the
same* GradientPaint.

FIGURE 13.4

*Two rectangles using the
same* GradientPaint.

A call to the GradientPaint constructor method takes the following format:

```
GradientPaint(x1, y1, color1, x2, y2, color2);
```

The point x1,y1 is where the color represented by color1 begins, and x2,y2 is where the shift ends at color2.

If you want to use a cyclic gradient shift, an extra argument is added at the end:

```
GradientPaint(x1, y1, color1, x2, y2, color2, true);
```

The last argument is a Boolean value that is true for a cyclic shift. A false argument can be used for acyclic shifts, or you can omit this argument; acyclic shifts are the default behavior.

After you have created a GradientPaint object, set it as the current paint attribute by using the setPaint() method. The following statements create and select a gradient:

```
GradientPaint pat = new GradientPaint(0f,0f,Color.white,
    100f,45f,Color.blue);
comp2D.setPaint(pat);
```

All subsequent drawing operations to the comp2D object will use this fill pattern until another one is chosen.

Setting a Drawing Stroke

In previous versions of Java, the lines drawn in all graphics operations were 1 pixel wide. Java2D offers the capability to vary the width of the drawing line by using the setStroke() method with a BasicStroke.

A simple BasicStroke constructor takes three arguments:

- A float value representing the line width, with 1.0 as the norm
- An int value determining the style of cap decoration drawn at the end of a line
- An int value determining the style of juncture between two line segments

NEW TERM The endcap- and juncture-style arguments use `BasicStroke` class variables. *Endcap* styles apply to the ends of lines that do not connect to other lines. *Juncture* styles apply to the ends of lines that join other lines.

Possible endcap styles are `CAP_BUTT` for no endpoints, `CAP_ROUND` for circles around each endpoint, and `CAP_SQUARE` for squares. Figure 13.5 shows each endcap style. As you can see, the only visible difference between the `CAP_BUTT` and `CAP_SQUARE` styles is that `CAP_SQUARE` is longer because of the added square endcap.

FIGURE 13.5

Endpoint cap styles.

CAP_BUTT   CAP_ROUND   CAP_SQUARE

Possible juncture styles include `JOIN_MITER`, which joins segments by extending their outer edges, `JOIN_ROUND`, which rounds off a corner between two segments, and `JOIN_BEVEL`, which joins segments with a straight line. Figure 13.6 shows examples of each juncture style.

FIGURE 13.6

Endpoint juncture styles.

JOIN_MITER   JOIN_ROUND   JOIN_BEVEL

The following statements create a `BasicStroke` object and make it the current stroke:

```
BasicStroke pen = BasicStroke(2.0f,
    BasicStroke.CAP_BUTT,
    BasicStroke.JOIN_ROUND);
comp2D.setStroke(pen);
```

The stroke has a width of 2 pixels, plain endpoints, and rounded segment corners.

Creating Objects to Draw

After you have created a `Graphics2D` object and specified the rendering attributes, the final two steps are to create the object and draw it.

A drawn object in Java2D is created by defining it as a geometric shape using a class in the `java.awt.geom` package. You can draw lines, rectangles, ellipses, arcs, and polygons.

The `Graphics2D` class does not have different methods for each of the shapes you can draw. Instead, you define the shape and use it as an argument to `draw()` or `fill()` methods.

13

Lines

Lines are created using the Line2D.Float class. This class takes four arguments: the x,y coordinate of one endpoint followed by the x,y coordinate of the other. Here's an example:

```
Line2D.Float ln = new Line2D.Float(60F,5F,13F,28F);
```

This statement creates a line between 60,5 and 13,28. Note that an F is used with the literals sent as arguments. Otherwise, the Java compiler would assume that the values were integers.

Rectangles

Rectangles are created by using the Rectangle2D.Float class or Rectangle2D.Double class. The difference between the two is that one takes float arguments and the other takes double arguments.

Rectangle2D.Float takes four arguments: x coordinate, y coordinate, width, and height. The following is an example:

```
Rectangle2D.Float rc = new Rectangle2D.Float(10F,13F,40F,20F);
```

This creates a rectangle at 10,13 that is 40 pixels wide and 20 pixels tall.

Ellipses

Ellipses, which were called ovals in early versions of Java, can be created with the Ellipse2D.Float class. It takes four arguments: x coordinate, y coordinate, width, and height.

The following statement creates an ellipse at 113,25 with a width of 22 pixels and a height of 40 pixels:

```
Ellipse2D.Float ee = new Ellipse2D.Float(113,25,22,40);
```

Arcs

Of all the shapes you can draw in Java2D, arcs are the most complex to construct.

Arcs are created with the Arc2D.Float class, which takes seven arguments:

- The x,y coordinate of an invisible ellipse that would include the arc if it were drawn
- The width and height of the ellipse
- The starting degree of the arc
- The number of degrees it travels on the ellipse
- An integer describing how the arc is closed

The number of degrees traveled by the arc is specified in a counterclockwise direction by using negative numbers.

Figure 13.7 shows where degree values are located when determining the starting degree of an arc. The arc's starting angle ranges from 0 to 359 degrees counterclockwise. On a circular ellipse, 0 degrees is at the 3 o'clock position, 90 degrees is at 12 o'clock, 180 degrees is at 9 o'clock, and 270 degrees is at 6 o'clock.

FIGURE 13.7

Determining the starting degree of an arc.

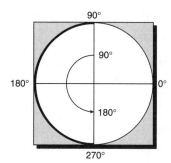

The last argument to the `Arc2D.Float` constructor uses one of three class variables: `Arc2D.OPEN` for an unclosed arc, `Arc2D.CHORD` to connect the arc's endpoints with a straight line, and `Arc2D.PIE` to connect the arc to the center of the ellipse like a pie slice. Figure 13.8 shows each of these styles.

FIGURE 13.8

Arc closure styles.

Arc2D.OPEN   Arc2D.CHORD   Arc2D.PIE

 Note

> The `Arc2D.OPEN` closure style does not apply to filled arcs. A filled arc that has `Arc2D.OPEN` as its style will be closed using the same style as `Arc2D.CHORD`.

13

The following statement creates an `Arc2D.Float` object:

```
Arc2D.Float = new Arc2D.Float(27F, 22F, 42F, 30F, 33F, 90F, Arc2D.PIE);
```

This creates an arc for an oval at 27,22 that is 42 pixels wide and 30 pixels tall. The arc begins at 33 degrees, extends 90 degrees clockwise, and will be closed like a pie slice.

Polygons

Polygons are created in Java2D by defining each movement from one point on the polygon to another. A polygon can be formed from straight lines, quadratic curves, or bezier curves.

The movements to create a polygon are defined as a GeneralPath object, which also is part of the java.awt.geom package.

A GeneralPath object can be created without any arguments, as shown here:

```
GeneralPath polly = new GeneralPath();
```

The moveTo() method of GeneralPath is used to create the first point on the polygon. The following statement would be used if you wanted to start polly at the coordinate 5,0:

```
polly.moveTo(5f, 0f);
```

After creating the first point, the lineTo() method is used to create lines that end at a new point. This method takes two arguments: the x,y coordinate of the new point.

The following statements add three lines to the polly object:

```
polly.lineTo(205f, 0f);
polly.lineTo(205f, 90f);
polly.lineTo(5f, 90f);
```

The lineTo() and moveTo() methods require float arguments to specify coordinate points.

If you want to close a polygon, the closePath() method is used without any arguments, as shown here:

```
polly.closePath();
```

This method closes a polygon by connecting the current point with the point specified by the most recent moveTo() method. You can close a polygon without this method by using a lineTo() method that connects to the original point.

Once you have created an open or closed polygon, you can draw it like any other shape using the draw() and fill() methods. The polly object is a rectangle with points at 5,0, 205,0, 205,90, and 5,90.

Drawing Objects

After you have defined the rendering attributes, such as color and line width, and have created the object to be drawn, you're ready to draw something in all its 2D glory.

All drawn objects use the same Graphics2D methods: draw() for outlines and fill() for filled objects. These take an object as their only argument.

Drawing a Map

The next project you will create is an application that draws a simple map using 2D drawing techniques. Enter the text of Listing 13.2 using your editor and save the file as Map.java.

LISTING 13.2   The Full Text of Map.java

```
 1: import java.awt.*;
 2: import java.awt.geom.*;
 3: import javax.swing.*;
 4:
 5: public class Map extends JFrame {
 6:     public Map() {
 7:         super("Map");
 8:         setSize(350, 350);
 9:         setDefaultCloseOperation(JFrame.EXIT_ON_CLOSE);
10:         MapPane map = new MapPane();
11:         Container content = getContentPane();
12:         content.add(map);
13:         setVisible(true);
14:     }
15:
16:     public static void main(String[] arguments) {
17:         Map frame = new Map();
18:     }
19:
20: }
21:
22: class MapPane extends JPanel {
23:     public void paintComponent(Graphics comp) {
24:         Graphics2D comp2D = (Graphics2D)comp;
25:         comp2D.setColor(Color.blue);
26:         Rectangle2D.Float background = new Rectangle2D.Float(
27:             0F, 0F, (float)getSize().width, (float)getSize().height);
28:         comp2D.fill(background);
29:         // Draw waves
30:         comp2D.setColor(Color.white);
31:         BasicStroke pen = new BasicStroke(2F,
32:         BasicStroke.CAP_BUTT, BasicStroke.JOIN_ROUND);
33:         comp2D.setStroke(pen);
34:         for (int ax = 0; ax < 340; ax += 10)
35:             for (int ay = 0; ay < 340; ay += 10) {
36:                 Arc2D.Float wave = new Arc2D.Float(ax, ay,
37:                     10, 10, 0, -180, Arc2D.OPEN);
38:                 comp2D.draw(wave);
39:             }
40:         // Draw Florida
41:         GradientPaint gp = new GradientPaint(0F, 0F, Color.green,
```

13

continues

Listing 13.2 Continued

```
42:             350F,350F, Color.orange, true);
43:         comp2D.setPaint(gp);
44:         GeneralPath fl = new GeneralPath();
45:         fl.moveTo(10F, 12F);
46:         fl.lineTo(234F, 15F);
47:         fl.lineTo(253F, 25F);
48:         fl.lineTo(261F, 71F);
49:         fl.lineTo(344F, 209F);
50:         fl.lineTo(336F, 278F);
51:         fl.lineTo(295F, 310F);
52:         fl.lineTo(259F, 274F);
53:         fl.lineTo(205F, 188F);
54:         fl.lineTo(211F, 171F);
55:         fl.lineTo(195F, 174F);
56:         fl.lineTo(191F, 118F);
57:         fl.lineTo(120F, 56F);
58:         fl.lineTo(94F, 68F);
59:         fl.lineTo(81F, 49F);
60:         fl.lineTo(12F, 37F);
61:         fl.closePath();
62:         comp2D.fill(fl);
63:         // Draw ovals
64:         comp2D.setColor(Color.black);
65:         BasicStroke pen2 = new BasicStroke();
66:         comp2D.setStroke(pen2);
67:         Ellipse2D.Float e1 = new Ellipse2D.Float(235, 140, 15, 15);
68:         Ellipse2D.Float e2 = new Ellipse2D.Float(225, 130, 15, 15);
69:         Ellipse2D.Float e3 = new Ellipse2D.Float(245, 130, 15, 15);
70:         comp2D.fill(e1);
71:         comp2D.fill(e2);
72:         comp2D.fill(e3);
73:     }
74: }
```

Some observations about the Map application:

- Line 2 imports the classes in the java.awt.geom package. This statement is required because import java.awt.*; in line 1 handles only classes, not packages, available under java.awt.

- Line 24 creates the comp2D object that is used for all 2D drawing operations. It's a cast of the Graphics object that represents the panel's visible surface.

- Lines 31–33 create a BasicStroke object that represents a line width of 2 pixels and then makes this the current stroke with the setStroke() method of Graphics2D.

- Lines 34–39 use two nested `for` loops to create waves from individual arcs.

- Lines 41–42 create a gradient fill pattern from the color green at 0,0 to orange at 50,50. The last argument to the constructor, `true`, causes the fill pattern to repeat itself as many times as needed to fill an object.

- Line 43 sets the current gradient fill pattern using the `setPaint()` method and the `gp` object that was just created.

- Lines 44–62 create the polygon shaped like the state of Florida and draw it. This polygon will be filled with a green-to-orange gradient pattern.

- Line 64 sets the current color to black. This replaces the gradient fill pattern for the next drawing operation because colors are also fill patterns.

- Line 65 creates a new `BasicStroke()` object with no arguments, which defaults to a 1-pixel line width.

- Line 66 sets the current line width to the new `BasicStroke` object `pen2`.

- Lines 67–69 create three ellipses at 235,140, 225,130, and 245,130. Each is 15 pixels wide and 15 pixels tall, making them circles.

Figure 13.9 shows the application running.

FIGURE 13.9

The Map *application.*

Summary

You now have some tools to improve the looks of a Java program. You can draw with lines, rectangles, ellipses, polygons, fonts, colors, and patterns onto a frame, a panel, and other user-interface components using Java2D.

Java2D uses the same two methods for each drawing operation—`draw()` and `fill()`. Different objects are created using classes of the `java.awt.geom` package, and these are used as arguments for the drawing methods of `Graphics2D`.

13

Tomorrow on Day 14, "Writing Java Applets," you'll work with another user-interface component that can be used for drawing operations: the applet window.

Q&A

Q I am confused by what the uppercase "F" is referring to in source code today. It is added to coordinates, as in the method `polly.moveTo(5F, 0F)`. Why is the "F" used for these coordinates and not others, and why is a lowercase "F" used elsewhere?

A The F and f indicate that a number is a floating-point number rather than an integer, and uppercase and lowercase can be used interchangeably. If you don't use one of them, the Java compiler will assume that the number is an int value. Many methods and constructors in Java require floating-point arguments but can handle integers because an integer can be converted to floating-point without changing its value. For this reason, constructors like `Arc2D.Float()` can use arguments such as 10 and 180 instead of 10F and 180F.

Quiz

Review today's material by taking this three-question quiz.

Questions

1. What object is required before you can draw something in Java?

    (a.) `Graphics` or `Graphics2D`

    (b.) `WindowListener`

    (c.) `JFrame`

2. Which of the following three fonts should not be used in a Java 2 program?

    (a.) `serif`

    (b.) `Courier`

    (c.) monospaced

3. What does `getSize().width` refer to?

    (a.) The width of the interface component's window

    (b.) The width of the frame's window

    (c.) The width of any graphical user interface component in Java

Answers

1. (a.)

2. (b.) Choosing specific font names, as opposed to font descriptors like serif and monospaced, limits the flexibility of Java in selecting which font to use on a specific platform.

3. (c.) You can call getSize().width and getSize().height on any component in Java.

Certification Practice

The following question is the kind of thing you could expect to be asked on a Java programming certification test. Answer it without looking at today's material or using the Java compiler to test the code.

Given:

```java
import java.awt.*;
import javax.swing.*;

public class Result extends JFrame {
    public Result() {
        super("Result");
        Container pane = getContentPane();
        JLabel width = new JLabel("This frame is " +
            getSize().width + " pixels wide.");
        pane.add("North", width);
        setSize(220, 120);
    }

    public static void main(String[] arguments) {
        Result r = new Result();
        r.setVisible(true);
    }
}
```

What will be the reported width of the frame, in pixels, when the application runs?

(a.) 0 pixels

(b.) 120 pixels

(c.) 220 pixels

(d.) the width of the user's monitor

13

The answer is available on the book's Web site at http://www.java21days.com. Visit the Day 13 page and click the Certification Practice link.

Exercises

To extend your knowledge of the subjects covered today, try the following exercises:

- Create an application that draws a circle with its radius, x,y position, and color all determined by parameters.
- Create an application that draws a pie graph.

Where applicable, exercise solutions are offered on the book's Web site at http://www.java21days.com.

DAY 14

Writing Java Applets

For most people, their first exposure to the Java programming language was in late 1995, when Netscape Navigator began running *applets*—small Java programs that ran within a World Wide Web browser.

At the time, this was a revolutionary development for the Web, because applets were the first interactive content that could be delivered as part of a Web page.

Although you can do similar things with Macromedia Flash, Microsoft ActiveX, and other technology today, Java remains an effective choice for Web-based programming.

Today, you will start with the basics of applet programming:

- The differences between applets and applications
- How to create a simple applet
- How to put an applet onto a Web page
- How to send information from a Web page to an applet
- How to store an applet in an archive for faster download off a Web page
- How to create applets that are run by the Java Plug-in, a virtual machine that improves a Web browser's Java support

How Applets and Applications Are Different

The difference between Java applets and applications lies in how they are run.

Applications are run by loading the application's main class file with a Java interpreter, such as the java tool in the Java 2 SDK.

Applets, on the other hand, are run on any browser that supports Java. This includes current versions of Netscape Navigator, Microsoft Internet Explorer, Opera, and Sun's HotJava browser. Applets also can be tested by using the SDK's appletviewer tool.

For an applet to run, it must be included on a Web page using HTML tags in the same way images and other elements are presented.

When a user with a Java-capable browser loads a Web page that includes an applet, the browser downloads the applet from a Web server and runs it on the Web user's own system using a Java interpreter.

For many years, browsers used their own built-in Java interpreters to run applets. However, Sun also offers its own browser interpreter, the Java Plug-in, which can be configured to run applets in Internet Explorer, Navigator, and Opera.

Like an application, a Java applet includes a class file and any other helper classes that are needed to run the applet. Java's standard class library is included automatically.

Because Java applets run inside a Java browser, some of the work of creating a user interface is already done for the applet programmer. There's an existing window for the applet to run in, a place to display graphics and receive information, and the browser's interface.

 Note

> It is possible for a single Java program to function as both an applet and an application. Although different procedures are used to create these types of programs, they do not conflict with each other. The features specific to applets will be ignored when the program runs as an application, and vice versa.

Applet Security Restrictions

Because Java applets are run on a Web user's system, there are some serious restrictions to what an applet is capable of doing. If these restrictions were not in place, a malicious Java programmer could easily write an applet to delete users' files, collect private information from the system, and commit other security breaches.

As a general rule, Java applets run under a "better safe than sorry" security model. Applets cannot do any of the following:

- They cannot read or write files on the user's file system.
- They cannot communicate with an Internet site other than the one that served the Web page that included the applet.
- They cannot run any programs on the reader's system.
- They cannot load programs stored on the user's system, such as executable programs and shared libraries.

These security measures are in effect for all Java applets run by the built-in interpreters in Internet Explorer and Navigator.

Java applications have none of these restrictions. They can take full advantage of Java's capabilities.

Restrictive security rules also are in place for all applets run by the Java Plug-in, unless they have been digitally signed to verify the identity of the applet publisher. Digitally signed applets have the same access to your computer as Java applications. You'll learn more about them later today.

Caution

Although Java's security model makes it extremely difficult for a malicious applet to do harm to a user's system, it will never be 100 percent secure. Search the Web for "hostile applets," and you'll find discussion of security issues in different versions of Java and how they have been addressed. Java is more secure than other Web programming solutions, such as ActiveX, but all browser users should acquaint themselves with the issue.

Choosing a Java Version

A Java programmer who writes applets must address this issue: For which Java version should I write?

At the time of this writing, Java 1.1 is the most up-to-date version of the language supported by the built-in Java interpreter available for Internet Explorer 6.0 and Internet Explorer 5.0, the browsers used by more than 80 percent of all Web users.

However, with the introduction of Windows XP in fall 2001, Microsoft stopped including the Java interpreter with Internet Explorer. Users must choose to install it when they try to load an applet on a Web page, a process that can take 30 minutes or more on a dial-up modem connection (or around 5 minutes on a cable or DSL connection).

14

To provide a way for applet programmers to make use of current versions of Java, Sun offers the Java Plug-in, a Java interpreter that can be installed as a replacement to other applet interpreters.

Applet programmers generally choose one of the following three options:

- Write an applet using only Java 1.0 features so it will run on all Java-capable browsers.
- Write an applet using only Java 1.0 or 1.1 features so it will run on Navigator 4.0 and higher, Internet Explorer 4 and higher, and Opera 3.6 and higher.
- Write an applet using all Java features and provide a way for users to download and install the Java Plug-in so they can run the applet.

Java 2 has been designed so that in almost all circumstances a program using only Java 1.0 features can compile and run successfully on a Java 1.0 interpreter or 1.0-capable browser. Similarly, an applet using Java 1.1 features can run on a browser supporting that language version.

If an applet uses any feature that was introduced with Java 2, the program won't run successfully on a browser that doesn't support that version of the language, unless the browser has been equipped with the Java Plug-in. The only test environment that always supports the most current version of Java is the latest `appletviewer` from the corresponding SDK.

This is a common source of errors for Java applet programmers. If you write a Java 2 applet and run it on a browser without the plug-in, you will get security errors, class-not-found errors, and other problems that prevent the applet from running.

 Note

> In this book, Java 2 techniques are used for all programs, even applets. There's a wealth of information available in previous editions of this book for applet programmers who don't want to use Java 2, and Sun also offers full documentation for prior versions at http://java.sun.com/infodocs.

One of the enhancements available with the Java Plug-in is a more sophisticated security model. If a Web user accepts a signed applet's security certificate, the applet can run without restriction on the user's system, just as an application can.

Creating Applets

The Java programs you've created up to this point have been Java applications—programs with a main() method that is used to create objects, set instance variables, and call other methods.

Applets do not have a main() method that automatically is called to begin the program. Instead, there are several methods that are called at different points in the execution of an applet. You will learn about these methods today.

All Java 2 applets are subclasses of the JApplet class in the javax.swing package. Applets are graphical user interface components similar to windows. They can contain other components and have layout managers applied to them.

By inheriting from JApplet, your applet has the following built-in behaviors:

- It works as part of a Web browser and can respond to occurrences, such as the browser page being reloaded.
- It can present a graphical user interface and take input from users.

Although an applet can make use of as many other classes as needed, the JApplet class is the main class that triggers the execution of the applet. The subclass of JApplet that you create takes the following form:

```
public class yourApplet extends javax.swing.JApplet {
    // Applet code here
}
```

All applets must be declared public because the JApplet class is a public class. This requirement is true only of your main JApplet class, and any helper classes can be public or private.

When a browser's built-in Java interpreter encounters a Java applet on a Web page, that applet's class is loaded along with any other helper classes it uses. The browser automatically creates an instance of the applet's class and calls methods of the JApplet class when specific events take place.

Different applets that use the same class use different instances, so you could place more than one copy of the same type of applet on a page, and each could behave differently.

Major Applet Activities

Instead of a main() method, applets have methods that are called when specific things occur as the applet runs.

14

An example of a method is `paint()`, which is called whenever the applet's window needs to be displayed or redisplayed.

By default, these methods do nothing. For example, the `paint()` method that is inherited from `JApplet` is an empty method. The `paint()` method is similar to the `paintComponent()` method you worked with on Day 13, "Color, Fonts, and Graphics." For anything to be displayed on the applet window, the `paint()` method must be overridden with behavior to display text, graphics, and other things.

The following sections describe five of the more important methods in an applet's execution: initialization, starting, stopping, destruction, and painting.

Initialization

Initialization occurs when the applet is loaded. *Initialization* might include creating the objects the applet needs, setting up an initial state, loading images or fonts, or setting parameters. To provide behavior for the initialization of an applet, you override the `init()` method as follows:

```
public void init() {
    // Code here
}
```

One useful thing to do when initializing an applet is to set the color of its background window. Colors are represented in Java by the `Color` class, part of the `java.awt` package. Call `setBackground(Color)` in an applet to make the background of the applet window the specified color.

The `Color` class has class variables that represent the most commonly used colors: `black`, `blue`, `cyan`, `darkGray`, `gray`, `green`, `lightGray`, `magenta`, `orange`, `pink`, `red`, `white`, and `yellow`. You can use one of these variables as the argument to the `setBackground()` method, as in the following example:

```
setBackground(Color.green);
```

If used in an applet's `init()` method, the preceding statement makes the entire applet window green.

You also can create your own `Color` objects using integer values for red, green, and blue as three arguments to the constructor:

```
Color avocado = new Color(102, 153, 102);
setBackground(avocado)
```

This code sets the background to avocado green.

Starting

An applet is started after it is initialized. *Starting* also can occur if the applet was previously stopped. For example, an applet is stopped if the browser user follows a link to a different page, and it is started again when the user returns to the page containing the applet.

Starting can occur several times during an applet's life cycle, but initialization happens only once. To provide startup behavior for your applet, override the start() method as follows:

```
public void start() {
    // Code here
}
```

Functionality that you put in the start() method might include starting a thread to control the applet, sending the appropriate messages to helper objects, or in some way telling the applet to begin running.

Stopping

Stopping and starting go hand in hand. *Stopping* occurs when the user leaves the page that contains a running applet, or when an applet stops itself by calling stop() directly. By default, any threads the applet had started continue running even after the user leaves a page. By overriding stop(), you can suspend execution of these threads and restart them if the applet is viewed again. The following shows the form of a stop() method:

```
public void stop() {
    // Code here
}
```

Destruction

Destruction sounds harsher than it is. The destroy() method enables the applet to clean up after itself just before it is freed from memory or the browser exits. You can use this method to kill any running threads or to release any other running objects. Generally, you won't want to override destroy() unless you have specific resources that need to be released, such as threads that the applet has created. To provide cleanup behavior for your applet, override the destroy() method as follows:

```
public void destroy() {
    // Code here
}
```

14

Note
> You might be wondering how destroy() is different from finalize(), which was described on Day 5, "Creating Classes and Methods." The destroy() method applies only to applets; finalize() is a more general-purpose way for a single object of any type to clean up after itself.

Java has an automatic garbage collector that manages memory for you. The collector reclaims memory from resources after the program is done using them, so you don't normally have to use methods such as destroy().

Painting

Painting is how an applet displays something onscreen, be it text, a line, a colored background, or an image. Painting can occur many hundreds of times during an applet's life cycle: once after the applet is initialized, again if the browser window is brought out from behind another window onscreen, again if the browser window is moved to a different position onscreen, and so on. You must override the paint() method of your JApplet subclass to display anything. The paint() method looks like the following:

```
public void paint(Graphics screen) {
    Graphics2D screen2D = (Graphics2D)screen;
    // Code here
}
```

Note that unlike other methods described in this section paint() takes an argument: an instance of the class Graphics. This object is created and passed to paint() by the browser. As you did yesterday with the paintComponent() method, you use casting to create a Graphics2D object from this Graphics object.

You should import the Graphics and Graphics2D classes (part of the java.awt package) into your applet code, usually through an import statement at the top of your Java source file, as in the following:

```
import java.awt.*;
```

The paint() method is called automatically by the environment that contains the applet—normally a Web browser—whenever the applet window must be redrawn.

There are times in an applet when you do something that requires the window to be repainted. For example, if you call setBackground() to change the applet's background to a new color, this won't be shown until the applet window is redrawn.

To request that the window be redrawn in an applet, call the applet's repaint() method without any arguments:

```
repaint();
```

The `Graphics2D` object created in the applet's `paint()` method is required for all text and graphics you will draw in the applet window using Java2D.

A `Graphics2D` object represents an area being drawn to—in this case, an applet window. You can use this object to draw text to the window and handle other simple graphical tasks.

An Example Applet

The `Watch` applet displays the current date and time and updates the information roughly once a second.

This project uses objects of several classes:

- `GregorianCalendar`—A class in the `java.util` package that represents date/time values in the Gregorian calendar system, which is in use throughout the Western world
- `Font`—A `java.awt` class that represents the size, style, and family of a display font
- `Color` and `Graphics2D`—Two `java.awt` classes described in the previous section

Listing 14.1 shows the source code for the applet.

LISTING 14.1 The Full Text of `Watch.java`

```
 1: import java.awt.*;
 2: import java.util.*;
 3:
 4: public class Watch extends javax.swing.JApplet {
 5:     private Color butterscotch = new Color(255, 204, 102);
 6:     private String lastTime = "";
 7:
 8:     public void init() {
 9:         setBackground(Color.black);
10:     }
11:
12:     public void paint(Graphics screen) {
13:         Graphics2D screen2D = (Graphics2D)screen;
14:         Font type = new Font("Monospaced", Font.BOLD, 20);
15:         screen2D.setFont(type);
16:         GregorianCalendar day = new GregorianCalendar();
17:         String time = day.getTime().toString();
18:         screen2D.setColor(Color.black);
19:         screen2D.drawString(lastTime, 5, 25);
20:         screen2D.setColor(butterscotch);
21:         screen2D.drawString(time, 5, 25);
22:         try {
23:             Thread.sleep(1000);
```

14

continues

LISTING 14.1 Continued

```
24:            } catch (InterruptedException e) {
25:                // do nothing
26:            }
27:            lastTime = time;
28:            repaint();
29:        }
30: }
```

After you have created this program, you can compile it but won't be able to try it out yet. The applet overrides the init() method in lines 8–10 to set the background color of the applet window to black.

The paint() method is where this applet's real work occurs. The Graphics object passed into the paint() method holds the graphics state, which keeps track of the current attributes of the drawing surface. The state includes details about the current font and color to use for any drawing operation, for example. By using casting in line 13, a Graphics2D object is created that contains all this information.

Lines 14–15 set up the font for this graphics state. The Font object is held in the type instance variable and set up as a bold, monospaced, 20-point font. The call to setFont() in line 15 establishes this font as the one that will be used for subsequent drawing operations in lines 19 and 21.

Lines 16–17 create a new GregorianCalendar object that holds the current date and time. The getTime() method of this object returns the date and time as a Date object, another class of the java.util package. Calling toString() on this object returns the date and time as a string you can display.

Lines 18–19 set the color for drawing operations to black and then calls drawString() to display the string lastTime in the applet window at the x,y position 5,25. Because the background is black, nothing will appear. You'll see soon why this is done.

Lines 20–21 set the color using a Color object called butterscotch and then display the string time using this color.

Lines 22–26 use a class method of the Thread class to make the program do nothing for 1000 milliseconds (one second). Because the sleep() method will generate an InterruptedException error if anything occurs that should interrupt this delay, the call to sleep() must be enclosed in a try-catch block.

Lines 27–28 make the lastTime variable refer to the same string as the time variable and then call repaint() to request that the applet window be redrawn.

Calling `repaint()` causes the applet's `paint()` method to be called again. When this occurs, `lastTime` is displayed in black text in line 19, overwriting the last `time` string that was displayed. This clears the screen so the new value of `time` can be shown.

 Caution

> Calling `repaint()` within an applet's `paint()` method is not the ideal way to handle animation; it's suitable here primarily because the applet is a simple one. A better technique is to use threads and to devote a thread to the task of animation.

Note that the `0` point for x,y is at the top left of the applet's drawing surface, with positive *y* moving downward, so `50` is at the bottom of the applet. Figure 14.1 shows how the applet's bounding box and the string are drawn on the page.

FIGURE 14.1

Drawing the applet.

If you implement the right applet methods in your class (`init()`, `start()`, `stop()`, `paint()`, and so on), your applet works seamlessly without needing an explicit jumping-off point.

Including an Applet on a Web Page

After you create the class or classes that compose your applet and compile them into class files, you must create a Web page on which to place the applet.

Applets are placed on a page by using the `<APPLET>` tag, an HTML markup tag that works like other HTML elements. There also are numerous Web-page development tools, such as Claris Home Page and Macromedia Dreamweaver, that can be used to add applets to a page without using HTML.

The purpose of the `<APPLET>` tag is to place an applet on a Web page and control how it looks in relation to other parts of the page.

Java-capable browsers use the information contained in the tag to find and execute the applet's compiled class files. In this section, you will learn how to put Java applets on a Web page and how to serve the executable Java files to the Web at large.

14

Note The following section assumes that you have at least a passing understanding of writing HTML pages or know how to use a Web-development tool to approximate HTML. If you need help in this area, one of the co-authors of this book, Laura Lemay, has written *Sams Teach Yourself Web Publishing with HTML and XHTML in 21 Days* with Denise Tyler.

The <APPLET> Tag

The <APPLET> tag is a special extension to HTML for including Java applets in Web pages; the tag is supported by all browsers that handle Java programs. Listing 14.2 shows a simple example of the code for a Web page that includes an applet.

LISTING **14.2**   The Full Text of Watch.html

```
 1: <html>
 2: <head>
 3: <title>Watch Applet</title>
 4: </head>
 5: <body>
 6: <applet code="Watch.class" height="50" width="345">
 7: This program requires a Java-enabled browser.
 8: </applet>
 9: </body>
10: </html>
```

In Listing 14.2, the <APPLET> tag is contained in lines 6–8. In this example, the <APPLET> tag includes three attributes:

- CODE—Specifies the name of the applet's main class file
- WIDTH—Specifies the width of the applet window on the Web page
- HEIGHT—Specifies the height of the applet window

The class file indicated by the CODE attribute must be in the same folder as the Web page containing the applet, unless you use a CODEBASE attribute to specify a different folder. You will learn how to do that later today.

WIDTH and HEIGHT are required attributes because the Web browser needs to know how much space to devote to the applet on the page. It's easy to draw to an area outside the applet window in a program, so you must be sure to provide a window that is large enough.

Text, images, and other Web page elements can be included between the <APPLET> tag and the </APPLET> tag. These are displayed only on browsers that cannot handle Java programs, and including them is a good way to let people know they're missing out on a Java applet because their browser doesn't offer support for applets. If you don't specify anything between <APPLET> and </APPLET>, browsers that don't support Java display nothing in place of the applet.

In its simplest form, the <APPLET> tag uses CODE, WIDTH, and HEIGHT attributes to create a space of the appropriate size, and then loads and runs the applet in that space. The <APPLET> tag also includes several other attributes that can help you better integrate an applet into a Web page's overall design.

Note The attributes available for the <APPLET> tag are almost identical to those for the HTML <IMG> tag.

The ALIGN Attribute

The ALIGN attribute defines how the applet will be aligned on a Web page in relation to other parts of the page. This attribute can have one of eight values:

- ALIGN="Left" aligns the applet to the left of the text that follows the applet on the page.
- ALIGN="Right" aligns the applet to the right of the text that follows the applet on the page.
- ALIGN="TextTop" aligns the top of the applet with the top of the tallest text in the line.
- ALIGN="Top" aligns the applet with the topmost item in the line (which can be another applet, an image, or the top of the text).
- ALIGN="AbsMiddle" aligns the middle of the applet with the middle of the largest item in the line.
- ALIGN="Middle" aligns the middle of the applet with the middle of the text's baseline.
- ALIGN="Baseline" aligns the bottom of the applet with the text's baseline.
- ALIGN="AbsBottom" aligns the bottom of the applet with the lowest item in the line (which can be the text's baseline or another applet or image).

14

To end the formatting that is specified with the ALIGN attribute, you can use the HTML line break tag (<BR>) with the CLEAR attribute. This takes three values:

- <BR CLEAR="Left">—Continues displaying the rest of the Web page at the next clear left margin.
- <BR CLEAR="Right">—Continues displaying the rest of the Web page at the next clear right margin.
- <BR CLEAR="All">—Continues displaying the rest of the Web page at the next clear left and right margin.

Figure 14.2 shows the various alignment options, in which the smiley face in sunglasses is an applet.

FIGURE 14.2

Applet alignment options.

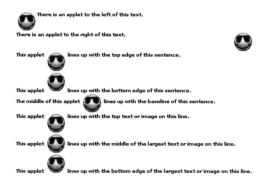

If you are using a Web-development tool that enables you to place Java applets on a page, you should be able to set the ALIGN attribute by choosing "Left", "Right", or one of the other values from within the program.

The HSPACE and VSPACE Attributes

The HSPACE and VSPACE attributes are used to set the amount of space, in pixels, between an applet and its surrounding text. HSPACE controls the horizontal space to the left and right of the applet, and VSPACE controls the vertical space above and below the applet. For example, here's that sample snippet of HTML with vertical space of 50 and horizontal space of 10:

```
<APPLET CODE="ShowSmiley.class" WIDTH=45 HEIGHT=42
ALIGN="Left" VSPACE=50 HSPACE=10>
This applet requires Java.
</APPLET>
```

Figure 14.3 shows how this applet, which displays a smiley face on a white background, would be displayed with other elements of a Web page. The background of the page is a grid, and each grid is 10 × 10 pixels in size. You can use the grid to measure the amount of space between the applet and the text on the page.

FIGURE 14.3

Vertical and horizontal space.

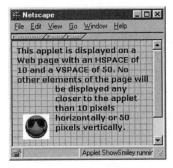

The CODE and CODEBASE Attributes

The CODE and CODEBASE attributes are used to indicate where the applet's main class file and other files can be found. They are used by a Java-capable browser when it attempts to run an applet after downloading it from a Web server.

CODE indicates the filename of the applet's main class file. If CODE is used without an accompanying CODEBASE attribute, the class file will be loaded from the same folder as the Web page containing the applet.

You must specify the .class file extension with the CODE attribute. The following is an example of an <APPLET> tag that loads an applet called Bix.class from the same folder as the Web page:

```
<APPLET CODE="Bix.class" HEIGHT=40 WIDTH=400>
</APPLET>
```

The CODEBASE attribute is used to cause the browser to look in a different folder for the applet and any other files it uses. CODEBASE indicates an alternative folder, or even an alternative World Wide Web site, from which to load the class and other files. The following loads a class called Bix.class from a folder called Torshire:

```
<APPLET CODE="Bix.class" CODEBASE="Torshire" HEIGHT=40 WIDTH=400>
</APPLET>
```

Here's an example in which the Java class files are loaded from a different Web site from the one containing the page:

```
<APPLET CODE="Bix.class" CODEBASE="http://www.java21days.com/javaclasses"
HEIGHT=40 WIDTH=400>
</APPLET>
```

14

Loading an Applet

After you have a main applet class file and an HTML file that uses the applet, you can load the HTML file with a Web browser.

Load the Watch.html page created from Listing 14.2 in a Web browser. One of three things may happen:

- If the browser is equipped with the Java Plug-in, the applet will be loaded and will begin running.
- If the browser does not offer any Java support, the following text will be displayed in place of the applet: "This program requires a Java-enabled browser."
- If the browser is not equipped with the Java Plug-in, but it does have its own built-in Java interpreter, the applet will not be loaded. An empty gray box will be displayed in its place.

If you installed the Java 2 SDK, it's likely you saw the applet running. The Java Plug-in can be installed along with the SDK and configured to replace the built-in Java interpreter in Internet Explorer and other Web browsers.

> **Tip**
>
> If you are using the SDK, you can use the `appletviewer` tool to view applets. Unlike a browser, `appletviewer` displays only the applets that are included on a Web page. It does not display the Web page itself.

Figure 14.4 shows the Watch.html page loaded in Internet Explorer 6 after it was configured to use the Java Plug-in.

FIGURE 14.4

Running an applet on a Web page with the Java Plug-in.

You should try to load this Web page with each of the browsers installed on your computer.

If you can't get the applet to load in a Web browser, but you can load it with the SDK's `appletviewer` tool, the likeliest reason is that the browser isn't equipped with the Java 2 Plug-In yet.

This is a circumstance that will be faced by many of the people using your applet. They must download and install the Java Plug-in before they can view any Java 2 applets, such as Watch, in their browser.

The <OBJECT> Tag

The <APPLET> tag is an HTML extension introduced specifically to present Java programs on Web pages. Today there are other types of programs that can run interactively on a page, including ActiveX controls, NetRexx applets, and Python programs. In order to deal with all these program types without requiring a different tag for each, the <OBJECT> tag has been added to the HTML specification.

To encourage users to install the plug-in, you can use a different HTML tag to load the applet: the <OBJECT> tag.

The <OBJECT> tag is used for all objects—interactive programs and other external elements—that can be presented as part of a Web page. It is supported by versions 4.0 and higher of Netscape Navigator and Microsoft Internet Explorer as well as by appletviewer.

It uses several of the same attributes as the <APPLET> tag, including WIDTH, HEIGHT, ALIGN, HSPACE, and VSPACE.

There are also some differences. Instead of using the CODE attribute to identify the name of the applet's class file, the <OBJECT> tag requires a new <PARAM> tag that takes the following format:

```
<PARAM NAME="Code" VALUE="Classname">
```

If the name of your applet's main class file is Adventure.class, the tag would be

```
<PARAM NAME="Code" VALUE="Adventure.class">
```

The <PARAM> tag is used to specify parameters that are sent to an applet when it runs. They're comparable to command-line arguments, but they also do double duty in <OBJECT> tags. You can have several <PARAM> tags within an applet, and all of them must be located between the <OBJECT> and </OBJECT> tags.

 Note   You'll take a longer look at the <PARAM> tag later today and will create an applet that makes use of it.

14

Another attribute required by the <OBJECT> tag is classid. It identifies the Java Plug-in as the interpreter that should be used to run the applet. This attribute should have a specific value:

```
clsid:8AD9C840-044E-11D1-B3E9-00805F499D93
```

This value is a string that identifies the Java Plug-in. You'll learn more about how to use it later today.

The <OBJECT> tag also has a CODEBASE attribute that contains an URL from which the Java Plug-in can be downloaded. For Java 2 version 1.4, the CODEBASE attribute should have this value:

```
http://java.sun.com/products/plugin/autodl/jinstall-1_4_0-win.cab
```

Listing 14.3 contains a Web page that loads the Watch applet using the <OBJECT> tag:

LISTING 14.3 The Full Text of Watch2.html.

```
 1: <html>
 2: <head>
 3: <title>Watch Applet</title>
 4: </head>
 5: <body>
 6: <object height="50" width="345" classid="clsid:8AD9C840-044E-11D1-B3E9-00805F499D93"
 7: codebase="http://java.sun.com/products/plugin/autodl/jinstall-1_4_0-win.cab">
 8:   <param name="Code" value="Watch.class">
 9: This program requires a Java-enabled browser.
10: </object>
11: </body>
12: </html>
```

If this Web page is loaded by current versions of Internet Explorer or Netscape Navigator, the browser checks for the existence of version 1.4 of the Java Plug-in on the computer running the browser. If it is found, it runs the applet instead of the browser's Java interpreter.

If the plug-in is not found, a dialog box opens asking the user whether the Java Plug-in should be downloaded and installed. The plug-in is around 9M in size and takes 30 to 45 minutes to download on a dial-up modem connection and around 5 to 10 minutes to download on a DSL or cable modem connection.

After the plug-in has been installed, the Watch applet will be run by the plug-in when it is encountered on a Web page. All subsequent Java 2 applets will be run by the Java Plug-in, whether they use the <APPLET> tag or the <OBJECT> tag.

Putting Applets on the Web

After you have an applet that works successfully when you test it locally on your system, you can make the applet available on the World Wide Web.

Java applets are presented by a Web server in the same way that HTML files, images, and other media are. You store the applet in a folder accessible to the Web server—often the same folder that contains the Web page that features the applet. The Web server should be configured to offer Java applets to browsers that support the language.

There are certain files you need to upload to a Web server:

- The HTML page containing the applet
- All `.class` files used by the applet that aren't part of Java's standard class library

If you know how to publish Web pages, image files, and other multimedia files, you don't have to learn any new skills to publish Java applets on your site.

The most common ways to publish on the Web are by sending files through FTP (File Transfer Protocol) or using Web-design software, such as Microsoft FrontPage or Macromedia Dreamweaver, that can publish files to the Web.

Java Archives

The standard way to place a Java applet on a Web page is to use the `<APPLET>` tag or the `<OBJECT>` tag to indicate the primary class file of the applet. A Java-enabled browser then downloads and runs the applet. Any other classes and any other files needed by the applet are downloaded from the Web server.

The problem with running applets in this way is that every file an applet needs—be it another helper class, image, audio file, text file, or anything else—requires a separate connection from a Web browser to the server containing the file. Because a fair amount of time is needed just to make the connection, this can increase the amount of time it takes to download an applet and everything it needs to run.

The solution to this problem is a Java archive, or JAR file. A *Java archive* is a collection of Java classes and other files packaged into a single file. By using a Java archive, the browser makes only one connection to the server rather than several. By reducing the number of files the browser has to load from the server, you can download and run your applet more quickly. Java archives also can be compressed, making the overall file size smaller and therefore faster to download—although it will take some time on the browser side for the files to be decompressed before they can run.

Versions 4.0 and higher of the Navigator and Internet Explorer browsers include support for JAR files. To create these archives, the SDK includes a tool called `jar` that can pack files into Java archives and can unpack them. JAR files can be compressed using the Zip format or packed without using compression. The following command packs all of a folder's class and GIF image files into a single Java archive called `Animate.jar`:

```
jar cf Animate.jar *.class *.gif
```

14

The argument cf specifies two command-line options that can be used when running the jar program. The c option indicates that a Java archive file should be created, and f indicates that the name of the archive file will follow as one of the next arguments.

You also can add specific files to a Java archive with a command, such as

```
jar cf AudioLoop.jar AudioLoop.class beep.au loop.au
```

This creates an AudioLoop.jar archive containing three files: AudioLoop.class, loop.au, and beep.au.

Run jar without any arguments to see a list of options that can be used with the program.

An applet's archive file is specified differently with the <APPLET> and <OBJECT> tags.

In <APPLET> tags, the ARCHIVE attribute is used to show where the archive can be found, as in the following example:

```
<applet code="AudioLoop.class" archive="AudioLoop.jar" width=45 height=42>
</applet>
```

This tag specifies that an archive called AudioLoop.jar contains files used by the applet. Browsers and browsing tools that support JAR files will look inside the archive for files that are needed as the applet runs.

 Caution   Although a Java archive can contain class files, the ARCHIVE attribute does not remove the need for the CODE attribute. A browser still needs to know the name of the applet's main class file in order to load it.

In <OBJECT> tags, the applet's archive file is specified as a parameter using the <PARAM> tag. The tag should have the name attribute with the value "archive" and a value attribute with the name of the archive file.

The following example is a rewrite of the preceding example to use <OBJECT> instead of <APPLET>:

```
<object code="AudioLoop.class" width=45 height=42>
    <param name="archive" value="AudioLoop.jar">
</object>
```

Passing Parameters to Applets

With Java applications, you can pass parameters to the main() method by using arguments on the command line. You then can parse those arguments inside the body of your class, and the application acts accordingly based on the arguments it is given.

Applets, however, don't have command lines. Applets can get different input from the HTML file that contains the <APPLET> or <OBJECT> tag through the use of applet parameters. To set up and handle parameters in an applet, you need two things:

- A special parameter tag in the HTML file
- Code in your applet to parse those parameters

Applet parameters come in two parts: a name, which is simply a name you pick, and a value, which determines the value of that particular parameter. For example, you can indicate the color of text in an applet by using a parameter with the name color and the value red. You can determine an animation's speed using a parameter with the name speed and the value 5.

In the HTML file that contains the embedded applet, you indicate each parameter using the <PARAM> tag, which has two attributes for the name and the value called (surprisingly enough) NAME and VALUE. The <PARAM> tag goes inside the opening and closing <APPLET> tags, as in the following:

```
<APPLET CODE="QueenMab.class" WIDTH=100 HEIGHT=100>
<PARAM NAME=font VALUE="TimesRoman">
<PARAM NAME=size VALUE="24">
A Java applet appears here.
</APPLET>
```

This example defines two parameters to the QueenMab applet: one named font with a value of TimesRoman, and one named size with a value of 24.

The usage of the <PARAM> tag is the same for applets that use the <OBJECT> tag instead of the <APPLET> tag.

Parameters are passed to your applet when it is loaded. In the init() method for your applet, you can retrieve these parameters by using the getParameter() method. The getParameter() method takes one argument, a string representing the name of the parameter you're looking for, and returns a string containing the corresponding value of that parameter. (As with arguments in Java applications, all parameter values are returned as strings.) To get the value of the font parameter from the HTML file, you might have a line such as the following in your init() method:

```
String theFontName = getParameter("font");
```

Note

The names of the parameters as specified in the <PARAM> tag and the names of the parameters in getParameter() must match, including the same case. In other words, <PARAM NAME="eecummings"> is different from <PARAM NAME="EECummings">. If your parameters are not being properly passed to your applet, make sure the parameter cases match.

14

Note that if a parameter you expect has not been specified in the HTML file, getParameter() returns null. Most often, you will want to test for a null parameter and supply a reasonable default, as shown:

```
if (theFontName == null)
    theFontName = "Courier";
```

Keep in mind that getParameter() returns strings; if you want a parameter to be some other object or type, you have to convert it yourself. For example, consider the HTML file for the QueenMab applet. To parse the size parameter and assign it to an integer variable called theSize, you might use the following lines:

```
int theSize;
String s = getParameter("size");
if (s == null)
    theSize = 12;
else theSize = Integer.parseInt(s);
```

Listing 14.4 contains a modified version of the Watch applet that enables the background color to be specified as a parameter called background.

LISTING 14.4   The Full Text of NewWatch.java

```
 1: import java.awt.*;
 2: import java.util.*;
 3:
 4: public class NewWatch extends javax.swing.JApplet {
 5:     private Color butterscotch = new Color(255, 204, 102);
 6:     private String lastTime = "";
 7:     Color back;
 8:
 9:     public void init() {
10:         String in = getParameter("background");
11:         back = Color.black;
12:         if (in != null) {
13:             try {
14:                 back = Color.decode(in);
15:             } catch (NumberFormatException e) {
16:                 showStatus("Bad parameter " + in);
17:             }
18:         }
19:         setBackground(back);
20:     }
21:
22:     public void paint(Graphics screen) {
23:         Graphics2D screen2D = (Graphics2D)screen;
24:         Font type = new Font("Monospaced", Font.BOLD, 20);
25:         screen2D.setFont(type);
26:         GregorianCalendar day = new GregorianCalendar();
27:         String time = day.getTime().toString();
```

LISTING 14.4 Continued

```
28:            screen2D.setColor(back);
29:            screen2D.drawString(lastTime, 5, 25);
30:            screen2D.setColor(butterscotch);
31:            screen2D.drawString(time, 5, 25);
32:            try {
33:                Thread.sleep(1000);
34:            } catch (InterruptedException e) {
35:                // do nothing
36:            }
37:            lastTime = time;
38:            repaint();
39:        }
40: }
```

The NewWatch method contains only a few changes beyond the init() method. A Color object is declared in line 7, and line 28 is changed so it uses this object to set the current color instead of Color.black.

The init() method in lines 9–20 has been rewritten to work with a parameter called background. This parameter should be specified as a hexadecimal string—a pound character ("#") followed by three hexadecimal numbers that represent the red, green, and blue values of a color. Black is #000000, red is #FF0000, green is #00FF00, blue is #0000FF, white is #FFFFFF, and so on. If you are familiar with HTML, you have probably used hexadecimal strings before.

The Color class has a decode(String) class method that creates a Color object from a hexadecimal string. This occurs in line 14; the try-catch block handles the NumberFormatException error that occurs if in does not contain a valid hexadecimal string.

Line 19 sets the applet window to the color represented by the back object. To try this program, create the HTML document in Listing 14.5.

LISTING 14.5 The Full Text of NewWatch.html

```
 1: <html>
 2: <head>
 3: <title>Watch Applet</title>
 4: </head>
 5: <body bgcolor="#996633">
 6: <p>The current time:<br>
 7: <object height="50" width="345" classid="clsid:8AD9C840-044E-11D1-B3E9-00805F499D93"
 8: codebase="http://java.sun.com/products/plugin/autodl/jinstall-1_4_0-win.cab">
 9:    <param name="Code" value="NewWatch.class">
10:    <param name="background" value="#996633">
```

continues

14

LISTING 14.5 Continued

```
11: This program requires a Java-enabled browser.
12: </object>
13: </body>
14: </html>
```

The <OBJECT> tag on this page contains the same classid and codebase attributes you should include with all Java 2 applets. It also has HEIGHT and WIDTH attributes to specify the size of the applet window.

Two parameters are specified on lines 9–10: The first specifies the name of the applet's class file: NewWatch.class. The second has the name background and the value #996633. This string value is the hexadecimal color value for a shade of brown. In Listing 14.4, line 5 of the applet sets the background color of the page using three decimal values.

Loading this HTML file produces the result shown in Figure 14.5.

FIGURE 14.5

Viewing the NewWatch.html page in a browser.

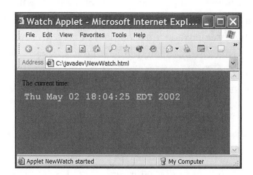

Because the applet window and Web page have the same background color, the edges of the applet are not visible in Figure 14.5. If no background parameter is specified in the HTML code loading the NewWatch applet, the default is black.

Sun's HTML Converter

At this point, you have learned how to use two tags to present applets: <APPLET> and <OBJECT>. There is also a third tag that has been supported on some versions of Netscape Navigator: <EMBED>.

Creating a Web page that supports all of these options is difficult, even for experienced Web developers.

To make the process easier, Sun has created a Java application called HTMLConverter that converts an existing Web page so all its applets are run by the Java Plug-in.

This application is included with the Java 2 SDK and can be run at a command-line.

To make use of the converter, first create a Web page that loads an applet using an <APPLET> tag. The HTMLConverter application will load this page and convert its HTML to use the Plug-In.

After you have created a page, run HTMLConverter with the name of the page as an argument. For example:

```
HTMLConverter Watch3.html
```

The preceding command will convert all applets contained in Watch3.html to be run by the Java Plug-in.

 Caution
> The HTMLConverter application overwrites the existing HTML code on the page. If you also want the non-plug-in version of the page, you should copy the HTML document and run HTMLConverter on that copy.

Summary

Although applets are no longer the focus of Java development, they are still the element of Java technology that reaches the most people. There are applets on thousands of World Wide Web sites; more than 4.6 million Web pages contain an applet, according to the AltaVista search engine at http://www.altavista.com.

Because they are executed and displayed within Web pages, applets can use the graphics, user interface, and event structure provided by the Web browser. This capability provides the applet programmer with a lot of functionality without a lot of extra toil.

Today you learned the basics of applet creation, including the following:

- All Java 2 applets are subclasses of the javax.swing.JApplet class, which provides the behavior the program needs to run within a Web browser.
- Applets have five main methods that cover activities an applet performs as it runs: init(), start(), stop(), destroy(), and paint(). These methods are overridden to provide functionality in an applet.
- Applets are placed on Web pages using the <APPLET> tag or the <OBJECT> tag in HTML, and the <PARAM> tag can be used to specify parameters that customize how the applet functions.

14

- To reduce the time it takes to download an applet from a Web server, you can use Java archive files.

- Applets can receive information from a Web page by using the <PARAM> tag in association with an applet. Inside the body of your applet, you can gain access to those parameters using the getParameter() method.

- If you want to use Java 2 features in your applets, you can create HTML documents that use the Java Plug-in rather than a browser's built-in interpreter.

Q&A

Q **I have an applet that takes parameters and an HTML file that passes it those parameters, but when my applet runs, all I get are null values. What's going on here?**

A Do the names of your parameters (in the NAME attribute) exactly match the names you're testing for in getParameter()? They must be exact, including case, for the match to be made. Also make sure that your <PARAM> tags are inside the opening and closing <APPLET> tags and that you haven't misspelled anything.

Q **Because applets don't have a command line or a standard output stream, how can I do simple debugging output like System.out.println() in an applet?**

A Depending on your browser or other Java-enabled environment, you might have a console window in which debugging output (the result of System.out.println()) appears, or it might be saved to a log file. (Netscape has a Java Console under the Options menu; Internet Explorer uses a Java log file that you must enable by choosing Options, Advanced.)

You can continue to print messages using System.out.println() in your applets—just remember to remove them after you're done so they don't confuse your users.

Q **An applet I am trying to run doesn't work—all I see is a gray box. Is there a place I can view any error messages generated by this applet?**

A If you're using the Java Plug-in to run applets, you can view error messages and other information by opening the Java Console. In Windows, double-click the Java cup icon in the System Tray. Some versions of Netscape Navigator make the Java output window available as a pull-down menu. As for Microsoft Internet Explorer on Windows, version 4.0 saves a log in the text file javalog.txt in your main \WINDOWS\JAVA folder (often C:\WINDOWS\JAVA).

Quiz

Review today's material by taking this three-question quiz.

Questions

1. Which class should an applet inherit from if Swing features will be used in the program?

   (a.) `java.applet.Applet`

   (b.) `javax.swing.JApplet`

   (c.) Either one

2. What method is called whenever an applet window is obscured and must be redrawn?

   (a.) `start()`

   (b.) `init()`

   (c.) `paint()`

3. What happens if you put a Java 2 applet on a Web page using the `<APPLET>` tag and it is loaded by a copy of Internet Explorer 6 that does not include the Java Plug-in?

   (a.) It runs correctly.

   (b.) It doesn't run and an empty gray box is displayed.

   (c.) The user is offered a chance to download and install the Java Plug-in.

Answers

1. (b.) If you're going to use Swing's improved interface and event-handling capabilities, the applet must be a subclass of `JApplet`.

2. (c.) You also can request that the applet window be redisplayed by calling the applet's `repaint()` method.

3. (b.) The applet won't run because Internet Explorer's Java interpreter doesn't support Java 2 applets. The user won't be given a chance to download and install the Java Plug-in unless you use the <OBJECT> tag.

Certification Practice

The following question is the kind of thing you could expect to be asked on a Java programming certification test. Answer it without looking at today's material or using the Java compiler to test the code.

14

If you want to create an applet with a graphical user interface, which method should you override to create interface components and add them to the applet?

(a.) `paint(Graphics)`

(b.) `start()`

(c.) `stop()`

(d.) `init()`

The answer is available on this book's Web site at `http://www.java21days.com`. Visit the Day 14 page and click the Certification Practice link.

Exercises

To extend your knowledge of the subjects covered today, try the following exercises:

- Enhance the `NewWatch` applet so you can set the color of the text with a parameter.
- Create an applet that takes two numbers using text fields and adds them together when an Add button is pushed, displaying the result on a label.

Where applicable, exercise solutions are offered on this book's Web site at `http://www.java21days.com`.

WEEK 3

Java Programming

15

16

17

18

19

20

21

DAY **15**

Working with Input and Output

Many of the programs you create with Java will need to interact with some kind of data source. There are countless ways in which information can be stored on a computer, including files on a hard drive or CD-ROM, pages on a Web site, and even the computer's memory.

You might expect to need a different technique to handle each different storage device. Fortunately, that isn't the case.

In Java, information can be stored and retrieved using a communications system called streams, which are implemented in the `java.io` package.

Today you will learn how to create input streams to read information and output streams to store information. You'll work with each of the following:

- Byte streams, which are used to handle bytes, integers, and other simple data types
- Character streams, which handle text files and other text sources

You can deal with all data the same way once you know how to work with an input stream, whether the information is coming from a disk, the Internet, or even another program. The same holds for using output streams to transmit data.

> Java 2 version 1.4 introduces `java.nio`, a new package for advanced input and output programming. Because this package is most useful in network programming, it will be discussed during Day 17, "Communicating Across the Internet."

Introduction to Streams

In Java all data are written and read using streams. Streams, like the bodies of water that share the same name, carry something from one place to another.

NEW TERM A *stream* is a path traveled by data in a program. An *input stream* sends data from a source into a program, and an *output stream* sends data from a program to a destination.

You will deal with two types of streams today: byte streams and character streams. *Byte streams* carry integers with values that range from 0 to 255. A diverse assortment of data can be expressed in byte format, including numerical data, executable programs, Internet communications, and bytecode—the class files that are run by a Java virtual machine.

In fact, every kind of data imaginable can be expressed using either individual bytes or a series of bytes combined with each other.

NEW TERM *Character streams* are a specialized type of byte stream that handles only textual data. They're distinguished from byte streams because Java's character set supports Unicode, a standard that includes many more characters than could be expressed easily using bytes.

Any kind of data that involves text should use character streams, including text files, Web pages, and other common types of text.

Using a Stream

The procedure for using either a byte stream or a character stream in Java is largely the same. Before you start working with the specifics of the `java.io` classes, it's useful to walk through the process of creating and using streams.

For an input stream, the first step is to create an object that is associated with the data source. For example, if the source is a file on your hard drive, a `FileInputStream` object could be associated with this file.

15

After you have a stream object, you can read information from that stream by using one of the object's methods. FileInputStream includes a read() method that returns a byte read from the file.

When you're done reading information from the stream, you call the close() method to indicate that you're done using the stream.

For an output stream, you begin by creating an object that's associated with the data's destination. One such object can be created from the BufferedWriter class, which represents an efficient way to create text files.

The write() method is the simplest way to send information to the output stream's destination. For instance, a BufferedWriter write() method can send individual characters to an output stream.

As with input streams, the close() method is called on an output stream when you have no more information to send.

Filtering a Stream

The simplest way to use a stream is to create it and then call its methods to send or receive data, depending on whether it's an output stream or an input stream.

Many of the classes you will work with today achieve more sophisticated results when a filter is associated with a stream before reading or writing any data.

NEW TERM   A *filter* is a type of stream that modifies the way an existing stream is handled. Think of a dam on a mountain stream. The dam regulates the flow of water from the points upstream to the points downstream. The dam is a type of filter—remove it, and the water would flow in a much less controlled fashion.

The procedure for using a filter on a stream is as follows:

- Create a stream associated with a data source or a data destination.
- Associate a filter with that stream.
- Read or write data from the filter rather than the original stream.

The methods you call on a filter are the same as the methods you would call on a stream. There are read() and write() methods, just as there would be on an unfiltered stream.

You can even associate a filter with another filter, so the following path for information is possible: an input stream associated with a text file, which is filtered through a Spanish-to-English translation filter, which is then filtered through a no-profanity filter, and is finally sent to its destination—a human being who wants to read it.

If this is confusing in the abstract, you will have opportunities to see the process in practice in the following sections.

Handling Exceptions

There are several exceptions in the `java.io` package that may occur when you are working with files and streams.

A `FileNotFound` exception occurs when you try to create a stream or file object using a file that couldn't be located.

An `EOFException` indicates that the end of a file has been reached unexpectedly as data was being read from the file through an input stream.

These exceptions are subclasses of `IOException`. One way to deal with all of them is to enclose all input and output statements in a `try-catch` block that catches `IOException` objects. Call the exception's `toString()` method in the `catch` block to find out more about the problem.

Byte Streams

All byte streams are either a subclass of `InputStream` or `OutputStream`. These classes are abstract, so you cannot create a stream by creating objects of these classes directly. Instead, you create streams through one of their subclasses, such as the following:

- `FileInputStream` and `FileOutputStream`—Byte streams stored in files on disk, CD-ROM, or other storage devices
- `DataInputStream` and `DataOutputStream`—A filtered byte stream from which data such as integers and floating-point numbers can be read

`InputStream` is the superclass of all input streams.

File Streams

The byte streams you will work with most often are likely to be file streams, which are used to exchange data with files on your disk drives, CD-ROMs, or other storage devices you can refer to by using a folder path and filename.

You can send bytes to a file output stream and receive bytes from a file input stream.

File Input Streams

A file input stream can be created with the `FileInputStream(String)` constructor. The `String` argument should be the name of the file. You can include a path reference with

15

the filename, which enables the file to be in a different folder from the class loading it. The following statement creates a file input stream from the file scores.dat:

```
FileInputStream fis = new FileInputStream("scores.dat");
```

After you create a file input stream, you can read bytes from the stream by calling its read() method. This method returns an integer containing the next byte in the stream. If the method returns a -1, which is not a possible byte value, this signifies that the end of the file stream has been reached.

To read more than one byte of data from the stream, call its read(byte[], *int*, *int*) method. The arguments to this method are as follows:

1. A byte array where the data will be stored
2. The element inside the array where the data's first byte should be stored
3. The number of bytes to read

Unlike the other read() method, this does not return data from the stream. Instead, it returns either an integer that represents the number of bytes read or -1 if no bytes were read before the end of the stream was reached.

The following statements use a while loop to read the data in a FileInputStream object called diskfile:

```
int newByte = 0;
while (newByte != -1) {
    newByte = diskfile.read();
    System.out.print(newByte + " ");
}
```

This loop reads the entire file referenced by diskfile one byte at a time and displays each byte, followed by a space character. It also will display a -1 when the end of the file has been reached; you could guard against this easily with an if statement.

The ReadBytes application in Listing 15.1 uses a similar technique to read a file input stream. The input stream's close() method is used to close the stream after the last byte in the file is read. This must be done to free system resources associated with the open file.

LISTING 15.1 The Full Text of ReadBytes.java

```
1: import java.io.*;
2:
3: public class ReadBytes {
4:     public static void main(String[] arguments) {
5:         try {
6:             FileInputStream file = new
7:                 FileInputStream("class.dat");
```

continues

LISTING 15.1 Continued

```
 8:              boolean eof = false;
 9:              int count = 0;
10:              while (!eof) {
11:                  int input = file.read();
12:                  System.out.print(input + " ");
13:                  if (input == -1)
14:                      eof = true;
15:                  else
16:                      count++;
17:              }
18:              file.close();
19:              System.out.println("\nBytes read: " + count);
20:          } catch (IOException e) {
21:              System.out.println("Error -- " + e.toString());
22:          }
23:      }
24: }
```

If you run this program, you'll get the following error message:

```
Error -- java.io.FileNotFoundException: class.dat (The system
cannot find the file specified).
```

This error message looks like the kind of exception generated by the compiler, but it's actually coming from the catch block in lines 20–22 of the ReadBytes application. The exception is being thrown by lines 6–7 because the class.dat file cannot be found.

You need a file of bytes in which to read. This can be any file; a suitable choice is the program's class file, which contains the bytecode instructions executed by the Java virtual machine. Create this file by making a copy of ReadBytes.class and renaming the copy class.dat. Don't rename the ReadBytes.class file or you won't be able to run the program.

Tip

> Windows users can use MS-DOS in a command-line window to create
> class.dat. Go to the folder that contains ReadBytes.class and use the fol-
> lowing command:
>
> copy ReadBytes.class class.dat
>
> UNIX users can type the following at a command line:
>
> cp ReadBytes.class class.dat

When you run the program, each byte in `class.dat` will be displayed, followed by a count of the total number of bytes. If you used `ReadBytes.class` to create `class.dat`, the last several lines of output should resemble the following:

```
177 0 1 0 0 0 96 0 99 0 17 0 1 0 25 0 0 0 62 0 15 0 0 0 6 0 10 0 8
0 12 0 9 0 14 0 10 0 17 0 11 0 23 0 12 0 49 0 13 0 55 0 14 0 60 0
16 0 63 0 10 0 67 0 18 0 71 0 19 0 96 0 20 0 99 0 21 0 128 0 23 0
1 0 28 0 0 0 2 0 29 -1
Bytes read: 953
```

The number of bytes displayed on each line of output depends on the column width that text can occupy on your system. The bytes shown depend on the file used to create `class.dat`.

File Output Streams

A file output stream can be created with the `FileOutputStream(String)` constructor. The usage is the same as the `FileInputStream(String)` constructor, so you can specify a path along with a filename.

You have to be careful when specifying the file associated with an output stream. If it's the same as an existing file, the original will be wiped out when you start writing data to the stream.

You can create a file output stream that appends data after the end of an existing file with the `FileOutputStream(String, boolean)` constructor. The string specifies the file, and the Boolean argument should equal `true` to append data instead of overwriting existing data.

The file output stream's `write(int)` method is used to write bytes to the stream. After the last byte has been written to the file, the stream's `close()` method closes the stream.

To write more than one byte, the `write(byte[], int, int)` method can be used. This works in a manner similar to the `read(byte[], int, int)` method described previously. The arguments to this method are the byte array containing the bytes to output, the starting point in the array, and the number of bytes to write.

The `WriteBytes` application in Listing 15.2 writes an integer array to a file output stream.

LISTING 15.2   The Full Text of `WriteBytes.java`

```
1: import java.io.*;
2:
3: public class WriteBytes {
4:     public static void main(String[] arguments) {
5:         int[] data = { 71, 73, 70, 56, 57, 97, 15, 0, 15, 0,
6:             128, 0, 0, 255, 255, 255, 0, 0, 0, 44, 0, 0, 0,
```

continues

LISTING 15.2   Continued

```
 7:                0, 15, 0, 15, 0, 0, 2, 33, 132, 127, 161, 200,
 8:                185, 205, 84, 128, 241, 81, 35, 175, 155, 26,
 9:                228, 254, 105, 33, 102, 121, 165, 201, 145, 169,
10:                154, 142, 172, 116, 162, 240, 90, 197, 5, 0, 59 };
11:        try {
12:            FileOutputStream file = new
13:                FileOutputStream("pic.gif");
14:            for (int i = 0; i < data.length; i++)
15:                file.write(data[i]);
16:            file.close();
17:        } catch (IOException e) {
18:            System.out.println("Error -- " + e.toString());
19:        }
20:    }
21: }
```

The following things are taking place in this program:

- Lines 5–10—Create an integer array called data with 66 elements
- Lines 12 and 13—Create a file output stream with the filename pic.gif in the same folder as the WriteBytes.class file
- Lines 14 and 15—Use a for loop to cycle through the data array and write each element to the file stream
- Line 16—Closes the file output stream

After you run this program, you can display the pic.gif file in any Web browser or graphics-editing tool. It's a small image file in the GIF format, as shown in Figure 15.1.

FIGURE 15.1

The pic.gif *file (enlarged).*

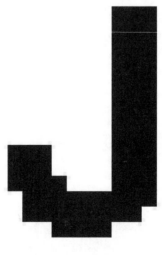

Filtering a Stream

 Filtered streams are streams that modify the information sent through an existing stream. They are created using the subclasses `FilterInputStream` and `FilterOutputStream`.

These classes do not handle any filtering operations themselves. Instead, they have subclasses, such as `BufferInputStream` and `DataOutputStream`, that handle specific types of filtering.

Byte Filters

Information is delivered more quickly if it can be sent in large chunks, even if those chunks are received faster than they can be handled.

As an example of this, consider which of the following book-reading techniques is faster:

- A friend lends you a book in its entirety and you read it.
- A friend lends you a book one page at a time and doesn't give you a new page until you have finished the previous one.

Obviously, the first technique is going to be faster and more efficient. The same benefits are true of buffered streams in Java.

 A *buffer* is a storage place where data can be kept before it is needed by a program that reads or writes that data. By using a buffer, you can get data without always going back to the original source of the data.

Buffered Streams

A buffered input stream fills a buffer with data that hasn't been handled yet. When a program needs this data, it looks to the buffer first before going to the original stream source.

Buffered byte streams use the `BufferedInputStream` and `BufferedOutputStream` classes.

A buffered input stream is created using one of the following two constructors:

- `BufferedInputStream(InputStream)`—Creates a buffered input stream for the specified *InputStream* object
- `BufferedInputStream(InputStream, int)`—Creates the specified *InputStream* buffered stream with a buffer of *int* size

The simplest way to read data from a buffered input stream is to call its `read()` method with no arguments, which normally returns an integer from 0 to 255 representing the next byte in the stream. If the end of the stream has been reached and no byte is available, -1 is returned.

You also can use the read(*byte[]*, *int*, *int*) method available for other input streams, which loads stream data into a byte array.

A buffered output stream is created using one of these two constructors:

- BufferedOutputStream(*OutputStream*)—Creates a buffered output stream for the specified *OutputStream* object
- BufferedOutputStream(*OutputStream*, *int*)—Creates the specified *OutputStream* buffered stream with a buffer of *int* size

The output stream's write(*int*) method can be used to send a single byte to the stream, and the write(*byte[]*, *int*, *int*) method writes multiple bytes from the specified byte array. The arguments to this method are the byte array, array starting point, and number of bytes to write.

Note

> Although the write() method takes an integer as input, the value should be from 0 to 255. If you specify a number higher than 255, it will be stored as the remainder of the number divided by 256. You can test this when running the project you will create later in this day.

When data is directed to a buffered stream, it will not be output to its destination until the stream fills or the buffered stream's flush() method is called.

The next project, the BufferDemo application, writes a series of bytes to a buffered output stream associated with a text file. The first and last integers in the series are specified as two arguments, as in the following SDK command:

```
java BufferDemo 7 64
```

After writing to the text file, BufferDemo creates a buffered input stream from the file and reads the bytes back in. Listing 15.3 contains the source code.

LISTING 15.3   The Full Text of BufferDemo.java

```
 1: import java.io.*;
 2:
 3: public class BufferDemo {
 4:     public static void main(String[] arguments) {
 5:         int start = 0;
 6:         int finish = 255;
 7:         if (arguments.length > 1) {
 8:             start = Integer.parseInt(arguments[0]);
 9:             finish = Integer.parseInt(arguments[1]);
10:         } else if (arguments.length > 0)
11:             start = Integer.parseInt(arguments[0]);
```

LISTING 15.3   Continued

```
12:             ArgStream as = new ArgStream(start, finish);
13:             System.out.println("\nWriting: ");
14:             boolean success = as.writeStream();
15:             System.out.println("\nReading: ");
16:             boolean readSuccess = as.readStream();
17:         }
18: }
19:
20: class ArgStream {
21:     int start = 0;
22:     int finish = 255;
23:
24:     ArgStream(int st, int fin) {
25:         start = st;
26:         finish = fin;
27:     }
28:
29:     boolean writeStream() {
30:         try {
31:             FileOutputStream file = new
32:                 FileOutputStream("numbers.dat");
33:             BufferedOutputStream buff = new
34:                 BufferedOutputStream(file);
35:             for (int out = start; out <= finish; out++) {
36:                 buff.write(out);
37:                 System.out.print(" " + out);
38:             }
39:             buff.close();
40:             return true;
41:         } catch (IOException e) {
42:             System.out.println("Exception: " + e.getMessage());
43:             return false;
44:         }
45:     }
46:
47:     boolean readStream() {
48:         try {
49:             FileInputStream file = new
50:                 FileInputStream("numbers.dat");
51:             BufferedInputStream buff = new
52:                 BufferedInputStream(file);
53:             int in = 0;
54:             do {
55:                 in = buff.read();
56:                 if (in != -1)
57:                     System.out.print(" " + in);
58:             } while (in != -1);
59:             buff.close();
```

continues

LISTING 15.3 Continued

```
60:                 return true;
61:             } catch (IOException e) {
62:                 System.out.println("Exception: " + e.getMessage());
63:                 return false;
64:             }
65:     }
66: }
```

This program's output depends on the two arguments specified when it was run. If you use 4 and 13, the following output is shown:

```
Writing:
 4 5 6 7 8 9 10 11 12 13
Reading:
 4 5 6 7 8 9 10 11 12 13
```

This application consists of two classes: BufferDemo and a helper class called ArgStream. BufferDemo gets the two arguments' values, if they are provided, and uses them in the ArgStream() constructor.

The writeStream() method of ArgStream is called in line 14 to write the series of bytes to a buffered output stream, and the readStream() method is called in line 16 to read those bytes back.

Even though they are moving data in two directions, the writeStream() and readStream() methods are substantially the same. They take the following format:

- The filename, numbers.dat, is used to create a file input or output stream.
- The file stream is used to create a buffered input or output stream.
- The buffered stream's write() method is used to send data, or the read() method is used to receive data.
- The buffered stream is closed.

Because file streams and buffered streams throw IOException objects if an error occurs, all operations involving the streams are enclosed in a try-catch block for this exception.

> The boolean return values in writeStream() and readStream() indicate whether the stream operation was completed successfully. They aren't used in this program, but it's good practice to let callers of these methods know if something goes wrong.

Console Input Streams

One of the things many experienced programmers miss when they begin learning Java is the ability to read textual or numeric input from the console while running an application. There is no input method comparable to the output methods `System.out.print()` and `System.out.println()`.

Now that you can work with buffered input streams, you can put them to use receiving console input.

The `System` class, part of the `java.lang` package, has a class variable called `in` that is an `InputStream` object. This object receives input from the keyboard through the stream.

You can work with this stream as you would any other input stream. The following statement creates a new buffered input stream associated with the `System.in` input stream:

```
BufferedInputStream command = new BufferedInputStream(System.in);
```

The next project, the `ConsoleInput` class, contains a class method you can use to receive console input in any of your Java applications. Enter the text of Listing 15.4 in your editor, and save the file as `ConsoleInput.java`.

LISTING 15.4   The Full Text of `ConsoleInput.java`

```
 1: import java.io.*;
 2:
 3: public class ConsoleInput {
 4:     public static String readLine() {
 5:         StringBuffer response = new StringBuffer();
 6:         try {
 7:             BufferedInputStream buff = new
 8:                 BufferedInputStream(System.in);
 9:             int in = 0;
10:             char inChar;
11:             do {
12:                 in = buff.read();
13:                 inChar = (char) in;
14:                 if (in != -1) {
15:                     response.append(inChar);
16:                 }
17:             } while ((in != -1) & (inChar != '\n'));
18:             buff.close();
19:             return response.toString();
20:         } catch (IOException e) {
21:             System.out.println("Exception: " + e.getMessage());
22:             return null;
23:         }
24:     }
```

continues

LISTING 15.4 Continued

```
25:
26:     public static void main(String[] arguments) {
27:         System.out.print("\nWhat is your name? ");
28:         String input = ConsoleInput.readLine();
29:         System.out.println("\nHello, " + input);
30:     }
31: }
```

The ConsoleInput class includes a main() method that demonstrates how it can be used. When you compile and run it as an application, the output should resemble the following:

```
What is your name? Amerigo Vespucci

Hello, Amerigo Vespucci
```

Data Streams

If you need to work with data that isn't represented as bytes or characters, you can use data input and data output streams. These streams filter an existing byte stream so each of the following primitive types can be read or written directly from the stream: boolean, byte, double, float, int, long, and short.

A data input stream is created with the DataInputStream(*InputStream*) constructor. The argument should be an existing input stream, such as a buffered input stream or a file input stream.

A data output stream requires the DataOutputStream(*OutputStream*) constructor, which indicates the associated output stream.

The following list indicates the read and write methods that apply to data input and output streams, respectively:

- readBoolean(), writeBoolean(*boolean*)
- readByte(), writeByte(*integer*)
- readDouble(), writeDouble(*double*)
- readFloat(), writeFloat(*float*)
- readInt(), writeInt(*int*)
- readLong(), writeLong(*long*)
- readShort(), writeShort(*int*)

Each input method returns the primitive data type indicated by the name of the method. For example, the readFloat() method returns a float value.

15

There also are `readUnsignedByte()` and `readUnsignedShort()` methods that read in unsigned `byte` and `short` values. These are not data types supported by Java, so they are returned as `int` values.

Note

> Unsigned bytes have values ranging from 0 to 255. This differs from Java's `byte` variable type, which ranges from -128 to 127. Along the same line, an unsigned `short` value ranges from 0 to 65,535, instead of the -32,768 to 32,767 range supported by Java's `short` type.

A data input stream's different read methods do not all return a value that can be used as an indicator that the end of the stream has been reached.

As an alternative, you can wait for an `EOFException` (end-of-file exception) to be thrown when a read method reaches the end of a stream. The loop that reads the data can be enclosed in a `try` block, and the associated `catch` statement should handle only `EOFException` objects. You can call `close()` on the stream and take care of other cleanup tasks inside the `catch` block.

This is demonstrated in the next project. Listings 15.5 and 15.6 contain two programs that use data streams. The `WritePrimes` application writes the first 400 prime numbers as integers to a file called `400primes.dat`. The `ReadPrimes` application reads the integers from this file and displays them.

LISTING 15.5   The Full Text of `WritePrimes.java`

```
 1: import java.io.*;
 2:
 3: class WritePrimes {
 4:     public static void main(String[] arguments) {
 5:         int[] primes = new int[400];
 6:         int numPrimes = 0;
 7:         // candidate: the number that might be prime
 8:         int candidate = 2;
 9:         while (numPrimes < 400) {
10:             if (isPrime(candidate)) {
11:                 primes[numPrimes] = candidate;
12:                 numPrimes++;
13:             }
14:             candidate++;
15:         }
16:
17:         try {
18:             // Write output to disk
```

continues

LISTING 15.5   Continued

```
19:                    FileOutputStream file = new
20:                        FileOutputStream("400primes.dat");
21:                    BufferedOutputStream buff = new
22:                        BufferedOutputStream(file);
23:                    DataOutputStream data = new
24:                        DataOutputStream(buff);
25:
26:                    for (int i = 0; i < 400; i++)
27:                        data.writeInt(primes[i]);
28:                    data.close();
29:                } catch (IOException e) {
30:                    System.out.println("Error -- " + e.toString());
31:                }
32:        }
33:
34:        public static boolean isPrime(int checkNumber) {
35:            double root = Math.sqrt(checkNumber);
36:            for (int i = 2; i <= root; i++) {
37:                if (checkNumber % i == 0)
38:                    return false;
39:            }
40:            return true;
41:        }
42: }
```

LISTING 15.6   The Full Text of ReadPrimes.java

```
 1: import java.io.*;
 2:
 3: class ReadPrimes {
 4:     public static void main(String[] arguments) {
 5:         try {
 6:             FileInputStream file = new
 7:                 FileInputStream("400primes.dat");
 8:             BufferedInputStream buff = new
 9:                 BufferedInputStream(file);
10:             DataInputStream data = new
11:                 DataInputStream(buff);
12:
13:             try {
14:                 while (true) {
15:                     int in = data.readInt();
16:                     System.out.print(in + " ");
17:                 }
18:             } catch (EOFException eof) {
19:                 buff.close();
```

15

LISTING 15.6   Continued

```
20:               }
21:          } catch (IOException e) {
22:               System.out.println("Error -- " + e.toString());
23:          }
24:     }
25: }
```

Most of the WritePrimes application is taken up with logic to find the first 400 prime numbers. After you have an integer array containing the first 400 primes, it is written to a data output stream in lines 17–31.

This application is an example of using more than one filter on a stream. The stream is developed in a three-step process:

- A file output stream that is associated with a file called 400primes.dat is created.
- A new buffered output stream is associated with the file stream.
- A new data output stream is associated with the buffered stream.

The writeInt() method of the data stream is used to write the primes to the file.

The ReadPrimes application is simpler because it doesn't need to do anything regarding prime numbers—it just reads integers from a file using a data input stream.

Lines 6–11 of ReadPrimes are nearly identical to statements in the WritePrimes application, except that input classes are used instead of output classes.

The try-catch block that handles EOFException objects is in lines 13–20. The work of loading the data takes place inside the try block.

The while(true) statement creates an endless loop. This isn't a problem; an EOFException will automatically occur when the end of the stream is encountered at some point as the data stream is being read. The readInt() method in line 15 reads integers from the stream.

The last several output lines of the ReadPrimes application should resemble the following:

```
2137 2141 2143 2153 2161 2179 2203 2207 2213 2221 2237 2239 2243 22
51 2267 2269 2273 2281 2287 2293 2297 2309 2311 2333 2339 2341 2347
 2351 2357 2371 2377 2381 2383 2389 2393 2399 2411 2417 2423 2437 2
441 2447 2459 2467 2473 2477 2503 2521 2531 2539 2543 2549 2551 255
7 2579 2591 2593 2609 2617 2621 2633 2647 2657 2659 2663 2671 2677
2683 2687 2689 2693 2699 2707 2711 2713 2719 2729 2731 2741
```

Character Streams

After you know how to handle byte streams, you have most of the skills needed to handle character streams as well. Character streams are used to work with any text that is represented by the ASCII character set or Unicode, an international character set that includes ASCII.

Examples of files that you can work with through a character stream are plain text files, HTML documents, and Java source files.

The classes used to read and write these streams are all subclasses of Reader and Writer. These should be used for all text input instead of dealing directly with byte streams.

Reading Text Files

FileReader is the main class used when reading character streams from a file. This class inherits from InputStreamReader, which reads a byte stream and converts the bytes into integer values that represent Unicode characters.

A character input stream is associated with a file using the FileReader(*String*) constructor. The string indicates the file, and it can contain path folder references in addition to a filename.

The following statement creates a new FileReader called look and associates it with a text file called index.txt:

```
FileReader look = new FileReader("index.txt");
```

After you have a file reader, you can call the following methods on it to read characters from the file:

- read() returns the next character on the stream as an integer.
- read(*char[], int, int*) reads characters into the specified character array with the indicated starting point and number of characters read.

The second method works like similar methods for the byte input stream classes. Instead of returning the next character, it returns either the number of characters that were read or -1 if no characters were read before the end of the stream was reached.

The following method loads a text file using the FileReader object text and displays its characters:

```
FileReader text = new
    FileReader("readme.txt");
int inByte;
do {
```

```
        inByte = text.read();
        if (inByte != -1)
            System.out.print( (char)inByte );
    } while (inByte != -1);
    System.out.println("");
    text.close();
```

Because a character stream's `read()` method returns an integer, you must cast this to a character before displaying it, storing it in an array, or using it to form a string. Every character has a numeric code that represents its position in the Unicode character set. The integer read off the stream is this numeric code.

If you want to read an entire line of text at a time instead of reading a file character by character, you can use the `BufferedReader` class in conjunction with a `FileReader`.

The `BufferedReader` class reads a character input stream and buffers it for better efficiency. You must have an existing `Reader` object of some kind to create a buffered version. The following constructors can be used to create a `BufferedReader`:

- `BufferedReader(Reader)`—Creates a buffered character stream associated with the specified `Reader` object, such as `FileReader`

- `BufferedReader(Reader, int)`—Creates a buffered character stream associated with the specified `Reader` and with a buffer of *int* size

A buffered character stream can be read using the `read()` and `read(char[], int, int)` methods described for `FileReader`. You can read a line of text using the `readLine()` method.

The `readLine()` method returns a `String` object containing the next line of text on the stream, not including the character or characters that represent the end of a line. If the end of the stream is reached, the value of the string returned will be equal to `null`.

An end-of-line is indicated by any of the following:

- A newline character (`'\n'`)
- A carriage return character (`'\r'`)
- A carriage return followed by a newline (`"\n\r"`)

The project contained in Listing 15.7 is a Java application that reads its own source file through a buffered character stream.

LISTING **15.7**   The Full Text of `ReadSource.java`

```
 1: import java.io.*;
 2:
 3: public class ReadSource {
 4:     public static void main(String[] arguments) {
 5:         try {
 6:             FileReader file = new
 7:                 FileReader("ReadSource.java");
 8:             BufferedReader buff = new
 9:                 BufferedReader(file);
10:             boolean eof = false;
11:             while (!eof) {
12:                 String line = buff.readLine();
13:                 if (line == null)
14:                     eof = true;
15:                 else
16:                     System.out.println(line);
17:             }
18:             buff.close();
19:         } catch (IOException e) {
20:             System.out.println("Error -- " + e.toString());
21:         }
22:     }
23: }
```

Much of this program is comparable to projects created earlier today, as illustrated:

- Lines 6 and 7—An input source is created: the `FileReader` object associated with the file `ReadSource.java`.

- Lines 8 and 9—A buffering filter is associated with that input source: the `BufferedReader` object `buff`.

- Lines 11–17—A `readLine()` method is used inside a `while` loop to read the text file one line at a time. The loop ends when the method returns the value `null`.

The `ReadSource` application's output is the text file `ReadSource.java`.

Writing Text Files

The `FileWriter` class is used to write a character stream to a file. It's a subclass of `OutputStreamWriter`, which has behavior to convert Unicode character codes to bytes.

There are two `FileWriter` constructors: `FileWriter(String)` and `FileWriter(String, boolean)`. The string indicates the name of the file that the character stream will be directed into, which can include a folder path. The optional Boolean argument should equal `true` if the file is to be appended to an existing text file. As with other stream-writing classes, you must take care not to accidentally overwrite an existing file when you're appending data.

Three methods of `FileWriter` can be used to write data to a stream:

- `write(int)`—Writes a character
- `write(char[], int, int)`—Writes characters from the specified character array with the indicated starting point and number of characters written
- `write(String, int, int)`—Writes characters from the specified string with the indicated starting point and number of characters written

The following example writes a character stream to a file using the `FileWriter` class and the `write(int)` method:

```
FileWriter letters = new FileWriter("alphabet.txt");
for (int i = 65; i < 91; i++)
    letters.write( (char)i );
letters.close();
```

The `close()` method is used to close the stream after all characters have been sent to the destination file. The following is the `alphabet.txt` file produced by this code:

```
ABCDEFGHIJKLMNOPQRSTUVWXYZ
```

The `BufferedWriter` class can be used to write a buffered character stream. This class's objects are created with the `BufferedWriter(Writer)` or `BufferedWriter(Writer, int)` constructors. The `Writer` argument can be any of the character output stream classes, such as `FileWriter`. The optional second argument is an integer indicating the size of the buffer to use.

`BufferedWriter` has the same three output methods as `FileWriter`: `write(int)`, `write(char[], int, int)`, and `write(String, int, int)`.

Another useful output method is `newLine()`, which sends the preferred end-of-line character (or characters) for the platform being used to run the program.

Tip

> The different end-of-line markers can create conversion hassles when transferring files from one operating system to another, such as when a Windows XP user uploads a file to a Web server that's running the Linux operating system. Using `newLine()` instead of a literal (such as `'\n'`) makes your program more user-friendly across different platforms.

The `close()` method is called to close the buffered character stream and make sure all buffered data is sent to the stream's destination.

Files and Filename Filters

In all of the examples thus far, a string has been used to refer to the file that's involved in a stream operation. This often is sufficient for a program that uses files and streams, but if you want to copy files, rename files, or handle other tasks, a `File` object can be used.

`File`, which also is part of the `java.io` package, represents a file or folder reference. The following `File` constructors can be used:

- `File(String)`—Creates a `File` object with the specified folder; no filename is indicated, so this refers only to a file folder.
- `File(String, String)`—Creates a `File` object with the specified folder path and the specified name.
- `File(File, String)`—Creates a `File` object with its path represented by the specified `File` and its name indicated by the specified `String`.

You can call several useful methods on a `File` object.

The `exists()` method returns a Boolean value indicating whether the file exists under the name and folder path established when the `File` object was created. If the file exists, you can use the `length()` method to return a `long` integer indicating the size of the file in bytes.

The `renameTo(File)` method renames the file to the name specified by the `File` argument. A Boolean value is returned, indicating whether the operation was successful.

The `delete()` or `deleteOnExit()` method should be called to delete a file or a folder. The `delete()` method attempts an immediate deletion (returning a Boolean value indicating whether it worked). The `deleteOnExit()` method waits to attempt deletion until the rest of the program has finished running. This method does not return a value—you couldn't do anything with the information—and the program must finish at some point for it to work.

The `mkdir()` method can be used to create the folder specified by the `File` object it is called on. It returns a Boolean value indicating success or failure. There is no comparable method to remove folders because `delete()` can be used on folders as well as files.

As with any file-handling operations, these methods must be handled with care to avoid deleting the wrong files and folders or wiping out data. There's no method available to undelete a file or folder.

Each of the methods will throw a `SecurityException` if the program does not have the security to perform the file operation in question, so these exceptions need to be dealt with through a `try-catch` block or a `throws` clause in a method declaration.

The program in Listing 15.8 converts all the text in a file to uppercase characters. The file is pulled in using a buffered input stream, and one character is read at a time. After the character is converted to uppercase, it is sent to a temporary file using a buffered output stream. File objects are used instead of strings to indicate the files involved, which makes it possible to rename and delete files as needed.

15

LISTING 15.8   The Full Text of `AllCapsDemo.java`

```
 1: import java.io.*;
 2:
 3: public class AllCapsDemo {
 4:     public static void main(String[] arguments) {
 5:         AllCaps cap = new AllCaps(arguments[0]);
 6:         cap.convert();
 7:     }
 8: }
 9:
10: class AllCaps {
11:     String sourceName;
12:
13:     AllCaps(String sourceArg) {
14:         sourceName = sourceArg;
15:     }
16:
17:     void convert() {
18:         try {
19:             // Create file objects
20:             File source = new File(sourceName);
21:             File temp = new File("cap" + sourceName + ".tmp");
22:
23:             // Create input stream
24:             FileReader fr = new
25:                 FileReader(source);
26:             BufferedReader in = new
27:                 BufferedReader(fr);
28:
29:             // Create output stream
30:             FileWriter fw = new
31:                 FileWriter(temp);
32:             BufferedWriter out = new
33:                 BufferedWriter(fw);
34:
35:             boolean eof = false;
36:             int inChar = 0;
37:             do {
38:                 inChar = in.read();
39:                 if (inChar != -1) {
40:                     char outChar = Character.toUpperCase( (char)inChar );
```

continues

LISTING 15.8 Continued

```
41:                          out.write(outChar);
42:                      } else
43:                          eof = true;
44:                  } while (!eof);
45:                  in.close();
46:                  out.close();
47:
48:                  boolean deleted = source.delete();
49:                  if (deleted)
50:                      temp.renameTo(source);
51:          } catch (IOException e) {
52:              System.out.println("Error -- " + e.toString());
53:          } catch (SecurityException se) {
54:              System.out.println("Error -- " + se.toString());
55:          }
56:      }
57: }
```

After you compile the program, you need a text file that can be converted to all capital letters. One option is to make a copy of AllCapsDemo.java and give it a name like TempFile.java.

The name of the file to convert is specified at the command line when running AllCapsDemo, as in the following SDK example:

```
java AllCapsDemo TempFile.java
```

This program does not produce any output. Load the converted file into a text editor to see the result of the application.

Summary

Today you learned how to work with streams in two directions: pulling data into a program over an input stream and sending data from a program using an output stream.

You used byte streams for many types of nontextual data and character streams to handle text. Filters were associated with streams to alter the way information was delivered through a stream, or to alter the information itself.

Today's lesson covers most java.io package classes, but there are other types of streams you might want to explore. Piped streams are useful when communicating data among different threads, and byte array streams can connect programs to a computer's memory.

Because the stream classes in Java are so closely coordinated, you already possess most of the knowledge you need to use these other types of streams. The constructors, read methods, and write methods are largely identical.

Streams are a powerful way to extend the functionality of your Java programs because they offer a connection to any kind of data you might want to work with.

Tomorrow you will use streams to read and write Java objects.

Q&A

Q A C program that I use creates a file of integers and other data. Can I read this using a Java program?

A You can, but one thing you have to consider is whether your C program represents integers in the same manner that a Java program represents them. As you might recall, all data can be represented as an individual byte or a series of bytes. An integer is represented in Java using four bytes that are arranged in what is called big-endian order. You can determine the integer value by combining the bytes from left-to-right. A C program implemented on an Intel PC is likely to represent integers in little-endian order, which means the bytes must be arranged from right-to-left to determine the result. You might have to learn about advanced techniques, such as bit shifting, to use a data file created with a programming language other than Java.

Q The `FileWriter` class has a `write(int)` method that's used to send a character to a file. Shouldn't this be `write(char)`?

A The `char` and `int` data types are interchangeable in many ways; you can use an `int` in a method that expects a `char`, and vice versa. This is possible because each character is represented by a numeric code that is an integer value. When you call the `write()` method with an `int`, it outputs the character associated with that integer value. When calling the `write()` method, you can cast an `int` value to a `char` to ensure that it's being used as you intended.

Quiz

Review today's material by taking this three-question quiz.

Questions

1. What happens when you create a `FileOutputStream` using a reference to an existing file?

   (a.) An exception is thrown.

   (b.) The data you write to the stream are appended to the existing file.

   (c.) The existing file is replaced with the data you write to the stream.

2. What two primitive types are interchangeable when you're working with streams?

   (a.) byte and boolean

   (b.) char and int

   (c.) byte and char

3. In Java, what is the maximum value of a byte variable and the maximum value of an unsigned byte in a stream?

   (a.) Both are 255

   (b.) Both are 127

   (c.) 127 for a byte variable and 255 for an unsigned byte

Answers

1. (c.) That's one of the things to look out for when using output streams; you can easily wipe out existing files.

2. (b.) Because a char is represented internally by Java as an integer value, you can often use the two interchangeably in method calls and other statements.

3. (c.) The byte primitive data type has values ranging from -128 to 127, whereas an unsigned byte can range from 0 to 255.

Certification Practice

The following question is the kind of thing you could expect to be asked on a Java programming certification test. Answer it without looking at today's material or using the Java compiler to test the code.

Given:

```
import java.io.*;

public class Unknown {
    public static void main(String[] arguments) {
        String command = "";
        BufferedReader br = new BufferedReader(new
            InputStreamReader(System.in));
        try {
            command = br.readLine();
        }
        catch (IOException e) { }
    }
}
```

Will this program successfully store a line of console input in the `String` object named `command`?

(a.) Yes

(b.) No, because a buffered input stream is required to read console input.

(c.) No, because it won't compile successfully.

(d.) No, because it reads more than one line of console input.

The answer is available on this book's Web site at `http://www.java21days.com`. Visit the Day 15 page and click the Certification Practice link.

Exercises

To extend your knowledge of the subjects covered today, try the following exercises:

- Write a modified version of the `HexRead` program from Day 7, "Threads and Exceptions," that reads two-digit hexadecimal sequences from a text file and displays their decimal equivalents.

- Write a program that reads a file to determine the number of bytes it contains, and then overwrites all those bytes with zeroes (`0`). (For obvious reasons, don't test this program on any file you intend to keep; the data in the file will be wiped out.)

Where applicable, exercise solutions are offered on this book's Web site at `http://www.java21days.com`.

DAY 16

Serializing and Examining Objects

An essential concept of object-oriented programming is the way data are represented. In an object-oriented language such as Java, an object represents two things:

- Behavior—The things an object can do
- Attributes—The data that differentiate the object from other objects

Combining behavior and attributes is a departure from many other programming languages. A program has typically been defined as a set of instructions that manipulate data. The data are a separate thing, as in word-processing software. Most word processors are considered programs that are used to create and edit text documents.

Object-oriented programming and other techniques are blurring the line between program and data. An object in a language such as Java encapsulates both instructions (behavior) and data (attributes).

Today you will discover three ways that a Java program can take advantage of this representation:

- Object serialization—The capability to read and write an object using streams
- Reflection—The capability of one object to learn details about another object
- Remote method invocation—The capability to query another object to investigate its features and call its methods

Object Serialization

As you learned yesterday during Day 15, "Working with Input and Ouput," Java handles access to external data via the use of a class of objects called streams. A *stream* is an object that carries data from one place to another. Some streams carry information from a source into a Java program. Others go the opposite direction and take data from a program to a destination.

A stream that reads a Web page's data into an array in a Java program is an example of the former. A stream that writes a `String` array to a disk file is an example of the latter.

Two types of streams were introduced during Day 15:

- *Byte streams*, which read and write a series of integer values ranging from `0` to `255`
- *Character streams*, which read and write textual data

These streams separate the data from the Java class that works with it. To use the data at a later time, you must read it in through a stream and convert it into a form the class can use, such as a series of variables or objects.

A third type of stream, an *object stream*, makes it possible for data to be represented as part of an object rather than something external to it.

Object streams, like byte and character streams, are part of the `java.io` package. Working with them requires many of the same techniques you used during Day 15.

For an object to be saved to a destination such as a disk file, it must be converted to serial form.

Note

Serial data are sent one element at a time, like a line of cars on an assembly line. You might be familiar with the *serial port* on a computer, which is used to send information as a series of bits one after the other. Another way to send data is in *parallel*, transferring more than one element simultaneously.

An object indicates that it can be used with streams by implementing the `Serializable` interface. This interface, which is part of the `java.io` package, differs from other interfaces with which you have worked; it does not contain any methods that must be included in the classes that implement it. The sole purpose of the `Serializable` interface is to indicate that objects of that class can be stored and retrieved in serial form.

Objects can be serialized to disk on a single machine or can be serialized across a network, such as the Internet, even in a case in which different operating systems are involved. You can create an object on a Windows machine, serialize it to a UNIX machine, and load it back into the original Windows machine without introducing any errors. Java transparently works with the different formats for saving data on these systems when objects are serialized.

A programming concept involved in object serialization is *persistence*—the capability of an object to exist and function outside the program that created it.

Normally, an object that is not serialized is not persistent. When the program that uses the object stops running, the object ceases to exist.

Serialization enables object persistence because the stored object continues to serve a purpose even when no Java program is running. The stored object contains information that can be restored in a program so it can resume functioning.

When an object is saved to a stream in serial form, all objects to which it contains references are saved also. This makes it easier to work with serialization; you can create one object stream that takes care of numerous objects at the same time.

You also can exclude some of an object's variables from serialization, which might be necessary to save disk space or prevent information that presents a security risk from being saved. As you will see later today, this requires the use of the `transient` modifier.

Object Output Streams

An object is written to a stream via the `ObjectOutputStream` class.

An object output stream is created with the `ObjectOutputStream(OutputStream)` constructor. The argument to this constructor can be either of the following:

- An output stream representing the destination where the object should be stored in serial form
- A filter that is associated with the output stream leading to the destination

As with other streams, you can chain more than one filter between the output stream and the object output stream.

The following code creates an output stream and an associated object output stream:

```
FileOutputStream disk = new FileOutputStream(
    "SavedObject.dat");
ObjectOutputStream obj = new ObjectOutputStream(disk);
```

The object output stream created in this example is called `obj`. Methods of the `obj` class can be used to write serializable objects and other information to a file called `SavedObject.dat`.

After you have created an object output stream, you can write an object to it by calling the stream's `writeObject(Object)` method.

The following statement calls this method on `disk`, the stream created in the previous example:

```
disk.writeObject(userData);
```

This statement writes an object called `userData` to the `disk` object output stream. The class represented by `userData` must be serializable in order for it to work.

An object output stream also can be used to write other types of information with the following methods:

- `write(int)`—Writes the specified integer to the stream, which should be a value from 0 to 255
- `write(byte[])`—Writes the specified byte array
- `write(byte[], int, int)`—Writes a subset of the specified byte array. The second argument specifies the first array element to write and the last argument represents the number of subsequent elements to write.
- `writeBoolean(boolean)`—Writes the specified `boolean`
- `writeByte(int)`—Writes the specified integer as a byte value
- `writeBytes(String)`—Writes the specified string as a series of bytes
- `writeChar(int)`—Writes the specified character
- `writeChars(String)`—Writes the specified string as a series of characters
- `writeDouble(double)`—Writes the specified `double`
- `writeFloat(float)`—Writes the specified `float`
- `writeInt(int)`—Writes the specified `int`, which, unlike the argument to `write(int)`, can be any int value
- `writeLong(long)`—Writes the specified `long`
- `writeShort(short)`—Writes the specified `short`

The `ObjectOutputStream` constructor and all methods that write data to an object output stream throw `IOException` objects. These must be accounted for using a `try-catch` block or a `throws` clause.

Listing 16.1 contains a Java application that consists of two classes: `ObjectToDisk` and `Message`. The `Message` class represents a message that one person could send to another, perhaps as electronic mail or a short note in a private chat. This class has `from` and `to` objects that store the names of the sender and recipient, a `now` object that holds a `Date` value representing the time it was sent, and a `text` array of `String` objects that holds the message. There also is an `int` called `lineCount` that keeps track of the number of lines in the message.

When designing a program that transmits and receives electronic messages, it makes sense to use some kind of stream to save these messages to disk. The information that constitutes the message must be saved in some form as it is transmitted from one place to another; it also might need to be saved until the recipient is able to read it.

Messages can be preserved by saving each message element separately to a byte or character stream. In the example of the `Message` class, the `from` and `to` objects could be written to a stream as strings and the `text` object could be written as an array of strings. The `now` object is a little trickier because there isn't a way to write a `Date` object to a character stream. However, it could be converted into a series of integer values representing each part of a date: hour, minute, second, and so on. Those could be written to the stream.

Using an object output stream makes it possible to save `Message` objects without first translating them into another form.

The `ObjectToDisk` class in Listing 16.1 creates a `Message` object, sets up values for its variables, and saves it to a file called `Message.obj` via an object output stream.

LISTING 16.1 The Full Text of `ObjectToDisk.java`

```
 1: import java.io.*;
 2: import java.util.*;
 3:
 4: public class ObjectToDisk {
 5:     public static void main(String[] arguments) {
 6:         Message mess = new Message();
 7:         String author = "Sam Wainwright, London";
 8:         String recipient = "George Bailey, Bedford Falls";
 9:         String[] letter = { "Mr. Gower cabled you need cash. Stop.",
10:             "My office instructed to advance you up to twenty-five",
11:             "thousand dollars. Stop. Hee-haw and Merry Christmas." };
12:         Date now = new Date();
```

continues

LISTING **16.1**   Continued

```
13:            mess.writeMessage(author, recipient, now, letter);
14:            try {
15:                FileOutputStream fo = new FileOutputStream(
16:                    "Message.obj");
17:                ObjectOutputStream oo = new ObjectOutputStream(fo);
18:                oo.writeObject(mess);
19:                oo.close();
20:                System.out.println("Object created successfully.");
21:            } catch (IOException e) {
22:                System.out.println("Error -- " + e.toString());
23:            }
24:        }
25: }
26:
27: class Message implements Serializable {
28:        int lineCount;
29:        String from, to;
30:        Date when;
31:        String[] text;
32:
33:        void writeMessage(String inFrom,
34:            String inTo,
35:            Date inWhen,
36:            String[] inText) {
37:
38:            text = new String[inText.length];
39:            for (int i = 0; i < inText.length; i++)
40:                text[i] = inText[i];
41:            lineCount = inText.length;
42:            to = inTo;
43:            from = inFrom;
44:            when = inWhen;
45:        }
46: }
```

You should see the following output after you compile and run the `ObjectToDisk`
application:

```
Object created successfully.
```

Object Input Streams

An object is read from a stream using the `ObjectInputStream` class. As with other
streams, working with an object input stream is very similar to working with an object
output stream. The primary difference is the change in the data's direction.

An object input stream is created with the ObjectInputStream(*InputStream*) constructor. Two exceptions are thrown by this constructor: IOException and StreamCorruptionException. IOException, common to stream classes, occurs whenever any kind of input/output error occurs during the data transfer. StreamCorruptionException is specific to object streams, and it indicates that the data in the stream are not a serialized object.

An object input stream can be constructed from an input stream or a filtered stream.

The following code creates an input stream and an object input stream to go along with it:

```
try {
    FileInputStream disk = new FileInputStream(
        "SavedObject.dat");
    ObjectInputStream obj = new ObjectInputStream(disk);
} catch (IOException ie) {
    System.out.println("IO error -- " + ie.toString());
} catch (StreamCorruptionException se) {
    System.out.println("Error - data not an object.");
}
```

This object input stream is set up to read from an object that is stored in a file called SavedObject.dat. If the file does not exist or cannot be read from disk for some reason, an IOException is thrown. If the file isn't a serialized object, a thrown StreamCorruptionException indicates this problem.

An object can be read from an object input stream by using the readObject() method, which returns an Object. This object can be immediately cast into the class it belongs to, as in the following example:

```
WorkData dd = (WorkData)disk.readObject();
```

This statement reads an object from the disk object stream and casts it into an object of the class WorkData. In addition to IOException, this method throws OptionalDataException and ClassNotFoundException errors.

OptionalDataException indicates that the stream contains data other than serialized object data, which makes it impossible to read an object from the stream.

ClassNotFoundException occurs when the object retrieved from the stream belongs to a class that could not be found. When objects are serialized, the class is not saved to the stream. Instead, the name of the class is saved to the stream, and the Java interpreter loads when the object is loaded from a stream.

Other types of information can be read from an object input stream with the following methods:

- read()—Reads the next byte from the stream, which is returned as an int
- read(byte[], int, int)—Reads bytes into the specified byte array. The second argument specifies the first array element where a byte should be stored. The last argument represents the number of subsequent elements to read and store in the array.
- readBoolean()—Reads a boolean value from the stream
- readByte()—Reads a byte value from the stream
- readChar()—Reads a char value from the stream
- readDouble()—Reads a double value from the stream
- readFloat()—Reads a float value from the stream
- readInt()—Reads an int value from the stream
- readLine()—Reads a String from the stream
- readLong()—Reads a long value from the stream
- readShort()—Reads a short value from the stream
- readUnsignedByte()—Reads an unsigned byte value and returns it as an int
- readUnsignedShort()—Reads an unsigned short value and returns it as an int

Each of these methods throws an IOException if an input/output error occurs as the stream is being read.

When an object is created by reading an object stream, it is created entirely from the variable and object information stored in that stream. No constructor method is called to create variables and set them up with initial values. There's no difference between this object and the one that was originally serialized.

Listing 16.2 contains a Java application that reads an object from a stream and displays its variables to standard output. The ObjectFromDisk application loads the object that was serialized to the file message.obj.

This class must be run from the same folder that contains the file message.obj and the Message class.

LISTING 16.2   The Full Text of ObjectFromDisk.java

```
1: import java.io.*;
2: import java.util.*;
3:
4: public class ObjectFromDisk {
```

LISTING 16.2 Continued

```
 5:     public static void main(String[] arguments) {
 6:         try {
 7:             FileInputStream fi = new FileInputStream(
 8:                 "message.obj");
 9:             ObjectInputStream oi = new ObjectInputStream(fi);
10:             Message mess = (Message) oi.readObject();
11:             System.out.println("Message:\n");
12:             System.out.println("From: " + mess.from);
13:             System.out.println("To: " + mess.to);
14:             System.out.println("Date: " + mess.when + "\n");
15:             for (int i = 0; i < mess.lineCount; i++)
16:                 System.out.println(mess.text[i]);
17:             oi.close();
18:         } catch (Exception e) {
19:             System.out.println("Error -- " + e.toString());
20:         }
21:     }
22: }
```

The output of this program is as follows:

```
Message:

From: Sam Wainwright, London
To: George Bailey, Bedford Falls
Date: Thu Jun 13 00:19:23 EDT 2002

Mr. Gower cabled you need cash. Stop.
My office instructed to advance you up to twenty-five
thousand dollars. Stop. Hee-haw and Merry Christmas.
```

Transient Variables

When creating an object that can be serialized, one design consideration is whether all of the object's instance variables should be saved.

In some cases, an instance variable must be created from scratch each time the object is restored. A good example is an object referring to a file or input stream. Such an object must be created anew when it is part of a serialized object loaded from an object stream, so it doesn't make sense to save this information when serializing the object.

It's a good idea to exclude from serialization a variable that contains sensitive information. If an object stores the password needed to gain access to a resource, that password is more at risk if serialized into a file. The password also might be detected if it is part of an object that was restored over a stream that exists on a network.

A third reason not to serialize a variable is to save space on the storage file that holds the object. If its values can be established without serialization, you might want to omit the variable from the process.

To prevent an instance variable from being included in serialization, the transient modifier is used.

This modifier is included in the statement that creates the variable, preceding the class or data type of the variable. The following statement creates a transient variable called limit:

```
public transient int limit = 55;
```

Inspecting Classes and Methods with Reflection

On Day 3, "Working with Objects," you learned how to create Class objects that represent the class to which an object belongs. Every object in Java inherits the getClass() method, which identifies the class or interface of that object. The following statement creates a Class object named keyclass from an object referred to by the variable key:

```
Class keyClass = key.getClass();
```

By calling the getName() method of a Class object, you can find out the name of the class:

```
String keyName = keyClass.getName();
```

These features are part of Java's support for reflection, a technique that enables one Java class—such as a program you write—to learn details about any other class.

Through reflection, a Java program can load a class it knows nothing about, find the variables, methods, and constructors of that class, and work with them.

Inspecting and Creating Classes

The Class class, which is part of the java.lang package, is used to learn about and create classes, interfaces, and even primitive types.

In addition to using getClass(), you can create Class objects by appending .class to the name of a class, interface, array, or primitive type, as in the following examples:

```
Class keyClass = KeyClass.class;
Class thr = Throwable.class;
Class floater = float.class;
Class floatArray = float[].class;
```

You also can create Class objects by using the forName() class method with a single argument: a string containing the name of an existing class. The following statement creates a Class object representing a JLabel, one of the classes of the javax.swing package:

```
Class lab = Class.forName("javax.swing.JLabel");
```

The forName() method throws a ClassNotFoundException if the specified class cannot be found, so you must call forName() within a try-catch block or handle it in some other manner.

To retrieve a string containing the name of a class represented by a Class object, call getName() on that object. For classes and interfaces, this name will include the name of the class and a reference to the package to which it belongs. For primitive types, the name will correspond to the type's name (such as int, float, or double).

Class objects that represent arrays are handled a little differently when getName() is called on them. The name begins with one left bracket character ([) for each dimension of the array; float[] would begin with [, int[][] with [[, KeyClass[][][] with [[[, and so on.

If the array is of a primitive type, the next part of the name is a single character representing the type, as shown in Table 16.1.

TABLE 16.1 Type Identification for Primitive Types

Character	Primitive Type
B	byte
C	char
D	double
F	float
I	int
J	long
S	short
Z	boolean

For arrays of objects, the brackets are followed by an L and the name of the class. For example, if you called getName() on a String[][] array, the result would be [[Ljava.lang.String.

You also can use the `Class` class to create new objects. Call the `newInstance()` method on a `Class` object to create the object and cast it to the correct class. For example, if you have a `Class` object named `thr` that represents the `Throwable` interface, you can create a new object as follows:

```
Throwable thr2 = (Throwable)thr.newInstance();
```

The `newInstance()` method throws several kinds of exceptions:

- `IllegalAccessException`—You do not have access to the class, either because it is not `public` or because it belongs to a different package.
- `InstantiationException`—You cannot create a new object because the class is abstract.
- `SecurityViolation`—You do not have permission to create an object of this class.

When `newInstance()` is called and no exceptions are thrown, the new object is created by calling the constructor of the corresponding class with no arguments.

> You cannot use this technique to create a new object that requires arguments to its constructor method. Instead, you must use a `newInstance()` method of the `Constructor` class, as you will see later today.

Working with Each Part of a Class

Although `Class` is part of the `java.lang` package, the primary support for reflection is the `java.lang.reflect` package, which includes the following classes:

- `Field`—Manages and finds information about class and instance variables
- `Method`—Manages class and instance methods
- `Constructor`—Manages constructors, the special methods for creating new instances of classes
- `Array`—Manages arrays
- `Modifier`—Decodes modifier information about classes, variables, and methods (which were described on Day 6, "Packages, Interfaces, and Other Class Features")

Each of these reflection classes has methods for working with an element of a class.

A `Method` object holds information about a single method in a class. To find out about all methods contained in a class, create a `Class` object for that class and call `getDeclaredMethods()` on that object. An array of `Method[]` objects will be returned that represents all methods in the class that were not inherited from a superclass. If no methods meet that description, the length of the array will be `0`.

The Method class has several useful instance methods:

- getParameterTypes()—This method returns an array of Class objects representing each argument contained in the method signature.
- getReturnType()—This method returns a Class object representing the return type of the method, whether it's a class or primitive type.
- getModifiers()—This method returns an int value that represents the modifiers that apply to the method, such as whether it is public, private, and the like.

Because the getParameterTypes() and getReturnType() methods return Class objects, you can use getName() on each object to find out more about it.

The easiest way to use the int returned by getModifiers() is to call the Modifier class method toString() with that integer as an argument. For example, if you have a Method object named current, you can display its modifiers with the following code:

```
int mods = current.getModifiers();
System.out.println(Modifier.toString(mods));
```

The Constructor class has some of the same methods as the Method class, including getModifiers() and getName(). One method that's missing, as you might expect, is getReturnType(); constructors do not contain return types.

To retrieve all constructors associated with a Class object, call getConstructors() on that object. An array of Constructor objects will be returned.

To retrieve a specific constructor, first create an array of Class objects that represents every argument sent to the constructor. When this is done, call getConstructors() with that Class array as an argument.

For example, if there is a KeyClass(String, int) constructor, you can create a Constructor object to represent this with the following statements:

```
Class kc = KeyClass.class;
Class[] cons = new Class[2];
cons[0] = String.class;
cons[1] = int.class;
Constructor c = kc.getConstructor(cons);
```

The getConstructor(Class[]) method throws a NoSuchMethodException if there isn't a constructor with arguments that match the Class[] array.

After you have a Constructor object, you can call its newInstance(Object[]) method to create a new instance using that constructor.

Inspecting a Class

To bring all this material together, Listing 16.3 is a short Java application named SeeMethods that uses reflection to inspect the methods in a class.

LISTING 16.3 The Full Text of SeeMethods.java

```
 1: import java.lang.reflect.*;
 2:
 3: public class SeeMethods {
 4:     public static void main(String[] arguments)  {
 5:         Class inspect;
 6:         try {
 7:             if (arguments.length > 0)
 8:                 inspect = Class.forName(arguments[0]);
 9:             else
10:                 inspect = Class.forName("SeeMethods");
11:             Method[] methods = inspect.getDeclaredMethods();
12:             for (int i = 0; i < methods.length; i++) {
13:                 Method methVal = methods[i];
14:                 Class returnVal = methVal.getReturnType();
15:                 int mods = methVal.getModifiers();
16:                 String modVal = Modifier.toString(mods);
17:                 Class[] paramVal = methVal.getParameterTypes();
18:                 StringBuffer params = new StringBuffer();
19:                 for (int j = 0; j < paramVal.length; j++) {
20:                     if (j > 0)
21:                         params.append(", ");
22:                     params.append(paramVal[j].getName());
23:                 }
24:                 System.out.println("Method: " + methVal.getName() + "()");
25:                 System.out.println("Modifiers: " + modVal);
26:                 System.out.println("Return Type: " + returnVal.getName());
27:                 System.out.println("Parameters: " + params + "\n");
28:             }
29:         } catch (ClassNotFoundException c) {
30:             System.out.println(c.toString());
31:         }
32:     }
33: }
```

The SeeMethods application displays information about the public methods in the class you specify at the command line (or SeeMethods itself, if you don't specify a class). To try the program, enter the following at a command line:

```
java SeeMethods java.util.Random
```

If you run the application on the `java.util.Random` class, the program's output is the following:

```
Method: next()
Modifiers: protected synchronized
Return Type: int
Parameters: int

Method: nextDouble()
Modifiers: public
Return Type: double
Parameters:

Method: nextInt()
Modifiers: public
Return Type: int
Parameters: int

Method: nextInt()
Modifiers: public
Return Type: int
Parameters:

Method: setSeed()
Modifiers: public synchronized
Return Type: void
Parameters: long

Method: nextBytes()
Modifiers: public
Return Type: void
Parameters: [B

Method: nextLong()
Modifiers: public
Return Type: long
Parameters:

Method: nextBoolean()
Modifiers: public
Return Type: boolean
Parameters:

Method: nextFloat()
Modifiers: public
Return Type: float
Parameters:

Method: nextGaussian()
Modifiers: public synchronized
Return Type: double
Parameters:
```

16

By using reflection, the SeeMethods application can learn every method of a class.

A Class object is created in lines 7–10 of the application. If a class name is specified as a command-line argument when SeeMethods was run, the Class.forName() method is called with that argument. Otherwise, SeeMethods is used as the argument.

After the Class object is created, its getDeclaredMethods() method is used in line 11 to find all the methods contained in the class (with the exception of methods inherited from a superclass). These methods are stored as an array of Method objects.

The for loop in lines 12–28 cycles through each method in the class, storing its return type, modifiers, and arguments and then displaying them.

Displaying the return type is straightforward: Each method's getReturnType() method is stored as a Class object in line 14, and that object's name is displayed in line 26.

When a method's getModifiers() method is called in line 15, an integer is returned that represents all modifiers used with the method. The class method Modifier.toString() takes this integer as an argument and returns the names of all modifiers associated with it.

Lines 19–23 loop through the array of Class objects that represents the arguments associated with a method. The name of each argument is added to a StringBuffer object named params in line 22.

Reflection is most commonly used by tools such as class browsers and debuggers as a way to learn more about the class of objects being browsed or debugged. It also is needed with JavaBeans, where the capability for one object to query another object about what it can do (and then ask it to do something) is useful when building larger applications. You will learn more about JavaBeans during Day 19, "Creating and Using JavaBeans."

Reflection is an advanced feature that you might not be using in your programs. It becomes most useful when you're working on object serialization, JavaBeans, and other programs that need runtime access to Java classes.

Remote Method Invocation

Remote method invocation (RMI) creates Java applications that can talk to other Java applications over a network. To be more specific, RMI allows an application to call methods and access variables inside another application, which might be running in a different Java environment or different operating system, and to pass objects back and forth over a network connection. RMI is a more sophisticated mechanism for communicating among distributed Java objects than a simple socket connection; the mechanisms and protocols by which you communicate among objects are defined and standardized. You can talk to another Java program by using RMI without having to know beforehand what protocol to speak to or how to speak it.

Note

Another form of communicating among objects is called RPC (*remote procedure calls*), which allows you to call methods or execute procedures in other programs over a network connection. Although RPC and RMI have a lot in common, the major difference is that RPC sends only procedure calls over the wire, with the arguments either passed along or described in such a way that they can be reconstructed at the other end. RMI actually passes whole objects back and forth over the Internet, and is therefore better suited for a fully object-oriented distributed object model.

16

Although the concept of RMI might bring up visions of objects all over the world merrily communicating with each other, RMI is most commonly used in a more traditional client/server situation: A single server application receives connections and requests from a number of clients. RMI is simply the mechanism by which the client and server communicate.

RMI Architecture

The goals for RMI were to integrate a distributed object model into Java without disrupting the language or the existing object model and to make interacting with a remote object as easy as interacting with a local one. Using RMI, a programmer should be able to do the following:

- Use remote objects in precisely the same ways as local objects (assign them to variables, pass them as arguments to methods, and so on)

- Call methods in remote objects the same way that local calls are accomplished

In addition, RMI includes more sophisticated mechanisms for calling methods on remote objects to pass whole objects or parts of objects either by reference or by value; it also includes additional exceptions for handling network errors that might occur during a remote operation.

RMI uses several layers to accomplish all these goals, and a single method call crosses many of these layers to get where it's going (see Figure 16.1). There are actually three layers:

- The Stub and Skeleton Layers on the client and server, respectively. These layers behave as surrogate objects on each side, hiding the remoteness of the method call from the actual implementation classes. For example, in your client application you can call remote methods in precisely the same way that you call local methods; the stub object is a local surrogate for the remote object.

- The Remote Reference Layer, which handles packaging of a method call and its parameters and returns values for transport over the network
- The Transport Layer, which is the actual network connection from one system to another

FIGURE 16.1

RMI layers.

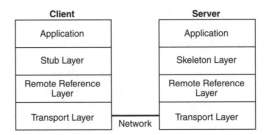

Having three layers for RMI allows each layer to be independently controlled or implemented. Stubs and skeletons allow the client and server classes to behave as if the objects they were dealing with were local and to use exactly the same Java language features to access those objects. The Remote Reference Layer separates the remote object processing into its own layer, which can then be optimized or implemented independently of the applications that depend on it. Finally, the Network Transport Layer is used independently of the other two so you can use different kinds of socket connections for RMI (TCP, UDP, or TCP with some other protocol, such as SSL).

When a client application makes a remote method call, the call passes to the stub and then onto the Remote Reference Layer, which packages the arguments if necessary. That layer then passes the call via the Network Layer to the server, where the Remote Reference Layer on the server side unpackages the arguments and passes them to the skeleton and then to the server implementation. The return values for the method call then take the reverse trip back to the client side.

The packaging and passing of method arguments is one of the more interesting aspects of RMI because objects have to be converted into something that can be passed over the network by using serialization. As long as an object can be serialized, RMI can use it as a method parameter or a return value.

Remote Java objects used as method parameters or return values are passed by reference, just as they would be locally. Other objects, however, are copied. Note that this behavior affects how you write your Java programs when they use remote method calls; you cannot, for example, pass an array as an argument to a remote method, have the remote object change that array, and expect the local copy to be modified. This is not how local objects behave, where all objects are passed as references.

Creating RMI Applications

To create an application that uses RMI, you use the classes and interfaces defined by the java.rmi packages, which include the following:

- java.rmi.server—For server-side classes
- java.rmi.registry—Which contains the classes for locating and registering RMI servers on a local system
- java.rmi.dgc—For garbage collection of distributed objects

The java.rmi package contains the general RMI interfaces, classes, and exceptions.

To implement an RMI-based client/server application, you first define an interface that contains all the methods your remote object will support. The methods in that interface must all include a throws RemoteException statement, which handles potential network problems that might prevent the client and server from communicating.

Listing 16.4 contains a simple interface that can be used with a remote object.

LISTING 16.4   The Full Text of PiRemote.java

```
1: package com.prefect.pi;
2:
3: import java.rmi.*;
4:
5: interface PiRemote extends Remote {
6:     double getPi() throws RemoteException;
7: }
```

An RMI interface like this must be part of a package for it to be accessible from a remote client program.

 Caution

Using a package name causes the Java compiler and interpreter to be pickier about where a program's Java and class files are located. A package's root folder should be a folder in your system's CLASSPATH, and each part of a package name is used to create a subfolder. If the folder C:\j2sdk1.4 is on your system's CLASSPATH, the PiRemote.java file could be saved in a folder called C:\j2sdk1.4\com\prefect\pi. If you don't have a folder matching the package name, you should create it.

This interface doesn't do anything, requiring a class to implement it. For now, you can compile it by entering the following command from the folder where PiRemote is located:

```
javac PiRemote.java
```

Although the package name is required when compiling the file, it isn't needed when compiling the interface.

The next step is to implement the remote interface in a server-side application, which usually extends the `UnicastRemoteObject` class. You implement the methods in the remote interface inside that class, and you also create and install a security manager for that server (to prevent random clients from connecting and making unauthorized method calls). You can, of course, configure the security manager to allow or disallow various operations. The Java class library includes a class called `RMISecurityManager`, which can be used for this purpose.

In the server application, you also register the remote application, which binds it to a host and port.

Listing 16.5 contains a Java server application that implements the `PiRemote` interface:

LISTING 16.5   The Full Text of `Pi.java`

```
 1: package com.prefect.pi;
 2:
 3: import java.net.*;
 4: import java.rmi.*;
 5: import java.rmi.registry.*;
 6: import java.rmi.server.*;
 7:
 8: public class Pi extends UnicastRemoteObject
 9:     implements PiRemote {
10:
11:     public double getPi() throws RemoteException {
12:         return Math.PI;
13:     }
14:
15:     public Pi() throws RemoteException {
16:     }
17:
18:     public static void main(String[] arguments) {
19:         System.setSecurityManager(new
20:             RMISecurityManager());
21:         try {
22:             Pi p = new Pi();
23:             Naming.bind("//Default:1010/Pi", p);
24:         } catch (Exception e) {
25:             System.out.println("Error -- " +
26:                 e.toString());
27:                 e.printStackTrace();
28:         }
29:     }
30: }
```

In the call to the `bind()` method in line 23, the text `Default:1010` identifies the machine name and port for the RMI registry. If you were running this application from a Web server of some kind, the name `Default` would be replaced with an URL. The name `Default` should be changed to your machine's real name.

Tip

> On a Windows 95 or 98 system, you can find your system's name by selecting Start, Settings, Control Panel, Network. Click the Identification tag to see the machine name, which is located in the Computer Name field. On a Windows XP system, right-click My Computer, choose Properties, and then click the Computer Name tab.

16

On the client side, you implement a simple application that uses the remote interface and calls methods in that interface. A `Naming` class (in `java.rmi`) allows the client to transparently connect to the server. Listing 16.6 contains `OutputPi.java`.

LISTING 16.6 The Full Text of `OutputPi.java`

```
 1: package com.prefect.pi;
 2:
 3: import java.rmi.*;
 4: import java.rmi.registry.*;
 5:
 6: public class OutputPi {
 7:     public static void main(String[] arguments) {
 8:         System.setSecurityManager(
 9:             new RMISecurityManager());
10:         try {
11:             PiRemote pr =
12:                 (PiRemote)Naming.lookup(
13:                     "//Default:1010/Pi");
14:             for (int i = 0; i < 10; i++)
15:                 System.out.println("Pi = " + pr.getPi());
16:         } catch (Exception e) {
17:             System.out.println("Error -- " + e.toString());
18:             e.printStackTrace();
19:         }
20:     }
21: }
```

At this point, you can compile these programs using the standard Java compiler. Before you can use these programs, you must use the `rmic` command-line program to generate the Stub and Skeleton Layers so RMI can actually work between the two sides of the process.

To create the stubs and skeletons files for the current project, go to the root folder of your packages and enter the following command:

```
rmic com.prefect.pi.Pi
```

Two files are created: `Pi_Stub.class` and `Pi_Skel.class`.

Finally, the `rmiregistry` program connects the server application to the network and binds it to a port so that remote connections can be made.

The `rmiregistry` program does not work correctly if the `Pi_Stub.class` and `Pi_Skel.class` files are located on your system's `CLASSPATH`. This is because the program assumes you don't need remote implementations of these files if they can be found locally.

The easiest way to avoid this problem is to run `rmiregistry` after temporarily disabling your `CLASSPATH`. This can be done on a Windows system by opening a new MS-DOS window and entering the following command:

```
set CLASSPATH=
```

Because the client and server applications use port 1010, you should start the `rmiregistry` program with the following command:

```
start rmiregistry 1010
```

After starting the RMI registry, you should run the server program `Pi`. Because this application is part of a package, you must include its full package name when running the application with the Java interpreter.

You also must indicate where all the class files associated with the application can be found, including `Pi_Stub.class` and `Pi_Skel.class`. This is done by setting the `java.rmi.server.codebase` property.

If the application's class files were stored at `http://www.java21days.com/java/`, the following command could be used to run the application from the same folder that contains `Pi.class`:

```
java -Djava.rmi.server.codebase=http://www.java21days/java/
          com.prefect.pi.Pi
```

The last step is to run the client program `OutputPi`. Switch to the folder that contains `OutputPi.class` and enter the following:

```
java com.prefect.pi.OutputPi
```

This program produces the following output:

```
Pi = 3.141592653589793
Pi = 3.141592653589793
Pi = 3.141592653589793
Pi = 3.141592653589793
Pi = 3.141592653589793
Pi = 3.141592653589793
Pi = 3.141592653589793
Pi = 3.141592653589793
Pi = 3.141592653589793
Pi = 3.141592653589793
```

RMI and Security

RMI generates security errors when you attempt to run the `Pi` and `OutputPi` programs on some systems.

If you get `AccessControlException` error messages associated with calls to the `Naming.bind()` and `Naming.lookup()` methods, your system needs to be configured so these RMI calls can execute successfully.

One way to do this is to set up a simple file that contains the most lax security policy possible for Java and use this file to set the `java.security.policy` property when you run `Pi` and `OutputPi`.

Listing 16.7 contains a text file that can be used for this purpose. Create this file using a text editor and save it as `policy.txt` in the same folder as `OutputPi.class` and `Pi.class`.

LISTING 16.7 The Full Text of `policy.txt`

```
1: grant {
2:     permission java.security.AllPermission;
3:     // Allow everything for now
4: };
```

Security policy files of this kind are used to grant and deny access to system resources. In this example, all permissions are granted, which prevents the `AccessControlException` error from occurring as you run the RMI client and server programs.

The `-Djava.security.policy=policy.txt` option can be used with the Java interpreter. The following examples show how this can be done:

```
java -Djava.rmi.server.codebase=http://www.java21days.com/
        java/ -Djava.security.policy=policy.txt com.prefect.pi.Pi
java -Djava.security.policy=policy.txt com.prefect.pi.OutputPi
```

Summary

Although Java has always been a network-centric language, with applets running on Web browsers since version 1.0, the topics covered today show how the language is extending in two directions.

Object serialization shows how objects created with Java have a lifespan beyond that of a Java program. You can create objects in a program that are saved to a storage device such as a hard drive and recreated later, long after the original program has ceased to run.

RMI shows how Java's method calls have a reach beyond a single machine. By using RMI's techniques and command-line tools, you can create Java programs that can work with other programs no matter where they're located, whether in another room or another continent.

Although both of these features can be used to create sophisticated networked applications, object serialization is suitable for many other tasks. You might see a need for it in some of the first programs that you create; persistence is an effective way to save elements of a program for later use.

Q&A

Q Are object streams associated with the `Writer` and `Reader` classes that are used to work with character streams?

A The `ObjectInputStream` and `ObjectOutputStream` classes are independent of the byte stream and character stream superclasses in the `java.io` package, although they function similarly to many of the byte classes.

There shouldn't be a need to use `Writer` or `Reader` classes in conjunction with object streams because you can accomplish the same things via the object stream classes and their superclasses (`InputStream` and `OutputStream`).

Q Are `private` variables and objects saved when they are part of an object that's being serialized?

A They are saved. As you might recall from today's discussion, no constructor methods are called when an object is loaded into a program using serialization. Because of this, all variables and objects that are not declared `transient` are saved to prevent the object from losing something that might be necessary to its function.

Saving `private` variables and objects might present a security risk in some cases, especially when the variable is being used to store a password or some other sensitive data. Using `transient` prevents a variable or object from being serialized.

Quiz

Review today's material by taking this three-question quiz.

Questions

1. What is returned when you call `getName()` on a `Class` object that represents a `String[]` array?

   (a.) `java.lang.String`

   (b.) `[Ljava.lang.String`

   (c.) `[java.lang.String`

2. What is persistence?

   (a.) The capability of an object to exist after the program that created it has stopped running

   (b.) An important concept of object serialization

   (c.) The ability to work through 16 days of a programming book and still be determined enough to answer these end-of-chapter questions

3. What `Class` method is used to create a new `Class` object using a string containing the name of a class?

   (a.) `newInstance()`

   (b.) `forName()`

   (c.) `getName()`

Answers

1. (b.) The bracket indicates the depth of the array, the `L` indicates that it is an array of objects, and the class name that follows is self-explanatory.

2. (a.), (b.), or (c.)

3. (b.) If the class is not found, a `ClassNotFoundException` will be thrown.

Certification Practice

The following question is the kind of thing you could expect to be asked on a Java programming certification test. Answer it without looking at today's material or using the Java compiler to test the code.

16

Given:

```
public class ClassType {
    public static void main(String[] arguments) {
        Class c = String.class;
        try {
            Object o = c.newInstance();
            if (o instanceof String)
                System.out.println("True");
            else
                System.out.println("False");
        } catch (Exception e) {
            System.out.println("Error");
        }
    }
}
```

What will be the output of this application?

(a.) True

(b.) False

(c.) Error

(d.) The program will not compile

The answer is available on this book's Web site at http://www.java21days.com. Visit the Day 16 page and click the Certification Practice link.

Exercises

To extend your knowledge of the subjects covered today, try the following exercises:

- Use reflection to write a Java program that takes a class name as a command-line argument and checks whether it is an application; all applications have a main() method with public static as modifiers, void as a return type, and String[] as the only argument.

- Write a program that creates a new object using Class objects and the newInstance() method that serializes the object to disk.

Where applicable, exercise solutions are offered on this book's Web site at http://www.java21days.com.

DAY 17

Communicating Across the Internet

Java was developed initially as a language that would control a network of interactive consumer devices. Connecting machines was one of the main purposes of the language when it was designed, and that remains true today.

The `java.net` package makes it possible to communicate over a network with your Java programs. The package provides cross-platform abstractions for simple networking operations, including connecting and retrieving files by using common Web protocols and creating basic Unix-like sockets.

Used in conjunction with input and output streams, reading and writing files over the network becomes almost as easy as reading or writing files on disk.

The `java.nio` package introduced in Java 2 version 1.4 is an expansion of Java's input and output classes that enhances the networking capabilities of the language.

Today you will write networking Java programs, creating applications that load a document over the World Wide Web, mimic a popular Internet service, and serve information to clients.

Networking in Java

 Networking is the capability of different computers to make connections with each other and to exchange information.

In Java, basic networking is supported by classes in the `java.net` package, including support for connecting and retrieving files by HTTP and FTP, as well as working at a lower level with basic Unix-like sockets.

The easiest way to use Java's network capabilities is to create applications, which aren't subject to the same default security policies as applets. Applets cannot connect to any networked machine other than the one that hosts the server they were loaded from.

There are three simple ways you can communicate with systems on the Net:

- Loading a Web page and any other resource with a URL from an applet
- Using the socket classes, `Socket` and `ServerSocket`, which open standard socket connections to hosts and read to and write from those connections
- Calling `getInputStream()`, a method that opens a connection to a URL and can extract data from that connection

Creating Links Inside Applets

Because applets run inside Web browsers, it's often useful to direct the browser to load a new Web document.

Before you can load anything, you must create a new instance of the class `URL` that represents the address of the resource you want to load. *URL* is an acronym for *uniform resource locator*, and it refers to the unique address of any document or other resource that is accessible on the Internet.

`URL` is part of the `java.net` package, so you must import the package or refer to the class by its full name in your programs.

To create a new `URL` object, use one of four constructors:

- `URL(String)` creates a URL object from a full Web address such as `http://www.java21days.com` or `ftp://ftp.netscape.com`.

- URL(*URL*, *String*) creates a URL object with a base address provided by the specified *URL* and a relative path provided by the *String*. When specifying the address, you can call getDocumentBase() for the URL of the page containing your applet or getCodeBase() for the URL of the applet's class file. The relative path will be tacked onto the base address.
- URL(*String*, *String*, *int*, *String*) creates a new URL object from a protocol (such as "http" or "ftp"), host name (such as "www.cnn.com" or "web.archive.org"), port number (80 for HTTP), and a filename or path name.
- URL(*String*, *String*, *String*) is the same as the previous constructor minus the port number.

When you use the URL(*String*) constructor, you must deal with MalformedURLException objects, which are thrown if the *String* does not appear to be a valid URL. These objects can be handled in a try-catch block:

```
try {
    URL load = new URL("http://www.samspublishing.com");
} catch (MalformedURLException e) {
    System.out.println("Bad URL");
}
```

After you have a URL object, you pass it to the browser by calling the showDocument() method of the AppletContext class in your applet. AppletContext is an interface that represents the environment in which an applet runs—the Web browser and the page in which it is contained.

Call getAppletContext() in your applet to get an AppletContext object to work with, then call showDocument(*URL*) on that object:

```
AppletContext ct = getAppletContext();
ct.showDocument(load);
```

These lines cause the browser presenting the applet to load and display the document at the URL represented by load.

Listing 17.1 contains two classes: WebMenu and a helper class called WebButton. The WebMenu applet displays three buttons that contain links to Web sites, as shown in Figure 17.1. Clicking the buttons causes the document to be loaded from the locations to which those buttons refer.

FIGURE 17.1

Running the WebMenu
applet in Internet
Explorer 6.

LISTING 17.1   The Full Text of WebMenu.java

```
 1: import java.net.*;
 2: import java.awt.*;
 3: import java.awt.event.*;
 4: import javax.swing.*;
 5:
 6: public class WebMenu extends JApplet implements ActionListener {
 7:     WebButton[] choices = new WebButton[3];
 8:
 9:     public void init() {
10:         choices[0] = new WebButton("Obscure Store",
11:             "http://www.obscurestore.com/");
12:         choices[1] = new WebButton("Need to Know",
13:             "http://www.ntk.net/");
14:         choices[2] = new WebButton("Bleat",
15:             "http://www.lileks.com/bleats");
16:
17:         FlowLayout flo = new FlowLayout();
18:         Container pane = getContentPane();
19:         pane.setLayout(flo);
20:         for (int i = 0; i < choices.length; i++) {
21:             choices[i].addActionListener(this);
22:             pane.add(choices[i]);
23:         }
24:         setContentPane(pane);
25:     }
26:
27:     public void actionPerformed(ActionEvent evt) {
28:         WebButton clicked = (WebButton)evt.getSource();
29:         try {
30:             URL load = new URL(clicked.address);
31:             getAppletContext().showDocument(load);
32:         } catch (MalformedURLException e) {
33:             showStatus("Bad URL:" + clicked.address);
34:         }
35:     }
```

LISTING 17.1 Continued

```
36: }
37:
38: class WebButton extends JButton {
39:     String address;
40:
41:     WebButton(String iLabel, String iAddress) {
42:         super(iLabel);
43:         address = iAddress;
44:     }
45: }
```

This applet can be tested using the following HTML on a Web page:

```
<applet code="WebMenu.class" height="100" width="125">
</applet>
```

17

Note

> This applet must be run from a Web browser rather than `appletviewer` for the buttons to load new pages. Because it uses event-handling techniques introduced after Java 1.0, it requires a Web browser equipped with the Java Plug-in.

Two classes make up this project: `WebMenu`, which implements the applet, and `WebButton`, a user-interface component that extends the `JButton` class to add an instance variable that holds a Web address.

This applet creates three `WebButton` instances (lines 10–15) and stores them in an array. Each button is assigned a name, which is used as a label, and a Web address, which is stored as a `String` rather than a `URL`.

After each button is set up, a container is created to represent the applet's content pane and set up to use the `FlowLayout` layout manager (lines 17–19).

In lines 20–23, an `ActionListener` is attached to each button before it is added to the container. This container is designated as the applet's content pane in line 24.

Because of the action listeners, the `actionPerformed()` method in lines 27–35 is called when a button is pressed. This method determines which button was clicked and then uses the `address` variable of that button to construct a new `URL` object. After you have a `URL` object, the call to `showDocument()` in line 31 tells the browser to load that Web page in the current window.

> **Tip**
>
> You can also load a URL in a new browser window or a specific frame. For a new window, call showDocument(*URL, String*) with "_blank" as the second argument. For a frame, use its name as the second argument.

Because the Web page information is stored in the applet, you must recompile the class file every time you add, remove, or modify an address. A better way to implement this program would be to store the Web page names and URLs as parameters in an HTML document, a technique described in Day 14, "Writing Java Applets."

Opening Web Connections

As you have seen when working with applets, it is easy to load a Web page or anything else with an URL. If the file you want to grab is stored on the Web and can be accessed by using the more common URL forms (HTTP, FTP, and so on), your Java program can use the URL class to get it.

For security reasons, by default applets can connect only to the same host from which they originally loaded. That means that if you have your applets stored on a system called http://www.java21days.com, the only machine to which your applet can open a connection will be that same host—and that same hostname. If the file that the applet wants to retrieve is on that same system, using URL connections is the easiest way to get it.

This restriction will change how you write and test applets that load files through their URLs. Because you haven't been dealing with network connections, you've been able to do all your testing on the local disk simply by opening the HTML files in a browser or with the appletviewer tool. You cannot do this with applets that open network connections. For those applets to work correctly, you must do one of two things:

- Run your browser on the same machine on which your Web server is running. If you don't have access to your Web server, you can often install and run a Web server on your local machine.

- Upload your class and HTML files to your Web server each time you want to test them. You then run the applet off the uploaded Web page instead of running it locally.

You'll know when you're not doing things correctly: If you try to load an applet or a file from a different server, you get a security exception, along with a lot of other error messages printed to your screen or to the Java console. Because of this, you might want to work with applications when you're connecting to the Internet and using its resources.

Opening a Stream over the Net

As you learned during Day 15, "Working with Input and Output," there are several ways you can pull information through a stream into your Java programs. The classes and methods you choose depend on the format of the information and what you want to do with it.

One of the resources you can reach from your Java programs is a text document on the World Wide Web, whether it's an HTML file or some other kind of plain text document.

You can use a four-step process to load a text document off the Web and read it line by line:

1. Create a URL object that represents the resource's World Wide Web address.
2. Create a URLConnection object that can load the URL and make a connection to the site hosting it.
3. Use the getInputStream() method of that URLConnection object to create an InputStreamReader that can read a stream of data from the URL.
4. Using that input stream reader, create a BufferedReader object that can efficiently read characters from an input stream.

There's a lot of interaction going on between Point A (the Web document) and Point B (your Java program). The URL is used to set up a URL connection, which is used to set up an input stream reader, which is used to set up a buffered input stream reader. The need to catch any exceptions that occur along the way adds more complexity to the process.

This can be confusing, so it's useful to step through a program that implements this procedure. The GetFile application in Listing 17.2 uses the four-step technique to open a connection to a Web site and read an HTML document from it. When the document is fully loaded, it is displayed in a text area.

LISTING 17.2   The Full Text of GetFile.java

```
1: import javax.swing.*;
2: import java.awt.*;
3: import java.awt.event.*;
4: import java.net.*;
5: import java.io.*;
6:
7: public class GetFile {
8:     public static void main(String[] arguments) {
9:         if (arguments.length == 1) {
10:             PageFrame page = new PageFrame(arguments[0]);
```

continues

LISTING 17.2 Continued

```
11:                     page.show();
12:             } else
13:                 System.out.println("Usage: java GetFile url");
14:         }
15: }
16:
17: class PageFrame extends JFrame {
18:     JTextArea box = new JTextArea("Getting data ...");
19:     URL page;
20:
21:     public PageFrame(String address) {
22:         super(address);
23:         setSize(600, 300);
24:         JScrollPane pane = new JScrollPane(box);
25:         getContentPane().add(pane);
26:         WindowListener l = new WindowAdapter() {
27:             public void windowClosing(WindowEvent evt) {
28:                 System.exit(0);
29:             }
30:         };
31:         addWindowListener(l);
32:
33:         try {
34:             page = new URL(address);
35:             getData(page);
36:         } catch (MalformedURLException e) {
37:             System.out.println("Bad URL: " + address);
38:         }
39:     }
40:
41:     void getData(URL url) {
42:         URLConnection conn = null;
43:         InputStreamReader in;
44:         BufferedReader data;
45:         String line;
46:         StringBuffer buf = new StringBuffer();
47:         try {
48:             conn = this.page.openConnection();
49:             conn.connect();
50:             box.setText("Connection opened ...");
51:
52:             in = new InputStreamReader(conn.getInputStream());
53:             data = new BufferedReader(in);
54:
55:             box.setText("Reading data ...");
56:             while ((line = data.readLine()) != null)
57:                 buf.append(line + "\n");
58:
```

LISTING 17.2   Continued

```
59:                box.setText(buf.toString());
60:            } catch (IOException e) {
61:                System.out.println("IO Error:" + e.getMessage());
62:            }
63:        }
64:
65: }
```

To run the GetFile application, specify a URL as the only command-line argument. For example:

```
java GetFile http://tycho.usno.navy.mil/cgi-bin/timer.pl
```

Any URL can be chosen; try http://www.samspublishing.com for the Sams Publishing Web site or http://random.yahoo.com/bin/ryl for a random link from the Yahoo! directory. The preceding example loads a page from the U.S. Naval Observatory's official timekeeping site, as shown in Figure 17.2.

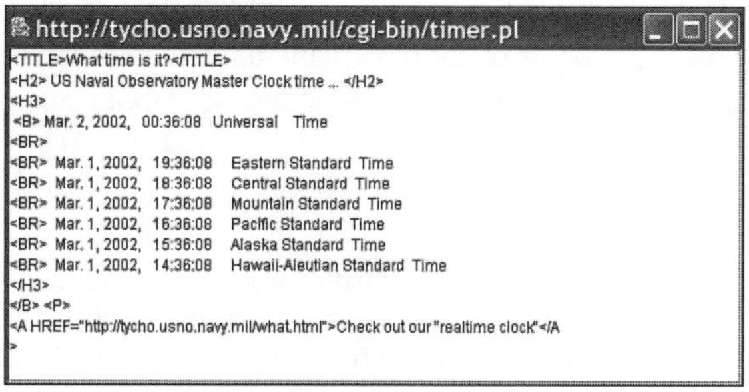

FIGURE 17.2

Running the GetFile *application.*

Two-thirds of Listing 17.2 is devoted to running the application, creating the user interface, and creating a valid URL object. The only thing that's new in this project is the getData() method in lines 41–63, which loads data from the resource at a URL and displays it in a text area.

First, three objects are initialized: a URLConnection, InputStreamReader, and BufferedReader. These will be used together to pull the data from the Internet to the Java application. In addition, two objects are created to actually hold the data when it arrives: a String and a StringBuffer.

Lines 48–49 open a URL connection, which is necessary to get an input stream from that connection.

Line 52 uses the URL connection's getInputStream() method to create a new input stream reader.

Line 53 uses that input stream reader to create a new buffered input stream reader—a `BufferedReader` object called `data`.

After you have this buffered reader, you can use its `readLine()` method to read a line of text from the input stream. The buffered reader puts characters in a buffer as they arrive and pulls them out of the buffer when requested.

The `while` loop in lines 56–57 reads the Web document line by line, appending each line to the `StringBuffer` object that was created to hold the page's text. A string buffer is used instead of a string because you can't modify a string at runtime in this manner.

After all the data have been read, line 59 converts the string buffer into a string with the `toString()` method and then puts that result in the program's text area by calling the component's `append(String)` method.

A `try-catch` statement surrounds the section of the program that opened a network connection, read from the file, and created a string.

Sockets

For networking applications beyond what the `URL` and `URLConnection` classes offer (for example, for other protocols or for more general networking applications), Java provides the `Socket` and `ServerSocket` classes as an abstraction of standard TCP socket programming techniques.

> **Note**
>
> Java also provides facilities for using datagram (UDP) sockets, which are not covered here. See the Java class library documentation for the `java.net` package if you're interested in working with datagrams. This documentation is available on Sun's Java Web site at `http://java.sun.com/j2se/1.4/docs/api/`.

The `Socket` class provides a client-side socket interface similar to standard Unix sockets. Create a new instance of `Socket` to open a connection (where `hostName` is the host to connect to and `portNumber` is the port number):

```
Socket connection = new Socket(hostName, portNumber);
```

After you create a socket, you should set its timeout value, which determines how long the application will wait for data to arrive. This is handled by calling the socket's `setSoTimeOut(int)` method with the number of milliseconds to wait as the only argument:

```
connection.setSoTimeOut(50000);
```

By using this method, any efforts to read data from the socket represented by `connection` will wait for only 50,000 milliseconds (50 seconds). If the timeout is reached, an `InterruptedIOException` will be thrown, which gives you an opportunity in a `try-catch` block to either close the socket or try to read from it again.

If you don't set a timeout in a program that uses sockets, it might hang indefinitely waiting for data.

Tip

This problem is usually avoided by putting network operations in their own thread and running them separately from the rest of the program, a technique used with animation on Day 7, "Threads and Exceptions."

After the socket is open, you can use input and output streams to read and write from that socket:

```
BufferedInputStream bis = new
    BufferedInputStream(connection.getInputStream());
DataInputStream in = new DataInputStream(bis);

BufferedOutputStream bos = new
    BufferedOutputStream(connection.getOutputStream());
DataOutputStream out = new DataOutputStream(bos);
```

You really don't need names for all of these objects; they are used only to create a stream or stream reader. For an efficient shortcut, combine several statements as in this example using a `Socket` object named `sock`:

```
DataInputStream in = new DataInputStream(
    new BufferedInputStream(
    sock.getInputStream()));
```

In this statement, the call to `sock.getInputStream()` returns an input stream associated with that socket. This stream is used to create a `BufferedInputStream`, and the buffered input stream is used to create a `DataInputStream`. The only variables you are left with are `sock` and `in`, the two objects needed as you receive data from the connection and close it afterward. The intermediate objects—a `BufferedInputStream` and an `InputStream`—are needed only once.

After you're done with a socket, don't forget to close it by calling the `close()` method. This also closes all the input and output streams you might have set up for that socket. For example:

```
connection.close();
```

17

Socket programming can be used for a large number of services that are delivered using TCP/IP networking, including telnet, SMTP (incoming mail), NNTP (Usenet news), and finger.

The last of these, finger, is a protocol for asking a system about one of its users. By setting up a finger server, a system administrator enables an Internet-connected machine to answer requests for user information. Users can provide information about themselves by creating .plan files, which are sent to anyone who uses finger to find out more about them.

Although it has fallen into disuse in recent years because of security concerns, finger was the most popular way that Internet users published facts about themselves and their activities before the World Wide Web was introduced. You could use finger on a friend's account at another college to see if that person was online and read the person's current .plan file.

Note

> Today, there's still one community that actively spreads personal messages by finger—the game-programming community. The GameFinger Web site, which acts as a gateway between the Web and finger, has links to dozens of these throwbacks at http://finger.planetquake.com/.

As an exercise in socket programming, the Finger application is a rudimentary finger client (see Listing 17.3).

LISTING 17.3 The Full Text of Finger.java

```
 1: import java.io.*;
 2: import java.net.*;
 3: import java.util.*;
 4:
 5: public class Finger {
 6:     public static void main(String[] arguments) {
 7:         String user;
 8:         String host;
 9:         if ((arguments.length == 1) && (arguments[0].indexOf("@") > -1)) {
10:             StringTokenizer split = new StringTokenizer(arguments[0],
11:                 "@");
12:             user = split.nextToken();
13:             host = split.nextToken();
14:         } else {
15:             System.out.println("Usage: java Finger user@host");
16:             return;
```

LISTING 17.3 Continued

```
17:        }
18:        try {
19:            Socket digit = new Socket(host, 79);
20:            digit.setSoTimeout(20000);
21:            PrintStream out = new PrintStream(digit.getOutputStream());
22:            out.print(user + "\015\012");
23:            BufferedReader in = new BufferedReader(
24:                new InputStreamReader(digit.getInputStream()));
25:            boolean eof = false;
26:            while (!eof) {
27:                String line = in.readLine();
28:                if (line != null)
29:                    System.out.println(line);
30:                else
31:                    eof = true;
32:            }
33:            digit.close();
34:        } catch (IOException e) {
35:            System.out.println("IO Error:" + e.getMessage());
36:        }
37:    }
38: }
```

When making a finger request, specify a username followed by an at sign ("@") and a host name, the same format as an e-mail address. One real-life example is johnc@idsoftware.com, the finger address of id Software founder John Carmack. You can request his .plan file by running the Finger application as follows:

```
java Finger johnc@idsoftware.com
```

If johnc has an account on the idsoftware.com finger server, the output of this program will be his .plan file and perhaps other information. The server also will let you know if a user can't be found.

The GameFinger site includes addresses for other game designers who provide .plan updates, including Chris Hargrove (chrish@finger.3drealms.com), Kenn Hoekstra (khoekstra@ravensoft.com), and Pat Lipo (plipo@ravensoft.com).

The Finger application uses the StringTokenizer class to convert an address in *user@host* format into two String objects: user and host (lines 10–13).

The following socket activities are taking place:

- Lines 19–20: A new `Socket` is created using the host name and port 79, the port that is traditionally reserved for finger services, and a timeout of 20 seconds is set.
- Line 21: The socket is used to get an `OutputStream`, which feeds into a new `PrintStream` object.
- Line 22: The finger protocol requires that the username be sent through the socket, followed by a carriage return ('\015') and linefeed ('\012'). This is handled by calling the `print()` method of the new `PrintStream`.
- Lines 23–24: After the username has been sent, an input stream must be created on the socket to receive input from the finger server. A `BufferedReader` stream, `in`, is created by combining several stream-creation expressions together. This stream is well suited for finger input because it can read a line of text at a time.
- Lines 26–32: The program loops as lines are read from the buffered reader. The end of output from the server causes `in.readLine()` to return `null`, ending the loop.

The same techniques used to communicate with a finger server through a socket can be used to connect to other popular Internet services. You could turn it into a telnet or Web-reading client with a port change in line 19 and little other modification.

Socket Servers

Server-side sockets work similarly to client sockets, with the exception of the `accept()` method. A server socket listens on a TCP port for a connection from a client; when a client connects to that port, the `accept()` method accepts a connection from that client. By using both client and server sockets, you can create applications that communicate with each other over the network.

To create a server socket and bind it to a port, create a new instance of `ServerSocket` with a port number as an argument to the constructor, as in the following example:

```
ServerSocket servo = new ServerSocket(8888);
```

Use the `accept()` method to listen on that port (and to accept a connection from any clients if one is made):

```
servo.accept();
```

After the socket connection is made, you can use input and output streams to read from and write to the client.

To extend the behavior of the socket classes—for example, to allow network connections to work across a firewall or a proxy—you can use the abstract class `SocketImpl` and the interface `SocketImplFactory` to create a new transport-layer socket implementation.

This design fits with the original goal of Java's socket classes: to allow those classes to be portable to other systems with different transport mechanisms. The problem with this mechanism is that although it works for simple cases, it prevents you from adding other protocols on top of TCP (for example, to implement an encryption mechanism such as SSL) and from having multiple socket implementations per Java runtime.

For these reasons, sockets were extended after Java 1.0 so the `Socket` and `ServerSocket` classes are not final and extendable. You can create subclasses of these classes that use either the default socket implementation or your own implementation. This allows much more flexible network capabilities.

Designing a Server Application

Here's an example of a Java program that uses the `Socket` classes to implement a simple network-based server application.

The `TimeServer` application makes a connection to any client that connects to port 4413, displays the current time, then closes the connection.

For an application to act as a server, it must monitor at least one port on the host machine for client connections. Port 4413 was chosen arbitrarily for this project, but it could be any number from 1024 to 65535.

Note

> The Internet Assigned Numbers Authority controls the usage of ports 0 to 1023, but claims are staked to the higher ports on a more informal basis. When choosing port numbers for your own client/server applications, it's a good idea to do research on what ports are being used by others. Search the Web for references to the port you want to use and plug the terms "Registered Port Numbers" and "Well-Known Port Numbers" into search engines to find lists of in-use ports. A good guide to port usage is available on the Web at `http://www.sockets.com/services.htm`.

When a client is detected, the server creates a `Date` object that represents the current date and time, then sends it to the client as a `String`.

In this exchange of information between the server and client, the server does almost all of the work. The client's only responsibility is to establish a connection to the server and display messages received from the server.

Although you could develop a simple client for a project like this, you also can use any telnet application to act as the client, as long as it can connect to a port you designate. Windows includes a command-line application called `telnet` that you can use for this purpose.

Listing 17.4 contains the full source code for the server application.

LISTING 17.4 The Full Text of `TimeServer.java`

```
 1: import java.io.*;
 2: import java.net.*;
 3: import java.util.*;
 4:
 5: public class TimeServer extends Thread {
 6:     private ServerSocket sock;
 7:
 8:     public TimeServer() {
 9:         super();
10:         try {
11:             sock = new ServerSocket(4413);
12:             System.out.println("TimeServer running ...");
13:         } catch (IOException e) {
14:             System.out.println("Error: couldn't create socket.");
15:             System.exit(1);
16:         }
17:     }
18:
19:     public void run() {
20:         Socket client = null;
21:
22:         while (true) {
23:             if (sock == null)
24:                 return;
25:             try {
26:                 client = sock.accept();
27:                 BufferedOutputStream bos = new BufferedOutputStream(
28:                     client.getOutputStream());
29:                 PrintWriter os = new PrintWriter(bos, false);
30:                 String outLine;
31:
32:                 Date now = new Date();
33:                 os.println(now);
34:                 os.flush();
35:
36:                 os.close();
37:                 client.close();
38:             } catch (IOException e) {
39:                 System.out.println("Error: couldn't connect to client.");
40:                 System.exit(1);
41:             }
42:         }
43:     }
44:
45:     public static void main(String[] arguments) {
46:         TimeServer server = new TimeServer();
47:         server.start();
48:     }
49:
50: }
```

Testing the Server

The TimeServer application must be running in order for a client to be able to connect to it. To get things started, you must first run the server:

```
java TimeServer
```

The server will display only one line of output if it is running successfully:

```
TimeServer running ...
```

With the server running, you can connect to it using a telnet program, such as the one that's included with Windows.

To run telnet on Windows 95, 98, Me, NT, or 2000, click Start, Run to open the Run dialog, and then type **telnet** in the Open text field and press Enter. A telnet window will open.

To make a telnet connection using this program, choose the menu command Connect, Remote System. A Connect dialog box will open, as shown in Figure 17.3. Enter **localhost** in the Host Name field, 4413 in the Port field, and leave the default value—vt100—in the TermType field.

FIGURE 17.3

Making a telnet *connection.*

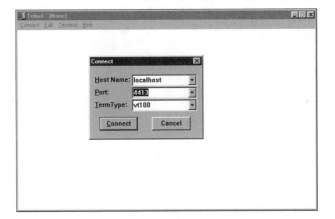

To use telnet on Windows XP, choose Start, Run to open the Run dialog, type telnet localhost 4413 in the Open text field, and then press Enter.

The host name localhost represents your own machine—the system running the application. You can use it to test server applications before deploying them permanently on the Internet.

Depending on how Internet connections have been configured on your system, you might need to log on to the Internet before a successful socket connection can be made between a telnet client and the TimeServer application.

If the server is on another computer connected to the Internet, you would specify that computer's host name or IP address instead of localhost.

When you use telnet to make a connection with the TimeServer application, it displays the server's current time and closes the connection. The output of the telnet program should be something like the following:

```
Thu Jun 13 18:41:10 EST 2002
Connection to host lost.
Press any key to continue...
```

The java.nio Package

Java 2 version 1.4 introduces the java.nio package, a group of classes that expands the networking capabilities of the language.

The new input/output package has features that are useful for reading and writing data; working with files, sockets, and memory; and handling text.

There are also two related packages that are used often when you are working with the new input/output features: java.nio.channels and java.nio.charset.

Buffers

The java.nio package includes support for *buffers*, objects that represent data streams stored in memory.

Buffers are often used to improve the performance of programs that read input or write output. They enable a program to put a lot of data in memory, where it can be used or altered more quickly.

There is a buffer that corresponds with each of the primitive data types in Java:

- ByteBuffer
- CharBuffer
- DoubleBuffer
- FloatBuffer
- IntBuffer
- LongBuffer
- ShortBuffer

Each of these classes has a static method called wrap() that can be used to create a buffer from an array of the corresponding data type. The only argument to the method should be the array.

For example, the following statements create an array of integers and an `IntBuffer` that holds the integers in memory as a buffer:

```
int[] temperatures = { 90, 85, 87, 78, 80, 75, 70, 79, 85, 92, 99 };
IntBuffer tempBuffer = IntBuffer.wrap(temperatures);
```

A buffer keeps track of how it is used, storing the position where the next item will be read or written. After the buffer is created, its `get()` method can be called to return the item at the current position in the buffer. The following statements extend the previous example and display everything in the integer buffer:

```
for (int i = 0; tempBuffer.remaining() > 0; i++)
    System.out.println(tempBuffer.get());
```

Another way to create a buffer is to set up an empty buffer and then put data into it. To create the buffer, call the static method `allocate(int)` of the buffer class with the size of the buffer as an argument.

There are five `put()` methods you can use to store data in a buffer (or replace the data that are already there). The arguments used with these methods depend on the kind of buffer you're working with. For an integer buffer

- `put(int)`—Stores the integer at the current position in the buffer, and then increments the position
- `put(int, int)`—Stores an integer (the second argument) at a specific position in the buffer (the first argument)
- `put(int[])`—Stores all the elements of the integer array in the buffer, beginning at the first position of the buffer
- `put(int[], int, int)`—Stores all or a portion of an integer array in the buffer. The second argument specifies the position in the buffer where the first integer in the array should be stored. The third argument specifies the number of elements from the array to store in the buffer.
- `put(IntBuffer)`—Stores the contents of an integer buffer in another buffer, beginning at the first position of the buffer

As you put data in a buffer, you must often keep track of the current position so you know where the next data will be stored.

To find out the current position, call the buffer's `position()` method. An integer is returned that represents the position. If this is 0, you're at the start of the buffer.

Call the `position(int)` method to change the position to the argument specified as an integer.

Another important position to track when using buffers is the limit—the last place in the buffer that contains data.

17

It isn't necessary to figure out the limit when the buffer is always full; in that case, you know the last position of the buffer has something in it.

However, if there's a chance your buffer might contain less data than you have allocated, you should call the buffer's flip() method after reading data into the buffer. This sets the current position to the start of the data you just read and sets the limit to the end.

Later today, you'll use a byte buffer to store data loaded from a Web page on the Internet. This is a place where flip() becomes necessary, because you don't know how much data the page contains when you request it.

If the buffer is 1,024 bytes in size and the page is 1,500 bytes, the first attempt to read data will load the buffer with 1,024 bytes, filling it.

The second attempt to read data will load the buffer with only 476 bytes, leaving the rest empty. If you call flip() afterward, the current position is set to the beginning of the buffer and the limit is set to 476.

The following code creates an array of Fahrenheit temperatures, converts them to Celsius, and then stores the Celsius value in a buffer:

```
int[] temps = { 90, 85, 87, 78, 80, 75, 70, 79, 85, 92, 99 };
IntBuffer tempBuffer = IntBuffer.allocate(temperatures.length);
for (int i = 0; i < temps.length; i++) {
    float celsius = ( (float)temps[i] - 32 ) / 9 * 5;
    tempBuffer.put( (int)celsius );
};
tempBuffer.position(0);
for (int i = 0; tempBuffer.remaining() > 0; i++)
    System.out.println(tempBuffer.get());
```

After the buffer's position is set back to the start, the contents of the buffer are displayed.

Byte Buffers

You can use the buffer methods introduced thus far with byte buffers, but byte buffers also offer additional useful methods.

For starters, byte buffers have methods to store and retrieve data that isn't a byte:

- putChar(char)—Stores two bytes in the buffer that represent the specified char value
- putDouble(double)—Stores eight bytes in the buffer that represent the double value
- putFloat(float)—Stores four bytes in the buffer that represent the float value
- putInt(int)—Stores four bytes in the buffer that represent the int value
- putLong(long)—Stores eight bytes in the buffer that represent the long value
- putShort(short)—Stores two bytes in the buffer that represent the short value

Each of these methods puts more than one byte in the buffer, moving the current position forward the same number of bytes.

There's also a corresponding group of methods to retrieve nonbytes from a byte buffer: `getChar()`, `getDouble()`, `getFloat()`, `getInt()`, `getLong()`, and `getShort()`.

Character Sets

Character sets, which are offered in the `java.nio.charset` package, are a set of classes used to convert data between byte buffers and character buffers.

There are three main classes:

- `Charset`—A Unicode character set with a different byte value for each different character in the set
- `Decoder`—A class that transforms a series of bytes into a series of characters
- `Encoder`—A class that transforms a series of characters into a series of bytes

Before you can do any transformations between byte and character buffers, you must create a `CharSet` object that maps characters to their corresponding byte values.

To create a character set, call the `forName(String)` static method of the `Charset` class, specifying the name of the set's character encoding.

Java 2 version 1.4 includes support for eight character encodings:

- US-ASCII—The 128-character ASCII set that makes up the Basic Latin block of Unicode (also called ISO646-US)
- ISO-8859-1—The 256-character ISO Latin Alphabet No. 1.a. character set (also called ISO-LATIN-1)
- UTF-8—A character set that includes US-ASCII and the Universal Character Set (also called Unicode), a set comprising thousands of characters used in the world's languages
- UTF-16BE—The Universal Character Set represented as 16-bit characters with bytes stored in big-endian byte order
- UTF-16LE—The Universal Character Set represented as 16-bit characters with bytes stored in little-endian byte order
- UTF-16—The Universal Character Set represented as 16-bit characters with the order of bytes indicated by an optional byte-order mark

17

The following statement creates a `Charset` object for the ISO-8859-1 character set:

```
Charset isoset = Charset.forName("ISO-8859-1");
```

Once you have a character set object, you can use it to create encoders and decoders. Call the object's `newDecoder()` method to create a `CharsetDecoder` and the `newEncoder()` method to create a `CharsetEncoder`.

To transform a byte buffer into a character buffer, call the decoder's `decode(ByteBuffer)` method, which returns a `CharBuffer` containing the bytes transformed into characters.

To transform a character buffer into a byte buffer, call the encoder's `encode(CharBuffer)` method. A `ByteBuffer` is returned containing the byte values of the characters.

The following statements convert a byte buffer called `netBuffer` into a character buffer using the ISO-8859-1 character set:

```
Charset set = Charset.forName("ISO-8859-1");
CharsetDecoder decoder = set.newDecoder();
netBuffer.position(0);
CharBuffer netText = decoder.decode(netBuffer);
```

 Caution Before the decoder is used to create the character buffer, the call to `position(0)` resets the current position of the `netBuffer` to the start. When working with buffers for the first time, it's easy to overlook this and leave a buffer with a lot less data than you expected.

Channels

A common use for a buffer is to associate it with an input or output stream. You can fill a buffer with data from an input stream or write a buffer to an output stream.

To do this, you must use a *channel*, an object that connects a buffer to the stream. Channels are part of the `java.nio.channels` package.

Channels can be associated with a stream by calling the `getChannel()` method available in some of the stream classes in the `java.io` package.

The `FileInputStream` and `FileOutputStream` classes have `getChannel()` methods that return a `FileChannel` object. This file channel can be used to read, write, and modify the data in the file.

The following statements create a file input stream and a channel associated with that file:

```
try {
    String source = "prices.dat";
    FileInputStream inSource = new FileInputStream(source);
    FileChannel inChannel = inSource.getChannel();
} catch (FileNotFoundException fne) {
    System.out.println(fne.getMessage());
}
```

After you have created the file channel, you can find out how many bytes the file contains by calling its size() method. This will be necessary if you want to create a byte buffer to hold the contents of the file.

Bytes are read from a channel into a ByteBuffer with the read(*ByteBuffer*, *long*) method. The first argument is the buffer. The second argument is the current position in the buffer, which determines where the file's contents will begin to be stored.

The following statements extend the last example by reading a file into a byte buffer using the inChannel file channel:

```
long inSize = inChannel.size();
ByteBuffer data = ByteBuffer.allocate( (int)inSize );
inChannel.read(data, 0);
data.position(0);
for (int i = 0; data.remaining() > 0; i++)
    System.out.print(data.get() + " ");
```

The attempt to read from the channel generates an IOException error if a problem occurs. Although the byte buffer is the same size as the file, this isn't a requirement. If you are reading the file into the buffer so you can modify it, you can allocate a larger buffer.

The next project you will create incorporates the new input/output features you have learned about thus far: buffers, character sets, and channels.

The ChangeBuffer application reads a small file into a byte buffer, displays the contents of the buffer, converts it to a character buffer, and then displays the characters.

Enter the text of Listing 17.5 and save it as ChangeBuffer.java.

17

LISTING 17.5   The Full Text of `ChangeBuffer.java`

```
 1: import java.nio.*;
 2: import java.nio.channels.*;
 3: import java.nio.charset.*;
 4: import java.io.*;
 5:
 6: public class ChangeBuffer {
 7:     public static void main(String[] arguments) {
 8:         try {
 9:             // read byte data into a byte buffer
10:             String data = "friends.dat";
11:             FileInputStream inData = new FileInputStream(data);
12:             FileChannel inChannel = inData.getChannel();
13:             long inSize = inChannel.size();
14:             ByteBuffer source = ByteBuffer.allocate( (int)inSize );
15:             inChannel.read(source, 0);
16:             source.position(0);
17:             System.out.println("Original byte data:");
18:             for (int i = 0; source.remaining() > 0; i++)
19:                 System.out.print(source.get() + " ");
20:
21:             // convert byte data into character data
22:             source.position(0);
23:             Charset ascii = Charset.forName("US-ASCII");
24:             CharsetDecoder toAscii = ascii.newDecoder();
25:             CharBuffer destination = toAscii.decode(source);
26:             destination.position(0);
27:             System.out.println("\n\nNew character data:");
28:             for (int i = 0; destination.remaining() > 0; i++)
29:                 System.out.print(destination.get());
30:         } catch (FileNotFoundException fne) {
31:             System.out.println(fne.getMessage());
32:         } catch (IOException ioe) {
33:             System.out.println(ioe.getMessage());
34:         }
35:     }
36: }
```

After you compile the file, you need a copy of `friends.dat`, the small file of byte data that's used in the application. To download it from this book's Web site at `http://www.java21days.com`, open the Day 17 page, click the `friends.dat` hyperlink, and save the file in the same place as `ChangeBuffer.class`.

 Tip

You can also create your own file. Open a text editor, type a sentence or two in the document, and save it as `friends.dat`.

If you use the copy of `friends.dat` from the book's Web site, the output of the `ChangeBuffer` application is the following:

```
Original byte data:
70 114 105 101 110 100 115 44 32 82 111 109 97 110 115 44 32
99 111 117 110 116 114 121 109 101 110 44 32 108 101 110 100
32 109 101 32 121 111 117 114 32 101 97 114 115 46 13 10 13
10

New character data:
Friends, Romans, countrymen, lend me your ears.
```

The `ChangeBuffer` application uses the techniques introduced today to read data and represent it as bytes and characters, but you could have accomplished the same thing with the old input/output package, `java.io`.

For this reason, you might wonder why it's worth learning the new package at all.

One reason is that buffers enable you to manipulate large amounts of data much more quickly. You'll find out another reason in the next section.

Network Channels

The most popular feature of the `java.nio` package is likely to be the support for non-blocking input and output over a networking connection.

In Java, *blocking* refers to a statement that must complete execution before anything else happens in the program. All of the socket programming you have done up to this point has used blocking methods exclusively. For example, in the `TimeServer` application, when the server socket's `accept()` method is called, nothing else happens in the program until a client makes a connection.

As you can imagine, it's problematic for a networking program to wait until a particular statement is executed, because numerous things can go wrong. Connections can be broken. A server could go offline. A socket connection could appear to be stalled because a blocked statement is waiting for something to happen.

For example, an application that reads data using an HTTP connection and buffers the data might be waiting for a buffer to be filled even though no more data remains to be sent. The program will appear to have halted because the blocked statement never finishes executing.

With the `java.nio` package, you can create networking connections and read and write from them using nonblocking methods.

Here's how it works:

- You associate a socket channel with an input or output stream.
- You configure the channel to recognize the kind of networking events you want to monitor: new connections, attempts to read data over the channel, and attempts to write data.
- You call a method to open the channel.
- Because the method is nonblocking, the program continues execution so you can handle other tasks.
- If one of the networking events you are monitoring takes place, your program is notified by calling a method associated with the event.

This is comparable to how user-interface components are programmed in Swing. An interface component is associated with one or more event listeners and placed in a container. If the interface component receives input that is being monitored by a listener, an event-handling method is called. Until that happens, the program can handle other tasks.

To use nonblocking input and output, you must work with channels instead of streams.

Nonblocking Socket Clients

The first step in the development of a client is to create an object that represents the Internet address to which you are making a connection. This task is handled by the new `InetSocketAddress` class in the `java.net` package.

If the server is identified by a host name, call `InetSocketAddress(String, int)` with two arguments: the name of the server and its port number.

If the server is identified by its IP address, use the `InetAddress` class in `java.net` to identify the host. Call the static method `InetAddress.getByName(String)` with the IP address of the host as the argument. The method returns an `InetAddress` object representing the address, which you can use in calling `InetSocketAddress(InetAddress, int)`. The second argument is the server's port number.

Nonblocking connections require a socket channel, another of the new classes in the `java.nio` package. Call the `open()` static method of the `SocketChannel` class to create the channel.

A socket channel can be configured for blocking or nonblocking communication. To set up a nonblocking channel, call the channel's `configureBlocking(boolean)` method with an argument of `false`. Calling it with `true` makes it a blocking channel.

Once the channel has been configured, call its `connect()` method to connect the socket.

On a blocking channel, the `connect()` method will attempt to establish a connection to the server and wait until it is complete, returning a value of `true` to indicate success.

On a nonblocking channel, the `connect()` method returns immediately and returns a value of `false`. To figure out what's going on over the channel and respond to events, you must use a channel-listening object called a `Selector`.

A `Selector` is an object that keeps track of things that happen to a socket channel (or another channel in the package that is a subclass of `SelectableChannel`).

To create a `Selector`, call its `open()` method, as in the following statement:

```
Selector monitor = Selector.open();
```

When you use a `Selector`, you must indicate the events you are interested in monitoring. This is handled by calling a channel's `register(Selector, int, Object)` method.

The three arguments to `register()` are the following:

- The `Selector` object you have created to monitor the channel
- An `int` value that represents the events being monitored (also called selection keys)
- An `Object` that can be delivered along with the key, or `null` otherwise

Instead of using an integer value as the second argument, it's easier to use one or more class variables from the `SelectionKey` class: `SelectionKey.OP_CONNECT` to monitor connections, `SelectionKey.OP_READ` to monitor attempts to read data, and `SelectionKey.OP_WRITE` to monitor attempts to write data.

The following statements create a `Selector` to monitor a socket channel called `wire` for reading data:

```
Selector spy = Selector.open();
channel.register(spy, SelectionKey.OP_READ, null);
```

To monitor more than one kind of key, add the `SelectionKey` class variables together. For example:

```
Selector spy = Selector.open();
channel.register(spy, SelectionKey.OP_READ + SelectionKey.OP_WRITE, null);
```

Once the channel and selector have been set up, you can wait for events by calling the selector's `select()` or `select(long)` methods.

The `select()` method is a blocking method that waits until something has happened on the channel.

The `select(long)` method is a blocking method that waits until something has happened or the specified number of milliseconds has passed, whichever comes first.

Both select() methods return the number of events that have taken place, or 0 if nothing has happened. You can use a while loop with a call to the select() method as a way to loop until something happens on the channel.

Once an event has taken place, you can find out more about it by calling the selector's selectedKeys() method, which returns a Set object containing details on each of the events.

Use this Set object as you would any other set, creating an Iterator to move through the set by using its hasNext() and next() methods.

The call to the set's next() method returns an object that should be cast to a SelectionKey. This object represents an event that took place on the channel.

There are three methods in the SelectionKey class that can be used to identify the key in a client program: isReadable(), isWriteable(), and isConnectible(). Each returns a boolean value. (A fourth method is used when you're writing a server: isAcceptable().)

After you have retrieved a key from the set, call the key's remove() method to indicate that you are going to do something with it.

The last thing to find out about the event is the channel on which it took place. Call the key's channel() method, which returns the associated SocketChannel.

If one of the events identifies a connection, you must make sure the connection has been completed before using the channel. Call the key's isConnectionPending() method, which returns true if the connection is still in progress and false if it is complete.

To deal with a connection that is still in progress, you can call the socket's finishConnect() method, which will make an attempt to complete the connection.

Using a nonblocking socket channel involves the interaction of numerous new classes from the java.nio and java.net packages.

To give you a more complete picture of how these classes work together, the last project of the day is LoadURL, a Web application that uses a nonblocking socket channel to load the contents of a URL.

Enter the text of Listing 17.6, save it as LoadURL.java and compile the application.

LISTING 17.6 The Full Text of LoadURL.java

```
 1: import java.nio.*;
 2: import java.nio.channels.*;
 3: import java.nio.charset.*;
 4: import java.io.*;
 5: import java.net.*;
 6: import java.util.*;
 7:
 8: public class LoadURL {
 9:
10:     public LoadURL(String urlRequest) {
11:         SocketChannel sock = null;
12:         try {
13:             URL url = new URL(urlRequest);
14:             String host = url.getHost();
15:             String page = url.getPath();
16:             InetSocketAddress address = new InetSocketAddress(host, 80);
17:             Charset iso = Charset.forName("ISO-8859-1");
18:             CharsetDecoder decoder = iso.newDecoder();
19:             CharsetEncoder encoder = iso.newEncoder();
20:
21:             ByteBuffer byteData = ByteBuffer.allocate(16384);
22:             CharBuffer charData = CharBuffer.allocate(16384);
23:
24:             sock = SocketChannel.open();
25:             sock.configureBlocking(false);
26:             sock.connect(address);
27:
28:             Selector listen = Selector.open();
29:             sock.register(listen, SelectionKey.OP_CONNECT +
30:                 SelectionKey.OP_READ);
31:
32:             while (listen.select(500) > 0) {
33:                 Set keys = listen.selectedKeys();
34:                 Iterator i = keys.iterator();
35:                 while (i.hasNext()) {
36:                     SelectionKey key = (SelectionKey) i.next();
37:                     i.remove();
38:                     SocketChannel keySock = (SocketChannel) key.channel();
39:                     if (key.isConnectable()) {
40:                         if (keySock.isConnectionPending()) {
41:                             keySock.finishConnect();
42:                         }
43:                         CharBuffer httpReq = CharBuffer.wrap(
44:                             "GET " + page + "\n\r\n\r");
45:                         ByteBuffer request = encoder.encode(httpReq);
46:                         keySock.write(request);
47:                     } else if (key.isReadable()) {
48:                         keySock.read(byteData);
```

continues

LISTING 17.6   Continued

```
49:                              byteData.flip();
50:                              charData = decoder.decode(byteData);
51:                              charData.position(0);
52:                              System.out.print(charData);
53:
54:                              byteData.clear();
55:                              charData.clear();
56:                      }
57:                  }
58:              }
59:          sock.close();
60:          } catch (MalformedURLException mue) {
61:              System.out.println(mue.getMessage());
62:          } catch (UnknownHostException uhe) {
63:              System.out.println(uhe.getMessage());
64:          } catch (IOException ioe) {
65:              System.out.println(ioe.getMessage());
66:          }
67:      }
68:
69:      public static void main(String arguments[]) {
70:          LoadURL app = new LoadURL(arguments[0]);
71:      }
72: }
```

Run the LoadURL application with one argument: The URL of a Web page, XML file, or another kind of text file on the Web:

```
java LoadURL http://www.jabbercentral.com/rss.php
```

The output of the application is either the contents of the file or an error message generated by the Web server. The preceding example loads an XML file containing the latest headlines from the Jabber Central instant messaging news site.

The LoadURL application uses the techniques that have been employed in several examples today.

One exception: In lines 13–15, a URL object is created using the URL passed to the application as an argument. This isn't necessary to use the socket, but it's an easy way to check the validity of a user-submitted URL and divide the URL into two parts: the host of the URL and the file being requested.

The application creates a nonblocking socket channel and registers two kinds of keys for a selector to look for: connection and read events.

The `while` loop that begins on line 32 checks to see if the selector has received any keys. When it has, `select(500)` returns the number of keys and the statements inside the loop are executed.

If the key relates to a connection, the application checks in line 40 if the connection is still pending. If it is, the call to `finishConnect()` in line 41 attempts to complete the connection.

Once the connection has been made, a character buffer is created to hold a request for a Web file. The request uses HTTP, the protocol employed on the World Wide Web; the command `GET` is followed by a space, the name of the file being requested, and some newline and carriage returns to signify the end of the request.

Before the request can be sent, it is converted to a byte buffer in line 45. The call to `write(ByteBuffer)` in line 46 sends the request over the socket channel.

If the key relates to reading data, the application makes use of the 16K byte buffer and character buffer created in lines 21–22.

These buffers are designed to be reused; one of the advantages of using buffers is that they require fewer objects, causing a program to run more quickly.

In lines 48–49, up to 16K is read into the `byteData` buffer and the call to `flip()` does two things: It sets the current position to the start of the buffer and sets the limit to the last byte read into the buffer. The limit will be at position 16384 if a full 16K was read from the socket or smaller if the end of the file was reached and less data was available from the Web server.

In line 50, the `charData` character buffer is loaded by decoding the byte buffer using the ISO-8859-1 character set specified in lines 17–19.

The call to `position(0)` in line 51 moves the current position to the start of the buffer, and its contents are displayed in line 52.

In lines 54–55, the buffers are emptied so they can be reused as more data is read from the socket.

Summary

Networking has many applications that your programs can use. You might not have realized it, but the `GetFile` and `LoadURL` projects are both rudimentary Web browsers. They can load a Web page's text into a Java program and display it, though they don't do anything to make sense of the HTML tags, presenting the raw text delivered by a Web server.

Today you learned how to use URLs, URL connections, and input streams in conjunction to pull data from the World Wide Web into your program.

You created a socket application that implements the basics of the finger protocol, a method for retrieving user information on the Internet.

You also learned how client and server programs are written in Java using the old blocking techniques that were available prior to Java 1.4 and the new nonblocking techniques that have been introduced with the `java.nio` package.

To make use of nonblocking techniques, you learned about the fundamental classes of Java's new networking package: buffers, character encoders and decoders, socket channels, and selectors.

Tomorrow, during Day 18, "JavaSound," you'll work with JavaSound, another package that was introduced in a recent version of the language.

Q&A

Q How can I mimic an HTML form submission in a Java applet?

A Currently, applets make it difficult to do this. The best (and easiest way) is to use `GET` notation to get the browser to submit the form contents for you.

HTML forms can be submitted two ways: either by using the `GET` request or by using `POST`. If you use `GET`, your form information is encoded in the URL itself, something like this:

```
http://www.blah.com/cgi-bin/myscript?foo=1&bar=2&name=Laura
```

Because the form input is encoded in the URL, you can write a Java applet to mimic a form, get input from the user, and then construct a new `URL` object with the form data included on the end. Then just pass that URL to the browser by using `getAppletContext()` and `showDocument()`, and the browser will submit the form results itself. For simple forms, this is all you need.

Q How can I do `POST` form submissions?

A You have to mimic what a browser does to send forms using `POST`. Create a `URL` object for the form-submission address, such as `http://www.cadenhead.info/cgi-bin/mail2rogers.cgi`, and then call this object's `openConnection()` method to create a `URLConnection` object. Call the connection's `setDoOutput()` method to indicate that you will be sending data to this URL, and then send the connection a series of name-value pairs that hold the data, separated by ampersand characters (`"&"`).

For instance, the `mail2rogers.cgi` form is a CGI program that sends mail to Rogers Cadenhead, the co-author of this book. It transmits `name`, `subject`, `email`, `comments`, `who`, `rcode`, and `scode` data. If you have created a `PrintWriter` stream called pw that is connected to this CGI program, you can post information to it using the following statement:

```
pw.print("name=YourName&subject=Your+Book&email=you@yourdomain.com&"
    + "comments=Your+POST+example+works.+I+owe+you+$1,000&"
    + "who=preadm&rcode=2java21&scode=%2Fmailsent.html");
```

Quiz

Review today's material by taking this quiz.

Questions

1. What network action is not permitted in an applet under the default security level for Java?

(a.) Loading a graphic from the server that hosts the applet

(b.) Loading a graphic from a different server

(c.) Loading a Web page from a different server in the browser containing the applet

2. In the finger protocol, which program makes a request for information about a user?

(a.) The client

(b.) The server

(c.) Both can make that request

3. Which method is preferred for loading the data from a Web page into your Java application?

(a.) Creating a `Socket` and an input stream from that socket

(b.) Creating a `URL` and a `URLConnection` from that object

(c.) Loading the page using the applet method `showDocument()`

Answers

1. (b.) Applets cannot make network connections to any machine other than the one from which they were served.

2. (a.) The client requests information and the server sends something back in response. This is traditionally how client/server applications function, although some programs can act as both client and server.

3. (b.) Sockets are good for low-level connections, such as when you are implementing a new protocol. For existing protocols such as HTTP, there are classes that are better suited to that protocol—`URL` and `URLConnection`, in this case.

17

Certification Practice

The following question is the kind of thing you could expect to be asked on a Java programming certification test. Answer it without looking at today's material or using the Java compiler to test the code.

Given:

```
import java.nio.*;

public class ReadTemps {
    public ReadTemps() {
        int[] temperatures = { 78, 80, 75, 70, 79, 85, 92, 99, 90, 85, 87 };
        IntBuffer tempBuffer = IntBuffer.wrap(temperatures);
        int[] moreTemperatures = { 65, 44, 71 };
        tempBuffer.put(moreTemperatures);
        System.out.println("First int: " + tempBuffer.get());
    }
}
```

What will be the output when this application is run?

(a.) First int: 78

(b.) First int: 71

(c.) First int: 70

(d.) none of the above

The answer is available on this book's Web site at http://www.java21days.com. Visit the Day 17 page and click the Certification Practice link.

Exercises

To extend your knowledge of the subjects covered today, try the following exercises:

- Modify the WebMenu program so it generates 10 URLs that begin with http://www., end with .com, and contain three random letters or numbers in between (such as http://www.mcp.com, http://www.cbs.com, and http://www.eod.com). Use these URLs in 10 WebButton objects on an applet.

- Write a program that takes finger requests, looks for a .plan file matching the username requested, and sends it if found. Send a "user not found" message otherwise.

Where applicable, exercise solutions are offered on this book's Web site at http://www.java21days.com.

JavaSound

All the different ways in which a program can be visually interesting—the user interface, graphics, images, and animation—involve the classes of the Swing and Abstract Windowing Toolkit packages.

For programs that are audibly interesting, Java 2 supports sound using applet methods that have been available since the introduction of the language and an extensive new class library called JavaSound.

Today you will make Java programs audible in two ways.

First, you will use methods of the `Applet` class, the superclass of all Java applets. You can use these methods to retrieve and play sound files in programs using a large number of formats, including `WAV`, `AU`, and `MIDI`.

Next, you will work with JavaSound, several packages that enable the playback, recording, and manipulation of sound.

Retrieving and Using Sounds

Java supports the playback of sound files through the `Applet` class, and you can play a sound one time or as a repeating sound loop.

Prior to Java 2, the language could handle only one audio format: 8KHz mono AU with mu-law encoding (named for the Greek letter μ, or mu). If you wanted to use something that was in a format such as WAV, you had to translate it to mu-law AU, often at a loss of quality.

Java 2 adds much fuller support for audio. You can load and play digitized sound files in AIFF, AU, and WAV. Three MIDI-based song file formats also are supported: Type 0 MIDI, Type 1 MIDI, and RMF. The greatly improved sound support can handle 8- or 16-bit audio data in mono or stereo, and the sample rates can range from 8KHz to 48KHz.

The simplest way to retrieve and play a sound is through the play() method of the Applet class. The play() method, like the getImage() method, takes one of two forms:

- play() with one argument—an URL object—loads and plays the audio clip stored at that URL.
- play() with two arguments—a base URL and a folder pathname—loads and plays that audio file. The first argument often will be a call to getDocumentBase() or getCodeBase(), as you have seen with getImage().

The following statement retrieves and plays the sound zap.au, which is stored in the same place as the applet:

```
play(getCodeBase(), "zap.au");
```

The play() method retrieves and plays the given sound as soon as possible after it is called. If the sound file can't be found, the only indication you'll receive of a problem is the silence. No error message will be displayed.

To play a sound repeatedly, start and stop the sound, or play it repeatedly as a loop, you must load it into an AudioClip object by using the applet's getAudioClip method. AudioClip is part of the java.applet package, so it must be imported to be used in a program.

The getAudioClip() method takes one or two arguments in the same fashion as the play() method. The first (or only) argument is an URL argument identifying the sound file, and the second is a folder path reference.

The following statement loads a sound file into the clip object:

```
AudioClip clip = getAudioClip(getCodeBase(),
    "audio/marimba.wav");
```

In this example, the filename includes a folder reference, so the file marimba.wav will be loaded from the subfolder audio.

The getAudioClip() method can be called only within an applet. As of Java 2, applications can load sound files by using newAudioClip(), a class method of the java.awt.Applet class. Here's the previous example rewritten for use in an application:

```
AudioClip clip = Applet.newAudioClip("audio/marimba.wav");
```

After you have created an AudioClip object, you can call the play() (plays the sound), stop() (halts playback), and loop()(plays repeatedly) methods.

If the getAudioClip() or newAudioClip() methods can't find the sound file indicated by their arguments, the value of the AudioClip object will be null. Trying to play a null object results in an error, so test for this condition before using an AudioClip object.

More than one sound can play simultaneously; they will be mixed together during playback.

When using a sound loop in an applet, note that it won't stop automatically when the applet's running thread is stopped. If a Web user moves to another page, the sound continues playing, which isn't likely to win you any friends among the Web-surfing public.

You can fix this problem by using the stop() method on the looping sound at the same time the applet's thread is being stopped.

Listing 18.1 is an applet that plays two sounds: a looping sound named train.wav and another sound called whistle.wav that plays every 5 seconds.

18

LISTING 18.1   The Full Text of Looper.java

```
 1: import java.awt.*;
 2: import java.applet.AudioClip;
 3:
 4: public class Looper extends javax.swing.JApplet implements Runnable {
 5:     AudioClip bgSound;
 6:     AudioClip beep;
 7:     Thread runner;
 8:
 9:     public void init() {
10:         bgSound = getAudioClip(getCodeBase(),"train.wav");
11:         beep = getAudioClip(getCodeBase(), "whistle.wav");
12:     }
13:
14:     public void start() {
15:         if (runner == null) {
16:             runner = new Thread(this);
17:             runner.start();
18:         }
19:     }
20:
21:     public void stop() {
22:         if (runner != null) {
```

continues

LISTING 18.1 Continued

```
23:                    if (bgSound != null)
24:                        bgSound.stop();
25:                    runner = null;
26:            }
27:        }
28:
29:        public void run() {
30:            if (bgSound != null)
31:                bgSound.loop();
32:            Thread thisThread = Thread.currentThread();
33:            while (runner == thisThread) {
34:                try {
35:                    Thread.sleep(9000);
36:                    if (beep != null)
37:                        beep.play();
38:                } catch (InterruptedException e) { }
39:            }
40:        }
41:
42:        public void paint(Graphics screen) {
43:            Graphics2D screen2D = (Graphics2D)screen;
44:            screen2D.drawString("Playing Sounds ...", 10, 10);
45:        }
46: }
```

To test `Looper`, create a Web page with an applet window of any height and width. The audio files `train.wav` and `whistle.wav` can be copied from the book's Web site (`http://www.java21days.com`) into the `\J21work` folder on your system. When you run the applet, the only visual output is a single string, but you should hear two sounds playing as the applet runs.

The `init()` method in lines 9–12 loads the two sound files. No attempt is made in this method to make sure that the files were actually loaded; if they cannot be found, the `bgsound` and `beep` variables will equal `null`. Testing for `null` values in these variables will occur elsewhere before the sound files are used, such as in lines 30 and 36, when the `loop()` and `play()` methods are used on the `AudioClip` objects.

Lines 23–24 turn off the looping sound if the thread is also stopped.

JavaSound

The new version of Java includes several packages that greatly expand the sound playback and creation capabilities of the language.

JavaSound, an official part of the Java class library since Java 2 version 1.3, is made up primarily of two packages:

- `javax.sound.midi`—Classes for playing, recording, and synthesizing sound files in `MIDI` format
- `javax.sound.sampled`—Classes for playing, recording, and mixing recorded audio files

The JavaSound library supports all the audio formats available for playback in applets and applications: `AIFF`, `AU`, `MIDI`, and `WAV`. It also supports `RMF`, a standard for Rich Media Format music files.

MIDI Files

The `javax.sound.midi` package offers extensive support for `MIDI` music files. `MIDI`, which stands for Musical Instrument Digital Interface, is a format for storing sound as a series of notes and effects to be produced by computer synthesized instruments.

Unlike sampled files representing actual sound recorded and digitized for computer presentation, such as `WAV` and `AU`, `MIDI` is closer to a musical score for a synthesizer than a realized recording. `MIDI` files are stored instructions that tell `MIDI` sequencers how to reproduce sound, which synthesized instruments to use, and other aspects of presentation. The sound of a `MIDI` file depends on the quality and variety of the instruments available on the computer or output device.

`MIDI` files are generally much smaller than recorded audio, and they're not suited to representing voices and some other types of sound. However, because of compactness and effects-capability, `MIDI` is used in many different ways, such as computer game background music, Muzak-style versions of pop songs, or the preliminary presentations of classical composition for composers and students.

`MIDI` files are played back by using a sequencer—which can be a hardware device or software program—to play a data structure called a sequence. A sequence is made up of one or more tracks, each containing a series of time-coded `MIDI` notes and effect instructions called `MIDI` events.

Each of these elements of MIDI presentation is represented by an interface or class in the `javax.sound.midi` package: the `Sequencer` interface and the `Sequence`, `Track`, and `MidiEvent` classes.

There also is a `MidiSystem` class that provides access to the `MIDI` playback and storage resources on a computer system.

18

Playing a `MIDI` File

To play a `MIDI` file using JavaSound, you must create a `Sequencer` object based on the MIDI-handling capability of a particular system.

The `MidiSystem` class method `getSequencer()` returns a `Sequencer` object that represents a system's default sequencer:

```
Sequencer midi = MidiSystem.getSequencer();
```

This class method generates an exception—an object indicating an error—if the sequencer is unavailable for any reason. A `MidiUnavailableException` is generated in this circumstance.

You worked with exceptions briefly yesterday during Day 17, "Communicating Across the Internet," enclosing calls to `Thread.sleep()` in `try-catch` blocks because that method generates `InterruptedException` errors if the method is interrupted.

You can handle the exception generated by `getSequencer()` with the following code:

```
try {
    Sequencer.midi = MidiSystem.getSequencer();
    // additional code to play a MIDI sequence ...
} catch (MidiUnavailableException exc) {
    System.out.println("Error: " + exc.getMessage());
}
```

In this example, if a sequencer is available when `getSequencer()` is called, the program continues to the next statement inside the `try` block. If the sequencer can't be accessed because of a `MidiUnavailableException`, the program executes the `catch` block, displaying an error message.

Several methods and constructors involved in playing a MIDI file generate exceptions. Rather than enclosing each one in its own `try-catch` block, it can be easier to handle all possible errors by using `Exception`, the superclass of all exceptions, in the `catch` statement:

```
try {
    Sequencer.midi = MidiSystem.getSequencer();
    // additional code to play a MIDI sequence ...
} catch (Exception exc) {
    System.out.println("Error: " + exc.getMessage());
}
```

This example doesn't just handle `MidiUnavailableException` problems in the `catch` block. When you add additional statements to load and play a MIDI sequence inside the `try` block, any exceptions generated by those statements will cause the `catch` block to be executed.

After you have created a `Sequencer` object that can play MIDI files, you call another class method of `MidiSystem` to retrieve a MIDI sequence from a data source:

- `getSequence(File)`—Loads a sequence from the specified file
- `getSequence(URL)`—Loads a sequence from the specified Internet address
- `getSequence(InputStream)`—Loads a sequence from the specified data input stream, which can come from a file, input device, or another program

To load a `MIDI` sequence from a file, you must first create a `File` object using its filename or a reference to its filename and the folder where it can be found.

If the file is in the same folder as your Java program, you can create it using the `File(String)` constructor with that name. The following statement creates a `File` object for a `MIDI` file called `nevermind.mid`:

```
File sound = new File("nevermind.mid");
```

You can also use relative file references that include subfolders:

```
File sound = new File("tunes/nevermind.mid");
```

The `File` constructor generates a `NullPointerException` if the argument to the constructor has a `null` value.

After you have a `File` object associated with a `MIDI` file, you can call `getSequence(File)` to create a sequence:

```
File sound = new File("aboutagirl.mid");
Sequence seq = MidiSystem.getSequence(sound);
```

If all goes well, the `getSequence()` class method will return a `Sequence` object. If not, two kinds of errors can be generated by the method: `InvalidMidiDataException` if the system can't handle the MIDI data (or it isn't MIDI data at all) and `IOException` if file input was interrupted or failed for some reason.

At this point, if your program has not been derailed by an error, you have a `MIDI` sequencer and a sequence to play. You are ready to play the file; you don't have to deal with tracks or `MIDI` events just to play back an entire `MIDI` file.

Playing a sequence involves the following steps:

- Call the sequencer's `open()` method so the device prepares to play something.
- Call the sequencer's `start()` method to begin playing the sequence.
- Wait for the sequence to finish playing (or for a user to stop playback in some manner).
- Call the sequencer's `close()` method to free the device for other things.

18

The only one of these methods that generates an exception is open(), which produces a MidiUnavailableException if the sequencer can't be readied for playback.

Calling close() stops a sequencer, even if it is playing one or more sequences. You can use the sequencer method isRunning(), which returns a boolean value, to check whether it is still playing (or recording) MIDI sequences.

The following example uses this method on a sequencer object called playback that has a sequence loaded:

```
playback.open();
playback.start();
while (playback.isRunning()) {
    try {
        Thread.sleep(1000);
    } catch (InterruptedException e) { }
}
playback.close();
```

The while loop prevents the sequencer from being closed until the sequence has completed playback. The call to Thread.sleep() inside the loop slows it down so isRunning() is checked only once per second (1,000 milliseconds)—otherwise, the program will use a lot of resources by calling isRunning() numerous times per second.

The PlayMidi application in Listing 18.2 plays a MIDI sequence from a file on your system. The application displays a frame that contains a user-interface component called MidiPanel, and this panel runs in its own thread and plays the file.

LISTING 18.2   The Full Text of PlayMidi.java

```
 1: import javax.swing.*;
 2: import javax.sound.midi.*;
 3: import java.awt.GridLayout;
 4: import java.io.File;
 5:
 6: public class PlayMidi extends JFrame {
 7:
 8:     PlayMidi(String song) {
 9:         super("Play MIDI Files");
10:         setSize(180, 100);
11:         setDefaultCloseOperation(JFrame.EXIT_ON_CLOSE);
12:         MidiPanel midi = new MidiPanel(song);
13:         JPanel pane = new JPanel();
14:         pane.add(midi);
15:         setContentPane(pane);
16:         show();
17:     }
18:
19:     public static void main(String[] arguments) {
20:         if (arguments.length != 1) {
```

LISTING 18.2 Continued

```
21:                     System.out.println("Usage: java PlayMidi filename");
22:             } else {
23:                 PlayMidi pm = new PlayMidi(arguments[0]);
24:             }
25:         }
26: }
27:
28: class MidiPanel extends JPanel implements Runnable {
29:     Thread runner;
30:     JProgressBar progress = new JProgressBar();
31:     Sequence currentSound;
32:     Sequencer player;
33:     String songFile;
34:
35:     MidiPanel(String song) {
36:         super();
37:         songFile = song;
38:         JLabel label = new JLabel("Playing file ...");
39:         setLayout(new GridLayout(2, 1));
40:         add(label);
41:         add(progress);
42:         if (runner == null) {
43:             runner = new Thread(this);
44:             runner.start();
45:         }
46:     }
47:
48:     public void run() {
49:         try {
50:             File file = new File(songFile);
51:             currentSound = MidiSystem.getSequence(file);
52:             player = MidiSystem.getSequencer();
53:             player.open();
54:             player.setSequence(currentSound);
55:             progress.setMinimum(0);
56:             progress.setMaximum((int)player.getMicrosecondLength());
57:             player.start();
58:             while (player.isRunning()) {
59:                 progress.setValue((int)player.getMicrosecondPosition());
60:                 try {
61:                     Thread.sleep(1000);
62:                 } catch (InterruptedException e) { }
63:             }
64:             progress.setValue((int)player.getMicrosecondPosition());
65:             player.close();
66:         } catch (Exception ex) {
67:             System.out.println(ex.toString());
68:         }
69:     }
70: }
```

18

You must specify the name of a MIDI file as a command-line argument when running this application. If you don't have any MIDI files, one is available from the book's Web site; visit http://www.java21days.com and open the Day 18 page.

Tip

> Hundreds of MIDI archives are on the World Wide Web. To find some of the most popular archives, visit the search engine Google at http://www.google.com and search for the term MIDI files. Google displays sites in the order of their popularity, so you should be able to quickly find a few great MIDI resources.

The following command runs the application with a MIDI file called betsy.mid (the 19th century folk song *Sweet Betsy from Pike*, available from this book's Web site):

```
java PlayMidi betsy.mid
```

Figure 18.1 shows the application in mid-playback.

FIGURE 18.1

The PlayMidi *application playing a MIDI file.*

The application includes a progress bar that displays how much of the sequence has been played. This is handled using the JProgressBar user-interface component and two sequencer methods:

- getMicrosecondLength()—The total length of the currently loaded sequence, expressed in microseconds as a long value
- getMicrosecondPosition()—The microsecond that represents the current position in the sequence, also a long value

A microsecond is equal to one-millionth of a second, so you can use these methods to get an astonishingly precise measurement of MIDI playback progress.

The progress bar is created as an instance variable of MidiPanel in line 27. Though you can create a progress bar with a minimum and maximum, there's no way to know the length of a sequence until it has been loaded.

The progress bar's minimum is set to 0 in line 55 and to the sequence's microsecond length in line 56.

Caution

The progress bar's setMinimum() and setMaximum() methods require integer arguments, so this application converts the microsecond values from long to int. Because of this loss of precision, the progress bar won't work correctly for files longer than 2.14 billion microseconds (around 35.6 minutes).

The run() method in lines 48–69 of Listing 18.2 loads the system sequencer and a MIDI file into a sequence and plays the sequence. The while loop in lines 58–63 uses the sequencer's isRunning() method to wait until the file finishes playing before doing anything else. This loop also updates the progress bar by calling its setValue() method with the current microsecond position of the sequence.

After the file finishes playback and the while loop terminates, the microsecond position of the sequence is reported as 0, which is used in line 64 to set the progress bar back to its minimum value.

Manipulating Sound Files

Up to this point, you have used JavaSound to recreate functionality that's already available in the audio methods of the Applet class, which can play MIDI files in addition to the other supported formats.

JavaSound's strength as an alternative becomes apparent when you manipulate the sound files with which you are working. You can change many aspects of the presentation and recording of audio using the JavaSound packages.

One way to change a MIDI file during playback is to alter its tempo, the speed at which the file is played.

To do this on an existing Sequencer object, call its setTempoFactor(float) method.

Tempo is represented as a float value from 0.0 upward. Every MIDI sequence has its own established tempo, which is represented by the value 1.0. A tempo of 0.5 is half as fast, 2.0 twice as fast, and so on.

To retrieve the current tempo, call getTempoFactor(), which returns a float value.

The next project you will create, MidiApplet, uses the same technique to load and play a MIDI file as the PlayMidi application—a panel is displayed that plays a MIDI file in its own thread. The MIDI file is loaded using a File object and played using a sequencer's open(), start(), and close() methods.

18

One difference in this project is that the MIDI file can be played over and over again, rather than just once.

Because this is an applet rather than an application, the MIDI file to play will be specified as a parameter. Listing 18.3 contains an example of an HTML document that can be used to load the applet.

LISTING **18.3**   The Full Text of MidiApplet.html

```
1: <applet code="MidiApplet.class" height="100" width="250">
2: <param name="file" value="camptown.mid">
3: </applet>
```

The MIDI file used in this example, a MIDI version of *Camptown Races,* is available from this book's Web site at http://www.java21days.com on the Day 18 page. You can, of course, substitute any other MIDI file.

The MidiApplet project has three user-interface components you can use to control how the file is played: play and stop buttons and a drop-down list for the selection of a tempo.

Figure 18.2 shows what the program looks like when loaded by appletviewer.

FIGURE **18.2**

The MidiApplet *program playing Camptown Races.*

Because applets will continue playing sound in a Web browser even after a user loads a different page, there must be a way to stop playback.

If you are running audio in its own thread, you can stop the audio by using the same thread-stopping techniques introduced for animation yesterday; run the thread in a Thread object, loop while that object and Thread.currentThread() represent the same object, and set runner to null when you are ready to stop the thread.

Listing 18.4 contains the MidiApplet project. The length of this program is primarily due to the creation of the graphical user interface and the event-handling methods to receive input from the user. The JavaSound-related aspects of the program will be introduced after you have created the applet.

LISTING 18.4 The Full Text of `MidiApplet.java`

```
 1: import javax.swing.*;
 2: import java.awt.event.*;
 3: import javax.sound.midi.*;
 4: import java.awt.GridLayout;
 5: import java.io.File;
 6:
 7: public class MidiApplet extends javax.swing.JApplet {
 8:     public void init() {
 9:         JPanel pane = new JPanel();
10:         MidiPlayer midi = new MidiPlayer(getParameter("file"));
11:         pane.add(midi);
12:         setContentPane(pane);
13:     }
14: }
15:
16: class MidiPlayer extends JPanel implements Runnable, ActionListener {
17:
18:     Thread runner;
19:     JButton play = new JButton("Play");
20:     JButton stop = new JButton("Stop");
21:     JLabel message = new JLabel();
22:     JComboBox tempoBox = new JComboBox();
23:     float tempo = 1.0F;
24:     Sequence currentSound;
25:     Sequencer player;
26:     String songFile;
27:
28:     MidiPlayer(String song) {
29:         super();
30:         songFile = song;
31:         play.addActionListener(this);
32:         stop.setEnabled(false);
33:         stop.addActionListener(this);
34:         for (float i = 0.25F; i < 7F; i += 0.25F)
35:             tempoBox.addItem("" + i);
36:         tempoBox.setSelectedItem("1.0");
37:         tempoBox.setEnabled(false);
38:         tempoBox.addActionListener(this);
39:         setLayout(new GridLayout(2, 1));
40:         add(message);
41:         JPanel buttons = new JPanel();
42:         JLabel tempoLabel = new JLabel("Tempo: ");
43:         buttons.add(play);
44:         buttons.add(stop);
45:         buttons.add(tempoLabel);
46:         buttons.add(tempoBox);
47:         add(buttons);
```

18

continues

LISTING **18.4** Continued

```
48:            if (songFile == null) {
49:                play.setEnabled(false);
50:            }
51:        }
52:
53:    public void actionPerformed(ActionEvent evt) {
54:        if (evt.getSource() instanceof JButton) {
55:            if (evt.getSource() == play)
56:                play();
57:            else
58:                stop();
59:        } else {
60:            String item = (String)tempoBox.getSelectedItem();
61:            try {
62:                tempo = Float.parseFloat(item);
63:                player.setTempoFactor(tempo);
64:                message.setText("Playing " + songFile + " at "
65:                    + tempo + " tempo");
66:            } catch (NumberFormatException ex) {
67:                message.setText(ex.toString());
68:            }
69:        }
70:    }
71:
72:    void play() {
73:        if (runner == null) {
74:            runner = new Thread(this);
75:            runner.start();
76:            play.setEnabled(false);
77:            stop.setEnabled(true);
78:            tempoBox.setEnabled(true);
79:        }
80:    }
81:
82:    void stop() {
83:        if (runner != null) {
84:            runner = null;
85:            stop.setEnabled(false);
86:            play.setEnabled(true);
87:            tempoBox.setEnabled(false);
88:        }
89:    }
90:
91:    public void run() {
92:        try {
93:            File song = new File(songFile);
94:            currentSound = MidiSystem.getSequence(song);
95:            player = MidiSystem.getSequencer();
```

LISTING 18.4   Continued

```
 96:            } catch (Exception ex) {
 97:                message.setText(ex.toString());
 98:            }
 99:            Thread thisThread = Thread.currentThread();
100:            while (runner == thisThread) {
101:                try {
102:                    player.open();
103:                    player.setSequence(currentSound);
104:                    player.setTempoFactor(tempo);
105:                    player.start();
106:                    message.setText("Playing " + songFile + " at "
107:                        + tempo + " tempo");
108:                    while (player.isRunning() && runner != null) {
109:                        try {
110:                            Thread.sleep(1000);
111:                        } catch (InterruptedException e) { }
112:                    }
113:                    message.setText("");
114:                    player.close();
115:                } catch (Exception ex) {
116:                    message.setText(ex.toString());
117:                    break;
118:                }
119:            }
120:        }
121: }
```

Run `MidiApplet` by loading it on an HTML document using `appletviewer` or a Web browser that's equipped with the Java Plug-in.

The tempo of the `MIDI` file is controlled by a drop-down list component called `tempoBox`. This component is created with a range of floating-point values from 0.25 to 6.75 in lines 34–35. The list's `addItem(Object)` method cannot be used with `float` values, so they are combined with an empty string—quote marks without any text inside—in line 35. This causes the combined argument to be sent to `addItem()` as a `String` object.

Though the tempo can be set using `tempoBox`, it is stored in its own instance variable, `tempo`. This variable is initialized in line 23 with a value of 1.0, the sequence's default playback speed.

If the drop-down list from which a user selects a value has an `ActionListener` associated with it, the listener's `actionPerformed` method will be called.

The `actionPerformed()` method in lines 53–70 handles all three kinds of possible user input:

- Clicking the Play button causes the `play()` method to be called.
- Clicking the Stop button causes the `stop()` method to be called.
- Choosing a new value from the drop-down list causes that value to become the new tempo.

Because all the items in `tempoBox` are stored as strings, you must convert them into floating-point values before you can use them to set the tempo.

This can be done by calling the class method `Float.parseFloat()`, which is comparable to the method `Integer.parseInt()` that you have used several times during the past two weeks to work with integers.

Like the other parse method, `parseFloat()` generates a `NumberFormatException` error if the string cannot be converted to a `float` value.

Note

When `tempoBox` was created, the only items added to it were strings that convert successfully to floating-point values, so there's no way a `NumberFormatException` can result from using this component to set the tempo. However, Java still requires that the exception be dealt with in a `try-catch` block.

Line 63 calls the sequencer's `setTempoFactor()` method with the tempo selected by the user. This takes effect immediately, so you can modify the tempo of a song with sometimes-maniacal results.

After the sequencer and sequence have been created in the `run()` method, the `while` loop in lines 100–119 keeps playing the song until the `Thread` object `runner` has been set to `null`.

Another `while` loop, which is nested inside this one, makes sure that the sequencer is not closed while the song is playing. This loop in lines 108–112 is a little different from the one used in the `PlayMidi` application. Instead of looping while `player.isRunning()` returns the value `true`, it requires two conditions to be met:

```
while (player.isRunning() && runner != null) {
    // statements in loop
}
```

The `&&` (and) operator causes the `while` loop to continue only if both expressions are `true`. If you did not test for the value of `runner` here, the thread would continue playing the `MIDI` file until the song ends, rather than stopping when `runner` has been set to `null`, which should signal the end of the thread.

The `MidiApplet` program does not stop the thread when the user goes to a different Web page.

Because `MidiPanel` has a `stop()` method that stops the thread, you can halt `MIDI` playback when the page is no longer being viewed by using the following two steps:

1. Create an instance variable in `MidiApplet` for the user-interface component `MidiPanel`.

2. Override the applet's `stop()` method and use it to call the panel's `stop()` method.

Summary

One of the strengths of the Java class library is how complex programming tasks such as sound playback and alteration are encapsulated within easy-to-create and workable classes. You can play a `MIDI` file that can be manipulated in real time using only a few objects and class methods, in spite of the extremely complex behind-the-scenes development work.

Today, you played sound in programs using simple and more sophisticated techniques.

If you are trying only to play an audio file, working with `getAudioClip()` and `newAudioClip()` methods in the `Applet` class is probably sufficient.

If you want to do more complex things with the audio, such as changing its tempo and making other dynamic modifications, JavaSound packages such as `javax.sound.midi` can be used.

18

Q&A

Q The method `getSequence(InputStream)` is mentioned in this day. What is an input stream, and how are they used with sound files?

A Input streams are objects that retrieve data as they are being sent from another source. The source can be a wide range of things capable of producing data—files, serial ports, servers, or even objects in the same program. You worked with streams extensively on Day 15, "Working with Input and Output."

Q What other things are possible in JavaSound, in addition to what's presented here?

A JavaSound is a set of packages that rivals Swing in complexity, and many of the classes involve sophisticated stream- and exception-handling techniques that will be covered next week. You can learn more about JavaSound and the things you can accomplish with the library on Sun's Web site at `http://java.sun.com/ products/java-media/sound`. Sun offers a Java application called the Java Sound Demo that collects some of the most impressive features of JavaSound: playback, recording, `MIDI` synthesis, and programmable `MIDI` instruments.

Quiz

Review today's material by taking this quiz.

Questions

1. Which `Applet` class method can be used to create an `AudioClip` object in an application?

   (a.) `newAudioClip()`

   (b.) `getAudioClip()`

   (c.) `getSequence()`

2. What class represents the `MIDI` resources that are available on a specific computer system?

   (a.) `Sequencer`

   (b.) `MIDISystem`

   (c.) `MIDIEvent`

3. How many microseconds does it take to cook a 3-minute egg?

   (a.) 180,000

   (b.) 180,000,000

   (c.) 180,000,000,000

Answers

1. (a.) It's a misnomer for this method to be included in the `Applet` class, but that's a quirk of Java 1.0 that remains in Java 2.0.

2. (b.) The `MIDISystem` class is used to create objects that represent sequencers, synthesizers, and other devices that handle `MIDI` audio.

3. (b.) One million microseconds are in a second, so 180 million microseconds equal 180 seconds.

Certification Practice

The following question is the kind of thing you could expect to be asked on a Java programming certification test. Answer it without looking at today's material or using the Java compiler to test the code.

Given:

```
public class Operation {
    public static void main(String[] arguments) {
        int x = 1;
        int y = 3;
        if ((x != 1) && (y++ == 3))
            y = y + 2;
    }
}
```

What is the final value of y?

(a.) 3

(b.) 4

(c.) 5

(d.) 6

The answer is available on this book's Web site at `http://www.java21days.com`. Visit the Day 18 page, and click the Certification Practice link.

Exercises

To extend your knowledge of the subjects covered today, try the following exercises:

- Create an application that uses `newAudioClip()` to play a sound file.
- Convert the `MidiApplet` project so you can specify more than one `MIDI` file as parameters on a Web page and play each one in succession.

Where applicable, exercise solutions are offered on the book's Web site at `http://www.java21days.com`.

18

DAY 19

Creating and Using JavaBeans

As you have learned, one of the advantages of object-oriented programming is the capability to reuse an object in different programs. If you have created a spellchecker object that works with your word-processing program, you should be able to use the same object with an e-mail program also.

Sun has extended this principle by offering JavaBeans: software objects that interact with other objects according to a strict set of guidelines—the JavaBeans Specification. After you know how to work with one JavaBean according to these guidelines, you know how to work with them all.

Several programming tools have been developed with beans in mind. These environments, including the free Sun ONE Studio Java development environment, make it possible to develop Java programs quickly by using existing beans and establishing the relationships among them.

Today, you'll explore the following subjects:

- Creating reusable software objects in Java
- How JavaBeans relates to the Java class library
- The JavaBeans API
- JavaBeans development tools
- Working with JavaBeans
- Creating an applet with JavaBeans

Reusable Software Components

A growing trend in the field of software development is the use of *reusable components*—elements of a program that can be used with more than one software package.

 A *software component* is a piece of software isolated into a discrete, easily reusable structure.

If you develop parts of a program so they are self-contained, it should be possible for these components to be assembled into programs with much greater efficiency. This notion of reusing carefully packaged software applies the assembly-line approach to software. The idea is to build small, reusable components and then reuse them as much as possible, thereby streamlining the development process.

Perhaps the greatest difficulty that component software has had to face is the wide range of disparate microprocessors and operating systems in use today. There have been several reasonable attempts at component software, but they've always been limited to a specific operating system. Microsoft's VBX and OCX component architectures have had great success in the Intel PC world, but they've done little to bridge the gap between PCs and other operating systems.

 Note

> Microsoft's ActiveX technology, which is based on its OCX technology, was designed to provide an all-purpose component technology that's compatible across a wide range of platforms. However, because ActiveX is dependent on 32-bit Windows code, it is not suitable to development on other operating systems.

Some component technologies also suffer from having been developed in a particular programming language or for a particular development environment. Just as platform-dependency cripples components at runtime, limiting component development to a particular programming language or development environment cripples components at the development end. Software developers want to decide for themselves which language is the most appropriate for a particular task. Likewise, they want to select the development environment that best fits their needs, rather than being forced to use an environment based on a component technology. Therefore, any realistic long-term component technology must deal with both platform-dependency and language-dependency.

Java has been a major factor in making platform-independent software development a reality, and it offers software-component development through JavaBeans.

JavaBeans is an architecture- and platform-independent set of classes for creating and using Java software components. It takes advantage of the portable Java platform to provide a component-software solution.

The Goal of JavaBeans

JavaBeans was designed to be compact because components will often be used in distributed environments in which entire components are transferred across a low-bandwidth Internet connection. The second part of this goal relates to the ease with which the components are built and used. It's not such a stretch to imagine components that are easy to use, but creating a component architecture that makes it easy to build components is a different issue altogether.

The second major goal of JavaBeans is to be fully portable. As a result, developers will not need to worry about including platform-specific libraries with their Java applets.

The existing Java architecture already offers a wide range of benefits that are easily applied to components. One of the more important (but rarely mentioned) features of Java is its built-in class-discovery mechanism, which allows objects to interact with each other dynamically. This results in a system in which objects can be integrated with each other, independent of their respective origins or development histories. The class-discovery mechanism is not just a neat Java feature; it is a necessary requirement in any component architecture.

NEW TERM Another example of JavaBeans inheriting existing Java functionality is *persistence,* which is the capability of an object to store and retrieve its internal state. Persistence is handled automatically in JavaBeans by using the serialization mechanism already present in Java. *Serialization* is the process of storing or retrieving information through a standard protocol. Alternatively, developers can create customized persistence solutions whenever necessary.

Although support for distributed computing is not a core element of the JavaBeans architecture, it is provided. JavaBeans component developers can select the distributed-computing approach that best fits their needs. Sun provides a distributed-computing solution in its Remote Method Invocation (RMI) technology, but JavaBeans developers

19

are in no way handcuffed to this solution. Other options include CORBA (Common Object Request Broker Architecture) and Microsoft's DCOM (Distributed Component Object Model), among others.

Distributed computing has been cleanly abstracted from JavaBeans to keep things tight while still giving a wide range of options to developers who require distributed support. JavaBeans's final design goal deals with design-time issues and how developers build applications by using JavaBeans components.

The JavaBeans architecture includes support for specifying design-time properties and editing mechanisms to better facilitate visual editing of JavaBeans components. The result is that developers will be able to use visual tools to assemble and modify JavaBeans components in a seamless fashion, much the way existing PC visual tools work with components such as VBX or OCX controls. In this way, component developers specify the way in which the components are to be used and manipulated in a development environment.

How JavaBeans Relates to Java

Although Java's object-oriented nature provides a means for objects to work in conjunction with each other, there are a few rules or standards governing how object interactions are conducted. These rules are needed for a robust component-software solution, and they are provided through JavaBeans.

JavaBeans specifies a rich set of mechanisms for interaction among objects, along with common actions that most objects will need to support, such as persistence and event handling. It also provides the framework by which this component communication can take place. Even more important is the fact that JavaBeans components can be easily tweaked via a standard set of well-defined properties.

JavaBeans components aren't limited to user-interface objects such as buttons, however. You can just as easily develop nonvisual JavaBeans components that perform some background function in concert with other components. In this way, JavaBeans merges the power of visual Java applets with nonvisual Java applications under a consistent component framework.

NEW TERM A *nonvisual component* is any component that doesn't have a visible output. If you think of components in terms of Swing components, such as buttons and menus, this might seem a little strange. However, keep in mind that a component is simply a tightly packaged program and doesn't need to be visual. A good example is a timer component, which fires timing events at specified intervals and is nonvisual. Timer components are very popular in other component-development environments, such as Microsoft Visual Basic.

With visual tools, you can use a variety of JavaBeans components together without necessarily writing any code. JavaBeans components expose their own interfaces visually, providing a means to edit their properties without programming. Furthermore, by using a visual editor, you can drop a JavaBeans component directly into an application without writing any code. This is an entirely new level of flexibility and reusability that was impossible with Java alone.

The JavaBeans API

JavaBeans is ultimately a programming interface, meaning that all its features are implemented as extensions to the standard Java class library. All the functionality provided by JavaBeans is actually implemented in the JavaBeans API, a suite of smaller APIs devoted to specific functions (services). The following is a list of the main component services in the JavaBeans API that are necessary for all the features you're learning about today:

- Graphical user interface merging
- Persistence
- Event handling
- Introspection
- Application builder support

If you understand these services and how they work, you'll have much more insight into exactly what type of technology JavaBeans is. These services are implemented as smaller APIs contained within the larger JavaBeans API.

The user-interface–merging APIs enable a component to merge its elements with a container. Most containers have menus and toolbars that display any special features provided by the component. The interface-merging APIs allow the component to add features to the container document's menu and toolbar. These APIs also define the mechanism that facilitates interface layout between components and their containers.

The persistent APIs specify the mechanism by which components can be stored and retrieved within the context of a containing document. By default, components inherit the automatic serialization mechanism provided by Java. Developers are also free to design more elaborate persistence solutions based on the specific needs of their components.

The event-handling APIs specify an event-driven architecture that defines how components interact with each other. Java already includes a powerful event-handling model, which serves as the basis for the event-handling component APIs. These APIs are critical in giving components the freedom to interact with each other in a consistent fashion.

19

The introspection APIs define the techniques by which components make their internal structure readily available at design time. These APIs allow development tools to query a component for its internal state, including the interfaces, methods, and member variables of which the component is composed.

These APIs are divided into two distinct sections, based on the level at which they are being used. For example, the low-level introspection APIs give development tools direct access to component internals, which is a function you wouldn't necessarily want in the hands of component users. This brings you to the high-level APIs, which use the low-level APIs to determine which parts of a component are exported for user modification. Although development tools will undoubtedly use both APIs, they will use the high-level APIs only when providing component information to the user.

The application builder support APIs provide the overhead necessary for editing and manipulating components at design time. These APIs are used largely by visual development tools to visually lay out and edit components while constructing an application. The section of a component that provides visual editing capabilities is specifically designed to be physically separate from the component itself. This is because standalone runtime components should be as compact as possible. In a purely runtime environment, components are transferred with only the necessary runtime component. Developers who want to use only the design-time portion of the component can do so.

 Note   More information on the JavaBeans specification is available from Sun's Java Web site. The JavaBeans Component API documentation is available at `http://java.sun.com/j2se/1.4/docs/guide/beans/`.

Development Tools

The best way to understand the JavaBeans interface is to work with it in a programming environment that supports bean development.

Bean programming requires an environment with a fairly sophisticated graphical user interface because much of the development work is done visually. In an integrated development environment such as WebGain Visual Café, you can establish a relationship between two beans in an interface by dragging a line between them with your mouse.

The tools in the Software Development Kit are almost exclusively used from the command line without a graphical interface. Because of this, you need a different programming tool to develop beans when using the SDK tools. Most of the commercially available Java development tools support JavaBeans, including Visual Café, Metrowerks CodeWarrior Professional, IBM VisualAge for Java, Borland JBuilder, and Oracle JDeveloper.

> **Caution** If you're shopping for a Java-integrated development environment that supports JavaBeans, an important thing to note is whether it supports Java 2 version 1.4 or a previous version of the language.

If you don't have a development tool that supports JavaBeans programming, you can use the free JavaBeans Development Kit from Sun.

JavaBeans Development Kit

Sun's JavaBeans Development Kit, also called the BDK, is a free tool that can be used to try out bean development if you don't have any other Java programming environment that supports beans.

If this sounds like damning the BDK with faint praise, it is. Sun makes the following recommendation on its Java Web site: "The BDK is not intended for use by application developers, nor is it intended to be a full-fledged application-development environment. Instead, application developers should consider the various Java application-development environments supporting JavaBeans."

When the BDK was released, it served a purpose similar to the original Java Development Kit: enabling programmers to work with a new technology when no alternative was available. With the arrival of numerous JavaBeans-capable programming tools, Sun has not focused its efforts on extending the functionality of the BDK and improving its performance. The BDK is now useful primarily as an introduction to JavaBeans development, and that's what it will be used for today.

The BDK is available for Windows and Solaris. It was developed using the Java language, so there also is a platform-independent version that you can use on other Java-enabled operating systems. It can be downloaded from `http://java.sun.com/beans/software/bdk_download.html`

> **Caution** If this page is not available, visit the main page at Sun's Java site at `http://java.sun.com`. The JavaBeans Development Kit is available in the "Products & APIs" section under the name JavaBeans Development Kit.

19

The BDK is around 2.4MB in size, requiring up to 15 minutes to download on a 56K dial-up Internet connection and less than two minutes on a high-speed connection. While you're waiting for the file transfer to finish, be sure to read the installation instructions and last-minute notes on the BDK download page. You might need to make changes to your system's CLASSPATH setting for the BDK to function properly.

The BDK is available as a single executable file that can be run to install the software or as a ZIP archive. If you download the ZIP archive, all of the files in the BDK are stored in a beans folder in the archive. Copy or move this folder from the archive to a folder on your computer (such as the main Java 2 installation folder).

During the installation from an .EXE file, you will select the Java virtual machine that the BDK will use. Choose the Java interpreter that you've been using to run Java 2 programs as you worked through the days in this book.

Caution

> The BDK's Windows installation program may be having compatibility problems with the current version of Java 2. If you can't install it, try the platform-independent version of the BDK instead, which is packaged as a ZIP archive.

The following things are included in the BDK:

- The BeanBox—A JavaBeans container that can be used to manipulate sample beans and work with those of your own creation
- More than a dozen sample beans, including a Juggler bean that displays a juggling animation, a Molecule bean that displays a 3D molecule, and OrangeButton, a user-interface component
- The complete Java source code of the BeanBox
- Makefiles—Configuration scripts that can be used to re-create the BDK
- A tutorial about JavaBeans and the BeanBox from Sun

Working with JavaBeans

As you work with JavaBeans in a development environment such as the BDK, you'll quickly discover how different beans are from Java classes that weren't designed to be beans.

JavaBeans differs from other classes in a major way: Beans can interact with a development environment, running inside it as if a user were running them. The development environment also can interact directly with the beans, calling their methods and setting up values for their variables.

If you have installed the BDK, you can use it in the following sections to work with existing beans and to create a new one. If not, you'll still learn more about how beans are used in conjunction with a development environment.

Bean Containers

JavaBeans shares something with Swing: the use of *containers*, user-interface components that hold other components.

JavaBeans development takes place within a bean container. The BDK includes the BeanBox, a rudimentary container that can be used to do the following:

- Save a bean
- Load a saved bean
- Drop beans into a window where they can be laid out
- Move and resize beans
- Edit a bean's properties
- Configure a bean
- Associate a bean that generates an event with an event handler
- Associate the properties of different beans with each other
- Convert a bean into an applet
- Add new beans from a Java archive (jar files)

To run the BeanBox application, go to the folder where the BDK was installed and open the beanbox subfolder. This subfolder contains two batch-command files that can be used to run the BeanBox: run.bat for Windows systems and run.sh for Linux and Solaris systems.

These batch files load the BeanBox application using the Java interpreter you selected during BDK installation, which is probably the Java 2 interpreter. Four windows will open, as shown in Figure 19.1.

19

FIGURE **19.1**

*The windows that
make up the BeanBox
application.*

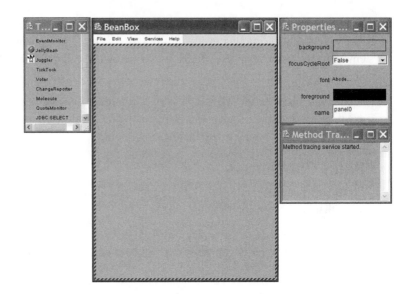

The largest window is the BeanBox composition window, which arranges beans and creates their associations with each other.

The other two windows along the top are the Toolbox window (on the left), which lists several beans that can be selected for placement in the composition window, and a Properties window (on the right), which is used to configure the bean. The fourth window, in the lower-right corner, is the Method Tracer window, which provides more information on how components are interacting in the BeanBox.

Most of the work will be done within the composition window, which is comparable to the main window of a drawing program, such as Adobe Illustrator. All beans are placed, rearranged, lined up, and selected for editing within this window.

Placing a Bean

The first step in placing a bean in the BeanBox is to select it in the Toolbox window. When you do this, your cursor will switch to a crosshairs symbol. With the crosshairs, you can click anywhere in the main composition window to place the selected type of bean in it. When you place a bean, it's best to choose someplace near the middle of the composition window. You can use the Edit, Cut and Edit, Paste menu commands to move the bean if needed. You also can move a bean by placing your cursor over the edge of the bean until the cursor becomes a set of compass-direction arrows, dragging the bean to a new location, and releasing the mouse.

Try this by clicking the `Juggler` label in the Toolbox window and then clicking somewhere in the middle of the main composition window. An animation of a juggling bicuspid will appear in the main window (see Figure 19.2). You may recognize the juggler; it's Duke, the official mascot of the Java language. Appropriately, the objects he's tossing around are giant beans.

FIGURE 19.2

Duke juggles some giant beans in the main BeanBox window.

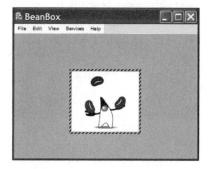

In Figure 19.2, the striped line around the `Juggler` bean indicates that it is selected for editing. You can select the BeanBox window by clicking anywhere other than the `Juggler` bean, and you can select the Juggler bean again by clicking it. You can edit, copy, cut, and paste a bean only if it has been selected for editing.

Adjusting a Bean's Properties

When a bean has been selected in the main composition window of the BeanBox, its editable properties, if any, are displayed in the Properties window. This window for the current project is shown in Figure 19.3.

FIGURE 19.3

Editable properties of a bean, shown in the Properties window.

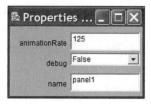

As shown in Figure 19.3, the `Juggler` bean has three editable properties: `debug`, `animationRate`, and `name`.

Changes to a JavaBean's properties will be reflected in the bean. If you give the `Juggler` bean's `animationRate` property a higher integer value, there will be a longer pause between each frame of the animation. If you decrease the property, the animation will speed up.

19

After you change the `animationRate` property, the bean will change accordingly after you skip to a different property by either pressing the Tab key or clicking a different property's value. Try entering extreme values such as 1 and 1,000 for the animation speed to see the response in the `Juggler` bean.

A bean's editable properties can be established by public methods within the bean. Each property that can be set has a `set()` method whose full name matches the name of the property in the Properties window of the BeanBox. Likewise, each property whose value can be read has a corresponding `get()` method. A JavaBeans development environment such as the BeanBox uses reflection to find these methods and then makes it possible for you to work with the properties at design time or as a program is running.

For example, the `animationRate` property of the `Juggler` bean could have two methods, such as the following:

```
public int getAnimationRate(){
    return animRate;
}

public void setAnimationRate(int newRate) {
    animRate = newRate;
}
```

In these two methods, `animRate` is a private variable that determines the pause between frames of the juggling animation.

By using the prefixes `set` and `get` for these method names, the `Juggler` bean developer indicates that the `animationRate` property can be altered from within a JavaBeans development environment such as the BeanBox.

The BeanBox, like all bean-development tools that follow the standards established by Sun, calls the public `get()` methods of the bean to determine which properties to include in the Properties window. When one of the properties is changed, a `set()` method is called with the changed value as an argument.

The developer of a bean can override this behavior by providing a `BeanInfo` class that indicates the methods, properties, events, and other things that should be accessible from a bean-development environment.

Tip

Keeping a variable private and using `get()` and `set()` methods to read and change it is a good principle in all object-oriented programming, even when you're not trying to develop a bean. This practice is called *encapsulation*, and it is used to control how an object can be accessed by other objects. The more encapsulated an object is, the harder it becomes for other objects to use it incorrectly.

Creating Interactions Among Beans

Another purpose of the BeanBox is to establish interactions among different beans.

To see how this works, first place two ExplicitButton beans anywhere in the main composition window of the BeanBox. If they overlap with the Juggler bean or with each other, move the beans farther away from each other.

 Caution

There appear to be two bugs in the beans included with the Bean Development Kit, though the problem may be limited to Windows XP users. If you can't find the ExplicitButton bean listed in the Toolbox window, you need to update several of the JAR archive files included with the BDK.

To fix the problem, go to the Day 19 page of this book's Web site at http://www.java21days.com/, download the files buttons.jar and test.jar, and save them in the jars subfolder of your BDK installation. (For example, if you installed the BDK into the c:\j2sdk1.4.0\beans folder, save the two jar files in c:\j2sdk1.4.0\beans\jars). After downloading the files, shut down the BeanBox and run it again.

To move a bean, first click it so a striped line appears around it in the BeanBox window. Then place your cursor above the lower edge of the bean until the cursor changes to a four-sided arrow. After this happens, drag the bean to a new location. Figure 19.4 shows two buttons along the bottom edge of the Juggler bean.

FIGURE 19.4

Two ExplicitButton *beans and a* Juggler *bean in the main BeanBox window.*

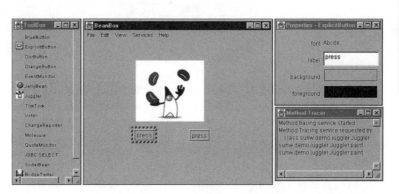

19

ExplicitButton beans are similar to the JButton components that you have used in graphical user interfaces. They have a background color, a foreground color, and a text label with configurable fonts.

After placing the buttons, give one the label "Stop!" and change its background color to red. Give the other the label "Go!" and change its background color to green.

To change a button's label, click the button in the BeanBox and then edit the label field in the Properties window. To change the background color, click the panel next to the label Background in the Properties window. A new Color Editor dialog box will open, enabling you to select a color by entering numeric values for red, green, and blue or by using a list box. The changes that you make will be reflected instantly in the bean.

At this point, the purpose of these buttons should be fairly obvious: One will stop the animation, and the other will start it. For these things to take place, you must establish a relationship between the buttons and the Juggler bean.

The first step is to select the bean that is causing something to take place. In the current example, that bean would be either of the ExplicitButton beans. Clicking one of these should cause something to happen to the Juggler bean.

After selecting the bean, choose the menu command Edit, Events, button push, actionPerformed. A red line will connect the button and the cursor, as shown in Figure 19.5.

FIGURE 19.5

Establishing an event association between two beans.

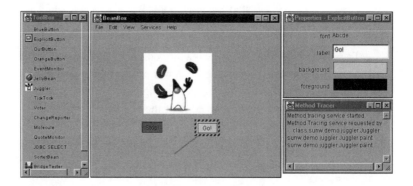

This red line should connect the ExplicitButton bean with the Juggler bean. Drag the line to the Juggler bean, and then click it to establish the association between the two beans.

When this association has been established, you'll see an EventTargetDialog window that lists different methods in the target bean, as shown in Figure 19.6. The method that is chosen will be called automatically when the specified ExplicitButton bean fires an actionPerformed event. (This event occurs when the button is clicked or the Enter key is pressed while the button has the input focus on the interface.)

FIGURE 19.6

Choosing a method to call in the EventTargetDialog window.

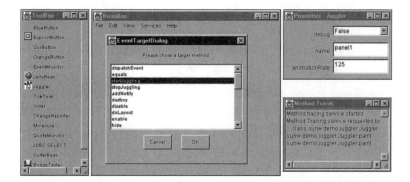

The Juggler bean contains two methods that are used to either stop or start the juggling animation. These are called stopJuggling() and startJuggling(), respectively. By separating behavior like this into its own method, the developer enables these methods to be useful in an interaction among beans. Organizing a bean's methods in this way, offering as many interactions as necessary, is one of the biggest tasks in JavaBeans development.

The Stop! button should be associated with the Juggler bean's stopJuggling() method, and the Go! button should be associated with startJuggling().

By establishing this interaction among three beans, you have created a simple, functional Java program that can display, start, and stop an animation.

Creating a JavaBeans Program

After you have placed one or more beans on a shared interface, set up their properties, and established interactions among them, you have created a Java program.

To save a project in the BeanBox, use the File, Save menu command. This enables you to save the following information to a file:

- The beans as they are currently configured
- The arrangement of the beans
- The size of the window the beans occupy
- The interactions among the beans

This does not save the project as a Java program that you can run outside the BeanBox. To save a project in a form that you can run, use the File, MakeApplet command. This command requires two things: the name to give the applet's main class file, and the name of the jar archive that will hold all files needed to run the applet, including class files and other data.

19

After you specify these items, an applet will be created with a sample HTML page that loads it. The HTML file will be placed in the same folder that contains the applet's jar archive. You can load this page by using appletviewer or any Web browser that is equipped with the Java 2 Plug-in.

These applets are distributed using jar archives for the applet itself and any beans in it. Listing 19.1 contains the applet tag generated by BeanBox for the applet, which was named JugglingFool.

LISTING 19.1 The Applet Tag Generated by BeanBox

```
 1: <html>
 2: <head>
 3: <title>Test page for JugglingFool as an APPLET</Title>
 4: </head>
 5: <body>
 6: <h1>Test for JugglingFool as an APPLET</h1>
 7: This is an example of the use of the generated
 8: JugglingFool applet.  Notice the Applet tag requires several
 9: archives, one per JAR used in building the Applet
10: <p>
11: <applet
12:     archive="./JugglingFool.jar,./support.jar
13:         ,./buttons.jar
14:         ,./juggler.jar
15:     "
16:     code="JugglingFool"
17:     width=382
18:     height=513
19: >
20: Trouble instantiating applet JugglingFool!!
21: </applet>
```

Figure 19.7 shows the JugglingFool animation applet running in the appletviewer tool.

FIGURE 19.7

A JavaBeans applet running in appletviewer.

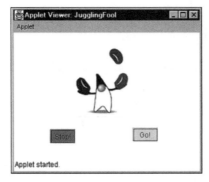

> **Note**
>
> The size of the applet's window will be determined by the size of the main composition window in the BeanBox. To resize the window, select it by clicking outside all beans inside the window and then resize it as you would a bean.

Working with Other Beans

Developing software by using prepackaged components like this is a form of *rapid application development*. Unlike many of the terms you have learned in this book, rapid application development, also called RAD, is self-explanatory jargon. It's often used to quickly create a working version of software for demonstration or prototype purposes.

A common example of RAD is using Microsoft Visual Basic to create a prototype of a Visual C++ program. One of the strengths of Visual Basic is its speedy graphical user interface design, which makes it a more effective solution for prototyping than the more complex Visual C++.

JavaBeans makes RAD development more commonplace in Java software development. A programmer can swiftly cobble together a working program by using existing JavaBeans components.

Hundreds of beans are available from Sun and other developers, including those at the following sites:

- JARS, the Java Applet Ratings Service, includes a JavaBeans resource section at `http://www.jars.com/jars_resources_javabeans.html`
- *JavaWorld* Magazine's Developer Tools Guide: `http://www.javaworld.com/javaworld/tools/jw-tools-index.html`
- Sun's JavaBeans home page: `http://java.sun.com/beans`

Beans are packaged into `jar` archives. If you have downloaded a bean and would like it to show up in the Toolbox window of the BeanBox, save the bean's `jar` archive in BDK's `jars` folder, a subfolder of the folder where the BDK was installed on your system.

19

Summary

When combined with an integrated development environment that supports them, beans enable rapid application development of Java programs.

Today, you learned about the underlying principles of reusable software components and how these principles are realized in Java. Putting these ideas into practice, you saw how Sun's JavaBeans Development Kit (BDK) can be used to work with existing beans, establish relationships among them, and create full Java programs.

Although you should seek a real development tool before developing your own programs with JavaBeans, you can use the BDK to evaluate the applicability of beans to your own programming tasks.

You also should use the JavaBeans resources on the World Wide Web. Many of the beans that are available over the Web already accomplish tasks you'll try to handle in your own programs. By using beans, you can reduce the number of things you must create from scratch.

Q&A

Q Will the JavaBeans Development Kit be upgraded into a fully featured bean-programming tool?

A On its Web site, Sun states that development of the BeanBox ended in 1999 and that it should now be used "for educational and demonstration purposes only." Sun continues to state that the BDK is intended for testing beans and providing a reference version of how beans should be used inside development environments. It appears that professional programming tools, such as Visual Café, Sun ONE Studio, and others, are going to remain the best choice for JavaBeans development.

Q In the `JugglingFool` example, the `animationRate` property has a different capitalization in the `setAnimationRate()` and `getAnimationRate()` methods. What accounts for this difference?

A The capitalization is different because of the following naming conventions for Java programs: All variables and method names begin with a lowercase letter, and all words but the first in a variable name begin with a single uppercase letter.

Quiz

Review today's material by taking this quiz.

Questions

1. If you develop a bean that has a `getWindowHeight()` method that returns an integer and a `setWindowHeight(int)` method, what property will show up in a bean-development environment?

(a.) `WindowHeight`

(b.) windowHeight

(c.) Nothing unless you also set something up in a `BeanInfo` file

2. When can you modify a bean's properties?

(a.) At design time

(b.) At runtime

(c.) Both

3. How do you change the size of an applet created using the BDK?

(a.) Edit the HTML generated by the BDK after you create the applet.

(b.) Edit a property of the BeanBox.

(c.) Resize the BeanBox before creating the applet.

Answers

1. (b.) Although you can also use a `BeanInfo` file to exclude `windowHeight` from showing up as a property in a bean-development environment.

2. (c.) As you have seen with the `Juggler` example, beans will even run as they are being designed.

3. (c.) Although answer "a" is also true because you can edit the HTML directly and modify the `HEIGHT` and `WEIGHT` attributes of the `APPLET` tag.

Certification Practice

The following question is the kind of thing you could expect to be asked on a Java programming certification test. Answer it without looking at today's material or using the Java compiler to test the code.

Given:

```
public class NameDirectory {
    String[] names;
    int nameCount;

    public NameDirectory() {
        names = new String[20];
        nameCount = 0;
    }

    public void addName(String newName) {
        if (nameCount < 20)
            // answer goes here
    }
}
```

19

The `NameDirectory` class must be able to hold 20 different names. What statement should replace `// answer goes here` in order for the class to function correctly?

(a.) `names[nameCount] = newName;`

(b.) `names[nameCount] == newName;`

(c.) `names[nameCount++] = newName;`

(d.) `names[++nameCount] = newName;`

The answer is available on this book's Web site at `http://www.java21days.com`. Visit the Day 19 page and click the Certification Practice link.

Exercises

To extend your knowledge of the subjects covered today, try the following exercises:

- Download a bean from the JARS JavaBean resource section and make use of it in the BeanBox.

- Add a `TickTock` bean—a bean that causes something to happen at set intervals—to the `Juggler` project. Experiment with the bean and see whether you can make it restart the juggling bean every 30 seconds.

Where applicable, exercise solutions are offered on this book's Web site at `http://www.java21days.com`.

DAY 20

Reading and Writing Data Using JDBC and XML

Almost all Java programs deal with data in some way. You have used primitive types, objects, arrays, linked lists, and other data structures to represent data up to this point.

As you develop more sophisticated programs, those might not be the best choices. Today, you will work with data in more sophisticated ways.

You will begin by exploring Java Database Connectivity (JDBC), a class library that connects Java programs to relational databases developed by Microsoft, Sybase, Oracle, Informix, and other sources. By using a driver as a bridge to the database source, you can store and retrieve data directly from Java.

Next, you will learn how to read data files that have been created using XML (Extensible Markup Language), a format for storing and organizing data that is independent of any software program that works with the data.

This independence gives XML something in common with Java: It's completely portable, so XML files can be easily read, written, and exchanged by different software on different operating systems.

Java Database Connectivity

Java Database Connectivity (JDBC) is a set of classes that can be used to develop client/server database applications using Java.

Client/server software connects a user of information with a provider of that information, and it's one of the most commonplace forms of programming. You use it every time you surf the Web: A client program called a Web browser requests Web pages, image files, and other documents using a Uniform Resource Locator, or URL. Different server programs provide the requested information, if it can be found, for the client.

One of the biggest obstacles faced by database programmers is the wide variety of database formats in use, each with its own proprietary method of accessing data.

To simplify using relational database programs, a standard language called SQL (Structured Query Language) has been introduced. This language supplants the need to learn different database-querying languages for each database format.

Today as you work with JDBC you will

- Use JDBC drivers to work with different relational databases
- Access a database with SQL
- Move through the records that result from an SQL database operation
- Set up a JDBC data source

In database programming, a request for records in a database is called a *query*. Using SQL, you can send complex queries to a database and get the records you're looking for in any order you specify.

Consider the example of a database programmer at a student loan company who has been asked to prepare a report on the most delinquent loan recipients. The programmer could use SQL to query a database for all records in which the last payment was more than 180 days ago and the amount due is more than $0.00. SQL also can be used to control the order in which records are returned, so the programmer can get the records in the order of Social Security number, recipient name, amount owed, or another field in the loan database.

All this is possible with SQL, and the programmer hasn't used any of the proprietary languages associated with popular database formats.

Caution SQL is strongly supported by many database formats, so in theory you should be able to use the same SQL commands for each database tool that supports the language. However, you still might need to learn some idiosyncrasies of a specific database format when accessing it through SQL.

SQL is the industry-standard approach to accessing relational databases. JDBC supports SQL, enabling developers to use a wide range of database formats without knowing the specifics of the underlying database. It also enables the use of database queries that are specific to a database format.

The JDBC class library's approach to accessing databases with SQL is comparable to existing database-development techniques, so interacting with an SQL database by using JDBC isn't much different than using traditional database tools. Java programmers who already have some database experience can hit the ground running with JDBC. The JDBC API has already been widely endorsed by industry leaders, including some development-tool vendors who have announced future support for JDBC in their development products.

The JDBC library includes classes for each of the tasks that are commonly associated with database usage:

- Making a connection to a database
- Creating a statement using SQL
- Executing that SQL query in the database
- Viewing the resulting records

These JDBC classes are all part of the `java.sql` package in Java 2.

Database Drivers

Java programs that use JDBC classes can follow the familiar programming model of issuing SQL statements and processing the resulting data. The format of the database and the platform it was prepared on don't matter.

20

This platform- and database-independence is made possible by a driver manager. The classes of the JDBC class library are largely dependent on driver managers, which keep track of the drivers required to access database records. You'll need a different driver for each database format that's used in a program, and sometimes you might need several drivers for versions of the same format.

JDBC database drivers can be written either entirely in Java or implemented using native methods to bridge Java applications to existing database-access libraries.

JDBC also includes a driver that bridges JDBC and another database-connectivity standard, called ODBC.

The JDBC-ODBC Bridge

ODBC, Microsoft's common interface for accessing SQL databases, is managed on a Windows system by the ODBC Data Source Administrator.

This is run from the Control Panel on a Windows system; to get there on most versions of Windows, click Start, Settings, Control Panel, ODBC Data Sources. On Windows XP, choose Start, Control Panel, Performances and Maintenance, Administrative Tools, Data Sources (ODBC).

The administrator adds ODBC drivers, configures drivers to work with specific database files, and logs SQL use. Figure 20.1 shows the ODBC Data Source Administrator on a Windows system.

FIGURE 20.1

The ODBC Data Source Administrator on a Windows XP system.

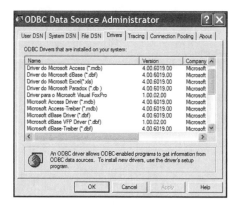

In Figure 20.1, the Drivers tabbed dialog box lists all the ODBC drivers that are present on the system. Many of the drivers are specific to a database company's format, such as the Microsoft Access Driver.

The JDBC-ODBC bridge allows JDBC drivers to be used as ODBC drivers by converting JDBC method calls into ODBC function calls.

Using the JDBC-ODBC bridge requires three things:

- The JDBC-ODBC bridge driver included with Java 2:
  `sun.jdbc.odbc.JdbcOdbcDriver`
- An ODBC driver
- An ODBC data source that has been associated with the driver using software such as the ODBC Data Source Administrator

ODBC data sources can be set up from within some database programs. For example, when a new database file is created in Lotus Approach, users have the option of associating it with an ODBC driver.

All ODBC data sources must be given short descriptive names. The name will be used inside Java programs when a connection is made to the database that the source refers to.

After an ODBC driver is selected and the database is created on a Windows system, they will show up in the ODBC Data Source Administrator. Figure 20.2 shows an example of this for a data source named `WorldEnergy`.

FIGURE 20.2

A listing of data sources in the ODBC Data Sources Administrator.

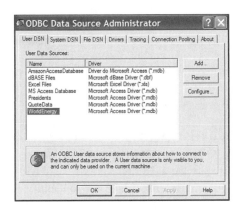

The data source `WorldEnergy` is associated with a Microsoft Access driver, according to Figure 20.2.

> **Note**
>
> Microsoft Access includes ODBC drivers that can be used to connect to an Access database file. Most Windows database programs will include one or more ODBC drivers that correspond to the format.

Connecting to an ODBC Data Source

Your first project today is a Java application that uses a JDBC-ODBC bridge to connect to a Microsoft Access file.

The Access file for this project is `world20.mdb`, a database of world energy statistics published by the U.S. Energy Information Administration. The Coal table in this database includes these fields:

- Country
- Year
- Anthracite Production

20

The database used in this project is included on this book's official Web site at
`http://www.java21days.com`.

To use this database, you must have an ODBC driver on your system that supports
Microsoft Access files. Using the ODBC Data Source Administrator (or a similar program if you're on a non-Windows system), you must create a new ODBC data source
that is associated with `world20.mdb`.

Other setup work might be needed depending on the ODBC drivers that are present
on your system, if any. Consult the documentation included with the ODBC driver.

 Caution

> Though the process of using a Microsoft Access database on a Windows sys-
> tem via ODBC is fairly straightforward, with other database formats and
> systems you might need to install an ODBC driver and learn more about its
> use before you try to create a JDBC-ODBC application.

After you have downloaded `world20.mdb` to your computer or found another database
that's compatible with the ODBC drivers on your system, the final step in getting the file
ready for JDBC-ODBC is to create a data source associated with it. Unlike other input-
output classes in Java, JDBC doesn't use a filename to identify a data file and use its
contents. Instead, a tool such as the ODBC Data Source Administrator is used to name
the ODBC source and indicate the file folder whereit can be found.

In the ODBC Data Source Administrator, click the User DSN tab to see a list of data
sources that are available. To add a new one associated with `world20.mdb` (or your own
database), click the Add button, choose an ODBC driver, and then click the Finish button.

A Setup window will open that you can use to provide a name, short description, and other
information about the database. Click the Select button to find and choose the database file.

Figure 20.3 shows the Setup window used to set up `world20.mdb` as a data source in
the ODBC Data Source Administrator.

FIGURE 20.3

*The driver Setup
window.*

After a database has been associated with an ODBC data source, working with it in a Java program is relatively easy if you are conversant with SQL.

The first task in a JDBC program is to load the driver (or drivers) that will be used to connect to a data source. A driver is loaded with the `Class.forName(String)` method. `Class`, part of the `java.lang` package, can be used to load classes into the Java interpreter. The `forName(String)` method loads the class named by the specified string. A `ClassNotFoundException` may be thrown by this method.

All programs that use an ODBC data source will use `sun.jdbc.odbc.JdbcOdbcDriver`, the JDBC-ODBC bridge driver that is included with Java 2. Loading this class into a Java interpreter requires the following statement:

```
Class.forName("sun.jdbc.odbc.JdbcOdbcDriver");
```

After the driver has been loaded, you can establish a connection to the data source by using the `DriverManager` class in the `java.sql` package.

The `getConnection(String, String, String)` method of `DriverManager` can be used to set up the connection. It returns a reference to a `Connection` object representing an active data connection.

The three arguments of this method are as follows:

- A name identifying the data source and the type of database connectivity used to reach it
- A username
- A password

The last two items are needed only if the data source is secured with a username and a password. If not, these arguments can be null strings (`""`).

The name of the data source is preceded by the text `jdbc:odbc:` when using the JDBC-ODBC bridge, which indicates the type of database connectivity in use.

The following statement could be used to connect to a data source called `Payroll` with a username of `Doc` and a password of `Notnow`:

```
Connection payday = DriverManager.getConnection(
    "jdbc:odbc:Payroll", "Doc", "Notnow");
```

Once you have a connection, you can reuse it each time you want to retrieve or store information from that connection's data source.

20

The getConnection() method and all others called on a data source will throw
SQLException errors if something goes wrong as the data source is being used.
SQL has its own error messages, and they will be passed along as part of
SQLException objects.

Retrieving Data from a Database using SQL

An SQL statement is represented in Java by a Statement object. Statement is an
interface, so it can't be instantiated directly. However, it is returned by the
createStatement() method of a Connection object, as in the following example:

```
Statement lookSee = payday.CreateStatement();
```

After you have a Statement object, you can use it to conduct an SQL query by calling
the object's executeQuery(*String*) method. The String argument should be an SQL
query that follows the syntax of that language.

> **Caution**
>
> It's beyond the scope of this day to teach SQL, a rich data retrieval and stor-
> age language that has its own book in this series: *Teach Yourself SQL in 21
> Days* by Ryan Stephens and Ronald Plew. Although you need to learn SQL to
> do any extensive work with it, a lot of the language is easy to pick up from
> any examples you can find, such as those you will work with today.

The following is an example of an SQL query that could be used on the Coal table of the
world20.mdb database:

```
SELECT Country, Year, Anthracite Production FROM Coal
    WHERE (Country Is Not Null) ORDER BY Year
```

This SQL query retrieves several fields for each record in the database for which the
Country field is not equal to null. The records that are returned are sorted according to
their Country field, so Afghanistan would precede Burkina Faso.

If the SQL query has been phrased correctly, the executeQuery() method will
return a ResultSet object holding all the records that have been retrieved from the
data source.

> **Note**
>
> To add records to a database instead of retrieving them, the statement's
> executeUpdate() method should be called. You will work with this later.

When a `ResultSet` is returned from `executeQuery()`, it is positioned at the first record that has been retrieved. The following methods of `ResultSet` can be used to pull information from the current record:

- `getDate(String)`—Returns the `Date` value stored in the specified field name
- `getDouble(String)`—Returns the `double` value stored in the specified field name
- `getFloat(String)`—Returns the `float` value stored in the specified field name
- `getInt(String)`—Returns the `int` value stored in the specified field name
- `getLong(String)`—Returns the `long` value stored in the specified field name
- `getString(String)`—Returns the `String` stored in the specified field name

These are just the simplest methods that are available in the `ResultSet` interface. The methods you should use depend on the form that the field data took when the database was created, although methods such as `getString()` and `getInt()` can be more flexible in the information they retrieve from a record.

You also can use an integer as the argument to any of these methods, such as `getString(5)`, instead of a string. The integer indicates which field to retrieve (1 for the first field, 2 for the second field, and so on).

An `SQLException` will be thrown if a database error occurs as you try to retrieve information from a result set. You can call this exception's `getSQLState()` and `getErrorCode()` methods to learn more about the error.

After you have pulled the information you need from a record, you can move to the next record by calling the `next()` method of the `ResultSet` object. This method returns a `false` Boolean value when it tries to move past the end of a result set.

You also can move through the records in a result set with these other methods:

- `afterLast()`—Moves to a place immediately after the last record in the set
- `beforeFirst()`—Moves to a place immediately before the first record in the set
- `first()`—Moves to the first record in the set
- `last()`—Moves to the last record in the set
- `previous()`—Moves to the previous record in the set

With the exception of `afterLast()` and `beforeFirst()`, these methods return a `false` Boolean value if no record is available at that position in the set.

20

When you're done using a connection to a data source, you can close it by calling the connection's `close()` method with no arguments.

Listing 20.1 contains the `CoalTotals` application, which uses the JDBC-ODBC bridge and an SQL statement to retrieve some records from an energy database. Four fields are retrieved from each record indicated by the SQL statement: `FIPS`, `Country`, `Year`, and `Anthracite Production`. The result set is sorted according to the `Year` field, and these fields are displayed to standard output.

LISTING 20.1   The Full Text of `CoalTotals.java`

```
 1: import java.sql.*;
 2:
 3: public class CoalTotals {
 4:     public static void main(String[] arguments) {
 5:         String data = "jdbc:odbc:WorldEnergy";
 6:         try {
 7:             Class.forName("sun.jdbc.odbc.JdbcOdbcDriver");
 8:             Connection conn = DriverManager.getConnection(
 9:                 data, "", "");
10:             Statement st = conn.createStatement();
11:             ResultSet rec = st.executeQuery(
12:                 "SELECT * " +
13:                 "FROM Coal " +
14:                 "WHERE " +
15:                 "(Country='" + arguments[0] + "') " +
16:                 "ORDER BY Year");
17:             System.out.println("FIPS\tCOUNTRY\t\tYEAR\t" +
18:                 "ANTHRACITE PRODUCTION");
19:             while(rec.next()) {
20:                 System.out.println(rec.getString(1) +  "\t"
21:                     + rec.getString(2) + "\t\t"
22:                     + rec.getString(3) + "\t"
23:                     + rec.getString(4));
24:             }
25:             st.close();
26:         } catch (SQLException s) {
27:             System.out.println("SQL Error: " + s.toString() + " "
28:                 + s.getErrorCode() + " " + s.getSQLState());
29:         } catch (Exception e) {
30:             System.out.println("Error: " + e.toString()
31:                 + e.getMessage());
32:         }
33:     }
34: }
```

This program must be run with a single argument specifying the Country field in the database from which to pull records. If the application were run with an argument of Poland, the output from the sample database would be the following:

```
FIPS  COUNTRY  YEAR    ANTHRACITE PRODUCTION
PL    Poland   1990    0.0
PL    Poland   1991    0.0
PL    Poland   1992    0.0
PL    Poland   1993    174.165194805424
PL    Poland   1994    242.50849909616
PL    Poland   1995    304.237935229728
PL    Poland   1996    308.64718066784
PL    Poland   1997    319.67029426312
PL    Poland   1998    319.67029426312
```

Try running the program with other countries that produce anthracite, such as France, Swaziland, and New Zealand. For any country that has a space in the name, remember to put quotation marks around the country name when running the program.

Writing Data to a Database Using SQL

In the CoalTotals application, you retrieved data from a database using an SQL statement that was prepared as a string, like this:

```
SELECT * FROM Coal WHERE (Country='Swaziland') ORDER BY YEAR
```

This is a common way to use SQL. You could write a program that asks a user to enter an SQL query and then displays the result (though this probably isn't a good idea—SQL queries can be used to delete records, tables, and even entire databases).

The java.sql package also supports another way to create an SQL statement: a prepared statement.

A prepared statement, which is represented by the PreparedStatement class, is an SQL statement that is compiled before it is executed. This enables the statement to return data more quickly and is a better choice if you are executing an SQL statement repeatedly in the same program.

20

Tip

Prepared statements also have another advantage over Windows systems: They make it possible to write data to a Microsoft Access database using the JDBC-ODBC driver. For several years, I've had no luck at all writing data from Java to Access using statements, but I can use prepared statements without any trouble. I can't figure out why. I'm hoping another author writes a book titled *Teach Yourself Why Microsoft Access Hates My Unprepared SQL Statements in 21 Days*.

To create a prepared statement, call a connection's prepareStatement(*String*) method with a string that indicates the structure of the SQL statement.

To indicate the structure, you write an SQL statement in which parameters have been replaced with question marks.

Here's an example for a connection object called cc:

```
PreparedStatement ps = cc.prepareStatement(
    "SELECT * FROM Coal WHERE (Country='?') ORDER BY YEAR");
```

Here's another example with more than one question mark:

```
PreparedStatement ps = cc.prepareStatement(
    "INSERT INTO BOOKDATA VALUES(?, ?, ?, ?, ?, ?, ?)");
```

The question marks in these SQL statements are placeholders for data. Before you can execute the statement, you must put data in each of these places using one of the methods of the PreparedStatement class.

To put data into a prepared statement, you must call a method with the position of the placeholder followed by the data to insert.

For example, to put the string "Swaziland" in the first prepared statement, call the setString(*int*, *String*) method:

```
ps.setString(1, "Swaziland");
```

The first argument indicates the position of the placeholder, numbered from left to right. The first question mark is 1, the second is 2, and so on.

The second argument is the data to put in the statement at that position.

The following methods are available:

- setAsciiStream(*int*, *InputStream*, *int*)—At the position indicated by the first argument, inserts the specified InputStream, which represents a stream of ASCII characters. The third argument indicates how many bytes from the input stream to insert.

- setBinaryStream(*int*, *InputStream*, *int*)—At the position indicated by the first argument, inserts the specified InputStream, which represents a stream of bytes. The third argument indicates the number of bytes to insert from the stream.

- setCharacterStream(*int*, *Reader*, *int*)—At the position indicated by the first argument, inserts the specified Reader, which represents a character stream. The third argument indicates the number of characters to insert from the stream.

- setBoolean(*int*, *boolean*)—Inserts a boolean value at the position indicated by the integer

- setByte(*int*, *byte*)—Inserts a byte value at the indicated position
- setBytes(*int*, *byte[]*)—Inserts an array of bytes at the indicated position
- setDate(*int*, *Date*)—Inserts a Date object (from the java.sql package) at the indicated position
- setDouble(*int*, *double*)—Inserts a double value at the indicated position
- setFloat(*int*, *float*)—Inserts a float value at the indicated position
- setInt(*int*, *int*)—Inserts an int value at the indicated position
- setLong(*int*, *long*)—Inserts a long value at the indicated position
- setShort(*int*, *short*)—Inserts a short value at the indicated position
- setString(*int*, *String*)—Inserts a String value at the indicated position

There's also a setNull(*int*, *int*) method that stores SQL's version of a null (empty) value at the position indicated by the first argument.

The second argument to setNull() should be a class variable from the Types class in java.sql to indicate what kind of SQL value belongs in that position.

There are class variables for each of the SQL data types. This list, which is not complete, includes some of the most commonly used variables: BIGINT, BIT, CHAR, DATE, DECIMAL, DOUBLE, FLOAT, INTEGER, SMALLINT, TINYINT, and VARCHAR.

The following code puts a null CHAR value at the fifth position in a prepared statement called ps:

```
ps.setNull(5, Types.CHAR);
```

The next project demonstrates the use of a prepared statement to add stock quote data to a database.

As a service to people who follow the stock market, the Yahoo! Web site offers a Download Spreadsheet link on its main stock quote page for each ticker symbol.

To see this link, look up a stock quote on Yahoo! or go directly to a page such as this one:

```
http://quote.yahoo.com/q?s=msft&d=v1
```

Below the table of price and volume information, you can find a Download Spreadsheet link.

Here's what the link looks like for Microsoft:

```
http://quote.yahoo.com/d/quotes.csv?s=MSFT&f=sl1d1t1c1ohgv&e=.csv
```

20

You can click this link to open the file or save it to a folder on your system. The file, which is only one line long, contains the stock's price and volume data saved at the last market close. Here's an example of what Microsoft's data looked like on March 22, 2002:

```
"MSFT",60.45,"3/22/2002","4:00pm",-0.91,61.05,61.14,60.22,20670700
```

The fields in these data, in order, are the ticker symbol, closing price, date, time, price change since yesterday's close, daily low, daily high, daily open, and volume.

The QuoteData application uses each of these fields except one: the time, which isn't particularly useful because it's always the time the market closed.

The following takes place in the program:

- The ticker symbol of a stock is taken as a command-line argument.
- A QuoteData object is created with the ticker symbol as an instance variable called ticker.
- The object's retrieveQuote() method is called to download the stock data from Yahoo! and return it as a String.
- The object's storeQuote() method is called with that String as an argument. It saves the stock data to a database using a JDBC-ODBC connection.

The last task requires a stock quote database, which can be reached through JDBC-ODBC, set up to collect these data.

Windows users can download quotedata.mdb, a Microsoft Access 2000 database created to hold Yahoo!'s stock quote data, from the book's Web site: Visit http://www.java21days.com and open the Day 20 page. After you download the database (or create one of your own), use the ODBC Data Source administrator to create a new data source associated with the database. This application assumes the name of the source is QuoteData.

Enter the text of Listing 20.2 into your editor and save the file as QuoteData.java.

LISTING 20.2   The Full Text of QuoteData.java

```
 1: import java.io.*;
 2: import java.net.*;
 3: import java.sql.*;
 4: import java.util.*;
 5:
 6: public class QuoteData {
 7:     private String ticker;
 8:
 9:     public QuoteData(String inTicker) {
10:         ticker = inTicker;
11:     }
```

LISTING 20.2 Continued

```
12:
13:     private String retrieveQuote() {
14:         StringBuffer buf = new StringBuffer();
15:         try {
16:             URL page = new URL("http://quote.yahoo.com/d/quotes.csv?s=" +
                        ticker
17:                 + "&f=sl1d1t1c1ohgv&e=.csv");
18:             String line;
19:             URLConnection conn = page.openConnection();
20:             conn.connect();
21:             InputStreamReader in= new
                        InputStreamReader(conn.getInputStream());
22:             BufferedReader data = new BufferedReader(in);
23:             while ((line = data.readLine()) != null) {
24:                 buf.append(line + "\n");
25:             }
26:         } catch (MalformedURLException mue) {
27:             System.out.println("Bad URL: " + mue.getMessage());
28:         } catch (IOException ioe) {
29:             System.out.println("IO Error:" + ioe.getMessage());
30:         }
31:         return buf.toString();
32:     }
33:
34:     private void storeQuote(String data) {
35:         StringTokenizer tokens = new StringTokenizer(data, ",");
36:         String[] fields = new String[9];
37:         for (int i = 0; i < fields.length; i++) {
38:             fields[i] = stripQuotes(tokens.nextToken());
39:         }
40:         String datasource = "jdbc:odbc:QuoteData";
41:         try {
42:             Class.forName("sun.jdbc.odbc.JdbcOdbcDriver");
43:             Connection conn = DriverManager.getConnection(
44:                 datasource, "", "");
45:             PreparedStatement pstmt = conn.prepareStatement(
46:                 "INSERT INTO Stocks VALUES(?, ?, ?, ?, ?, ?, ?, ?)");
47:             pstmt.setString(1, fields[0]);
48:             pstmt.setString(2, fields[1]);
49:             pstmt.setString(3, fields[2]);
50:             pstmt.setString(4, fields[4]);
51:             pstmt.setString(5, fields[5]);
52:             pstmt.setString(6, fields[6]);
53:             pstmt.setString(7, fields[7]);
54:             pstmt.setString(8, fields[8]);
55:             pstmt.executeUpdate();
56:             conn.close();
57:         } catch (SQLException sqe) {
```

20

continues

LISTING 20.2 Continued

```
58:                     System.out.println("SQL Error: " + sqe.getMessage());
59:             } catch (ClassNotFoundException cnfe) {
60:                 System.out.println(cnfe.getMessage());
61:             }
62:     }
63:
64:     private String stripQuotes(String input) {
65:         StringBuffer output = new StringBuffer();
66:         for (int i = 0; i < input.length(); i++) {
67:             if (input.charAt(i) != '\"') {
68:                 output.append(input.charAt(i));
69:             }
70:         }
71:         return output.toString();
72:     }
73:
74:     public static void main(String[] arguments) {
75:         if (arguments.length < 1) {
76:             System.out.println("Usage: java QuoteData tickerSymbol");
77:             System.exit(0);
78:         }
79:         QuoteData qd = new QuoteData(arguments[0]);
80:         String data = qd.retrieveQuote();
81:         qd.storeQuote(data);
82:     }
83: }
```

After you compile the QuoteData application, connect to the Internet and run the program. Remember to specify a valid ticker symbol as a command-line argument. To load the current quote for MSFT (Microsoft):

```
java QuoteData MSFT
```

The retrieveQuote() method (lines 13–32) downloads the quote data from Yahoo! and saves it as a string. The techniques used in this method were covered on Day 17, "Communicating Across the Internet."

The storeQuote() method (lines 34–62) makes use of the SQL techniques covered in this section.

The method begins by splitting up the quote data into a set of string tokens, using the , character as the delimiter between each token. The tokens are then stored in a String array with nine elements.

The array contains the same fields as the Yahoo! data in the same order: ticker symbol, closing price, date, time, price change, low, high, open, and volume.

In lines 40–44, a data connection to the QuoteData data source is created using the JDBC-ODBC driver.

This connection is then used in lines 45–46 to create a prepared statement. This statement uses the INSERT INTO SQL statement, which causes data to be stored in a database. In this case, the database is quotedata.mdb, and the INSERT INTO statement refers to the Stocks table in that database.

There are eight placeholders in the prepared statement. Only eight are needed, instead of nine, because the application does not make use of the time field from the Yahoo! data.

In lines 47–54, a series of setString() methods puts the elements of the String array into the prepared statement, in the same order that the fields exist in the database: ticker symbol, closing price, date, price change, low, high, open, and volume.

Some of the fields in the Yahoo! data are dates, floating-point numbers, and integers, so you might think it would be better to use setDate(), setFloat(), and setInt() for those data.

However, Microsoft Access 2000 does not support some of these methods when you are using SQL to work with the database, even though they exist in Java. If you try to use an unsupported method, such as setFloat(), an SQLException error occurs.

It's easier to send Access strings and let the database program convert them automatically into the right format. This is likely to be true when you are working with other databases; the level of SQL support varies based on the product and ODBC driver involved.

After the prepared statement has been prepared and all the placeholders are gone, the statement's executeUpdate() method is called in line 55. This will either add the quote data to the database or throw an SQL error. (One easy way to cause an error is to run the program twice on the same day with the same ticker symbol; quotedata.mdb won't allow duplicate stock entries for the same day.

The private method stripQuotes() is used to remove quotation marks from Yahoo!'s stock data. This method is called on line 38 to take care of three fields that contain extraneous quotes: the ticker symbol, date, and time.

JDBC Drivers

Creating a Java program that uses a JDBC driver is similar to creating one that uses the JDBC-ODBC bridge.

The first step is to acquire and install a JDBC driver. Sun does not include a JDBC driver with Java 2, but more than a dozen companies, including Informix, Oracle, Symantec, IBM, and Sybase, sell drivers or package them with commercial products. A list of available JDBC drivers can be found on Sun's JDBC site at http://java.sun.com/products/jdbc/jdbc.drivers.html.

Some of these drivers are available to download for evaluation. You can use one of them, NetDirect's JDataConnect Server, for today's next project. The JDataConnect Server is available for trial download from http://www.j-netdirect.com/.

The steps for setting up a data source for JDBC are the same as with the JDBC-ODBC bridge:

- Create the database.
- Associate the database with a JDBC driver.
- Establish a data source, which may include selecting a database format, database server, username, and password.

NetDirect's JDataConnect Server uses the ODBC Data Source Administrator to create a new data source associated with a database.

 Caution   On Windows NT, 2000, and XP, you must set up the data source using the System DSN tab rather than the User DSN tab. This is required because the JDataConnect server connects to the database outside of your account, so it must be available to all users on your computer.

Listing 20.3 is a Java application that uses the JDataConnect JDBC driver to access a database file called People.mdb. This database is a Microsoft Access file with contact information for U.S. presidents.

LISTING 20.3   The Full Text of Presidents.java

```
 1: import java.sql.*;
 2:
 3: public class Presidents {
 4:     public static void main(String[] arguments) {
 5:         String data = "jdbc:JDataConnect://127.0.0.1/Presidents";
 6:         try {
 7:             Class.forName("JData2_0.sql.$Driver");
 8:             Connection conn = DriverManager.getConnection(
 9:                 data, "", "");
10:             Statement st = conn.createStatement();
11:             ResultSet rec = st.executeQuery(
12:                 "SELECT * FROM Contacts ORDER BY NAME");
13:             while(rec.next()) {
14:                 System.out.println(rec.getString("NAME") +  "\n"
15:                     + rec.getString("ADDRESS1") + "\n"
16:                     + rec.getString("ADDRESS2") + "\n"
17:                     + rec.getString("PHONE") + "\n"
```

LISTING 20.3 Continued

```
18:                          + rec.getString("E-MAIL") + "\n");
19:                 }
20:             st.close();
21:         } catch (Exception e) {
22:             System.out.println("Error -- " + e.toString());
23:         }
24:     }
25: }
```

Before this program will run successfully, the JDataConnect Server must be started, unless it is already running (on a Windows NT or Windows XP system, it is set up as a service during JDataConnect installation and does not need to be started manually). The reference to 127.0.0.1 in line 6 refers to this server; 127.0.0.1 is a substitute for the name of your own machine.

The JDataConnect Server can be used to connect remotely to servers on the Internet, so 127.0.0.1 could be replaced with an Internet address, such as db.naviseek.com:1150, if a JDataConnect Server is running at that location and port.

Line 5 creates the database address that will be used when creating a Connection object representing the connection to the Presidents data source. This address includes more information than the one used with the JDBC-ODBC bridge driver, as shown:

```
jdbc:JDataConnect://127.0.0.1/Presidents
```

Line 7 of the Presidents application loads the JDBC driver included with the JDataConnect Server:

```
JData2_0.sql.$Driver
```

Configuration information for the data source and driver will be provided by the company that developed the JDBC driver. The database address can vary widely from one JDBC driver implementation to another, although there should always be a reference to a server, a database format, and the name of the data source.

If the People.mdb database exists, the database has been associated with an ODBC data source, and the JDBC driver has been set up correctly, the output of the Presidents application should be similar to the following (depending on the records in the database):

```
Gerald Ford
Box 927
Rancho Mirage, CA 92270
(734) 741-2218
library@fordlib.nara.gov
```

20

```
Jimmy Carter
Carter Presidential Center
1 Copenhill, Atlanta, GA 30307
(404) 727-7611
carterweb@emory.edu

Ronald Reagan
11000 Wilshire Blvd.
Los Angeles, CA 90024
library@reagan.nara.gov

George Bush
Box 79798
Houston, TX 77279
(409) 260-9552
library@bush.nara.gov

Bill Clinton
15 Old House Lane
Chappaqua, NY 10514
(501) 370-8000
info@clintonpresidentialcenter.com

George W. Bush
White House, 1600 Pennsylvania Ave.
Washington, DC 20500
(202) 456-1414
president@whitehouse.gov
```

Using XML

One of the main selling points of Java is that the language produces programs that can run on different operating systems without modification.

The portability of software is a big convenience in today's computing environment, where Windows, Linux, MacOS, and a half-dozen other operating systems are in wide use, and many people work with multiple systems.

About 18 months after Java was introduced, a portable standard for data was introduced: XML, which stands for Extensible Markup Language.

XML enables data to be completely portable, read and written by different software on different operating systems without compatibility problems.

Today, you'll explore XML and learn about the following features of the markup language:

- How to represent data as XML
- Why XML is a useful way to store data
- How to use XML to create a new data format

- How to document the elements of your new format
- How to read XML data using Java

Data that are compliant with XML is easier to reuse for several reasons.

First, the data are structured in a standard way, making it possible for software programs to read and write the data as long as they support XML. If you create an XML file that represents your company's employee database, there are several dozen XML parsers that can read the file and make sense of its contents.

This is true no matter what kind of information you collect about each employee. If your database contains only the employee's name, ID number, and current salary, XML parsers can read it. If it contains 25 items, including birthday, blood type, and hair color, parsers can read that, too.

Second, the data are self-documenting, making it easier for people to understand the purpose of a file just by looking at it in a text editor. Anyone who opens your XML employee database should be able to figure out the structure and content of each employee record without any assistance from you.

This is evident in Listing 20.4, which contains an XML file.

LISTING 20.4   The Full Text of `collection.librml`

```
 1: <?xml version="1.0"?>
 2: <!DOCTYPE Library SYSTEM "librml.dtd">
 3: <Library>
 4:    <Book>
 5:       <Author>Joseph Heller</Author>
 6:       <Title>Catch-22</Title>
 7:       <PublicationDate edition="Trade"
                isbn="0684833395">09/1996</PublicationDate>
 8:       <Publisher>Simon and Schuster</Publisher>
 9:       <Subject>Fiction</Subject>
10:       <Review>heller-catch22.html</Review>
11:    </Book>
12:    <Book>
13:       <Author>Kurt Vonnegut</Author>
14:       <Title>Slaughterhouse-Five</Title>
15:       <PublicationDate edition="Paperback"
                isbn="0440180295">12/1991</PublicationDate>
16:       <Publisher>Dell</Publisher>
17:       <Subject>Fiction</Subject>
18:    </Book>
19: </Library>
```

20

Enter this text using a word processor or text editor and save it as plain text under the name `collection.librml`. (You can also download a copy of it from the book's Web site at `http://www.java21days.com` on the Day 20 page.)

Can you tell what the data represent? Although the `?xml` and `!DOCTYPE` tags at the top may be indecipherable, the rest is clearly a book database of some kind.

The `?xml` tag in the first line of the file has an attribute called `version` that has a value of 1.0. All XML files must begin with an `?xml` tag like this.

Data in XML are surrounded by tag elements that describe the data. Start tags begin with a < character followed by the name of the tag and a > character. End tags begin with the </ characters followed by a name and a > character. In Listing 20.4, for example, `<Book>` on line 12 is a start tag and `</Book>` on line 18 is an end tag. Everything within those tags is considered to be the value of that element.

Tags can be nested within other tags, creating a hierarchy of XML data that establishes relationships within those data. In Listing 20.4, everything in lines 13–17 is related; each tag defines something about the same book.

XML also supports tag elements that are defined by a single tag rather than a pair of tags. These tags begin with a < character followed by the name of the tag and the /> characters. For example, the book database could include a `<outOfPrint/>` tag that indicates a book isn't presently available for sale.

Tag elements also can include attributes, which are made up of data that supplement the rest of the data associated with the tag. Attributes are defined within a start tag element. The name of an attribute is followed by an equal sign and text within quotation marks. In line 7 of Listing 20.4, the `PublicationDate` tag includes two attributes: `edition`, which has a value of `"Trade"`, and `isbn`, which has a value of `"0684833395"`.

XML encourages the creation of data that are understandable and usable even if the user doesn't have the program that created it and cannot find any documentation that describes it.

By insisting upon well-formed markup, XML simplifies the task of writing programs that work with the data.

One of the major motivations behind the development of XML in 1996 was the inconsistency of HTML. It's a wildly popular way to organize data for presentation to users, but Web browsers have always been designed to allow for inconsistent use of HTML tags. Web page designers can break numerous rules of valid HTML, as it's defined by the World Wide Web Consortium, and their work still loads normally into a browser such as Netscape Navigator. Millions of people are putting content on the Web without paying heed to valid HTML at all. They test their content to make sure it's viewable in Web browsers, but they don't worry whether it's structured according to all the rules of HTML.

 Note

> The World Wide Web Consortium, founded by Web inventor Tim Berners-Lee, is the group that developed HTML and maintains the standard version of the language. You can find out more from the consortium Web site at http://www.w3.org. If you'd like to validate a Web page to see whether it follows all the rules of standard HTML, visit http://validator.w3.org.

There's strong demand on the World Wide Web for software that collects data from Web pages and interacts with services offered over the Internet, such as e-commerce shopping agents that collect price and availability data from online stores, enabling customers to do price comparisons. The developers of services like this quickly run into the inconsistency in how HTML is used to organize Web content. Even if you can write software that puzzles through the markup tags on a page to extract information, any changes to the site's design can stop your program from working correctly.

Designing an XML Dialect

Although XML is described as a language and is compared with HTML, it's actually much larger in scope than that. XML is a markup language that defines how to define a markup language.

That's an odd distinction to make, and it sounds like the kind of thing you'd encounter in a philosophy textbook. This concept is important to understand, though, because it explains how XML can be used to define data as varied as health care claims, genealogical records, newspaper articles, and molecules.

The "X" in XML stands for Extensible, and it refers to organizing data for your own purposes. Data that are organized using the rules of XML can represent anything you like:

- A programmer at a telemarketing company can use XML to store data on each outgoing call, saving the time of the call, the number, the operator who made the call, and the result.

- A hobbyist can use XML to keep track of the annoying telemarketing calls she receives, noting the time of the call, the company, and the product being peddled.

- A programmer at a government agency can use XML to track complaints about telemarketers, saving the name of the marketing firm and the number of complaints.

20

Each of these examples uses XML to define a new language that suits a specific purpose. Although you could call them XML languages, they're more commonly described as XML dialects or XML document types.

When a new XML dialect is created, the formal way to document it is to create a document type definition (DTD). This determines the rules that the data must follow to be considered well-formed in that dialect.

Listing 20.5 contains the DTD for the book database listed earlier.

LISTING 20.5   The Full Text of `librml.dtd`

```
1: <!ELEMENT Library (Book?)+ >
2: <!ELEMENT Book (Author?, Title, PublicationDate?, Publisher?, Subject?,
        Review?)* >
3: <!ELEMENT Author (#PCDATA)>
4: <!ELEMENT Title (#PCDATA)>
5: <!ELEMENT PublicationDate (#PCDATA)>
6: <!ATTLIST PublicationDate edition CDATA "" isbn CDATA "">
7: <!ELEMENT Publisher (#PCDATA)>
8: <!ELEMENT Subject (#PCDATA)>
9: <!ELEMENT Review (#PCDATA)>
```

In Listing 20.4, the XML file contained the following line:

```
<!DOCTYPE Library SYSTEM "librml.dtd">
```

The `!DOCTYPE` tag is used to identify the DTD that applies to the data. When a DTD is present, many XML tools can read XML created for that DTD and determine if the data follow all the rules correctly. If they don't, they will be rejected with a reference to the line that caused the error. This process is called *validating the XML*.

One thing you'll run into as you work with XML is data that have been structured as XML but weren't defined using a DTD. These data can be parsed (presuming they're well-formed), so you can read them into a program and do something with them, but you can't check their validity to make sure they're organized correctly according to the rules of their dialect.

Tip

To get an idea of what kind of XML dialects have been created, visit the Schema.Net Web site at `http://www.schema.net`. The site includes a directory of XML dialects covering science, commerce, multimedia, the Internet, and many other subjects.

Processing XML with Java

With the release of Java 2 version 1.4, Sun Microsystems has made support for XML a standard part of the Java class library.

Sun supports XML through the Java Application Programming Interface for XML Processing, a set of Java classes for reading, writing, and manipulating XML data currently in version 1.1. To find out more about these classes and other related XML technology from Sun, visit the company's Java Web site at `http://java.sun.com/xml/`.

The Java API for XML Processing includes nine packages:

- `javax.xml.parsers`
- `javax.xml.transform`
- `javax.xml.transform.dom`
- `javax.xml.transform.sax`
- `javax.xml.transform.stream`
- `org.w3c.dom`
- `org.xml.sax`
- `org.xml.sax.ent`
- `org.xml.sax.helpers`

The `javax.xml.parsers` package is the entry point to all the other packages. You can use the classes of this package to parse and validate XML data using two techniques: the Simple API for XML (SAX) and the Document Object Model (DOM).

Before getting too bogged down in any more TLAs (three-letter acronyms), it will be useful to look at how to use SAX with the `javax.xml.parsers` package and see XML parsing in action.

Reading an XML File

As you learned on Day 15, "Working with Input and Output," in order to read a file from disk in Java, you must set up a series of stream or reader objects that work in conjunction with each other. For instance, to read a buffered stream of bytes from a file, a `File` object is used to create a `FileInputStream` object, which is then used to create a `BufferedInputStream`.

Parsing an XML file using SAX and the `javax.xml.parsers` package requires the same kind of relationship among classes. First, you create a `SAXParserFactory` object by calling the class method `SAXParserFactory.newInstance()`, as in this statement:

```
SAXParserFactory factory = SAXParserFactory.newInstance();
```

20

The purpose of a SAX parser factory is to create a SAX parser according to your specifications. One specification is whether or not the SAX parser should validate XML with a DTD. To support validation, call the parser factory's `setValidating(Boolean)` method with an argument of `true`:

```
factory.setValidating(true);
```

After you've set up the factory to produce the parser you want, call the factory's `newSaxParser()` method to create a `SAXParser` object:

```
SAXParser sax = factory.newSAXParser();
```

This method generates a `ParserConfigurationException` if the factory cannot create a parser that meets your specifications, so you must deal with it in a `try-catch` block or a `throws` statement in the method where `newSAXParser()` is called.

The SAX parser can read XML data from files, input streams, and other sources. To read from a file, the parser's `parse(File, DefaultHandler)` method is called. This method throws two kinds of exceptions: `IOException` if an error occurs as the file is being read and `SAXException` if the SAX parser runs into some kind of problem parsing data.

`SAXException` is a class in the `org.xml.sax` package, one of three packages created by the XML industry group XML.Org that's included in the Java 2 class library. This exception is the superclass of all SAX exceptions, and you can call the exception object's `getMessage()` method in a `catch` block to display more information about the specific problem that triggered the exception.

The second argument to the `parse()` method is an object of the class `DefaultHandler`, part of the `org.xml.sax.helpers` package. The `DefaultHandler` class is a do-nothing class that implements four interfaces of the `org.xml.sax` package: `ContentHandler`, `DTDHandler`, `EntityResolver`, and `ErrorHandler`. These four interfaces are implemented by classes that want to be notified of specific events that occur as the `parse()` method reads XML data.

To implement all of these interfaces, the `DefaultHandler` class includes the following methods:

- `startDocument()`—The parser has reached the beginning of XML data.
- `endDocument()`—The parser has reached the end of XML data.
- `startElement(String, String, String, Attributes)`—The parser has read a start tag element.
- `characters(char[], int, int)`—The parser has read character data located between a start tag and an end tag.
- `endElement(String, String, String)`—The parser has read an end tag element.

Each of these methods throws `SAXException` exceptions.

In order to do something with XML data that are being parsed, you create a subclass of
DefaultHandler that overrides the methods you want to deal with.

Counting XML Tags

Listing 20.6 contains CountTag, a Java application that counts the number of times a starting
tag element appears in an XML file. You specify the filename and tag as command-line
arguments, so it can work with any XML file you'd like to inspect.

LISTING 20.6   The Full Text of CountTag.java

```
 1: import javax.xml.parsers.*;
 2: import org.xml.sax.*;
 3: import org.xml.sax.helpers.*;
 4: import java.io.*;
 5:
 6: public class CountTag extends DefaultHandler {
 7:
 8:     public static void main(String[] arguments) {
 9:         if (arguments.length > 1) {
10:             CountTag ct = new CountTag(arguments[0], arguments[1]);
11:         } else {
12:             System.out.println("Usage: java CountTag filename tagName");
13:         }
14:     }
15:
16:     CountTag(String xmlFile, String tagName) {
17:         File input = new File(xmlFile);
18:         SAXParserFactory factory = SAXParserFactory.newInstance();
19:         factory.setValidating(false);
20:         try {
21:             SAXParser sax = factory.newSAXParser();
22:             CountTagHandler cth = new CountTagHandler(tagName);
23:             sax.parse(input, cth);
24:             System.out.println("The " + cth.tag + " tag appears "
25:                 + cth.count + " times.");
26:         } catch (ParserConfigurationException pce) {
27:             System.out.println("Could not create that parser.");
28:             System.out.println(pce.getMessage());
29:         } catch (SAXException se) {
30:             System.out.println("Problem with the SAX parser.");
31:             System.out.println(se.getMessage());
32:         } catch (IOException ioe) {
33:             System.out.println("Error reading file.");
34:             System.out.println(ioe.getMessage());
35:         }
36:     }
37: }
38:
```

20

continues

LISTING 20.6   Continued

```
39: class CountTagHandler extends DefaultHandler {
40:     String tag;
41:     int count = 0;
42:
43:     CountTagHandler(String tagName) {
44:         super();
45:         tag = tagName;
46:     }
47:
48:     public void startElement(String uri, String localName,
49:         String qName, Attributes attributes) {
50:
51:         if (qName.equals(tag))
52:             count++;
53:     }
54: }
```

Two classes are defined in Listing 20.6: `CountTag`, which creates a SAX parser and tells it to parse a `File` object, and `CountTagHandler`, which counts tags.

This application includes a helper class, `CountTagHandler`, which is a subclass of `DefaultHandler`. To count the number of times a start tag appears in an XML file, the `startElement(String, String, String, Attributes)` method is overridden.

When a SAX parser calls `startElement()`, the arguments to the method provide information about the tag:

- The first argument is the tag's Uniform Resource Indicator (URI).
- The second argument is the tag's local name.
- The third argument is the tag's qualified name.
- The fourth argument is an `Attributes` object that contains information about the attributes associated with a tag.

A tag's URI and qualified name refer to XML namespaces, which make it possible to identify XML tags and attributes in a way that's globally unique across the Internet. This prevents two different tags from being accessible using the same URI and qualified name.

The only name that the `CountTagHandler` class looks for is the qualified name of a tag. In an XML file that doesn't use namespaces, the qualified name is the text that falls between the < and > characters on the tag.

If CountTag.class is in the same folder as collection.librml, you can run it with the following command:

```
java CountTag collection.librml Book
```

The output of this application should be the following:

```
The Book tag appears 2 times.
```

The CountTag application uses a nonvalidating parser, so you can try it with any XML file stored on your system. If you'd like to test it with a longer file, the Day 20 page of this book's Web site at http://www.java21days.com includes the file history.opml.

 Note   Outliner Processor Markup Language (OPML) is an XML dialect created by UserLand Software to represent information that's stored as an outline. You can find out more about this dialect at http://www.opml.org.

Reading XML Data

As you work with a subclass of DefaultHandler, you can keep track of start tags by overriding the startElement() method. When a parser detects a start tag, you don't know anything about the data that follow the tag. If you're trying to extract data from an XML file, you must override a few more methods inherited from DefaultHandler.

Retrieving data from an XML tag is a three-step process:

1. Override the startElement() method to find out when a new start tag is parsed.
2. Override the characters() method to find out what a tag contains.
3. Override the endElement() method to find out when an end tag is reached.

A parser calls the characters(char[], int, int) method when a tag contains character data—in other words, text. The first argument is an array of characters that holds the data.

You don't use this entire character array, however. The data within the tag are contained in a portion of the array. The second argument to characters() indicates the first element of the array to read data from, and the third argument indicates the number of characters to read.

20

The following character() method uses character data to create a String object and then displays it:

```
public void characters(char[] text, int first, int length) {
    String data = new String(text, first, length);
    System.out.println(data);
}
```

A parser calls the endElement(*String*, *String*, *String*) method when an end tag is reached. The three arguments to this method are the same as the first three arguments of the startElement() method—the URI, qualified name, and local name of the tag.

The SAX parser doesn't consider </ or > to be a part of a tag's name. If the parser reads an end tag called </Source>, it will call the endElement() method with Source as its third argument.

The last two methods you may want to override in a DefaultHandler subclass are startDocument() and endDocument(), which don't have any arguments.

Validating XML Data

Today's last project is ReadLibrary, a Java application that reads the XML file created with the dialect introduced earlier today—the book database format used in the file collection.librml and defined in the file librml.dtd.

Because a DTD is available for this dialect, the SAX parser you create with a SAXParserFactory object should be validating. This is accomplished by calling the factory's setValidating(*Boolean*) method with an argument of true.

The ReadLibrary project is organized in much the same way as the last project; there's a main application class called ReadLibrary.class, a helper called LibraryHandler.class, and a helper class called Book.class.

The ReadLibrary class loads a file specified by a command-line argument, creates a SAX parser, and tells it to parse the file.

The LibraryHandler class, a subclass of DefaultHandler, contains the methods that keep track of what the parser is doing and take actions at different steps of the XML-parsing process.

When you're reading XML data using SAX, the characters() method needs to know the last start tag read by the parser. Otherwise, there's no way to find out which tag contains the data. To keep track of this, the LibraryHandler class has an instance variable called currentActivity that stores the current parsing activity as an integer value.

The integer value assigned to currentActivity will be one of six class variables, which are set up in the following statements:

```
static int READING_TITLE = 1;
static int READING_AUTHOR = 2;
static int READING_PUBLISHER = 3;
static int READING_PUBLICATION_DATE = 4;
static int READING_SUBJECT = 5;
static int READING_REVIEW = 6;
static int READING_NOTHING = 0;
```

Using class variables for integer values makes the class easier for a programmer to understand and minimizes the chance that incorrect values will be used in a statement.

The `LibraryHandler` class also has a variable called `libraryBook` that's an instance of the `Book` class. Here are the statements that make up that class:

```
class Book {
    String title;
    String author;
    String publisher;
    String publicationDate;
    String edition;
    String isbn;
    String subject;
    String review;
}
```

The `Book` class is used to hold the different elements of each library book as they're read from an XML file.

Inside the `startElement()` method, a tag's local name is stored in the `localName` variable. The following statement is used in the method:

```
if (localName.equals("Title"))
    currentActivity = READING_TITLE;
```

This statement sets the `currentActivity` variable to the value of the class variable `READING_TITLE` when the SAX parser encounters the `<Title>` tag.

When character data have been received in the `characters()` method, the `currentActivity` variable is used to figure out which tag contains the data. The following statements appear in the method:

```
String value = new String(ch, start, length);
if (currentActivity == READING_TITLE)
    libraryBook.title = value;
```

The first statement creates a string called `value` that contains the character data within the tag. If the parser is reading the title tag, `value` is assigned to the `libraryBook` object's `title` variable.

The last thing that you must set up in the `LibraryHandler` class is displaying the information about each book when all of its XML data has been parsed. This takes place in the `endElement()` method, which stores each ending tag's local name in a variable called `localName`. When `localName` is equal to `"Book"`, the parser has reached the `</BOOK>` tag in the XML file. This tag signifies that no more information about the current book has been defined.

20

The following statement appears in the method:

```
if (localName.equals("Book"))
    System.out.println("\nTitle: " + libraryBook.title);
```

Listing 20.7 contains the full source code of the ReadLibrary application.

LISTING 20.7   The Full Text of ReadLibrary.java

```
 1: import javax.xml.parsers.*;
 2: import org.xml.sax.*;
 3: import org.xml.sax.helpers.*;
 4: import java.io.*;
 5:
 6: public class ReadLibrary extends DefaultHandler {
 7:
 8:     public static void main(String[] arguments) {
 9:         if (arguments.length > 0) {
10:             ReadLibrary read = new ReadLibrary(arguments[0]);
11:         } else {
12:             System.out.println("Usage: java ReadLibrary filename");
13:         }
14:     }
15:
16:     ReadLibrary(String libFile) {
17:         File input = new File(libFile);
18:         SAXParserFactory factory = SAXParserFactory.newInstance();
19:         factory.setValidating(true);
20:         try {
21:             SAXParser sax = factory.newSAXParser();
22:             sax.parse(input, new LibraryHandler() );
23:         } catch (ParserConfigurationException pce) {
24:             System.out.println("Could not create that parser.");
25:             System.out.println(pce.getMessage());
26:         } catch (SAXException se) {
27:             System.out.println("Problem with the SAX parser.");
28:             System.out.println(se.getMessage());
29:         } catch (IOException ioe) {
30:             System.out.println("Error reading file.");
31:             System.out.println(ioe.getMessage());
32:         }
33:     }
34: }
35:
36: class LibraryHandler extends DefaultHandler {
37:     static int READING_TITLE = 1;
38:     static int READING_AUTHOR = 2;
39:     static int READING_PUBLISHER = 3;
40:     static int READING_PUBLICATION_DATE = 4;
41:     static int READING_SUBJECT = 5;
```

LISTING 20.7 Continued

```
42:    static int READING_REVIEW = 6;
43:    static int READING_NOTHING = 0;
44:    int currentActivity = READING_NOTHING;
45:    Book libraryBook = new Book();
46:
47:    LibraryHandler() {
48:        super();
49:    }
50:
51:    public void startElement(String uri, String localName,
52:        String qName, Attributes attributes) {
53:
54:        if (qName.equals("Title"))
55:            currentActivity = READING_TITLE;
56:        else if (qName.equals("Author"))
57:            currentActivity = READING_AUTHOR;
58:        else if (qName.equals("Publisher"))
59:            currentActivity = READING_PUBLISHER;
60:        else if (qName.equals("PublicationDate"))
61:            currentActivity = READING_PUBLICATION_DATE;
62:        else if (qName.equals("Subject"))
63:            currentActivity = READING_SUBJECT;
64:        else if (qName.equals("Review"))
65:            currentActivity = READING_REVIEW;
66:
67:        if (currentActivity == READING_PUBLICATION_DATE) {
68:            libraryBook.isbn = attributes.getValue("isbn");
69:            libraryBook.edition = attributes.getValue("edition");
70:        }
71:    }
72:
73:    public void characters(char[] ch, int start, int length) {
74:        String value = new String(ch, start, length);
75:        if (currentActivity == READING_TITLE)
76:            libraryBook.title = value;
77:        if (currentActivity == READING_AUTHOR)
78:            libraryBook.author = value;
79:        if (currentActivity == READING_PUBLISHER)
80:            libraryBook.publisher = value;
81:        if (currentActivity == READING_PUBLICATION_DATE)
82:            libraryBook.publicationDate = value;
83:        if (currentActivity == READING_SUBJECT)
84:            libraryBook.subject = value;
85:        if (currentActivity == READING_REVIEW)
86:            libraryBook.review = value;
87:    }
88:
89:    public void endElement(String uri, String localName, String qName) {
```

20

continues

LISTING 20.7 Continued

```
 90:          if (qName.equals("Book")) {
 91:              System.out.println("\nTitle: " + libraryBook.title);
 92:              System.out.println("Author: " + libraryBook.author);
 93:              System.out.println("Publisher: " + libraryBook.publisher);
 94:              System.out.println("Publication Date: "
 95:                  + libraryBook.publicationDate);
 96:              System.out.println("Edition: " + libraryBook.edition);
 97:              System.out.println("ISBN: " + libraryBook.isbn);
 98:              System.out.println("Review: " + libraryBook.review);
 99:              libraryBook = new Book();
100:          }
101:      }
102: }
103:
104: class Book {
105:      String title;
106:      String author;
107:      String publisher;
108:      String publicationDate;
109:      String edition;
110:      String isbn;
111:      String subject;
112:      String review;
113: }
```

The ReadLibrary application reads an XML file that uses the library book dialect shown in Listings 20.4 and 20.5. To read the collection.librml file with the application, type the following at a command line:

```
java ReadLibrary collection.librml
```

The program will display the following output:

```
Title: Catch-22
Author: Joseph Heller
Publisher: Simon and Schuster
Publication Date: 09/1996
Edition: Trade
ISBN: 0684833395
Review: heller-catch22.html

Title: Slaughterhouse-Five
Author: Kurt Vonnegut
Publisher: Dell
Publication Date: 12/1991
Edition: Paperback
ISBN: 0440180295
Review: null
```

Summary

In today's lesson, you learned about working with data stored in popular database formats such as Microsoft Access, MySQL, and xBase. Using either Java Database Connectivity (JDBC) or a combination of JDBC and ODBC, you can incorporate existing data-storage solutions into your Java programs.

You also learned several ways to work with data that don't exist yet, by using some of the data structures that are more sophisticated than arrays and linked lists.

These standard data structures provide a range of options that cover many practical programming scenarios.

In many ways Extensible Markup Language is the data equivalent of the Java language. It liberates data from the software used to create them and the operating system the software ran on, just as Java can liberate software from a particular operating system.

You learned the basics of XML and how to use the Java API for XML Processing to retrieve data from an XML file. Writing XML data in Java doesn't require this API. You can create XML files simply by writing strings to a file, output stream, or another medium.

One of the biggest advantages to representing data using XML is that you will always be able to get those data back. If you decide to move the data into a relational database, a MySQL database, or some other form, you can easily retrieve the information.

You also can transform XML into other forms, such as HTML, through a variety of technology, both in Java and through tools developed in other languages.

Q&A

Q Can the JDBC-ODBC bridge driver be used in an applet?

A The default security in place for applets does not allow the JDBC-ODBC bridge to be used because the ODBC side of the bridge driver employs native code rather than Java. Native code can't be held to the security restrictions in place for Java, so there's no way to ensure that this code is secure.

JDBC drivers that are implemented entirely in Java can be used in applets, and they have the advantage of requiring no configuration on the client computer.

Q Why is Extensible Markup Language called XML instead of EML?

A None of the founders of the language appears to have documented the reason for choosing XML as the acronym. The general consensus in the XML community is that it was chosen because it "sounds cooler" than EML. Before anyone snickers at that distinction, Sun Microsystems chose the name Java for its programming

20

language using the same criteria, turning down more technical-sounding alternatives such as DNA and WRL.

There is a possibility that the founders of XML were trying to avoid confusion with a programming language called EML (Extended Machine Language), which predates Extensible Markup Language.

Quiz

Review today's material by taking this quiz.

Questions

1. What does a `Statement` object represent in a database program?

(a.) A connection to a database

(b.) A database query written in Structured Query Language

(c.) A data source

2. What kind of driver is not included with Java 2 SDK 1.4?

(a.) A JDBC driver

(b.) A JDBC-ODBC driver

(c.) Both

3. When all the start element tags, end element tags, and other markup are applied consistently in a document, what adjective describes the document?

(a.) Validating

(b.) Parsable

(c.) Well-formed

4. What class in the `javax.xml.parsers` package is used to create SAX parsers?

(a.) `SAXParserFactory`

(b.) `SAXParser`

(c.) `DefaultHandler`

5. Which of the following would be an acceptable end element tag in XML?

(a.) `</Category>`

(b.) `<Category/>`

(c.) `<Category>`

Answers

1. (b.) The class, part of the `java.sql` package, represents an SQL statement.

2. (a.) Many relational database programs include a JDBC driver, but one is not shipped with the SDK at this writing.

3. (c.) In order for data to be considered XML, the data must be well-formed.

4. (a.) The `SAXParserFactory` class is used to create a SAX parser according to your specifications.

5. (a.) Every end element tag must be a name surrounded by the characters "</" and ">". Answer b, `<Category/>`, would be acceptable as an element tag that does not surround any data.

Certification Practice

The following question is the kind of thing you could expect to be asked on a Java programming certification test. Answer it without looking at today's material or using the Java compiler to test the code.

Given:

```java
public class ArrayClass {

    public static ArrayClass newInstance() {
        count++;
        return new ArrayClass();
    }

    public static void main(String arguments[]) {
        new ArrayClass();
    }

    int count = -1;
}
```

Which line in this program will prevent it from compiling successfully?

(a) `count++;`

(b) `return new ArrayClass();`

(c) `public static void main(String arguments[]) {`

(d) `int count = -1;`

The answer is available on this book's Web site at `http://www.java21days.com`. Visit the Day 20 page and click the Certification Practice link.

20

Exercises

To extend your knowledge of the subjects covered today, try the following exercises:

- Modify the CoalTotals application to pull fields from the Country Oil Totals table instead of the Coal table.
- Create two applications: one that retrieves records from a database and produces an XML file that contains the same information and a second application that reads data from that XML file and displays them.

Where applicable, exercise solutions are offered on this book's Web site at http://www.java21days.com.

DAY 21

Writing Java Servlets and JavaServer Pages

One of the most exciting areas of Java development has become Web application programming. Thousands of developers are writing servlets (applications run by a server) and using a complementary technology called JavaServer Pages.

Servlets employ Java on the Web without the prohibitive security restrictions in place for applets. They run on a server rather than on user computers, so they can use all the features of the language.

JavaServer Pages are a way to execute Java statements that are contained in an HTML document. They enable Web sites to use Java for interactive aspects of a page and use HTML and other Web technology for the rest.

Today, you'll learn about the following topics:

- How to write servlets and run them on a Web server to generate Web content dynamically
- How to use Sun's servlet class library

- How to use servlets to receive data from a Web form
- How to store and retrieve cookies
- How to create a JavaServer Page
- How to use servlets on a page
- How to include Java expressions, statements, and variables on a page

Using Web Servlets

Although servlets were designed for use with different kinds of Internet servers, Sun and other servlet developers are focusing on how to employ servlets on the World Wide Web.

Java servlets are run by a Web server that has an interpreter that supports the Java Servlet specification. This interpreter, which is often called a *servlet engine*, is optimized to run servlets with a minimum of the Web server's resources.

Java servlets serve the same purpose as programs that are implemented using the Common Gateway Interface, which is a protocol for writing software that sends and receives information through a Web server. CGI programming has been supported on the Web for most of its existence. Most CGI programs, which are also called CGI *scripts*, have been written using languages such as Perl, Python, PHP, and C.

You've used hundreds of CGI programs as you browsed the Web. CGI is used for these purposes:

- Collecting data from a form on a Web page
- Receiving information from fields in an URL
- Running programs on the computer that runs the Web server
- Storing and retrieving configuration information for each user of a Web page—a feature commonly known as "browser cookies"
- Sending data back to a Web user in the form of an HTML document, a GIF file, or another common format

Java servlets can do all these things, and they also support some behavior that's extremely difficult to implement using most CGI scripting languages.

Servlets offer full support for sessions, which are a way to keep track of how a Web user navigates the parts of a Web site, opening and closing pages over a period of time. They also can communicate directly with a Web server using a standard interface. As long as the server supports Java servlets, it can exchange information with those programs.

Java servlets have the same portability advantages as the language itself. Although Sun's official implementation of servlets was created with the designers of the Apache Web server, other server developers also have introduced tools to support Java servlets, including IBM WebSphere Application Server, BEA WebLogic, Jetty, and the Microsoft Internet Information Server.

Servlets also run efficiently in memory. If 10 people are simultaneously using the same CGI script, a Web server will have 10 copies of that script loaded into memory. If 10 people are using a Java servlet, however, only one copy of the servlet will be loaded, and this servlet will spawn threads to handle each user.

Supporting Servlets

Java servlets and JavaServer Pages are supported by Sun Microsystems through Tomcat, which was developed by Sun Microsystems and the Apache Software Foundation, the group that oversees the Apache Web server.

Tomcat includes two Java class libraries, `javax.servlet` and `javax.servlet.http`, and software that adds servlet functionality to the Apache Web server. There also is a stand-alone servlet interpreter you can use to test servlets before deploying them on the Web.

You can find out more about Tomcat from two Web sites:

- Sun's Java servlet site at `http://java.sun.com/products/servlet/`
- Apache's Tomcat site at `http://jakarta.apache.org/tomcat/`

Before you can use servlets, you must have a Web server that offers support for these programs. If you have an Apache Web server and are conversant in how to extend its functionality, you can add Tomcat support to the server. Your current Web server or Web application server may already include support for servlets.

If you don't have a server but you'd like to begin developing servlets, there are several companies that offer commercial Web hosting with Java servlet support. These companies have already installed Tomcat and configured it to work with their servers, leaving you to focus on writing servlets using the classes of the `javax.servlet` and `javax.servlet.http` packages.

The Open Directory Project lists more than a dozen companies that offer built-in servlet hosting. Visit `http://www.dmoz.org` and search for "servlet hosting."

21

Note

> For the past several years, I've been using Motivational Marketing Associates to host servlets and JavaServer Pages on the official Web sites for my books. MMA offers Java servlet hosting on an Apache Web server running Linux. You can find out more about its commercial hosting services by visiting http://www.mmaweb.com/.

Servlets are supported by several Web servers, each of which has its own installation, security, and administration procedures. This day is devoted to what you do with a server after it's installed—creating and compiling Java servlets and JavaServer Pages programming.

To compile servlets on your computer, you must install the two Java servlet packages, `javax.servlet` and `javax.servlet.http`. These packages are not part of the standard Java class library included with Java 2 version 1.4.

At the time of this writing, the last full release of these packages is Java Servlet 2.3, which is supported by Tomcat version 4.0.

To download Java Servlet 2.3, visit the Java Servlet site at `http://java.sun.com/products/servlet/` and click the Download link. (You also may be able to go directly to `http://java.sun.com/products/servlet/download.html`, though Sun moves pages around from time to time on its Java site.)

These packages are available as `ZIP` archive files, which you must open using software that can extract ZIP files (such as WinZIP on a Windows system). When you are extracting files to your computer, choose the option to use the existing folder names in the archive.

Caution

> There are several things you can download from that page, including different versions of the packages, documentation, and technical specifications. The file you want to download is in the "2.3 Final Release" section of the page and is next to the heading "Download class files 2.3."

Version 2.3 includes all of the class files in the two packages, Javadoc documentation for the classes, and a `jar` file that also contains all of the classes.

This Java archive is named `servlet.jar`, and it will be installed into a `lib` subfolder. Add this file to your computer's CLASSPATH.

Developing Servlets

Java servlets are created and compiled just like any other Java application. After you have installed the two servlet JAR files and added them to your CLASSPATH setting, you can compile them with the Java compiler included with SDK 1.4 or any other tool that supports Java 2 version 1.4.

To create a servlet, create a subclass of the `HttpServlet` class, which is part of the `javax.servlet` package. This class includes methods that represent the life cycle of a servlet and methods that receive information from the Web server running the servlet.

The `init(ServletConfig)` method is called automatically when a Web server first brings a servlet online to handle a user's request. As mentioned earlier, one Java servlet can handle multiple requests from different Web users. The `init()` method is called only once, when a servlet comes online. If a servlet is already online when another request to use the servlet is received, the `init()` method won't be called again.

The `init()` method has one argument—`ServletConfig`, an interface in the `javax.servlet` package that contains methods to find out more about the environment in which a servlet is running.

The `destroy()` method is called when a Web server takes a servlet offline. Like the `init()` method, this is called only once, when all users have finished receiving information from the servlet. If this doesn't take place in a specified amount of time, `destroy()` will be called automatically, which prevents a servlet from being hung up while it waits for information to be exchanged with a user.

One of the main tasks of a servlet is to collect information from a Web user and present something back in response. You can collect information from a user by using a *form*, which is a group of text boxes, radio buttons, text areas, and other input fields on a Web page.

Figure 21.1 shows a Web form on a page loaded with Microsoft Internet Explorer 6.

21

FIGURE **21.1**

Collecting information with a Web form.

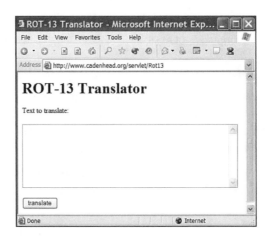

The form displayed in Figure 21.1 contains two fields: a text area and a clickable button labeled "translate." The HyperText Markup Language (HTML) tags used to display this page are the following:

```
<html>
<body>
<head><title>ROT-13 Translator</title></head>
<h1>ROT-13 Translator</h1>
<p>Text to translate:
<form action="Rot13" method="POST">
<textarea name="text" ROWS=8 COLS=55>
</textarea>
<p><input type="submit" value="translate">
</form>
</body>
</html>
```

The form is contained within the `<form>` and `</form>` HTML tags. Each field on the form is represented by its own tags: `<textarea>` and `</textarea>` for the text area and `<input>` for the "translate" button. The text area is given a name, `text`.

Tip

> Web servlets require you to have a basic familiarity with HTML because the only user interface for a servlet is a Web page running in a browser. Two books that are good for learning HTML are *Sams Teach Yourself HTML in 24 Hours* by Dick Oliver and *Sams Teach Yourself Web Publishing with HTML and XHTML in 21 Days, Third Edition* by Laura Lemay (one of the authors of this book).

Each field on a form stores information that can be transmitted to a Web server and then sent to a Java servlet. Web browsers communicate with servers by using Hypertext Transfer Protocol (HTTP). Form data can be sent to a server using two kinds of HTTP requests: GET and POST.

When a Web page calls a server using GET or POST, the name of the program that will handle the request must be specified as a Web address, also called a uniform resource locator (URL).

A GET request affixes all data on a form to the end of an URL, as in this example:

```
http://www.java21days.com/servlets/beep?number=5551220&repeat=no
```

A POST request includes form data as a header that is sent separately from the URL. This is generally preferred, and it's required when confidential information is being collected on the form. Also, some Web servers and browsers do not support URLs longer than 255 characters, which limits the amount of information that can be sent in a GET request.

Java servlets handle both of these requests through methods inherited from the HttpServlet class: doGet(*HttpServletRequest*, *HttpServletResponse*) and doPost(*HttpServletRequest*, *HttpServletResponse*). These methods throw two kinds of exceptions: ServletException, which is part of the javax.servlet package, and IOException, an exception in the standard java.io package that involves input and output streams.

These methods function identically within Java, so a common technique in Java servlet programming is to use one method to call the other, as in the following:

```
public void doGet(HttpServletRequest request,
    HttpServletResponse response) throws ServletException, IOException {

    doPost(request, response);
}
```

The doGet() and doPost() methods have two arguments: an HttpServletRequest object and an HttpServletResponse object. These objects belong to classes in the javax.servlet.http package. A servlet receives information about how it was run by calling methods of the HttpServletRequest class. For example, when a Web form is submitted to a servlet, each field on the form is stored as a string by the HttpServletRequest class.

You can retrieve these fields in a servlet by calling the getParameter(*String*) method with the name of the field as an argument. This method returns null if no field of that name exists.

21

A servlet communicates with the user by sending back an HTML document, an image file, or another type of information supported by a Web browser. It sends this information by calling the methods of the HttpServletResponse class.

The first thing you must do when preparing a response is define the kind of content the servlet is sending to a browser. Call the setContentType(*String*) method with the content type as an argument.

The most common form for a response is HTML, which is set by calling setContentType("text/html"). You can also send a response as text ("text/plain"), graphics files ("image/gif", "image/jpeg"), and application-specific formats such as "application/msword".

To send data to a browser, you create a servlet output stream associated with the browser and then call the println(*String*) method on that stream. Servlet output streams are represented by the ServletOutputStream class, which is part of the javax.servlet package. You can get one of these streams by calling the getOutputStream() method of the HttpServletResponse class.

The following example creates a servlet output stream from an HttpServletResponse object called response and then sends a short Web page to that stream:

```
ServletOutputStream out = response.getOutputStream();
out.println("<html>");
out.println("<body>");
out.println("<h1>Hello World!</h1>");
out.println("</body>");
out.println("</html>");
```

Listing 21.1 contains a Java servlet that receives data from the form displayed in Figure 21.1.

LISTING 21.1   The Full Text of Rot13.java

```
 1: import java.io.*;
 2:
 3: import javax.servlet.*;
 4: import javax.servlet.http.*;
 5:
 6: public class Rot13 extends HttpServlet {
 7:
 8:     public void doPost(HttpServletRequest req, HttpServletResponse res)
 9:         throws ServletException, IOException {
10:
11:         String text = req.getParameter("text");
12:         String translation = translate(text);
13:         res.setContentType("text/html");
14:         ServletOutputStream out = res.getOutputStream();
15:         out.println("<html>");
```

LISTING 21.1 Continued

```
16:            out.println("<body>");
17:            out.println("<head><title>ROT-13 Translator</title></head>");
18:            out.println("<h1>ROT-13 Translator</h1>");
19:            out.println("<p>Text to translate:");
20:            out.println("<form action=\"Rot13\" method=\"POST\">");
21:            out.println("<textarea name=\"text\" ROWS=8 COLS=55>");
22:            out.println(translation);
23:            out.println("</textarea>");
24:            out.println("<p><input type=\"submit\" value=\"translate\">");
25:            out.println("</form>");
26:            out.println("</body>");
27:            out.println("</html>");
28:        }
29:
30:        public void doGet(HttpServletRequest req, HttpServletResponse res)
31:            throws ServletException, IOException {
32:
33:            doPost(req, res);
34:        }
35:
36:        String translate(String input) {
37:            StringBuffer output = new StringBuffer();
38:            if (input != null) {
39:                for (int i = 0; i < input.length(); i++) {
40:                    char inChar = input.charAt(i);
41:                    if ((inChar >= 'A') & (inChar <= 'Z')) {
42:                        inChar += 13;
43:                        if (inChar > 'Z')
44:                            inChar -= 26;
45:                    }
46:                    if ((inChar >= 'a') & (inChar <= 'z')) {
47:                        inChar += 13;
48:                        if (inChar > 'z')
49:                            inChar -= 26;
50:                    }
51:                    output.append(inChar);
52:                }
53:            }
54:            return output.toString();
55:        }
56: }
```

After saving the servlet, compile it with the Java compiler.

The Rot13 servlet receives text from a Web form, translates it using ROT-13, and then displays the result in a new Web form. ROT-13 is a simple method of encrypting text

21

through letter substitution. Each letter of the alphabet is replaced with the letter that's 13 places away: A becomes N, N becomes A, B becomes O, O becomes B, C becomes P, P becomes C, and so on.

Because the ROT-13 encryption scheme is easy to decode, it isn't used when it's important to keep information secret. Instead, it's used casually on Internet discussion forums such as Usenet newsgroups. For example, if someone on a movie newsgroup wants to share a "spoiler" that reveals a plot detail about an upcoming movie, she can encode it in ROT-13 to prevent people from reading it accidentally.

> **Note**
>
> Want to know the big secret from the 1973 film *Soylent Green*? Decode this ROT-13 text: Fbba gurl'yy or oerrqvat hf yvxr pnggyr! Lbh'ir tbg gb jnea rirelbar naq gryy gurz! Fblyrag terra vf znqr bs crbcyr! Lbh'ir tbg gb gryy gurz! Fblyrag terra vf crbcyr!

To make the ROT-13 servlet available, you must publish its class files in a folder on your Web server that has been designated for Java servlets. On an Apache server equipped with Tomcat, servlets are often put in a `WEB-INF/classes` subfolder of your main Web folder. (For instance, if `/htdocs` is the root folder of your Web site, servlets would be in `/htdocs/WEB-INF/classes`.)

You run a servlet by typing its URL, such as `http://www.cadenhead.info/servlet/Rot13`, into a Web browser's address bar. Replace the first part of the URL with the name or IP address of your own Web server.

> **Tip**
>
> You can try out a working ROT-13 servlet on the book's Web site; visit `http://www.java21days.com` and open the Day 21 page.

Using Cookies

Many Web sites can be customized to keep track of information about you and the features you want the site to display. This customization is possible because of a Web browser feature called *cookies*. These are small files containing information that a Web site wants to remember about a user, such as his username, the number of times he's visited, and the like. The files are stored on the user's computer, and a Web site can read only the cookies on the user's system that the site has created.

Because of privacy considerations, most Web browsers can be configured to reject all cookies or ask permission before allowing a site to create a cookie. The default behavior for most browsers is to accept all cookies.

With servlets, you can easily create and retrieve cookies as a user runs your program. Cookies are supported by the Cookie class in the javax.servlet.http package.

To create a cookie, call the Cookie(*String*, *String*) constructor. The first argument is the name you want to give the cookie, and the second is the cookie's value.

One use for cookies is to count the number of times someone has loaded a servlet. The following statement creates a cookie named visits and gives it the initial value of 1:

```
Cookie visitCookie = new Cookie("visits", "1");
```

When you create a cookie, you must decide how long it should remain valid on a user's computer. Cookies can be valid for an hour, a day, a year, or any time in between. When a cookie is no longer valid, the Web browser will delete it automatically.

Call a cookie's setMaxAge(*int*) method to set the amount of time the cookie will remain valid, in seconds. If you use a negative value as an argument, the cookie will remain valid only while the user's Web browser is open. If you use 0 as a value, the cookie will not be stored on a user's computer.

Note
The purpose of creating a cookie with a maximum age of 0 is to tell the Web browser to delete the cookie if it already has one.

Cookies are sent to a user's computer along with the data that are displayed by the Web browser. To send a cookie, call the addCookie(*Cookie*) method of an HttpServletResponse object.

You can add more than one cookie to a response. When cookies are stored on a user's computer, they're associated with the URL of the Web page or program that created the cookie. You can associate several cookies with the same URL.

When a Web browser requests a URL, the browser checks to see whether any cookies are associated with that URL. If there are, the cookies are sent along with the request.

In a servlet, call the getCookies() method of an HttpServletRequest object to receive an array of Cookie objects. You can call each cookie's getName() and getValue() methods to find out about that cookie and do something with the data.

Listing 21.2 contains SetColor, a servlet that enables a user to select the background color of the page that the servlet displays. The color is stored as a cookie called color, and the servlet requests the cookie from a Web browser every time the servlet is loaded.

21

LISTING 21.2   The Full Text of `SetColor.java`

```
 1: import java.io.*;
 2:
 3: import javax.servlet.*;
 4: import javax.servlet.http.*;
 5:
 6: public class SetColor extends HttpServlet {
 7:
 8:     public void doPost(HttpServletRequest req, HttpServletResponse res)
 9:         throws ServletException, IOException {
10:
11:         String pageColor;
12:         String colorParameter = req.getParameter("color");
13:         if (colorParameter != null) {
14:             Cookie colorCookie = new Cookie("color", colorParameter);
15:             colorCookie.setMaxAge(31536000);
16:             res.addCookie(colorCookie);
17:             pageColor = colorParameter;
18:         } else {
19:             pageColor = retrieveColor(req.getCookies());
20:         }
21:         ServletOutputStream out = res.getOutputStream();
22:         res.setContentType("text/html");
23:         out.println("<html>");
24:         out.println("<body bgcolor=\"" + pageColor + "\">");
25:         out.println("<head><title>The U.S. Constitution</title></head>");
26:         out.println("<h1>The U.S. Constitution</h1>");
27:         displayFile("constitution.html", out);
28:         out.println("<h5>Choose a new color</h5>");
29:         out.println("<form action=\"SetColor\" method=\"POST\">");
30:         out.println("<input type=\"text\" name=\"color\" value=\"" +
31:             pageColor + "\" SIZE=40>");
32:         out.println("<p><input type=\"submit\" value=\"Change Color\">");
33:         out.println("</form>");
34:         out.println("</body>");
35:         out.println("</html>");
36:     }
37:
38:     public void doGet(HttpServletRequest req, HttpServletResponse res)
39:         throws ServletException, IOException {
40:
41:         doPost(req, res);
42:     }
43:
44:     String retrieveColor(Cookie[] cookies) {
45:         String inColor = "#FFFFFF";
46:         for (int i = 0; i < cookies.length; i++) {
47:             String cookieName = cookies[i].getName();
48:             if (cookieName.equals("color")) {
```

Listing 21.2 Continued

```
49:                    inColor = cookies[i].getValue();
50:                }
51:            }
52:        return inColor;
53:    }
54:
55:    void displayFile(String pageName, ServletOutputStream out) {
56:        try {
57:            ServletContext servletContext = getServletContext();
58:            String filename = servletContext.getRealPath(pageName);
59:            FileReader file = new FileReader(filename);
60:            BufferedReader buff = new BufferedReader(file);
61:            boolean eof = false;
62:            while (!eof) {
63:                String line = buff.readLine();
64:                if (line == null)
65:                    eof = true;
66:                else
67:                    out.println(line);
68:            }
69:            buff.close();
70:        } catch (IOException e) {
71:            log("Error -- " + e.toString());
72:        }
73:    }
74: }
```

The `SetColor` servlet displays the contents of an HTML file along with the rest of the page. This example uses `constitution.html`, a copy of the U.S. Constitution in HTML format. You can download this file from this book's Web site at `http://www.java21days.com` (open the Day 21 page). You also can use any other HTML file by changing Lines 25–27 of the program.

After you compile the servlet and put it on your Web server in the servlets folder, you can run it by loading the servlet's URL into a browser, such as `http://www.cadenhead.info/servlet/SetColor`.

Figure 21.2 shows the bottom of the page displayed by the servlet.

21

FIGURE 21.2

A Web page generated by the SetColor *servlet.*

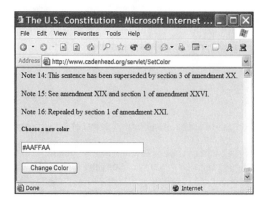

To change the page's background color, type a new value into the "Choose a new color" text field and click the Change Color button.

Colors are expressed as a # sign followed by three two-digit hexadecimal numbers (in Figure 21.2, the numbers are AA, FF, and AA). These numbers represent the amount of red, green, and blue the color contains, ranging from a minimum of 00 to a maximum of FF. If you aren't familiar with hexadecimal colors, you can try these out while testing the servlet:

- #FF0000: Bright red
- #00FF00: Bright green
- #0000FF: Bright blue
- #FFAAAA: Light red
- #AAFFAA: Light green
- #AAAAFF: Light blue
- #FFCC66: Butterscotch

JavaServer Pages

Java servlets make it easy to generate HTML text dynamically, producing pages that change in response to user input and data. However, servlets make it hard to generate HTML text that never changes, because it's cumbersome and tedious to use Java statements to output HTML.

Servlets also require the services of a Java programmer whenever the HTML needs to be changed. The servlet must be edited, recompiled, and deployed on the Web, and very few organizations are comfortable handing that task to a nonprogrammer.

The solution to this problem is JavaServer Pages, which create documents that mix static HTML with the output of servlets and elements of the Java language, such as expressions and Java statements.

JavaServer Pages are part of the Tomcat specification from Sun Microsystems and the Apache Software Foundation. JavaServer Pages are a complement to servlets, rather than a replacement. They make it easy to separate two kinds of Web content:

- Static content, the portions of a Web page that don't change, such as an online store's description of each product
- Dynamic content, the portions of a Web page that are generated by a servlet, such as the store's pricing and availability data for each product, which can change as items sell out

When you use only servlets on a project, it becomes extremely difficult to make minor changes, such as correcting a typo in text, rewording a paragraph, or altering some HTML tags to change how the page is presented. Any kind of change requires the servlet to be edited, compiled, tested, and redeployed on the Web server.

With JavaServer Pages, you can put the static content of a Web page in an HTML document and call servlets from within that content. You also can use other parts of the Java language on a page, such as expressions, `if-then` blocks, and variables. A Web server that supports the Tomcat specification knows how to read these pages and execute the Java code they contain, generating an HTML document as if you wrote a servlet to handle the whole task. In actuality, JavaServer Pages do use servlets for everything.

You create a JavaServer Page as you would create an HTML document—in a text editor or Web publishing program such as Microsoft FrontPage 2002 or Macromedia Dreamweaver. When you save the page, use the `.jsp` file extension to indicate that the file is a JavaServer Page instead of an HTML document. Then the page can be published on a Web server like an HTML document (although the server must support Tomcat).

When a user requests the JavaServer Page for the first time, the Web server compiles a new servlet that presents the page. This servlet combines everything that has been put into the page:

- Text marked up with HTML
- Calls to Java servlets
- Java expressions and statements
- Special JavaServer Pages variables

21

Writing a JavaServer Page

A JavaServer Page consists of three kinds of elements, each with its own special markup tag that's similar to HTML:

- Scriptlets—Java statements executed when the page is loaded. Each of these statements is surrounded by <% and %> tags.

- Expressions—Java expressions that are evaluated, producing output that's displayed on the page. These are surrounded by <%= and %> tags.

- Declarations—Statements to create instance variables and handle other setup tasks required in the presentation of the page. These are surrounded by <%! and %> tags.

Using Expressions

Listing 21.3 contains a JavaServer Page that includes one expression, a call to the `java.util.Date()` constructor. This constructor produces a string containing the current time and date. Enter this file with any text editor that can save files as plain text. (The editor you've been using to create Java source code will work for this purpose as well.)

LISTING 21.3   The Full Text of `time.jsp`

```
1: <html>
2: <head>
3: <title>Clock</title>
4: </head>
5: <body>
6: <h1 align="Center">
7: <%= new java.util.Date() %>
8: </h1>
9: </body>
10: </html>
```

After saving the file, upload it to your Web server in a folder where other Web pages are stored. Unlike Java servlets, which must be in a folder that has been designated for servlets, JavaServer Pages can be placed in any folder that's accessible on the Web.

When you load the page's URL for the first time, the Web server will compile the JavaServer Page into a servlet. This causes the page to load slowly, but it won't happen again because the server keeps this servlet around for all subsequent requests.

The output of `time.jsp` is shown in Figure 21.3.

FIGURE 21.3

Using an expression in a JavaServer Page.

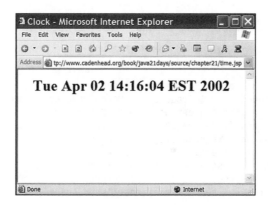

When a JavaServer Page includes an expression, it's evaluated to produce a value and displayed on the page. If the expression produces different values each time it's run, as `time.jsp` does, this will be reflected in the page when it's loaded in a Web browser.

There are several servlet variables you can refer to in expressions and other elements of a JavaServer Page:

- `application`—The servlet context used to communicate with the Web server
- `config`—The servlet configuration object used to see how the servlet was initialized
- `out`—The servlet output stream
- `request`—The HTTP servlet request
- `response`—The HTTP servlet responses
- `session`—The current HTTP session

Each of these variables refers to an object you worked with earlier today in Java servlets, and you can call the same methods from within a JavaServer Page that were available in a servlet.

The next page you'll create, `environment.jsp`, shows how the `request` variable can be used on a page. This variable represents an object of the `HttpServletRequest` class, and you can call the object's `getHeader(String)` method to retrieve HTTP headers that describe the request in more detail. Listing 21.4 shows the text of `environment.jsp`.

LISTING 21.4 The Full Text of `environment.jsp`

```
1: <html>
2: <head>
3: <title>Environment Variables</title>
```

continues

21

LISTING 21.4 Continued

```
 4: </head>
 5: <body>
 6: <ul>
 7: <li>Accept: <%= request.getHeader("Accept") %>
 8: <li>Accept-Encoding: <%= request.getHeader("Accept-Encoding") %>
 9: <li>Connection: <%= request.getHeader("Connection") %>
10: <li>Content-Length: <%= request.getHeader("Content-Length") %>
11: <li>Content-Type: <%= request.getHeader("Content-Type") %>
12: <li>Cookie: <%= request.getHeader("Cookie") %>
13: <li>Host: <%= request.getHeader("Host") %>
14: <li>Referer: <%= request.getHeader("Referer") %>
15: <li>User-Agent: <%= request.getHeader("User-Agent") %>
16: </ul>
17: </body>
18: </html>
```

In lines 7–15 of the environment.jsp page, each line contains a call to getHeader() that retrieves a different HTTP request header. An example of the output is shown in Figure 21.4. The values reported for each header depend on your Web server and the Web browser you're using, so you won't see the same values for User-Agent, Referer, and other headers.

FIGURE 21.4

Using servlet variables on a JavaServer Page.

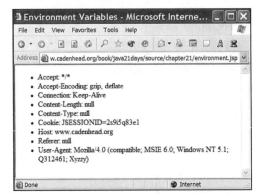

Using Scriptlets

You can also use Java statements in your JavaServer Page—calling methods, assigning values to variables, creating conditional statements, and so on. These statements begin with the <% tag and end with the %> tag. More than one statement can be enclosed within these tags.

Statements that appear inside a JavaServer Page are called *scriptlets*. You can use any of the servlet variables that were available for expressions.

Listing 21.5 contains the code for shopforbooks.jsp, a Web page that displays a list of books, with hyperlinks to each book's page at an online bookstore.

LISTING 21.5   The Full Text of shopforbooks.jsp

```
 1: <html>
 2: <head>
 3: <title>Shop for Books</title>
 4: </head>
 5: <body>
 6: <h2 align="Left">Favorite Books</h2>
 7: <%
 8: String[] bookTitle = { "Catch-22", "Something Happened",
 9:     "Good as Gold" };
10: String[] isbn = { "0684833395", "0684841215", "0684839741" };
11: String amazonLink = "http://www.amazon.com/exec/obidos/ASIN/";
12: String bnLink = "http://shop.bn.com/booksearch/isbnInquiry.asp?isbn=";
13:
14: String store = request.getParameter("store");
15: if (store == null) {
16:     store = "Amazon";
17: }
18: for (int i = 0; i < bookTitle.length; i++) {
19:     if (store.equals("Amazon"))
20:         out.println("<li><a href=\"" + amazonLink + isbn[i] + "\">" +
21:             bookTitle[i] + "</a>");
22:     else
23:         out.println("<li><a href=\"" + bnLink + isbn[i] + "\">" +
24:             bookTitle[i] + "</a>");
25: }
26: %>
27: <p>Preferred Bookstore:
28: <form action="shopforbooks.jsp" method="POST">
29: <p><input type="radio" value="Amazon" <%= (store.equals("Amazon") ?
            "checked" : "") %>
30: name="store"> Amazon.Com
31: <p><input type="radio" value="BN" <%= (store.equals("BN") ? " checked" : "")
        %>
32: name="store"> Barnes & Noble
33: <p><input type="submit" value="Change Store">
34: </form>
35: </body>
36: </html>
```

21

This JavaServer Page includes a form at the bottom of the page that lets users pick which bookstore they like to use for online shopping.

In line 28, the form is being submitted to the URL of the JavaServer Page. Because pages are actually servlets, they can also receive form data that's sent by POST or GET.

This page uses the `store` field to hold `"Amazon"` if Amazon.com is the preferred store and `"BN"` if Barnes & Noble is the preferred store.

One thing to note as you test the server page is how the radio buttons on the form always match the store you've chosen. This occurs because of expressions that appear on lines 29 and 31. Here's one of those expressions:

```
<%= (store.equals("Amazon") ? " checked" : "") %>
```

This expression uses the ternary operator with the conditional `store.equals("Amazon")`. If this condition is true, the word "checked" is the value of the expression. Otherwise, an empty string ("") is the value.

The value of expressions is displayed as part of the JavaServer Page. Figure 21.5 shows what this page looks like in a Web browser.

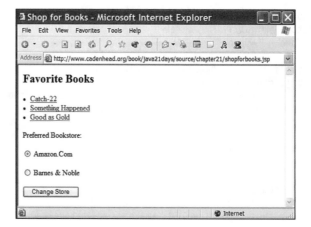

FIGURE 21.5

Displaying dynamic content using scriptlets.

Using Declarations

The last element you can insert into a JavaServer Page is a declaration, which is a statement that sets up a variable or method that will be defined in the page when it's compiled into a servlet. This feature is primarily used in conjunction with expressions and servlets.

Declarations are surrounded by `<%!` and `%>` tags, as in the following example:

```
<!% boolean noCookie = true %>
<!% String userName = "New user" %>
```

These declarations create two instance variables: `noCookie` and `userName`. When the JavaServer Page is compiled into a servlet, these variables will be part of the definition of that class.

Listing 21.6 contains a JavaServer Page that uses a declaration to present a counter.

LISTING 21.6 The Full Text of `counter.jsp`

```
 1: <%@ page import="counter.*" %>
 2: <html>
 3: <head>
 4: <title>Counter Example</title>
 5: </head>
 6: <body>
 7: <h1>JSP Stats</h1>
 8: <%! Counter visits; %>
 9: <%! int count; %>
10:
11: <%
12: visits = new Counter(application.getRealPath("counter.dat"));
13: count = visits.getCount() + 1;
14: %>
15:
16: <p>This page has been loaded <%= count %> times.
17:
18: <% visits.setCount(count); %>
19: </body>
20: </html>
```

Before you can try this page, you need to create a helper class that's called by statements in lines 8, 12, 13, and 18 of the page.

The `Counter` class in Listing 21.7 represents a Web counter that tallies each hit to a page.

LISTING 21.7 The Full Text of `counter.java`

```
 1: package counter;
 2:
 3: import java.io.*;
 4: import java.util.*;
 5:
 6: public class Counter {
 7:     private int count;
 8:     private String filepath;
 9:
10:     public Counter(String inFilepath) {
11:         count = 0;
12:         filepath = inFilepath;
13:     }
14:
15:     public int getCount() {
16:         try {
```

continues

21

LISTING 21.7 Continued

```
17:                  File countFile = new File(filepath);
18:                  FileReader file = new FileReader(countFile);
19:                  BufferedReader buff = new BufferedReader(file);
20:                  String current = buff.readLine();
21:                  count = Integer.parseInt(current);
22:                  buff.close();
23:             } catch (IOException e) {
24:                  // do nothing
25:             } catch (NumberFormatException nfe) {
26:                  // do nothing
27:             }
28:             return count;
29:         }
30:
31:         public void setCount(int newCount) {
32:             count = newCount;
33:             try {
34:                  File countFile = new File(filepath);
35:                  FileWriter file = new FileWriter(countFile);
36:                  BufferedWriter buff = new BufferedWriter(file);
37:                  String output = "" + newCount;
38:                  buff.write(output, 0, output.length());
39:                  buff.close();
40:             } catch (IOException e) {
41:                  // do nothing
42:             }
43:         }
44: }
```

After you compile this class successfully, store it in the same folder on your Web server as the Java servlets you created earlier today. The Counter class isn't a servlet, but Tomcat looks in that folder for classes that are referenced on a JavaServer Page.

The Counter class loads an integer value from a file called counter.dat that is stored on the Web server. The getCount() method retrieves the current value of the counter, and the setCount(*int*) method sets the current value. After the value is set, it's saved to the file so the counter continues to incrementally increase.

Figure 21.6 shows counter.jsp being loaded in a Web browser.

FIGURE 21.6

Using servlets to count visits to a Web page.

Creating a Web Application

By combining Java classes, servlets, and JavaServer Pages, you can create interactive Web applications—sites that dynamically generate content in response to user input in a sophisticated, cohesive way.

Every time you shop on an e-commerce site such as Amazon.com or use an online reference such as the Internet Movie Database (IMDB), you are running a Web application.

To see how several aspects of Java technology can work together on the Web, you will create Guestbook, a Web application that enables visitors to leave a message for the creator of a site.

The Guestbook project is made up of three things:

- guestbook.jsp, a JavaServer Page that displays guest book entries from a text file on a Web server and provides a form where a visitor can add an entry
- guestbookpost.jsp, a JavaServer Page that saves a new guest book entry to the text file
- Guestbook.java, a class that is used to filter out some characters before they are saved in the guest book

The JavaServer Pages in this project make heavy use of scriptlets and expressions. Listing 21.8 contains the source code for guestbook.jsp.

LISTING 21.8 The Full Text of guestbook.jsp

```
1: <%@ page import="java.util.*,java.io.*" %>
2: <html>
3: <head>
4: <title>Visitors Who Signed our Guestbook</title>
5: </head>
6: <body>
7: <h3>Visitors Who Signed our Guestbook</h3>
```

21

continues

LISTING 21.8 Continued

```
 8: <%
 9: String id = request.getParameter("id");
10: boolean noSignatures = true;
11: try {
12:     String filename = application.getRealPath(id + ".gbf");
13:     FileReader file = new FileReader(filename);
14:     BufferedReader buff = new BufferedReader(file);
15:     boolean eof = false;
16:     while (!eof) {
17:         String entry = buff.readLine();
18:         if (entry == null)
19:             eof = true;
20:         else {
21:             StringTokenizer entryData = new StringTokenizer(entry, "^");
22:             String name = (String) entryData.nextElement();
23:             String email = (String) entryData.nextElement();
24:             String url = (String) entryData.nextElement();
25:             String entryDate = (String) entryData.nextElement();
26:             String ip = (String) entryData.nextElement();
27:             String comments = (String) entryData.nextElement();
28:             out.print("<p>From: " + name);
29:             if (!email.equals("None"))
30:                 out.println(" <" + email + "><br>");
31:             else
32:                 out.println("<br>");
33:             if (!url.equals("None"))
34:                 out.println("Home Page: <a href=\"" + url + "\">" + url +
                        "</a><br>");
35:             out.println("Date: " + entryDate + "<br>");
36:             out.println("IP: " + ip);
37:             out.println("<blockquote>");
38:             out.println("<p>" + comments);
39:             out.println("</blockquote>");
40:             noSignatures = false;
41:         }
42:     }
43:     buff.close();
44: } catch (IOException e) {
45:     out.println("<p>This guestbook could not be read because of an error.");
46:     log("Guestbook Error: " + e.toString());
47: }
48: if (noSignatures)
49:     out.println("<p>No one has signed our guestbook yet.");
50: %>
51: <h3>Sign Our Guestbook</h3>
```

LISTING 21.8 Continued

```
52: <form method="POST" action="guestbookpost.jsp">
53:   <table border="0" cellpadding="5" cellspacing="0" width="100%">
54:     <tr>
55:       <td width="15%" valign="top" align="right">Your Name:</td>
56:       <td width="50%"><input type="text" name="name" size="40"></td>
57:     </tr>
58:     <tr>
59:       <td width="15%" valign="top" align="right">Your E-mail Address:</td>
60:       <td width="50%"><input type="text" name="email" size="40"></td>
61:     </tr>
62:     <tr>
63:       <td width="15%" valign="top" align="right">Your Home Page:</td>
64:       <td width="50%"><input type="text" name="url" size="40"></td>
65:     </tr>
66:     <tr>
67:       <td width="15%" valign="top" align="right">Your Comments:</td>
68:       <td width="50%"><textarea rows="6" name="comments"
                   cols="40"></textarea></td>
69:     </tr>
70:   </table>
71:   <p align="center"><input type="submit" value="Submit" name="B1">
72:   <input type="reset" value="Reset" name="Reset"></p>
73: <input type="hidden" name="id" value="<%= id %>">
74: </form>
75: </body>
76: </html>
```

After you save this page, store it in any folder on your Tomcat-equipped Web server where pages can be stored. You can test this even before anything else in the project is done, as long as you have an empty guest book file.

To create this file, save an empty text file on your system and give it the name cinema.gbf. Store it on the Web in the same folder as guestbook.jsp.

When you load this JavaServer Page, you must include a parameter that specifies the ID of the guest book to load, as in this URL:

```
http://www.java21pro.com/guestbook.jsp?id=cinema
```

The server name and folder depend on where you have published guestbook.jsp.

Figure 21.7 shows what your guest book should look like when your JavaServer Page compiles successfully and tries to display the contents of the cinema.gbf file.

21

FIGURE 21.7

Testing the
guestbook.jsp *page.*

The guest book file stores each guest book entry on its own line, with a caret ('^') separating each field in the entry. Visitors can provide their name, e-mail address, home page address, and a comment. Two other things are saved for each entry: the date and time it was written and the IP address of the visitor.

The following text is an example of a guest book file that contains two entries:

```
John Smith^jsmith@prefect.com^http://www.tvguide.com^Thu Apr 25
        01:19:27 EST 2002^65.80.105.19^Your Web site is great.
D. James^deejay@naviseek.com^http://www.imdb.com^ Thu Apr 25
        01:19:53 EST 2002^165.40.10.18^Thanks for the information.
```

The next JavaServer Page to create is guestbookpost.jsp, the page that updates the guest book with new entries submitted by visitors. Listing 21.9 contains the source code for this JavaServer Page.

LISTING 21.9   The Full Text of guestbookpost.jsp

```
 1: <%@ page import="java.util.*,java.io.*,guestbook.*" %>
 2: <html>
 3: <head>
 4: <title>Thank You For Signing Our Guestbook</title>
 5: </head>
 6: <body>
 7: <h3>Thank You For Signing Our Guestbook</h3>
 8: <%
 9: String id = request.getParameter("id");
10: String[] entryFields = { "name", "email", "url", "comments" };
11: String[] entry = new String[4];
```

LISTING 21.9 Continued

```
12: for (int i = 0; i < entryFields.length; i++) {
13:     entry[i] = Guestbook.filterString(request.getParameter(entryFields[i]));
14: }
15: Date now = new Date();
16: String entryDate = now.toString();
17: String ip = request.getRemoteAddr();
18: %>
19:
20: <p>Your entry looks like this:
21: <p>From: <%= entry[0] %><%= (!entry[1].equals("None") ? "<"+entry[1]+">" :
            "") %><br>
22: <% if (!entry[2].equals("None")) { %>
23: Home Page: <a href="<%= entry[2] %>"><%= entry[2] %></a><br>
24: <% } %>
25: Date: <%= entryDate %><br>
26: IP: <%= ip %>
27: <blockquote>
28: <p><%= entry[3] %>
29: </blockquote>
30:
31: <%
32: try {
33:     boolean append = true;
34:     String filename = application.getRealPath(id + ".gbf");
35:     FileWriter fw = new FileWriter(filename, append);
36:     BufferedWriter fileOut = new BufferedWriter(fw);
37:     String newEntry = entry[0] + "^" + entry[1] + "^" + entry[2] + "^"
38:         + entryDate + "^" + ip + "^" + entry[3];
39:     fileOut.write(newEntry, 0, newEntry.length());
40:     fileOut.newLine();
41:     fileOut.close();
42: } catch (IOException e) {
43:     out.println("<p>This guestbook could not be updated because of an
                error.");
44:     log("Guestbook Error: " + e.toString());
45: }
46: %>
47:
48: <p><a href="guestbook.jsp?id=<%= id %>">View the Guestbook</a>
49: </body>
50:
51: </html>
```

21

The guestbookpost.jsp JavaServer Page collects data from a Web form, removes characters from the data that can't be put in the guest book, and stores the result in a text file.

Each guest book has its own file with a name that begins with the ID parameter of the book and ends with the `.gbf` file extension. If the guest book has the ID of `cinema`, the filename is `cinema.gbf`.

Like the other JavaServer Page included in this Web application, `guestbookpost.jsp` can be stored in any folder on your Web server where HTML documents are kept. For this project, store the page in the same folder as `guestbook.jsp` and `cinema.gbf`.

Before you can try the `Guestbook` application, you must create a Java class that will be used to filter some unwanted text from guest book entries before they are posted.

There are three characters that cannot be included in the guest book because of the way entries are stored in a file:

- Caret characters ('^')
- Return characters, which have the integer value of 13 in Java
- Linefeed characters, which have the integer value of 10

To remove these characters before they are saved in a guest book, a helper class called `Guestbook` will be created. This class has a static method called `filterString(String)` that removes those three characters from a string.

Listing 21.10 contains the source code for this class.

LISTING 21.10   The Full Text of `Guestbook.java`

```
 1: package guestbook;
 2:
 3: public class Guestbook {
 4:     public static String filterString(String input) {
 5:         input = replaceText(input, '^', ' ');
 6:         input = replaceText(input, (char)13, ' ');
 7:         input = replaceText(input, (char)10, ' ');
 8:         return input;
 9:     }
10:
11:     private static String replaceText(String inString, char oldChar,
12:         char newChar) {
13:
14:         while (inString.indexOf(oldChar) != -1) {
15:             int oldPosition = inString.indexOf(oldChar);
16:             StringBuffer data = new StringBuffer(inString);
17:             data.setCharAt(oldPosition, newChar);
18:             inString = data.toString();
19:         }
20:         return inString;
21:     }
22: }
```

The replaceText() method in lines 11–21 of Listing 21.10 does most of the work in the class. It takes three arguments:

- A string that might contain unwanted characters
- A character that should be removed
- A character that should be added in its place

When you compile the Guestbook class, put it on your Web server in the same place where servlets are stored. On an Apache Web Server equipped with Tomcat, the folder is probably /WEB-INF/classes or /htdocs/WEB-INF/classes.

To test the guestbookpost.jsp server page, open the page that displays guest book entries using an ID parameter of cinema again, as in this example:

```
http://www.java21days.com/guestbook.jsp?id=cinema
```

When you add an entry to the guest book and click the Submit button, you should see a page resembling Figure 21.8.

FIGURE 21.8

Adding an entry to a guest book.
Go ahead and add a few guest book entries to see how they are displayed in the guest book.

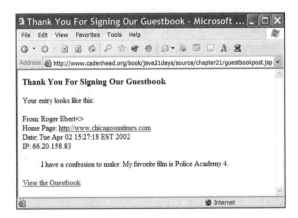

Summary

The main purpose of the classes in the javax.servlet and javax.servlet.http packages is to exchange information with a Web server. Java servlets are an alternative to the Common Gateway Interface, which is the most popular way that programming languages are used to retrieve and present data on the Web. Because servlets can use all features of the Java language (with the exception of a graphical user interface), you can use them to create sophisticated Web applications.

21

Servlets are being used to run e-commerce storefronts, take orders from users, connect to databases of products, and collect billing information when a purchase is made. They're also used to run discussion boards, content-management systems, and many other types of dynamically generated Web sites.

JavaServer Pages are an effective way to separate static content on Web pages from the dynamic content generated by servlets for those pages. This technique makes it easier to modify the text and presentation of a Web page without requiring changes to the servlet and other classes the page uses.

This brings you to the main event: the conclusion of your three-week trip through the Java language. Now that you've had a chance to work with the syntax and the core classes that make up Java, you're ready to tackle the really hard stuff: your own programs.

This book has an official Web site at `http://www.java21days.com`. It features answers to frequently asked questions, all the book's source code, error corrections, and supplementary material.

Congratulations! Now that you have learned Java, you've acquired some of the potential I talked about 21 days ago. As you spend more days on your own programs, learning new language features, developing your own classes and extending existing ones, you will learn another reason why the name of the language is an inspired choice.

Java, like its caffeinated counterpart, is habit-forming.

Q&A

Q Is there a way to make a Java applet communicate with a servlet?

A If you want the applet to continue running after it contacts the servlet, the servlet must be on the same machine as the Web page that contains the applet. For security reasons, applets cannot make a network connection to any machine other than the one that hosts the applet.

If you want an applet to load a servlet in the Web browser, you can call the applet's `getAppletContext()` method to get an `AppletContext` object, and then call that object's `showDocument(URL)` method with the servlet's URL as the argument.

Q **Why do servlets and JavaServer Pages require the `getRealPath()` method to determine where a file is located on the Web server? Can't you store the file in the same folder as a servlet and use the filename without referring to a path?**

A Tomcat doesn't support relative filenames inside servlets or JavaServer Pages. You must know the exact location of a file on the Web server in order to read or write data in the file. Because this information isn't always available to you in a live Web-hosting environment, the `ServletContext` interface includes the `getRealPath()` method. This method asks the Web server for the full pathname of a file. One of the biggest advantages of using Tomcat rather than Common Gateway Interface scripts is that you can communicate directly with the server.

In the `counter.jsp` example earlier today, the `counter.dat` file was created in the same folder where `counter.jsp` is stored. Tomcat doesn't store files in the same folder as servlets.

Quiz

Review today's material by taking this quiz.

Questions

1. If a servlet is run at the same time by five Web users, how many times is the servlet's `init()` method called?

    (a.) 5

    (b.) 1

    (c.) 0–1

2. What technology is *not* included as part of Tomcat?

    (a.) Java servlets

    (b.) JavaServer Pages

    (c.) Java API for XML Processing

3. When data are submitted from a form on a Web page and they show up in the browser's address bar as part of an URL, what kind of request is being used?

    (a.) A `GET` request

    (b.) A `POST` request

    (c.) A `HEAD` request

21

4. If you see a `request` variable on a JavaServer Page, what class in `javax.servlets.http` is it referring to?

   (a.) `HttpServletResponse`

   (b.) `HttpServletRequest`

   (c.) `ServletContext`

5. Which tools do you need on your computer to create a JavaServer Page?

   (a.) A Java interpreter and compiler

   (b.) A Java interpreter, compiler, and appletviewer

   (c.) None of the above

6. Which of the JavaServer Pages elements uses the `<%=` and `%>` tags?

   (a.) Declarations

   (b.) Expressions

   (c.) Statements

Answers

1. (c.) The `init()` method is called when the Web server first loads the servlet. This may have taken place before all five of these users requested the servlet, so it could call `init()` one time or not at all.

2. (c.) The Java API for XML Processing

3. (a.) A `GET` request encodes fields from a form into an URL and then submits that URL to a Web browser as a request.

4. (b.) `HttpServletRequest`

5. (c.) All you need is a text editor. When you publish the page, Tomcat will compile it into a servlet and then run the program.

6. (b.) The expression inside the tags will be evaluated and its value will be displayed on the page at the expression's location.

Certification Practice

The following question is the kind of thing you could expect to be asked on a Java programming certification test. Answer it without looking at today's material or using the Java compiler to test the code.

Given:

```
public class BadClass {
    String field[] = new String[10];
    int i = 0;
```

```
        public BadClass() {
            for ( ; i < 10; i++)
                field[i] = packField(i);
        }

        private String packField(int i) {
            StringBuffer spaces = new StringBuffer();
            for (int j = 0; j < i; j++) {
                spaces.append(' ');
            }
            return spaces;
        }
    }
```

Which line in this program will prevent it from compiling successfully?

(a.) `String field[] = new String[10];`

(b.) `for ( ; i < 10; i++)`

(c.) `StringBuffer spaces = new StringBuffer();`

(d.) `return spaces;`

The answer is available on this book's Web site at `http://www.java21days.com`. Visit the Day 21 page and click the Certification Practice link.

Exercises

To extend your knowledge of the subjects covered today, try the following exercises:

- Create a modified version of the `SetColor` servlet that also lets you choose a different color for the text on the page.

- Create a servlet that stores the data entered in a form in a file.

- Create a version of the `SetColor` servlet that uses JavaServer Pages.

- Write a JavaServer Page that displays one greeting for Internet Explorer users and another greeting for everyone else.

Where applicable, exercise solutions are offered on this book's Web site at `http://www.java21days.com`.

21

Appendices

A

B

C

D

E

F

APPENDIX A

Choosing Java

The 21 days of this book cover a cross section of Java's most popular capabilities, including multithreaded programming, Internet networking, file input and output, graphical user interface design, event handling, XML processing, JavaBeans component programming, and database connectivity.

The programs you write with Java can run on a diverse number of computing environments, such as desktop systems, Web browsers, Internet servers, hand-held computers, home appliances, and smartcards.

In this appendix, you'll learn more about why more than two million other programmers have used the language. If you're unfamiliar with the origins of Java, or if you're still unsure about whether it will be suitable for the kind of software development you undertake, this primer addresses the following questions:

- Where Java is today and how it got there
- Why Java is worth learning
- Why Java is being chosen for software projects
- What you need to start writing Java programs

Java's Past, Present, and Future

Based on the enormous amount of press Java has received over the past several years and the huge number of books about Java, you might have an inflated impression of what Java is capable of.

Java is a programming language that's well suited to designing software that works in conjunction with the Internet. It's also an object-oriented programming language, making use of a methodology that is becoming increasingly useful in the world of software design. Additionally, it's a cross-platform language, which means its programs are designed to run without modification on Microsoft Windows, Apple Macintosh, Linux, Solaris, and other systems. Java extends beyond desktops to run on devices such as televisions, smart cards, and cellular phones.

Java is closer to programming languages such as C, C++, Python, Visual Basic, and Delphi than it is to a page-description language such as HTML, a Web scripting language such as JavaScript, or a data description language such as XML.

Interactive Web Programming

Java first became popular because of its capability to run on World Wide Web pages. Using a plug-in, Netscape Navigator, Microsoft Internet Explorer, and other browsers can download a Java program included on a Web page and run it locally on the Web user's system.

These programs, which are called *applets*, appear on a Web page in a similar fashion to images. Unlike images, applets can be interactive—taking user input, responding to it, and presenting ever-changing content.

Applets can be used to create animation, charts, graphs, games, navigational menus, multimedia presentations, and other interactive effects.

Figure A.1 shows an applet running in the Internet Explorer 6.0 Web browser. This applet, Every Icon, is an interactive work of art implemented as a Java program by John F. Simon, Jr., an artist and programmer who has taught at the School of Visual Arts in Manhattan. It has been shown at the 2000 Whitney Biennial art exhibition and purchased by the Guggenheim Museum and the San Francisco Museum of Modern Art.

FIGURE A.1

A Java applet running on a Web page displayed in Internet Explorer 6.0.

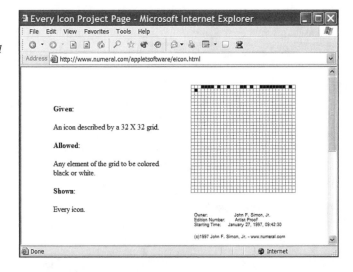

A

> **Note**
>
> The Every Icon applet is designed to display every possible icon that can be drawn using black or white squares in a simple 32 × 32 grid. Although the applet displays icons quickly, it takes more than 16 months on a Pentium-equipped computer to display all 4.29 billion variations possible on the top line of the grid alone. Displaying all variations on the top two lines would take around 16 billion years. Displaying all icons would take more years than there are atoms in the universe. You can find Every Icon and Simon's other art projects by visiting `http://www.numeral.com`.

Applets are downloaded over the World Wide Web just like HTML-formatted pages, graphics, and any other element of a Web site. On a Web browser that is equipped to handle Java, the applet will begin running when it finishes downloading.

Applets are written with the Java language, compiled into a form that can be run as a program, and placed on a Web server.

Until recently, most applets were written using Java 1.0 or Java 1.1, the first two versions of the language, because the leading browser developers did not add built-in support for subsequent versions of Java.

When it released Windows XP, Microsoft stopped offering Java support as a built-in feature of Internet Explorer. This change should increase the use of the Java Plug-in, a free browser enhancement offered by Sun Microsystems that runs Java applets. If a user visits a page containing a Java 2 applet with a browser that cannot run Java, a dialog box appears, asking whether the Java Plug-in should be downloaded and installed.

 Note   You can learn more about applets, browsers, and the Java Plug-in during Day 14, "Writing Java Applets."

Like Visual C++, Visual Basic, and Delphi, Java is a robust language that can be used to develop a wide range of software, supporting graphical user interfaces, networking, database connectivity, and other sophisticated functionality.

Java programs that don't run within a Web browser are called *applications*.

Java Grew from a Little Oak

The Java language was developed at Sun Microsystems in December 1990 as part of a project code-named Green, a small research effort into consumer electronics. Researchers were working on a programming language for smart appliances of the future to talk to each other, in the tradition of *The Jetsons* TV series—step one in realizing a society in which giant glass bubbles drop down over your body and dress you every morning.

To put its research into action, Green developed a prototype device called the Star 7, a handheld gadget resembling the later Palm Pilot, that could communicate with others of its own kind.

The original idea was to develop the Star 7 operating system in C++, the hugely popular object-oriented programming language created by Bjarne Stroustrup. However, Green project member James Gosling became fed up with how C++ was performing on the task, so he barricaded himself in his office and wrote a new language to handle the Star 7 better.

The language was named Oak in honor of a tree Gosling could see out his office window. It was later renamed Java after Sun's lawyers found out about another product called Oak and didn't want Sun to go out on a limb.

Because Java was designed for embedded electronic devices instead of state-of-the-art PCs, it had to be small, efficient, and easily portable to a wide range of hardware devices. It also had to be reliable. People have learned to live with occasional system crashes and lockups in a 30MB software application. However, there aren't many people willing to debug an elevator while its programmers work out the kinks.

A

Java wasn't catching on as an appliance development tool, but just as things were looking grim for the Green project, the World Wide Web started to take off. Many of the things that made Java good for the Star 7 turned out to be good for the Web:

- Java was small—programs loaded quickly on a Web page.
- Java was secure—safeguards prevented programs from causing damage, whether accidental or intentional.
- Java was portable—owners of Windows, Macintosh, Linux, and other operating systems could run the same program in their Web browsers without modification.

In order to demonstrate Java's potential, in 1994 project members created HotJava, a Web browser that could run Java applets. The browser demonstrated two things about Java: what it offered the World Wide Web, and what kind of program Java could create. Green programmers had used their new language to create the browser, rather than implementing it in C++.

Netscape became the first company to license the Java language in August 1995, incorporating a Java interpreter in its industry-leading Navigator Web browser. Microsoft followed by licensing Java for Internet Explorer, and millions of people could run interactive programs in their browsers for the first time.

Spurred by this huge audience of Web users, more than 300,000 people learned Java programming from 1995 to 1996. Sun added hundreds of employees to its Java effort, believing that the language was ideally suited for a wide variety of desktop, portable, and network computing platforms beyond the Web.

Versions of the Language

Sun has released five major versions of the Java language:

- Java 1.0, a small Web-centered version uniformly available in all popular Web browsers
- Java 1.1, a 1997 release with improvements to the user interface, event handling, and a component technology called JavaBeans
- Java 2 version 1.2, a significantly expanded version released in 1998 with retooled graphical user interface features, database connectivity, and many other improvements
- Java 2 version 1.3, a 2000 release that added new core features such as improved multimedia, more accessibility, and faster compilation
- Java 2 version 1.4, an early 2002 release that adds enhanced Java support in Web browsers, XML processing, and three long-requested features: assertions, regular expressions, and user preference support

The features described in the preceding list are part of the Java 2 Standard Edition, the most popular edition of the language, which has a target audience of software developers writing for personal computers in a variety of corporate, academic, and governmental environments.

There are also two other editions:

- The Java 2 Platform Enterprise Edition, an expanded edition for the developers of enterprise systems—large-scale, computing-intensive projects with increased requirements for scalability, portability, and the need to work in conjunction with older hardware and software
- The Java 2 Platform Micro Edition, a smaller edition designed to run on personal digital assistants, smart cards, and other consumer devices—returning Java to its roots

This book covers the Standard Edition, which is the best mix of features for the largest audience of Java developers and the people they write software for.

It gives special emphasis to the Java 2 Software Development Kit (SDK), a free development tool that is available from Sun's Java Web site at `http://java.sun.com`.

The kit has always been available at no cost since the introduction of the language, and this availability is one of the factors behind the language's rapid growth. It is the first development tool that supports new versions of Java, sometimes six months to a year before other Java development software. According to Sun, the kit has been downloaded more than three million times since 1995.

In addition to the SDK, there are more than two dozen commercial development tools available for Java programmers. The following are some of the most popular:

- WebGain's (formerly Symantec's) Visual Café
- Borland's JBuilder
- IBM's Visual Age for Java
- Sun ONE Studio
- Visual SlickEdit

If you are going to use something other than SDK 1.4 to create Java programs as you read this book, you need to make sure that your development tool is up-to-date in its support for Java 2.

Java's Outlook

Anyone who can accurately predict the future of Java should be going after venture capital instead of writing a book. The technology firm Kleiner, Perkins, Caufield and Byers

A

(KPCB) created a fund to invest $100 million in start-up companies on the basis of their future plans involving Java, and has already given millions to Active Software, Marimba, Resonate, Viant, and a dozen other companies.

With the caveat that neither author of this book is pursuing venture capital, we predict a bright future for Java over the coming decade.

The new version of Java 2 incorporates the following key improvements:

- Java Web Start—A way to launch Java programs from a Web browser, making installation and deployment of Java software easier
- Assertions—A new keyword, `assert`, and new exceptions that can be used to make programs more reliable
- Regular expressions—A new package that offers sophisticated pattern matching, a feature in Perl and other languages that's extremely useful when processing text and working with XML
- Preferences—A way to store user preferences and other customization information in a common database comparable to the Windows Registry

You work with several of these new features in this book.

Why Choose Java

Java applets were a breakthrough in interactive content on the Web, and many top sites used them to deliver news, present information, and attract visitors. Today, ESPN.com uses Java applets for live events in its fantasy sports leagues, which have more than 100,000 subscribers.

Although there are still thousands of applets on the Web today, the most exciting Java-related developments are occurring elsewhere. Sun has extended the language far beyond its roots as an interesting Web technology.

A great example of this is Jini, Sun's Java-based technology for connecting computers and other devices together. The goal of Jini is effortless networking—connect two Jini devices together and they instantly form a network without the need to run any special installation or configuration programs.

Jini, which ironically returns Java to the original goals of the Green project, is just one of the new areas where the language is being employed.

Another is support for Java programs that run on Internet servers, either as Web applications called *servlets* or as JavaServer Pages—Web documents that combine Java code with HTML markup tags and content. Java's server technology is being used on thousands of Web sites to generate dynamic content in response to user input. One of the most popular implementations is the travel site Trip.Com.

> Trip.Com also features one of the most amazing Java applets I have seen in six years of writing about the language: FlightTracker. The applet can track the progress of any U.S. flight, displaying a map that shows the movement of the plane and reporting its altitude, speed, and heading.
>
> To try the applet, visit the Web site http://www.trip.com.

Regardless of where you find it running, Java's strengths remain its object-oriented nature, ease of learning, and platform neutrality.

Java Is Object-Oriented

If you're not yet familiar with object-oriented programming, you get plenty of chances to become so during the first week of this book.

Object-oriented programming (OOP) is a way of conceptualizing a computer program as a set of separate objects that interact with each other. An object contains both information and the means of accessing and changing that information—an efficient way to create computer programs that can be improved easily and used later for other tasks.

Java inherits many of its object-oriented concepts from C++ and borrows concepts from other object-oriented languages as well.

Java Is Easy to Learn

In part, Java was first created at the Green project in rejection of the complexity of C++. C++ is a language with numerous features that are powerful but easy to employ incorrectly.

Java was intended to be easier to write, compile, debug, and learn than other object-oriented languages. It was modeled strongly after C++ and takes much of its syntax from that language.

Note
> The similarity to C++ is so strong that many Java books make frequent comparisons between the features of the two languages. Today, it's more common for a Java programmer to learn the language before or in place of C++. For this reason, there aren't many references to C++ in this book.

Despite Java's similarities to C++, the most complex and error-prone aspects of that language have been excluded from Java. You won't find pointers or pointer arithmetic because those features are easy to use incorrectly in a program and even harder to fix. Strings and arrays are objects in Java, as is everything else except a few simple data structures such as integers, floating-point numbers, and characters.

Additionally, memory management is handled automatically by Java rather than requiring the programmer to allocate and deallocate memory, and multiple inheritance is not supported.

Experienced C++ programmers will undoubtedly miss these features as they start to use Java, but everyone else will learn Java more quickly because of their absence.

Although Java is easier to learn than many other programming languages, a person with no programming experience at all will find Java challenging. It is more complicated than working in something such as HTML or JavaScript, but definitely something a beginner can accomplish.

Note
> Sams Publishing publishes another Java tutorial aimed directly at beginning programmers: *Sams Teach Yourself Java 2 in 24 Hours, Third Edition,* by Rogers Cadenhead, one of the coauthors of this book.

Java Is Platform Neutral

Because it was created to run on a wide variety of devices and computing platforms, Java was designed to be platform neutral, working the same no matter where it runs.

This was a huge departure in 1995, when Visual C++, Visual Basic, and other leading programming environments were designed almost exclusively to support Microsoft Windows 95 or Windows NT.

The original goal for Java programs to run without modification on all systems has not been realized. Java developers routinely test their programs on each environment they expect them to be run on, and sometimes they are forced into cumbersome workarounds as a result. Even different versions of the same Web browser can require this kind of testing. Java game programmer Karl Hörnell calls it a "hopeless situation."

However, Java's platform-neutral design still makes it much easier to employ Java programs in a diverse range of different computing situations.

As with all high-level programming languages, Java programs are originally written as *source code*, a set of programming statements entered into a text editor and saved as a file.

When you compile a program written in most programming languages, the compiler translates your source file into *machine code*—instructions that are specific to the processor your computer is running. If you compile your code on a Windows system, the resulting program will run on other Windows systems but not on Macs, Palm Pilots, and other machines. If you want to use the same program on another platform, you must transfer your source code to the new platform and recompile it to produce machine code specific to that system. In many cases, changes to the source will be required before it will compile on the new machine, because of differences in its processors or operating system functionality and other factors.

Java programs, on the other hand, are compiled into machine code for a *virtual machine*—a program that acts as a sort of computer within a computer. This machine code is called *bytecode*, and the virtual machine takes this code as input and carries out each instruction.

The virtual machine is commonly known as the *Java interpreter*, and every environment that supports Java must have an interpreter tailored to its own operating system and processor.

Java is also platform neutral at the source level. Java programs are saved as text files before they are compiled, and these files can be created on any platform that supports Java. For example, you could write a Java program on a Windows XP machine, upload it to a Linux machine over the Internet, and then compile it.

Java interpreters can be found in several places. For applets, the interpreter is either built into a Java-enabled browser, such as older versions of Internet Explorer, or installed separately as a browser plug-in.

If you're used to the way other languages create platform-specific code, you might think the Java interpreter adds an unnecessary layer between your source file and the compiled machine code.

The interpreter does cause some significant performance issues—as a rule, Java bytecode executes more slowly than platform-specific machine code produced by a compiled language such as C or C++.

Sun, IBM, WebGain, and other Java developers are addressing this with technology such as HotSpot, a faster virtual machine included with Java 2, and compilers that turn byte-code into platform-specific machine code. Every new generation of processors also increases Java's sometimes laggard performance.

For some Java programs, speed might not be as much of an issue as portability and ease of development. The widespread deployment of Java in large business and government projects shows that the loss in speed is less of an issue than it was for early versions of the language.

Summary

Java is a different language today than it was in 1995.

This has a good side—a proven market for Java programmers exists at present, and the skills are in strong demand. Six years ago you couldn't find "Java" in a classified ad out-side of Silicon Valley, and even there the market consisted of Sun Microsystems and only a few others.

This also has a bad side—Java is at least 13 times as large today as it was upon its first release, so there's much more to learn.

APPENDIX B

Using the Java 2 Software Development Kit

When the Java programming language was introduced to the public in 1995, Sun Microsystems also made available a free tool to develop Java programs: the Java 2 Software Development Kit.

The Software Development Kit is a set of command-line programs that are used to create, compile, and run Java programs. Every new release of Java is accompanied by a new release of the development kit: The current version is Java 2 SDK version 1.4.

Although more sophisticated Java programming tools such as Borland JBuilder, WebGain Visual Café, and IBM VisualAge for Java are now available, many programmers continue to use the Software Development Kit. I've been using it as my primary Java programming tool for years.

This appendix covers how to download and install the Software Development Kit, set it up on your computer, and use it to create, compile, and run a simple Java program.

It also describes how to correct the most common cause of problems for a beginning Java programmer—a misconfigured Software Development Kit.

Choosing a Java Development Tool

If you're using a Microsoft Windows or Apple MacOS system, you probably have a Java interpreter installed that can run Java programs. For several years, an interpreter was included with the Microsoft Internet Explorer and Netscape Navigator Web browsers.

To develop Java programs, you need more than an interpreter. You also need a compiler and other tools that are used to create, run, and test programs.

The Software Development Kit includes a compiler, interpreter, debugger, file archiving program, and several other programs.

The kit is simpler than other development tools. It does not offer a graphical user interface, text editor, or other features that many programmers rely on.

To use the kit, you type commands at a text prompt. MS-DOS, Linux, and UNIX users will be familiar with this prompt, which is also called a command line.

Here's an example of a command you might type while using the Software Development Kit:

```
javac RetrieveMail.java
```

This command tells the `javac` program (the Java compiler included with Java 2 SDK 1.4) to read a source code file called `RetrieveMail.java` and to create one or more class files. These files contain compiled bytecode that can be executed by a Java interpreter. When `RetrieveMail.java` is compiled, one of the files will be named `RetrieveMail.class`. If the class file was set up to function as an application, a Java interpreter can run it.

People who are comfortable with command-line environments will be at home using the Software Development Kit. Everyone else must become accustomed to the lack of a graphical point-and-click environment as they develop programs.

If you have another Java development tool and you're certain it is compatible with version 1.4 of the Java language, you don't need to use the Software Development Kit. Many development tools can be used to create the tutorial programs in this book.

 Caution   If you have any doubts regarding compatibility, or this book is your first experience with the Java language, you should probably use SDK 1.4 or a tool described in Appendix D, "Using Sun ONE Studio."

Installing the Software Development Kit

You can download version 1.4 of the Java 2 Software Development Kit from Sun's Java Web site at `http://java.sun.com`.

The Web site's Downloads section offers links to several versions of the Java Software Development Kit, and it also offers Sun ONE Studio and other products related to the language. The product you should download is called the Java 2 Software Development Kit, Standard Edition, version 1.4.

SDK 1.4 is available for the following platforms:

- Windows 95, 98, Me, NT (with Service Pack 4), 2000, and XP
- Solaris SPARC and Intel
- Linux

The kit requires a computer with a Pentium processor that is 166 MHz or faster, 32MB of memory, and 70MB of free disk space. Sun recommends at least 48MB of memory if you're going to work with Java 2 applets (which you will do on Day 14, "Writing Java Applets").

> **Tip**
>
> SDK 1.4 for the Macintosh is available directly from Apple. To find out more about Apple's kit and download the tool, visit the Web site `http://devworld.apple.com/java/`. SDK 1.3 and other Java development tools were included as part of Mac OS X Developers Tools.
>
> If you're using another platform, you can check to see whether it has a tool that supports Java 1.4 by visiting Sun's site at `http://java.sun.com/cgi-bin/java-ports.cgi/`.

When you're looking for this product, you might find that the Software Development Kit's version number has a third number after 1.4, such as "SDK 1.4.1." To fix bugs and address security problems, Sun periodically issues new releases of the kit and numbers them with an extra period and digit after the main version number. Choose the most advanced version of SDK 1.4 that's offered, whether it's numbered 1.4.0, 1.4.1, 1.4.2, or higher.

> **Caution**
>
> Take care not to download two similarly named products from Sun by mistake: the Java 2 Runtime Environment, Standard Edition, version 1.4 or the Java 2 Software Development Kit, Standard Edition, Source Release.

To go directly to the kit's download page, the current address is `http://java.sun.com/j2se/1.4/`.

To set up the kit, you must download and run an installation program (or install it from a CD). On Sun's Web site, after you choose the version of the kit that's designed for your operating system, you can download it as a single file that's around 35–40MB in size.

After you have downloaded the file, you will be ready to set up the development kit.

Windows Installation

Before installing SDK 1.4, you should make sure that no other Java development tools are installed on your system (assuming, of course, that you don't need any other tool at the moment). Having more than one Java programming tool installed on your computer can often cause configuration problems with the Software Development Kit.

To set up the program on a Windows system, double-click the installation file or click Start, Run from the Windows taskbar to find and run the file.

The InstallShield Wizard will guide you through the process of installing the software. If you accept Sun's terms and conditions for using the kit, you'll be asked where to install the program, as shown in Figure B.1.

FIGURE B.1

Choose a destination folder for SDK 1.4.

The wizard will suggest a folder where the kit should be installed. In Figure B.1, the wizard is suggesting the folder C:\j2sdk1.4.0-rc. When you install the kit, the suggested name might be different.

Tip

Before continuing, write down the name of the folder you have chosen. You'll need it later to configure the kit and fix any configuration problems that may occur.

Click the Next button to use the suggested folder. If you want to pick a different folder, click Browse and use the Windows File Open dialog box to select a location.

Next, you will be asked what parts of the Software Development Kit to install. This dialog box is shown in Figure B.2.

FIGURE B.2

Selecting components of SDK 1.4 to install.

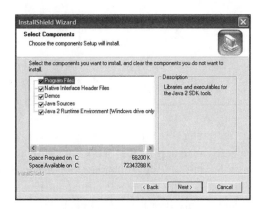

By default, the wizard will install all components of the SDK:

- Program Files—The executable programs needed to create, compile, and test your Java projects.
- Native Interface Header Files—Files used when combining Java programs with programs written in other languages. You can omit these for the tutorials in this book.
- Demos—Java 2 programs you can run and the source code files used to create them, which you can examine to learn more about the language.
- Java Sources—The source code for the thousands of classes that make up the Java 2 class library.
- Java 2 Runtime Environment—A Java interpreter you can distribute with the programs you create.

If you accept the default installation, you need around 72MB of free hard disk space. You can save space by omitting everything but the program files. However, the demo programs and Java 2 runtime environment are extremely useful, so if you have the room, it's a good idea to install them.

Neither the native header files nor Java source files are needed for any of the material in this book; both are primarily of interest to experienced Java programmers.

After you choose the components to install, click the Next button to continue. You'll be asked whether to set up the Java Plug-in to work with the Web browsers on your system (see Figure B.3).

FIGURE B.3

*Setting up the Java
Plug-in with Web
browsers.*

The Java Plug-in is an interpreter that runs Java programs incorporated into Web pages.
These programs, which are called applets, can work with different interpreters. Sun
offers the plug-in, which has the advantage of supporting the current version of the Java
language. A popular alternative is the Microsoft virtual machine, which works with
Internet Explorer but can run only Java 1.0 and 1.1 applets.

Choose the browsers that will use the Java Plug-in and click Next, then click Finish on
the last dialog box. The InstallShield Wizard will install SDK 1.4 on your system.

Configuring the Software Development Kit

After the InstallShield Wizard installs SDK 1.4, you must edit your computer's environment variables to include references to the kit.

Experienced MS-DOS users can finish setting up the SDK by adjusting two variables
and then rebooting the computer:

- Edit the computer's PATH variable and add a reference to the Software Development
  Kit's bin folder (which is C:\j2sdk1.4.0-rc\bin if you installed the kit into the
  C:\j2sdk1.4.0-rc folder).

- Edit or create a CLASSPATH variable so it contains a reference to the current folder—
  a period character and semicolon (".;" without the quotation marks)—followed by a
  reference to the tools.jar file in the kit's lib folder (which is C:\j2sdk1.4.0-rc\
  lib\tools.jar if the kit was installed into C:\j2sdk1.4.0-rc).

For inexperienced MS-DOS users, the following section covers in detail how to set the
PATH and CLASSPATH variables on a Windows system.

Users of other operating systems should follow the instructions provided by Sun on its
Software Development Kit download page.

Using a Command-Line Interface

The Java Software Development Kit requires the use of a command line to compile Java programs, run them, and handle other tasks.

A command line is a way to operate a computer by typing commands at your keyboard, rather than by using a mouse. Very few programs designed for Windows users require the command line today.

B

Note

To get to a command line in Windows:

- On Windows 95, 98, or Me, click the Start button, choose Programs, then click MS-DOS Prompt (as shown in Figure B.4).

- On Windows NT or 2000, click the Start button, choose Programs, choose Accessories, then click Command Prompt.

- On Windows XP, click the Start button, choose All Programs, choose Accessories, then click Command Prompt.

FIGURE B.4

Finding a command line from the Windows 95, 98, or Me taskbar.

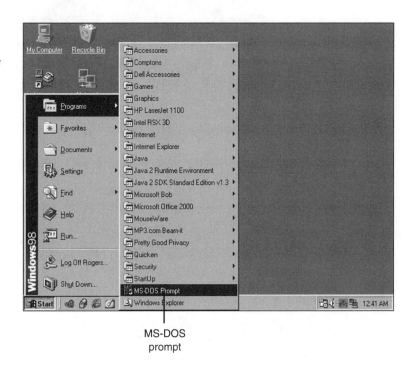

MS-DOS
prompt

When you open a command line in Windows, a new window in which you can type commands opens.

The command line in Windows uses commands borrowed from MS-DOS, the Microsoft operating system that preceded Windows. MS-DOS supports the same functions as Windows—copying, moving, and deleting files and folders; running programs; scanning and repairing a hard drive; formatting a floppy disk; and so on.

A command-line window is shown in Figure B.5.

Figure B.5

Using a newly opened command-line window.

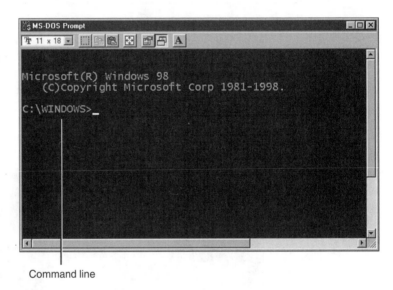

Command line

In the window, a cursor will blink on the command line whenever you can type a new command. In Figure B.5, C:\WINDOWS> is the command line.

Because MS-DOS can be used to delete files and even format your hard drive, you should learn something about the operating system before experimenting with its commands. If you'd like to learn a lot about MS-DOS, a good book is *Special Edition Using MS-DOS 6.22, Third Edition*, published by Que.

However, you need to know only a few things about MS-DOS to use the Software Development Kit: how to create a folder, how to open a folder, and how to run a program.

Opening Folders in MS-DOS

When you are using MS-DOS on a Windows system, you will have access to all of the folders you normally use in Windows. For example, if you have a Windows folder on your C: hard drive, the same folder is accessible as C:\Windows from a command line.

To open a folder in MS-DOS, type the command CD followed by the name of the folder and press Enter. Here's an example:

```
CD C:\TEMP
```

When you enter this command, the TEMP folder on your system's C: drive will be opened, if it exists. After you open a folder, your command line will be updated with the name of that folder, as shown in Figure B.6.

B

FIGURE B.6

Opening a folder in a command-line window.

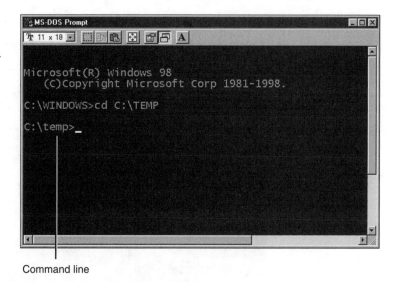

Command line

You also can use the CD command in other ways:

- Type CD \ to open the root folder on the current hard drive.

- Type CD *foldername* to open a subfolder matching the name you've used in place of *foldername*, if that subfolder exists.

- Type CD .. to open the folder that contains the current folder. For example, if you are in C:\Windows\Fonts and you use the CD .. command, C:\Windows will be opened.

One of the book's suggestions is to create a folder called J21work where you can create the tutorial programs described in the book. If you have already done this, you can switch to that folder by using the following commands:

1. CD \

2. CD J21work

If you haven't created that folder yet, you can accomplish the task within MS-DOS.

Creating Folders in MS-DOS

To create a folder from a command line, type the command MD followed by the name of
the folder and press Enter, as in the following example:

    MD C:\STUFF

The STUFF folder will be created in the root folder of the system's C: drive. To open a
newly created folder, use the CD command followed by that folder's name, as shown in
Figure B.7.

FIGURE B.7

*Creating a new folder
in a command-line
window.*

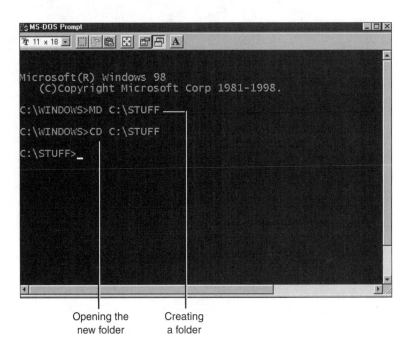

Opening the   Creating
new folder   a folder

If you haven't already created a J21work folder, you can do it from a command line:

- Change to the root folder (using the CD \ command).
- Type the command MD J21work and press Enter.

After J21work has been created, you can go to it at any time from a command line by
using this command:

    CD \J21work

The last thing you need to learn about MS-DOS to use the Software Development Kit is
how to run programs.

Running Programs in MS-DOS

The simplest way to run a program at the command line is to type its name and press Enter. For example, type DIR and press Enter to see a list of files and subfolders in the current folder.

You also can run a program by typing its name followed by a space and some options that control how the program runs. These options are called *arguments*.

To see an example of this, change to the root folder (using CD \) and type DIR J21work. You'll see a list of files and subfolders contained in the J21work folder, if it contains any.

After you have installed the Software Development Kit, you should run the Java interpreter to see that it works. Type the following command at a command line:

```
java -version
```

In the preceding example, java is the name of the Java interpreter program and -version is an argument that tells the interpreter to display its version number.

You can see an example of this in Figure B.8, but your version number might be different depending on which version of the SDK you have installed.

FIGURE B.8

Running the Java interpreter in a command line window.

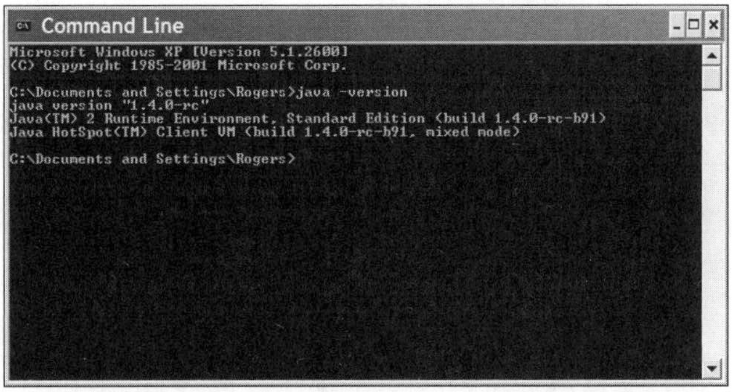

If java -version works and you see a version number, it should begin with 1.4 because you are using SDK 1.4. Sun sometimes tacks on a third number, but as long as it begins with 1.4 you are using the correct version of the Software Development Kit.

If you see an incorrect version number or a Bad command or file name error after running java -version, you need to make some changes to how the Software Development Kit is configured on your system.

Correcting Configuration Errors

When you are writing Java programs for the first time, the most likely source of problems is not typos, syntax errors, or other programming mistakes. Most errors result from a misconfigured Software Development Kit.

If you type java -version at a command line and your system can't find the folder that contains java.exe, you will see one of the following error messages or something similar (depending on your operating system):

```
Bad command or file name

'java' is not recognized as an internal or external command, operable
        program, or batch file
```

To correct this, you must configure your system's PATH variable.

Setting the PATH on Windows 95, 98, or Me

On a Windows 95, 98, or Me system, you configure the PATH variable by editing the AUTOEXEC.BAT file in the root folder of the main hard drive. This file is used by MS-DOS to set environment variables and configure how some command-line programs function.

AUTOEXEC.BAT is a text file you can edit with Windows Notepad. Start Notepad by clicking Start, Programs, Accessories, Notepad from the Windows taskbar.

The Notepad text editor will open. Choose File, Open from Notepad's menu bar, go to the root folder on your main hard drive, then open the file AUTOEXEC.BAT.

When you open the file, you'll see a series of MS-DOS commands, each on its own line, as shown in Figure B.9.

FIGURE B.9

Editing the
AUTOEXEC.BAT *file*
with Notepad.

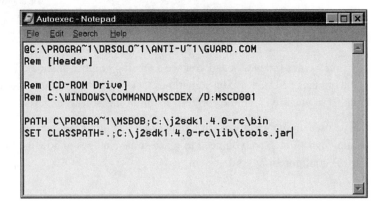

```
@C:\PROGRA~1\DRSOLO~1\ANTI-U~1\GUARD.COM
Rem [Header]

Rem [CD-ROM Drive]
Rem C:\WINDOWS\COMMAND\MSCDEX /D:MSCD001

PATH C\PROGRA~1\MSBOB;C:\j2sdk1.4.0-rc\bin
SET CLASSPATH=.;C:\j2sdk1.4.0-rc\lib\tools.jar
```

The only commands you need to look for are any that begin with PATH.

The PATH command is followed by a space and a series of folder names separated by semicolons. It sets up the PATH variable, a list of folders that contain command-line programs you use.

PATH is used to help MS-DOS find programs when you run them at a command line. In the preceding example, the PATH command in Figure B.9 includes two folders:

```
C:\PROGRA~1\MSBOB

C:\j2sdk1.4.0-rc\bin
```

You can see what PATH has been set to by typing the following command at a command line:

```
PATH
```

To set up the Software Development Kit correctly, the folder that contains the Java interpreter must be included in the PATH command in AUTOEXEC.BAT.

The interpreter has the filename java.exe. If you installed SDK 1.4 in the C:\j2sdk1.4.0-rc folder on your system, java.exe is in C:\jdk1.4.0-rc\bin.

If you can't remember where you installed the kit, you can look for java.exe: Choose Start, Find, Files or Folders. You might find several copies in different folders. To see which one is correct, open a command-line window and do the following for each copy you have found:

1. Use the CD command to open a folder that contains java.exe.

2. Run the command java -version in that folder.

When you know the correct folder, create a blank line at the bottom of the AUTOEXEC.BAT file and add the following:

```
PATH rightfoldername;%PATH%
```

For example, if c:\j2sdk1.4.0\bin is the correct folder, the following line should be added at the bottom of AUTOEXEC.BAT:

```
PATH c:\j2sdk1.4.0\bin;%PATH%
```

The %PATH% text keeps you from wiping out any other PATH commands in AUTOEXEC.BAT.

After making changes to AUTOEXEC.BAT, save the file and reboot your computer. When this is done, try the java -version command.

If it displays the correct version of the Software Development Kit, your system is probably configured correctly. You'll find out for sure when you try to create a sample program later in this appendix.

B

Setting the `Path` on Windows NT, 2000, or XP

On a Windows NT, 2000, or XP system, you configure the `Path` variable using the Environment Variables dialog box, one of the features of the system's Control Panel.

To open this dialog box

1. Right-click the My Computer icon on your desktop or Start menu and choose Properties. The System Properties dialog box opens.

2. Click the Advanced tab to bring it to the front.

3. Click the Environment Variables button. The Environment Variables dialog box opens (Figure B.10).

FIGURE B.10

Setting environment variables in Windows NT, 2000, or XP.

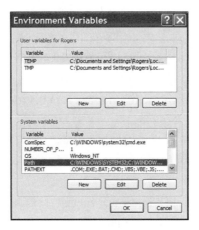

There are two kinds of environment variables you can edit: system variables, which apply to all users on your computer, and user variables, which apply only to you.

`Path` is a system variable that helps MS-DOS find programs when you run them at a command line. It contains a list of folders separated by semicolons.

To set up the Software Development Kit correctly, the folder that contains the Java interpreter must be included in the `Path`. The interpreter has the filename `java.exe`. If you installed SDK 1.4 in the `C:\j2sdk1.4.0-rc` folder on your system, `java.exe` is in `C:\jdk1.4.0-rc\bin`.

If you can't remember where you installed the kit, you can look for `java.exe`: Choose Start, Search. You might find several copies in different folders. To see which one is correct, open a command-line window and do the following for each copy you have found:

1. Use the `CD` command to open a folder that contains `java.exe`.

2. Run the command `java -version` in that folder.

When you know the correct folder, return to the Environment Variables dialog box, select Path in the System variables list, then click Edit. The Edit System Variables dialog box opens with Path in the Variable name field and a list of folders in the Variable value field (Figure B.11).

FIGURE B.11

Changing your system's Path *variable.*

To add a folder to the Path, click the Variable value field and move your cursor to the end without changing anything. At the end, add a semicolon followed by the name of the folder that contains the Java interpreter.

For example, if c:\j2sdk1.4.0\bin is the correct folder, the following text should be added to the end of the Path variable:

```
c:\j2sdk1.4.0\bin
```

After making the change, click OK twice: once to close the Edit System Variable dialog box and another time to close the Environment Variables dialog box.

Try it: Open a command-line window and type the command java -version.

If it displays the right version of the Software Development Kit, your system is probably configured correctly, though you won't know for sure until you try to use the kit later in this appendix.

Using a Text Editor

Unlike more sophisticated Java development tools, the Software Development Kit does not include a text editor to use when you create source files.

For an editor or word processor to work with the kit, it must be able to save text files with no formatting.

This feature has different names in different editors. Look for a format option, such as one of the following, when you save a document or set the properties for a document:

- Plain text
- ASCII text
- DOS text
- Text-only

If you're using Windows, there are several editors included with the operating system.

Windows Notepad is a no-frills text editor that works only with plain-text files. It can handle only one document at a time. Click Start, All Programs, Accessories, Notepad to run it on Windows XP or Start, Programs, Accessories, Notepad to run it on other Windows systems.

Windows WordPad is a step above Notepad. It can handle more than one document at a time and can handle both plain-text and Microsoft Word formats. It also remembers the last several documents it has worked on and makes them available from the File pull-down menu. It's also on the Accessories menu with Notepad.

Windows users can also use Microsoft Word, but you must save files as text rather than in Word's proprietary format. UNIX and Linux users can author programs with emacs, pico, and vi; Macintosh users have SimpleText for Java source file creation.

One disadvantage of using simple text editors such as Notepad or WordPad is that they do not display line numbers as you edit.

Seeing the line number helps in Java programming because many compilers indicate the line number at which an error occurred. Take a look at the following error generated by the SDK compiler:

```
Palindrome.java:2: Class Font not found in type declaration.
```

The number 2 after the name of the Java source file indicates the line that triggered the compiler error. With a text editor that supports numbering, you can go directly to that line and start looking for the error.

Usually there are better ways to debug a program with a commercial Java programming package, but kit users must search for compiler-generated errors using the line number indicated by the javac tool. This is one of the best reasons to move on to an advanced Java development program after learning the language with the Software Development Kit.

Tip

Another alternative is to use the kit with a programmer's text editor that offers line numbering and other features. One of the most popular for Java is jEdit, a free editor available for Windows, Linux, and other systems at the Web site http://www.jedit.org/.

Creating a Sample Program

Now that you have installed and set up the Software Development Kit, you're ready to create a sample Java program to make sure it works.

Java programs begin as source code—a series of statements created using a text editor and saved as a text file. You can use any program you like to create these files, as long as it can save the file as plain, unformatted text.

The Software Development Kit does not include a text editor, but most other Java development tools include a built-in editor for creating source code files.

Run your editor of choice and enter the Java program in Listing B.1. Make sure all the parentheses, braces, and quotation marks in the listing are entered correctly and capitalize everything in the program exactly as shown. If your editor requires a filename before you start entering anything, call it `HelloUser.java`.

LISTING B.1 Source Code of `HelloUser.java`

```
1: public class HelloUser {
2:     public static void main(String[] arguments) {
3:         String username = System.getProperty("user.name");
4:         System.out.println("Hello, " + username);
5:     }
6: }
```

The line numbers and colons along the left side of Listing 1.1 are not part of the program; they're included so I can refer to specific lines by number in each program. If you're ever unsure about the source code of a program in this book, you can compare it to a copy on the book's official World Wide Web site at the following address:

    http://www.java21days.com

After you finish typing the program, save the file somewhere on your hard drive with the name `HelloUser.java`. Java source files must be saved with the extension `.java`.

Tip

> If you have created a folder called J21work, save `HelloUser.java` and all other Java source files from this book in that folder. This makes it easier to find them while using a command-line window.

If you're using Windows, a text editor such as Notepad might add an extra .txt file extension to the filename of any Java source files you save. For example, HelloUser.java is saved as HelloUser.java.txt. As a workaround to avoid this problem, place quotation marks around the filename when saving a source file. Figure B.12 shows this technique being used to save a file called Ellsworth.java from Windows Notepad.

FIGURE B.12

Saving a source file from Windows Notepad.

A better solution is to permanently associate .java files with the text editor you'll be using. In Windows, open the folder that contains HelloUser.java and double-click the file. If you have never opened a file with the .java extension, you'll be asked what program to use when opening files of this type. Choose your preferred editor and select the option to make your choice permanent. From this point on, you can open a source file for editing by double-clicking the file.

The purpose of this project is to test the Software Development Kit; none of the Java programming concepts used in the five-line HelloUser program are described in this appendix.

You'll learn the basics of the language on Day 1, "Getting Started with Java." If you have figured out anything about Java simply by typing in the source code of Listing B.1, that's entirely your fault. I didn't teach you anything yet.

Compiling and Running the Program in Windows

Now you're ready to compile the source file with the Software Development Kit's Java compiler, a program called javac. The compiler reads a .java source file and creates one or more .class files that can be run by a Java interpreter.

Open a command-line window, then open the folder where you saved HelloUser.java.

If you saved the file in the J21work folder inside the root folder on your main hard drive, the following MS-DOS command will open the folder:

```
cd \J21work
```

When you are in the correct folder, you can compile HelloUser.java by entering the following at a command prompt:

```
javac HelloUser.java
```

Figure B.13 shows the MS-DOS commands used to switch to the \J21work folder and compile HelloUser.java.

FIGURE B.13

Compiling a Java program in a command-line window.

The Software Development Kit compiler does not display any message if the program compiles successfully. If there are problems, the compiler lets you know by displaying each error along with the line that triggered the error.

If the program compiled without any errors, a file called HelloUser.class is created in the same folder that contains HelloUser.java.

The class file contains the Java bytecode that will be executed by a Java interpreter. If you get any errors, go back to your original source file and make sure that you typed it exactly as it appears in Listing B.1.

After you have a class file, you can run that file using a Java interpreter. The SDK's interpreter is called java, and it also is run from the command line.

Run the HelloUser program by switching to the folder containing HelloUser.class and entering the following:

```
java HelloUser
```

You should see the word "Hello" followed by a comma and your user name.

B

Note

When running a Java class with the kit's Java interpreter, don't specify the .class file extension after the name of the class. If you do, you'll see an error like the following:

```
Exception in thread "main" java.lang.NoClassDefFoundError:
HelloUser/class
```

Figure B.14 shows the successful output of the HelloUser application along with the commands used to get to that point.

FIGURE B.14

Compiling and running a Java application.

If you can compile the program and run it successfully, your Software Development Kit is working and you are ready to start Day 1 of this book.

If you cannot get the program to compile successfully, even though you have typed it exactly as it appears in the book, there may be one last problem with how the Software Development Kit is configured on your system: the CLASSPATH environment variable might need to be configured.

Setting Up the **CLASSPATH** Variable

All of the Java programs that you write rely on two kinds of class files: the classes you create and the Java class library, a set of hundreds of classes that represent the functionality of the Java language.

The Software Development Kit needs to know where to find Java class files on your system. In many cases, the kit can figure this out on its own by looking in the folder where it was installed.

You also can set it up yourself by creating or modifying another environment variable: CLASSPATH.

Setting the CLASSPATH on Windows 95, 98, or Me

If you have compiled and run the HelloUser program successfully, the Software Development Kit has been configured successfully. You don't need to make any more changes to your system.

On the other hand, if you see a Class not found error or NoClassDefFound error whenever you try to run a program, you need to make sure your CLASSPATH variable is set up correctly.

To do this, run Windows Notepad, choose File, Open, go to the root folder on your system, and then open the file AUTOEXEC.BAT. A file containing several MS-DOS commands is opened in the editor, as shown in Figure B.15.

FIGURE B.15

Editing your system's environment variables.

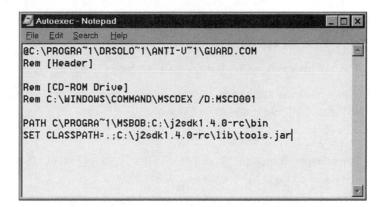

```
Autoexec - Notepad
File   Edit   Search   Help
@C:\PROGRA~1\DRSOLO~1\ANTI-U~1\GUARD.COM
Rem [Header]

Rem [CD-ROM Drive]
Rem C:\WINDOWS\COMMAND\MSCDEX /D:MSCD001

PATH C\PROGRA~1\MSBOB;C:\j2sdk1.4.0-rc\bin
SET CLASSPATH=.;C:\j2sdk1.4.0-rc\lib\tools.jar
```

Look for a line in the file that contains the SET CLASSPATH= command followed by a series of folder and filenames separated by semicolons.

CLASSPATH is used to help the Java compiler find the class files that it needs. The SET CLASSPATH= command in Figure B.15 included two things with a semicolon between them:

.

```
c:\j2sdk1.4.0-rc\lib\tools.jar
```

A CLASSPATH can contain folders or files. It also can contain a period character (". "), which is another way to refer to the current folder in MS-DOS.

You can see your system's CLASSPATH variable by typing the following command at a command line:

```
ECHO %CLASSPATH%
```

If your CLASSPATH includes folders or files that you know are no longer on your computer, you should remove the references to them on the SET CLASSPATH= line in AUTOEXEC.BAT. Make sure to remove any extra semicolons also.

To set up the Software Development Kit correctly, the file containing the Java class library must be included in the SET CLASSPATH= command. This file has the filename tools.jar. If you installed the kit in the C:\jdk1.4.0 folder on your system, tools.jar is probably in the folder C:\jdk1.4.0\lib.

If you can't remember where you installed the kit, you can look for tools.jar by clicking Start, Find, Files or Folders from the Windows taskbar. If you find several copies, you should be able to find the correct one using this method:

1. Use CD to open the folder that contains the Java interpreter (java.exe)
2. Enter the command CD ..
3. Enter the command CD lib

The lib folder normally contains the right copy of tools.jar.

When you know the correct location, create a blank line at the bottom of the AUTOEXEC.BAT file and add the following:

```
SET CLASSPATH=%CLASSPATH%;.;rightlocation
```

For example, if the tools.jar file is in the c:\j2sdk1.4.0\lib folder, the following line should be added at the bottom of AUTOEXEC.BAT:

```
SET CLASSPATH=%CLASSPATH%;.;c:\j2sdk1.4.0\lib\tools.jar
```

After making changes to AUTOEXEC.BAT, save the file and reboot your computer. After this is done, try to compile and run the HelloUser sample program again. You should be able to accomplish this once the CLASSPATH variable has been set up correctly.

Setting the Classpath on Windows NT, 2000, or XP

On a Windows NT, 2000, or XP system, you also configure the Classpath variable using the Environment Variables dialog.

To open it

1. Right-click the My Computer icon on your desktop or Start menu and choose Properties. The System Properties dialog box opens.
2. Click the Advanced tab to bring it to the front.
3. Click the Environment Variables button. The Environment Variables dialog box opens (Figure B.16).

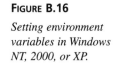

FIGURE B.16

Setting environment variables in Windows NT, 2000, or XP.

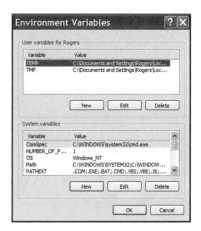

If your system has a Classpath variable, it will probably be one of the system variables. Your system may not have a Classpath variable; the Software Development Kit can normally find class files without the variable.

However, if your system has a Classpath, it must be set up with at least two things: a reference to the current folder (a period) and a reference to a file that contains the Java class library (tools.jar).

If you installed the kit in the C:\jdk1.4.0 folder, tools.jar is in the folder C:\jdk1.4.0\lib.

If you can't remember where you installed the kit, you can look for tools.jar by clicking Start, Search from the Windows taskbar. If you find several copies, you should be able to find the correct one using this method:

1. Use CD to open the folder that contains the Java interpreter (java.exe)

2. Enter the command CD ..

3. Enter the command CD lib

The lib folder normally contains the right copy of tools.jar.

When you know the correct folder, return to the Environment Variables dialog box shown in Figure B.16.

If your system does not have a Classpath variable, click the New button under the System variables list. The New System Variable dialog box opens.

If your system has a Classpath variable, choose it and click the Edit button. The Edit System Variable dialog box opens.

Both boxes contain the same thing: a Variable Name field and a Variable Value field.

Enter Classpath in the Variable Name field and the correct value for your Classpath in the Variable Value field.

For example, if you installed the Software Development Kit in c:\j2sdk1.4.0, your Classpath should contain the following:

```
.;C:\j2sdk1.4.0\lib\tools.jar
```

Figure B.17 shows how I set up the Classpath for my system, which has the Software Development Kit installed in C:\j2sdk1.4.0-rc.

FIGURE B.17

Setting up a Classpath *in Windows XP.*

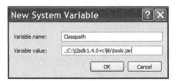

After setting up your Classpath, click OK twice: once to close the Edit or New System Variable dialog box and another time to close the Environment Variables dialog box.

Unlike Windows 95, 98, and Me users, you don't have to reboot the system before you can try it out. Open a command-line window and type the command java -version.

If it displays the right version of the Software Development Kit, your system might be configured correctly and require no more adjustments. Try creating the sample HelloUser program again; it should work once the CLASSPATH variable has been set up correctly.

Troubleshooting Your Kit Installation

This book has a Web site where you can find solutions to problems, corrections, answers to readers' questions, and other useful material.

There's an online version of this appendix on the site and a way to contact coauthor Rogers Cadenhead if you are still having problems with the Software Development Kit. The site is available at http://www.java21days.com/.

APPENDIX C

Programming with the Java 2 Software Development Kit

The Java 2 Software Development Kit (SDK) can be used throughout this book to create, compile, and run Java programs.

The tools that make up the kit contain numerous features that many programmers don't explore at all, and some of the tools themselves might be new to you.

This appendix covers features of the SDK that you can use to create more reliable, better-tested, and faster-running Java programs.

The following topics will be covered:

- Running Java applications with the interpreter
- Compiling programs with the compiler
- Running Java applets with the applet viewer

- Creating documentation with the documentation tool
- Finding bugs in your program and learning more about its performance with the debugger
- Setting system properties with the interpreter and applet viewer

An Overview of the SDK

Although there are several dozen development environments you can use to create Java programs, the most widely used is the Software Development Kit (SDK) from Sun Microsystems. The kit is the set of command-line tools that are used to develop software with the Java language.

There are two main reasons for the popularity of the kit:

- It's free. You can download a copy at no cost from Sun's official Java World Wide Web site at `http://java.sun.com`.
- It's first. Whenever Sun releases a new version of the language, the first tools that support the new version are in the SDK.

The SDK uses the command line—also called the MS-DOS prompt, command prompt, or console under Windows or the shell prompt under Unix. Commands are entered using the keyboard, as in the following example:

```
javac VideoBook.java
```

This command compiles a Java program called `VideoBook.java` using the SDK compiler. There are two elements to the command: the name of the SDK compiler, `javac`, followed by the name of the program to compile, `VideoBook.java`. A space character separates the two elements.

Each SDK command follows the same format: the name of the tool to use, followed by one or more elements indicating what the tool should do. These elements are called *arguments*.

The following illustrates the use of command-line arguments:

```
java VideoBook add VHS "Bad Influence"
```

This command tells the Java interpreter to run a class file called `VideoBook` with three command-line arguments: the strings `add`, `VHS`, and `Bad Influence`.

Note

You might think there are four command-line arguments because of the space between the words Bad and Influence. The quotation marks around "Bad Influence" cause it to be considered one command-line argument rather than two. This makes it possible to include a space character.

Some arguments used with the SDK modify how a tool will function. These arguments are preceded by a hyphen character and are called *options*.

The following command shows the use of an option:

```
java -version
```

This command tells the Java interpreter to display its version number rather than trying to run a class file. It's a good way to find out whether the SDK is correctly configured to run Java programs on your system. Here's an example of the output run on a system equipped with SDK 1.4.0:

```
java version "1.4.0"
Java(TM) 2 Runtime Environment, Standard Edition (build1.4.0)
Java HotSpot(TM) Client VM (build 1.4.0, mixed mode)
```

In some instances, you can combine options with other arguments. For example, if you compile a Java class that uses deprecated methods, you can see more information on these methods by compiling the class with a -deprecation option, as in the following:

```
javac -deprecation OldVideoBook.java
```

The java Interpreter

java, the Java interpreter, is used to run Java applications from the command line. It takes as an argument the name of a class file to run, as in the following example:

```
java BidMonitor
```

Although Java class files end with the .class extension, this extension should not be specified when using the interpreter.

The class loaded by the Java interpreter must contain a class method called main() that takes the following form:

```
public static void main(String[] arguments) {
    // Method here
}
```

Some simple Java programs might consist of only one class—the one containing the main() method. In other cases, the interpreter automatically loads any other classes that are needed.

The Java interpreter runs bytecode—the compiled instructions that are executed by a Java virtual machine. After a Java program is saved in bytecode as a .class file, it can be run by different interpreters without modification. If you have compiled a Java 2 program, it should be compatible with any interpreter that fully supports Java 2.

 Note

Interestingly enough, Java is not the only language that you can use to create Java bytecode. NetRexx, JPython, JRuby, JudoScript, and several dozen other languages will compile into .class files of executable bytecode through the use of compilers specific to those languages. Robert Tolksdorf maintains a comprehensive list of these languages, currently available from the Web page at http://grunge.cs.tu-berlin.de/~tolk/vmlanguages.html.

There are two different ways to specify the class file that should be run by the Java interpreter. If the class is not part of any package, you can run it by specifying the name of the class, as in the preceding java BidMonitor example. If the class is part of a package, you must specify the class by using its full package and class name.

For example, consider a SellItem class that is part of the com.prefect.auction package. To run this application, the following command would be used:

```
java com.prefect.auction.SellItem
```

Each element of the package name corresponds to its own subfolder. The Java interpreter will look for the SellItem.class file in several different places:

- The com\prefect\auction subfolder of the folder where the java command was entered (if the command was made from the C:\J21work folder, for example, the SellItem.class file could be run successfully if it was in the C:\J21work\com\ prefect\auction folder)
- The com\prefect\auction subfolder of any folder in your CLASSPATH setting

If you're creating your own packages, an easy way to manage them is to add a folder to your CLASSPATH that's the root folder for any packages you create, such as C:\javapackages or something similar. After creating subfolders that correspond to the name of a package, place the package's class files in the correct subfolder.

Java 2 version 1.4 includes support for assertions, a new feature to improve the reliability of programs. To run a program using the Java interpreter and make use of any assertions that it contains, use the command line -ea, as in the following example:

```
java -ea Outline
```

The Java interpreter will execute all `assert` statements in the application's class and all other class files that it uses, with the exception of classes from the Java class library.

To remove that exception and make use of all assertions, run a class with the -esa option.

If you don't specify one of the options that turns on the assertions feature, all `assert` statements will be ignored by the interpreter.

The `javac` Compiler

`javac`, the Java compiler, converts Java source code into one or more class files of byte-code that can be run by a Java interpreter.

Java source code is stored in a file with the `.java` file extension. This file can be created with any text editor or word processor that can save a document without any special formatting codes. The terminology varies depending on the text-editing software being used, but these files are often called plain text, ASCII text, DOS text, or something similar.

A Java source code file can contain more than one class, but only one of the classes can be declared to be public. A class can contain no public classes at all if desired, although this isn't possible with applets because of the rules of inheritance.

If a source code file contains a class that has been declared to be public, the name of the file must match the name of that class. For example, the source code for a public class called `BuyItem` must be stored in a file called `BuyItem.java`.

To compile a file, the `javac` tool is run with the name of the source code file as an argument, as in the following:

```
javac BidMonitor.java
```

You can compile more than one source file by including each separate filename as a command-line argument, such as this command:

```
javac BidMonitor.java SellItem.java
```

You also can use wildcard characters such as * and ?. Use the following command to compile all .java files in a folder:

```
javac *.java
```

When you compile one or more Java source code files, a separate .class file will be created for each Java class that compiles successfully.

If you are compiling a program that makes use of assertions, you must use the -source 1.4 option, as in this command:

```
javac -source 1.4 Outline.java
```

The 1.4 argument refers to Java 2 version 1.4, the first version of the language that supports the assert statement. If the -source option is not used and you try to compile a program that contains assertions, javac displays an error message and won't compile the file.

Another useful option when running the compiler is -deprecation, which causes the compiler to describe any deprecated methods that are being employed in a Java program. Normally, the compiler will issue a single warning if it finds any deprecated methods in a program. The -deprecation option causes the compiler to list each method that has been deprecated, as in the following command:

```
javac -deprecation SellItem.java
```

If you're more concerned with the speed of a Java program than the size of its class files, you can compile its source code with the -0 option. This creates class files that have been optimized for faster performance. Methods that are static, final, or private might be compiled *inline*, a technique that makes the class file larger but causes the methods to be executed more quickly.

If you are going to use a debugger to look for bugs in a Java class, compile the source with the -g option to put all debugging information in the class file, including references to line numbers, local variables, and source code. (To keep all of this out of a class, compile with the -g:none option.)

Normally, the Java compiler doesn't provide a lot of information as it creates class files. In fact, if the source code compiles successfully and no deprecated methods are employed, you won't see any output from the compiler at all. No news is good news in this case.

If you'd like to see more information on what the javac tool is doing as it compiles source code, use the -verbose option. The more verbose compiler will describe the time it takes to complete different functions, the classes that are being loaded, and the overall time required.

The `appletviewer` Browser

`appletviewer`, the Java applet viewer, is used to run Java programs that require a Web browser and are presented as part of an HTML document.

The applet viewer takes an HTML document as a command-line argument, as in the following example:

```
appletviewer NewAuctions.html
```

If the argument is a Web address instead of a reference to a file, `appletviewer` will load the HTML document at that address. For example:

```
appletviewer http://www.javaonthebrain.com
```

When an HTML document is loaded by `appletviewer`, every applet on that document will begin running in its own window. The size of these windows depends on the `HEIGHT` and `WIDTH` attributes that were set in the applet's HTML tag.

Unlike a Web browser, `appletviewer` cannot be used to view the HTML document itself. If you want to see how the applet is laid out in relation to the other contents of the document, you must use a Java-capable Web browser.

> **Caution**
>
> The current versions of Netscape Navigator and Microsoft Internet Explorer do not offer built-in support for Java applets, but support for the language is available as a browser plug-in from Sun MicroSystems. The Java Plug-in from Sun can be used to run a Java 2 applet in a browser in place of the browser's Java interpreter. The Plug-in can be installed along with the Software Development Kit, so it may already be present on your system. You also can download it from Sun's Web site at `http://java.sun.com/products/plugin/`.

Using `appletviewer` is reasonably straightforward, but you may not be familiar with some of the menu options that are available as the viewer runs an applet. Figure C.1 shows the options on the `appletviewer` tool's Applet pull-down menu.

FIGURE C.1

The Applet pull-down menu of appletviewer.

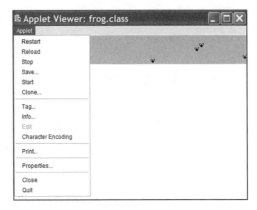

The following menu options are available:

- The Restart and Reload options are used to restart the execution of the applet. The difference between these two options is that Restart does not unload the applet before restarting it, whereas Reload does. The Reload option is equivalent to closing the applet viewer and opening it up again on the same Web page.
- The Start and Stop options are used to call the start() and stop() methods of the applet directly.
- The Clone option creates a second copy of the same applet running in its own window.
- The Tag option displays the program's <APPLET> or <OBJECT> tag, along with the HTML for any <PARAM> tags that configure the applet.

Another option on the Applet pull-down menu is Info, which calls the getAppletInfo() and getParameterInfo() methods of the applet. A programmer can implement these methods to provide more information about the applet and the parameters that it can handle. The getAppletInfo() method should return a string that describes the applet. The getParameterInfo() method should return an array of string arrays that specify the name, type, and description of each parameter.

Listing C.1 contains a Java 2 applet that demonstrates the use of these methods.

LISTING C.1   The Full Text of AppInfo.java

```
1: import java.awt.*;
2:
3: public class AppInfo extends javax.swing.JApplet {
4:     String name, date;
5:     int version;
6:
7:     public String getAppletInfo() {
8:         String response = "This applet demonstrates the "
```

LISTING C.1 Continued

```
 9:                    + "use of the Applet's Info feature.";
10:            return response;
11:        }
12:
13:        public String[][] getParameterInfo() {
14:            String[] p1 = { "Name", "String", "Programmer's name" };
15:            String[] p2 = { "Date", "String", "Today's date" };
16:            String[] p3 = { "Version", "int", "Version number" };
17:            String[][] response = { p1, p2, p3 };
18:            return response;
19:        }
20:
21:        public void init() {
22:            name = getParameter("Name");
23:            date = getParameter("Date");
24:            String versText = getParameter("Version");
25:            if (versText != null)
26:                version = Integer.parseInt(versText);
27:        }
28:
29:        public void paint(Graphics screen) {
30:            Graphics2D screen2D = (Graphics2D) screen;
31:            screen2D.drawString("Name: " + name, 5, 50);
32:            screen2D.drawString("Date: " + date, 5, 100);
33:            screen2D.drawString("Version: " + version, 5, 150);
34:        }
35: }
```

The main function of this applet is to display the value of three parameters: Name, Date, and Version. The getAppletInfo() method returns the following string:

```
This applet demonstrates the use of the Applet's Info feature.
```

The getParameterInfo() method is a bit more complicated if you haven't worked with multidimensional arrays. The following things are taking place:

- Line 13 defines the return type of the method as a two-dimensional array of String objects.

- Line 14 creates an array of String objects with three elements: "Name", "String", and "Programmer's Name". These elements describe one of the parameters that can be defined for the AppInfo applet. They describe the name of the parameter (Name in this case), the type of data that the parameter should hold (a string), and a description of the parameter ("Programmer's Name"). The three-element array is stored in the p1 object.

- Lines 15–16 define two more String arrays for the Date and Version parameters.

- Line 17 uses the `response` object to store an array that contains three string arrays: p1, p2, and p3.
- Line 18 uses the `response` object as the method's return value.

Listing C.2 contains a Web page that can be used to load the `AppInfo` applet.

LISTING C.2   The Full Text of `AppInfo.html`

```
1: <applet code="AppInfo.class" height=200 width=170>
2: <param name="Name" value="Rogers Cadenhead">
3: <param name="Date" value="03/01/02">
4: <param name="Version" value="3">
5: </applet>
```

Figure C.2 shows the applet running with the applet viewer, and Figure C.3 is a screen capture of the dialog box that opens when the viewer's Info menu option is selected.

FIGURE C.2

The `AppInfo` *applet running in* `appletviewer`.

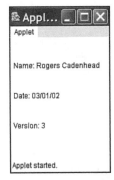

FIGURE C.3

The Info dialog box of the `AppInfo` *applet.*

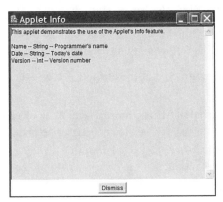

These features require a browser that makes this information available to users. The SDK's `appletviewer` handles this through the Info menu option, but browsers such as Internet Explorer do not offer anything like it at this time.

The `javadoc` Documentation Tool

`javadoc`, the Java documentation creator, takes a `.java` source code file or package name as input and generates detailed documentation in HTML format.

For `javadoc` to create full documentation for a program, a special type of comment statement must be used in the program's source code. Tutorial programs in this book use `//`, `/*`, and `*/` in source code to create *comments*—information for people who are trying to make sense of the program.

Java also has a more structured type of comment that can be read by the `javadoc` tool. This comment is used to describe program elements such as classes, variables, objects, and methods. It takes the following format:

```
/** A descriptive sentence or paragraph.
 * @tag1 Description of this tag.
 * @tag2 Description of this tag.
 */
```

A Java documentation comment should be placed immediately above the program element it is documenting and should succinctly explain what the program element is. For example, if the comment precedes a `class` statement, it should describe the purpose of the class.

In addition to the descriptive text, different items can be used to document the program element further. These items, called *tags,* are preceded by an @ sign and are followed by a space and a descriptive sentence or paragraph.

Listing C.3 contains a thoroughly documented version of the `AppInfo` applet called `AppInfo2`. The following tags are used in this program:

- `@author`—The program's author. This tag can be used only in documenting a class, and it will be ignored unless the `-author` option is used when `javadoc` is run.

- `@version` *text*—The program's version number. This also is restricted to class documentation, and it requires the `-version` option when you're running `javadoc` or the tag will be ignored.

- `@return` *text*—The variable or object returned by the method being documented.

- `@serial` *text*—A description of the data type and possible values for a variable or object that can be serialized. More information about serialization is presented during Day 16, "Serializing and Examining Objects."

LISTING C.3 The Full Text of `AppInfo2.java`

```
 1: import java.awt.*;
 2:
 3: /** This class displays the values of three parameters:
 4:  * Name, Date and Version.
 5:  * @author <a href="http://java21days.com">Rogers Cadenhead</a>
 6:  * @version 3.0
 7:  */
 8: public class AppInfo2 extends javax.swing.JApplet {
 9:     /**
10:      * @serial The programmer's name.
11:      */
12:     String name;
13:     /**
14:      * @serial The current date.
15:      */
16:     String date;
17:     /**
18:      * @serial The program's version number.
19:      */
20:     int version;
21:
22:     /**
23:      * This method describes the applet for any browsing tool that
24:      * requests information from the program.
25:      * @return A String describing the applet.
26:      */
27:     public String getAppletInfo() {
28:         String response = "This applet demonstrates the "
29:             + "use of the Applet's Info feature.";
30:         return response;
31:     }
32:
33:     /**
34:      * This method describes the parameters that the applet can take
35:      * for any browsing tool that requests this information.
36:      * @return An array of String[] objects for each parameter.
37:      */
38:     public String[][] getParameterInfo() {
39:         String[] p1 = { "Name", "String", "Programmer's name" };
40:         String[] p2 = { "Date", "String", "Today's date" };
41:         String[] p3 = { "Version", "int", "Version number" };
42:         String[][] response = { p1, p2, p3 };
43:         return response;
44:     }
45:
```

LISTING C.3   Continued

```
46:    /**
47:     * This method is called when the applet is first initialized.
48:     */
49:    public void init() {
50:        name = getParameter("Name");
51:        date = getParameter("Date");
52:        String versText = getParameter("Version");
53:        if (versText != null)
54:            version = Integer.parseInt(versText);
55:    }
56:
57:    /**
58:     * This method is called when the applet's display window is
59:     * being repainted.
60:     */
61:    public void paint(Graphics screen) {
62:        Graphics2D screen2D = (Graphics2D)screen;
63:        screen.drawString("Name: " + name, 5, 50);
64:        screen.drawString("Date: " + date, 5, 100);
65:        screen.drawString("Version: " + version, 5, 150);
66:    }
67: }
```

The following command will create HTML documentation from the source code file
AppInfo2.java:

```
javadoc -author -version AppInfo2.java
```

The Java documentation tool will create several different Web pages in the same folder
as AppInfo2.java. These pages will document the program in the same manner as Sun's
official documentation for the Java 2 class library.

Tip

> To see the official documentation for Java 2 SDK 1.4 and the Java class
> libraries, visit http://java.sun.com/j2se/1.4/docs/api/.

To see the documentation that javadoc has created for AppInfo2, load the newly created
Web page index.html on your Web browser. Figure C.4 shows this page loaded with
Internet Explorer 6.0.

FIGURE C.4

*Java documentation
for the* AppInfo2
program.

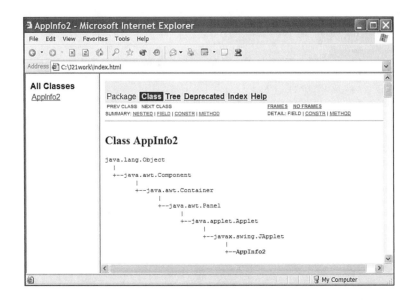

The javadoc tool produces extensively hyperlinked Web pages. Navigate through the pages to see where the information in your documentation comments and tags shows up.

If you're familiar with HTML markup, you can use HTML tags such as <A>, <TT>, and <B> within your documentation comments. Line 5 of the AppInfo2 program uses an <A> tag to turn the text "Rogers Cadenhead" into a hyperlink to this book's Web site.

The javadoc tool also can be used to document an entire package by specifying the package name as a command-line argument. HTML files will be created for each .java file in the package, along with an HTML file indexing the package.

If you would like the Java documentation to be produced in a different folder than the default, use the -d option followed by a space and the folder name.

The following command creates Java documentation for AppInfo2 in a folder called C:\JavaDocs\:

```
javadoc -author -version -d C:\JavaDocs\ AppInfo2.java
```

The following list details the other tags you can use in Java documentation comments:

- @deprecated *text*—A note that this class, method, object, or variable has been deprecated. This causes the javac compiler to issue a deprecation warning when the feature is used in a program that's being compiled.

- @exception *class description*—Used with methods that throw exceptions, this tag documents the exception's class name and its description.

- @param *name description*—Used with methods, this tag documents the name of an argument and a description of the values the argument can hold.

- @see *class*—This tag indicates the name of another class, which will be turned into a hyperlink to the Java documentation of that class. This can be used without restriction in comments.

- @see *class#method*—This tag indicates the name of a method of another class, which will be used for a hyperlink directly to the documentation of that method. This is usable without restriction.

- @since *text*—This tag indicates a note describing when a method or feature was added to its class library.

The jar Java File Archival Tool

When you deploy a Java program, keeping track of all the class files and other files required by the program can be cumbersome.

To make this easier, the SDK includes a tool called jar that can pack all of a program's files into a Java archive—also called a JAR file. The jar tool also can be used to unpack the files in one of these archives.

JAR files can be compressed using the Zip format or packed without using compression.

To use the tool, type the command jar followed by command-line options and a series of file names, folder names, or wildcards.

The following command packs all of a folder's class and GIF image files into a single Java archive called Animate.jar:

```
jar cf Animate.jar *.class *.gif
```

The argument cf specifies two command-line options that can be used when running the jar program. The c option indicates that a Java archive file should be created, and f indicates that the name of the archive file will follow as one of the next arguments.

You also can add specific files to a Java archive with a command such as the following:

```
jar cf AudioLoop.jar AudioLoop.class beep.au loop.au
```

This creates an AudioLoop.jar archive containing three files: AudioLoop.class, loop.au, and beep.au.

Run jar without any arguments to see a list of options that can be used with the tool.

One use for jar is to put all files necessary to run a Java applet in a single JAR file. This makes it much easier to deploy the applet on the Web.

The standard way of placing a Java applet on a Web page is to use <APPLET> or <OBJECT> to indicate the primary class file of the applet. A Java-enabled browser then downloads and runs the applet. Any other classes and any other files needed by the applet are downloaded from the Web server.

The problem with running applets in this way is that every single file an applet requires—helper classes, images, audio files, text files, or anything else—requires a separate connection from a Web browser to the server containing the file. This can significantly increase the amount of time it takes to download an applet and everything it needs to run.

If you can reduce the number of files the browser has to load from the server by putting many files into one Java archive, your applet can be downloaded and run by a Web browser more quickly. If the files in a Java archive are compressed, it loads even more quickly.

Versions 4.0 and higher of the Microsoft Internet Explorer and Netscape Navigator Web browsers support JAR files.

After you create a Java archive, the ARCHIVE attribute is used with the <APPLET> tag to show where the archive can be found. You can use Java archives with an applet with tags such as the following:

```
<applet code="AudioLoop.class" archive="AudioLoop.jar" width=45 height=42>
</applet>
```

This tag specifies that an archive called AudioLoop.jar contains files used by the applet. Browsers and browsing tools that support JAR files will look inside the archive for files that are needed as the applet runs.

 Caution Although a Java archive can contain class files, the ARCHIVE attribute does not remove the need for the CODE attribute. A browser still needs to know the name of the applet's main class file in order to load it.

When an <OBJECT> tag is used to display an applet that uses a JAR file, the applet's archive file is specified as a parameter using the <PARAM> tag. The tag should have the name attribute "archive" and a value attribute with the name of the archive file.

The following example is a rewrite of the preceding example to use <OBJECT> instead of <APPLET>:

```
<object code="AudioLoop.class" width=45 height=42>
    <param name="archive" value="AudioLoop.jar">
</object>
```

The `jdb` Debugger

`jdb`, the Java debugger, is a sophisticated tool that helps you find and fix bugs in Java programs. You can also use it to understand better what is taking place behind the scenes in the Java interpreter as a program is running. It has a large number of features, including some that might be beyond the expertise of a Java programmer who is new to the language.

You don't need to use the debugger to debug Java programs. This is fairly obvious, especially if you've been creating your own Java programs as you read this book. After the Java compiler generates an error, the most common response is to load the source code into an editor, find the line cited in the error message, and try to spot the problem. This dreaded compile-curse-find-fix cycle is repeated until the program compiles without complaint.

After using this debugging method for a while, you might think that the debugger isn't necessary to the programming process because it's such a complicated tool to master. This reasoning makes sense when you're fixing problems that cause compiler errors. Many of these problems are simple things such as a misplaced semicolon, unmatched { and } brackets, or the use of the wrong type of data as a method argument. However, when you start looking for logic errors—more subtle bugs that don't stop the program from compiling and running—a debugger is an invaluable tool.

The Java debugger has two features that are extremely useful when you're searching for a bug that can't be found by other means: single-step execution and breakpoints. *Single-step execution* pauses a Java program after every line of code is executed. *Breakpoints* are points where execution of the program will pause. Using the Java debugger, these breakpoints can be triggered by specific lines of code, method calls, or caught exceptions.

The Java debugger works by running a program using a version of the Java interpreter that it has complete control over.

Before you use the Java debugger with a program, you should compile the program with the -g option, which causes extra information to be included in the class file. This information greatly aids in debugging. Also, you shouldn't use the -0 option because its optimization techniques might produce a class file that does not directly correspond with the program's source code.

Debugging Applications

If you're debugging an application, the `jdb` tool can be run with a Java class as an argument. This is shown in the following:

```
jdb WriteBytes
```

This example runs the debugger with `WriteBytes.class`, an application that's available from the book's Web site at `http://www.java21days.com`. Visit the site, select the Appendix C page, and then save the files `WriteBytes.class` and `WriteBytes.java` in the same folder that you run the debugger from.

The `WriteBytes` application writes a series of bytes to disk to produce the file `pic.gif`.

The debugger loads this program but does not begin running it, displaying the following output:

```
Initializing jdb...
>
```

The debugger is controlled by typing commands at the > prompt.

To set a breakpoint in a program, the `stop in` or `stop at` commands are used. The `stop in` command sets a breakpoint at the first line of a specific method in a class. You specify the class and method name as an argument to the command, as in the following example:

```
stop in SellItem.SetPrice
```

This command sets a breakpoint at the first line of the `SetPrice` method. Note that no arguments or parentheses are needed after the method name.

The `stop at` command sets a breakpoint at a specific line number within a class. You specify the class and number as an argument to the command, as in the following example:

```
stop at WriteBytes:14
```

If you're trying this with the `WriteBytes` class, you'll see the following output after entering this command:

```
Deferring breakpoint WriteBytes:14
It will be set after the class is loaded.
```

You can set as many breakpoints as desired within a class. To see the breakpoints that are currently set, use the `clear` command without any arguments. The `clear` command lists all current breakpoints by line number rather than method name, even if they were set using the `stop in` command.

By using `clear` with a class name and line number as an argument, you can remove a breakpoint. If the hypothetical `SellItem.SetPrice` method was located at line 215 of `SellItem`, you could clear this breakpoint with the following command:

```
clear SellItem:215
```

Within the debugger, you can begin executing a program with the run command. The following output shows what the debugger displays after you begin running the WriteBytes class:

```
run WriteBytes
VM Started: Set deferred breakpoint WriteBytes:14

Breakpoint hit: "thread=main", WriteBytes.main(), line=14 bci=413

14                  for (int i = 0; i < data.length; i++)
```

After you have reached a breakpoint in the WriteBytes class, experiment with the following commands:

- list—At the point where execution stopped, this command displays the source code of the line and several lines around it. This requires access to the .java file of the class where the breakpoint has been hit, so you must have WriteBytes.java in either the current folder or one of the folders in your CLASSPATH.
- locals—This command lists the values for local variables that are currently in use or will soon be defined.
- print *text*—This command displays the value of the variable, object, or array element specified by *text*.
- step—This command executes the next line and stops again.
- cont—This command continues running the program at the point it was halted.
- !!—This command repeats the previous debugger command.

After trying out these commands within the application, you can resume running the program by clearing the breakpoint and using the cont command. Use the exit command to end the debugging session.

The WriteBytes application creates a file called pic.gif. You can verify that this file ran successfully by loading it with a Web browser or image-editing software. You'll see a small letter J in black and white.

After you have finished debugging a program and you're satisfied that it works correctly, recompile it without the -g option.

Debugging Applets

You can't debug an applet by loading it using the jdb tool. Instead, use the -debug option of the appletviewer, as in the following example:

```
appletviewer -debug AppInfo.html
```

This will load the Java debugger, and when you use a command such as run, the appletviewer will begin running also. Try out this example to see how these tools interact with each other.

Before you use the run command to execute the applet, set a breakpoint in the program at the first line of the getAppletInfo method. Use the following command:

```
stop in AppInfo.getAppletInfo
```

After you begin running the applet, the breakpoint won't be hit until you cause the getAppletInfo() method to be called. This is accomplished by selecting Applet, Info from the appletviewer's menu.

Advanced Debugging Commands

With the features you have learned about so far, you can use the debugger to stop execution of a program and learn more about what's taking place. This might be sufficient for many of your debugging tasks, but the debugger also offers many other commands. These include the following:

- up—This command moves up the stack frame so that you can use locals and print to examine the program at the point before the current method was called.

- down—This command moves down the stack frame to examine the program after the method call.

In a Java program, often there are places where a chain of methods is called. One method calls another method, which calls another method, and so on. At each point where a method is being called, Java keeps track of all the objects and variables within that scope by grouping them together. This grouping is called a *stack*, as if you were stacking these objects like a deck of cards. The various stacks in existence as a program runs are called the *stack frame*.

By using up and down along with commands such as locals, you can better understand how the code that calls a method interacts with that method.

You can also use the following commands within a debugging session:

- classes—This command lists the classes currently loaded into memory.

- methods—This command lists the methods of a class.

- memory—This command shows the total amount of memory and the amount that isn't currently in use.

- threads—This command lists the threads that are executing.

The `threads` command numbers all of the threads, which enables you to use the `suspend` command followed by that number to pause the thread, as in `suspend 1`. You can resume a thread by using the `resume` command followed by its number.

Another convenient way to set a breakpoint in a Java program is to use the `catch` *text* command, which pauses execution when the `Exception` class named by *text* is caught.

You can also cause an exception to be ignored by using the `ignore` *text* command with the `Exception` class named by *text*.

Using System Properties

One obscure feature of the SDK is that the command-line option `-D` can modify the performance of the Java class library.

If you have used other programming languages prior to learning Java, you might be familiar with environment variables, which provide information about the operating system in which a program is running. An example is the `CLASSPATH` setting, which indicates the folders in which the Java interpreter should look for a class file.

Because different operating systems have different names for their environment variables, they cannot be read directly by a Java program. Instead, Java includes a number of different system properties that are available on any platform with a Java implementation.

Some properties are used only to get information. The following system properties are among those that should be available on any Java implementation:

- `java.version`—The version number of the Java interpreter
- `java.vendor`—A string identifying the vendor associated with the Java interpreter
- `os.name`—The operating system in use
- `os.version`—The version number of that operating system

Other properties can affect how the Java class library performs when being used inside a Java program. An example of this is the `java2d.font.usePlatformFont` property. If this property has a value of `true`, a Java program will use the Java 1.1 style of font rendering rather than the system used in subsequent versions of the language. This property became useful with a beta version of Java 1.2 that had some bugs in how the `appletviewer` tool handled fonts.

A property can be set at the command line by using the `-D` option followed by the property name, an equal sign, and the new value of the property, as in this command:

```
java -Djava2d.font.usePlatformFont=true Auctioneer
```

The use of the system property in this example will cause the `Auctioneer` application to use 1.1-style fonts.

You also can create your own properties and read them using the `getProperty()` method of the `System` class, which is part of the `java.lang` package.

Listing C.4 contains the source code of a simple program that displays the value of a user-created property.

LISTING C.4   The Full Text of `ItemProp.java`

```
1: class ItemProp {
2:     public static void main(String[] arguments) {
3:         String n = System.getProperty("item.name");
4:         System.out.println("The item is named " + n);
5:     }
6: }
```

If this program is run without setting the `item.name` property on the command line, the output is the following:

```
The item is named null
```

The `item.name` property can be set using the `-D` option, as in this command:

```
java -Ditem.name="Microsoft Bob" ItemProp
```

The output is the following:

```
The item is named Microsoft Bob
```

The `-D` option is used with the Java interpreter. To use it with the `appletviewer` as well, all you have to do differently is precede the `-D` with `-J`. The following command shows how this can be done:

```
appletviewer -J-Djava2d.font.usePlatformFont=true AuctionSite.html
```

This example causes `appletviewer` to use Java 1.1-style fonts with all applets on the Web page `AuctionSite.html`.

Summary

This appendix explores several features of the SDK that are increasingly helpful as you develop more experience with Java:

- Using the Java debugger with applets and applications
- Creating an optimized version of a compiled class

- Writing applet methods that provide information to a browser upon request
- Using the Java documentation creation tool to describe a class, its methods, and other aspects of the program fully

These SDK features weren't required during the 21 days of this book because of the relative simplicity of the tutorial programs. Although it can be complicated to develop a Swing application or to work with threads and streams for the first time, your biggest challenge lies ahead: integrating concepts like these into more sophisticated Java programs.

Tools such as javadoc and the debugger really come into their own on complex projects.

When a bug occurs because of how two classes interact with each other, or similar subtle logic errors creep into your code, a debugger is the best way to identify and repair the problems.

As you create an entire library of classes, javadoc can easily document these classes and show how they are interrelated.

Q&A

Q The official Java documentation is filled with long paragraphs that describe classes and methods. How can these be produced using javadoc?

A In the Java documentation creator, there's no limit to the length of a description. Although they're often as brief as a sentence or two, they can be longer if necessary. End the description with a period, immediately followed by a new line with a tag of some kind or the end of the comment.

Q Do I have to document everything in my Java classes if I'm planning to use the javadoc tool?

A The Java documentation creator will work fine no matter how many or how few comments you use. Deciding which elements of the program need to be documented is up to you. You probably should describe the class and all methods, variables, and objects that aren't hidden from other classes.

The javadoc tool will display a warning each time a serializable object or variable is defined in a program without a corresponding Java documentation comment.

APPENDIX **D**

Using Sun ONE Studio

For most of Java's existence, programmers have learned the language using the Software Development Kit (SDK) from Sun Microsystems, a set of command-line tools used to create Java programs, described in Appendices B and C.

The SDK is highly popular, but it lacks some features most professional programmers take for granted—such as a built-in text editor, graphical user interface, and project management tools. These features, which are essential for everyday programming, are typically supplied in an integrated development environment (IDE).

One IDE you can choose for creating Java software is Sun ONE Studio, also offered by Sun MicroSystems.

This appendix covers how to download and install Sun ONE Studio and use it to create, compile, and run a simple Java program.

Choosing a Java Development Tool

Several different integrated development environments are available for Java programming.

Sun ONE Studio includes tools you will use all the time: a text editor, graphical user interface designer, Web page editor, file archival tool, and project manager.

The IDE also includes tools that aren't essential now, as you're getting started with the language, but may become indispensible later, including a debugger, Java servlet and JavaServer Pages editing and testing tool, and JDBC database connection developer.

There are two versions of Sun ONE Studio:

- The Community Edition, available for free from Sun's Web site.
- The Enterprise Edition, which currently sells for $1995 (or $995 if you bought a past edition of Forte or recent versions of Borland JBuilder, IBM VisualAge for Java, Microsoft Visual Basic, or WebGain Visual Café).

As you might expect from the price, the Enterprise Edition is targeted at professional Java programmers doing large-scale development for corporate and government enterprises.

The Community Edition contains most of the functionality of the Enterprise Edition—including everything you'll need to complete the tutorials in this book.

Sun ONE Studio supports Java 2 version 1.4 (and can be configured to support other versions), so you can continue using it as Sun releases new versions of Java.

Installing Sun ONE Studio

Sun ONE Studio, formerly known as Forte for Java, is available at several different places on Sun's Web site. To see what versions are available for download, visit the Web page http://forte.sun.com/ffj/downloads/.

The Downloads page includes the Community and Enterprise editions of Sun ONE Studio along with dozens of add-on programs that enhance the functionality of the software.

To use Sun ONE Studio, you must also install a compatible version of the Java 2 Software Development Kit. The easiest way to do this is to download and install a version of Sun ONE Studio Community Edition that includes the SDK.

On the Forte downloads page, this product is currently being called the Community Edition, v.3.0—J2SE 1.4 Cobundle.

> **Tip**
>
> By the time you visit the page, the name of this product may be different because of Sun's penchant for giving things laboriously complicated names and changing them around from time to time (something the author of this book has no business mocking). Anything that's called a Community Edition "Cobundle" is probably what you need.

The Sun ONE Studio cobundle is currently available for the following platforms:

- Windows 98, NT, and 2000 (with Service Pack 2)
- Solaris SPARC and Intel
- Linux

Though Sun ONE Studio doesn't officially support Windows XP yet, I've been able to use it on that operating system with only one unusual error (which will be explained later).

The Windows and Linux versions of Sun ONE Studio require a computer with a Pentium II processor that is 350 MHz or faster, 110MB of free disk space, and 128MB of memory. Sun recommends a more beefed-up machine: a 450 MHz Pentium III processor with 256MB of memory on Windows or 512MB of memory on Linux.

D

> **Tip**
>
> There is no Macintosh version of Sun ONE Studio, but the Solaris version runs on Mac OS X. Apple offers a free version of the SDK and a Project Builder integrated development environment. To find out more about Apple's Java programming tools, visit the Web site `http://devworld.apple.com/java/`.
>
> If you're using another platform, you can check to see whether it has a tool that supports Java 1.4 by visiting Sun's site at `http://java.sun.com/cgi-bin/java-ports.cgi/`.

To set up Sun ONE Studio, you must download and run an installation program (or install it from a CD). After you have downloaded the file, you're ready to set it up on your system.

Running the Installation Wizard

Before installing the Studio/SDK cobundle, you must remove any version of the kit that's presently installed on your system. Otherwise, Sun ONE Studio may have trouble finding the kit and using it to perform some of its tasks.

To set up the software on a Windows system, double-click the installation file icon or click Start, Run from the Windows taskbar to find and run the file.

An installation wizard will guide you through the process of setting up the software. If you accept Sun's terms and conditions for using Sun ONE Studio and a second set of terms and conditions for the SDK, you'll be asked where to install the program, as shown in Figure D.1.

FIGURE D.1

Choosing a destination folder for Sun ONE Studio (formerly Forte for Java) and the SDK.

The wizard will suggest a folder where the cobundle should be installed. In Figure D.1, the wizard is suggesting the folder C:\J2SDK_Forte.

If you want to pick a different folder, click Browse and use the Windows file open dialog box to select a location.

Click the Next button to review the folder where Forte and the kit will be installed. If it's acceptable, click Next to install the software and add Sun ONE Studio to your Start menu.

Configuring Sun ONE Studio

The first time you run Sun ONE Studio, you'll be asked several questions about how to configure the software.

Caution

Although the name of the software has been changed to Sun ONE Studio on Sun's Web site, at the time of this writing the version of the software available on the site hasn't been updated to reflect the name change. It still is titled Forte for Java.

To run the program:

- On Windows XP, choose Start, choose All Programs, open the Forte for Java CE folder, and click Forte for Java CE.
- On other Windows systems, choose Start, choose Programs, open the Forte for Java CE folder, and click Forte for Java CE.

The first question you're asked is where to store your programming projects (Figure D.2).

FIGURE D.2

Choosing a work folder for your Sun ONE Studio projects.

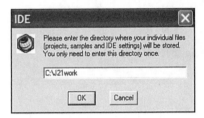

In Figure D.2, I've chosen C:\J21work.

Next, you are asked whether you want to import settings from a previous installation of Forte or NetBeans 3.0 or 3.1. Choose an option using the Yes or No radio button and click Next to import settings or Finish if you have no settings to import.

Caution

> After deciding whether to import settings, you may see an error message about a disk drive. During installation on a Windows XP system, an error dialog opened with this message: "There is no disk in the drive. Please insert a disk into drive \Device\Harddisk1\DR1."
>
> This appears to be a bug in the installation program rather than a problem that prevents the software from installing correctly. Click Continue to close the dialog and continue setting up Sun ONE Studio.

A setup wizard opens asking where iPlanet has been installed (Figure D.3).

Sun ONE Studio can be configured to work with iPlanet, an e-commerce Web server offered by Sun MicroSystems. If you own iPlanet, you can write JavaServer Pages and servlets in Sun ONE Studio and deploy them on the server.

D

FIGURE D.3

Setting up Sun ONE Studio to work with the iPlanet Web server.

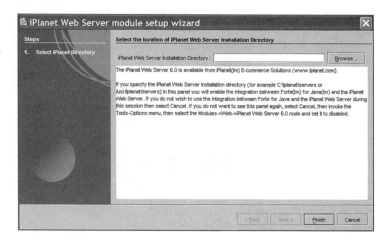

If you aren't using iPlanet, click Cancel to close this wizard, preventing it from showing up the next time you run Sun ONE Studio.

If you are an iPlanet user, click Browse, find the iPlanet folder on your system, and click OK. The folder name will appear in the iPlanet Web Server Installation Directory field. Click Finish to set up Sun ONE Studio to use this server.

Next, a Setup Wizard opens so that you can finish configuring the software (Figure D.4).

FIGURE D.4

Configuring Sun ONE Studio's proxy server, browser, and the user interface.

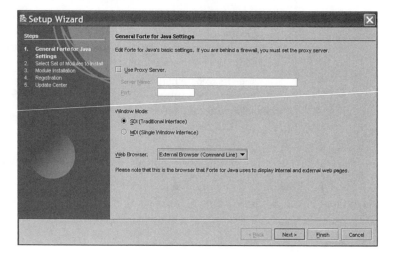

The default settings are as follows, shown in Figure D.4:

- Don't use a proxy server.
- Open different Sun ONE Studio projects in the same window—a feature also known as a single-document interface (SDI).
- Use the system's default Web browser to test Java applets.

These settings should be fine for most new users getting started with Sun ONE Studio, unless you're in a corporate or academic environment where you must use a firewall to connect to the Internet. In that case, select the Use Proxy Server option and provide the server name and port of your Internet firewall. Click Next to continue.

The Setup Wizard follows up by asking which modules you want to install (Figure D.5).

FIGURE D.5

Choosing which Sun ONE Studio modules to install.

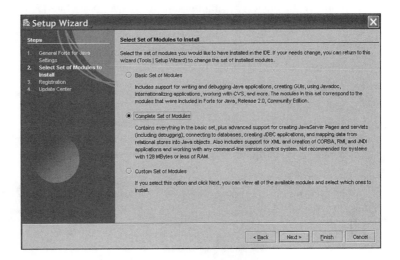

The wizard recommends that you install only the Basic Set of Modules if you're on a system with 128MB of memory. However, you're going to miss some of the features in the Complete Set of Modules when you get to the third week of this book—especially the XML, JDBC, JavaServer Pages, and servlet tools.

Choose the set of modules to install and click Next. The wizard will tell you to click Next for advanced setup options or click Finish. The advanced options relate to early-access beta releases of the software, which you can download and install automatically if you register a developer account with Sun. If you're using Sun ONE Studio primarily to learn Java, you probably should skip the advanced setup at this point.

Creating a Sample Program

Now that you have installed Sun ONE Studio and set up the software, you're ready to use it in the creation of a sample Java program.

If you have never used an integrated development environment before, you're likely to be a little shell-shocked when you close the software's Welcome window and see Sun ONE Studio for the first time. There are more than a hundred menu commands, toolbar buttons, and other interface components at your disposal.

Most IDEs are designed to make experienced programmers more productive rather than to help new programmers learn a language. Sun ONE Studio is no exception.

It can be difficult to learn how to use an IDE at the same time you are learning Java. This is probably the biggest selling point for the Java 2 Software Development Kit.

However, if you'd like to make use of the power and convenience of Sun ONE Studio while learning Java, this section and some supplementary reading should be enough to get started.

In this section, you'll create a short Java application and run it, displaying the output of the program.

To start, create a new project in Sun ONE Studio by selecting New from the File menu. The New from Template Wizard opens (Figure D.6).

FIGURE D.6

Selecting the template for a new project in Sun ONE Studio.

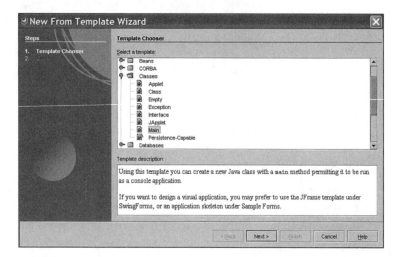

Sun ONE Studio offers templates for the most common programming projects you will undertake. This project is to create an application, which can be done with the Main template. In the Select a Template window, open the Classes folder and choose the Main template.

In the Template Description text area, the wizard describes the template you have chosen. Click the Next button to confirm your choice.

The next step is to choose a name for the application and a place where its files will be stored (Figure D.7).

FIGURE D.7

Entering the name for a new project in Sun ONE Studio.

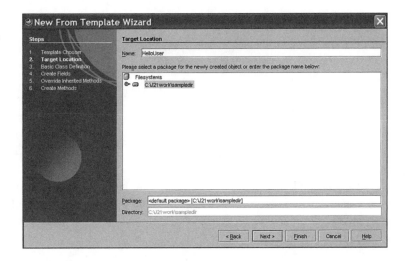

When you create a Java class, you can make it part of a group of classes by putting it in a package—one of the features of the language you'll learn about during Week 1 of the book.

The wizard suggests a default name and package for your new project, using the work folder you specified the first time you ran the software.

Enter the text HelloUser in the Name field and accept the package suggested by the wizard.

At this point, you could click Next to set up more aspects of the program. However, you don't need to on this project—click Finish. Sun ONE Studio creates the source code for a Java application called HelloUser and opens it for editing in a Source Editor window (Figure D.8).

FIGURE **D.8**

*The Source Editor
window in Sun ONE
Studio.*

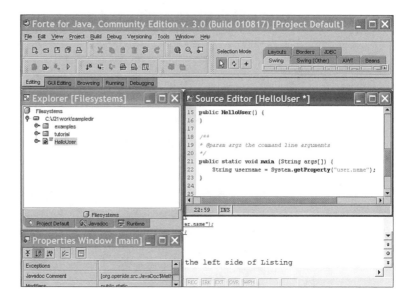

All Java programs begin as source code—a series of statements created using a text editor and saved as a text file.

The Sun ONE Studio Source Editor window numbers lines along the left edge of the window. When you create the HelloUser project, it contains the following Java statements as lines 21–22:

```
public static void main (String[] args) {
}
```

Insert a blank line between these two lines and enter the following statements at that place in the file:

```
String username = System.getProperty("user.name");
System.out.println("Hello, " + username);
```

When you're done, lines 21–24 should be the same as Listing D.1. Make sure all the parentheses, braces, and quotation marks in the listing are entered correctly and capitalize everything in the program exactly as shown.

LISTING D.1   Partial Source Code of the HelloUser Program

```
21:     public static void main (String[] args) {
22:         String username = System.getProperty("user.name");
23:         System.out.println("Hello, " + username);
24:     }
```

The line numbers and colons along the left side of Listing D.1 are not part of the program—they're included so that I can refer to specific lines by number in this book. If you're ever unsure about the source code of a program in this book, you can compare it to a copy on the book's official World Wide Web site at the following address:

```
http://www.java21days.com
```

After you finish typing in the program, save the project by choosing Save from the File menu.

Note

The purpose of this project is to try out Sun ONE Studio—none of the Java programming concepts used in the HelloUser program are described in this appendix. You'll learn the basics of the language on Day 1, "Getting Started with Java."

Running the Program

When you save source code, Sun ONE Studio saves it in your work folder and then compiles it, creating one or more class files that can be run by a Java interpreter.

To run the program, right-click the HelloUser icon in the Explorer window (Figure D.9) and choose Execute.

D

FIGURE D.9

Running a Java application in Sun ONE Studio.

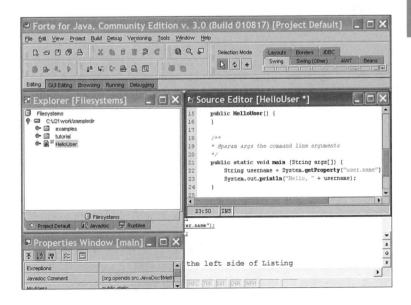

Figure D.10 shows the successful output of the HelloUser application.

FIGURE D.10

Viewing the output of the HelloUser *application.*

Additional Help for Beginners

Sun MicroSystems offers a tutorial for beginning Sun ONE Studio users in the developer resources section of the Studio Web site: the *Forte for Java Community Edition 3.0 Getting Started Guide*.

To find this tutorial and other online help, visit the Web page http://forte.sun.com/ffj/documentation/.

This book has a Web site where you can find solutions to problems, corrections, answers to reader questions, and other useful material.

There's an online version of this appendix on the site and a way to contact me (coauthor Rogers Cadenhead). The site is available at http://www.java21days.com/.

APPENDIX E

Where to Go from Here: Java Resources

Now that you have finished this book, you might be wondering where you can go to improve your Java programming skills. This appendix lists some books, World Wide Web sites, Internet discussion groups, and other resources that you can use to expand your Java knowledge.

Other Books to Consider

Sams Publishing publishes several books on Java programming topics, including many that follow up on the material covered in this book. The following list includes ISBN numbers, which will be needed at bookstores if they don't currently carry the book that you're looking for:

- *Sams Teach Yourself J2EE in 21 Days* by Martin Bond and others. ISBN: 0-67232-384-2. A tutorial for Java developers who want to use the Java 2 Enterprise Edition (J2EE).

- *JXTA: Java P2P Programming* by Daniel Brookshier and others. ISBN: 0-67232-366-4. An introduction to Sun Microsystem's JXTA classes, which support peer-to-peer networked programming.

- *MySQL and JSP Web Applications: Data-Driven Programming Using Tomcat and MySQL* by James Turner. ISBN: 0-67232-309-5. Advice and programming tutorials for JavaServer Pages programmers using the MySQL database with their Web applications.

- *Developing Java Servlets, Second Edition,* by James Goodwill and Samir Mehta. ISBN: 0-67232-107-6. A tutorial on Java servlet and JavaServer Pages programming and how to use them with XML, Enterprise JavaBeans, and the Java 2 Enterprise Edition.

- *Jini and JavaSpaces Application Development* by Robert Flenner. ISBN: 0-67232-258-7. A guide to wireless networked programming using JINI, Sun's technology for connecting different disconnected devices using Java.

Chapters and other material from many Sams Publishing Java books have been made available for free on the World Wide Web at InformIT, a Web site for information technology professionals produced in collaboration with Sams at `http://www.informit.com`.

InformIT also includes chapters from upcoming books, a Linux resource called InfoBase, and new articles by computer book authors and IT professionals.

The Sams Publishing Web site, `http://www.samspublishing.com`, includes an online catalog, a list of upcoming releases, and links to author Web sites. It's a good place to see what's coming up from Sams Publishing and other parts of the Pearson Technology Group.

Sun's Official Java Site

The Java software division of Sun Microsystems Inc. maintains an active Web site at `http://java.sun.com`.

This site is the first place to visit when looking for Java-related information. New versions of the Java 2 Software Development Kit and other programming resources are available for downloading, along with documentation for the entire Java class library.

The site includes the following features:

- **Products and APIs**—This area is a directory of all the development tools, Java class libraries, and new Java technologies that can be downloaded from the Java division, including the Software Development Kit, language documentation, and more than 50 other products and new Java class libraries. API is an acronym for Application Programming Interface, and the term is analogous to class library in Java.

- **Developer Connection**—This area is a consolidated resource for all technical information of interest to Java programmers, including complete documentation for the Java language in HTML format. You can find information on language conferences, a searchable database of Java bug reports, and a discussion forum for Java developers and people learning the language.

- **Docs and Training**—You can find thousands of pages of free documentation here, covering the Software Development Kit, the Java class library for Java 2 and all previous versions, and information on Sun's official Java books.

- **Online Support**—This area contains technical support, customer service, and sales assistance for purchasers of Java products and users of Java development tools.

- **Community Discussion**—Sun's Java division hosts a large number of Web-based discussion areas on topics for beginners and experienced pros alike. Sun gives out prizes for participants who earn the most "Duke dollars," which are given out by members of the discussion community when someone provides helpful information.

- **Industry News**—This area contains announcements related to upcoming product releases and Java-related events such as JavaOne, the yearly conference for Java programmers. There are also press releases from Sun's Java software division and "success stories," examples of how the language is being used professionally.

- **Solutions Marketplace**—In this area you can find a database of information about products and services of interest to Java developers. If you're shopping for JavaBeans components, development tools, consultants, or new class libraries, you can find them here.

- **Case Studies**—Like the "success stories" area of the Industry News section, this area touts how Java is being employed. Company press releases and more in-depth analysis of technology solutions are published, describing how Java was used and some of the issues the developers faced.

This site is continually updated with free resources useful to Java programmers.

Java 2 Version 1.4 Class Documentation

Perhaps the most useful part of Sun's Java site is the documentation for every class, variable, and method in Java 2's class library. Thousands of pages are online at no cost to show you how to use the classes in your programs.

To visit the class documentation for Java 2 version 1.4, visit the Web page at `http://java.sun.com/j2se/1.4/docs/api/`.

Other Java Web Sites

Because so much of the Java phenomenon was originally inspired by its use on Web pages, a large number of Web sites focus on Java and Java programming.

This Book's Official Site

This book has an official Web site at `http://www.java21days.com`. This site is described fully in Appendix F, "This Book's Web Site."

Café au Lait

Elliotte Rusty Harold, the author of several excellent books on Java programming, offers Café au Lait, a frequently updated weblog covering Java news, product releases, and other sites of interest to programmers. The site is an invaluable resource for people interested in Java and is published at `http://www.ibiblio.org/javafaq/`. Harold also offers a list of frequently asked questions related to Java, as well as some unofficial documentation compiled by programmers over the past several years.

Workbench

I also publish a weblog called Workbench. It covers Java, Internet technology, computer books, and similar topics. Though I won't go as far as calling it an "invaluable resource," I'm pretty sure that my mother would. It's published at `http://workbench.cadenhead.info`.

Java Review Service

The Java Review Service reviews new programs, components, and tools that are published on the Web, recognizing some as "Top 1%," "Top 5%," or "Top 25%." Resources are also categorized by topic, with a description of each resource and links to download the source code, if it is available. To access the Java Review Service (JARS) Web site, which is another directory that rates Java applets, direct your Web browser to `http://www.jars.com`.

JavaWorld Magazine

One of the best magazines that serves the Java programming community is also the cheapest. *JavaWorld* is available for free on the World Wide Web at `http://www.javaworld.com`.

JavaWorld publishes frequent tutorial articles along with Java development news and other features, which are updated monthly. The Web-only format provides an advantage over some of its print competitors, such as *Java Report,* in the area of how-to articles. When an article is teaching a particular concept or type of programming, *JavaWorld* can offer a Java applet that demonstrates the lesson.

Gamelan: Earthweb's Java Directory

Because Java is an object-oriented language that offers JavaBeans as a means to create self-contained programming components, it is easy to use resources created by other developers in your own programs. Before you start a Java project of any significance, you should scan the World Wide Web for resources that you might be able to use in your program.

A good place to start is Gamelan, Earthweb's Java directory. This site catalogs Java programs, programming resources, and other information at `http://softwaredev.earthweb.com/java`.

Gamelan is one of the most comprehensive Web resources of its kind, surpassing even Sun's official site in the depth of its coverage related to applets, JavaBeans, and useful Web sites.

Lists of Java Books

Those of us who write Java books like to think that you're forsaking all others by choosing our work. However, anecdotal studies (and the number of Java books on *our* shelves) indicate that you might benefit from other books devoted to the language.

Elliotte Rusty Harold maintains a list of Java- and JavaScript-related books at `http://www.ibiblio.org/javafaq/books.html`.

Java Newsgroups

One of the best resources for both novice and experienced Java programmers is Usenet, the international network of discussion groups that is available to most Internet users through either an Internet service provider or a news service, such as Google Groups, `http://groups.google.com/`, or NewsGuy, `http://www.newsguy.com`. The following are descriptions of some of the Java discussion groups that are available on Usenet:

- `comp.lang.java.programmer`—Because this group is devoted to questions and answers related to Java programming, it is the place for all subjects that don't belong in one of the other groups. Any Java-related topic is suitable for discussion here.
- `comp.lang.java.advocacy`—This group is devoted to any Java discussions that are likely to inspire heated or comparative debate. If you want to argue the merits of

E

Java against another language, this is the place for it. This group can be a good place to consult if you want to see whether Java is the right choice for a project on which you're working.

- `comp.lang.java.announce`—This group, which has been relatively inactive in recent years, is a place to read announcements, advertisements, and press releases of interest to the Java development community. It is moderated, so all postings must be submitted for approval before they are posted to the group.

- `comp.lang.java.beans`—This group is devoted to discussions related to JavaBeans programming, announcements of Beans that have been made available, and similar topics concerning component software development.

- `comp.lang.java.corba`—This advanced discussion group is devoted to Java-language implementations of CORBA, the Common Object Request Broker Architecture.

- `comp.lang.java.databases`—This group is used for talk related to JDBC, the Java Database Connectivity libraries, and other solutions for connecting Java programs to databases.

- `comp.lang.java.gui`—This group is devoted to the Abstract Windowing Toolkit, Swing, and other graphical user interface class libraries and development tools.

- `comp.lang.java.help`—This group provides a place to discuss installation problems related to Java programming tools and similar issues that bedevil beginners.

- `comp.lang.java.machine`—The most advanced of the Java discussion groups, this group is devoted to discussing the implementation of the language, issues with porting it to new machines, the specifics of the Java Virtual Machine, and similar subjects.

- `comp.lang.java.programmer`—This group contains questions and answers related to Java programming, which makes it another good place for new programmers to frequent.

- `comp.lang.java.security`—This discussion group is devoted to security issues related to Java, especially in regard to running Java programs and other executable content on the World Wide Web.

Job Opportunities

If you're one of those folks who are learning Java as a part of your plan to become a captain of industry, several of the resources listed in this appendix have a section devoted to job opportunities. Check out some of the Java-related job openings that may be available.

If you are interested in joining Sun's Java division itself, visit `http://java.sun.com/jobs`.

Although it isn't specifically a Java employment resource, the World Wide Web site Career Builder enables you to search the job classifieds of more than two dozen job databases, including newspaper classifieds and many other sources. You have to register to use the site, but it's free, and there are more than 100,000 job postings that you can search using keywords such as *Java* or *Internet* or *snake charmer*. Go to `http://www.careerbuilder.com`.

E

APPENDIX F

This Book's Web Site

As much as the author would like to think otherwise, there are undoubtedly some things you're not clear about after completing the 21 days of this book. Programming is a specialized technical field that throws strange concepts and jargon—such as "instantiation," "ternary operators," and "big- and little-endian byte order"—at the reader.

If you're unclear about any of the topics covered in this book, or if I was unclear about a topic (shrug), visit this book's Web site at `http://www.java21days.com` for assistance.

I use the Web site to offer each of the following:

- Error corrections and clarifications: When errors are brought to my attention, they will be described on the site with the corrected text and any other material that will help.

- Answers to reader questions: If readers have questions that aren't covered in this book's Q&A sections, many will be presented on the site.

- The source code and compiled class files for all programs you create during the 21 days of this book.

- Sample Java programs: Working versions of some programs featured in this book are available on the site.

- Solutions, including source code, for activities suggested at the end of each day.

- Updated links to the sites mentioned in this book; if sites mentioned in the book have changed addresses and I know about the new URL, I'll offer it here.

You can also send e-mail to me by visiting the book's site. Click the Feedback link and you'll be taken to a page where you can send e-mail directly from the Web or find out my current e-mail address for comments related to the book.

This doesn't have to be said, as I learned from past editions of this book, but it's offered anyway: Feel free to voice all opinions, positive, negative, indifferent, or undecided.

I have been a user of the Internet and online services long enough to have my parentage questioned in seven spoken languages and one particularly memorable nonverbal one. Any criticism you send will be interpreted as "tough love," and nothing you say could be rougher than what my music teacher said after my audition for the lead in the Yale Elementary School production of *Jesus Christ Superstar.*

Rogers Cadenhead

INDEX